Intelligent Information Systems 2002

Advances in Soft Computing

Editor-in-chief
Prof. Janusz Kacprzyk
Systems Research Institute
Polish Academy of Sciences
ul. Newelska 6
01-447 Warsaw, Poland
E-mail: kacprzyk@ibspan.waw.pl
http://www.springer.de/cgi-bin/search-bock.pl?series=4240

Esko Turunen
Mathematics Behind Fuzzy Logic
1999. ISBN 3-7908-1221-8

Robert Fullér
Introduction to Neuro-Fuzzy Systems
2000. ISBN 3-7908-1256-0

Robert John and Ralph Birkenhead (Eds.)
Soft Computing Techniques and Applications
2000. ISBN 3-7908-1257-9

Mieczysław Kłopotek, Maciej Michalewicz and Sławomir T. Wierzchoń (Eds.)
Intelligent Information Systems
2000. ISBN 3-7908-1309-5

Peter Sinčák, Ján Vaščák, Vladimír Kvasnička and Radko Mesiar (Eds.)
The State of the Art in Computational Intelligence
2000. ISBN 3-7908-1322-2

Bernd Reusch and Karl-Heinz Temme (Eds.)
Computational Intelligence in Theory and Practice
2001. ISBN 3-7908-1357-5

Robert John and Ralph Birkenhead (Eds.)
Developments in Soft Computing
2001. ISBN 3-7908-1361-3

Mieczysław A. Kłopotek, Maciej Michalewicz and Sławomir T. Wierzchoń (Eds.)
Intelligent Information Systems 2001
2001. ISBN 3-7908-1407-5

Antonio Di Nola and Giangiacomo Gerla (Eds.)
Lectures on Soft Computing and Fuzzy Logic
2001. ISBN 3-7908-1396-6

Tadeusz Trzaskalik and Jerzy Michnik (Eds.)
Multiple Objective and Goal Programming
2002. ISBN 3-7908-1409-1

James J. Buckley and Esfandiar Eslami
An Introduction to Fuzzy Logic and Fuzzy Sets
2002. ISBN 3-7908-1447-4

Ajith Abraham and Mario Köppen (Eds.)
Hybrid Information Systems
2002. ISBN 3-7908-1480-6

Lech Polkowski
Rough Sets
2002. ISBN 3-7908-1510-1

Mieczysław A. Kłopotek
Sławomir T. Wierzchoń
Maciej Michalewicz
Editors

Intelligent Information Systems 2002

Proceedings of the IIS' 2002 Symposium, Sopot, Poland, June 3–6, 2002

With 147 Figures
and 64 Tables

Physica-Verlag
A Springer-Verlag Company

Prof. Dr. Mieczysław A. Kłopotek
Prof. Dr. Sławomir T. Wierzchoń
Dr. Maciej Michalewicz
Polish Academy of Sciences
Institute of Computer Science
ul. Ordona 21
01-237 Warsaw
Poland
klopotek@ipipan.waw.pl
stw@ipipan.waw.pl
michalew@ipipan.waw.pl

ISSN 1615-3871
ISBN 978-3-7908-1509-2 ISBN 978-3-7908-1777-5 (eBook)
DOI 10.1007/978-3-7908-1777-5

Library of Congress Cataloging-in-Publication Data
IIS 2002 Symposium (2002: Sopot, Poland)
Intelligent information systems 2002: proceedings of the IIS' 2002 Symposium, Sopot, Poland, June 3–6, 2002 / Mieczyslaw A. Kłopotek, Slawomir T. Wierzchon, Maciej Michalewicz, editors.
p. cm. – (Advances in soft computing)
Includes bibliographical references.
ISBN 978-3-7908-1509-2
1. Expert systems (Computer science) – Congresses. 2. Artificial intelligence – Congresses I. Kłopotek, Mieczyslaw. II. Wierzchon, Slawomir T. III. Michalewicz, Maciej. IV. Title. V. Series.

Physica-Verlag Heidelberg New York
a member of BertelsmannSpringer Science+Business Media GmbH

Softcover Design: Erich Kirchner, Heidelberg

SPIN 10882860 88/2202-5 4 3 2 1 0 – Printed on acid-free paper

Preface

This volume contains articles accepted for presentation during The Intelligent Information Systems Symposium IIS'2002 which was held in Sopot, Poland, on June 3-6, 2002. This is eleventh, in the order, symposium organized by the Institute of Computer Science of Polish Academy of Sciences and devoted to new trends in (broadly understood) Artificial Intelligence.

The meetings started back to 1992. With small initial audience, workshops in the series grew to an important meeting of Polish and foreign scientists working at the universities in Europe, Asia and the Northern America. Over years, the workshops transformed into regular symposia devoted to latest trends in such fields like Machine Learning, Knowledge Discovery, Natural Language Processing, Knowledge Based Systems and Reasoning, and Soft Computing (i.e. Fuzzy and Rough Sets, Bayesian Networks, Neural Networks and Evolutionary Algorithms). At present, about 50-60 papers are accepted each year. Besides, for several years now, the symposia are accompanied by a number of tutorials, given by the outstanding scientists in their domain.

The main topics of this year symposium included:

- decision trees and other classifier systems
- neural network and biologiccally motivated systems
- clustering methods
- handling imprecision and uncertainty
- deductive, distributed and agent-based systems

We were pleased to see the continuation of the last year trend towards an increase in the number of co-operative contributions and in the number and diversity of practical applications of theoretical research.

Application areas of presented methods and systems included medical and mechanical diagnosis, decision making, motion and scene synthesis, military systems. Practical issues were investigated from various theoretical points of view like automated and semi-automated learning procedures, non-standard statistical, evolutionary, immunological and rough set theoretic approaches to learning and knowledge representation, agent technology. New algorithms for optimization, reasoning, learning from large data bases and other were presented. New possibilities of exploitation of Internet as a medium for enhancing fuctionality of intelligent tools were suggested.

As a result, interesting practical solutions were proposed and challenging new research issues were suggested. Questions of efficiency of proposed and existing algorithms were studied by means of logical analysis and simulation studies. Overlapping of diverse branches of AI research was strikingly visible.

On behalf of the Program Committee and of the Organizing Committee we would like to thank all participants: computer scientists, mathematicians, engineers, logicians and other interested researchers who found excitement in advancing the area of intelligent systems. We hope that this volume of IIS'2002 Proceeding will be a valuable reference work in your further research.

The editors would like to thank Dr. Krzysztof Trojanowski, Mrs. Mrs. Alicja Aloksa, Anna Monkiewicz and Anna Bittner. for the support in preparing this volume.

Warsaw,
June, 2002

Mieczysław A. Kłopotek
Sławomir T. Wierzchoń
Maciej Michalewicz

Contents

Decision Trees and Other Classifier Systems

A Comparison of Six Discretization Algorithms Used for Prediction of Melanoma

Stanislaw Bajcar[1], Jerzy W. Grzymala-Busse[2], Zdzislaw S. Hippe[3]

[1] Regional Dermatology Center, 35-310 Rzeszow, Poland

[2] Department of Electrical Engineering and Computer Science, University of Kansas, Lawrence, KS 66045, USA

[3] Department of Expert Systems and Artificial Intelligence, University of Information Technology and Management, 35-225 Rzeszow, Poland

Abstract. *Melanoma is a very serious and lethal skin cancer. In this paper six discretization algorithms, used for preprocessing of melanoma data, were compared using criteria of rule set complexity, total number of errors, and expert's evaluation. The best discretization method was based on divisive clustering technique. An additional experiment in which the best rules from all six rule sets, selected by an expert, were used for melanoma prediction, was additionally conducted. Our conclusion is that in the original data set, cases with suspicious melanoma were not well represented.*

Keywords: prediction of melanoma, rough set theory, LERS data mining system, LEM2 rule induction algorithm, discretization, clustering techniques.

1 Introduction

In this paper we study melanoma prediction using data mining techniques. Melanoma is a very serious skin and lethal cancer. It is a disease of contemporary time, the number of melanoma cases is constantly increasing, due to, among other factors, sun exposure and a thinning layer of ozone over the Earth [1, 4, 5, 8, 9, 10, 15]. Our data on melanoma were collected in the Regional Dermatology Center in Rzeszow, Poland. The data consist of 146 cases of *benign nevus*, 78 cases of *blue nevus*, 92 cases of *suspicious melanoma* and 94 cases of *malignant melanoma*, a total of 410 cases. Attributes of the data are divided into five categories: Asymmetry, Border, Color, Diversity, and TDS. The variable *Asymmetry* has three different values: *symmetric spot*, *one axial symmetry*, and *two axial symmetry*. *Border* is a numerical attribute, with values from 0 to 8. *Asymmetry* and *Border* are single-value attributes. The remaining two attributes, *Color* and *Diversity*, are many-value attributes. *Color* has six possible values: *black*, *blue*, *dark brown*, *light brown*, *red* and *white*. Similarly, *Diversity* has five values: *pigment dots*, *pigment globules*, *pigment network*, *structureless areas* and *branched stricks*. We introduced six single-valued variables describing color: C_BLACK, C_BLUE, C_d_BROWN, C_l_BROWN, C_RED and C_WHITE and five single-valued variables describing diversity: D_PIGM_DOTS, D_PIGM_GLOB, D_PIGM_NETW, D_SLESS_ARS and D_b_STRICKS. In all of these 11 attributes the values are 0 or 1, 0 meaning lack of the corresponding property and 1 meaning the occurrence of the property. Thus, every case is characterized by the values of 13 attributes. On the basis of those 13 attributes the TDS is computed using the following formula (known as the ABCD formula):

$$\text{TDS} = 1.3 * \text{Asymmetry} + 0.1 * \text{Border} + 0.5 * \Sigma\ \text{Colors} + \Sigma\ \text{Diversities},$$

where for *Asymmetry* the value *symmetric spot* counts as 0, *one axial symmetry* counts as 1, and *two axial symmetry* counts as 2, Σ Colors represent the sum of all values of the six color attributes and Σ Diversities represent the sum of all values of the five diversity attributes.

2 Discretization

The attributes Asymmetry and Border have integers as values, attribute TDS is a real-value type of a variable. All three attributes should be discretized before or during rule induction, i.e., numerical values of these attributes should be converted into symbolic. Let *A* be a numerical attribute, with domain $[a, b]$. As a result of discretization, interval [a, b] is replaced by a set of the following *k* subintervals

$$[a_0, a_1), [a_1, a_2), \ldots, [a_{k-1}, a_k],$$

where $a_0 = a$, $a_{i-1} < a_i$, for $i = 1, 2, \ldots, k$, and $a_k = b$. In rules these intervals are denoted $a_0..a_1$, $a_1..a_2, \ldots, a_{k-1}..a_k$. Numbers $a_1, a_2, \ldots, a_{k-1}$ are called *cutpoints*.

In general, discretization methods can be categorized as *local* or *global* [3]. Local methods operate on only one attribute. Global methods consider all attributes at once. All six discretization methods used in our experiments were global. Among these six discretization methods, two methods based on cluster analysis and one method used in C4.5 [14], are inherently global. The remaining three methods, *Equal Interval Width*, *Equal Frequency Interval*, and *Minimal Class Entropy*, are local. However, we used a special technique, called *Globalization of a Local Method* [3], to convert these three local methods into global. Using the Globalization of a Local Method, first all numerical attributes are discretized once using chosen local discretization method, i.e., a single cutpoint is selected for each numerical attribute. Then, using entropy as a criterion of quality, the worst interval (interval with the largest entropy) among all numerical attributes is selected and the corresponding numerical attribute is subject to re-discretization. The process is continued until each elementary set, defined by all attributes, is contained in some concept or all attributes define the same indiscernibility relation as the original data set. Both ideas, of the elementary set and indiscernibility relation are taken from rough set theory [12, 13].

Equal Interval Width discretization method selects cutpoints in such a way that the attribute domain is divided into equal width intervals. If the cutpoints are selected in such a way that each interval contains approximately equal number of attribute values, the discretization method is called Equal Frequency Interval. Using minimal class entropy discretization, all possible cutpoints for a numerical attribute are considered, then the cutpoint for which the sum of entropies for both subintervals (classes) is minimal is selected. The class with the larger entropy is subdivided again. Then the largest entropy class indicates the class to be subdivided again and so on.

In discretization based on cluster analysis, first clusters are formed, using a similarity criterion, then the clusters are projected on numerical attributes and initial intervals are created, finally, these intervals are merged together using the same criterion to stop as in the process of converting local discretization methods into global. Forming clusters may be either top-down (divisive) or bottom-up (agglomerative). In divisive techniques, initially all cases are grouped in one cluster, then this cluster is gradually divided into smaller and smaller clusters. In agglomerative techniques, initially each case is a single cluster, then they are fused together, forming larger and larger clusters.

System C4.5 has its own discretization scheme, used with forming a tree at the same time. In our experiments we identified all cutpoint, created by C4.5, and formed a new data set, in which all attributes were discretized by C4.5.

3 Rule Induction and Classification

For rule induction, classification, and validation we used the data mining system LERS (Learning from Examples based on Rough Sets). After discretization, in the next step of processing the input data file, LERS checks if the input data file is *consistent* (i.e., if the file does not contain conflicting cases). If the input data file is inconsistent, LERS computes *lower* and *upper approximations* of all concepts. Any subset of the set of all cases, defined by the same value of the decision is called a *concept*. The ideas of lower and upper approximations are fundamental for rough set theory [12, 13]. In our experiments rules were induced by the algorithm LEM2 (Learning from Examples Module, version 2). LEM2 is a part of the system LERS.

In general, LERS uses two different approaches to rule induction: one is used in machine learning, the other in knowledge acquisition. In machine learning, or more specifically, in learning from examples (cases), the usual task is to learn *discriminant description*, i.e., to learn the smallest set of minimal rules, describing the concept. To accomplish this goal, i.e., to learn discriminant description, LERS uses two algorithms: LEM1 and LEM2 (LEM1 and LEM2 stand for Learning from Examples Module, version 1 and 2, respectively). In our experiments we used only LEM2 algorithm since, in general, LEM2 induces simpler and more accurate rule sets.

To classify (predict) unseen cases LERS uses a modification of the *bucket brigade algorithm* [2, 11]. The decision to which concept a case belongs is made on the basis of three factors: strength, specificity, and support. They are defined as follows: *Strength* is the total number of cases correctly classified by the rule during training. *Specificity* is the total number of attribute-value pairs on the left-hand side of the rule. The matching rules with a larger number of attribute-value pairs are considered more specific. The third factor, *support*, is defined as the sum of scores of all matching rules from the concept. The concept *C* for which the support, i.e., the following expression

$$\sum_{Matching\_rules\_R\_describing\_C} Strength(R) \times Specificity(R)$$

is the largest is the winner and the case is classified as being a member of *C*.

For description of other classification systems see, e.g., [16].

In the classification system of LERS, if complete matching is impossible, all partially matching rules are identified. These are rules with at least one attribute-value pair matching the corresponding attribute-value pair of a case. For any partially matching rule *R*, the additional factor, called *Matching factor* (*R*), is computed. Matching_factor is defined as the ratio of the number of matched attribute-value pairs of a rule with a case to the total number of attribute-value pairs of the rule. In partial matching, the concept *C* for which the following expression is the largest

$$\sum_{Matching\_rules\_R\_describing\_C} Matching\_factor(R) \times Strength(R) \times Specificity(R)$$

is the winner and the case is classified as being a member of *C*.

Every rule is preceded by three numbers: specificity, strength, and the total number of training cases matching the left-hand side of the rule.

4 Experiments

Results of experiments with the melanoma data set are presented in Tables 1–5. Table 1 shows the number of intervals determined by the six discretization techniques. Peculiar is the data set discretized by the system C4.5. First of all, during discretization C4.5 deleted all attributes except Border, Color_blue, Color_red, Color_white and TDS. Thus, C4.5 ignored attributes Asymmetry, the three Color attributes, and all attributes related with Diversity. As a result, the melanoma data set processed by C4.5 was inconsistent (there were conflicting cases, with all attribute values the same, yet differently diagnosed). All five remaining discretization techniques outputted consistent discretized data sets. In the data set discretized by C4.5, the total number of conflicting cases was 82 (out of 410), i.e., 20%. The attribute TDS was the most extensively used, hence the largest number (5) of intervals for TDS—the largest among all six used discretization techniques. All remaining five discretization techniques outputted data sets with all 14 attributes, though—in general—they, potentially, may also reduce the total number of attributes. Some of the discretization techniques did not discretize attribute Asymmetry (all three values were unchanged), while other discretization techniques did not discretize attribute Border (all nine possible values were unchanged).

Table 1. Number of Intervals for Numerical Attributes

Discretization Algorithm	Assymetry	Border	TDS
C4.5	-	3	5
Equal Interval Width	3	6	4
Equal Interval Frequency	3	9	4
Minimal Class Entropy	3	9	3
Agglomerative Cluster Analysis	2	4	3
Divisive Cluster Analysis	2	3	3

Table 2. Intervals for TDS

Discretization Algorithm	Intervals for TDS
C4.5	1..2.8, 2.8..4.9, 4.9..5.5, 5.5..5.7, 5.7..8.7
Equal Interval Width	1..2.925, 2.925..4.85, 4.85..6.775, 6.775..8.7
Equal Interval Frequency	1..3.6, 3.6..4.85, 4.85..5.65, 5.65..8.7
Minimal Class Entropy	1..4.85, 4.85..5.45, 5.45..8.7
Agglomerative Cluster Analysis	1..4.9, 4.9..5.7, 5.7..8.7
Divisive Cluster Analysis	1..4.9, 4.9..5.5, 5.5..8.7

Table 3 presents the total number of rules and the total number of conditions for rule sets induced by algorithm LEM2 of LERS. Since the data set discretized by C4.5 was inconsistent, Table 3 presents numbers characterizing the certain rule set.

Table 3. Complexity of Rule Sets

Discretization Algorithm	Number of Rules	Number of Conditions
C4.5	16	40
Equal Interval Width	44	167
Equal Interval Frequency	37	124
Minimal Class Entropy	24	76
Agglomerative Cluster Analysis	31	118
Divisive Cluster Analysis	23	84

Table 4 shows the total number of errors, the result of ten-fold cross validation. In the case of C4.5 the certain rule set was used for validation. Also, an experienced diagnostician (expert) evaluated stronger rules for all six rule sets. In the case of C4.5, the rule set evaluated by the expert was the original, unpruned rule set produced by C4.5. The expert graded every rule as very good (4.0), good (3.0), weak (2.0), insufficient (1.0) and wrong (0.0). The average of all graded rules is reported in Table 4 as the Expert's Score.

Table 4. Quality of Rule Sets

Discretization Algorithm	Number of Errors	Expert's Score
C4.5	30	2.00
Equal Interval Width	28	2.85
Equal Interval Frequency	19	2.62
Minimal Class Entropy	13	2.38
Agglomerative Cluster Analysis	17	2.33
Divisive Cluster Analysis	15	2.67

Table 5 presents the Error Rank and the Expert's Rank (the best is number one, the worst is number six). The Final Score was computed using the same methodology as in the ranking tests of non-parametric statistical test, i.e., as the sum of the Error Rank and the Expert's rank. The rightmost column of Table 5 presents the Final Rank, determined on the basis of the Final Score. The winner is the discretization based on Divisive Cluster Analysis. We did not take into account complexity of rule sets in the final ranking since complexity of rule sets is far less important.

Table 5. Ranking of Discretization Algorithms

Discretization Algorithm	Error Rank	Expert's Rank	Final Score	Final Ranking
C4.5	6	6	12	6
Equal Interval Width	5	1	6	3
Equal Interval Frequency	4	3	7	4
Minimal Class Entropy	1	4	5	2
Agglomerative Cluster Analysis	3	5	8	5
Divisive Cluster Analysis	2	2	4	1

An additional experiment was conducted. A new rule set was created, consisting of all rules graded as very good by the expert from all six rule sets. This new rule set consisted of 28 rules. Then the original melanoma data set, before discretization, was used as a testing data set. As a result, 67 errors were reported. The dominant error was associated with the suspicious melanoma (51 cases) because the expert qualified only two rules characterizing suspicious melanoma as very good. Note that for five rule sets (all with exception of the rule set induced from data discretized by C4.5) the error rate against the original melanoma data set was equal to zero. Thus, most likely, the original melanoma data set did not contain the most representative cases from this class, consequently, LEM2 was unable to discover a sufficient number of very good rules.

5 Conclusions

Six discretization schemes used for data mining on melanoma data set were compared experimentally. The simplest discretized data set was produced by C4.5. However, this data set was inconsistent and the rule set induced from it was the most inaccurate, producing the largest number of errors during validation. Also, the expert estimated the rule set induced by C4.5 as the worst.

In general, many strong rules induced from the melanoma data set were positively evaluated by the expert, e.g., the following rule (that flawlessly diagnosed 98 patients)

(TDS, 1..4.85) & (C_BLUE, 0) & (C_d_BROWN, 1) & (D_PIGM_DOTS, 1) -> (MELANOMA, Benign_nev)

was graded as very good (4.0). On the other hand, the following rule

(TDS, 4.85..5.45) -> (MELANOMA, Suspicious)

diagnosed correctly 90 patients. In spite of this fact this rule was graded as insufficient (1.0). Most likely, this rule fits very well into the input data used for our experiments and is not specific enough for other data. On the other hand, the following rule

(D_b_STRICKS, 0) & (D_PIGM_NETW, 0) & (D_PIGM_DOTS, 0) & (C_WHITE, 0) & (ASYMMETRY, 0..0.5) -> (MELANOMA, Blue_nevus)

was graded as wrong (0.0). However, this rule diagnosed correctly 37 patients and is specific (having five conditions). All of these rules cited above were induced by LEM2 from the data discretized by the Divisive Cluster Analysis technique.

The best discretization algorithm overall, taking into account the total number of errors in ten-fold cross validation and the final grade given by the expert was the Divisive Cluster Analysis discretization technique.

Acknowledgment. This research has been partially supported by the State Committee for Research (KBN) of the Republic of Poland under the grant 7 T11E 030 21.

References

1. Bajcar, S. and Hippe, Z. S.: Risk estimate of melanoma diagnosis on the basis of assessment of dermatoscopic patterns. *Proc. of the National Conference Telemedycyna*, Lodz, Poland, August 17–19, 1999, 175–178.
2. Booker, L. B., Goldberg, D. E., and Holland, J. F.: Classifier systems and genetic algorithms. In *Machine Learning. Paradigms and Methods*. Carbonell, J. G. (Ed.), The MIT Press, Boston, MA, 1990, 235–282.
3. Chmielewski, M. R. and Grzymala-Busse, J. W.: Global discretization of continuous attributes as preprocessing for machine learning. *Int. Journal of Approximate Reasoning* **15** (1996) 319–331.
4. Friedman, R. J. Rigel, D. S., and Kopf, A. W.: Early detection of malignant melanoma: the role of physician examination and self-examination of the skin. *CA Cancer J. Clin.* **35** (1985) 130–151.
5. Grzymala-Busse, J. P., Grzymala-Busse, J. W., and Hippe, Z. S.: Melanoma prediction using data mining system LERS. *Proc. of the 25th Anniversary Annual International Computer Software and Applications Conference COMPSAC* 2001, Oct. 8–12, 2001, Chicago, IL, 615–620.
6. Grzymala-Busse, J. W.: LERS—A system for learning from examples based on rough sets. In *Intelligent Decision Support. Handbook of Applications and Advances of the Rough Sets Theory*. Slowinski, R. (ed.), Kluwer Academic Publishers, Dordrecht, Boston, London, 1992, 3–18.
7. Grzymala-Busse, J. W.: A new version of the rule induction system LERS. *Fundamenta Informaticae* **31** (1997) 27–39.
8. Grzymala-Busse, J. W. and Hippe, Z. S.: Melanoma prediction using k-Nearest Neighbor and LEM2 algorithms. *Proc. of the Tenth International Symposium on Intelligent Information Systems*, Zakopane, Poland, June 18–22, 2001, 43–55.
9. Hippe, Z. S.: Computer database NEVI on endargement by melanoma. *Task Quarterly* **4** (1999) 483–488.
10. Hippe, Z. S., Grzymala-Busse, J. W., Bajcar, S., Kinczyk, B., and Klubek, K.: A comparison of covering and induction algorithms for generation of rules identifying melanocyte changes (in Polish). *Proc. of the Telemedicine Conference*, September 24–26, 2001, Lodz, Poland, 37–41.
11. Holland, J. H., Holyoak, K. J., and Nisbett, R. E.: *Induction. Processes of Inference, Learning, and Discovery*. The MIT Press, Boston, MA, 1986.
12. Pawlak, Z.: Rough Sets. *International Journal of Computer and Information Sciences*, **11** (1982) 341–356.
13. Pawlak, Z. *Rough Sets. Theoretical Aspects of Reasoning about Data*. Kluwer Academic Publishers, Dordrecht, Boston, London, 1991.
14. Quinlan, J. R.: *C4.5: Programs for Machine Learning*. San Mateo, CA: Morgan Kaufmann Publishers, 1993.
15. Rigel, D. S., Friedman, R. J., Kopf, A. W., Weltman, R., Prioleau, P. G., Safai, B., Lebwohl, M. G., Elizeri, Y., Torre, D. P., Bonford, T. T., *et al.*: Importance of complete cutaneous examination for the detection of malignant melanoma. *J. Am. Acad. Dermatol.* **14** (1986) 857–860.

16. Stefanowski, J.: On rough set based approaches to induction of decision rules. In Polkowski L., Skowron A. (eds.) *Rough Sets in Data Mining and Knowledge Discovery*. Physica Verlag, Heidelberg New York (1998) 500–529.

Appendix. The rule set induced by LEM2 using discretization based on Divisive Cluster Analysis

4, 98, 98
(TDS, 1..4.85) & (C_BLUE, 0) & (C_d_BROWN, 1) & (D_PIGM_DOTS, 1) -> (MELANOMA, Benign_nev)

3, 78, 78
(TDS, 1..4.85) & (C_BLUE, 0) & (D_b_STRICKS, 1) -> (MELANOMA, Benign_nev)

5, 10, 10
(C_BLUE, 0) & (C_BLACK, 0) & (ASYMMETRY, 0..0.5) & (D_PIGM_DOTS, 0) & (BORDER, 0..2.5) -> (MELANOMA, Benign_nev)

3, 73, 73
(TDS, 1..4.85) & (C_BLUE, 0) & (D_PIGM_NETW, 1) -> (MELANOMA, Benign_nev)

3, 13, 13
(D_PIGM_NETW, 0) & (C_BLUE, 0) & (D_PIGM_GLOB, 0) -> (MELANOMA, Benign_nev)

4, 7, 7
(D_PIGM_NETW, 0) & (D_b_STRICKS, 0) & (C_BLUE, 0) & (BORDER, 2.5..3.5) -> (MELANOMA, Benign_nev)

4, 31, 31
(C_l_BROWN, 1) & (TDS, 1..4.85) & (D_PIGM_DOTS, 1) & (C_RED, 1) -> (MELANOMA, Benign_nev)

6, 2, 2
(BORDER, 3.5..8) & (C_BLACK, 1) & (D_PIGM_NETW, 0) & (C_WHITE, 0) & (C_BLUE, 1) & (D_PIGM_DOTS, 1) -> (MELANOMA, Benign_nev)

4, 22, 22
(BORDER, 3.5..8) & (C_BLACK, 1) & (TDS, 1..4.85) & (C_BLUE, 0) -> (MELANOMA, Benign_nev)

3, 59, 59
(TDS, 1..4.85) & (C_BLUE, 1) & (C_BLACK, 0) -> (MELANOMA, Blue_nevus)

3, 51, 51
(TDS, 1..4.85) & (C_BLUE, 1) & (D_PIGM_DOTS, 0) -> (MELANOMA, Blue_nevus)

5, 18, 18
(D_b_STRICKS, 0) & (D_PIGM_NETW, 0) & (D_PIGM_GLOB, 1) & (BORDER, 0..2.5) & (C_l_BROWN, 0) -> (MELANOMA, Blue_nevus)

5, 37, 37
(D_b_STRICKS, 0) & (D_PIGM_NETW, 0) & (D_PIGM_DOTS, 0) & (C_WHITE, 0) & (ASYMMETRY, 0..0.5) -> (MELANOMA, Blue_nevus)

5, 1, 1
(BORDER, 0..2.5) & (D_PIGM_NETW, 0) & (C_d_BROWN, 0) & (C_WHITE, 1) & (D_PIGM_DOTS, 1) -> (MELANOMA, Blue_nevus)

4, 7, 7
(D_PIGM_DOTS, 0) & (C_RED, 1) & (BORDER, 0..2.5) & (D_PIGM_NETW, 0) -> (MELANOMA, Blue_nevus)

1, 90, 90
(TDS, 4.85..5.45) -> (MELANOMA, Suspicious)

4, 1, 1
(TDS, 5.45..8.7) & (C_RED, 0) & (C_WHITE, 0) & (BORDER, 2.5..3.5) -> (MELANOMA, Suspicious)

4, 1, 1
(TDS, 5.45..8.7) & (C_BLACK, 0) & (C_RED, 0) & (C_WHITE, 0) -> (MELANOMA, Suspicious)

4, 49, 49
(TDS, 5.45..8.7) & (C_BLUE, 0) & (C_BLACK, 1) & (BORDER, 3.5..8) -> (MELANOMA, Malignant)

2, 51, 51
(TDS, 5.45..8.7) & (C_WHITE, 1) -> (MELANOMA, Malignant)

3, 12, 12
(TDS, 5.45..8.7) & (D_PIGM_NETW, 1) & (C_BLUE, 1) -> (MELANOMA, Malignant)

3, 39, 39
(TDS, 5.45..8.7) & (D_PIGM_NETW, 1) & (C_RED, 1) -> (MELANOMA, Malignant)

2, 13, 13
(TDS, 5.45..8.7) & (BORDER, 0..2.5) -> (MELANOMA, Malignant)

Meta-learning via Search Combined with Parameter Optimization

Włodzisław Duch and Karol Grudziński

Department of Informatics, Nicholas Copernicus University,
Grudziądzka 5, 87-100 Toruń, Poland.
www.phys.uni.torun.pl/kmk

Abstract. Framework for Similarity-Based Methods (SBMs) allows to create many algorithms that differ in important aspects. Although no single learning algorithm may outperform other algorithms on all data an almost optimal algorithm may be found within the SBM framework. To avoid tedious experimentation a meta-learning search procedure in the space of all possible algorithms is used to build new algorithms. Each new algorithm is generated by applying admissible extensions to the existing algorithms and the most promising are retained and extended further. Training is performed using parameter optimization techniques. Preliminary tests of this approach are very encouraging.

1 Introduction

There is no single learning algorithm that is inherently superior to all other algorithms. This fact is known as the 'no free lunch' theorem [1]. Yet most efforts in the computational intelligence field goes into the improvement of individual methods. For example, in the neural network field model selection efforts are restricted to selection of architectures (number of nodes, each performing the same type of functions) and improvements of the training schemes, while in the decision tree field branching criteria and pruning strategies are discussed. A notable exception in the machine learning field is the multistrategy learning introduced by Michalski [2]. Our own efforts in this direction include the introduction of heterogeneous adaptive systems of decision tree [3] and of different neural networks types [4].

In real world applications a good strategy is to find the best algorithm that works for a given data trying many different approaches. This may not be easy. First, not all algorithms are easily available, for example there is no research or commercial software for some of the best algorithms used in the StatLog project [5]. Second, each program requires usually a different data format. Third, programs have many parameters and it is not easy to master them all. Our "meta-learning" strategy here is to use recently introduced framework for Similarity-Based Methods (SBM) [6] to construct automatically the best model of the given data. A search for the best model in the space of all models that may be generated within SBM framework is performed. Simplest model are created at the beginning and new types of parameters and procedures are added, allowing to explore more complex models. Neural networks increase model complexity by adding the same type of parameters, generating different models within a single method. This is not a good strategy if the bias of the method (in this case coming from particular type of transfer functions used by the network) does not match the structure of the data. Creating different models of the data using algorithms that have different biases should allow overcome the "no free lunch" theorem and lead to relatively simple models that may be easily understood.

Although the meta-learning approach is quite general and may be used for any association, approximation and unsupervised learning tasks, this paper is focused on methods useful for classification. In the next section the SBM framework is briefly introduced, the third section presents the meta-learning approach used to select the best method, and the fourth section contains our preliminary experiences in analyzing a few datasets. Conclusions and plans for future developments close this paper.

2 A framework for meta-learning

By **an algorithm**, or **a method**, a certain well-defined computational procedure is meant, for example a k-NN method or an RBF neural network. **A model** is an instance of a method with specific values of parameters. The SBM framework [6] covers all methods based on computing similarity between the new case and cases in the training set. It includes such well-known methods as the k–Nearest Neighbor (k-NN) algorithm and it's extensions, originating mainly from machine learning and pattern recognition fields, as well as neural methods such as the popular multilayer perceptron networks (MLP) and networks based on radial–basis functions (RBF).

A function or a procedure to estimate the posterior probability $p(C_i|\mathbf{X};M), i = 1..K$ of assigning vector $\mathbf{X}$ to class C_i, depends on the choice of the model M, that involves various procedures, parameters and optimization methods. Let N be the number of attributes, K be the number of classes, vectors are written in bold face while vector components are in italics. Given a set of objects (cases) $\{\mathbf{O}^p\}, p = 1..n$ and their symbolic labels $C(\mathbf{O}^p)$, define useful numerical features $X_j^p = X_j(\mathbf{O}^p), j = 1...N$ characterizing these objects. This preprocessing step involves computing various characteristics of images, spatio-temporal patterns, replacing symbolic features by numerical values etc. Using a function suitable for evaluation of similarity or dissimilarity of objects represented by vectors in the feature space, $D(\mathbf{X},\mathbf{Y})$ create a reference (or prototype) vectors $\mathbf{R}$ in the feature space using the similarity measure and the training set $\mathcal{T} = \{\mathbf{X}^p\}$ (a subset of all cases given for classification). The set of reference vectors, similarity measure, the feature space and procedures employed to compute probability define the classification model M.

Once the model has been selected it should be optimized. For this purpose define a cost function $E[\mathcal{T};M]$ measuring the performance accuracy of the system on a training set $\mathcal{T}$ of vectors; a validation set $\mathcal{V}$ composed of cases that are not used directly to optimize model M may also be defined and performance $E[\mathcal{V};M]$ measuring generalization abilities of the model assessed. Optimize parameters of the model M_a until the cost function $E[\mathcal{T};M_a]$ reaches minimum on the set $\mathcal{T}$ or on the validation set $E[\mathcal{V};M_a]$. If the model produced so far is not sufficiently accurate add new procedures/parameters creating more complex model M_{a+1}. If a single model is not sufficient create several local models $M_a^{(l)}$ and use an interpolation procedure to select the best model or combine results creating ensembles of models. All these steps are mutually dependent and involve many choices described below in some details.

The final classification model M is build by selecting a combination of all available elements and procedures. A general similarity-based classification model may include all or some of the following elements:
$M = \{\mathbf{X}(\mathbf{O}), \Delta(\cdot,\cdot), D(\cdot,\cdot), k, G(D), \{\mathbf{R}\}, \{p_i(R)\}, E[\cdot], K(\cdot), \mathcal{S}(\cdot)\}$, where:
$\mathbf{X}(\mathbf{O})$ is the mapping defining the feature space and selecting the relevant features;
$\Delta_j(X_j;Y_j)$ calculates similarity of X_j, Y_j features, $j = 1..N$;
$D(\mathbf{X},\mathbf{Y}) = D(\{\Delta_j(X_j;Y_j)\})$ is a function that combines similarities defined for each attribute to compute similarities of vectors; if the similarity function selected has metric properties the SBM may be called the minimal distance (MD) method.
k is the number of reference vectors taken into account in the neighborhood of $\mathbf{X}$;
$G(D) = G(D(\mathbf{X},\mathbf{R}))$ is the weighting function estimating contribution of the reference vector $\mathbf{R}$ to the classification probability of $\mathbf{X}$;
$\{\mathbf{R}\}$ is a set of reference vectors created from the set of training vectors $\mathcal{T} = \{\mathbf{X}^p\}$ by some selection and optimization procedure;
$p_i(\mathbf{R}), i = 1..K$ is a set of class probabilities for each reference vector;
$E[\mathcal{T};M]$ or $E[\mathcal{V};M]$ is a total cost function that is minimized at the training stage; it may include a misclassification risk matrix $\mathcal{R}(C_i,C_j), i,j = 1..K$;
$K(\cdot)$ is a kernel function, scaling the influence of the error, for a given training example, on the total cost function;
$\mathcal{S}(\cdot)$ is a function (or a matrix) evaluating similarity (or more frequently dissimilarity) of the classes; if class labels are soft, or if they are given by a vector of probabilities $p_i(\mathbf{X})$, classification task is in fact a mapping. $\mathcal{S}(C_i,C_j)$ function allows to include a large number of classes, "softening" the labeling of objects that are given for classification.

Various choices of parameters and procedures in the context of network computations leads to a large number of similarity-based classification methods. Some of these models are well known and some have not yet been used. We have explored so far only a few aspects of this framework, describing various procedures of feature selection, parameterization of similarity functions for objects and single features, selection and weighting of reference vectors, creation of ensembles of models and estimation of classification probability using ensembles, definitions of cost functions, choice of optimization methods, and various network realizations of the methods that may be created by combination of all these procedures [6–8].

The k-NN model $p(C_i|\mathbf{X};M)$ is parameterized by $p(C_i|\mathbf{X};k,D(\cdot),\{\mathbf{X}\})$, i.e. the whole training dataset is used as the reference set, k nearest prototypes are included with the same weight, and a typical distance function, such as the Euclidean or the Manhattan distance, is used. Probabilities are $p(C_i|\mathbf{X};M) = N_i/k$, where N_i is the number of neighboring vectors belonging to the class C_i. The most probable class is selected as the winner. Many variants of this basic model may be created [6,7].

Neural-like network realizations of the RBF and MLP types are also special cases of this framework.

The SBM framework allows for so many choices that exploring all the choices will be almost impossible. Instead an automatic search for the best model for a given data within the space of all possible models is pursued below.

3 Search for the best model

A search tree in the space of all models M_a for the simplest and most accurate model that accounts for the data requires a reference model that should be placed in the root of the tree. The reference model should be the simplest possible. In the SBM framework the k-NN model with k=1 and Euclidean distance function applied to standardized data is a good reference model. Not all extensions may be applied to all models. Instead of creating an expert system based on abstract description of models and checking the conditions for applicability of extensions algorithms, an "interaction matrix" defining possible extensions is defined. Interaction defines how to combine models in order to create more complex models. Consider two extensions of the basic model, one using an optimization of the number of nearest neighbors k and the other using attribute selection method. The interaction in the first algorithm says: 'If the attribute selection method is preceding the optimization of k in a model chain, optimize k with the attributes found by the earlier method'. Interaction in the second algorithm says that if optimization of k is followed by the attribute selection, the optimal k found earlier should be used to search for attributes. Without interaction the meta-learning algorithm reduces to the single-level ranking of basic models and does not create more complex methods.

Optimization should be done using validation sets (for example in crossvalidation tests) to improve generalization. Starting from the simplest model, such as the nearest neighbor model, qualitatively new "optimization channel" is opened by adding the most promising new extension, a set of parameters or a procedure that leads to greatest improvements. The model may be more or less complex than the previous one (for example, feature selection or selection of reference vectors may simplify the model). If several models give similar results the one with the lowest complexity is selected. For example, feature selection should be prefered over feature weighting. The search in the space of all SBM models is stopped when no significant improvements are achieved by new extensions.

The evaluation function $C(M_l)$ returns the classification accuracy of the model M_l calculated on a validation set or in the crossvalidation test. Let n denote the initial number of possible extensions of the reference model. The model sequence selection algorithm proceeds as follows:

1. Take the initial reference model as the best mode M_b.
2. Repeat until the pool of possible extensions is empty:
3. Create a pool of n initial models, $\mathcal{M} = \{M_l\}, l = 1 \ldots n$ applying all extensions to the best mode M_b.

4. Optimize all models in the pool.
5. Evaluate all these models $C(M_l)$ and arrange them in a decreasing order of accuracy $C_a(M_i) \geq C_a(M_j)$ for $i > j$.
6. Select the best model M_b from the $\mathcal{M}$ pool as the reference; if several models have similar performance select the one with lowest complexity.
7. If there is no significant improvement stop and return the current best model.
8. Otherwise remove the extension used to create this model from the list of available extensions; set $n = n - 1$.

The interaction between the current "best model" and all possible extension determines whether these extensions are applicable at a given stage. The number of model optimizations is equal to the number of initial extensions n and does not exceed $n(n-1)/2)$.

The result of this algorithm is a sequence of models of increasing complexity, without re-optimization of previously created models. This "best-first" algorithm finds a sequence of models that give the highest classification accuracy on validation partition or in crossvalidation tests. In case of k-NN-like models validation partition is rarely used since the leave-one-out calculations are easy to perform; for more complex models crossvalidation calculations are performed. Such approach may actually be preferable because rarely the data sets are sufficiently large to use validation sets, and using only the training set makes comparison with other methods easier.

The algorithm described above is prone to local minima, as any "best-first" or search algorithm. The beam search algorithm for selection of the best sequence of models is more computationally expensive but it has a better chance to find a good sequence of models. Since the SBM scheme allows to add many parameters and procedures, new models may also be created on demand if adding models created so far does not improve results. Some model optimizations, such as the minimization of the weights of attributes in the distance function, may be relatively expensive. Re-optimization of models in the pool may be desirable but it would increase the computational costs significantly. Therefore we will investigate below only the simplest "best-first" sequence selection algorithm, as described above.

4 Numerical experiments

We have performed preliminary numerical tests on several datasets. The models taken into account include optimization of k, optimization of distance function, feature selection, and optimization of the scaled distance functions:

$$D(\mathbf{X},\mathbf{Y})^{\alpha} = \sum_{i=1}^{n} s_i |X_i - Y_i|^{\alpha} \tag{1}$$

In the present implementation of the program α is changed from 0.25 to 10 in 0.25 steps; this covers Euclidean ($\alpha = 2$) and Manhattan ($\alpha = 1$) weighted functions. Two other distance function, Chebyschev ($\alpha = \inf$) and Canberra,

$$D_C(\mathbf{X},\mathbf{Y}) = \frac{|X_j, Y_j|}{|X_j, -Y_j|} \tag{2}$$

$$D_{Ch}(\mathbf{X},\mathbf{Y}) = \max_{i=1,\ldots,N} |X_i - Y_i| \tag{3}$$

are also included.

Various methods of learning by parameter optimization may be used. We have used the multisimplex method, adaptive simulated annealing (ASA) method [9] and a discretized search methods with progressive decreasing of quantization step (tuning). One of the scaling coefficients s_i should be fixed to 1, since only relative distances play role in the similarity-based methods. Starting parameters are another issue; initial scaling factors may start from zero or from one. Application of simplex or ASA methods may lead to models with relatively large variance; one way to stabilize these models is to create a number of models and use them in a committee [10].

4.1 Monk problems

The artificial dataset Monk-1 [11] is designed for rule-based symbolic machine learning algorithms (the data was taken from the UCI repository [12]). The nearest neighbor algorithms usually do not work well in such cases. 6 symbolic attributes are given as input, 124 cases are given for training and 432 cases for testing. We are interested here in the performance of the model selection procedures.

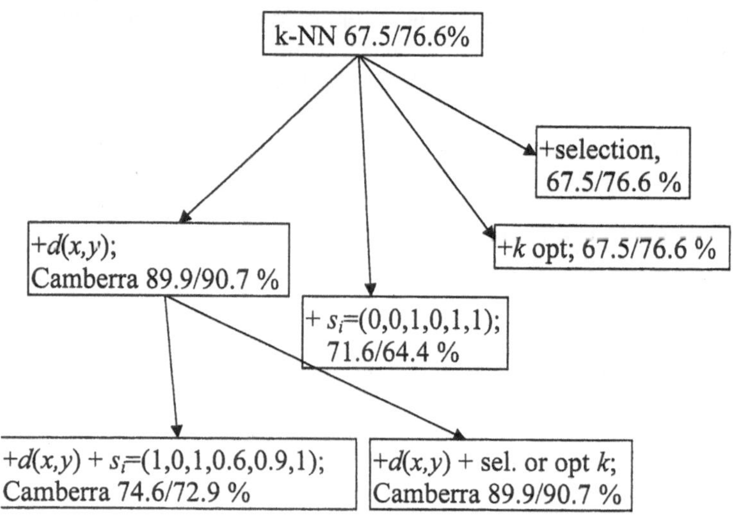

Fig. 1. Search for the best Monk2 data model.

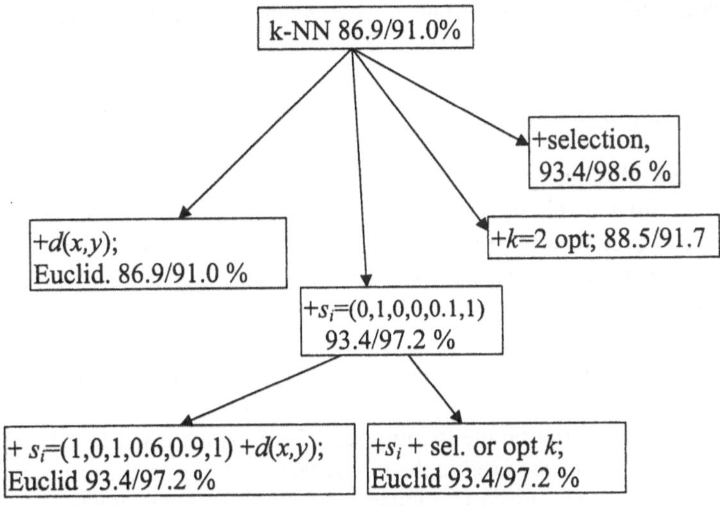

Fig. 2. Search for the best Monk3 data model.

The meta-learning algorithm starts from the reference model, a standard k-NN, with $k = 1$ and Euclidean function. The leave-one-out training accuracy is 76.6% (on test 85.9%). At the first level the choice is: optimization of k, optimization of the type of similarity function, selection of features and weighting of features. Results are summarized in the Table below. Feature weighting (1, 1, 0.1, 0, 0.9, 0), implemented here using a search procedure with 0.1 quantization step, already at the first level of search for the best extension of the reference model achieves 100% accuracy on the test set and 99.2%, or just a single error, in the leave-one-out estimations on the training set. Additional complexity may not justify further search. Selection of the optimal distance for the weighted k-NN reference model achieves 100% on both training and the test set, therefore the search procedure is stopped.

Table 1. Results for the Monk-1 problem with k-NN as reference model.

Method	Acc. Train %	Test %
ref = k-NN, k=1, Euclidean	76.6	85.9
ref + k=3	82.3	80.6
ref + Canberra distance	79.8	88.4
ref + feature selection 1, 2, 5	96.8	100.0
ref + feature weights	99.2	100.0
ref = k-NN, Euclid, weights	99.2	100.0
ref + Canberra distance	100.0	100.0

In the Monk 2 problem the best combination sequence of models was k-NN with Canberra distance function, giving the training accuracy of 89.9% and test set accuracy of 90.7%. In the Monk 3 case weighted distance with just 2 non-zero coefficients gave training accuracy of 93.4% and test result of 97.2%.

4.2 Hepatobiliary disorders

The data contain four types of hepatobiliary disorders found in 536 patients of a university affiliated Tokyo-based hospital; 163 cases were used as the test data [13]. Each case is described by 9 biochemical tests and a sex of the patient. The class distribution in the training partition is 34.0%, 23.9%, 22.3% and 19.8%. This dataset has strongly overlapping classes and is rather difficult. With 49 crisp logic rules only about 63% accuracy on the test set was achieved [14], and over 100 fuzzy rules based on Gaussian or triangular membership functions give about 75-76% accuracy.

The reference *k*-NN model with k=1, Euclidean distance function gave 72.7% in the leave-one-out run on the training set (77.9% on the test set). Although only the training set results are used in the model search results on the test set are given here to show if there is any correlation between the training and the test results. The search for the best model proceeded as follows:

First level

1. Optimization of *k* finds the best result with *k*=1, accuracy 72.7% on training (test 77.9%).
2. Optimization of the distance function gives training accuracy of 79.1% with Manhattan function (test 77.9%).
3. Selection of features removed feature "Creatinine level", giving 74.3% on the training set; (test 79.1%).
4. Weighting of features in the Euclidean distance function gives 78.0% on training (test 78.5%). Final weights were [1.0, 1.0, 0.7, 1.0, 0.2, 0.3, 0.8, 0.8, 0.0].

The best training result 79.1% (although 77.9% is not the best test result) is obtained by selecting the Manhattan function, therefore at the **second level** this becomes the reference model:

1. Optimization of *k* finds the best result with *k*=1, accuracy 72.7% on training (test 77.9%).
2. Selection of features did not remove anything, leaving 79.1% on the training (test 77.9%).
3. Weighting of features in the Manhattan distance function gives 80.1% on training (final weights are [1.0, 0.8, 1.0, 0.9, 0.4, 1.0, 1.0, 1.0, 1.0]; (test 80.4%).

At the **third level** weighted Manhattan distance giving 80.1% on training (test 80.4%) becomes the reference model and since optimization of *k* nor the selection of features does not improve the training (nor test) result this becomes the final model. Comparison of results on this data set is given below:

Since classes strongly overlap the best one can do in such cases is to identify the cases that can be reliable classified and assign the remaining cases to pairs of classes.

Table 2. Results for the hepatobiliary disorders. Accuracy on the training and test sets.

Method	Training set	Test set
Model optimization	80.1	80.4
FSM, Gaussian functions	93	75.6
FSM, 60 triangular functions	93	75.8
IB1c (instance-based)	–	76.7
C4.5 decision tree	94.4	75.5
Cascade Correlation	–	71.0
MLP with RPROP	–	68.0
Best fuzzy MLP model	75.5	66.3
LDA (statistical)	68.4	65.0
FOIL (inductive logic)	99	60.1
1R (rules)	58.4	50.3
Naive Bayes	–	46.6
IB2-IB4	81.2-85.5	43.6-44.6

4.3 Other data

We have tried the metalearning procedure on the ionosphere data [12]. Unfortunately there was no correlation between the results on the training and on the test set, so any good results in this case must be fortuitous.

The hypothyroid data [12] has 3772 cases for training, 3428 cases for testing, 22 attributes (15 binary, 6 continuous), and 3 classes: primary hypothyroid, compensated hypothyroid and normal (no hypothyroid). The class distribution in the training set is 93, 191, 3488 (92.5%) vectors and in the test set 73, 177, 3178 (92.7%). k-NN gives on standardized data slightly more than the base rate, but the search procedure finds first $k = 4$, then Canberra distance function and finally a set of weights for each attribute, leading to 98.89% accuracy on the test set. This is better than the best neural networks although still worse than logical rules for this data set [14].

5 Discussion

Although in this paper meta-learning was applied only to classification problems the SBM framework is also useful for associative memory algorithms, pattern completion, missing values [6], approximation and other computational intelligence problems. Although only a few extensions to the reference k-NN model were used the search in the model space automatically created quite accurate models. For hepatobiliary disorders a model with highest accuracy for real medical data has been found. Although the use of a validation set (or the use of the crossvalidation partitions) to guide the search process for the new models should prevent them from overfitting the data, at the same time enabling them to discover the best bias for the data other ways of model selection, such as the minimum description length (cf. [1]), should be investigated.

Similarity Based Learner (SBL) software developed in our laboratory includes many procedures belonging to the SBM framework. Methods implemented so far provide many similarity functions with different parameters, include several methods of feature selection, methods that weight attributes (based on minimization of the cost function or based on searching in the quantized weight space), methods of selection of interesting prototypes in the batch and on-line versions, and methods implementing partial-memory of the evolving system. Many optimization channels have not yet been programmed in our software, network models are still missing, but even at this preliminary stage results are very encouraging.

Acknowledgments: Support by the Polish Committee for Scientific Research, grant no. 8 T11C 006 19, is gratefully acknowledged.

References

1. Duda, R.O., Hart, P.E and Stork, D.G. (2001): Pattern classification. 2nd ed, John Wiley and Sons, New York (2001)
2. Michalski, R.S. (Ed.) (1993): Multistrategy Learning. Kluwer Academic Publishers.
3. Duch, W., and Grąbczewski, K. (2001): Heterogeneous adaptive systems. World Congress of Computational Intelligence, Honolulu, May 2001 (submitted).
4. Duch, W. and Jankowski N. (2001): Transfer functions: hidden possibilities for better neural networks. 9th European Symposium on Artificial Neural Networks (ESANN), Brugge 2001. De-facto publications, pp. 81-94
5. Michie, D., Spiegelhalter, D. J. and Taylor, C.C. (1994): Machine learning, neural and statistical classification. Elis Horwood, London
6. Duch, W., Adamczak, R., and Diercksen, G.H.F. (2000): Classification, Association and Pattern Completion using Neural Similarity Based Methods. Applied Mathematics and Computer Science **10**, 101–120
7. Duch W. (2000): Similarity-Based Methods. Similarity based methods: a general framework for classification, approximation and association, Control and Cybernetics 29 (4), 937-968.
8. Duch W., Grudziński K. (1999): Search and global minimization in similarity-based methods. In: Int. Joint Conference on Neural Networks (IJCNN), Washington, July 1999, paper no. 742
9. Ingberg, L. (1996): Adaptive simulated annealing (ASA): Lessons learned. J. Control and Cybernetics 25, 33-54
10. Grudziński, K., Duch, W. (2001): Ensembles of Similarity-Based Models. Inteligent Information Systems 2001, Advances in Soft Computing, Physica Verlag (Springer), pp. 75-85
11. Thrun, S.B. *et al.* (1991): The MONK's problems: a performance comparison of different learning algorithms. Carnegie Mellon University, Tech.Rep. CMU-CS-91-197
12. Mertz, C. J. and Murphy, P.M. UCI repository of machine learning datasets, http://www.ics.uci.edu/AI/ML/MLDBRepository.html
13. Hayashi, Y. , Imura, A., and Yoshida, K. (1990): Fuzzy neural expert system and its application to medical diagnosis. In: 8th International Congress on Cybernetics and Systems, New York, pp. 54-61
14. Duch, W., Adamczak, R., Grabczewski, K. (2001) A new methodology of extraction, optimization and application of crisp and fuzzy logical rules. IEEE Transactions on Neural Networks 12, 277-306

Flexible Multidiscretizer Based on Measures which are Used in Induction of Decision Trees

Cezary Ko•mider, cezary.kosmider@plusnet.pl

Systems Research Institute, Polish Academy of Sciences

Abstract. Discretization of continuous attributes offers a number of benefits for a machine learning process. Fundamental benefits are: a significant decreasing of learning time, a possible improvement of knowledge quality in case of noisy data, an increasing of knowledge legibility. In this paper we show analysis of a multi-discretizer which allows to apply a wide range of supervised discretization algorithms and which has very good abilities of tuning. Designed multidiscretizer allows to generate new supervised discretization algorithms and also variants similar to well known classic discretization algorithms such as e.g., ChiMerge. The multi-discretizer is based on top-down method and bottom-up one. It uses many measures which are mainly used in induction of decision trees and a few stop criterions. In this paper we study quality of the discretization generated by the multidiscretizer through evaluation of decision trees' accuracy. We focus on comparison of top-down method with bottom-up one and also the measures for the configuration presented below. For discretization research we use decision tree induction algorithms C4.5 and ID3.

Keywords: machine learning, learning from examples, discretization of continuous attributes, supervised discretization, measures, induction of decision trees.

Introduction

In most cases in machine learning systems, *top-down* approach dominates with relation to *bottom-up* one. E.g., algorithms which use top-down method are: top-down minimization of entropy (Fayyad and Irani 1993), D-2 (Catlett 1991), C4 (Quinlan et al. 1987), C4.5 (Quinlan 1993), CART (Breiman et al. 1984), PVM (Weiss et al. 1990). Algorithms which use bottom-up are e.g., ChiMerge (Kerber 1992), StatDisc (Richeldi and Rossotto 1995).

Measures are heart of many machine learning algorithms. In this paper these heuristics evaluate possible splits of attribute's values and they use information about instances' class. Their quality has fundamental impact on discretization quality generated by *supervised discretization algorithms*. They can be used in many machine learning problems, e.g., in decision tree induction algorithms, in rule induction algorithms, in discretization algorithms, for defining stop criterions.

As we said that a measure should create proper splits of attribute's values, similarly a *stop criterion* should in proper moment stop the algorithm to agree to compromise with reference to accuracy and speed of the learning process. Too many created intervals can make discretization useless because the learning time will not much decrease in comparison with the learning time on raw data. Moreover, the tree will be too big and characterized by a worse accuracy. On the other hand too few created intervals can cause that the learning time will be very short but with a big waste of accuracy.

The main idea of the multidiscretizer

The simplified schema of the multidiscretizer is presented below on figure 1:

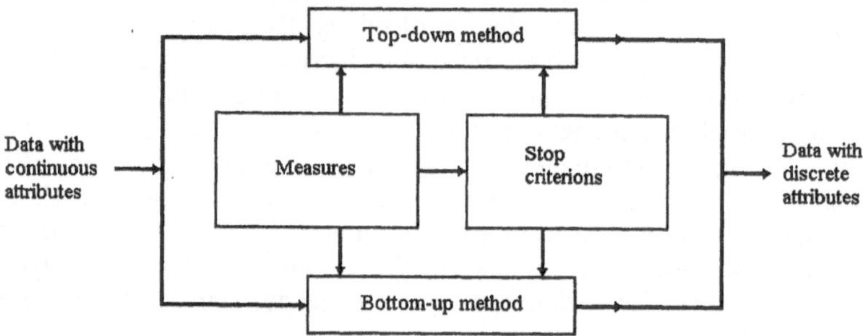

Fig. 1. The schema of the multidiscretizer

Data with continuous attributes represents a data set in which attributes have numeric values. The product of the multidiscretizer is *Data with discrete attributes* which represents a data where attributes have values from usually finite and a small set. Below we list the most important fundamental elements (figure 1) on which the *multidiscretizer* is based:

- *Methods*: *top-down*, *bottom-up*,
- *Measures* evaluating splits of attribute's values: *information gain* (Quinlan 1986), *gain ratio* (Quinlan 1986), *distance measure D* (Mantaras 1989, 1991), *chi square* (Kerber 1992), *G statistic* (Mingers 1987, 1989), *gini index* (Breiman et al. 1984), *relevance* (Baim 1988), *average absolute weight of evidence* (Michie 1989), *J measure* (Smyth and Goodman 1990), *twoing* (Breiman et al. 1984), *minimum description length (MDL)* (Kononenko 1995), *orthogonality metric (angular disparity)* (Fayyad and Irani 1992),
- *Stop criterions*: *value of measure*, *number of intervals*, *number of examples in interval*, *value of measure equals zero* for all split points (criterion built in, a user cannot manipulate this parameter - it is specific to top-down method).

The multidiscretizer represents following division of discretization algorithms:

- *Global discertization* – the whole range of attribute's values is taken into account during discretization,

- *Static discretization* – each attribute is processed in turn without taking into account a correlation between attributes,
- *Binary splitting* of attribute's values for top-down method (or merging *two* intervals during each iteration for bottom-up one).

The configuration of the multidiscertizer can be freely chosen from the options mentioned above. The system allows to generate new discertization algorithms and variants similar to discretization algorithms which appear in machine learning literature.

The main idea of research

Following figure 2 presents the schema of the multidiscretizer research:

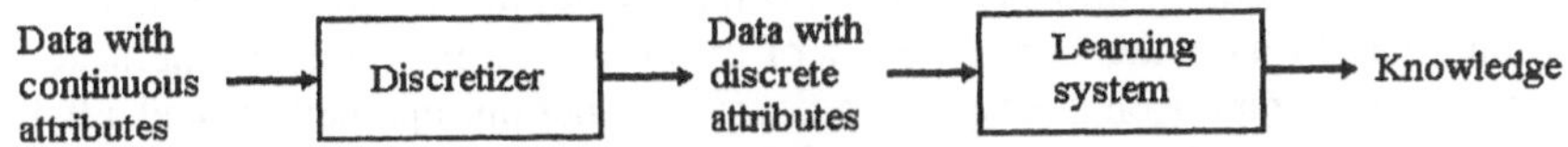

Fig. 2. The schema of the multidiscretizer research

Data with continuous attributes are discretized by *Discretizer* which represents one of many algorithms possible to generate by the multidiscretizer. The result of discretization i.e., *Data with discrete attributes* is directed to *Learning system* which represents a knowledge discovery algorithm. The product of *Learning system* is *Knowledge* evaluated from accuracy perspective. The accuracy of *Knowledge* generated by *Learning system* relies heavily on the accuracy of discretization created by a discretization algorithm.

In order to evaluate the discretization accuracy, as *Learning system* we used *ID3* (Quinlan 1986) and *C4.5* (Quinlan 1993) decision tree induction algorithms. These algorithms were taken from machine learning application WEKA 3.1.8 (developed by researchers from University of Waikato from New Zealand). In our research we used *diabetes*, *glass*, *iris*, *vehicle* data sets taken from UCI Machine Learning Repository.

As we said above it is important to realize that a discretization cannot be evaluated directly, but by evaluation of the results of learning algorithms. In that case the evaluation of discretization algorithms relies on many factors:

- A way of training and testing set creation,
- A way of data set split on training and testing set, e.g., 10-fold cross-validation,
- A way of decision tree induction algorithm working,
- A parameter needed to estimate the accuracy of the classifier (e.g., error ratio).

In our research the data set after discretization process was divided on a *training set* and a *testing set*. The training set was used to create a decision tree. Then the testing set was used to test the decision tree previously created. The estimating parameter was *error ratio*. C4.5 algorithm (ver. 8) always classifies all instances in contrast to ID3 algorithm (taken from WEKA 3.1.8). In that case the results should be fairly estimated, thus error ratio was defined as follows:

$$ER = \frac{I+U}{N} \cdot 100\%$$

where:

I – number of incorrectly classified examples,

U – number of unclassified examples,

N – number of all examples.

During evaluation of the knowledge accuracy we were using *stratified 10-fold cross-validation.*

Investigation of the knowledge accuracy

The knowledge accuracy generated by the decision tree induction algorithms was researched with taking into account following assumptions. We assume that each attribute has to have the same number of discretization intervals for the sake of necessity of comparison between top-down and bottom-up method and all the measures which evaluate possible splits of attribute's values. The main purpose of such configuration was reliable research of designed discretization algorithms, not creation of the best discretizer. In the first part of our research the number of discretization intervals was set to 7 (for data sets: diabetes, glass, iris, vehicle). In the second part the number of discretization intervals was set to 4 (for data sets: glass, iris) to observe the level of differences. We used following decision tree induction algorithms: C4.5, C4.5 without pruning, ID3. The pruning algorithm was switched off because it can disturb a little bit the comparison of the methods and the measures. For comparative reasons we present the discretization results of C4.5 algorithm for continuous attributes and also the results of unsupervised algorithms i.e., equal frequency intervals, equal width intervals. Below we present tables (1-6) which include the results of the research:

Table 1. Error ratio for *diabetes* data set, for 7 discretization intervals

	C4.5		C4.5, no pruning		ID3	
	t-down	b-up	t-down	b-up	t-down	b-up
Chi square	20,31%	23,44%	24,74%	26,56%	35,29%	37,11%
Gini index	23,44%	23,05%	23,44%	24,48%	38,28%	29,82%
MDL	21,74%	23,70%	24,48%	23,70%	33,59%	33,46%
J measure	23,05%	25,78%	26,17%	27,21%	38,02%	32,29%
Distance measure D	24,87%	31,38%	28,52%	31,90%	37,24%	32,94%
Orthogonality metric	24,74%	25,65%	26,04%	26,30%	29,43%	32,16%
Information gain	23,05%	25,78%	26,17%	27,21%	38,02%	32,29%
Twoing	27,08%	24,61%	29,43%	29,95%	42,84%	43,10%
Average absolute...	22,92%	25,52%	26,04%	29,43%	34,64%	38,15%
G statistic	20,96%	24,09%	24,35%	25,13%	34,38%	34,90%
Gain ratio	23,18%	23,83%	25,13%	25,00%	26,82%	29,17%
Relevance	22,92%	25,26%	24,87%	27,86%	34,11%	33,72%
Equal frequency...	24,87%		31,90%		42,97%	

Table 1 continued

Equal width intervals	26,95%	31,77%	39,19%
Continuous attributes	25,52%	26,04%	

Table 2. Error ratio for *glass* data set, for 7 discretization intervals

	C4.5		C4.5, no pruning		ID3	
	t-down	b-up	t-down	b-up	t-down	b-up
Chi square	28,97%	26,17%	30,84%	25,23%	32,71%	36,45%
Gini index	26,64%	44,86%	28,97%	42,99%	34,11%	46,26%
MDL	29,91%	31,78%	27,57%	28,97%	30,37%	35,51%
J measure	35,51%	44,86%	33,64%	42,99%	38,79%	45,79%
Distance measure D	32,24%	44,39%	32,24%	44,86%	36,45%	49,07%
Orthogonality metric	45,79%	49,53%	44,86%	50,93%	46,26%	52,34%
Information gain	35,51%	44,86%	33,64%	42,99%	38,79%	45,79%
Twoing	34,11%	29,44%	31,78%	30,37%	38,79%	39,25%
Average absolute...	30,37%	35,98%	31,31%	41,59%	35,98%	49,07%
G statistic	27,57%	28,04%	27,57%	28,04%	29,44%	28,50%
Gain ratio	41,12%	44,86%	40,65%	41,59%	43,46%	49,53%
Relevance	35,51%	64,49%	35,05%	65,42%	43,46%	66,36%
Equal frequency...	39,25%		38,32%		48,13%	
Equal width intervals	33,18%		33,18%		41,12%	
Continuous attributes	34,58%		35,05%			

Table 3. Error ratio for *iris* data set, for 7 discretization intervals

	C4.5		C4.5, no pruning		ID3	
	t-down	b-up	t-down	b-up	t-down	b-up
Chi square	4,67%	4,67%	5,33%	3,33%	6,67%	6,67%
Gini index	7,33%	7,33%	7,33%	6,67%	9,33%	6,67%
MDL	4,67%	5,33%	3,33%	3,33%	6,67%	6,67%
J measure	4,67%	4,67%	3,33%	3,33%	6,67%	9,33%
Distance measure D	4,67%	4,67%	3,33%	3,33%	6,67%	8,67%
Orthogonality metric	7,33%	8,67%	7,33%	8,67%	9,33%	8,00%
Information gain	4,67%	4,67%	3,33%	3,33%	6,67%	9,33%
Twoing	6,67%	6,67%	5,33%	5,33%	10,00%	8,00%
Average absolute...	5,33%	7,33%	5,33%	6,67%	6,67%	9,33%
G statistic	4,67%	4,67%	3,33%	3,33%	6,67%	6,67%
Gain ratio	4,67%	4,67%	3,33%	3,33%	8,00%	8,67%
Relevance	13,33%	5,33%	18,67%	3,33%	20,67%	4,00%
Equal frequency...	5,33%		6,67%		8,67%	
Equal width intervals	5,33%		6,00%		8,67%	
Continuous attributes	4,67%		4,67%			

Table 4. Error ratio for *vehicle* data set, for 7 discretization intervals

	C4.5		C4.5, no pruning		ID3	
	t-down	b-up	t-down	b-up	t-down	b-up
Chi square	32,27%	30,02%	30,14%	31,09%	37,35%	36,88%

Table 4 continued

Gini index	30,14%	28,49%	30,73%	31,09%	33,33%	34,63%
MDL	30,73%	30,14%	30,38%	30,50%	33,45%	36,64%
J measure	30,02%	29,43%	31,32%	33,69%	36,05%	36,29%
Distance measure D	29,91%	29,08%	33,33%	30,85%	34,28%	33,92%
Orthogonality metric	36,29%	31,80%	37,23%	33,45%	40,54%	36,76%
Information gain	30,02%	29,43%	31,32%	33,69%	36,05%	36,29%
Twoing	34,52%	31,80%	34,40%	32,98%	41,37%	39,13%
Average absolute...	30,38%	31,09%	32,03%	30,26%	38,89%	39,01%
G statistic	27,90%	30,38%	29,91%	31,09%	35,70%	35,93%
Gain ratio	30,38%	31,21%	30,61%	33,22%	37,35%	38,42%
Relevance	36,52%	42,32%	36,52%	42,44%	39,48%	45,63%
Equal frequency...	32,27%		32,86%		39,95%	
Equal width intervals	35,46%		36,29%		42,08%	
Continuous attributes	28,13%		27,78%			

Table 5. Error ratio for *glass* data set, for 4 discretization intervals

	C4.5		C4.5, no pruning		ID3	
	t-down	b-up	t-down	b-up	t-down	b-up
Chi square	28,04%	20,56%	28,97%	22,43%	27,57%	19,63%
Gini index	27,10%	47,66%	27,10%	47,66%	28,04%	42,52%
MDL	25,70%	34,58%	25,70%	31,31%	29,44%	28,04%
J measure	32,71%	51,40%	31,78%	50,93%	31,78%	46,73%
Distance measure D	33,18%	49,07%	30,84%	48,13%	29,91%	42,99%
Orthogonality metric	46,26%	49,53%	47,20%	54,21%	43,93%	49,07%
Information gain	32,71%	51,40%	31,78%	50,93%	31,78%	46,73%
Twoing	30,37%	30,37%	30,37%	33,64%	24,30%	28,04%
Average absolute...	27,57%	35,51%	29,44%	34,11%	25,70%	31,31%
G statistic	28,97%	25,70%	26,64%	25,23%	21,03%	23,36%
Gain ratio	48,13%	50,00%	47,20%	49,53%	41,59%	43,46%
Relevance	33,64%	64,49%	31,31%	64,49%	30,84%	59,81%
Equal frequency...	24,77%		27,10%		25,23%	
Equal width intervals	40,19%		40,65%		37,85%	
Continuous attributes	34,58%		35,05%			

Table 6. Error ratio for *iris* data set, for 4 discretization intervals

	C4.5		C4.5, no pruning		ID3	
	t-down	b-up	t-down	b-up	t-down	b-up
Chi square	3,33%	4,00%	3,33%	3,33%	6,67%	5,33%
Gini index	3,33%	4,00%	3,33%	2,67%	6,67%	6,00%
MDL	3,33%	5,33%	2,67%	3,33%	6,00%	6,67%
J measure	4,00%	4,00%	2,67%	4,00%	4,00%	5,33%
Distance measure D	4,00%	4,00%	3,33%	4,00%	4,67%	5,33%
Orthogonality metric	7,33%	4,00%	7,33%	2,67%	7,33%	6,67%
Information gain	4,00%	4,00%	2,67%	4,00%	4,00%	5,33%
Twoing	6,67%	6,67%	5,33%	7,33%	4,67%	6,67%
Average absolute...	7,33%	7,33%	8,00%	6,67%	5,33%	8,00%

Table 6 continued

<table>
<tr><td>G statistic</td><td>4,00%</td><td>4,00%</td><td>2,67%</td><td>3,33%</td><td>4,00%</td><td>5,33%</td></tr>
<tr><td>Gain ratio</td><td>4,00%</td><td>4,00%</td><td>2,67%</td><td>3,33%</td><td>5,33%</td><td>4,00%</td></tr>
<tr><td>Relevance</td><td>14,00%</td><td>14,67%</td><td>19,33%</td><td>13,33%</td><td>20,00%</td><td>13,33%</td></tr>
<tr><td>Equal frequency...</td><td colspan="2">8,00%</td><td colspan="2">8,00%</td><td colspan="2">10,00%</td></tr>
<tr><td>Equal width intervals</td><td colspan="2">8,00%</td><td colspan="2">9,33%</td><td colspan="2">9,33%</td></tr>
<tr><td>Continuous attributes</td><td colspan="2">4,67%</td><td colspan="2">4,67%</td><td colspan="2"></td></tr>
</table>

Conclusions

Comparison of the top-down and the bottom-up methods

Basing on the results presented above we can say that the algorithms top-down driven obtain better results than the algorithms bottom-up driven as regards accuracy of the decision trees. E.g., for glass data set (table 2, table 5) superiority is very clear. For diabetes data set (table 1), basing mainly on the results obtained by C4.5 and C4.5 without pruning, superiority is also visible but not so big as it was in the previous example. Similar situation we can see for vehicle data set (table 4) basing in this case on the results obtained by C4.5 without pruning and ID3. For iris data set, for 7 discretization intervals (table 3) it is hard to say which algorithms, based on which methods return better results. However for the same data set for 4 discretization intervals, algorithms top-down driven have superiority in accuracy (table 6).

Comparison of the measures

The best results as regards accuracy of the decision trees obtain the discretization algorithms based on the following measures: chi square, G statistic, MDL. E.g., the best results of the discretization algorithms based on chi square and G statistic can be showed for glass data set in table 2 and table 5. Similarly, the algorithms which use G statistic and MDL obtained the best results for vehicle data set (table 4). Chi square contributed to get the record results for a one of the two methods. E.g., the discretization algorithm based on top-down method and chi square measure allowed C4.5 (without pruning) to generate the decision tree characterizing by error ratio equals 25.23% (glass data set, table 2). MDL was also contributing to obtain very good results. This measure was in the lead of the best measures. Especially good results we can observe for ID3 algorithm. E.g., very good results of MDL are presented for following data sets: glass (table 2), iris (table 3), vehicle (table 4).

The worst results as regards accuracy of the decision trees obtain the discretization algorithms based on the following measures: relevance, orthogonality metric and twoing. Particularly the algorithms based on relevance very often obtained very high error level and were unforeseeable. E.g., for iris data set (table 3) (discretized by the algorithm based on top-down method and relevance measure) C4.5 without pruning and ID3 generated the decision trees with very poor accuracy. However for the algorithm based on bottom-up method the results were very good (also table 3).

Sometimes the differences between the algorithms based on the best and the worst measures were very big. E.g., for glass data set (table 2) we can see that error ratio for the algorithm based on relevance was twice greater than error ratio for the algorithm based on chi square. However for iris data set (table 6) the algorithm using relevance contributed to obtain error ratio over 4-5 times greater than error ratio obtained by the algorithms based on the best measures.

It is interesting that statistic G which is a measure based on information gain like gain ratio and distance measure D for the established configuration contributed to achieve better results than these obtained by algorithms based on modified information gain (gain ratio, distance measure D) and also on information gain. Thus the measures which are especially prepared to minimize overestimating of attributes with many values in case of binary attributes create different discretization than the discretization achieved by information gain (Kononenko 1995). It is also interesting that orthogonality metric which is especially prepared for binary attributes achieved poor results.

Comparison of the decision tree induction algorithms

Switching off the pruning algorithm in C4.5 did not make significant differences in the evaluation of the discretization methods. Only one example shows such disturbances. It was for vehicle data set (table 4) where after switching off the pruning it turned out that bottom-up method had superiority in accuracy in comparison with top-down one.

Our research also shows how used decision tree induction algorithms influenced on the change of the error level. C4.5 algorithm and its version without pruning achieved similar results as regards accuracy of the trees. Sometimes switching off the pruning worsened the results, e.g., see the results for diabetes data set presented in table 1. Sometimes switching off the pruning improved the results. Proper example we can see for iris data set (table 6), when it caused to achieve the best results for this data set. Thus if we want to get the best results we should experiment with the pruning in C4.5. Sometimes the error level obtained by the all of decision tree algorithms was very similar. A very good example can be the results for glass data set in table 5. Sometimes the differences were quite big - e.g., see the results for diabetes data set in table 1. ID3 algorithm usually obtained worse results than C4.5 and C4.5 without pruning.

Comparison of the results between 7 and 4 discretization intervals

The number of discretization intervals was changed from 7 to 4 intervals and the research was repeated. The results for 4 discretization intervals for glass data set are presented in table 5 and for iris data set in table 6. The distribution of the results was not changed significantly in comparison with the results for 7 discretization intervals, however the error level was lower - see the results presented in table 2 (glass) and table 3 (iris). Thus decreasing of the number of intervals contributed to achieve better results.

Comparison of designed discretization algorithms with discretization algorithm built in C4.5 and with the unsupervised algorithms

The most valuable point of reference towards designed algorithms, more valuable that mentioned below discretization of unsupervised algorithms is discretization performed by C4.5 on the basis of a data set with continuous attributes. Designed discretization algorithms based on the better part of the measures usually achieved better results than the discretization algorithm built in C4.5. Domination of these algorithms was not so big as towards unsupervised algorithms, however it was very clear. E.g., we can see the results for glass data set included in table 2 where a few designed algorithms were better than the discretization algorithm built in C4.5. In this example our algorithms were based on chi square, G statistic, MDL. The results were better about 5% of error ratio. Even better results we obtained for the same data set but for 4 discretization intervals (table 5). Then the algorithm based on chi square achieved the result better about 15% of error ratio than the algorithm built in C4.5.

Sometimes discretization of C4.5 also was very good. E.g., for vehicle data set, the discretization algorithm built in C4.5 obtained the best result in comparison with designed discretization algorithms researched for 7 discretization intervals (table 4).

The results of the unsupervised discretization algorithms were almost always worse than the results of the best supervised algorithms, but sometimes the unsupervised discretization algorithms obtained very good results. E.g., see the results of equal frequency intervals algorithm for glass data set showed in table 5. Such results are only coincidences because such simply algorithms are class-blind.

Further work

In this paper we assumed the fixed number of discretization intervals for an each attribute. Such approach was good only for comparison of the all algorithms. In order to achieve the best results in discretization it is neccessary to use appropriate stop criterion. It can be the value of a measure with a strong limit of discretization intervals. Also a good example can be top-down minimization of entropy where MDL was used as the stop criterion (Fayyad and Irani 1993). Static discretization, global discretization and binary splitting is useful for speed up of the discretization process, but the best results can be obtained by *dynamic* discretization algorithms. However then computation cost will increase significantly.

References

Baim PW (1988) A method for attribute selection in inductive learning systems. In: IEEE Trans. On PAMI. vol. 10, pp 888-896

Breiman L, Friedman JH, Olshen RA, Stone CJ (1984) Classification and Regression Trees. Wadsworth International Group

Catlett J (1991) On Changing Continuous Attributes Into Ordered Discrete Attributes. In: Kondratoff Y (ed) Proceedings of the European Working Session on Learning. Springer-Verlag, Berlin, pp 164-178

Fayyad U, Irani KB (1992) The attribute selection problem in decision tree generation. In: Proceedings of Tenth National Conference on Artificial Intelligence. MIT-Press, Cambridge, pp 104-110

Fayyad U, Irani KB (1993) Multi-Interval Discretization of Continuous-Valued Attributes for Classification Learning. In: Proceedings of the Thirteenth International Joint Conference on AI. vol.2, pp 1022-1027

Kerber R (1992) ChiMerge: Discretization of Numeric Attributes. In: Proceedings - Tenth National Conference on AI. pp 123-128

Kononenko I (1995) On Biases in Estimating Multi-Valued Attributes. In: Proceedings of the Fourteenth International Joint Conference on Artificial Intelligence. vol. 2

Lopez de Mantaras R (1989) ID3 Revisited: A distance-based criterion for attribute selection. In: Methodologies for Intelligent systems. vol. 4, pp 342-350

Lopez de Mantaras R (1991) A Distance-Based Attribute Selection Measure for Decision Tree Induction. In: Machine Learning. vol. 6, pp 81-92

Mitche D (1989) Personal Models of Rationality. In: Journal of Statistical Planning and Inference. vol. 21

Mingers J (1997) Expert systems – rule induction with statistical data. In: Journal of the Operational Research Society. vol. 38, pp 39-47

Mingers J (1989) An empirical comparison of selection measures for decision-tree induction. In: Machine Learning. vol. 3, pp 319-342

Quinlan JR (1986) Induction of Decision Trees. In: Machine Learning. vol. 1, pp 81-106

Quinlan JR (1993) C4.5: Programs for Machine Learning. Morgan Kaufmann

Quinlan JR, Compton PJ, Horn KA, Lazarus L (1987) Inductive knowledge acquisition: a case study. In: Quinlan JR (ed) Applications of Expert Systems. Turing Institute Press with Addison Wesley, Glasgow

Richeldi M, Rossotto M (1995) Class-Driven Statistical Discretization of Continuous Attributes (Extended Abstract). In: ECML 95. Iraklion, Greece, pp 335-338

Smyth P, Goodman RM (1990) Rule induction using information theory. In: Piatetsky-Shapiro G, Frawley W (eds) Knowledge Discovery in Databases. MIT Press

Weiss SM, Galen RS, Tadepalli PV (1990) Maximzing the predictive value of production rules. In: Artificial Intelligence. vol. 45, pp 47-71

Waikato's homepage: www.cs.waikato.ac.nz

Decision Tree Builder and Visualizer

Halina Kwaśnicka, Marcin Doczekalski,

Wrocław University of Technology, Department of Computer Science, Poland

Abstract. The paper presents computer system, named Decision Tree Builder and Visualizer (DTB&V), that allows to use large databases as source for whole process of decision tree generation and visualization. The system works with discrete and continuous attributes. DTB&V is a general tool allowing for: data preprocessing, generation of decision tree using developed algorithm, post processing (cutting the tree), and visualization of the obtained tree. DTB&V was tested using a number of databases commonly used for such tasks.

Keywords: Data mining, Decision Tree generation

Introduction

Computer systems of many companies contain terabytes of collected data. It is potentially a large source of knowledge useful for managers, but this knowledge must be drawn out from databases in the readable for people form. Traditional methods of data analysis and exploration are not suitable. There is a kind of paradox: having more collected data we have less useful information. The new, automated and intelligent methods for extracting useful knowledge from databases are needed. In the end of 1980s, the new discipline called ***Knowledge Discovery in Databases*** (**KDD**) emerged on the boundaries of artificial intelligence and databases. This area is still in the phase of intensive growth, although some commercial systems supporting **KDD** process are in the market. After Piatetsky-Shapiro, Frawley (1991) and Fayyad et all (1996), we can define **KDD** as:

> Knowledge Discovery in Databases is a nontrivial process of identification of real, new, potentially useful and maximally comprehensible patterns in a set of data.

Above defined, iterative and nontrivial process consists of a number of stages:

1. Understanding of problem domain, identification of final goal of **KDD** process,
2. Data gathering,
3. Preprocessing of data, data consolidation and refining,
4. Selection of adequate data (data reduction) and enrichment,
5. Encoding the data,
6. Data mining (exploration the data):
7. Interpretation, presentation and explanation of 'mined' knowledge,
8. Consolidation and practical exploitation of the uncovered knowledge.

Classification, clustering and regression are (among others) the tasks of data mining. Presentation of obtained knowledge covers analysis of 'mined' knowledge and verification concerning input requirements, and practical application. Visualization techniques are very useful during knowledge analysis.

The paper is structured as follow. The first part after introduction contains general description of the computer system *Decision Tree Builder and Visualizer*. In the next section we describe techniques used in the system. The system has been tested using commonly acceptable testing sets. Obtained results are presented and discussed in the fourth section. Short summary ends the paper.

DTB&V – Decision Tree Builder and Visualizer

The computer system, named *Decision Tree Builder and Visualizer* (**DTB&V**) have been developed as a classification tool. To develop classifier in the form of computer program, we need:

- a set of m attributes $A=\{A_1, A_2, ..., A_m\}$,
- a set of all classes ($C=\{C_1, C_2, ..., C_k\}$,
- a set of n cases, called a training set: $S=\{S_1, S_2, ..., S_n\}$,
- each case S_i ($i=1,2,...,n$) has a form: $\{a_{1,i}, a_{2,i}, ..., a_{m,i}: C_r\}$, where $a_{p,i}$ is a value of pth attribute of ith case, C_r is a class to which i^{th} case belongs.

A training set should be representative, it means that collected cases should cover all classes. We build our classifier by *supervised learning*, as a result we obtain a set of classification rules in the form: *if* $A_1=a_1$ and $A_2=a_2$ and ... and $A_m=a_m$ *then* class is C_r.

In the literature we can meet different approaches and algorithms of classification (Holsheimer, Siebes 1996, Michie et all 1994, Quinlan 1986, Mehta et all 1996, Shafer et all 1996). Decision tree seems to be the most popular technique. They have a number of advantages: high accuracy, relatively short time of construction, comprehensibility of discovered knowledge, and short time of response.

Nodes of tree denote attributes (more precisely – decision attributes), arcs represents their potential values. Leaves are labeled as classes. Classification process lies on the passing by the tree starting from the root and ending in the leaf. In each node a value of decision attribute is controlled, it indicates a path on which algorithm comes down. A label of achieved leaf is a class of classified object.

System architecture

Developed system consists of the three functional layers: (1) access to database, (2) data mining – data preprocessing and construction of a classifier, and (3) presentation layer – visualization of developed decision tree.

RDBMS Interbase 6.01 is used as a database server. To enable fast access to data, we have implemented low-level engine that directly uses API server functions. Data are accessible from the SQL level. The engine contains buffer – questions are only once interpreted by the server and scheme of questions are stored in this buffer. This is very significant issue because access to the data usually consumes over 90% processing time. Operations flow in the **DTB&V** is shown in Fig. 1.

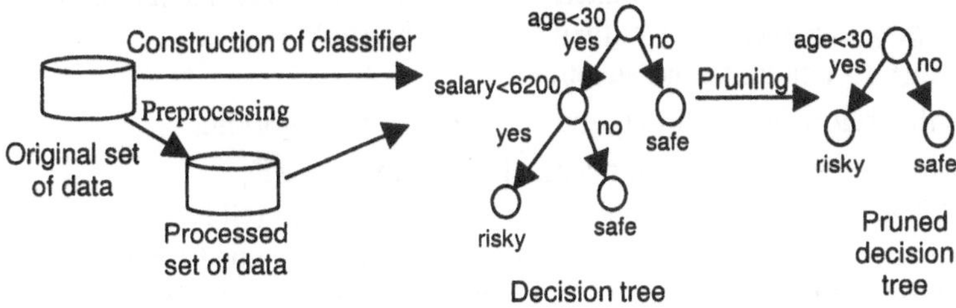

Fig. 1. Operations flow in the **DTB&V** system

Data preprocessing

DTB&V manages five types of attributes: INTEGER (32-bits number), SMALLINT (16-bits number), DOUBLE (real number), STRING, DATE. The first three types attributes can be discrete or continuous ones. For preprocessing we must define operation for each attribute, possible operations are presented in Table 1 and Table 2.

Table 1. Operations for continuous attributes

Operation	Description
Discretization	Exchange continuous attributes into discrete ones. Domain of attribute is divided into a number of ranges, each value is replaced by number of its range.
Coding	Values of attribute are sorted, each value is replaced by its position in the list

Table 2. Operations for discrete attributes

Operation	Description
Coding	Analogously to continuous attribute. For text attributes the lexicographic ordering is used, for date – chronological ordering.
Copying	Values of attribute are without changes.
Multiplication Division Addition Subtraction	Value of attribute is modified according to given number – operations are allowed only for numerical attributes.

Construction of classifier

DTB&V builds classifier as a decision tree. Algorithm is developed on the basis of SLIQ (Mehta et all 1996) and SPRINT (Shafer et all 1996). Our improvements of these approaches make algorithm more scalable, taking into account a size of database and a number of attributes. Pseudocode of proposed algorithm is presented in Fig. 2. In pseudocode we use following concepts:

- **temporary leaf** – a leaf that can become a node,
- **permanent leaf** – a leaf that cannot became a node,

- **IsPure(L)** – Boolean function, it returns TRUE when all records belonging to a node are from the same class,
- **IsSmall(L,L_{thr})** – Boolean function, it returns TRUE when a number of records belonging to a node is lower than assumed threshold L_{thr},
- **Depth(L)** – depth of generated tree.

One of the following conditions ends the work of the algorithm:

- Generated tree has assumed maximal admissible deep D_{max}
- Each leaf contains records belonging to the same class (all leaves are pure),
- A number of records in each leaf do not exceed assumed threshold T_{thr} (this value is assumed as percentage of number of records in a learning set).

```
Function Build_Tree(DataSet D): return Decision_Tree
Initialize tree T, all data records belong to its root;
while temporary leaves are in T and Depth T<MaxDepth do
for each attribute a do Make histogram H(a);
 for each temporary leaf L do
  for each value of attribute a a(i) do Compute
GINI(L,a(i));
  end for
 end for
end for
for each temporary leaf L do
   Find GINI with the smallest value for leaf L;
   Create temporary leaves - offsprings of L;
end for
for each temporary leaf L do
  if IsPure(L) or IsSmall(L,Lthr) then Mark L as permanent
  end if
end for
end while;
return T;
end function
```

Fig. 2. Pseudocode of algorithm of generation decision tree

Selection of suitable decision attribute for the node and values leaded to its offsprings is very significant issue in decision tree generation. In proposed algorithm we have used the GINI index (Mehta et all 1996). GINI shows how considered temporary leaf ought to be divided. Histograms containing information about class distribution in the data set are useful during computation the GINI index for each leaf. This method produces trees with similar accuracy as ID3 algorithm, but its complexity of computation is lower.

Pruning

Algorithm of pruning uses the Minimum Description Length (MDL) strategy and it is borrowed from (Mehta et all 1995, Wallace, Patrick 1993)). It assumes that the best model describing the data set minimizes a sum of costs of description the data. The method takes into account such variables as: a number of internal nodes, a number of leaves and proportion of internal nodes to the global number of nodes. Full description of the algorithm is presented in (Doczekalski 2001).

Visualization of decision tree

Visualization of decision tree is not trivial task – a size of tree is different for different sets of data therefore the coordinates of nodes and inscriptions must be automatically calculated. Calculation of coordinates of all nodes and leaves is the first step of the visualization procedure – it is done only if the tree has been modified (pruned). The second step is normalization of coordinates – whole tree is shifted in such way that all nodes and leaves must have positive values of coordinates. The algorithm and an example of visualization are presented in (Doczekalski 2001).

Experimental study of the DTB&V system

Developed system has been tested using a number of data sets commonly used by researches for evaluation of learning methods – benchmark sets. During experiments we take into account: accuracy of classification (original and pruned trees), scalability of algorithm (considering a number of records and attributes), influence of data preprocessing on the time of generation of decision tree.

STATLOG is often used as tests for classifiers. It consists of eight data sets presented in Table 3. Databases *Letter*, *Satimage* and *Shuttle* are originally divided into learning and testing sets, the other bases are randomly divided in relation 9:1.

Database TCPIP contains preprocessed (Stolfo et all 1999) data describing links with internet server. Original data have been collected during seven weeks – binary written package TCP/IP. Each connection has been classified as *normal* or one of 23 different attacks (24 classes). Final set consists of 4898430 records, 31 attributes. Testing set consists of 311029 records, it has different classes distribution than learning set, and contains attacks that are absent in the learning set. Such attacks cannot be properly classified by produced decision tree, therefore the authors (Stolfo et all 1999) have introduced hierarchy of classes. Response of classifier is recognized as correct if the returned class is in the same group as ex-

Table 3. Characteristic of data sets in STALOG benchmark

Data set	Domain	A number of attributes	A number of classes	A number of records (examples)
Australian	Credits analysis	14	2	690
Diabets	Medical diagnosis	8	2	768
DNA	Finding DNA sequences	180	3	3186
Letter	Hand writing recognition	16	26	15000+5000
Satimage	Satellite photo of arable land	36	6	4435+2000
Segment	Segmentation of screen images	19	7	2310
Shuttle	Radioactivity of space shuttle	9	7	43500+14500
Vehicle	Identification of vehicle	18	4	846

pected. There are 24 group of classes: normal connection (one class) and 23 sort of attacks, each contains one class from the learning set and 17 classes from a testing set. Distribution of classes in this database is very irregular. To test scalability of the proposed algorithm an artificial database has been created. Agraval and others (1992) have proposed a schema of database. All nine attributes (continuous and discrete) are generated randomly, only the last one – *output* is calculated using given function. The function is selected from five, defined by the authors. Obtained database is randomly disturbed. During study of scalability, the new attributes are added to the database (Mehta et all 1996). All tests have been made using Compaq Deskpro computer, Pentium III 667 MHz, 128 MB RAM, under Windows NT 4.0 Workstation with Service Pack 6. As a server of database we have used Interbase v. 6.0.1.

Experimental study of classification accuracy using STATLOG benchmark

DTB&V has been used to generate decision tree for all data sets from STATLOG base and accuracy of obtained classifiers has been analyzed. Obtained results – time of construction the tree, a size of obtained tree and accuracy of classification on the testing set are presented in Table 4. A size of tree is represented by three numbers: a number of nodes, a number of leaves, and a depth of tree. A time consumed for construction of decision tree depends almost linear on the number of access to the database. Testing phase consumes less than one second.

Table 4. Constructed tree by the **DTB&V** (time and obtained tree) using STALOG

Data set	Time [sec]	A size of tree	Accuracy (testing)
Australian	<1	155; 78; 12	81,16
Diabets	1	229; 115; 16	63,16
DNA	13	259; 130; 15	90,05
Letter	31	3697; 1849; 32	86,98
Satimage	13	765; 383; 22	85,30
Segment	4	133; 67; 17	96,97
Shuttle	18	63; 32; 10	99,98
Vehicle	1	251; 126; 16	66,67

Experimental study of pruning effect

All developed decision trees have been pruned, their accuracy is shown in Table 5.

Table 5. Accuracy of pruned tree on the original set of data

Data set	Accuracy for learning set	A size of tree	Accuracy for testing set
Australian	95,01	61; 31; 9	85,51
Diabets	91,62	89; 45; 11	64,47
DNA	98,05	155; 78; 14	91,82
Letter	93,68	1675; 838; 27	85,82
Satimage	95,78	327; 164; 17	86,60
Segment	98,56	75; 38; 14	95,67
Shuttle	99,96	41; 21; 10	99,92
Vehicle	92,13	121; 61; 14	73,81

Comparison of accuracy of original and pruned trees is shown in Fig.3. Pruning usually improves accuracy of classification. For 6 testing sets pruning decreases a number of nodes in decision tree up to 50%. A depth of tree decreases, in average, about 20%. Pruning is an efficient mechanism improving quality of generated trees. It does not prolong the processing time.

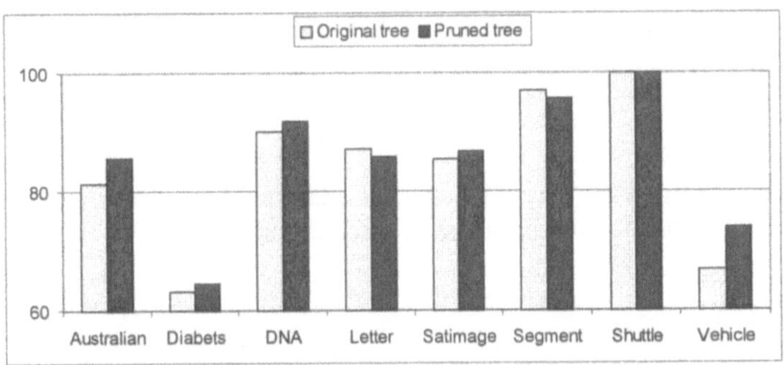

Fig. 3. Accuracy of developed tree and pruned tree

The **DTB&V** algorithm has been compared with others known techniques, SLIQ (Mehta et all 1996), IND-C4 and IND-CART (NASA 1992). The results are presented in Table 6 and Fig.4. **DTB&V** gives better result than SLIQ, both use GINI index, therefore pruning mechanism in **DTB&V** must be better. **DTB&V** gives good results, only for database Diabets the results are meaningful worse.

Table 6. The accuracy of classifiers

Data set	SLIQ	IND-C4	IND-Cart	DTB&V
Australian	84,9	84,4	85,3	**85,51**
Diabets	**75,4**	70,1	74,6	64,47
DNA	92,1	**92,5**	92,2	91,82
Letter	84,6	**86,8**	84,7	85,82
Satimage	86,3	85,2	85,3	**86,60**
Segment	94,6	**95,9**	94,9	95,67
Shuttle	99,9	99,9	99,9	**99,92**
Vehicle	70,3	71,1	68,8	**73,81**

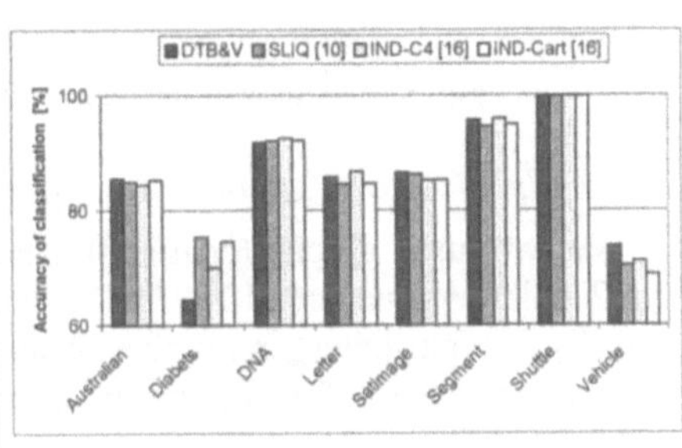

Fig. 4. Accuracy of different classifiers

A role of preprocessing – experimental study

All continuous attributes are discretized. DNA set does not contain continous values, therefore is not used in the experiments. Domain of each continuous attribute has been divided on the *r* ranges, *r*=Round(*number of different values of the attribute* /3+0,5) but no less than 40. The results are presented in Table 7 – raw tree, and Table 8 – pruned tree. Discretization in same cases does not improve classification, but deteriorates (see Fig. 5). It is caused probably by a loss of information carried by data (in *Letter* all attributes have 16 different values, therefore any information has been lost by discretizasion process). It is caused probably by a loss

Table 7. Constructed tree by the **DTB&V** with data preprocessing

Data set	Time [sec]	A size of tree	Accuracy (testing)
Australian	<1	181; 91; 14	78,26
Diabets	1	229; 115; 16	72,36
Letter	36	3697;1849;32	86,98
Satimage	11	765; 383; 22	84,25
Segment	3	133; 67; 17	97,84
Shuttle	31	63; 32; 10	98,92
Vehicle	1	251; 126; 16	76,19

Table 8. Constructed tree by the **DTB&V** with data preprocessing and pruning

Data set	Accuracy (learning)	A size of tree	Accuracy (testing)
Australian	93,39	57; 29; 10	82,61
Diabets	91,18	97; 49; 12	68,42
Letter	93,68	1675;838; 27	85,82
Satimage	95,58	343; 172; 18	85,05
Segment	98,61	81; 41; 15	96,96
Shuttle	98,95	73; 37; 13	98,90
Vehicle	91,60	125; 63; 16	78,57

of information carried by data (in *Letter* all attributes have 16 different values, therefore any information has been lost by discretizasion process).

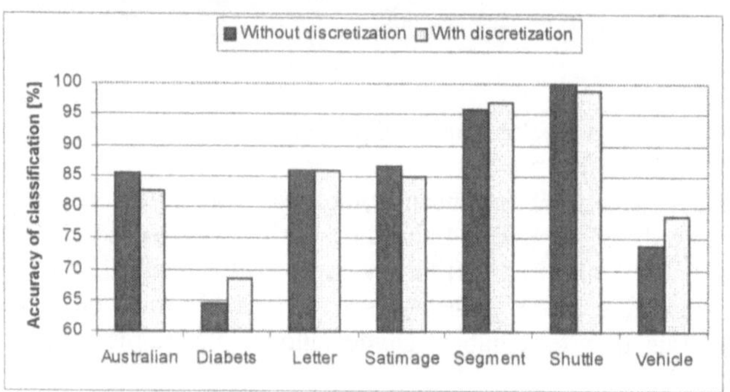

Fig. 5. Accuracy of the tree – without and with discretization

Scalability of DTB&V algorithm – experimental study

We have used special (artificial) databases and two different functions – number 2 and 5 (Agraval et all 1992). Databases contain 10^3 to 10^6 records (continuous and discrete attributes), a number of attributes varies from 9 to 400. **DTB&V** is quite good scalable for data generated using Function 2, but for Function 5 it is rather poor device: it cannot work with 250000 records – virtual memory turned out to be too small. For data set generated with Function 2, **DTB&V** generates small trees (depth is equal to 7 or 8, see Table 9). For discretized data the **DTB&V** produces small trees. Scalability of the algorithm in relation to number of attributes is satisfactory.

Building of classifiers on the base of TCPIP – simulation study of the DTB&V

TCPIP is difficult database for classification task. We assume that virtual memory is 500 MB. Our interest is: dependency of time of building and accuracy of generated tree in relation of assumed maximal depth. The results are collected in Table 11 and Table 12 (for pruned trees). System has been tested using traditional set of data and modified set – attacks are collected into groups.

Table 9. Results obtained using the **DTB&V** and artificial databases (in relation to number of records)

A number of records	Function 2	
	Time [sec]	A size of tree
10000	21	661;331; 26
25000	32	257;129; 20
50000	43	147; 74; 13
100000	44	29; 15; 7
250000	117	25; 13; 8
500000	250	23; 12; 7
1000000	858	28; 15; 8
	Function 5	
10000	10	243;122; 13
25000	33	437;219; 13
50000	260	699;350; 15
100000	1897	1101;551;16
≥250000	lack of memory	

Table 10. Results obtained using the **DTB&V** and artificial databases (in relation to number of attributes)

A number of attributes	Function 2	
	Time [sec]	A size of tree
9	14	41; 21; 9
20	15	23; 12; 7
50	148	901; 451; 18
100	47	25; 13; 7
200	113	25; 13; 8
400	901	1103; 12; 7
	Function 5	
9	35	409;205; 14
20	43	435;218; 14
50	61	407;204; 13
100	106	469;235; 14
200	197	403;202; 13
400	514	411;206; 13

Tree with 25 nodes and depth equal to 5 is good enough, its accuracy is about 92%. **DTB&V** needs no longer than one hour to generate such tree. Accuracy of classification is almost independent on a depth of tree (Table 11). Pruned trees are smaller, and a little bit better than original ones (Table 12). A number of accesses to the data strongly influence the time of tree construction and the time of classification (about 95% of all time).

Table 11. Results given by **DTB&V** using the TCPIP database

Max. depth	Time [sec]	Size of tree	Accuracy	Testing time [sec]	Accuracy on testing set	Accuracy on grouped set
5	3858	25;13;5	99,71	32	91,33	91,13
10	7787	213;107;10	99,92	32	91,89	92,54
20	14989	493;247;20	99,99	32	91,81	92,78
none	25326	735;368;32	99,99	32	92,07	93,76

Table 12. Results given by pruned trees – the TCPIP database

Max. depth	Size of tree	Accuracy (pruned)	Accuracy (test set)	Accuracy on grouped set	Max. depth	Size of tree	Accuracy (pruned)	Accuracy (test set)	Accuracy on grouped set
5	25;13;5	99,71	91,33	92,12	20	293;147;20	99,99	91,83	92,80
10	151;76;10	99,92	91,91	92,57	none	417;209;29	99,99	92,08	93,79

Interesting result are obtained when all abnormal connection are grouped. The accuracy of classification is not higher but classifiers distinguish *normal* connections from the attacks neglecting a kind of attack.

Summary

On the basis of all experiments we can say that proposed algorithm produces classifiers that give similar accuracy to the C4.5 and CART, but it is quicker due to used techniques of building the tree – *breadth-first*. Time of tree construction linearly depends on the number of access to the data, and access to the data consumes about 95% of all processing time, therefore algorithms that use strategy *depth-first* are not useful for large databases. Also scalability of proposed algorithm seems to be satisfactory. Very good effect give pruning – pruned trees are smaller and accuracy their classifications are usually a little bit better.

The **DTB&V** is not scalable regarded to continuous values of attributes. Discretization is the only solution of this situation. Inefficiency for continuous attributes is the weakest side of proposed algorithm. Future work ought to be focused on improvement of these deficiences.

Recently, large database servers often are multiprocessor computers. Therefore the possible development of the algorithm is its parallelisation.

References

Agraval R., Ghosh S., Imielinski T., Iyer B., Swami A., "An Interval Classifier for Database Mining Applications", *VLDB 92*, Vancouver, 1992, 560-573.

Agrawal R., Srikant R., "Fast algorithms for mining association rules in large databases", in *VLDB '94*, 1994.

Database TCPIP – http://kdd.ics.uci.edu/databases/kddcup99.

Databases STATLOG – http://www.ics.uci.edu/~mlearn/MLRepository.html.

Doczekalski M., "Techniki pozyskiwania wiedzy z baz danych" (Data Mining Techniques), Master Thesis, Department of Computer Science, Wrocław, 2001.

Fayyad U.M., Piatetetsky-Shapiro G., Smyth P., Uthurusamy R., "Advances in Knowledge Discovery and Data Mining", Cambridge MA, 1996.

Holsheimer M., Siebes A, "Data Mining. The Search for Knowledge in Databases", 1996.

IBM's Data Mining Technology, White Paper, 1996.

Mehta M., Agrawal R., Risanen J., "SLIQ: A fast scalable classifier for data mining", In *Proc. of the Fifth International Conference on Extending Database Technology*, Avignon, 1996.

Mehta M., Rissanen J., Agrawal R., "MDL-based decision tree pruning", in *International Conference on Knowledge Discovery in Databases and Data Mining*, Montreal, 1995.

Piatetsky-Shapiro G., Frawley W., "Knowledge Discovery from Databases", Cambridge, 1991.

Quinlan J. R., "Induction of decision trees", in *Machine Learning*, 1986.

Shafer J. C., Agrawal R., Mehta M., "SPRINT: A scalable parallel classifier for data mining", *Proc. of International Conference on Very Large Databases*, Bombay, 1996.

Srikant R., Agrawal R., "Mining Generalized Association Rules", w *Proceedings of the* 21st *International Conference on Very Large Databases*, September 1995.

Stolfo J. S., Fan W., Lee W., Prodromidis A., Chan P. K., "Cost-based Modeling and Evaluation for Data Mining With Application to Fraud and Intrusion Detection: Results from the JAM Project", 1999.

Wallace C., Patrick J., "Coding decision trees", in *Machine Learning*, 1993.

Modeling User Behavior by Integrating AQ Learning with a Database: Initial Results

Guido Cervone and Ryszard S. Michalski*

Machine Learning and Inference Laboratory
School Computational Sciences
George Mason University
Fairfax, VA, 22030
{gcervone, michalski}@gmu.edu

*Also with the Institute of Computer Science, Polish Academy of Sciences, Warsaw, Poland

Abstract: The paper describes recent results from developing and testing LUS methodology for user modeling. LUS employs AQ learning for automatically creating user models from datasets representing activities of computer users. The datasets are stored in a relational database and employed in the learning process through an SQL-style command that automatically executes the AQ20 rule learning program and generates user models. The models are in the form of *attributional rulesets* that are more expressive than conventional decision rules, and are easy to interpret and understand. Early experimental results from the testing of the LUS method gave highly encouraging results.

Keywords: User modeling, Computer intrusion detection, Machine learning, AQ learning, Inductive databases

1 Introduction

The rapidly growing global connectivity of computer systems creates a great need for effective methods that are able to detect unauthorized use of computers. Standard methods for assuring computer security, such as passwords, gateways, and firewalls not always provide sufficient protection from unauthorized accesses. Intruders typically exploit holes in the operating system or crack password files to gain access to the computer system and masquerade as legitimate users. As a result, detection of a sophisticated intruder is increasingly difficult, especially when there are many computer users or the intruder is an insider.

The approach discussed in this paper, called *Learning User Style* (*LUS*), applies symbolic learning, specifically AQ learning, to induce typical patterns of interactions between individual users and computers. Given records measuring various characteristics of the interaction between users and computers (in our project process LUS automatically creates models of user behavior (*symbolic user signatures*) by employing a machine learning program. The user models are in the form of rulesets relating the measured characteristics to the individual users.

The rulesets are expressed in *attributional calculus*, a highly expressive, logic-style language that can concisely represent complex relationships (Michalski, 2001). In the experiments described here, the rules are created by AQ20 learning program, which is the most recent implementation of AQ-type inductive learning. An important characteristic of AQ learning is that the generated rulesets (user signatures) are easy to interpret and understand. This means that they can be inspected and verified by experts, and hand-modified or extended, if desired.

To develop effective user models, large training and testing datasets may be needed for each user. If there are many users, the datasets to be handled may become massive. This creates an issue of how to handle such massive sets effectively both for user model creation and model testing. To address this problem, the learning system was integrated with a relational database and invoked through a *create* command of KQL, a knowledge generation language under development.

3 Basic Concepts and Terminology

To explain this research, we need to introduce some terminology. An *event* is a description of an entity or situation under consideration. In the context of user modeling, an event is vector of attribute-values that characterizes the use of computer by a user at a specific time or during a specific time period.

A *session* is a sequence of events characterizing a user's interaction with the computer from the login to the logoff. An *episode* is a sequence of events extracted from a session; it may contain just a few events, or all of the events in a session. In the training phase, it is generally desirable to use long episodes, or even whole sessions, as this helps to generate better user models. In the testing (or execution) phase, it is desirable to use short episodes, so that a user can be identified from as little information as possible.

The report by Goldring et al. (2000) indicated that one of the most relevant characteristics of the user behavior is the *mode* attribute. Therefore, in initial experiments, we have concentrated on the user model employing sequences of values of this attribute determined from the process table. Specifically, events were *n*-grams of the mode attribute, that is, sequences of *n* consecutive values of the mode attribute extracted from the data stream. The behavior of a user was characterized by a set of consecutive, overlapping *n*-grams (events) spanning a given period of user interaction with the computer.

The sequence of modes recorded in a session was transformed into a set of overlapping *n*-grams (events), each representing a sequence of *n* consecutive modes in the session's log. A set of events selected from one or more sessions of a specific user was used as a training set for learning this user's signature. In addition to a training set, a different set of testing events was created for each user for the purpose of testing the learned model. Both training and testing sets were stored in a relational database connected to ORACLE DB through Squirrel SQL client (see Section 6).

Training sets for each user were submitted to an AQ-type symbolic learning program, AQ20, described briefly in the next section. The program generated user profiles (symbolic user signatures) in the form of *attributional rulesets*—sets of attributional rules characterizing the behavior of one user.

4 The AQ20 Learning System

In this project, we used learning system AQ20, which is the latest implementation of the AQ learning methodology. Among AQ20 features that are most important for user modeling are:

1) generation of attributional rules that are more expressive than conventional ones, and this produces more compact models

2) ability to cope with noisy data

3) ability to work with continuous data without needing discretization. (This feature has been added specifically for this project)

4) ability to learn hypotheses according to a multi-criterion optimization function

5) scalable implementation that can work efficiently with large numbers of training examples (e.g., in this project AQ20 learned from several million examples).

A discussion of an initial (incomplete) AQ20 implementation, and the results from early experiments can be found in (Cervone, Panait, and Michalski, 2001).

5 The "Create ruleset" Command

In order to seamlessly integrate inductive learning and data mining capabilities with a database, a new language is being developed, called KQL (Knowledge Query Language), which includes SQL as a subset. A major command of KQL is *Create Ruleset* that calls a learning program to create rules from a dataset selected from the database. The general form of this command is:

Create Ruleset <Output-tableset> *from* <Input-tableset> *for* <Consequent> *Using* <Parameter-table>

where

<Output-table> is a relational table that will contain the ruleset to be learned. Individual rules in the ruleset are in the form:

> Consequent <= Premise, where PREMISE is a conjunction of conditions involving one or more attributes (such conditions are called *attributional conditions* (Michalski, 2001))

<Input-table> is a relational table that stores training examples

<Consequent> may specify just one value of the output attribute, in which case it is in the form of a simple condition [output-attribute=v], or all values of the output attribute, in which it is in the form [output-attribute=*], or, simply, output-attribute. In more general form, Consequent can be a product of *attributional conditions*.

<Parameter-table> specifies all control parameters of the learning program (in this case, AQ20).

In this project, the *ruleset create* command has been implemented so far in a somewhat more specialized form. It uses Squirrel/KQL (CREATE RULES, FROM, FOR and USING are terminators).

CREATE RULES [MULTIHEAD] RuleSetFamily FROM <DATA_TABLE>
FOR <TARGET-CONCEPT> USING <PARAM_SPEC>

<DATA_TABLE> : data_table

<TARGET> : Attributional_Complex {[x=1,4,6] & [y > 6]}

| Annotted_Attibute_list

| All_attributes [Except Attribute_list]

| Target_table

Annotated_Attribute_List : Annotated_Attribute_list Annotated_Attribute

| Annotated_attribute

Annotated_Attribute : Attribute [For <attribute_values>]

<PARAMETER_SPEC> : Table of parameters and values

| ID for parameter relational table

IN here Char or Discr mode would be defined

6 Squirrel SQL Client

In this research we employed Squirrel, a complete SQL client. Squirrel is a graphical Java program that allows one to view the structure of a JDBC database (Java Database Connection), browse the data stored in relational tables, issue SQL commands, etc. The distribution of Squirrel is handled by the sourceforge network (www.sourceforge.com). The home page for the Squirrel SQL client is at www.sourceforge.net/projects/squirrel-sql/. The modifications that we have done to the Squirrel code involved a modification of the Squirrel GUI and handling of SQL queries. An option was also added to the Squirrel that allows one to import raw data in form of comma separated format (CSV). Squirrel does not come with such an option, as it was designed primarily to browse and issue SQL commands rather than import data.

The Create-ruleset command was deeply integrated with the Squirrel program. A new Java class (KQL-adapter) was created that first checks if the query is a "create ruleset" command. If it is not, the control is passed back to Squirrel, which checks if the query is a valid SQL command. If it is, KQL-adapter creates SQL queries that retrieve target data and parameters from the database, store them in the AQ20 input file, and then runs AQ20 to generate rulesets. The resulting rules are displayed on the screen in text format.

In this project we used Oracle 8.1.7 working under the Irix operating system. The modified by us Squirrel client can be used, however, with any database for which a JDBC connection is supported, such as MySQL, mSQL, PostgreSQL, and others.

7. Datasets used in experiments

Datasets used in this experiment included information about 777 user sessions, collected from a Window operating system's process table, and characterized activities of 23 different users. The data were obtained from Dr. Thomas Goldring. Prior work done by Goldring et al. (2000) evaluated several existing methods for user modeling and indicated that an important attribute for user modeling is *mode* that characterizes the type of activity a user is engaged in at a given time, such as reading email, word processing, etc. Therefore, in our studies we also employed the *mode* attribute.

To be able to apply a learning program to a sequential data stream, the data were transformed to collections of n-grams. Given a sequence of items, an n-gram is constructed using a sliding window of size n. In our experiments we chose n=4, based on findings by Goldring et al. (2000).

The raw data were transferred into 4,808,024 4-grams characterizing 24 users, labeled from User0 to User23. A different number of sessions were extracted for each user, and each session had different length, which led to different numbers of n-grams for each users (Figure 1 and 2). Another characteristic feature of this data was that the number of distinct events (n-grams, in this case) was significantly different from the number of total events. This means is that there were many repetitions of the same n-grams in the data streams from different users.

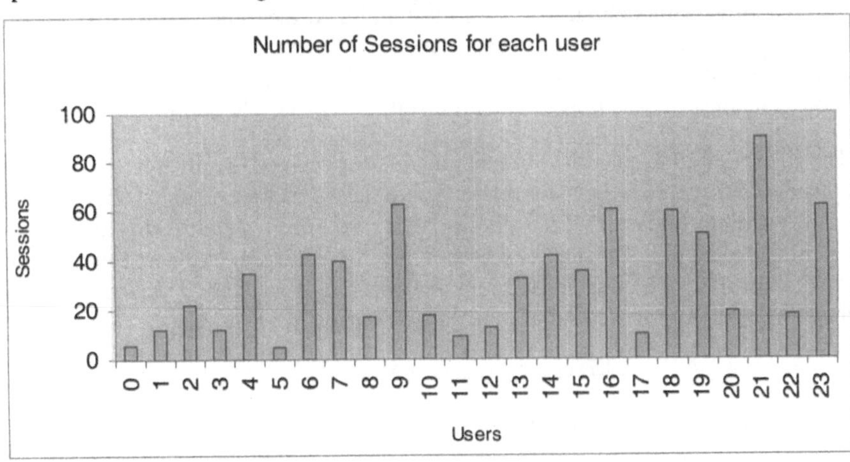

Figure 1: Number of sessions per user in the Windows dataset

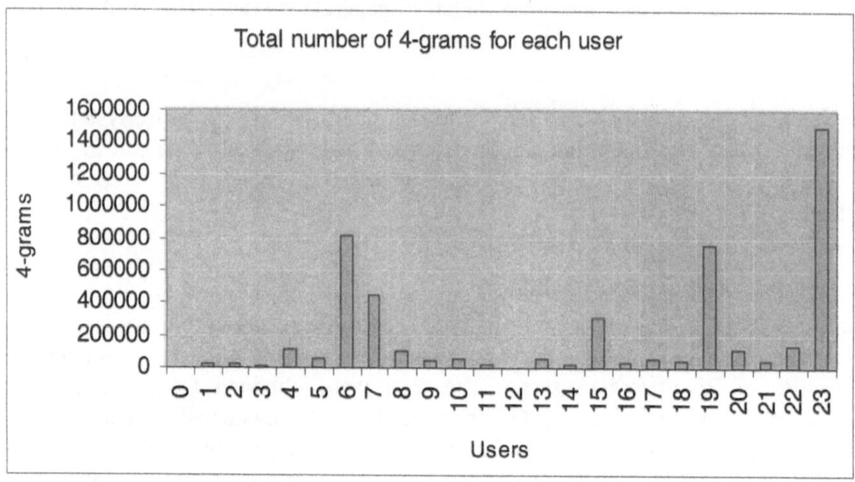

Figure 2: The number of different 4-grams per user in the dataset.

8 Creating user models and matching them against testing episodes

The original datasets were split into training and testing sets. The training set was subsequently split to different portions in order to determine the learning curve. Given a training set for each user, the AQ20 learning system learned rules models from them. These rules were subsequently tested on the testing set. The next section describes one of the experiments and obtained results.

Testing of rulesets typically involves matching single events against the learned rules. Attributional rules created by an AQ-type learning program are matched to events by the ATEST program (Reinke, 1984; Michalski and Kaufman, 2000). In the case of user modeling, to obtain meaningful results, one needs to match user models against a sequence of events (episode). To this end, a special method was developed that matches episodes with attributional rulesets and determines a score. The method was implemented in EPICn (Episode Classifier for n-grams).

The EPICn module calls the ATEST module for each of the distinct events in the episode, and for each decision class determines a degree of match between the corresponding ruleset R_i. and the episode. For each rule $R_{i,j}$ in ruleset i, it calculates a degree of match, c_{ijk}, between event k and rule R_{ij}, using the selected ATEST method. The degree of match between an event k and a ruleset R_i, called an *event score for class i and event k*, and denoted $\boldsymbol{EV}_{ik}$, is defined:

$$\boldsymbol{EV}_{ik} = \text{Max}_{j=1\ldots s(i)} (c_{ijk} \times t_{ij}) \quad (1)$$

where t_{ij} is the number of training examples satisfying R_{ij}.

The degree of match between an episode and the ruleset R_i, called the *episode score for class i* and denoted EP_i, is defined:

$$EP_i = \sum_{k=1}^{z} EV_{ik} \qquad (2)$$

EPICn classifies the episode to the class with the highest episode score, if the episode score is above the *score acceptance threshold* (SATH), and the difference between the highest and the next highest episode scores is greater than the *score acceptance tolerance (SATO).* The score acceptance threshold and score acceptance tolerance allow the program to avoid making definite decisions when the episode score or the difference between the highest and the next highest episode scores are too small. In such cases, the program classifies an episode as "unknown." Up to this point, EPICn has run only with the acceptance threshold and the acceptance tolerance of 0, so that no classifications have been assigned "unknown." Since EPICn calls upon ATEST, both EPICn and ATEST have been integrated within the same program, which leads to a faster execution of the testing process.

EPICn normalizes the scores defined in (2) so that for each episode, the sum total of degrees of match is 1. The definition of the episode score as stated in (2), is one of many possible such definitions.

9 Experiment 1 (7 users):

The AQ20 allows the user to tune the learning process to the problem at hand by specifying program control parameters (Michalski and Kaufman, 2000). In the experiment described below, the control parameters were:

ambiguity = empty
mode = Theory Formation and Pattern Discovery
maxstar = 1 & maxrule = 1
LEF = (MinNumSelectors, 0.3) (MaxNewPositives, 0.1)
LEF1 = (MaxQ)(MaxNewPositives, 0.0) (MinNumSelectors, 0.0)
LEF2 = (MaxTotalQ)(MaxNewPositives, 0.0) (MinNumSelectors, 0.0)

Several experiments were performed using different combinations of parameters. In every results (characterized by predictive accuracy on the testing set) were very similar. This means that AQ20 was not very sensitive to the input parameters in this application.

For this experiment the dataset was divided into two parts, the first 80% (chronologically) of the sessions for training and the last 20% for testing.

User	Distinct +	Distinct -	Total +	Total -
0	345	5236	3573	616828
1	348	5214	20858	671154
2	784	4497	19477	570508
3	226	5253	9351	627480
4	3006	2012	92626	545656
5	142	5537	59524	647063
6	865	4413	506532	84895

Table 1: Distribution of total and distinct events.

Initially, we experimented on a smaller dataset, consisting of the data from users 0-6 only. Testing was done both on the first 50% of the testing set, and then on the full testing set based on rules generated from training sessions that used 4%, 33%, 66% and 100% of the total training data. Table 1 illustrates the large difference between distinct events and total events, and it explains why some of the rules that have rather high rule quality according to the Q(*w*) measure (Kaufman and Michalski, 1999) when this is computed using the total events appear to be quite poor when the Q is compared using distinct events.

To illustrate results obtained in this experiment, below are the first two rules from the set of 17 rules generated as a User 1 model (the rules are represented in the form of *generalized n-grams*, in which each position is occupied not by a single value but by a set):

```
# -- This learning task took: 11.92 seconds of system time
# -- Number of rules for User 1 = 17
# -- Number of the distinct events in the target class:           348
# -- Number of the distinct events in the other class(es):       5214
# -- Number of the total training events in the target class:  20858
# -- Number of the total training in the other class(es):      671154

[User = 1]
← <{netscape,msie,telnet,explorer,web,acrobat,logon,rundll32,system,welcome,help},
   {netscape,msie,telnet,explorer,web,acrobat,logon,welcome,help}
   {netscape,msie,telnet,explorer,web,acrobat,logon,printing,welcome,dos,help}
   {netscape,msie,telnet,explorer,web,acrobat,logon,rundll32,welcome,dos,help}>
   : pd=262,nd=58,ud=118,pt=20718,nt=140,ut=3197,qd=0.607308,qt=0.986414

← <{netscape,telnet,office,acrobat,rundll32,welcome,help}
   {netscape,msie,telnet,web,acrobat,logon,printing,rundll32,dos,help}
   {netscape,msie,telnet,explorer,logon,rundll32,help}
   {netscape,msie,telnet,network,acrobat,printing}>
   : pd=74,nd=6,ud=6,pt=16565,nt=17,ut=7,qd=0.195631,qt=0.79334
```

The rules were learned by AQ20 from all events in the training set, running in the PD mode using LEF1 rule selection criterion. The first rule states that User 1 behavior is characterized by a set of 4-grams, in which the first position is occupied by any mode from the first set {netscape, msie, telnet, ...}, the second position is occupied by any mode from the second set {netscape, msie, ..help}, etc. This rule thus describes compactly 11979 4-grams.

The lines marked by # provide supplementary information about the experiment. The first line gives information about the system (kernel) time spent on learning the user model (from 20858 training examples). The next line specifies the number of rules learned for User 1. Lines 3-6 specify numbers of different example types used in the experiment.
Each rule is accompanied by annotations that represent various characteristics of the rule. Parameters pd and pt represent the number of distinct positive examples and the total positive examples, respectively, that are covered by the rule. Similarly, nd and nt represent the number of distinct negative and the total negative examples, respectively, covered by the rule. Parameters qd and qt indicate the rule quality measure, which takes into consideration both the number of positives covered out of all positives, and the number of negatives covered out of all negatives in the dataset. The difference between qd and qt is that qd is computed over distinct positives and distinct negatives, whereas qt is computed over the total positives and total negatives.

Figure 2 describes the performance of user models on the testing data. The darkened column indicates the matching score for the correct user model. As figure shows, in every testing case the correct user model was indicated.

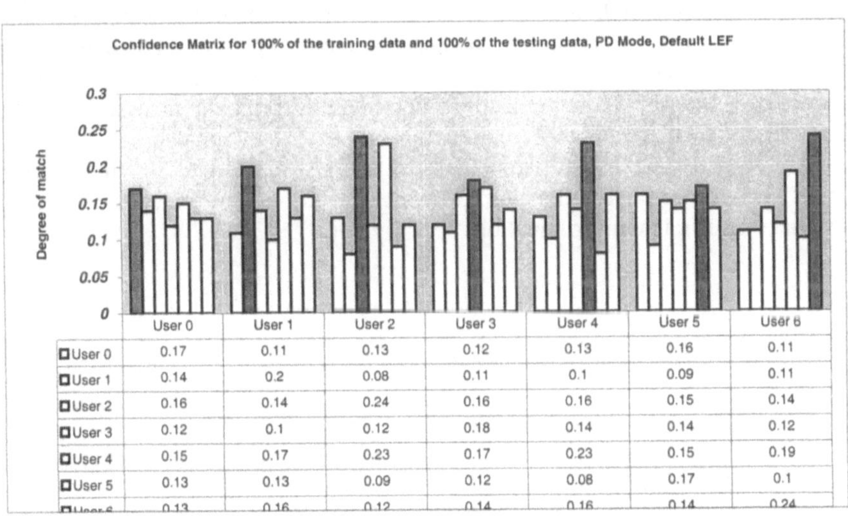

	User 0	User 1	User 2	User 3	User 4	User 5	User 6
User 0	0.17	0.11	0.13	0.12	0.13	0.16	0.11
User 1	0.14	0.2	0.08	0.11	0.1	0.09	0.11
User 2	0.16	0.14	0.24	0.16	0.16	0.15	0.14
User 3	0.12	0.1	0.12	0.18	0.14	0.14	0.12
User 4	0.15	0.17	0.23	0.17	0.23	0.15	0.19
User 5	0.13	0.13	0.09	0.12	0.08	0.17	0.1
User 6	0.13	0.16	0.12	0.14	0.16	0.14	0.24

Figure 3: Confidence matrix for rules learned from the complete training set.

In order to determine how sensitive is performance to the size of the training set, we have performed experiments in which the learning set was varied from 4%, 33%, 66% and 100% of the training data. The results are shown in Figure 3. As the figure shows, the perfomance was about .6 (60%) correct when the training set had only 4% of the events (random guessing is about 14% correct).

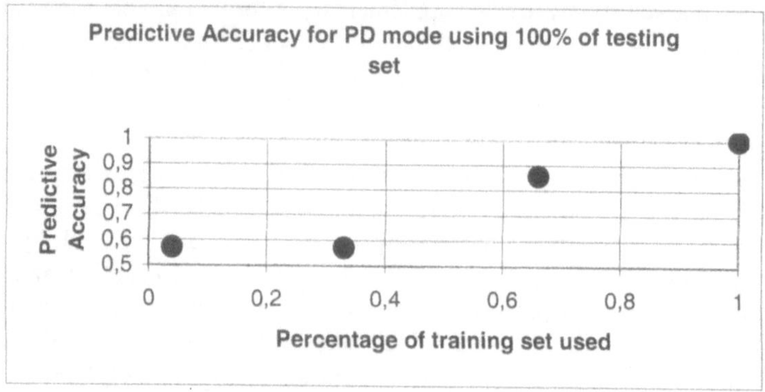

Figure 4: The learning curve for 7 users.

10 Experiment 2 (24 users)

The experiment involved learning user models for 24 users, using nearly 5 million training examples (the complete training set). Results were tested on approximately one million testing examples (the complete testing set). Results are illustrated in Figure 4. As before, darkened columns represent the matching score for the correct user model. As the figure shows, all users were classified correctly except one, User 11. This seems to be due to the fact that the dataset for user 11 had only a small number of sessions and a very small number of events per session (Figure 1 and 2). In some cases, e.g., for users 6 and 14, the matching score was the same for the correct models as for a few other models. This indicates insufficient discrimination.

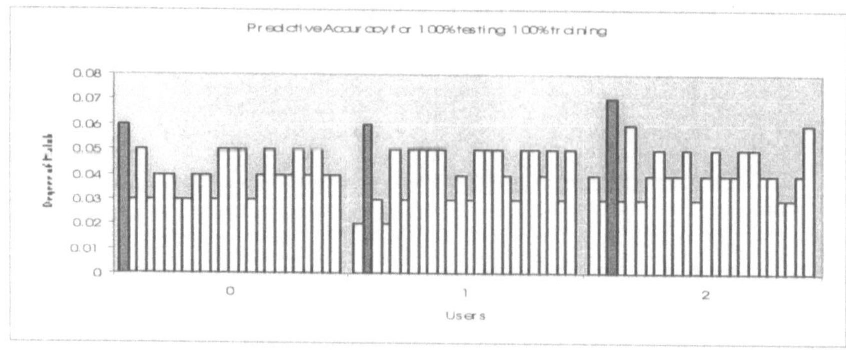

Figure 5: Results from testing 24 user models.

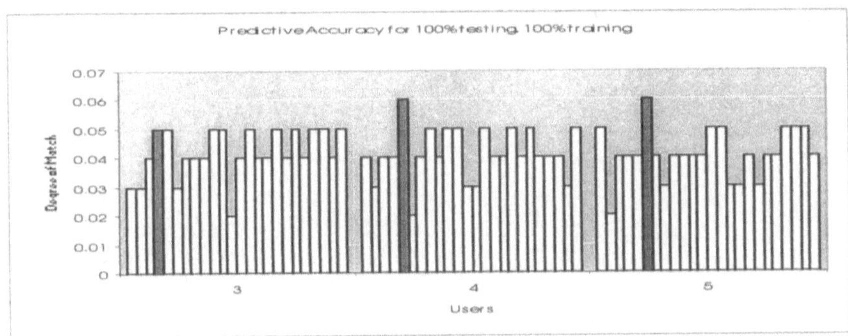

Figure 6: Results from testing 24 user models.

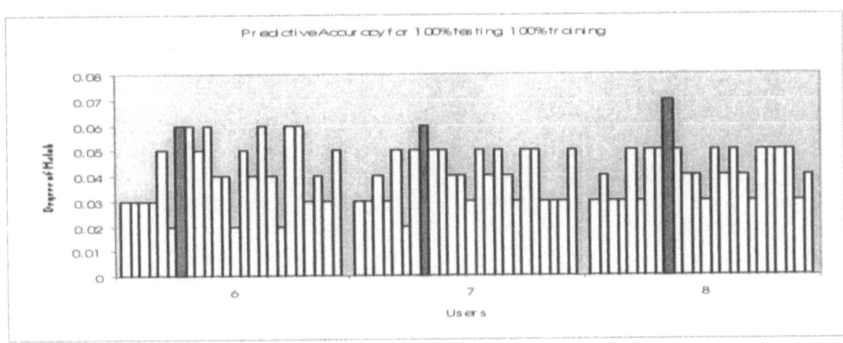

Figure 7: Results from testing 24 user models.

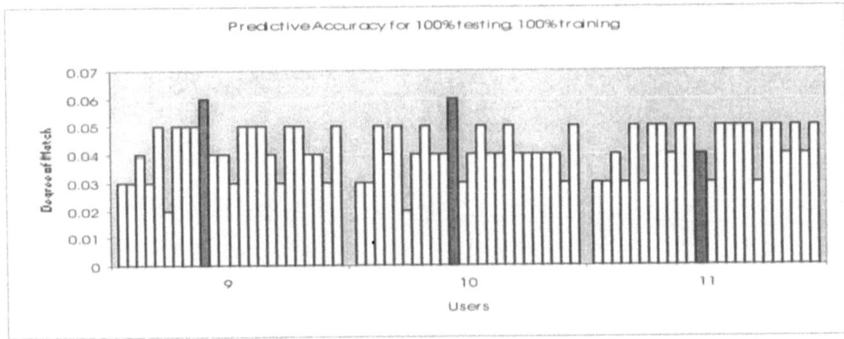

Figure 8: Results from testing 24 user models.

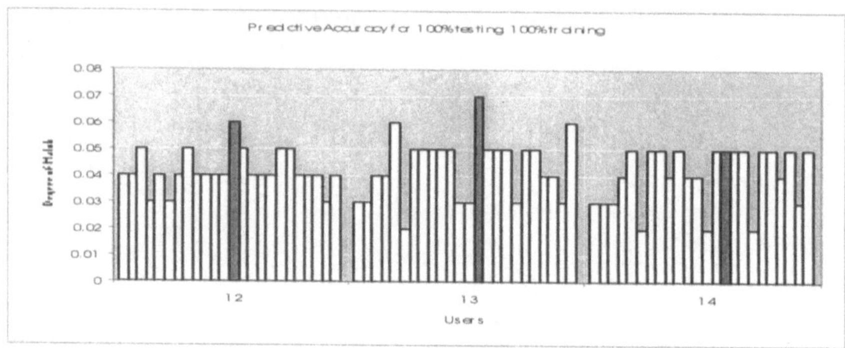

Figure 9: Results from testing 24 user models.

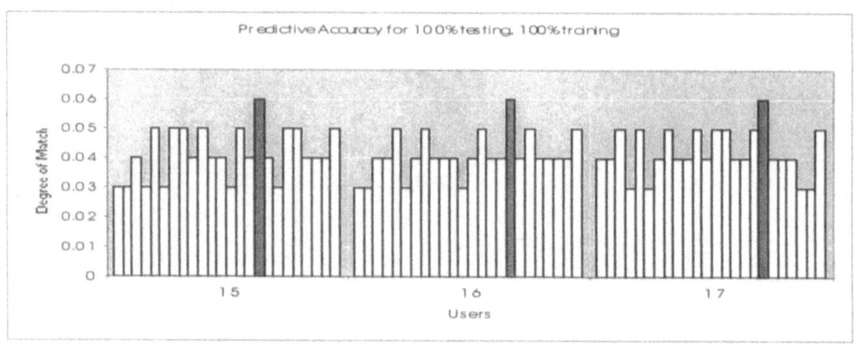

Figure 10: Results from testing 24 user models.

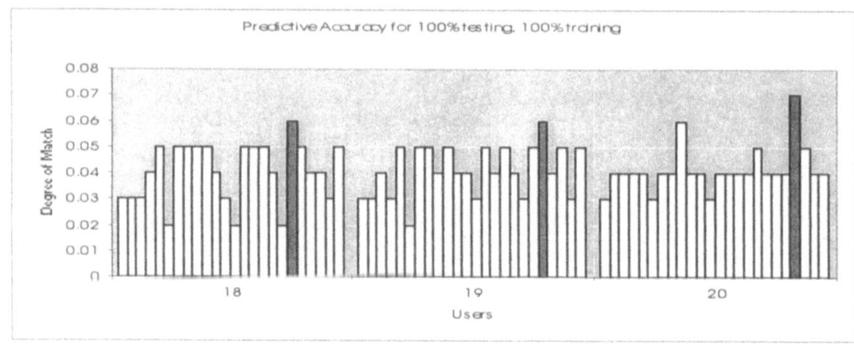

Figure 11: Results from testing 24 user models.

To illustrate the rules obtained in this experiment, below a selection of the rules learned for User 0. The learning time was larger in experiment 1, as expected, since have here 24 users rather than 7.

```
# -- This learning took:
# -- System time 767.15 sec
# -- Number of rules for this class = 52

# -- Number of distinct training events in the target class:     346
# -- Number of distinct training events in other classes:     71,931
# -- Total number of training events in the target class:      1,826
# -- Total number of training events in the other classes:3,750,169

[user=0]
    ← <{explorer,install,multimedia,system,time},
       {multimedia,system},
       {explorer,install,system},
       {explorer,install,multimedia,system},
       :pd=64,nd=31,ud=8,pt=916,nt=404,ut=11,qd=0.124322,qt=0.348035

    ← <{explorer,install,office,rundll32,system,time},
       {multimedia,system},
       {install,multimedia,rundll32,system,time},
       {explorer,install,rundll32,system,time}>
       :pd=68,nd=42,ud=9,pt=919,nt=73,ut=11,qd=0.121131,qt=0.466232

    ←
<{explorer,help,install,mail,multimedia,rundll32,system,time,web},
       {help,install,logon,mail,office,rundll32,system,time,web},
       {help,install,mail,office,printing,rundll32,system,time,web},
       {help,install,rundll32,system,time}

:pd=140,nd=343,ud=41,pt=1316,nt=701,ut=66,qd=0.1159,qt=0.470102

    ← <{install,office,printing,system},
       {install,rundll32,time},
       {install,multimedia,office,sql,system,web},
       {explorer,install,multimedia,rundll32,system,web}
       :pd=43,nd=4,ud=2,pt=397,nt=4,ut=2,qd=0.11,qt=0.21
```

10 Conclusion

The presented LUS method employs AQ20 learning program to learn user models from n-grams representing interactions between users and the computer. In view of the large datasets involved in this application, to make the learning and testing processes easier to handle, the learning systems was deeply integrated with a relational database, accessible through Squirrel, an SQL client. The obtained results for a small number of users (7) indicated perfect recognition rate. In the case of a larger number of users (24), there was one misclassification, which was likely due to a small number of training examples used.

Acknowledgments

Authors thank Dr. Goldring for providing datasets used in this study and for consultation on the n-gram approach to user modeling, and Dr. Kenneth A. Kaufman for his assistance and feedback in conducting this research. They also thank Dr. Menas Kafatos and Dr. Ruxin Yang for providing access to their mighty esip computer system that was used for storing datasets and running experiments.

Valuable help was also given by Colin Bell and all the members of the Squirrel development team. They helped solving many problems, and give valuable information on where to modify the code.

We also wish to thank the School of Computational Sciences for providing other computational equipment and logistic space that was used during the development of this project.

References

Bloedorn, E. and Michalski, R.S., "Data Driven Constructive Induction in AQ17-PRE: A Method and Experiments," *Proceedings of the Third International Conference on Tools for AI,* San Jose, CA, November 9-14, 1991.

Cervone G., Panait L. A., Michalski R.S., "The Development of the AQ20 Learning System and Initial Experiments," *Proceedings of the International Conference on Intelligent Systems (IIS 2000),* Poland, July 2001.

Michalski, R.S. and Kaufman, K., "Building Knowledge Scouts Using KGL Metalanguage," *Fundamenta Informaticae* 40, pp. 433-447, 2000a.

Kaufman, K.A. and Michalski, R.S., "An Adjustable Rule Learner for Pattern Discovery Using the AQ Methodology," *Journal of Intelligent Information Systems*, 14, pp. 199-216, 2000b.

Michalski, R.S, "A Theory and Methodology of Inductive Learning, in *Machine Learning: An Artificial Intelligence Approach*, Michalski, R.S, Carbonell, J.G. and Mitchell, T.M. (Eds.), Tioga Publishing Company, 1983, pp. 83-134.

Michalski, R.S., and Chilausky, R.L., "Learning By Being Told and Learning From Examples: An Experimental Comparison of the Two Methods of Knowledge Acquisition in the Context of Developing an Expert System for Soybean Disease Diagnosis," *Policy Analysis and Information Systems*, Vol. 4, No. 2, 1980.

Wnek, J. and Michalski, R.S., "Hypothesis-Driven Constructive Induction in AQ17: A Method and Experiments," *Reports of the Machine Learning and Inference Laboratory*, MLI 91-4, School of Information Technology and Engineering, George Mason University, Fairfax, VA, May 1991.

A Soft Decision Tree

Hung Son Nguyen

Institute of Mathematics,
Warsaw University,
Banacha 2, Warsaw 02095, Poland

Abstract. Searching for binary partition of attribute domains is an important task in Data Mining, particularly in decision tree methods. The most important advantage of decision tree methods are based on compactness and clearness of presented knowledge and high accuracy of classification. In case of large data tables, the existing decision tree induction methods often show to be inefficient in both computation and description aspects. The disadvantage of standard decision tree methods is also their instability, i.e., small deviation of data perhaps cause a total change of decision tree. We present the novel "soft discretization" methods using "soft cuts" instead of traditional "crisp" (or sharp) cuts. This new concept allows to generate more compact and stable decision trees with high classification accuracy. We also present an efficient method for soft cut generation from large data bases.

Key words: Data Mining, Rough set, Decision tree, Soft Discretization.

1 Introduction

The main step in methods of decision tree construction is to fine optimal partitions of the set of objects. The problem of searching for optimal partitions of real value attributes, defined by so called cuts, has been studied by many authors (see e.g. [1,2,10],[4]), where optimization criteria are defined by e.g. height of the obtained decision tree, the number of cuts or the classification accuracy of decision tree on new unseen objects. In general, all those problems are hard from computational point of view. Hence numerous heuristics have been investigated to develop approximate solutions of these problems. One of the major tasks of these heuristics is to define approximate measures estimating the quality of extracted cuts. In rough set and Boolean reasoning based methods, the quality is defined by the number of pairs of objects discerned by the partition.

One can mention some problems occurring in existing decision tree induction algorithms. The first is related to efficiency of searching for optimal partition of real value attributes assuming that the large data table is represented in relational data base. Using straightforward approach to the optimal partition selection (with respect to a given measure), the number of necessary queries is of order $O(N)$, where N is the number of pre-assumed partitions of the searching space. In such case, even the linear complexity is not acceptable because of the time needed for one step. The critical factor for time complexity of algorithms solving the discussed problem is the number of simple SQL queries like *SELECT COUNT FROM ... WHERE attribute BETWEEN ...* (related to some interval of attribute values) necessary to construct such partitions. Moreover, the existing (traditional) methods are using crisp conditions for object discerning. This can lead to misclassification of new objects which are, e.g., close to the separating boundary, and this fact can provide to low quality of new object classification.

The first problem is a big challenge for data mining researchers. Almost all existing methods are based on sampling technique, i.e., building a decision tree for small, randomly chosen subset of data, and then evaluate the quality of decision tree for whole data [3]. If the quality of generated decision tree is not sufficient enough, we have to repeat this step for new sample.

We propose a novel approach based on *soft cuts* which make possible to overcome the second problem. Decision trees using soft cuts as test functions are called *soft decision tree.* The new approach leads to new efficient strategies in searching for the best cuts (both soft and crisp cuts) using the whole data. We show some properties of considered optimization measures allowing to reduce the size of searching space. Moreover, we prove that using only $O(\log N)$ simple queries, one can construct the partition very close to optimal.

2 Basic notions

An *information system* [8] is a pair $\mathbb{A} = (U, A)$, where U is a non-empty, finite set called the *universe* and A is a non-empty finite set of *attributes*, i.e., $a : U \to V_a$ for $a \in A$, where V_a is called *the value set of* a. Elements of U are called *objects.* Two objects $x, y \in U$ are said to be *discernible* by attributes from A if there exists an attribute $a \in A$ such that $a(x) \neq a(y)$.

Any information system of the form $\mathbb{A} = (U, A \cup \{dec\})$ is called *decision table* where $dec \notin A$ is called *decision.* Without loss of generality we assume that $V_{dec} = \{1, \ldots, d\}$. Then the set $DEC_k = \{x \in U : dec(x) = k\}$ will be called the kth *decision class of* $\mathbb{A}$ for $1 \leq k \leq d$. Any pair (a, c), where a is an attribute and c is a real value, is called *a cut.* We say that *"the cut* (a, c) *discerns a pair of objects* x, y*"* if either $a(x) < c \leq a(y)$ or $a(y) < c \leq a(x)$.

2.1 Decision tree construction from Decision tables

The decision tree for a given decision table is (in simplest case) a binary directed tree with *test functions* (i.e. Boolean functions defined on the information vectors of objects) labeled in internal nodes and decision values labeled in leaves. In this paper, we consider decision trees using cuts as test functions. Every cut (a, c) is associated with test function $f_{(a,c)}$ such that for any object $u \in U$ the value of $f_{(a,c)}(u)$ is equal to 1 (true) if and only if $a(u) > c$. Every decision tree can be treated as a decision algorithm. The new object $u \in U$ can be classified by a given decision tree as follows: "*We start from root of decision tree. Let* (a, c) *be a cut labeling the root. If* $a(u) > c$

we go to the right subtree and if $a(u) \leq c$ *we go to the left subtree of the decision tree. The process will be continued for any node until we reach any external node.*" The decision tree is called *consistent* with the decision table

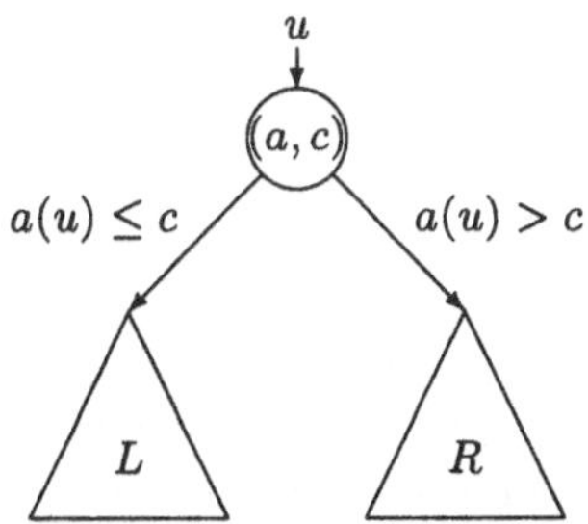

Fig. 1. Decision tree approach.

$\mathbb{A}$ if it classifies properly all objects from $\mathbb{A}$. The decision tree is called *optimal* with $\mathbb{A}$ if it has a smallest height among decision tree consistent with $\mathbb{A}$. The cut c on attribute a is called *optimal cut* if (a, c) labels one of internal nodes of optimal decision trees. Developing some decision tree induction methods [2,10] we should often solve the following problem: "*For a given set of candidate cuts* $\{c_1, ..., c_N\}$ *on an attribute* a*, find a cut* c_i *belonging to the set of optimal cuts with highest probability*". Usually, we use some *measure (or quality functions)* $F : \{c_1, ..., c_N\} \to \mathbb{R}$ to estimate the quality of cuts. For a given measure F, the *straightforward algorithm* should compute the values of F for all cuts: $F(c_1), .., F(c_N)$. The cut c_{Best} which optimizes the value of function F is selected as the result of searching process. The typical algorithm for decision tree induction can be described as follows:

1. For a given set of objects U, select a cut (a, c_{Best}) of high quality among all possible cuts and all attributes;
2. Induce a partition U_1, U_2 of U by (a, c_{Best}) ;
3. Recursively apply Step 1 to both sets U_1, U_2 of objects until some stopping condition is satisfied.

We consider the set of all relevant cuts $\mathbf{C}_a = \{c_1, ..., c_N\}$ on an attribute a.

Definition 1. The d-tuple of integers $\langle x_1, .., x_d \rangle$ is called class distribution of the set of objects $X \subset U$ iff $x_k = card(X \cap DEC_k)$ for $k \in \{1, ..., d\}$. If the set of objects X is defined by $X = \{u \in U : p \leq a(u) < q\}$ for some $p, q \in \mathbb{R}$ then the class distribution of X is called **the class distribution in** $[p; q)$.

In next sections we recall the most frequently used measures for decision tree induction like *"Entropy Measure" and "Discernibitity Measure"*, respectively.

Entropy measure uses class-entropy as a criterion to evaluate the list of best cuts which together with the attribute domain induce the desired intervals. The class information entropy of the set of N objects X with class distribution $\langle N_1, ..., N_d \rangle$, where $N_1 + ... + N_d = N$, is defined by $Ent(X) = -\sum_{j=1}^{d} \frac{N_j}{N} \log \frac{N_j}{N}$. Hence, the entropy of the partition induced by a cut point c on attribute a is defined by

$$E(a, c; U) = \frac{|U_L|}{n} Ent(U_L) + \frac{|U_R|}{n} Ent(U_R)$$

where $\{U_L, U_R\}$ is a partition of U defined by c. For a given feature a, the cut c_{min} which minimizes the entropy function over all possible cuts is selected see Figure 2. The methods based on information entropy are reported in [2,10].

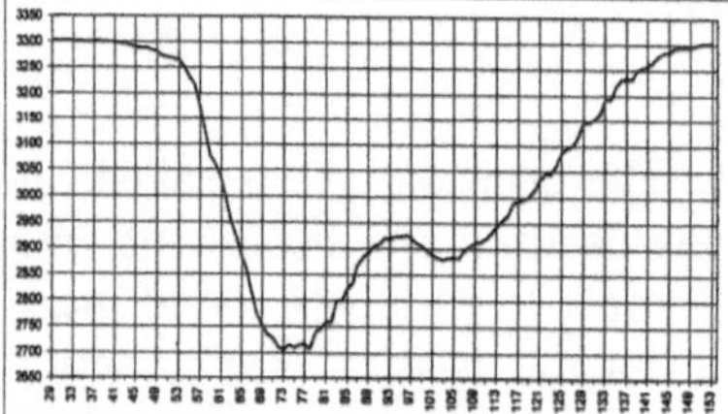

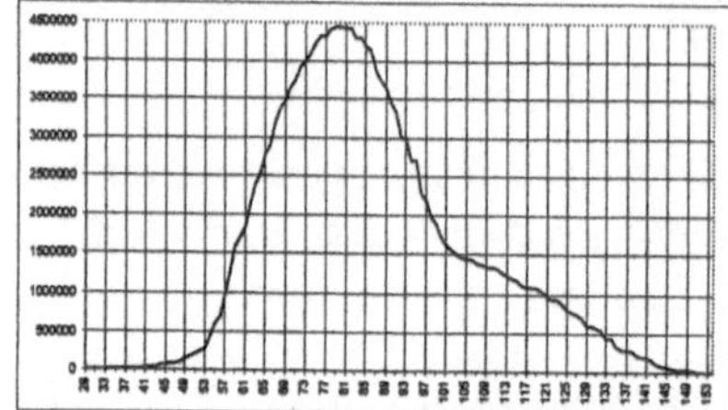

Fig. 2. The illustration of Entropy measure (left) discernibility measure(right) for the same data set. On horizontal axes: ID of consequent cuts; on vertical axes: values of corresponding measures

Discernibility measure is based on Rough Set and Boolean reasoning approach. Intuitively, energy of the set of objects $X \subset U$ can be defined by the number of pairs of objects from X to be discerned called $conflict(X)$. Let $\langle N_1, ..., N_d \rangle$ be a class distribution of X, then $conflict(X)$ can be computed by $conflict(X) = \sum_{i<j} N_i N_j$. The cut c which divides the set of objects U into U_1, and U_2 is evaluated by

$$W(c) = conflict(U) - conflict(U_1) - conflict(U_2)$$

i.e. the more is number of pairs of objects discerned by the cut (a, c), the larger is chance that c can be chosen to the optimal set of cut. This algorithm is called Maximal-Discernibility heuristics or *the MD-heuristics* for decision tree construction. Figures 2 illustrate the values of Entropy and Discernibility functions over set of possible cuts on one of attributes of SatImage data. One can see that the cuts preferred by both measures are quite similar. The high accuracy of decision trees constructed by using discernibility measure and their comparison with Entropy-based methods has been reported in [4].

2.2 Soft cuts

We have presented so far decision tree methods working with cuts treated as sharp classifiers such, that real values are partitioned by them into disjoint intervals. One can observe that in some situations objects which are close one to other, can be treated as very different. In this section we introduce some notions of *soft cuts* which discern two given values if those values are far enough from the cut. The formal definition of soft cuts is following:

Definition 2. A soft cut is any triple $p = \langle a, l, r \rangle$, where $a \in A$ is an attribute, $l, r \in \Re$ are called the left and right bounds of p $(l \leq r)$; the value $\varepsilon = \frac{r-l}{2}$ is called the uncertain radius of p. We say that a soft cut p discerns pair of objects x_1, x_2 if $a(x_1) < l$ and $a(x_2) > r$.

The intuitive meaning of $p = \langle a, l, r \rangle$ is such that there is a real cut somewhere between l and r. So we are not sure where one can place the real cut in the interval $[l, r]$. Hence for any value $v \in [l, r]$ we are not able to check if v is either on the left side or on the right side of the real cut. Then we say that the interval $[l, r]$ is an uncertain interval of the soft cut p. Any normal cut can be treated as soft cut of radius equal to 0.

Any set of soft cuts splits the real axis into intervals of two categories: the intervals corresponding to new nominal values and the intervals of uncertain values called boundary regions. The problem of searching for minimal set of soft cuts with a given uncertain radius can be solved in a similar way to the case of sharp cuts. We propose some heuristic for this problem in the last section of the paper. The problem becomes more complicated if we want to obtain as small as possible set of soft cuts with the radius as large as possible. We will discuss this problem in the next paper.

2.3 Soft decision tree

The test functions defined by cuts can be Here we propose two strategies being modifications of that method by using described above soft cuts (fuzzy separated cuts). They are called *fuzzy decision tree* and *rough decision tree.*

In fuzzy decision tree method instead of checking the condition $a(u) > c$ we have to check how strong is hypothesis that u is on the left or right side of the cut (a, c). This condition can be expressed by $\mu_L(u)$ and $\mu_R(u)$, where μ_L and μ_R are membership function of left and right intervals (respectively). The values of those membership functions can be treated as a probability distribution of u in the node labeled by soft cut $(a, c - \varepsilon, c + \varepsilon)$. Then one can compute the probability of the event that object u is reaching a leaf. The decision for u is equal to decision labeling the leaf with largest probability.

In the case of rough decision tree, when we are not able to decide to turn left or right (the value $a(u)$ is too close to c) we do not distribute the probability to children of considered node. We have to compare their answers taking into account the numbers of supported by them objects. The answer with most number of supported objects is a decision of given object.

3 Searching for best cuts in large data tables

In this section we present the efficient approach to searching for optimal cuts in large data tables. There are modifications of our MD-heuristic described in previous sections. We describe some techniques which have been presented in previous papers (see [5]).

3.1 Tail cuts can be eliminated

In [5] we have shown the following techniques for irrelevant cut eliminating. For given set of candidate cuts $\mathbf{C}_a = \{c_1, .., c_N\}$ on a such that $c_1 < c_2 ... < c_N$, by median of the kth decision class we mean the cut $c \in \mathbf{C}_a$ which minimizes the value $|L_k - R_k|$. The median of the kth decision class will be denoted by $Median(k)$. Let $c_{min} = \min_i\{Median(i)\}$ and $c_{max} = \max_i\{Median(i)\}$. We have shown in [5] the following theorem.

Theorem 1 *The quality function* $W : \{c_1,..,c_N\} \to \mathbb{N}$ *defined over the set of cuts is increasing in* $\{c_1, ..., c_{min}\}$ *and decreasing in* $\{c_{max}, ..., c_N\}$. *Hence* $c_{Best} \in \{c_{min}, ..., c_{max}\}$

This property is interesting because one can use only $O(d \log N)$ queries to determine the medians of decision classes by using Binary Search Algorithm. Hence the tail cuts can be eliminated by using using $O(d \log N)$ SQL queries. Let us also observe that if all decision classes have similar medians then almost all cuts can be eliminated.

3.2 Divide and conquer strategy

The main idea is to apply the *"divide and conquer"* strategy to determine the best cut $c_{Best} \in \{c_1, ..., c_n\}$ with respect to a given quality function. First we divide the set of possible cuts into k intervals (e.g. $k = 2, 3, ..$). Then we choose the interval to which the best cut may belong with the highest probability. We will use some approximating measures to predict the interval which probably contains the best cut with respect to discernibility measure. This process is repeated until the considered interval consists of one cut. Then the best cut can be chosen between all visited cuts.

The problem arises how to define the measure evaluating the quality of the interval $[c_L; c_R]$ having class distributions: $\langle L_1, ..., L_d\rangle$ in $(-\infty; c_L)$; $\langle M_1, ..., M_d\rangle$ in $[c_L; c_R)$; and $\langle R_1, ..., R_d\rangle$ in $[c_R; \infty)$. This measure should estimate the quality of the best cut among those belonging to the interval $[c_L; c_R]$.

In previous papers (see [5,7]) we proposed the following measures to estimate the quality of the best cut in $[c_L; c_R]$

$$Eval\left([c_L; c_R]\right) = \frac{W(c_L) + W(c_R) + conflict([c_L; c_R])}{2} + \Delta \qquad (1)$$

where the value of Δ is defined by:

$$\Delta = \frac{[W(c_R) - W(c_L)]^2}{8 \cdot conflict([c_L; c_R])} \quad \text{(in the dependent model)}$$

$$\Delta = \alpha \cdot \sqrt{D^2(W(c))} \qquad \text{for some } \alpha \in [0;1]; \quad \text{(in the independent model)}$$

The choice of Δ and the value of parameter α from $[0;1]$ can be tuned in learning process or are given by expert. One can see that to determine the value $Eval([c_L; c_R])$ we need only $O(d)$ simple SQL queries of the form:

```
SELECT COUNT
FROM data_table
WHERE (a BETWEEN c_L AND c_R) GROUPED BY d.
```

3.3 Local and Global Search

We present two strategies of searching for the best cut using formula 1 called *local* and *global search*. In local search algorithm, first we discover the best cuts on every attribute separately. Then we compare them to find out the global best one. The details of local algorithm can be described as follows:

ALGORITHM 1: Searching for semi-optimal cut
PARAMETERS: $k \in \mathbb{N}$ and $\alpha \in [0;1]$.
INPUT: attribute a; the set of candidate cuts $\mathbf{C}_a = \{c_1, .., c_N\}$ on a;
OUTPUT: The optimal cut $c \in \mathbf{C}_a$

begin
$Left \leftarrow \min$; $Right \leftarrow \max$; {see Theorem 1}
while $(Left < Right)$
1.Divide $[Left; Right]$ into k intervals with equal length by $(k+1)$ boundary points i.e.

$$p_i = Left + i * \frac{Right - Left}{k};$$

for $i = 0, .., k$.
2.For $i = 1, .., k$ compute $Eval([c_{p_{i-1}}; c_{p_i}], \alpha)$ using Formula (1). Let $[p_{j-1}; p_j]$ be the interval with maximal value of $Eval(.)$;
3.$Left \leftarrow p_{j-1}$; $Right \leftarrow p_j$;
endwhile;
Return the cut c_{Left};
end

Hence the number of queries necessary for running our algorithm is of order $O(dk \log_k N)$. In practice we set $k = 3$ because the function $f(k) = dk \log_k N$ has minimum over positive integers for $k = 3$. For $k > 2$, instead choosing the best interval $[p_{i-1}; p_i]$, one can select the best union $[p_{i-m}; p_i]$ of m consecutive intervals in every step for a predefined parameter $m < k$. The modified algorithm needs more – but still of order $O(\log N)$ – simple questions only.

The global strategy is searching for the best cut over all attributes. At the beginning, the best cut can belong to every attribute, hence for each attribute we keep the interval in which the best cut can be found (see Theorem 1), i.e. we have a collection of all potential intervals

$$\textbf{Interval\_Lists} = \{(a_1, l_1, r_1), (a_2, l_2, r_2), ..., (a_k, l_k, r_k)\}$$

Next we iteratively run the following procedure

- remove the interval $I = (a, c_L, c_R)$ having highest probability of containing the best cut (using Formula 1);
- divide interval I into smaller ones $I = I_1 \cup I_2 ... \cup I_k$;
- insert $I_1, I_2, ..., I_k$ to **Interval_Lists**.

This iterative step can be continued until we have one–element interval or the time limit of searching algorithm is exhausted. This strategy can be simply implemented using priority queue to store the set of all intervals, where priority of intervals is defined by Formula 1.

3.4 Example

We consider a randomly generated data table consisting of 12000 records. Objects are classified into 3 decision classes with the distribution $\langle 5000, 5600, 1400\rangle$, respectively. One real value attribute has been selected and $N = 500$ cuts on its domain has generated class distributions as shown in Figure 3. The medians of three decision classes are c_{166}, c_{414} and c_{189}, respectively. The median of every decision class has been determined by *binary search algorithm* using $\log N = 9$ simple queries. Applying Theorem 1 we conclude that it is enough to consider only cuts from $\{c_{166}, ..., c_{414}\}$. Thus 251 cuts have been eliminated by using 27 simple queries only.

In Figure 3 we show the graph of $W(c_i)$ for $i \in \{166, ..., 414\}$ and we illustrated the outcome of application of our algorithm to the reduce set of cuts for $k = 2$ and $\Delta = 0$. First the cut c_{290} is chosen and it is necessary to determine to which of the intervals $[c_{166}, c_{290}]$ and $[c_{290}, c_{414}]$ the best cut belongs. The values of function *Eval* on these intervals is computed: $Eval([c_{166}, c_{290}]) = 23927102$, $Eval([c_{290}, c_{414}]) = 24374685$. Hence, the best cut is predicted to belong to $[c_{290}, c_{414}]$ and the search process is reduced to the interval $[c_{290}, c_{414}]$. The above procedure is repeated recursively until the selected interval consists of single cut only. For our example, the best cut c_{296} has been successfully selected by our algorithm. In general the cut selected by the algorithm is not necessarily the best. However, numerous experiments on different large data sets shown that the cut c^* returned by the algorithm is close to the best cut c_{Best} (i.e. $\frac{W(c^*)}{W(c_{Best})} \cdot 100\%$ is about 99.9%).

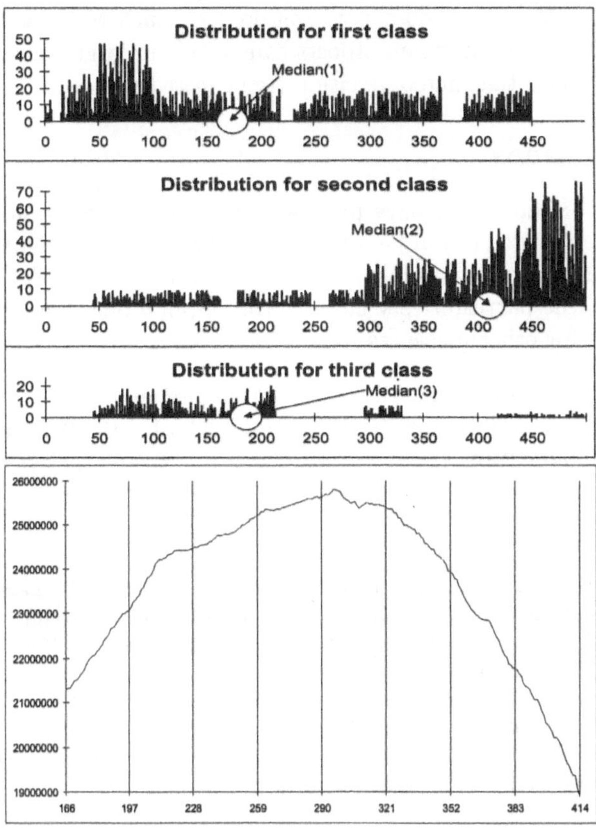

Fig. 3. Distributions for decision classes 1, 2, 3 and graph of $W(c_i)$ for $i \in \{166, .., 414\}$

3.5 Searching for soft cuts

One can modify the Algorithm 1 presented in the previous section to determine "soft cuts" in large data bases. The modification is based on changing the stop condition. In every iteration of the Algorithm 1, the current interval $[Left; Right]$ is divided equally into k smaller intervals and the best smaller interval will be chosen as the current interval. In the modified algorithm one can either select one of smaller intervals as the current interval or stop the algorithm and return the current interval as a result.

Intuitively, the Divide and Conquer Algorithm is stopped and results the interval $[c_L; c_R]$ if the following conditions hold:

- The class distribution in $[c_L; c_R]$ is too stable, i.e. there is no sub-interval of $[c_L; c_R]$ which is considerably better than $[c_L; c_R]$ him self;
- The interval $[c_L; c_R]$ is sufficiently small, i.e. it contains a small number of cuts;

- The interval $[c_L; c_R]$ does not contain too much objects; (because the large number of uncertain objects cans result in larger decision tree and then prolongs the time of decision tree construction)

4 Conclusions

The problem of optimal binary partition of continuous attribute domain for large data sets stored in *relational data bases* has been investigated. We show that one can reduce the number of simple queries from $O(N)$ to $O(\log N)$ to construct the partition very close to the optimal one. We plan to extend these results for other measures.

Acknowledgement: This paper has been partially supported by Polish State Committee of Research (KBN) grant No 8T11C02519 and grant of the Wallenberg Foundation.

References

1. Dougherty J., Kohavi R., Sahami M.: Supervised and unsupervised discretization of continuous features. In. Proc. of the 12th International Conference on Machine Learning, Morgan Kaufmann, San Francisco, CA, 1995, pp. 194–202.
2. Fayyad, U. M., Irani, K.B.: On the handling of continuous-valued attributes in decision tree generation. Machine Learning **8**, 1992, pp. 87–102.
3. John, G. H., Langley, P.: Static vs. dynamic sampling for data mining. Proceedings of the Second International Conference of Knowledge Discovery and Data Mining, Portland, AAAI Press 1996, pp. 367–370.
4. Nguyen, H. S.: Discretization Methods in Data Mining. In L. Polkowski, A. Skowron (Eds.): *Rough Sets in Knowledge Discovery* **1**, Springer Physica-Verlag, Heidelberg, 1998, pp. 451–482.
5. Nguyen, H. S.: Efficient SQL-Querying Method for Data Mining in Large Data Bases. Proc. of 16th International Joint Conference on Artificial Intelligence, IJCAI-99, Morgan Kaufmann Publishers, Stockholm, Sweden, 1999, pp. 806-811.
6. Nguyen, H. S.: On Efficient Construction of Decision tree from Large Databases. Proc. of the Second International Conference on Rough Sets and Current Trends in Computing (RSCTC'2000). Springer-Verlag, pp. 316-323.
7. Nguyen, H. S.: On Efficient Handling of Continuous Attributes in Large Data Bases, Fundamenta Informatica **48(1)**, pp. 61-81
8. Pawlak Z.: *Rough sets: Theoretical aspects of reasoning about data*, Kluwer Dordrecht, 1991.
9. Polkowski, L., Skowron, A. (Eds.): *Rough Sets in Knowledge Discovery* **Vol. 1,2**, Springer Physica-Verlag, Heidelberg, 1998.
10. Quinlan, J. R. *C4.5. Programs for machine learning*. Morgan Kaufmann, San Mateo CA, 1993.
11. Skowron, A., Rauszer, C.: The discernibility matrices and functions in information systems. In. R. Słowiński (ed.). Intelligent Decision Support – Handbook of Applications and Advances of the Rough Sets Theory, Kluwer Academic Publishers, Dordrecht, 1992, pp. 311–362

Agent-based Fuzzy Classifier System

Arkadiusz Niemiec, Robert Pająk, and Marek Kisiel-Dorohinicki

Department of Computer Science
University of Mining and Metallurgy, Kraków, Poland
e-mail: {niemiec,doroh}@agh.edu.pl

Abstract. This work presents a new evolutionary approach to data classification based on Holland's concept of a genetic-based classifier system. The novelty of the method proposed consists in the application of evolutionary multi-agent systems (EMAS) instead of classical genetic algorithms. In the paper the technique is described as well as preliminary experimental results are reported.

Keywords: data classification, fuzzy systems, evolutionary computation, multi-agent systems.

1 Introduction

Although plenty of classification algorithms have already been constructed, classification problems still arouse interests of many researchers and new solutions are being proposed. In general these problems include assigning certain membership classes to data sets (possibly describing some domain-specific objects). Among many different approaches (statistical, rule-based, neural) there is also a specific class of classification systems drove by evolutionary learning.

It is over 30 years since Holland published his first papers on the idea of a message passing, learning rule-based system – a *classifier system* [4]. By verifying answers to given questions, such a system could accumulate knowledge, which enabled it to formulate more and more correct responses. Learning was achieved at two levels: some kind of auction allowed for evaluation of particular *classifiers*, and a genetic algorithm transformed the whole population of classifiers based on their quality.

Since that time many variants of these ideas were described in literature, and also various applications were developed. Yet in many complex environments classical classifier systems could not prove useful because of their limitations concerning data representation, particularly representation of continuously changing, and often inexact values. This problem may be solved with the help of fuzzy systems theory – a fuzzy classifier system is a learning rule-based system, in which classifiers are (sets of) fuzzy rules [2]. The approach assumes integration of fuzzy rule base, a fuzzy inference system, and an evolutionary algorithm (e.g. each classifier is represented by a fuzzy rule, and the population represents a rule base). Thus it consists of similar elements as a classical classifier system, but these elements are *fuzzified.*

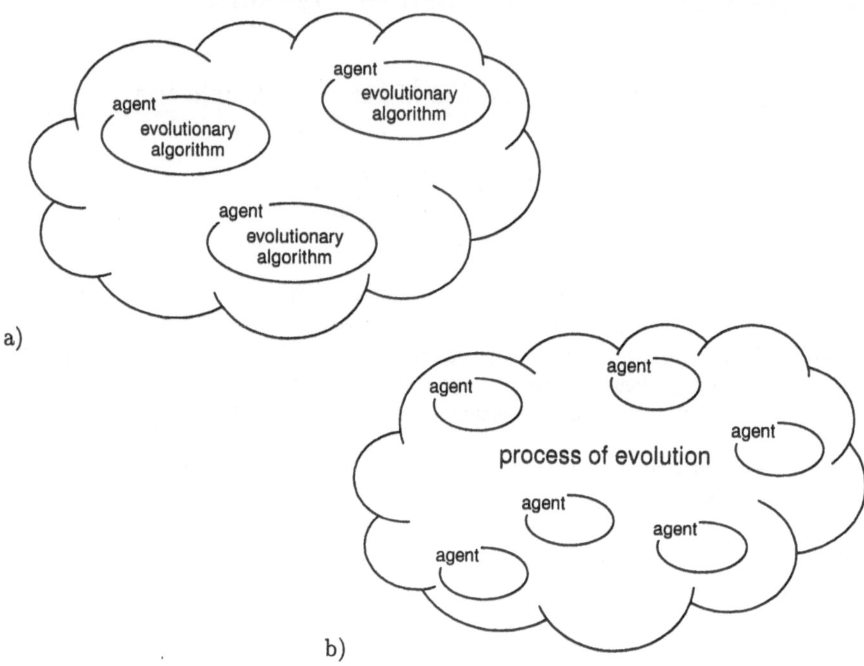

Fig. 1. Evolutionary algorithms supporting particular agents in MAS (a) and an evolutionary multi-agent system (b)

The novelty of the proposed approach to evolutionary fuzzy classification consists in application of an evolutionary multi-agent system (EMAS) instead of classical evolutionary computation. The key idea of EMAS is the incorporation of evolutionary processes into a multi-agent system (MAS) at a population level [1]. It means that besides interaction mechanisms typical for MAS (such as communication) agents are able to reproduce (generate new agents) and may die (be eliminated from the system). A decisive factor of an agent's activity is its fitness expressed by amount of possessed non-renewable resource called *life energy*. Selection is realised in such a way that agents with high energy are more likely to reproduce, while low energy increases the possibility of death.

Below the description of these ideas and their implementation is presented. As several tests have been performed, their results are also reported and preliminary conclusions are drawn.

2 Evolutionary Multi-agent Systems

During the last decade the idea of an intelligent autonomous agent and an agent-based system gains more and more interest. Agent technology is used in various domains, providing concepts and tools for development of intelligent decentralised systems [5]. Among lots of issues related to agent technology one can find also evolutionary computation present in multi-agent systems (MAS). In most such cases an evolutionary algorithm is used by an agent (fig. 1a) to aid realisation of some its tasks, mostly connected with learning or reasoning (e.g. [9]), or to support coordination of some group (team) activity (e.g. [3]). Yet it seems that interesting results may be achieved applying some model of evolution in MAS at a population level, i.e. among agents (fig. 1b). In this case variation operators together with selection/reproduction mechanism search for (near) optimal configuration of agents in the system. Such *evolutionary multi-agent systems* (EMAS) may be considered either a new class of adaptive multi-agent systems, where evolutionary processes help to accomplish population-level goals, or a new technique of evolutionary computation utilising a *decentralised* model of evolution, and thus extending classical evolutionary algorithms [1,7].

Following neodarwinian paradigms, two main components of the process of evolution are *inheritance* (with random changes of genetic information by means of mutation and recombination) and *selection*. They are realised by the phenomena of death and reproduction, which may be easily modelled as actions executed by agents:

→ the action of *death* results in the elimination of an agent from the system,
→ the action of *reproduction* is simply the production of a new agent from its parent(s).

Inheritance is to be accomplished by an appropriate definition of reproduction, which is similar to classical evolutionary algorithms. The set of parameters describing core properties of an agent (genotype) is inherited from its parent(s) – with the use of mutation and recombination. Besides, an agent may possess some knowledge acquired during its life, which is not inherited. Both inherited and acquired information determines the behaviour of an agent in the system (phenotype).

Selection is the most important and most difficult element of the model of evolution employed in EMAS. This is due to assumed lack of global knowledge (which makes it impossible to evaluate all individuals at the same time) and autonomy of agents (which causes that reproduction is achieved asynchronously). In such a situation selection mechanisms known from classical evolutionary computation cannot be used. The proposed principle of selection corresponds to its natural prototype and is based on the existence of non-renewable resource called *life energy*. The energy is gained and lost when the agent executes actions in the environment. Increase in energy is a reward for a 'good' behaviour of the agent, decrease – a penalty for a 'bad' behaviour (which behaviour is considered 'good' or 'bad' depends on the particular problem to be solved). At the same time the level of life energy determines actions an agent is able to execute. In particular low energy level should increase the possibility of death and high energy level should increase the possibility of reproduction.

A more precise description of this model and its advantages may be found in [1,7, and other]. In short, EMAS enables the following:

- local selection allows for intensive exploration of the search space, which is similar to parallel evolutionary algorithms,
- the way phenotype (behaviour of the agent) is developed from genotype (inherited information) depends on its interaction with the environment,
- self-adaptation of the population size is possible when appropriate selection mechanisms are used.

What is more, explicitly defined living space facilitates implementation in a distributed computational environment.

3 Fuzzy EMAS for Data Classification

The goal of the particular EMAS is data classification, which means that it should assign membership classes to supplied data sets – vectors of attributes, possibly describing some domain-specific objects, events or phenomena [6]. Of course before the system is able to give correct answers it should be given a representative set of examples: selected vectors of attributes with appropriate class membership assigned. Attribute vectors are supplied to the environment, where they become available for all agents. Each agent may perform its own analysis of incoming data and assign membership classes. During learning phase agents' answers are evaluated by comparison with correct membership classes, which allows for diversification of energy rewards. At the same time these answers constitute a base for generation of the response of the whole system.

In fact the system consists of two kinds of agents, namely *supervisor* and *classifier* agents, which are located on the islands. Supervisor agents are responsible for distributing input data and collecting answers. Each supervisor controls the process of creating the response of one island and together with other supervisors generates the system's response for a given data set. Classifier agents act according to the above-described rules of EMAS operation and carry out the classification of incoming data. A classification agent consist of:

- one or more classifiers; each classifier consists of a condition and a message, which are made of fuzzy concepts;
- parameters specifying its behaviour (life energy and several coefficients).

Each classifier may be created on the basis of another classifier or as a result of combination of two other classifiers in the *reproduction* process. New agents have the same value of energy, which may change during their life, while other coefficients are established at random for each agent.

Each cycle of processing begins when the system receives an *input message* (a vector of attributes describing a particular object, event or phenomenon). This message is transferred by means of supervisors to all islands and on each island an *auction* process begins. During auction agents determine the degree of similarity between conditions of their classifiers and the input message and choose one of their classifiers to generate a response (proposal of the solution). The supervisor selects the best agent, taking into consideration its energy and the degree of similarity of the selected classifier. The message generated by this classifier becomes the response of the island. As auction is finished, supervisors collect responses from all islands and — in order to generate a response of the whole system — look for the one which appears most frequently.

During learning phase the system receives also the information about correct class membership of each data set. It allows supervisors to give away energetic rewards to agents on the islands, which suggested a correct response. In the case of a wrong response agents located on the island are punished - the energy of these agents is decreased. During each cycle a supervisor also collects:

1. *life* tax — from all of agents; it affects weakening of these agents, which do not take part in auctions,
2. *auction* tax — from these agents, which took part in an auction; it prevents the same agents from dominating the population.

If energy of any agent falls to zero, the agent dies. The supervisor is a privileged agent: for the sake of actions, which it executes, its energy is never decreased or increased.

On each island some of classifier agents take a decision about reproduction. They communicate with each other in order to state which of them have energy level high enough to be able to reproduce. During simple reproduction (cloning) *mutation* of the created agents' classifiers may occur. Another possible way of agent reproduction is *crossover*. In that case an agent looks for other agents with high enough energy level and willing to take part in reproduction. An offspring agent created via crossover includes parts of agents-parents' classifiers, which can be also insignificantly changed as a result of mutation. Reproduction (cloning and crossover) process is limited only by available space on the island.

A classifier agent may also take a decision about changing the island on which it currently stays (*migration*). In order to do this it communicates with other agents on the island and obtains information about their life energy. It compares its energy with energy of other agents and on that basis it may state that actual conditions on this island are not suitable for its further development, because it does not take part in auction often enough. If so it tries to migrate to one of the neighbouring islands, in hope that it could find the environment, which would let it survive.

4 Experimental Studies

The tests were performed using the following methodology: as the sample of test data was loaded, for a certain number of iterations — greater then the size of the loaded sample — the data was passed to the system in random order. This step was then repeated requested number of times. The system's classification quality was expressed by the following formula:

$$\text{classification quality} = \frac{\text{number of correct responses}}{\text{number of iterations}}$$

The tests consisted of two parts:

1. Comparison of classification quality of the system and other algorithms tested on the same data sets.
2. Analysis of the influence of the system parameters on its classification quality — the behaviour of the system was tested changing the following parameters:
   - number of islands,
   - kind of membership function used for building classifiers (triangular or trapezoidal).

Data sets used in the tests were available from: *UCI Machine Learning Repository*, at *http://www.ics.uci.edu/~mlearn*. The following data sets were chosen: "BUPA liver disorders" (bupa), "Teaching assistant evaluation" (tae) "StatLog heart disease" (hea), "LED display" (led), "Waveform" (wav), "StatLog vehicle silhouette" (veh), "Congressional voting records" (vot).

Figure 2 shows the dependence of the system's classification quality on the number of iterations. One may notice that for most data sets the systems learns quite quickly, but for some of them a longer learning phase is needed. Also the results obtained to a large extent depend on the data set.

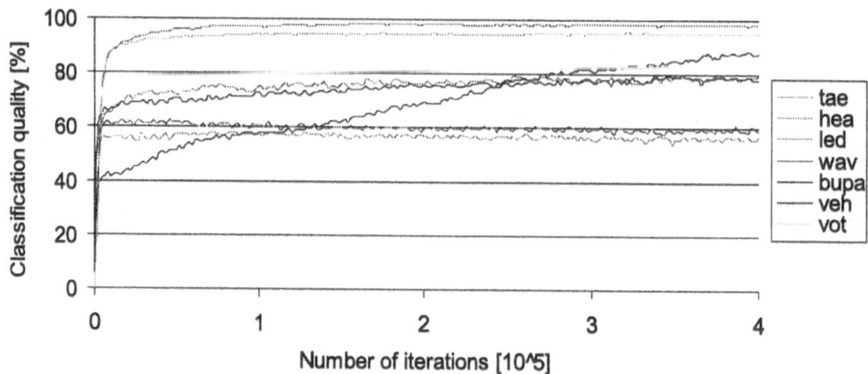

Fig. 2. Classification quality during learning phase for seven data sets

Algorithm	Data set						
	bupa	tae	hea	led	wav	veh	vot
FTL	0.413	0.693	0.148	0.271	0.179	0.410	0.0457
IB	0.328	0.373	0.222	0.276	0.285	0.260	0.0526
IB0	0.322	0.325	0.196	0.274	0.261	0.274	0.0386
IM	0.320	0.538	0.200	0.274	0.284	0.289	0.0503
IM0	0.312	0.492	0.204	0.274	0.243	0.278	0.0367
IC0	0.327	0.372	0.207	0.279	0.297	0.265	0.0480
IC1	0.319	0.537	0.219	0.286	0.313	0.298	0.0435
LMT	0.322	0.470	0.163	0.284	0.176	0.215	0.0483
T1	0.432	0.540	0.270	0.816	0.441	0.487	0.0435
LDA	0.326	0.411	0.141	0.271	0.178	0.224	0.0458
QDA	0.401	0.543	0.248	0.273	0.179	0.145	0.0549
NN	0.370	0.349	0.226	0.294	0.396	0.224	0.0526
LOG	0.309	0.450	0.159	0.269	0.154	0.196	0.0500
LVQ	0.329	0.628	0.341	0.313	0.170	0.374	0.0500
RBF	0.330	0.464	0.193	0.446	0.151	0.372	0.0523
EMAS	0.220	0.204	0.018	0.432	0.411	0.122	0.0475
Position	(1)	(1)	(1)	(14)	(15)	(1)	(7)

Table 1. Comparison of the percent learning error of 15 classification algorithms and the designed system

In order to compare the system's classification quality with other algorithms (tree and rule-based, statistical, neural nets) the results described in [8] were used. Table 1 presents the comparison of the percent error on the learning set of 15 various algorithms with the error of the designed system for each of seven data sets used in the tests. In order to reach the best system classification quality, the experiment was performed for 16 islands; on each island the maximum number of agents was 100. The error was given for 400000 iterations. Such a selection of the parameters caused the increase of computational expenditure of the system and for practical applications is surely too extravagant, but it allows to estimate learning abilities of the system. At the end of the table there is information about the position of the designed system in the ranking of all 16 algorithms (15 algorithms + the system).

The results presented show the high position of the system in comparison with other algorithms. What is interesting, worse results were obtained only for these data sets, which were generated artificially (led and wav). In these data sets the same values of attributes often appeared in many data vectors belonging to the data set, or they were disturbed on purpose. It is necessary to emphasize, that presented results concern only learning phase, because for the designed system it was hard to realise such a testing procedure, which could use testing data sets.

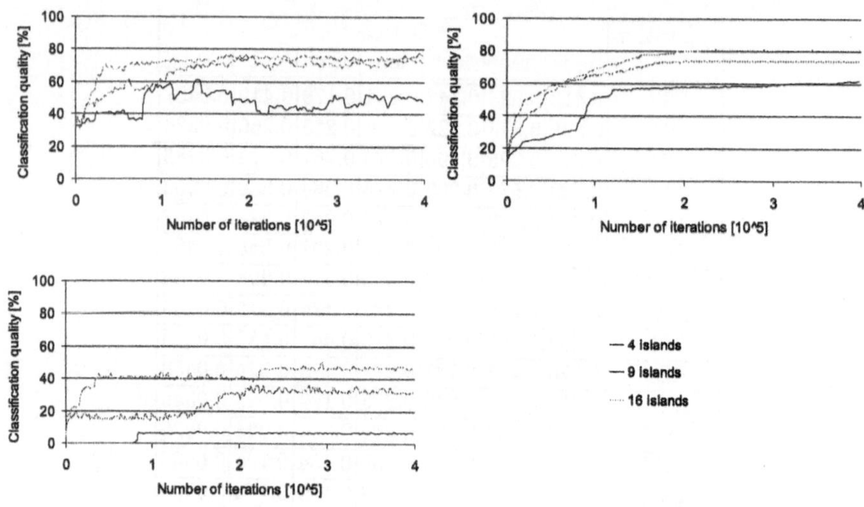

Fig. 3. Classification quality for four, nine and sixteen islands

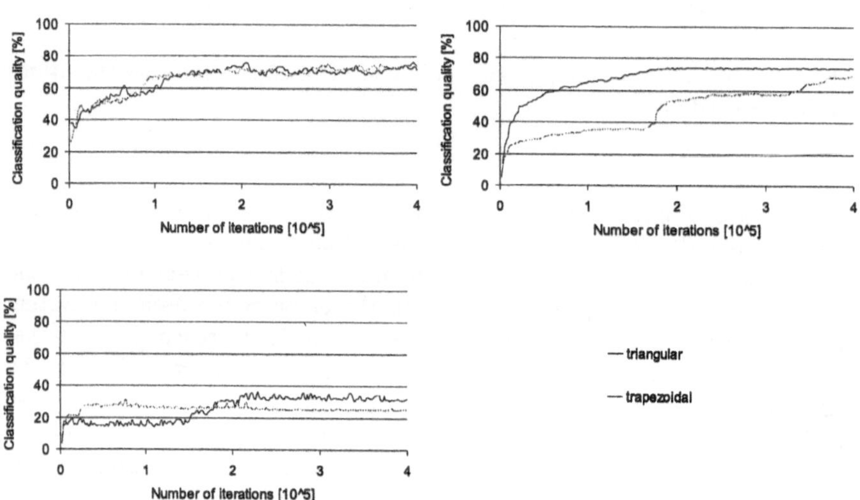

Fig. 4. Classification quality for triangular and trapezoidal membership functions applied in classifiers

Figures 3 and 4 show present the system's reaction for a change of one of two parameters. Each group consists of three plots showing the system's behaviour for three of the data sets mentioned above: "Teaching assistant evaluation" (tae), "StatLog heart disease" (hea), "LED display" (led). The tests were made for 9 islands and on each island the maximum number of agents was 50.

Plots in figure 3 present classification quality obtained for four, nine and sixteen islands. One may notice that increasing the number of islands always causes an improvement in classification quality. If there was only one island, there would be a chance for developing a certain group of agents with very high energy, which would prevent other agents from taking part in auction. This could cause weakening of these remaining agents leading to their death. Then only one trend of solutions could be developed in the system, which would lead to premature stopping of the evolution process (stasis). For a grater number of islands the system keeps simultaneously various trends of evolving solutions (like in parallel evolutionary algorithms). A greater number of solution trends makes easier adaptation to changing data, which should be classified.

Plots in figure 4 show classification quality for triangle and trapezoidal membership functions applied in classifiers. It may be observed that in most cases applying triangular membership functions in classifiers leads do higher system classification quality, than applying trapezoidal membership functions. It seems that classifiers with triangular membership functions are able to more precisely adapt to input data. It is caused by the fact, that triangular membership function has its maximum value only for one argument value, in contrast to trapezoidal membership function, which has maximum value for a range of argument values. Thus applying trapezoidal membership functions leads to assigning object described by similar (slightly different) attribute values to the same membership class.

5 Concluding Remarks

The proposed agent-based fuzzy classifier system seems to be an interesting application of the idea of an evolutionary multi-agent system. The preliminary results show very high adaptation of the system to the data during learning phase.

Further research should concern not only the system's classification quality (especially the realisation of the test phase) but also the effectiveness of the proposed approach, particularly in the case of large data sets. Also several extensions to the evolutionary process (such as aggregation) applied to EMAS in many other application domains should be considered.

References

1. K. Cetnarowicz, M. Kisiel-Dorohinicki, and E. Nawarecki. The application of evolution process in multi-agent world (MAW) to the prediction system. In M. Tokoro, editor, *Proc. of the 2nd Int. Conf. on Multi-Agent Systems (ICMAS'96)*. AAAI Press, 1996.
2. O. Cordón, F. Herrera, F. Hoffmann, and L. Magdalena. *Genetic Fuzzy Systems. Evolutionary Tuning and Learning of Fuzzy Knowledge Bases*, volume 19 of *Advances in Fuzzy Systems - Applications and Theory*. World Scientific, 2001.
3. M. Gordin, S. Sen, and N. Puppala. Evolving cooperative groups: Preliminary results. In *Working Papers of the AAAI-97 Workshop on Multiagent Learning*. AAAI, 1997.
4. J. H. Holland. Escaping britleness: The possibilities of general-purpose learning algorithms applied to parallel rule-based systems. In R. S. Michalski, J. G. Carbonell, and T. M. Mitchell, editors, *Machine Learning II*. Morgan Kaufmann Publishers, 1986.
5. N. R. Jennings, K. Sycara, and M. Wooldridge. A roadmap of agent research and development. *Journal of Autonomous Agents and Multi-Agent Systems*, 1(1), 1998.
6. N. K. Kasabov. *Foundations of Neural Networks, Fuzzy Systems, and Knowledge Engineering*. The MIT Press, 1996.
7. M. Kisiel-Dorohinicki, G. Dobrowolski, and E. Nawarecki. Evolutionary multi-agent system in multiobjective optimisation. In M. Hamza, editor, *Proc. of the IASTED Int. Symp. on Applied Informatics (AI 2001)*. IASTED/ACTA Press, 2001.
8. T.-S. Lim, W.-Y. Loh, and Y.-S. Shih. A comparison of prediction accuracy, complexity, and training time of thirty-three old and new classificaion algorithms. *Machine Learning*, 40:203–228, 2000.
9. J. Liu and H. Qin. Adaptation and learning in animated creatures. In W. L. Johnson and B. Hayes-Roth, editors, *Proc. of the 1st Int. Conf. on Autonomous Agents (Agents'97)*. ACM Press, 1997.

Decision Trees Learning System

Maciej Paliwoda

Faculty of Mathematics and Information Science,
Warsaw University of Technology

Abstract:
*This paper describes computer system – **Decision Trees Learning System (DTLS)** that was developed as a main part of the Master Thesis: "Implementation of the algorithms of learning decision trees, working on any SQL compatible database". Developed System is friendly, credible environment for searching and modeling knowledge stored in databases, using decision tree methodology. **DTLS** provides support for three most popular decision tree algorithms: C4.5, ID3 and CART. System also supports few variants of discretization for continuous attributes.*

Keywords: *C4.5, CART, Decision Trees, ID3, Learning System.*

1. Introduction

In today's world information is one of the most important "materials". In practice the information without "intelligent processing" is usually useless. Knowledge Discovery Systems are able to analyze and process raw data, find out the relationships and similarities among attributes (knowledge) and present them in readable and comprehensible form. But in many situations it is necessary to use such discovered knowledge to predict and classify new cases. This is a main task of Expert Systems.

One of the aims of my Master Thesis was to create universal Expert System, based on most popular decision tree learning algorithms, able to find knowledge in databases and classify new cases.
As a result of this project a windows application was developed, which:

- Uses one of three algorithms to construct decision tree – ID3, C4.5 and CART, with customizable parameters.
- Is able to handle continuous attributes – discretization using one of five implemented algorithms, with customizable parameters
- Estimates classification errors
- Can classify a new case
- Has a friendly GUI – clear presentation of the created tree, wizards methodology, that leads user through whole process.
- Allows user to define learning and test sample via friendly GUI

- Allows saving (and restoring) created tree to disk for future use.
- Can access any database that is ODBC compatible.

Currently application does not handle datasets with missing values.

2. Decision Trees – the basis

Decision tree is a way of modeling discovered knowledge, which allows showing dependencies between attributes (properties of the element) and the decision (class, the element belongs to) Decision trees can also be used to classify new cases.

Dependencies are presented as a tree – the coherent graph without any cycles. In such graph it is possible to point a root node, internal nodes and leaves. All internal nodes as well as root node, represent attributes (properties of the element). Leaves are indicating the decision (class) dependent on the value of attributes on the path from root node to a particular leaf. Each edge in graph, having the beginning in the specified node is labeled with the value of the attribute that is represented by this node.

Every decision tree is constructed recursively, using a learning sample. This process is also called *training phase*. In every recursive step whole learning sample (in the first step) or subset of this sample (in successive steps) is divided into smaller subsets depending on the value of the "best" attribute. "Best" means the attribute that maximizes the "information gain" over the current subset. There are many functions used to evaluate this "gain", many of them are native for algorithm that is selected to create tree from data. The more "information gain" attribute provides the closer[1] to root node it is.

When the tree is constructed it can be used for classification of the new cases (unknown in learning process). This allows finding a decision very quickly, performing only few comparisons on attribute values. Classification process starts at root node and moving down the tree until leaf is encountered. At each nonleaf node the case's outcome is determined and comparison shifts to the root of the subtree corresponding to this outcome.

Very important question is how to evaluate if tree is good or useless. There are some methods which estimate how big will be the overall classification error for unknown cases (percentage of misclassified cases). Two most popular methods and giving the best results are: independent testing sample and cross-validation. First uses an independent testing sample with known class attribute for each case and find out the number of misclassified cases by comparing true class value with class predicted from tree. The second method is more sophisticated, because it estimates error using only learning sample. In the first step it randomly divides the sample on N subsets (should have the same number of elements). Then tree is constructed N times using N-1 subsets, and every (of N) time other subset is put away. The subset that hasn't been used to create the tree is an independent testing

[1] path (in graph) from root node to this node is shorter

sample and partial classification error can be found using first method (independent testing sample). Cross-Validation classification Error is the arithmetic average of partial classification errors. Second method is used if separate testing sample is not available.

In the real life problems, many of the attributes can have any real value (like temperature or age), but many of the algorithms use only discrete-valued attributes, so it is necessary to transform from continuous-valued attributes to discrete ones. This process is called discretization. There are many algorithms performing discretization.

In the decision tree any path in the tree is a certain hypothesis describing the subset of learning sample. During training phase algorithm tries to create hypothesis that fits the learning sample as much as possible. This leads to quite significant errors during classification of the new cases. This is the main task of pruning process - decrease fitting to learning sample and do not increase overall classification error for the unknown cases at the same time. Many algorithms have special subalgorithms performing pruning.

3. Datasets

Application can access any database that is ODBC standard compatible. To make database visible for LDTS System, user must define ODBC connection in the MS Windows Environment.

To use a dataset (a sample) user has to define it. It is quite simple process. First step is selection of the database from defined ODBC Connections. Then user must authenticate himself in the selected database. After successful login all tables and views (with fields) defined in the database are displayed in the dialog window. The last step is to select fields that user wants to create view from.

Not all field types are allowed to create view from. It is not possible to use BLOB, and binary fields not being numbers or strings. All other field's types are labeled following mnemonics:

Mnemonic	Meanings
B	Logical fields (true/false)
C	One character length fields
D	Date/time type
F	Real numbers
N	Numeric (integer numbers)

S	Strings
X	Unsupported fields (like BLOB's and binary fields)
?	Fields with unknown type

Table 1. Fields' type mnemonics.

As a result of selection of the desired fields, SQL statement is generated. This statement describes the sample. Created dataset is used for learning or testing. Window that is used to define SQL statement is shown in the picture below:

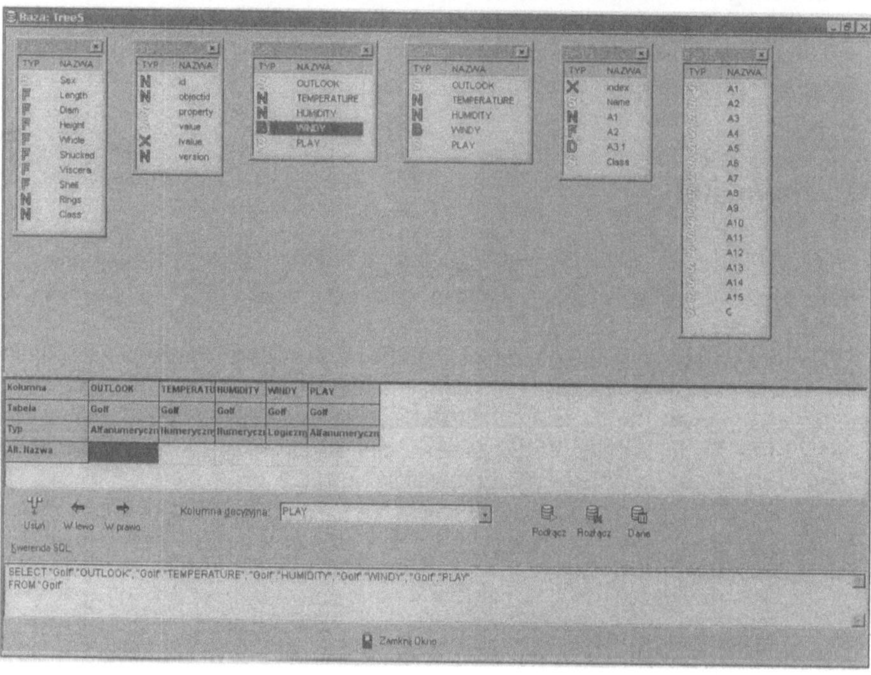

Figure 1. Dialog window for defining sample.

4. Decision Trees Algorithms

4.1 Discretization Algorithms

Many algorithms for learning decision trees work with attributes in discrete space. However, many real-world classification problems involve continuous features where such algorithms could not be applied unless the continuous attributes are first discretized. In the described System there were applied five discretization algorithms: Equal Interval Width, Chi-Merge, C4.5 Discretization, Fayyad-Irani MDLP and discretization from CART Algorithm.

Equal Interval Width [4] is the simplest method of discretization; it divides the range of observed values for a variable into **k** equal sized bins, where **k** is a user-supplied parameter.

The Chi-Merge [6] algorithm provides a statistically justified heuristic method for discretization. This algorithm begins by placing each observed real value into its own interval (bin) and proceeds by using the χ^2 test to determine when and which adjacent intervals can be merged. This method tests the hypothesis that the two adjacent intervals are statistically independent by making an empirical measure of the expected frequency of the classes represented in each of the intervals. Merging process lasts until maximum threshold value for χ^2 statistic is not exceeded or number of intervals is greater than assumed value.

The C4.5 discretization [10] divides attribute space on two subsets. All values of the attribute from the current subset that are less than assumed threshold are qualified to the first subset, to the second subset greater or equal ones. Threshold is selected only from the current set (not from whole space and all observed values) as an observed attribute value, which maximizes "information gain". To evaluate information gain Entropy heuristic is used, defined as:

$Ent(p_1,\dots,p_m) = -\sum_{i=1}^{m} p_i \log_2(p_i)$, where p_i is defined as probability that attribute has i-th value from the learning sample.

The Fayyad-Irani MDLP discretization [5] is a generalization of C4.5 discretization, because it finds all possible thresholds and creates all possible (giving maximum "information gain") subsets. It can be used globally (on the all space and observed values) and on the current subset as well. To find all thresholds it uses a sophisticated heuristic based on Minimum Description Length Principle. To evaluate "information gain" also entropy heuristic is used.

The last discretization is very similar to C4.5 discretization – also splits observed attribute space on two subsets; the main difference is heuristic evaluating "information gain". As in CART, this discretization uses heuristic GiniIndex: $i(p_1,\dots,p_m) = 1 - \sum_{j=1}^{m} p_j^2$.

4.2 Learning Decision Tree Algorithms

4.2.1 ID3 and C4.5

The ID3 algorithm [9] is the simplest algorithm. It handles only discrete spaced attributes, so discretization is necessary. If learning sample contains cases with missing values all such cases should be removed from sample[2].

Heuristic *Gain()* that is used for evaluating "information gain" is based on entropy (defined in previous section):

$$\Delta i(A;S) = Gain(A,S) = Ent(P_S) - Info(A,S), \text{where } Info(A,S) = \sum_{i=1}^{p} \frac{|S_i|}{|S|} Ent(P_{S_i}),$$

|S| is number of cases in current subset, $|S_i|$ - is a number of cases in current subset for which attribute A having i-th value. Main disadvantage of *Gain()* heuristic is fact that it prefers attributes having numerous set of values.

This algorithm select attribute that maximize value of the *Gain(A,S)* heuristic and set it as a splitting node in the tree.

The second algorithm C4.5 described in [10] is the improvement of the ID3. It also uses entropy heuristic for evaluation of information gain, but to avoid disadvantages of ID3 algorithm the *GainRatio()* heuristic is applied instead. It is defined as follow:

$$\Delta i'(A;S) = GainRatio(A,S) = \frac{Gain(A,S)}{Ent(P'')}, \text{ where } P''' = \left[\frac{|S_1|}{|S|}, \ldots, \frac{|S_p|}{|S|}\right].$$

C4.5 is able to handle continuous attributes – C4.5 Discretization sub-algorithm is used (see Section 4.1).

One of the most interesting features is ability to handle missing values. The idea is simple - algorithm evaluates *GainRatio()* using all cases from current subset, but result must be decreased by the fraction that is equal percentage of cases in current subset with missing values for particular attribute. Also if there are cases having missing value for the "best" (splitting) attribute, they are assigned to outcome subsets[3] with a probability (less then 1). So every case has a weight with is used in further calculations (i.e. |.| expression is counted as a sum of weights).

C4.5 uses pruning algorithm to improve prediction efficiency for the decision tree. It estimates error in the internal node and if it is smaller then sum of estimated errors in the leaves of the subtree for this node, whole subtree is pruned to this node. Pruning is done recursively from leaves to root node.

---

[2] In practice it leads to trees having significant classification errors, because learning sample is getting smaller, and cases with missing values can contain varying important information i.e. exceptions.

[3] Subsets that come into after splitting current subset according values of the "best" attribute

C4.5 has many other features described in details in [10] like: windowing (use subset of learning sample to create first nodes), Soft Thresholds (for continuous attributes) or Grouping of the attribute values.

This algorithm is treated as model algorithm and a base for comparison in many publications.

4.2.2 Classification and Regression Trees (CART)

CART algorithm (described in [1]) is very sophisticated algorithm. The main difference from other decision tree learning algorithms is that CART generates only binary trees (each internal node has always two children). Depending on type of the class attribute a classification tree is created (for discrete class attribute) or a regression tree (for continuous one). To evaluate "information gain" *GiniIndex()* heuristic are used:

$$i(S)=1-\sum_j p^2(j\mid S)$$

where S is a current subset of cases, and j goes through all values of the class attribute.

CART select as a splitting node attribute that maximizes value of the expression:

$$\Delta_G(\psi(A);S)=i(S)-p_L*i(S_L)-p_P*i(S_P)$$

or

$$\Delta_T(\psi(A);S)=\frac{p_L p_P}{4}\left[\sum_j \left|p(j|S_L)-p(j|S_P)\right|\right]^2$$

where S_L and S_P are outcome subsets after splitting current subset, and $p_{L,R}$ is a probability that case will be in left or right outcome, and $\psi(A)$ splitting criterion on attribute A.

When discrete attribute has more then two values CART groups values of the attribute in to two subsets. In general to select best splitting criterion all 2^{P-1} possibilities[4] must be searched, where **p** is a number of distinct values of the attribute.

To handle missing values "Surrogate Splits Method" [1] is used. The idea is to find the most similar attribute to the one having missing values and split current set according to its values.

Continuous attributes are handled as described in section 4.1.

Pruning in CART algorithm is also sophisticated and is called "*minimal cost-complexity pruning*". It is a compromise between size of the tree and its classification error. Pruning is done recursively from leaves to root node.

For CART it is possible to define cost matrix if misclassification cost is not equal in all situations. It lets better estimate overall classification error for the tree.

When the class attribute is continuous regression trees are constructed. In such case other heuristic is used for evaluating "information gain". There are also two parameters assigned with leaves – median from class attribute of cases covered by the node and its standard deviation.

---

[4] Because combinations are symmetric and trivial splits are ignored.

5. Using DTLS

Because of fact that process of creating decision tree requires specification of many parameters DLTS uses wizard methodology and user is guided step by step through whole process.

The first step in the process is selection of the algorithm that will be used for tree construction and specification of algorithm's parameters. In the next step user has to define learning sample, as described in the Section 2. When learning sample is named program displays information about it – name of the column, number of distinct values and number of cases with missing values. This step plays only informative role (no parameters are specified). In the fourth step user must select a discretization method for continuous attributes (if such attributes were discovered). For each continuous attribute control box is displayed that allows user to select one from the five possible discretization methods, specify additional parameters for selected one and decide if discretization is global (performed before construction of the decision tree on the all cases) or local (performed during construction process, on the current subset of the learning sample). In the next step user can select validation method. Two methods are available: independent testing sample and 10-fold cross-validation. Both methods can be selected. If method using independent testing sample is selected, user has to specify it. The next step allows user to match columns of learning and testing samples, if the last one was defined. Application tries to guess the proper matching and allows user to define his own assignment.

In the next step calculations are started and progress is shown on bars. Each part has its own bar: global discretization, calculations and tree building stage, validation processes. When calculations are finished, the report - containing information about overall classification error for the tree is generated. Information about error is also grouped by class value. The last step informs user that process has finished.

Wizard's windows are shown in the figure 3.

To display generated tree user has to close wizard windows, and press "tree button" on the toolbar. Sample tree is shown in the figure 2:

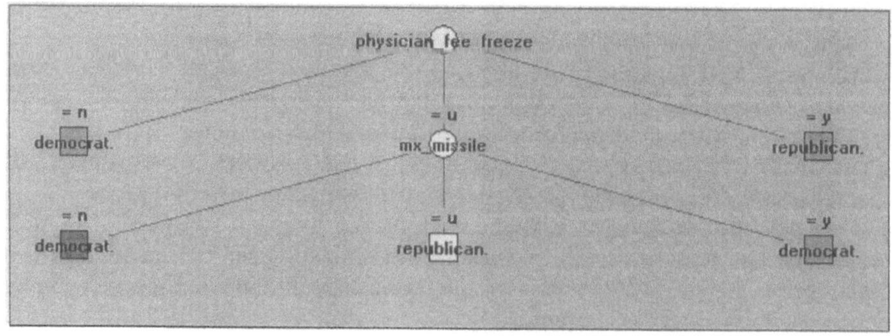

Figure 2. Sample tree generated by program.

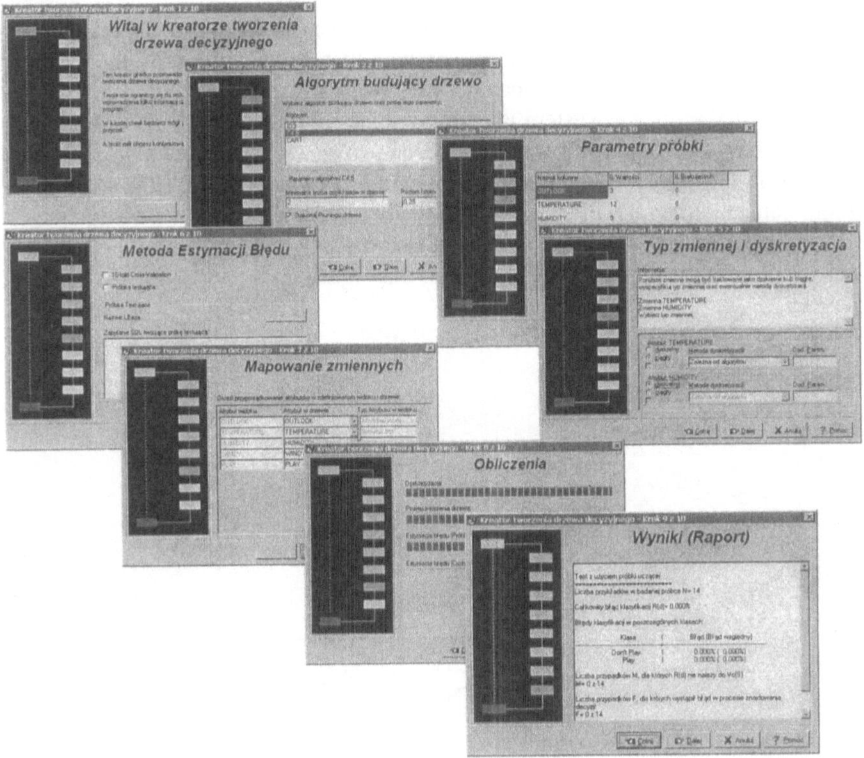

Figure 3. Decision Tree Creation Wizard's windows.

There is an assumed convention in displaying nodes in the tree. Internal nodes are represented as white circles labeled with attribute name. Leaves are represented as squares labeled with class name. If square is white then all cases in subset described by the path from root node to this leaf belong to the same class that node is labeled with. If color is gray then most popular class in subset is class this leaf is labeled with. Leaves having red color are representing root of the pruned tree. Node covers not empty subset, and the most popular class in subset is class this leaf is labeled with. If there is not possible to find out class name (i.e. empty set of cases) leaf has label: “>?<”.

Above each node (except the root one) there is an expression in the following form “*<operator>* *<value>*”, where *<operator>* is logical operand like: “=”, “<”, “>”, etc., and *<value>* is a value of “parent attribute”[5]. It describes what value should have parent attribute in considered case to move along the path in tree from parent node to particular child node or leaf.

Order of the tree nodes can be freely reorganized by user via drag & drop method.

[5] Parent attribute means attribute that is represented by node being parent to current node.

System also allows saving generated tree and restoring it from file. Tree is saved in the text file. There is special script language that is understood by the system and defines the tree. Using it user can define tree by himself.

The next feature of the System is ability to classify new cases. This is done using Classification Wizard. User is guided step by step through whole process: specification of sample to be classified, matching column names in this sample to column names in the tree. Results of classification are written in comma-separated file (specified by user) and also displayed on screen.

Main window of the application is shown in the Figure 4:

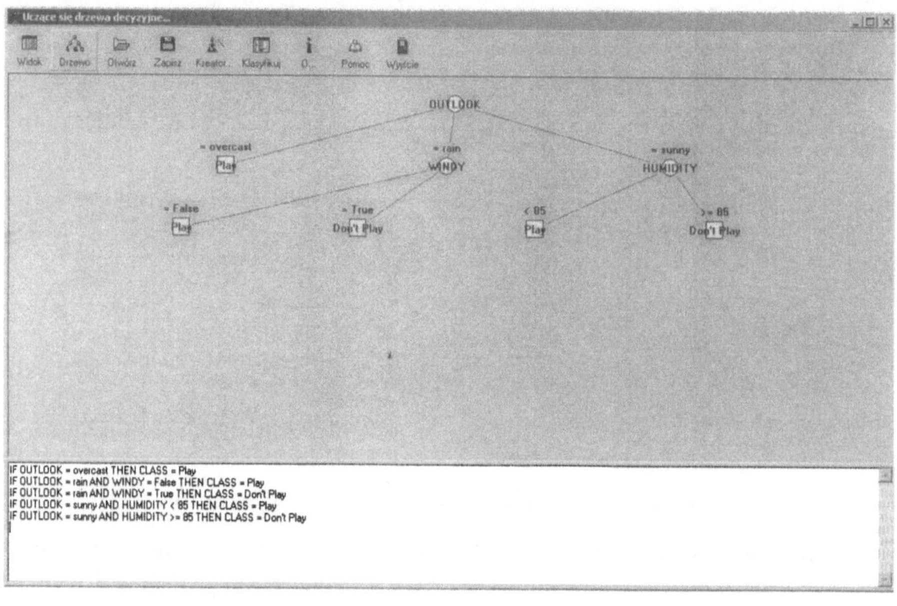

Figure 4. Main window of the Decision Tree Learning System.

6. Experimental Study

Using ***DTLS*** System experimental study comparing algorithms has been carried out.

First group of tests was comparison of the algorithms. There were three criteria: performance (time of the tree creation), overall classification error and tree size. Four algorithms were compared: ID3, CART, C4.5 and C4.5 with Fayyad-Iranii MDLP Discretization instead the default one. Charts below present all these parameters in dependency on algorithm and dataset:

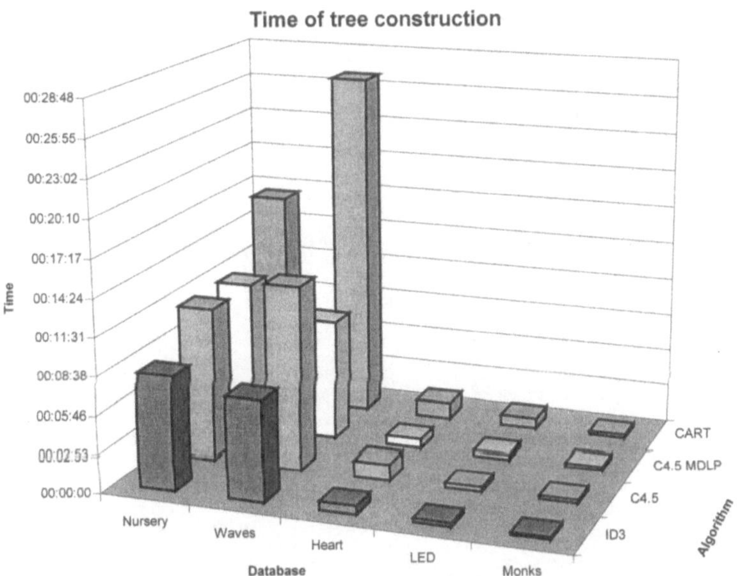

Chart 1. Time tree was constructed depending on algorithm.

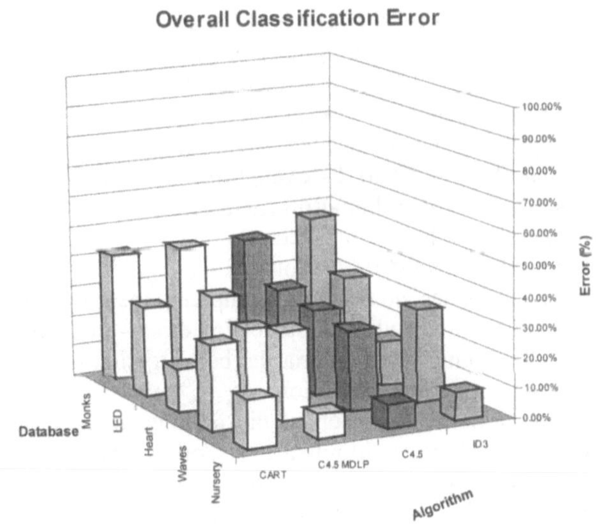

Chart 2. Overall classification error depending on algorithm.

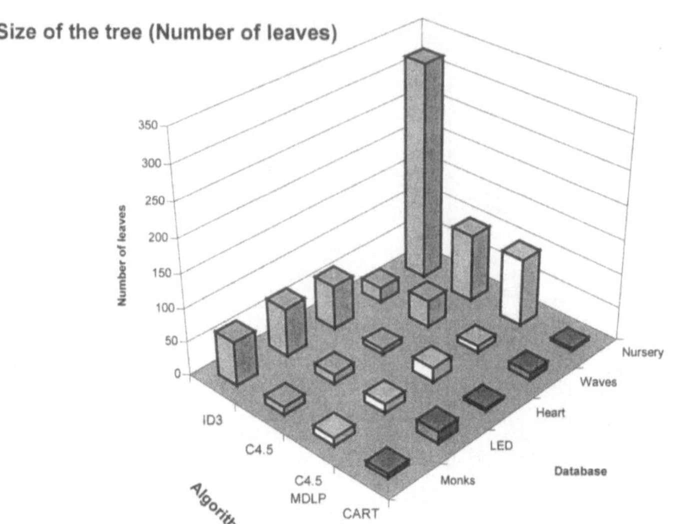

Chart 3. Size of the tree depending on algorithm.

Chart 1 shows tree creation times. The lower bar means the faster tree creation. From this chart it is straightforward to see that CART is the slowest algorithm, and ID3 is the fastest one. Differences in time creation (between CART and other algorithms) are quite significant for datasets: Nursery and Waves. That is because time of tree creation is proportional to number of continuous attributes[6] (all of them must be discretized, what is time consuming task). Also numerous set of class values causes longer creation time (as in database Nursery). Longer creation time for the CART algorithm is compensated by the smallest errors in tests with independent test sample (bars on Chart 2 – overall tree classification error are the shortest for all datasets). This algorithm also generates the smallest trees (bars on Chart 3 representing number of leaves in the created tree).

It is difficult to point the best algorithm. Some of them are better for one group of problems and other for the second ones. But comparing them we must take under consideration size of the tree and its classification error – things most important for the end-user. Assuming these criteria the best algorithm is CART algorithm in spite of quite long time of tree creation.

Second group of tests was comparison of the pruning methods: Pessimistic Pruning (used in C4.5 algorithm) and Minimal Cost Complexity Pruning (CART). Conclusions of comparison are: Pessimistic Pruning provides grater size gain (quotient of the number of leaves before and after pruning) and it is also faster then pruning deployed in CART. However CART (without pruning) generates smaller trees, so size gain is rather small. When comparing tree error before and after pruning, Minimal Cost Complexity Pruning is worse as well. But overall tree error is smaller when Minimal Cost Complexity Pruning is used.

[6] All 21 attributes in database Waves are continuous.

Third group of tests were comparison of discretization methods. To compare discretization methods C4.5 algorithm without pruning was applied. Time of tree creation and overall classification error were compared. Tree classification errors are shown on the chart below:

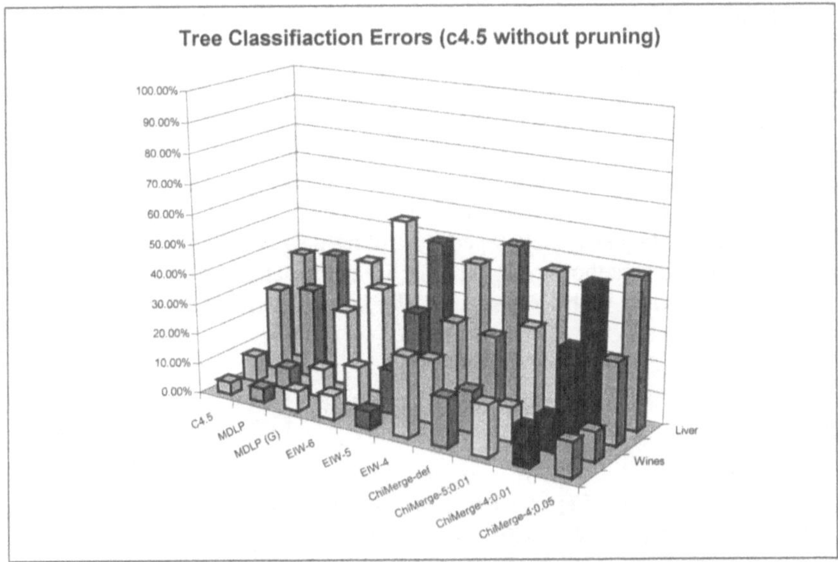

Chart 4. Comparison of the discretization methods according to classification error.

Performed tests show that global discretization leads to greater errors (usually 10-15%, longer bars on Chart 4). Global discretization causes creation of quite complex trees with many nodes describing empty subsets of learning sample. This situation is shown in the figure below:

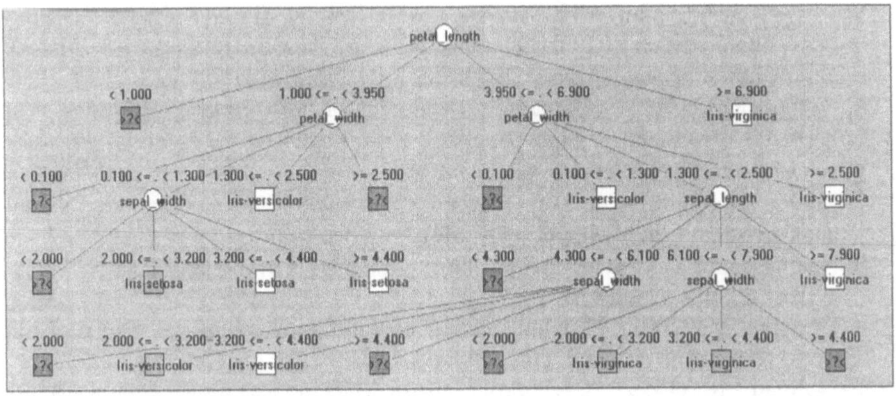

Figure 5. Tree grenerated by C4.5 algorithm with Equal Interval Width.

The fastest method is Equal Interval Width, and the slowest is ChiMerge. But the most universal (fast and giving smallest errors in trees) is Fayyad-Irani MDLP.

7. Summary

In this paper Decision Tree Learning System was described. Performed tests are consistent with results of the experiments presented in other publications [4,7]. This system can be used as an educational tool for students as well as a professional tool for searching knowledge written in database in practical application and representing it in the form of graphical structures.

This system can be easily developed by adding new functionality – new algorithms, discretization methods, etc. At least in can be changed to an engine that allow cooperation with Web Browsers and let it be part of the other Expert Systems.

References

1. Breiman L., Friedman J.H., Olshen R.A., Stone. C. J., (1984): "Classification and Regression Trees" Wadsworth and Brooks Monterey, Ca.
2. Catlett J., (1991): "Mega induction: machine learning on a very large data sets". PhD thesis. University of Sydney.
3. Catlett J., (1991): "On changing continuous attributes into ordered discrete attributes", in Y. Kodratoff, ed "Proceedings of the European Working Sessions on Learning", Berlin, Germany: Springer-Verlag, pp. 164-178.
4. Dougherty J., Kohavi R., Sahavi M., (1995): "Supervised and Unsupervised Discretization of Continuous Features." *In Proc. Twelfth International Conference on Machine Learning*. Morgan Kaufmann, Los Altos CA.
5. Fayyad U. M., Irani K. B., (1993): "Multi-interval discretization of continuous-valued attributes for classification learning", *In Proceedings of the 13th Int. Joint Conference on Artificial Intelligence,* pp. 1022-1027.
6. Kerber R., (1992): "Chimerge: Discretization of numeric attributes". *In AAAI-92, Proceedings Ninth National Conference on Artificial Intelligence*, AAAI Press/The MIT Press, pp. 123-128.
7. Michie D., Spiegelhalter D.J., Taylor C.C., (1994): "Machine Learning, Neural and Statistical Classification. (PDF file)
8. Nakhaeizadeh G., Taylor C.C., (1996): „Machine learning and Statistic", John Wileys & Sons, New York
9. Paliwoda M. (2001): "Implementation of the algorithms of learning decision trees, working on any SQL compatible database"; *Master Thesis*
10. Quinlan J.R., (1993): "C4.5: Programs for Machine Learning", Morgan Kaufmann Publishers, California.

Discovering Interesting Rules From Dense Data

Grzegorz Protaziuk, Przemyslaw Soldacki, and Lukasz Gancarz

Institute of Computer Science, Warsaw University of Technology
ul. .Nowowiejska 15/19, 00-665 Warszawa

Abstract Discovering association rules is one of the most important tasks in data mining and many efficient algorithms have been proposed in literature. However, the number of discovered rules is often so large, especially in dense data, that the user cannot analyze all discovered rules. To overcome that problem several methods for mining only interesting rules have been proposed. In this paper we describe efficient algorithm for finding maximal, unknown part of association with a given antecedent or consequent in databases with long patterns.

Keywords: data mining, association rules, interesting rules, maximal patterns, knowledge exploration

1 Introduction

In many cases the users are not interested in analyzing all association rules, which are present in databases, but they want to know in what relations chosen items occur. Certainly that output may be obtained by filtering previously found set of all association rules, but it can be done more efficiently if pruning methods are embedded in discovering process. In this paper we offer an extension to the Max-Miner algorithm, which realize that idea. We define an interesting association rule as a rule which has following properties: an antecedent or a consequent of the rule is given by the user, the rules meets user's support and confidence constraints, and the rule has maximal discovered part. That definition can be very useful in many practical cases. Let us consider a doctor looking for the best method of treatment (i.e. a method, which gives him the greatest chance of patient's curing) in a medical database. He is interested in a rule: "treatment" $\Rightarrow$ "patient cured", where "treatment" is a discovered method of treatment and a rule has the highest confidence i.e. the discovered method of treatment leads for patient's curing with high probability. From association rules with given consequent and the same support, rules with the maximal antecedents provide the highest confidence.
In case with given antecedent of rules the set of discovered rules has also useful property. That output implicitly and succinctly represents all association rules meeting constraints specified by the user. It is because each frequent itemset, which can be a consequent, is a subset of one of discovered maximal consequent.

The rest of this paper is organized in the following manner. Section 2 summarizes related work. Section 3 formally defines association rules and their properties.

Section 4 provides brief introduction of the Max-Miner algorithm and describes an extension of that algorithm for finding association rules with maximal unknown part. Some results of experiments are also presented. Section 5 concludes this paper.

2 Related Work

The efficient algorithms for finding all association rules were proposed in [2,12]. In [4,6] the problem of constraint-based mining in dense data was investigated. In [4] an algorithm for finding all maximal frequent itemsets was proposed. Some proposals of usage of that algorithm for generating association rules were also discussed. In [6] an algorithm for mining all association rules with given consequent meeting specified by the user conditions on minimal support, confidence and improvement was introduced. The *improvement* of a rule was defined as the minimum difference between its confidence and the confidence of any proper sub-rule with the same consequent.

For discovering the most interesting rules a variety of metrics including gain [7], chi-squared value [10], lift, or conviction were used. A new approach to the problem of finding the optimal rules, which involves a partial order on rules defined in terms of both rule support and confidence, was defined in [5]. That concept of rule interestingness captures the best rules according to previously mentioned measures.

Another approach to mining interesting association rules is finding such subset of all rules, which enables inferring all of them. In [8] a *cover operator* of rule was introduced. A *Cover* of rule $X \Rightarrow Y$, $X \neq \emptyset$, $Y \neq \emptyset$ is defined as following: cover($X \Rightarrow Y$) = $\{X \cup Z \Rightarrow V \mid Z, V \subseteq Y$ and $X \cap Y = \emptyset$ and $V \neq \emptyset\}$. By means of cover the set of representative rules can be defined as a set of rules where each rule r does not belong to cover of any other rule. The efficient algorithm for finding representative rules was presented in [8]. In [9,11] a concept of closed frequent itemsets has been used for generating non-redundant association rules. In [11] a rule r is non-redundant if there is no other rules r' having the same support and the same confidence, of which the antecedent is a subset of the antecedent of r and the consequent is a superset of the consequent of r. In [14] the definition of non redundant rules is very similar to one in [11]. The only difference is that both antecedent and consequent of a rule must be minimal.

In [13] a method for elimination of redundancy from set of previously generated association rules was presented. That algorithm generates from a given set of association rules with the same consequent a minimal subset that consists of rules with minimal antecedent, which describe the consequent in all the cases in the database that the original rule set does.

3 Association Rules and Their Properties

We begin with defining the necessary terminology. A database D is a set of transactions, which are sets over a finite item domain I. Let *k-itemset* be a set of k items from database.

The basic property of an itemset is *support*. It is defined as percentage of transactions in D database, which contain given itemset. It is referred as a *relative support*. Formal expression of that support is shown below:

$$support(A) = |\{T \in D \mid A \subseteq T\}| / |D|,$$

where: A – itemset, T – transaction, D - database
Sometimes an *absolute support* is used. It is defined as:

$$support_a(A) = |\{T \in D \mid A \subseteq T\}|$$

Frequent itemset is an itemset with support not less than a given minimal level called *minSup*. An itemset is maximal frequent if it have no frequent superset.

Association rule is an implication:

$$X \Rightarrow Y, \text{ where } X, Y \text{ are itemsets over } I \text{ and } X \neq \varnothing, Y \neq \varnothing \text{ and } X \cap Y = \varnothing.$$

X is called an antecedent of rule, Y is called a consequent of rule. The support of rule $X \Rightarrow Y$ is equal to the $support(X \cup Y)$.

Confidence of rule $X \Rightarrow Y$ denoted as confidence($X \Rightarrow Y$) is defined as:

$$confidence(X \Rightarrow Y) = \text{support}(X \Rightarrow Y) / \text{support}(X).$$

Parameter *minConf* is defined by the user and indicates minimal confidence that discovered rules have to have.

Support and confidence properties

Let A and B, be itemsets over D database. Then the following property is kept:

$$A \subseteq B \Rightarrow \text{support}(A) \geq \text{support}(B)$$

It is implied directly by support definition. The number of transactions containing an itemset is less or equal to the number of transactions containing its subset.
This property implies that every subset of a frequent itemset is also frequent. This fact is very important and useful for frequent itemset discovery, and is utilized by almost all algorithms.
Let r_A: $(X \cup L) \rightarrow Y$, r_B: $X \rightarrow (Y \cup L)$ be an association rule. The following property are kept:

$$\text{confidence}(r_A) \geq \text{confidence}(r_B)$$

It is also implied directly by confidence definition and the support property. The number of transactions containing the $(X \cup L)$ itemset is less or equal to the number of transactions containing the X itemset. Both rules have the same support because both are consist of the same itemset.

4 Presentation of the Max-Miner

In this section we present briefly the Max-Miner algorithm, which was introduced in [5]. That algorithm was designed for finding maximal frequent itemsets in dense databases. Then we describe modifications of that algorithm for finding interesting rules according to the definition in Section 2.

The main idea of the Max-Miner algorithm is to find maximal frequent itemsets as quickly as possible, what allows essential reduction of the search space. To perform pruning methods a structure called *candidate group* is used. A candidate group g consists of two itemsets: a head denoted by $g.h$ and a tail denoted by $g.t$, in which elements are set in the given order. The ordering applied to a tail of candidate groups is aimed to force the most frequent items to appear in the most candidate groups. This is because items with high frequency are more likely to be a part of long frequent itemsets.

From a given candidate group g descendant groups g' are created in the following manner: $g'.h = g.h \cup \{i\}$, $i \in g.t$, $g'.t = \{j \mid j \in g.t$ and j follows i in the ordering$\}$. In the presented algorithm a head of candidate group g is a frequent itemset (not necessary maximal) and each sum: $g.h$ with an element that is included in a tail of group g is potentially a frequent itemset.

```
C = Ø;
F = Gen_Initial_Groups(D,C);
while C ≠ Ø do
begin
   scan D to count the support for all groups g∈C;
   for each group g∈C such that g.h ∪ g.t is
   frequent do
      F = F ∪ {g.h ∪ g.t};
   Cnew = Ø;
   for each {group g∈C such that g.h ∪ g.t is
   infrequent do
      F = F ∪ {Gen_Cand_Groups(g,Cnew)};
   C = Cnew;
   F = f ∈ F | ¬∃ a ∈ F , a ⊃ f};
   remove from C any groups g such that g.h ∪ g.t
   has a superset in F;
end
result: F;
```

Figure 1: Main loop of the Max-Miner algorithm

The efficient pruning strategies are based on the following properties of candidate groups:

if $g.h \cup g.t$ is a frequent itemset then the sets: $g.h \cup \{i\}$, where $i \in g.t$, are also frequent but not maximal. In this case set $g.h \cup g.t$ is added to the set of potential maximal frequent itemsets and candidate group g is removed from the search space,

if for some element $i \in g.t$ set: $g.h \cup \{i\}$ is infrequent then the descendent group g' such that $g'.h = g.h \cup \{i\}$ is not created because all itemsets created from group g' will be infrequent too.
The *Gen_Sub_Nodes* and the *Gen_Cand_Groups* functions instead of creating a candidate group with an empty tail return it as a potentially maximal frequent itemset.

```
function Gen_Initial_Groups (D: transaction set, var C:
empty set of candidate groups): frequent set
    scan D to obtain F1- the set of frequent 1-
    itemsets;
    if F1 = Ø then
        return Ø;
    else
    begin
      order elements i in F1 by increasing value
      of support of elements i;
      for each element i ∈ F1, i ≠ the last element
      in ordered set F1 do
      begin
        create new candidate group g such that: g.h =
        i, h.t = {j|{j} follows i in the ordering};
        C = C ∪ {g};
      end
    end
    return the last element in ordered set F1;
```

Figure 2: Generating initial candidate groups

```
function Gen_Cand_Groups (g: candidate group, var Cnew:
set of new candidate groups):frequent itemset
    remove any element i ∈ g.t if g.h ∪ {i} is
    infrequent;
    order elements i in g.t by increasing value
    of support of set g.h ∪ {i};
    for each element i ∈ g.t, i ≠ the last element in
    ordered set g.t do
    begin
      create new candidate group g': such that: g'.h =
      g.h ∪ {i}, g'.t = {j|j follows i in the
      ordering};
      Cnew = Cnew ∪ {g};
    end
    return g.h ∪ {m}, where m is the last element in
    ordered set g.t;
```

Figure 3: Generating descendant groups

In the pseudo-code in Figures 1,2,3 we use the following additional notation: F – set of maximal frequent sets, C – set of candidate groups.

4.1. Introducing Modifications of the Max-Miner Algorithm

The presentation of the modifications of the Max-Miner algorithm we start from describing changes for mining rules with given antecedent.

An antecedent is given, consequent is searched

The first change is obvious – we add an input itemset, which is given by the user either a consequent (denoted as UC) or an antecedent (denoted as UA) of rules, to then main loop of algorithm and the Gen_Initial_Group function. The second change is a modification of the Gen_Initial_Group function. We add calculation of support of consequent/antecedent of rules during calculation of a set of 1-itemset. If the given UC or UA of rules is infrequent the algorithm ends. In this case in the database there is no rule, which meets the required conditions. Otherwise 1-itemsets, which consist of element that is included in the given UC or UA, are removed from the F_1 set. The last change related with considering function is that the function returns nothing.
The main loop of the Max-Miner algorithm must also be modified. The changes are following:

- during calculation of support of candidate groups we concern only those transactions in which the given antecedent of rules is included. This method causes that calculated support of output itemsets is not the support of those itemsets but is the support of union of sets: output itemset and the antecedent of rules.
- an itemset $z = g.h \cup g.t$ is added to the set of potentially maximal frequent itemsets when the following conditions are met: counted support of z is not less than *minSup* and the following formula is true: support($z \cup UA$) / support(UA) $\geq$ *minConf*. The last condition ensures that a rule: $UA \rightarrow z$ has required confidence,
- descendant group g' is created from a group g only if an additional condition is met, namely: the following formula has to be true: support($g.h \cup UA$) /support(UA) $\geq$ *minConf*.

A consequent is given, antecedent is searched

In this case the changes considering adding the new input parameter and the modification of *Gen_Initial_Group* function are the same as in the case with given antecedent. Specific modifications concern the main loop of the Max-Miner algorithm. The following changes are made:

- the parameter denoted by *sup_reg* is added to a candidate group and its elements. That parameter indicates the support of association rule that consists of sets, which that parameter concerns as it is shown in Figure 4. The *sup_reg* parameters related with group are calculated during calculation of the support of the group. The *sup_reg* parameter is also used to calculate the confidence of rules. That confidence is given in the following formula: *object.sup_reg* / support(*object*),

- an itemset $z = g.h \cup g.t$ is added to the set of potentially maximal frequent itemsets when the following conditions are met: 1) an itemset $r = g.h \cup g.t \cup UC$ is frequent, 2) a value of formula: *g.sup_reg*/support $(g.h \cup g.t)$ is not less than *minConf*. The first condition ensures that the support of discovered rules will be equal or greater than *minSup*, the second condition ensures that the confidence of rules $z \rightarrow UC$ will be greater or equal than *minConf*,
- a group g is an input parameter to the *Gen_Cand_Groups* function only if set $z = g.h \cup g.t$ is not added to the set of potentially maximal frequent itemsets.

g.sup_reg – a support of set $z = g.h \cup g.t \cup UC$
g.h.sup_reg – a support of set $z = g.h \cup UC$
g.t.i.sup_reg – a support of set $z = g.h \cup \{i\} \cup UC$, where $i \in g.t$

Figure 4: Meaning of the *sup_reg* parameter concerning particular parts of a candidate group.

Modification of the *Gen_Cand_Groups* function concerns three steps, namely:

- in the first step of this function each element $i \in g.t$, where g is an input group, for which an itemset $z = g.h \cup \{i\} \cup UC$ is infrequent, is removed from the tail of g group,
- in the second step of this function items included in the tail of an input group are ordered by the increasing value of the *sup_reg* parameter connected with them. It is because we are interested in the support of rules not the support of considered antecedent of the rule.
- the last modification is setting a condition on a return itemset. Itemset $z = g.h \cup \{m\}$ is returned only if a value of the following formula: support $(g.h \cup \{m\} \cup UC)$ /support$(g.h \cup \{m\})$ is not less than *minConf*. Otherwise this function returns an empty itemset.

Now we present simple algorithm, which generates association rules from an output of the modified Max-Miner algorithm (a set of discovered, maximal part of rules) and from the given part of rules

```
1)  F- set of maximal either consequent or antecedent
    of rules
2)  for each set i ∈ F do
3)  begin
4)     create rule i → UC with support= i.sup_reg and
       confidence = i.sup_reg / support(i); //or
4)     create rule UA → i  with support = support (i ∪
       UA) and confidence = support(i ∪ UA) /
       support(UA);
5)  end
```

Figure 5: Algorithm for generating association rules

4.2. Experiments

To analyze the performance of our modification of the Max-Miner algorithm we performed several experiments on the *mushroom* set, which is located on the ftp://ftp.ics.uci.edu/pub/machine-learning-databases/mushroom/ page. We used a PC with Pentium III 733MHz processor and 1 GB of main memory. The goal of our experiments was to find out how the time of execution of the modified Max-Miner algorithm and size of its output set change depending on the number of items in a given part of association rules.

Table 1 presents the number of discovered rules and the time of performance for different numbers of items in the given antecedent of rule. Tests were conducted for *minConf* parameter equal to 50% and three *minSup* parameters equal to: 0.2%, 0.5% and 1%. The given antecedents of rules consisted of randomly chosen frequent items.

Table 1: Number of rules and execution time with given antecedent

Number of items in antecedent	**Number of discovered rules**			**Time of performance in seconds**		
	sup=0.2%	sup=0,5%	sup=1%	sup=0.2%	sup=0,5%	sup=1%
1	12	12	12	3	3	3
2	12	12	12	2	2	2
3	3	3	3	2	2	2
4	7	7	7	2	2	2
5	6	6	6	1	1	1

where sup means *minSup*.

The number of discovered rules and the time of performance for different numbers of items in the given consequent of rules are presented on Figure 6 and Figure 7, respectively. Tests were conducted for *minConf* parameter equal to 50% and three *minSup* parameters equal to: 1%, 2% and 5%. The given consequents of rules consisted of randomly chosen frequent items.

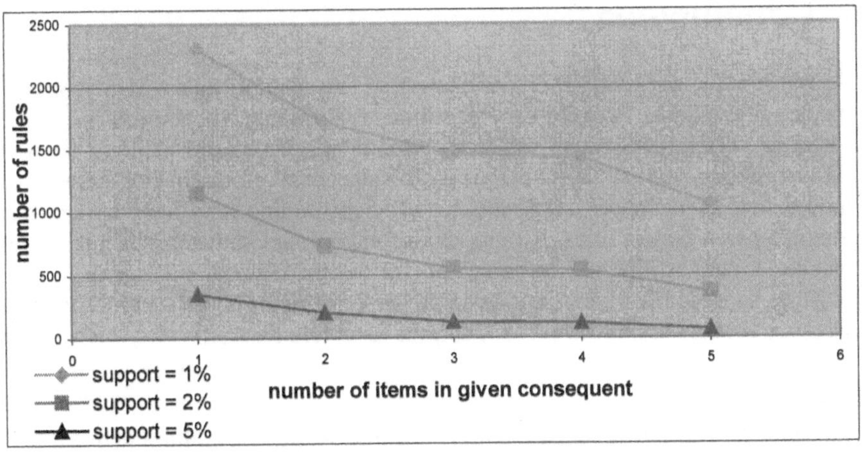

Figure 6: Number of rules with given consequent

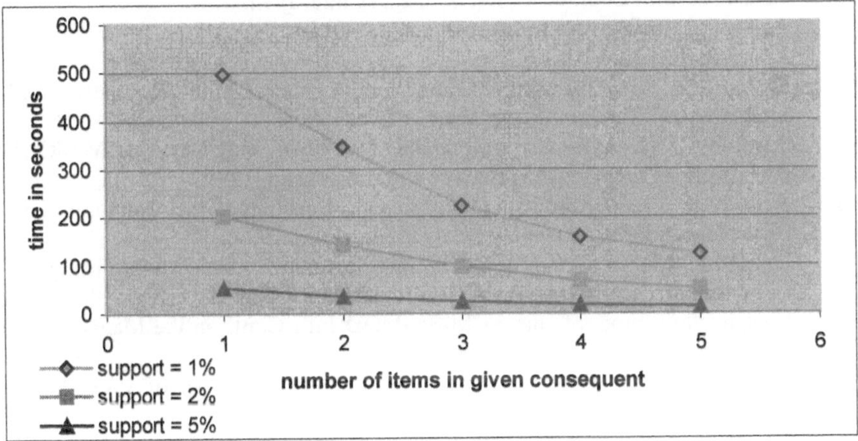

Figure 7: Execution time with given consequent

In both cases decreasing in time of execution were almost linear. The execution time in the case with known antecedent is much shorter than in the second case because we made only one pass over the database. In the next loop we read only those transactions, which included the given antecedent.

In the case with known antecedent changes in size of output set were irregular. That irregularity occurred because length of maximal consequents changed. In one case several itemsets, which pretended to be a maximal consequent had one superset, in another case those itemsets had no superset. In case with known consequent the size of output set decreased a little faster than linear.

5 Conclusions

We introduced the definition of interesting association rules and proposed an extension of the Max-Miner algorithm for finding such rules in dense databases. Our modification enables the user to specify the threshold of support and confidence and either consequent or antecedent of discovered rules. We showed how to use those constrains for efficient mining long itemsets and fast generating association rules. Results of our experiment showed that number of discovered rules still could be large. To reduce that size of the output set the measures such as lift or conviction can be used. Applying those measures to that discovery process seems to be a natural issue for future research.

References

1. Agrawal R., Imielinski T., Swami A.: Mining Associations Rules between Sets of Items in Large Databases, Proc. of the ACM SIGMOD Conf. on Management of Data. Washington DC 1993.
2. Agrawal R., Srikant R.: Fast Algorithms for Mining Association Rules in Large Databases, Int'l Conf. on VLDs; Santiago, Chile, 1994.
3. Agrawal R., Srikant R.: Mining Association Rules, Proc. of the 21st VLDB Conf. Zurich Switzerland 1995
4. Bayardo R.J. Jr.: Efficiently Mining Long Patterns from Databases, ACM-SIGMOD Int'l Conf. on Management of Data 1998.
5. Bayardo R.J. Jr., Agrawal R.: Mining the Most Interesting Rules, ACM SIGKDD Int'l Conf. on Knowledge Discovery and Data Mining1999.
6. Bayardo R.J. Jr., Agrawal R., Gunopulos D.: Constraint-Based Mining in Large, Dense Databases, Int'l Conf. on Data Engineering, 1999.
7. Fukuda T., Morimoto Y., Morishita S., Tokuyama T.: Data Mining using Two-Dimensional Optimized Association Rules: Scheme, Algorithms, and Visualization, Proc. of the ACM-SIGMOD Int'l Conf. on the Management of Data 1996.
8. Kryszkiewicz M.: Representative Association Rules; Proc. of PAKDD 1998 Melbourne, Australia
9. Kryszkiewicz M.: Representative Association Rules and Minimum Condition Maximum Consequence Association Rules; Proc. of PAKDD 1998 Nantes, France
10. Morishita S.: On Classification and Regresion, Proc. Of thr First Int'l Conf. on Discover Science, 1998.
11. Pasquier N., Taouli R., Stumme G.:Mining Minimal Non-redundant Association Rules using Frequent Closed Itemsets; Proc. of 6th Int'l Conf. on Rules and Objects in Databases London 2000
12 Savasere A., Omiecinski E., Navathe S.: An Efficient Algorithm for Mining Association Rules in Large Databases; In Proc. of the 21st Int'l Conf. on Very Large Data-Bases Zurich 1995.
13. Toivonen H., Klemettinen M., Ronkainen P., Hätönen K., Mannila H.: Pruning and Grouping Discovered Association Rules; Mlnet Workshop on Statistics, Machine Learning and Discovery in Databases; Heraklion, Create, Greece 1995
14. Zaki M.J.: Generating Non-Redundant Association Rules; KDD 2000 Boston MA USA

Action-Rules, Re-Classification of Objects and e-Commerce

Zbigniew W. Ras<1,2> and Shishir Gupta<1>

<1> UNC-Charlotte, Computer Science Dept., Charlotte, NC 28223, USA
<2> Polish Academy of Sciences, Institute of Computer Science, Ordona 21, 01-237 Warsaw, Poland
e-mail: ras@uncc.edu and shi2r@hotmail.com

Abstract: Consumers use electronic commerce to purchase a variety of goods and services online, including books, flowers, cars, food, banking, music and other forms of entertainment. Businesses also use these models to improve internal communication, help manage supply chains, conduct technical and market research, and locate potential customers and business partners. The U.S. Census Bureau of the U.S. Department of Commerce Web site (http://www.census.gov) is an example of an organization using many of these electronic commerce business models. Clearly, consumers decision to purchase some services or goods online is often dependent on satisfaction of previous buyers or features which for a current buyer are essential but they are not listed in the electronic commerce business model the customer wants to use. We claim that the query answering system for DKS proposed in [5] jointly with action rules proposed in [3] and extended in this paper to distributed agents framework can be effectively used to address this problem.

Keywords: knowledge discovery, distributed information systems, e-commerce.

1. Introduction

In the paper by Ras and Wieczorkowska (see [3]), the notion of an action rule was introduced. The main idea there was to generate, from a decision table, special type of rules which basically form a hint to business users showing a way to re-classify objects with respect to the decision attribute. In e-commerce application, this re-classification may just mean that a consumer not interested in a certain product, now may buy it. Decision table schema has a list of classification attributes used to classify consumers. Values of some of these attributes, for a given consumer, can be changed and this change can be influenced and controlled by a business user. However, some of these changes (for instance to the attribute "profit") can not be done directly to a chosen attribute. In this case, definitions of such an attribute in terms of other attributes have to be learned. These new definitions are used to construct action rules showing what changes in values of some attributes (called here flexible attributes), for a given consumer, are needed in order to re-classify this consumer the way business user wants. But, business user may be either unable or unwilling to proceed with actions leading to such changes. In all such cases we may search for definitions of these flexible attributes looking at either local or remote sites for help. If needed, this process can be continued leading to a chain of definitions of all these flexible attributes. This justifies that the distributed knowledge system framework, introduced in [4], can be a right vehicle for business users to generate action rules linking flexible attributes in several remote sites. These action rules are called in this paper global action rules.

2. Information Systems and Decision Tables

An information system is used for representing business knowledge. Its definition, given here, is due to Pawlak [2].

By an information system we mean a pair $S = (U, A)$, where:

1. U is a nonempty, finite set of objects (called customer identifiers),
2. A is a nonempty, finite set of attributes i.e. $a:U \rightarrow V_a$ for $a \in A$, where V_a is called the domain of a.

Information systems can be seen as generalizations of decision tables [2]. In any decision table together with the set of attributes a partition of that set into conditions and decisions is given. Additionally, we assume that the set of conditions is partitioned into stable conditions and flexible conditions [3]. Attribute a in A is called stable for the set U if its values assigned to objects from U are time dependent in a deterministic way. Otherwise, it is called flexible. Date of Birth is an example of a stable attribute. Interest rate on any customer account is an example of a flexible attribute. For simplicity reason, we will consider decision tables with only one decision. We adopt the following definition of a decision table:

By a decision table we mean any information system of the form $S = (U, A_1 \cup A_2 \cup \{d\})$, where $d \notin A_1 \cup A_2$ is a distinguished attribute called the decision. Elements of A_1 are called stable conditions, whereas the elements of $A_2 \cup \{d\}$ are called flexible conditions.

The assumption that attribute d is flexible is quite essential. We may want to re-classify an object x in U from the point of view of attribute d. In this case we may have to change values of some of its attributes from A_2, so the value of its attribute d might be changed as well. Before we proceed, certain relationships between values of attributes from A_2 and values of the attribute d will have to be discovered first.

3. Action Rules

In this section we recall a method proposed by Ras & Wieczorkowska (see [3]) to construct action rules from a decision table containing both stable and flexible attributes.

Before we introduce new definitions, assume that for any two collections of sets X, Y, we write, $X \subseteq Y$ if $(\forall x \in X)(\exists y \in Y)[\, x \subseteq y\,]$. Let $S = (U, A_1 \cup A_2 \cup \{d\})$ be a decision table and $B \subseteq A_1 \cup A_2$. We say that attribute d depends on B if $CLASS_S(B) \subseteq CLASS_S(d)$, where $CLASS_S(B)$ is a partition of U generated by B (see [2]). Assume now that attribute d depends on B where $B \subseteq A_1 \cup A_2$. The set B is called d-reduct in S if there is no proper subset C of B such that d depends on C. The concept of d-reduct in S was introduced in rough sets theory (see [2,6]) to identify minimal subsets of $A_1 \cup A_2$ such that rules describing the attribute d in terms of these subsets are the same as the rules describing d in terms of $A_1 \cup A_2$. Saying another words, it was shown that in order to induce rules in which THEN part consists of the decision attribute d and IF part consists of attributes belonging to $A_1 \cup A_2$, only subtables $(U, B \cup \{d\})$ of S where B is a d-reduct in S can be used for rules extraction.

By Dom(r) we mean all attributes listed in IF part of rule r. For example, if $r = [\,(a1,3)*(a2,4) \rightarrow (d,3)]$ is a rule then $Dom(r) = \{a1,a2\}$. By d(r) we denote the decision value of a rule r. In our example d(r) = 3.

If r1, r2 are rules and $B \subseteq A_1 \cup A_2$ is a set of attributes, then r1/B = r2/B means that the conditional parts of rules r1, r2 restricted to attributes B are the same. For example if $r1 = [(a1,3) \rightarrow (d,3)]$, then $r1/\{a1\} = r/\{a1\}$.

Example 1. Assume that S = ({x1,x2,x3,x4,x5,x6,x7,x8}, {**a**,**c**} {**b**} {**d**}) be a decision table represented by Figure 1. The set {**a**,**c**} contains stable attributes, **b** is a flexible attribute and **d** is a decision attribute.

It can be easily checked that {**b**,**c**}, {**a**,**b**} are the only two **d**-reducts in S.

Applying for instance LERS discovery system (developed by J. Grzymala-Busse), the following definitions are extracted from S:

(a,0) → (d,L), **(c,0) → (d,L)**,
(b,R) → (d,L), **(c,1) → (d,L)**,
(b,P) → (d,L), **(a,2)∧(b,S) → (d,H)**, **(b,S)∧(c,2) → (d,H)**.

Now, let us assume that (a, v → w) denotes the fact that the value of attribute a has been changed from v to w. Similarly, the term (a, v → w)(x) means that a(x)=v has been changed to a(x)=w. Saying another words, the property (a,v) of object x has been changed to property (a,w).

	a	b	c	d
x1	0	S	0	L
x2	0	R	1	L
x3	0	S	0	L
x4	0	R	1	L
x5	2	P	2	L
x6	2	P	2	L
x7	2	S	2	H
x8	2	S	2	H

Figure 1

Assume now that $S = (U, A_1 \cup A_2 \cup \{d\})$ is a decision table, where A_1 is the set of stable attributes and A_2 is the set of flexible attributes. Assume that rules r1, r2 have been extracted from S and $r1/A_1 = r2/A_1$, d(r1)=k1, d(r2)=k2 and k1< k2. Also, assume that (b1, b2,..., bp) is a list of all attributes in Dom(r1) $\cap$ Dom(r2) $\cap$ A_2 on which r1, r2 differ and r1(b1)= v1, r1(b2)= v2,..., r1(bp)= vp, r2(b1)= w1, r2(b2)= w2,..., r2(bp)= wp.

By (r1,r2)-action rule on $(x,y) \in U \times U$ we mean a formula **r**(x,y):
$[(b1, v1 \rightarrow w1) \wedge (b2, v2 \rightarrow w2) \wedge \ldots \wedge (bp, vp \rightarrow wp)](x) \Rightarrow [(d, k1 \rightarrow k2)](y)$.
If the value of the rule **r** on (x,y) is true then the rule **r** is valid for (x,y). Otherwise it is false. For simplicity reason, if x=y, we will say:

"value of the rule on x" instead of "value of the rule on (x,x)", and
"rule is valid for x" instead of "rule is valid for (x,x)".

Let us denote by $U^{<r1>}$ the set of objects in U supporting the rule r1. If (r1,r2)-action rule **r** is valid for $x \in U^{<r1>}$ then we say that the action rule **r** supports value $k2 \in Dom(d)$ in object x.

Example 2. Let $S = (U, A_1 \cup A_2 \cup \{\mathbf{d}\})$ be a decision table from Example 1, $A_2=\{\mathbf{b}\}$, $A_1 =\{\mathbf{a}, \mathbf{c}\}$. It can be checked that rules r1=[(**b**,**P**) $\rightarrow$ (**d**,**L**)], r2=[(**a**, **2**)$\wedge$(**b**, **S**) $\rightarrow$ (**d**,**H**)], r3=[(**b**, **S**)$\wedge$(**c**, **2**) $\rightarrow$ (**d**,**H**)] can be extracted from S. Clearly x5, x6 $\in U^{<r1>}$. Now, we can construct (r1,r2)-action rule **r** executed on x:

[(**b**, **P** $\rightarrow$ **S**)](x) $\Rightarrow$ [(**d**, **L** $\rightarrow$ **H**)](x).

Action rule **r** supports value **H** $\in$ Dom(**d**) in objects x5 and x6.

Example 3. Let $S = (U, A_1 \cup A_2 \cup \{\mathbf{d}\})$ be a decision table represented by Figure 2. Assume that $A_1= \{\mathbf{c}, \mathbf{b}\}$, $A_2 = \{\mathbf{a}\}$.

Clearly rules r1=[(**a**,**1**)$\wedge$(**b**,**1**) $\rightarrow$ (**d**,**L**)], r2=[(**c**,**2**)$\wedge$(**a**,**2**) $\rightarrow$ (**d**,**H**)] extracted from S are optimal. Also, $U^{<r1>} = \{x1, x4\}$.

It can be checked that (r1,r2)-action rule
[(**a**, **1** $\rightarrow$ **2**)](x) $\Rightarrow$ [(**d**, **L** $\rightarrow$ **H**)](x)

certainly supports new profit ranking **H** for **d** in object x1 but only possibly in x4.

	c	a	b	d
x1	2	1	1	L
x2	1	2	2	L
x3	2	2	1	H
x4	1	1	1	L

Figure 2

Algorithm for Constructing Action Rules was presented in [3].

4 Action Rules and Distributed Knowledge Systems

In this section we discuss the process of discovering action rules in distributed knowledge systems introduced in [4].

Let us assume that $S = (U,A)$ and $d \in A$ is a flexible attribute with $Dom(d)= \{d_1,d_2,d_3\}$. Also, assume that $A - \{d\} = A_1 \cup A_2$, where A_1 are stable attributes, A_2 are flexible attributes and,

$U_1= \{x : d_1 = d(x)\}$, $U_2= \{x : d_2 = d(x)\}$, $U_3= \{x : d_3 = d(x)\}$.

Our goal, if possible, is to change the classification of objects in U_1 from d_1 to either d_2 or d_3. To achieve this goal, first we extract rules from $S = (U,A)$ describing values of attribute d in terms of attributes from $A_1 \cup A_2$. Several situations can occur:

1. All d-reducts in S are subsets of A_2.
2. There is a reduct in S which is a subset of A_2.
3. All d-reducts have non-empty intersection with A_1.

In the first case we have the highest chance to change the classification of objects from U_1. The second case is similar assuming that the only reduct we want to consider is the one, which is a subset of A_2. In e-commerce scenario, the second case may describe situation when only one reduct is a subset of A_2 and it contains attributes which correspond to offers business user is willing to send out to customers. In the last case, we have the lowest chance to extract action rules from S because of the existence of stable attributes in a reduct. For instance, let us assume that *age* is a necessary condition for classification of objects from U with respect to the decision d. Now, if every person in U_1 is minimum 30 years old and every person in U_2 is maximum 20 years old, then objects from U_1 can not be reclassified to a group U_2 because the value of attribute *age* can not be changed.

In [4], we introduced the notion of a Distributed Knowledge Systems (DKS) framework. DKS is seen as a collection of knowledge systems where each knowledge system is initially defined as an information system coupled with a set of rules (called a knowledge base) extracted from that system. These rules are transferred between sites due to the requests of local query answering systems. Each rule transferred from one site of DKS to another remains at both sites so changes in the contents of knowledge bases may easily be handled. Useless rules (either of very low confidence or not used by query answering system for a long time) are removed from a knowledge base. Assume now that S, defined before, represents one of DKS sites. If rules extracted from S describing values of some flexible attribute d in terms of attributes from $A_1 \cup A_2$ do not lead us to any useful action rules (user is not willing to undertake actions leading to required changes of values of flexible attributes $B_2 \subset A_2$ within the classification part of a rule), we may:

1. find definitions of attributes from B_2 in terms of other local flexible attributes (local mining for rules),
2. find definitions of attributes from B_2 in terms of flexible attributes from other sites (mining for rules at a remote site),
3. find definitions of the decision attribute d in terms of flexible attributes from other sites (mining for rules at a remote site).

Now, we will discuss all three cases.

Example 4. Assume that $S_1 = (U_1, \{\mathbf{a}\} \cup \{\mathbf{b}, \mathbf{e}, \mathbf{d}\})$ is an information system, represented by Figure 3, where $\{\mathbf{a}\}$ is a set of stable attributes and $\{\mathbf{b}, \mathbf{e}, \mathbf{d}\}$ is a set of flexible attributes. Information system $S = (U, A_1 \cup A_2)$ where $A_2=\{\mathbf{b}, \mathbf{d}\}$, $A_1 =\{\mathbf{a}, \mathbf{c}\}$ is represented by Figure 1. These two systems represent two sites of DKS.

	a	b	e	d
y1	0	P	2	L
y2	0	P	2	H
y3	0	S	4	H
y4	2	S	4	H
y5	2	P	3	L
y6	2	P	3	H

Figure 3

From the rules describing attribute **d** and extracted from system S, the following action rule can be discovered: $[(\mathbf{b}, \mathbf{P} \rightarrow \mathbf{S})](x) \Rightarrow [(\mathbf{d}, \mathbf{L} \rightarrow \mathbf{H})](x)$, where $x \in U$.

Now, assume that the user would like to re-classify objects x5, x6 in the information system S with respect to attribute **d** but he does not know any appropriate action which can be taken to re-classify them with respect to attribute **b**. Attribute **b** is the only attribute in A_2 which is flexible so we can not search for a definition of **b** inside S. In this case, we have to look for another system S' in DKS in which attribute **b** is both local and it can be defined in terms of other flexible attributes in S'. In our example, it can be checked that the following action rule can be extracted from S_1 :

$[(\mathbf{e}, \mathbf{2} \rightarrow \mathbf{4})](y) \Rightarrow [\mathbf{b}, \mathbf{P} \rightarrow \mathbf{S})](y)$.

This rule is referring to objects y1, y2. The question is, how similar these two objects are to objects x5, x6? Clearly, higher similarity between objects x and y, where $x \in \{x5, x6\}$ and $y \in \{y1, y2\}$, will guarantee higher probabilty of success for the following action rule (called a global action rule because its classification attribute is at a remote site):

If $\rho(x,y) > \lambda$, then $[(\mathbf{e}, \mathbf{2} \rightarrow \mathbf{4})](y) \Rightarrow [(\mathbf{d}, \mathbf{L} \rightarrow \mathbf{H})](x)$

where $(x,y) \in U \times U_1$, $\rho(x,y)$ describes the similarity between objects x, y, and λ is some threshold value.

Locally, for the system S, this global action rule can be re-written as:

$[(\mathbf{e}, \mathbf{?} \rightarrow \mathbf{4})](x) \Rightarrow [(\mathbf{d}, \mathbf{L} \rightarrow \mathbf{H})](x)$ with confidence k, where k is calculated on the basis of $\rho(x,y)$ from the paragraph above.

The interpretation of the last rule is quite interesting. It is referring to reclassification of objects x5, x6 with respect to a remote attribute **e**. If this step is successful, these objects should be re-classified with respect to the decision attribute **d**. Two situations can still happen:

1. The user knows and is willing to undertake an appropriate action needed to verify and eventually change the value of the remote attribute **e** for objects x5, x6.
2. The user does not know such actions. In this case we have to search for a definition of attribute **e** either in terms of local or new global attributes for S (see [4]).

Finally, the last case, represents situation when the decision attribute **d** belongs to both local and remote site. It happens in the current example. The global action rule, we already learned, has the following local form for S:

$\mathbf{r1} = [[(\mathbf{e}, \mathbf{?} \rightarrow \mathbf{4})](x) \Rightarrow [(\mathbf{d}, \mathbf{L} \rightarrow \mathbf{H})](x)]$.

As we have stated before, this rule is a possible rule and its confidence is calculated on the basis of $\rho(x,y)$.

At site S_1, this rule is referring to objects y1, y2. The following two certain rules can be extracted from S_1:

$(\mathbf{b},\mathbf{S}) \rightarrow (\mathbf{d},\mathbf{H})$, $(\mathbf{e},\mathbf{4}) \rightarrow (\mathbf{d},\mathbf{H})$.

Clearly, the second rule "supports" our global action rule **r1** when it is seen as a local rule in S_1 and the same will increase our confidence in **r1** when applied in S.

References

1. Chmielewski M. R., Grzymala-Busse J. W., Peterson N. W., Than S., "The Rule Induction System LERS - a Version for Personal Computers", in *Foundations of Computing and Decision Sciences*, Vol. 18, No. 3-4, 1993, Institute of Computing Science, Technical University of Poznan, Poland, 181-212.
2. Pawlak Z., "Rough Sets and Decision Tables", in *Lecture Notes in Computer Science* 208, Springer-Verlag, 1985, 186-196.
3. Ras, Z., Wieczorkowska, A., "Action Rules: how to increase profit of a company", in *"Principles of Data Mining and Knowledge Discovery"*, (Eds. D.A. Zighed, J. Komorowski, J. Zytkow), Proceedings of PKDD'00, Lyon, France, LNCS/LNAI, No. 1910, Springer-Verlag, 2000, 587-592
4. Ras, Z., Zytkow, J.M., "Mining for attribute definitions in a distributed two-layered DB system", in *Journal of Intelligent Information Systems*, Kluwer, Vol. 14, No. 2/3, 2000, 115-130
5. Ras, Z., "Query Answering based on Distributed Knowledge Mining", Invited paper, in Proceedings of IAT'2001, Maebashi City, Japan, October 23-26
6. Skowron A., Grzymala-Busse J., "From the Rough Set Theory to the Evidence Theory", *in ICS Research Reports* 8/91, Warsaw University of Technology, October, 1991

Discovering Interesting Rules from Financial Data

Przemysław Sołdacki and Grzegorz Protaziuk

Institute of Computer Science, Warsaw University of Technology
e-mail: *{psoldack,gprotazi}@ii.pw.edu.pl*

Abstract: In this paper problem of mining data with weights and finding association rules is presented. Some applications are discussed, especially focused on financial data. Solutions of the problem are analyzed. A few approaches are proposed and compared. Pruning based on measures of rules interestingness is described and some measures proposed in literature are shown. Influence of data weights on these measures is also discussed.
Keywords: knowledge exploration, data mining, association rules, data with weights

1 Introduction

Discovering association rules is one of the most important tasks in data mining and many efficient algorithms were proposed in literature. However, the number of discovered rules is often so large, that the user cannot analyze all discovered rules. To overcome that problem several methods for mining interesting rules only have been proposed. One of them is pruning based on interestingness measures. Many measures have been proposed in literature. We describe and compare them.

Most of data mining algorithms assume equal data weights of all transactions. It is reasonable in most cases. However sometimes different data weights can increase applicability and accuracy of algorithms. Data weights influence on interestingness measures. In this paper we describe how weights of transaction items can be used for mining interesting rules, especially in financial data.

The rest of this paper is organized in the following manner. Section 2 summarizes related work. Section 3 formally defines association rules and their properties. Section 4 describes usage of weight of items in discovering frequent itemsets and association rules. Section 5 presents association rules interestingness measures proposed in literature. Section 6 concludes this paper.

2 Related Work

The efficient algorithms for finding all association rules were proposed in [2,4,6.9]. For discovering the most interesting rules varied metrics including coverage, lift, conviction or PS (Piatetsky-Shapiro measure) were used. A new approach to the problem of finding the optimal rules, which involves a partial order on rules defined in terms of both rule support and confidence, was defined in [5]. That concepts of rule interestingness capture the best rules according to previously mentioned measures. Many other interestingness measures have been proposed in literature. Some of them can be found in [6],[13],[14],[15],[16]. Some approaches to using data weights can also be found in [12].

Another approach facilitating mining of interesting association rules is based on finding such a subset of all rules, which enables inferring all of them. In [7] a *cover operator* of rule was introduced. A *Cover* of rule $X \Rightarrow Y$, $X \neq \emptyset$, $Y \neq \emptyset$ is defined as following: $Cover(X \Rightarrow Y) = \{X \cup Z \Rightarrow V \mid Z,V \subseteq Y \text{ and } X \cap Y = \emptyset \text{ and } V \neq \emptyset\}$. By means of cover the set of representative rules can be defined as set of rules where each rule r does not belong to cover of any other rule. The efficient algorithm for finding representative rules was presented in [8]. A concept of closed frequent itemsets and a method for generating non-redundant rules based on that concept was described in [10]. A rule r is redundant if there exists a rule with the same support and confidence as r and either its consequent is a subset of consequent of rule r or its antecedent is a subset of antecedent of rule r.

3 Association Rules and Their Properties

We begin with definition of necessary terminology. A database D is a set of transactions, which are sets over a finite item domain I. Let *k-itemset* be a set of k items from database.

The most basic property of an itemset is *support*. It is defined as percentage of transactions in D database, which contain given itemset. It is referred as a relative support. Formal expression is shown below:

$$support(A) = |\{T \in D \mid A \subseteq T\}| \,/\, |D|, \text{ where:}$$

A – itemset,
T – transaction,
D - database

Sometimes an absolute support is used. It is defined as: $support_a(A) = |\{T \in D \mid A \subseteq T\}|$

Frequent itemset is an itemset with support not less than a given minimal level called *minSup*. An itemset is maximal frequent if it have no frequent superset.

Association rule is an implication:

$$X \Rightarrow Y, \text{ where } X, Y \text{ are itemsets over } I \text{ and } X \neq \emptyset,\ Y \neq \emptyset \text{ and } X \cap Y = \emptyset.$$

X is called an antecedent of rule, Y is called consequent of rule. The support of rule $X \Rightarrow Y$ is equal to the $support(X \cup Y)$.

Confidence of rule $X \Rightarrow Y$ denoted as $confidence(X \Rightarrow Y)$ is defined as:

$$confidence(X \Rightarrow Y) = support(X \Rightarrow Y) \,/\, support(X).$$

Parameter *minConf* is defined by the users and indicates minimal confidence that discovered rules need to have.

3.1 Support Properties

Let A and B, be itemsets over D database. Then the following property is kept:

$$A \subseteq B \;\Rightarrow\; support(A) \geq support(B)$$

It is implied directly by support definition. A number of transactions containing an itemset is less or equal to a number of transactions containing its subset.

This property implies that every subset of a frequent itemset is also frequent. It is very important and useful fact for frequent itemset discovery and is utilized by almost all algorithms.

4 Data with Weights

4.1 Applications

One of classic knowledge exploration problems is purchase-basket analysis. Let us discover it from salesman point of view where income or profit is the key issue. Number of transactions is not so important. It is assumed that transactions giving higher income are more interesting than others. Consequently we presume that a day of highest income is more important than a day of maximal number of transactions.

Usually when analyzing purchase-basket we can easily get goods along with their prices and sometimes even with margin on every product. We can use all these information. We can use prices as data weights if we are more interested in income. Using margin we will set store by profit.

Certainly there are many other applications, where data with weights are very helpful. It includes almost all situations, when data being explored are associated with money.

Also other values and measures can be used as data weights, for instance: a time of activities, a size or physical weight of goods and so on.

4.2 Data Formats

There are two main approaches of data weighting depending on data formats:

- associating weights to transaction items
- associating weights to transactions

Let us present following examples in different data formats (X1 and L are some attributes we want to analyze):

Table 1. Data A. Relational format, weights associated to transactions

Transaction ID (TID)	X1	L	Weight
1	A	4	8
2	B	3	9
3	A	3	2
4	C	1	10
5	A	8	11

Table 2. Data B. Transactional format, weights associated to items

Transaction ID (TID)	Item	Weight
1	A	5
1	B	3
2	B	3
2	D	6
3	E	1
3	D	1

As we can see a data format naturally selects resolution of information about weights. Certainly there are also other possibilities. We can imagine some hybrid formats. Next two tables show such examples.

Table 3. Data C. Relational format, weights associated to items (weights after colon)

Transaction ID (TID)	X1	L
1	A:5	4:3
2	B:3	3:6
3	A:1	3:1
4	C:6	1:4
5	A:6	8:5

Table 4. Data D: Transactional format, weights associated to transaction (weight as value of WEIGHT attribute)

Transaction ID (TID)	Item
1	X1=A
1	L=4
1	WEIGHT =3
2	X1=B
2	L=3
2	WEIGHT =6
3	X1=A
3	L=3
3	WEIGHT =4

Let weights be combined by arithmetic adding. It is true in many kinds of weights, for example money. To have a weight of transaction we just need to add weights of all items contained in it. Certainly it is not easy and usually not even possible to get items weights from transaction weights. In certain cases analytical methods can be used.

4.3 Itemsets and Association Rules With Weights

Support is a relevance measure of an itemset. By modifying definition of support we can use information on data weights. Certainly it influences support and confidence of association rules, which are based on itemsets support.

4.4 Item Weights

Assume following support definition:

$$support(A) = \Sigma_{t \in D} \Sigma_{\{e \mid e \in t \cap A\}} weight(e),$$

where D – database, t – transaction, e – item

Such a definition represents sum of weights of all items contained in a set. Let us consider purchase data, for instance. In this situation the support shows total amount of money earned by selling goods contained in an itemset. Unfortunately such a definition is very inconvenient, because increasing cardinality of an itemset increases support. It violates one of main support's properties. We would like to have a definition where increasing cardinality of an itemset effects in equal or lower value of support. This property is very important and is used by almost all algorithms for finding frequent itemsets and association rules. Therefore we have to consider changes in this definition to achieve needed property.

4.5 Transaction Weights

Let us define itemset support as:

$$support(A) = \Sigma_{\{t \mid t \in D \wedge A \subseteq t\}} \Sigma_{e \in t}\, weight(e)$$

what is equivalent to

$$support(A) = \Sigma_{\{t \mid t \in D \wedge A \subseteq t\}}\, weight(t)$$

where

$$weight(t) = \Sigma_{e \in t}\, weight(e)$$

It means that support if itemset is a sum of weights of transactions containing given itemset. In purchase-basket example support represent summary sale of transactions that include items of given set. It is possible that a very cheap item is frequently present in very expensive transactions. However such information is also valuable, because maybe this cheap item increases sale of other expensive items, which appear in a same transaction. It can be a good reason to make a promotion and to give such cheap item for free.

An additional advantage of such a definition is that assuming all transaction weights equal to 1, we get classic support definition.

5 Interestingness Measures

Support and confidence are the most basic measures of rules interestingness. Usually interesting rules are defined as rules describing surprising uncommon situations. In such cases support and confidence are not sufficient. Many additional measures were proposed.

Please note that confidence definition is based on support of entire rule and of antecedent. It does not use support of a consequent. Thus we lost some information. It can cause some negative effects. For instance: if customers buy milk in 80% of transactions and it is an independent event on buying salmon then confidence of *salmon* $\Rightarrow$ *milk* rule is 80%. Certainly rule describing independent events is not interesting.

Most of measures are defined by combination of itemsets probabilities. Support of itemset describes probability of its appearance in transaction from database *D*. Itemsets of rule $A \Rightarrow B$ are shown in the Figure 1.

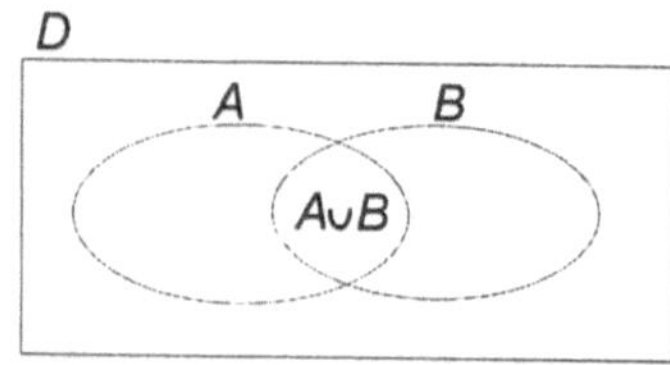

Fig. 1. Itemsets of rule $A \Rightarrow B$.

We can define probabilities of itemsets appearances in the following manner:

$P(A) = support(A)$
$P(B) = support(B)$
$P(A,B) = support(A \cup B)$
$P(B \mid A) = P(A,B) / P(A) = confidence(A \Rightarrow B)$
$P(\sim A) = 1 - P(A) = 1 - support(A)$, where ~ is a negation

Coverage [13]

$$coverage(A \Rightarrow B) = P(A,B) / P(B) = support(A \cup B) / support(B)$$

It shows what part of itemsets from consequent is covered by a rule. Its values are in range [0; 1].

Lift [6],[14]

This measure is also called *interest*. It is defined as follows:

$$lift(A \Rightarrow B) = P(A,B) / (P(A) \cdot P(B)) = support(A \cup B) / (support(A) \cdot support(B))$$

It is equal to proportion of real support of itemset $A \cup B$ to expected support (assuming independent events). Therefore it shows level of correlation between antecedent and consequent. However it does not let to determine direction of implication, because it is symmetric.

Lift can be also defined using *confidence*:

$$lift(A \Rightarrow B) = confidence(A \Rightarrow B) / support(B)$$

This form of definition leads to another interpretation. *Lift* shows proportion of conditional probability B (under condition of A) to unconditional probability of B. It is explained in the following example:

Let us presume that during exploration process rule *bread* ⇒ *milk* is found and its confidence is equal to 80%. It potentially holds useful knowledge. However, if 90% of all customers buy milk then this rule is not interesting. In such a case *lift* is a very helpful measure. In considered example its value is lower than 1.

If antecedent and consequent were independent then:

$$confidence(A \Rightarrow B) = support(A \cup B) / support(A) =$$
$$= (support(A) \cdot support(B)) / support(A) = support(B)$$

Thus expected confidence is equal to support of consequent. Then *lift* shows how unexpected is real *confidence*.

Its values are in range $[0;+\infty)$. Values lower than 1 mean, that satisfying condition of antecedent decreases probability of consequent in comparison to unconditional probability. Consequently, values higher than 1 mean, that satisfying condition of antecedent increases probability of consequent in comparison to unconditional probability. If antecedent and consequent are independent then *lift* is equal to 1.

Piatetsky-Shapiro [13]

$$PS(A \Rightarrow B) = P(A,B) - P(A) \cdot P(B) = support(A \cup B) - support(A) \cdot support(B)$$

Absolute value of this measure shows dependence between antecedent and consequent. Its values are in range <-1;+1>. Positive values mean that conditional probability of consequent (under condition from antecedent) is higher than unconditional one. If antecedent and consequent are independent *PS* measure is equal to 0.

Conviction [14]

$$conviction(A \Rightarrow B) = P(A)\ P(\sim B) \ /\ P(A, \sim B)$$

This measure was derived from implication definition. Implication $A \Rightarrow B$, can be presented in following form $\sim(A \wedge \sim B)$. This form was transformed by avoiding negation and whole term was transferred to denominator. Thus the measure shows level of dependence between A and $\sim B$. After some transformations we achieve:

$$conviction(A \Rightarrow B) = P(A)\ (1 - P(B)) \ /\ (P(A) - P(A,B))$$

Using supports instead of probabilities leads to formula shown below:

$$conviction(A \Rightarrow B) = support(A) \cdot (1 - support(B)) \ /\ (support(A) - support(A \cup B))$$

what is equivalent to:

$$conviction(A \Rightarrow B) = (1 - support(B)) \ /\ (1 - confidence(A \Rightarrow B))$$

Its values are in range $[0;+\infty]$. If antecedent and consequent are independent it is equal to 1. For implications occurring in all cases measure's value is equal to $+\infty$.

Interestingness [6]

This measure is extension of *lift* measure. It shows level of interestingness based on support of antecedent and consequent, correlations between them and two additional parameters. It is defined as:

$$I(A \Rightarrow B) = \left(\left(\frac{\sup(A \cup B)}{\sup(A) \cdot \sup(B)} \right)^k - 1 \right) \cdot (\sup(A) \cdot \sup(B))^m$$

where parameter

k – importance of event dependency
m – importance of support

J-measure [16]

This measure shows how much information is contained in a rule. It is defined as:

$$J(A \Rightarrow B) = P(B) \cdot \left[\mathit{coverage}(A \Rightarrow B) \cdot \log(\frac{\mathit{coverage}(A \Rightarrow B)}{P(A)}) + (1 - \mathit{coverage}(A \Rightarrow B)) \cdot \log(\frac{1 - \mathit{coverage}(A \Rightarrow B)}{1 - P(A)}) \right]$$

what is equivalent to:

$$J(A \Rightarrow B) = \sup(B) \cdot \left[\mathit{coverage}(A \Rightarrow B) \cdot \log(\frac{\mathit{coverage}(A \Rightarrow B)}{\sup(A)}) + (1 - \mathit{coverage}(A \Rightarrow B)) \cdot \log(\frac{1 - \mathit{coverage}(A \Rightarrow B)}{1 - \sup(A)}) \right]$$

Expressions in square brackets show relative entropy of rule, which is mean value of information capacity. Thus measure combining it with consequent support shows how much rule is interesting.

5.1 Interestingness Measures With Weights

Using support definition from section 4.5 we can calculate other measures of association rule interestingness. Let us consider measure values with and without weights for some data shown below. Transaction 3 is weighted 11, which is sum of item weights. Please notice that without weights these data are symmetric considering items A and B, but with weights they are not.

Table 5. Sample data

Transaction ID (TID)	Item	Weight
1	A	1
2	B	10
3	A	1
3	B	10
4	A	1
5	B	10

Table 6. Interestingness measures

Measure	Value without weights	Value with weights
Support(A)	60%	39%
Support(B)	60%	94%
Support(A∪B)	20%	33%
Confidence(A⇒B)	33%	85%
Confidence(B⇒A)	33%	35%
Coverage(A⇒B)	60%	35%
Coverage(B⇒A)	60%	85%
Lift(A⇒B)	0.56	0.9
Lift(B⇒A)	0.56	0.9
PS(A⇒B)	-16%	-3.66%
PS(B⇒A)	-16%	-3.66%
Conviction(A⇒B)	0.6	0.39
Conviction(B⇒A)	0.6	0.94

Very interesting are asymmetric measures: confidence and conviction. Confidence is higher for rules with implication from item with lower weight to item with higher weight. In many cases it is very reasonable. During purchase basket data mining implication from a cheap product to expensive one is more interesting than the opposite implication.

Unexpectedly conviction measure behaves the opposite way. Certainly it sometimes also can be useful, however it is important to keep it in mind.

6 Conclusions

We discussed some aspects of mining interesting association rules. We analyzed two approaches to processing data with weights and presented advantages and disadvantages of both. Basic and additional measures of rule interestingness was collected and presented. We also highlighted weights influence to interestingness measures. Also several applications were proposed especially focused on financial aspects.

Using weights is a very interesting approach in association rules discovery process. In this paper only financial data analysis was discussed. It seems that there are many other important applications and it is possible direction of future extensions.

References

1. Agrawal R., Imielinski T., Swami A.: Mining Associations Rules between Sets of Items in Large Databases; Proc. of the ACM SIGMOD Conf. on Management of Data. Washington DC 1993.
2. Agrawal R., Srikant R.: Fast Algorithms for Mining Association Rules in Large Databases Int'l Conf. on VLDs; Santiago, Chile, 1994.
3. Agrawal R., Srikant R.: Mining Association Rules. Proc. of the 21st VLDB Conf. Zurich Switzerland 1995
4. Bayardo R.J. Jr.: Efficiently Mining Long Patterns from Databases; ACM-SIGMOD Int'l Conf. on Management of Data 1998.
5. Bayardo R.J. Jr., Agrawal R.: Mining the Most Interesting Rules; ACM SIGKDD Int'l Conf. on Knowledge Discovery and Data Mining1999.
6. Bayardo R.J. Jr., Agrawal R., Gunopulos D.: Constraint-Based Mining in Large, Dense Databases; Int'l Conf. on Data Engineering, 1999.
7. Kryszkiewicz M.: Representative Association Rules; Proc. of PAKDD 1998 Melbourne, Australia
8. Kryszkiewicz M.: Representative Association Rules and Minimum Condition Maximum Consequence Association Rules; Proc. of PAKDD 1998 Nantes, France
9. Savasere A., Omiecinski E., Navathe S.: An Efficient Algorithm for Mining Association Rules in Large Databases; In Proc. of the 21st Int'l Conf. on Very Large Data-Bases Zurich 1995.
10. Toivonen H., Klemettinen M., Ronkainen P., Hätönen K., Mannila H.: Pruning and Grouping Discovered Association Rules; Mlnet Workshop on Statistics, Machine Learning and Discovery in Databases; Heraklion, Create, Greece 1995
11. Zaki M.J.: Generating Non-Redundant Association Rules; KDD 2000 Boston MA USA
12. Hilderman, R. J., & Hamilton, H. J. (2001). Evaluation of interestingness measures for ranking discovered knowledge. Proceedings of the Fifth Pacific-Asia Conference on Knowledge Discovery and Data Mining (pp. 247--259). Hong Kong, China: Springer-Verlag.
13. B. Iglesia "Induction of Interesting Rules from Large Datasets", University of East Anglia, 1999.
14. S. Brin, R. Motwani, J. D. Ullman, S. Tsur „Dynamic Itemset Counting and Implication Rules for Market Basket Data", 1997.
15. B. Gray, M.E. Orlowska "Clustering categorical attributes into interesting association rules". Proceedings of the Second Pacific-Asia Conference on PAKDD'1998.
16. P. Smyth and R.M. Goodman "Rule induction using information theory". "Knowledge Discovery in Databases", 1991.

Bagging and Induction of Decision Rules

Jerzy Stefanowski

Institute of Computing Science, Poznan University of Technology, Piotrowo 3A, 60-965 Poznan, Poland. E-mail *jerzy.stefanowski@cs.put.poznan.pl*

Abstract. An application of the rule induction algorithm MODLEM to bagging is discussed. Bagging is a recent approach to construct multiple classifiers that combines homogeneous classifiers generated from different distributions of training examples. The basic characteristics of bagging and the MODLEM are given. This paper reports an experimental study of using bagging composite classifier and the single MODLEM based classifier on a representative collection of datasets. The results show that bagging substantially improve predictive accuracy.

1 Introduction

Creating classification systems on the basis of a set of learning examples is one of the main problems considered in machine learning and knowledge discovery. Much of research in this problem has focused on improving *predictive accuracy*. It is easy to understand why this is so - accuracy is a primary concern in all applications of supervised learning systems and is easily measured [11].

Recently, there has been observed a growing interest in increasing accuracy by combining *multiple learning models* into one classification system, for some review see, e.g. [6,4,13]. The integration of multiple classification models has been approached in many ways. First of all, one can decide between using *homogeneous* or *heterogeneous classifiers*. In a case of heterogeneous classifiers, one can use different learning algorithms on the same dataset and their predictions could be combined in a different way, e.g. by stacked generalization or meta-learning. Further on, due to the selective superiority of single learning algorithms one can create a hybrid system using multistrategic learning principle that fits the data with different representations [10]. Yet another popular approach is to generate and combine multiple, homogeneous models by using different training distributions (e.g. boosting or bagging techniques [2,5]). Empirical evaluations showed that these kinds of integration lead to improving predictive accuracy, it means that the composite system could better classify new (or testing) objects than its component models used independently.

In this paper we focus attention on the *bagging* approach introduced by Breiman [2]. It manipulates the input data to get several different learning sets by using specific sampling with replacement of learning examples. Then, different classifiers are generated from these learning sets. Finally, the multiple classifiers are combined by simple voting to form a composite classifier.

The aim of this paper is to examine the application of bagging approach to MODLEM [12], which is an algorithm inducing decision rules. First motivation results from a literature observation that bagging has been already applied mainly to such learning techniques as decision trees, Bayesian classifier or discriminant function [2–4,11]. According to our best knowledge, the rule induction has not be used yet in this framework. The second motivation follows our personal interest in the development of the MODLEM algorithm. We have already showed in computational experiments that, from numerical data, this algorithm produces decision rules, which are of comparable or better quality than rules induced by standard rule induction algorithms which need prediscretization phase [9]. Therefore, we want to check whether this algorithm could also improve predictive accuracy in the bagging approach. More precisely, we want to experimentally compare on several datasets the performance of the composite bagging classifier against the single use of the basic MODLEM algorithm.

The paper is organized as follows. In Section 2, we begin with a brief description of the MODLEM algorithm. In Section 3, we describe the bagging approach. Results of comparative experiments are given in Section 4. Discussion of these results and conclusions are presented in the final section.

2 Rule induction algorithm MODLEM

2.1 Notation

Let us assume that learning examples are represented in *decision table* $DT = (U, A \cup \{d\})$, where U is a set of examples (objects), A is a set of *condition attributes* describing examples such that $a : U \to V_a$ for every $a \in A$. The set V_a is a domain of a. Let $a(x)$ denotes the value of attribute $a \in A$ taken by $x \in U$; $d \notin A$ is a decision attribute that partitions examples into a set of decision classes (concepts) $\{K_j : j = 1, \ldots, k\}$.

A decision rule r describing class K_j is represented in the following form: *if* P *then* Q, where $P = w_1 \wedge w_2 \wedge \ldots w_p$ is a condition part of the rule and Q is decision part of the rule indicating that example satisfying P should be assigned to class K_j. The elementary condition of the rule r is defined as $(a_i(x)\ rel\ v_{a_i})$, where rel is a relational operator from the set $\{=, <, \leq, >, \geq\}$ and v_{a_i} is a constant being a value of attribute a_i.

$[P]$ is a *cover* of the condition part of rule r in DT, i.e. it is a set of examples, which description satisfy elementary conditions in P. Let B be a set of examples belonging to class K_j. For a decision rules r we require that $[P] \cap B \neq \emptyset$. If $[P] = \bigcap [w_i] \subseteq B$, the set B depends on P. This rule is discriminant as it distinguishes positive examples of class K_j from its negative examples. P should be a minimal conjunction of elementary conditions satisfying this requirement. The set of decision rules R completely describes examples of class K_j, if each example is covered by at least one decision rules. Usually we require to construct such a description by a *minimal set* of rules. Formally, it is expressed by the concept of *local covering* [7]. Let $\mathbf{P}$ be a set of conjunctions P of rules indicating class K_j. $\mathbf{P}$ is a local covering of examples from B, if the following conditions are satisfied: (1) each conjunction P is minimal; (2) $\bigcup_{P \in \mathbf{P}}[P] = B$; (3) $\mathbf{P}$ is minimal, i.e. it has the smallest number of elements.

If decision tables contain inconsistent examples, then one can use either probabilistic approach or rough set approach. In the rough set approach the lower approximation and the upper approximation are computed for each decision class. Then, a set of certain rules is induced from the lower approximation and a set of possible rule from the upper approximation.

2.2 Algorithm MODLEM

The MODLEM algorithm has been introduced in [12] and it generates heuristicaly a minimal set of rules describing succeeding decision classes (or their rough approximations). Its extra specificity is handling directly numerical attributes during rule induction when elementary conditions of rules are created, without any preliminary discretization phase. The general schema of the MODLEM algorithm is given below. It is iteratively repeated for each set of examples B from a succeeding decision concept.

Procedure MODLEM (**input** B set of examples; *criterion* - evaluation measure; **output** $\mathbf{P}$ single local covering of B)
begin
    $G := B$; $\mathbf{P} := \emptyset$;   { examples not covered by conjunction from $\mathbf{P}$ }
    while $G \neq \emptyset$ **do begin**
        $P := \emptyset$;   {candidate for condition part of the rule}
        $S := U$;   {set of objects covered by P}
        while ($P = \emptyset$) or (not($[P] \subseteq B$)) **do begin**
            $w := \emptyset$;   {candidate for elementary condition}
            for each attribute $a \in C$ **do begin**
                $new\_p :=$ *Find_best_condition*(a, S);
                if *Better*$(new\_p, w, criterion)$ **then** $w := new\_p$;
                { evaluate if new condition new_p is better than previous w}
            end;
            $P := P \cup \{w\}$;   {add to the condition part }
            $S := S \cap [w]$;
        end; { while not($[P] \subseteq B$)}
        for each elementary condition $w \in P$ **do**
            if $[P - w] \subseteq B$ then $P := P - \{w\}$; { Test minimality of the rule }
        $\mathbf{P} := \mathbf{P} \cup \{P\}$;   { Add P to the local covering }
        $G := B - \bigcup_{P \in \mathbf{P}} [P]$;   { Remove examples covered by the induced rule}
    end; { while $G \neq \emptyset$ }
    for each $P \in \mathbf{P}$ **do** **if** $\bigcup_{P' \in \mathbf{P}-P} [P'] = B$ **then** $\mathbf{P} := \mathbf{P} - P$
end{procedure}

Let us comment how function *Find_best_condition* works – for more details see [9,12]. Elementary conditions are represented as either $(f(a,x) < v_a)$ or $(f(a,x) \geq v_a)$. For nominal attributes, these conditions are $(f(a,x) = v_a)$. We will shortly present how best conditions are chosen for numerical attributes. First, for a given set of objects $x \in S$ their attribute values are sorted in an increasing order. The candidates for the cut-point v_a are computed as mid-points between successive values in the sorted order, taking into account decision class assignment of objects. They are evaluated according to chosen evaluation measure - either *class entropy* or *Laplace accuracy*. The best point among all tested ones (function *Better*) is chosen to be further compared against other attributes. The best condition w for all compared attributes is chosen to be added to the condition part of the rule.

2.3 Classification of objects

The set of induced rules is applied to classify new or testing objects. In this paper we employ the classification strategy introduced by Grzymala in LERS [8]. The decision to which class an object belongs to is made on the basis of the following factors: strength and support. The *Strength* is the total number of learning examples correctly classified by the rule during training. The *support* is defined as the sum of scores of all matching rules from the concept. The class K_j for which the support, i.e., the following expression

$$\sum_{matching\ rules\ R\ describing\ K_i} Strength\_factor(R)$$

is the largest is the winner and the object is assigned to K_j.

If complete matching is impossible, all partially matching rules are identified. These are rules with at least one attribute-value pair matching the corresponding attribute-value pair of an object. For any partially matching rule R, the additional factor, called *Matching factor* (R), defined as a ratio of matching conditions to all conditions in the rule, is computed. In partial matching, the concept K_j for which the following expression is the largest

$$\sum_{partially\ matching\ rules\ R} Matching\_factor(R) * Strength\_factor(R)$$

is the winner and the object is classified as being a member of K_j.

3 Bagging

The bagging approach belongs to these methods that combine homogeneous classifiers generated by the same learning algorithm. *Diversity* is one of the requirement, when using multiple models [6]. Thus, such methods manipulate the training set. The learning algorithm is runned several times, each time using a different distribution of the training examples. The generated classifiers are, then, combined to create a final classifier that is used to classify testing examples.

The *Bagging* approach (**B**ootstrap **agg**regat**ing**) was introduced by Breiman [2]. It aggregates by voting classifiers generated from different bootstrap samples. The ***bootstrap sample*** is obtained by uniformly sampling objects from the training set with replacement. Each sample has the same size as the original set, however, some examples do not appear in it, while others may appear more than once. For a training set with m examples, the probability of an example being selected at least once is $1-(1-1/m)^m$. For a large m, this is about 1 - $1/e$. Each bootstrap sample contains, on the average, 63.2% unique examples from the training set.

Given the parameter T which is the number of repetitions, T bootstrap samples $S_1, S_2, \ldots, S_T$ are generated. From each sample S_i a classifier C_i is induced by the same algorithm and the final classifier C^* is formed by aggregating T classifiers. A final classification of object x is built by a uniform voting scheme on $C_1, C_2, \ldots, C_T$, i.e. is assigned to the class predicted most often by these sub-classifiers, with ties broken arbitrarily. The approach is presented briefly below. For more details see [2].

(**input** LS learning set; T number of bootstrap samples; LA learning algorithm
output C^* classifier)
begin
  for $i = 1$ **to** T **do**
  begin
    $S_i :=$ bootstrap sample from LS; {sample with replacement}
    $C_i := LA(S_i)$; { generate a sub-classifier }
  end; { end for }
  $C^*(x) = \arg\max_{y \in K_j} \sum_{i=1}^{T} (C_i(x) = y)$ {the most often predicted class}
end

We could ask why does bagging work? As some authors explain (see e.g. [4,6]) taking a majority of hypothesis about the target concept, has the effect of reducing random variability of individual hypothesis. Another observation is that this approach works especially well for *unstable* learning algorithms - i.e. algorithms whose output classifier undergoes major changes in response to small changes in the training data [2]. However, bagging may slightly degrade the performance of stable algorithms, e.g. k-nearest neighbour. Besides instability of the method, Breiman [2] also discussed that bagging can improve accuracy if the induced classifiers are good and not correlated. He also said that "poor predictors can be transformed into worse ones by bagging", i.e. one should not use learning algorithms that produce poor classifiers from the repeated samples. Breiman introduced also more formal justification by the concept of an order-correct classifier [2] – a learning system that over many different training sets, tends to predict the correct class of a test object more often than any other. Breiman claimed that aggregating classifiers produced by an order-correct learner results into a nearly optimal classifier. Moreover, other authors [6,4] say that bagging works because it is an approximation to Bayesian model averaging.

Using CART decision tress Breiman [2] reported a significant improvement of predictive accuracy on several datasets. Quinlan [11] performed an extensive computational study with C4.5 extended by bagging or boosting (another approach that manipulates data to obtain different training sets [5]). Yet another experimental study was performed by Bauer and Kohavi [3]. The obtained results show that both bagging and boosting lead to markedly more accurate classifiers. When comparing bagging and boosting "head to head", boosting led to greater increase in accuracy for some datasets. However, these authors also showed some datasets, where boosting increased error, when compared to the single classifier. Bauer and Kohavi concluded that although boosting is on average better than bagging, it is not uniformly better than bagging. Moreover, Quinlan [11] noted that "bagging is less risky".

Bagging, and also boosting, requires a considerable number of sub-classifiers because they relay on varying the data distribution to get the diverse set of classifiers from a single algorithm. The literature review shows that the ensemble of classifiers may containing various number components. For example, in [3] 25 classifiers were used, Breiman considered 50 repetitions of sampling. However, Quinlan [11] analyzed both bagging and boosting with much smaller ensembles of classifiers (standard T=10, but good performance were also obtained by versions using 3 classifiers). The choice of T will be also examined in an experimental part of this paper.

4 Experiments

The aim of experiments is to compare on a several datasets the single use of the basic MODLEM algorithm against bagging classifier composed of single sub-classifiers (also trained by MODLEM algorithm). The hypothesis, we want to check, says the bagging approach could improve the predictive accuracy.

The predictive accuracy was evaluated using standard k-fold cross validation technique. In our experiment we used number of folds $k = 10$. The implementation of both classifiers was constructed in such a way that the division of an example set into training and testing parts was the same for single MODLEM algorithm and bagging approach. Sampling of k folds could be done either in a stratified way (according to decision class distribution) or in a simple random way. Moreover, while constructing bagging composite system we could choose T – the number of repetitions for internal bootstrapping, i.e. the number of sub-classifier inside the ensemble. All sub-classifiers are induced by means of MODLEM algorithm. Both, for its use as a single classifier or inside a composite classifier, the same strategy is applied to clas-

Table 1. Description of datasets

Dataset	Number of examples	Number of classes	Number of attributes numerical	discrete
bank	66	2	5	0
buses	76	3	8	0
zoo	101	7	16	1
hsv	122	7	9	2
hepatitis	155	2	6	13
iris	150	3	4	0
auto	159	6	43	0
segmentation	210	7	19	0
glass	241	6	9	0
bricks	216	2	10	0
vote	300	2	0	16
bupa	345	2	6	0
election	444	2	1	29
urolog1	500	2	0	27
urolog2	500	2	0	27
german	666	2	7	13
crx	690	2	6	9
pima	768	2	8	0

sify testing examples (described in section 2.3). In a case of inconsistencies in the training sets, the rough sets theory was used, and MODLEM produces only certain decision rules, which were further applied to testing examples.

Both classifiers were evaluated using 18 datasets, summarized in Table 1. They were chosen because considerable diversity in size, number of classes, and number and type of attributes. Most of them are coming from the UCI Machine Learning Repository [1], others (*buses, hsv, bricks, election, urology1, urology2*) are coming from well known rough sets applications.

The parameter T being the number of sub-classifiers inside bagging was set at the following values: 3, 5, 7 and 10. Choosing these values was inspired by good results obtained by Quinlan for small numbers of T [11].

The results of these experiments are given in Table 2. For each dataset, the first column shows the classification accuracy obtained by a single classifier over the ten cross-validations. Standard deviation is also given. The next columns contain results for composite bagging classifiers with changing the number of sub-classifiers. An asterisk indicates that differences for compared classifiers and given datasets are not statistically significant. Results presented in Table 2 were obtained for stratified sampling. The similar experiments were obtained also for non-stratified sampling. However, in this case the increase of predictive accuracy for bagging was generally much smaller. Moreover, in this case the number of datasets, where single classifier over-

Table 2. Comparison of classification accuracies [%] obtained by single MODLEM and bagging approach

Dataset	Single MODLEM	Bagging - with different T 3	5	7	10
bank	93.81 ± 0.94	95.05 ± 0.91	94.95 ± 0.84	95.22 ± 1.02	93.95* ± 0.94
buses	97.20 ± 0.94	98.05* ± 0.97	99.54 ± 1.09	97.02* ± 1.15	97.45* ± 1.13
zoo	94.64 ± 0.67	93.82* ± 0.68	93.89* ± 0.71	93.47 ± 0.73	93.68 ± 0.70
hsv	54.52 ± 1.05	64.75 ± 1.21	65.94 ± 0.69	64.78 ± 0.57	64.53 ± 0.55
hepatitis	78.62 ± 0.93	82.00 ± 1.14	84.05 ± 1.1	81.05 ± 0.97	84.0 ± 0.49
iris	94.93 ± 0.5	95.13* ± 0.46	94.86* ± 0.54	95.06* ± 0.53	94.33* ± 0.59
auto	85.23 ± 1.1	82. 98 ± 0.86	83.0 ±0.99	82.74 ±0.9	81.39 ± 0.84
segmentation	85.71 ± 0.71	86.19* ± 0.82	87.62 ± 0.55	87.61 ± 0.46	87.14 ± 0.9
glass	72.41 ± 1.23	68.5 ± 1.15	74.81 ± 0.94	74.25 ± 0.89	76.09 ± 0.68
bricks	90.32* ± 0.82	90.3 * ± 0.54	89.84* ± 0.65	91.21* ± 0.48	90.77* ± 0.72
vote	92.67 ± 0.38	93.33* ± 0.5	94.34 ± 0.34	95.01 ± 0.44	96.01 ± 0.29
bupa	65.77 ± 0.6	64.98* ± 0.76	76.28 ± 0.44	70.74 ± 0.96	75.69 ± 0.7
election	88.96 ± 0.54	90.3 ± 0.36	91.2 ± 0.47	91.66 ± 0.34	90.75 ± 0.55
urolog1	62.4 ± 0.51	65.2 ± 0.25	63.1* ± 0.5	65.8 ± 0.35	65.2 ± 0.34
urolog2	63.80 ± 0.73	64.8 ± 0.83	65.0 ± 0.43	67.40 ± 0.46	67.0 ± 0.67
german	72.16 ± 0.27	73.07* ± 0.39	76.2 ± 0.34	75.62 ± 0.34	75.75 ± 0.35
crx	84.64 ± 0.35	84.74* ± 0.38	86.24 ± 0.39	87.1 ± 0.46	89.42 ± 0.44
pima	73.57 ± 0.67	75.78* ± 0.6	74.35* ± 0.64	74.88 ± 0.44	77.87 ± 0.39

performed bagging, was growing to 6. The greater increase of accuracy was observed for *hsv* dataset only.

Table 3. Increase of accuracy with respect to a number of sub-classifiers T

Dataset	Number of sub-classifiers T 3	5	7	10	15	20
glass	-3.91	2.40	1.84	3.68	7.06	6.09
pima	2.21	0.78*	1.31	4.30	5.47	3.66
election	1.34	2.24	2.70	1.79	1.8	0.1*
crx	0.1*	1.6	2.46	4.78	2.61	2.18
hsv	10.23	11.42	10.26	10.01	11.35	14.64
german	0.91*	4.04	3.46	3.59	1.21	2.42
vote	0.66*	1.67	2.34	3.34	2.0	3.0

Another question may refer to influence of the parameter T in the bagging approach on the changes of predictive accuracy. For some of these datasets, where we observed this influence in Table 2, we additionally computed the results for using larger number of sub-classifiers. Results are summarized in Table 3.

5 Conclusions

The results of the comparative experiments on several datasets have shown that the bagging composite approach produced more accurate classifiers than the single, standard version of the MODLEM rule induction algorithm. Bagging significantly outperformed the single algorithm on 14 datasets of total 18 ones. The difference between classifiers were non-significant on 2 datasets (*iris* and *bricks*), and the single classifier was better only in a case of 2 datasets (*auto* and *zoo*); remind that Quinlan has also obtained decreases for *iris* and *auto* [11]. The highest increase of predictive accuracy were obtained for *hsv* – over 10%, *bupa* – around 10% and *hepatitis* – 5.43%. Comparing two ways of sampling we noticed that stratified sampling should be used. Simple random sampling has not led to so high increasing predictive accuracy.

It is difficult to see the unique relationship between the number of repetitions T in bagging and the change of the predictive accuracy over all datasets. Clearly, we noticed a group of datasets, where the increase of repetions (subclassifiers) has influenced better accuracy; these are datasets *hsv, glass, pima, vote.* For some datasets, as e.g. *elections, crx, german,* the predictive accuracy increased with T changing up to 7 or 10, then it was stable or slightly decreased. For other datasets the highest accuracies were obtained for T smaller than 10. We also noticed that using $T = 3$ was inappropriate nearly for all datasets - see Table 2. We could repeat here Breiman intuition: "*more replicants are required with an increasing number of classes*" [2].

The result of the experiments confirmed that bagging substantially improved predictive accuracy for rule induction by means of the MODLEM algorithm. We could expect an improvement with bagging because this algorithm, similarly to decision trees, is the unstable algorithm in the sense of postulate of Breiman and Gama [2,6]. There are at least two situations inside the rule induction to be affected by bagging. The first is the choice of the best condition. If two attributes (elementary conditions) evaluate similarly with respect to the given evaluation function, a small change in the training data can change the chosen attribute/condition. Bagging also substantially affects the choice of cut-points for numerical attributes - which is a particular operation inside the MODLEM algorithm. Again, a small change in the training set can lead to different cut-points. As it has been also noticed by other researches [4,6] aggregating the diversified classifiers by voting could lead to a more complex decision surface approximating target concept than obtained by the single model.

Finally, let us notice that bagging is an interesting and a quite simple approach to improve a rule induction method. In fact, all we need is adding a technique that selects the bootstrap sample, sends it to the learning algorithms and another step of aggregating votes of component classifiers. The disadvantage of bagging are: loosing a simple and easy interpretable structure of knowledge represented in a form decision rules, and increasing computation costs. However, the extra computation that is required is known in advance,

i.e. if T classifiers are generated, than the approach requires T times the computational effort of the single learning algorithm. Moreover, bagging can be easily computed in a parallel way. On the other hand, one gains increased predictive accuracy. We think that in many applications, the improvement of this accuracy would be well worth the computational cost.
Acknowledgment: The author wants to acknowledge financial support from State Committee for Scientific Research, research grant no. 8T11F 006 19.

References

1. Blake C., Koegh E., Mertz C.J. (1999) Repository of Machine Learning, University of California at Irvine [URL: http://www.ics.uci.edu/ mlearn/MLRepositoru.html].
2. Breiman L. (1996) Bagging predictors. Machine Learning, **24** (2), 123–140
3. Bauer E., Kohavi R. (1999) An empirical comparison of voting classification algorithms: Bagging, boosting, and variants. Machine Learning **36** (1/2), 105–139.
4. Dietrich T.G. (2000) Ensemble methods in machine learning. In: Proc. of 1st Int. Workshop on Multiple Classifier Systems, 1–15 .
5. Freund Y., Schapire R.E. (1996) Experiments with a new boosting algorithm. In: Proc. 13th Int. Conference on Machine Learning, 148–156.
6. Gama J. (1999) Combining classification algorithms. Ph.D. Thesis, University of Porto.
7. Grzymala-Busse J.W. (1992) LERS - a system for learning from examples based on rough sets. In: Slowinski R. (Ed.), Intelligent Decision Support, Kluwer Academic Publishers, 3–18.
8. Grzymala-Busse J.W. (1994) Managing uncertainty in machine learning from examples. In: Proc. 3rd Int. Symp. in Intelligent Systems, Wigry, Poland, IPI PAN Press, 70–84.
9. Grzymala-Busse J.W., Stefanowski J. (2001) Three approaches to numerical attribute discretization for rule induction. International Journal of Intelligent Systems, **16** (1), 29–38.
10. Michalski R.S., Tecuci G. (Eds) (1994) Machine Learning. A multistrategy approach. Volume IV. Morgan Kaufmann
11. Quinlan J.R. (1996) Bagging, boosting and C4.5. In: Proceedings of the 13th National Conference on Artificial Intelligence, 725–730.
12. Stefanowski J. (1998) The rough set based rule induction technique for classification problems. In: Proceedings of 6th Euorpean Conference on Intelligent Techniques and Soft Computing Aaachen EUFIT 98, 7-10 Sept. 109–113.
13. Stefanowski J. (2001) Multiple and hybrid classifiers. In: Polkowski L. (Ed.) Formal Methods and Intelligent Techniques in Control, Decision Making, Multimedia and Robotics, Post-Proceedings of 2nd Int. Conference, Warszawa, 174–188.
14. Stefanowski J. (2001) Algorithims of rule induction for knowledge discovery. (In Polish), Habilitation Thesis published as Series Rozprawy no. 361, Poznan Univeristy of Technology Press, Poznan.

Storing Data in KDD Systems /from Inlen 3.0 to InlenStar. Evolution of Database/

Krzysztof Trojanowski[1)], Andrzej Jodłowski[1)], Krzysztof Skowroński[2)]

[1)] Institute of Computer Science, Polish Academy of Sciences, Warsaw, Poland.
Krzysztof.Trojanowski@ipipan.waw.pl, Andrzej.Jodlowski@ipipan.waw.pl
[2)] Warsaw University of Technology, Poland.
Krzysztof.Skowronski@elka.pw.edu.pl

Abstract: In this paper we discuss forms of data storage in knowledge systems. A set of selected software systems is analysed. Then a new system called InlenStar is briefly presented and its structure of database is widely discussed, as an example of the structure of knowledge database.
Keywords: Knowledge Discovery in Databases, Data Mining.

Introduction

Knowledge Discovery in Databases (KDD) is a very dynamically developing domain [Witten 96]. Roots of this research area can be found in four other independent scientific domains: (1) machine learning, (2) statistics, (3) database management, and (4) optimisation. The main task in KDD is effective finding of interesting and reliable dependencies (knowledge) in existing data [Fayyad 96]. Actually, there exist quite a lot of different methods of knowledge representation, and therefore there are many methods of searching data dependencies respectively to applied representations. The result is a large group of KDD systems of different functionality and complexity. We can divide this group into classes respectively to the form of representation of discovered knowledge into following categories [kdnuggets]:

- Rules-based approach (PolyAnalyst, SuperQuery, CN2, RIPPER)
- Associations discovery (IBM Intelligent Miner for Data, apriori, Clementine)
- Decision-tree approach (CART, SAS/DBMiner, C5.0/See5, PolyAnalyst)
- Bayesian and Dependency Networks discovery (HUGIN, MSBN: Microsoft Belief Network Tools, DBLearn)
- Sequential Patterns discovery
- linear and nonlinear regression models discovery (SAS/DBMiner, MARS, S-Plus, SPSS, STATISTICA)

The other taxonomy of KDD systems is based on method of knowledge exploration. We can divide them into two main groups [Mitchell 97]:

- systems for classification,
- systems for clustering.

Other important criterion of classification can be method of data management:

- storing knowledge in its own specific structures, where access to data and knowledge is performed with system specific operators,
- storing knowledge in database structures, where access to data and knowledge is performed with standard database methods (e.g. via SQL or extended SQL commands).

Main advantage of the second approach is in using advanced methods of data manipulation, which are available to fully scalable current databases dedicated to very large data sets, like [Weiss 98]:

- data preparation,
- data cleaning,
- data-mining tasks,
- knowledge validation,
- knowledge transformation,
- knowledge visualisation and presentation.

KDD process can be divided into three main tasks [Michalski 98]:

- data management,
- knowledge discovery,
- knowledge management.

Therefore, knowledge discovery languages usually extend data manipulation language, i.e. SQL [Michalski 00a][Han 01].Thus KDD systems can be also divided into those, with some internal language created to define complex KDD processes, and those, without such a language, where an environment with a set of methods is given to user who has to do everything with a set of built in KDD system functions.

The paper is organised as follows: in the second section a comparison of a few selected KDD system databases is presented. The third section presents InlenStar database structure, compares it with a structure of Inlen 3.0, and indicates advantages of database of the new version of the system. The last section of this paper presents some conclusions and indicates directions of the further progress.

Compared systems

In previous section, we proposed a set of classification criteria for KDD systems, which divide them into classes. We selected a group of systems to compare with InlenStar. Systems belong to many classes. Among them, there are complex systems being components of large software products and systems dedicated exclusively to data-mining tasks as well. However, there are also some similarities among them. All of them store the knowledge in the form easy to interpret by experts (in opposite to „black box" systems where explanation of knowledge returned by the system is not available). The selected systems are: PolyAnalyst Discovery 4.4 [megaputer], SuperQuery [azmy], CART 4.0 [salford-systems], DBMiner Analytical System 3.0 [dbminer], and SAS Enterprise Miner [sas].

In this paper we study only forms of storing data in systems supporting knowledge discovery process, and therefore we did not discuss all other features of selected systems. A set of criteria respective to the selected feature mentioned above was prepared. We were especially interested in following issues:

1. What sources of data are acceptable by the system (i.e. what type of database is employed, e.g. Microsoft Excel spreadsheet, or SAS data file, etc.),
2. What is a system platform necessary for the knowledge system execution,
3. What forms of discovered knowledge representation are employed (e.g. rules, decision trees, etc.)
4. Are there any limitations concerned with the selected method of knowledge storage both in the files and during the learning process.

The first and not surprising conclusion is that Microsoft system environment and Microsoft database formats are respected by most of KDD systems (e.g. PolyAnalyst, SuperQuery, CART, DBMiner, SAS Enterprise Miner). However other system platforms are also recognised (PolyAnalyst for UNIX, CART in command mode works in DOS, UNIX, and the MacOS, SAS - Solaris). The commonly accepted formats are Excel spreadsheet and Access database. In the selected group of systems all of them have versions working in Win32 environment and recognise both MS database formats mentioned above. Lists of accepted formats for the systems are presented below:

PolyAnalyst - flat CSV files (Comma Separated Values), Microsoft Excel 7.0/97/2000 spreadsheet, SAS data file, ORACLE Express database, IBM Visual Warehouse 2.0/3.0, and other external data trough ODBC and OLEDB.

SuperQuery - MS Access, dBASE III, dBASE IV, Paradox 3.x-5.x, Btrieve, FoxPro 2.x, Excel 3.0-7.0, Text, ODBC (irrespectively to format of analysed data, Microsoft DAO Object Library is always installed with the system).

CART - the Salford Systems' file format (fully compatible with the SYSTAT from SPSS Science), data stored in an SQL-based system, and other external data trough ODBC (with a direct link to DBMS-Copy™), e.g. statistical analysis packages (e.g., SAS, SPSS), databases (e.g., Oracle, Informix), and spreadsheets (e.g., Excel, Lotus).

DBMiner - Microsoft SQL Server's OLAP Server 7.0 or Analysis Server 2000, and Excel 2000.

SAS Enterprise Miner - SAS data file, Microsoft Excel 7.0/97/2000 spreadsheet, Access2000, Access97, dBASE File, Lotus 1, Lotus 3, Lotus 4, Delimited File (*.txt), CSV files (Comma Separated Values), and user-defined formats.

All of the systems represent knowledge as sets of rules (except CART which is a pure decision-tree system), however other forms like decision-trees (PolyAnalyst, SAS Enterprise Miner) also appear. Graphs and charts are available to the user in each of them.

Limitations of the systems are usually concerned with accepted database file formats. Sometimes they have their origin in general approach to algorithm implementation, e.g. CART is an extremely memory-intensive program, storing all data used for tree growing in RAM. We can assume that other systems have the same type of problems since they have to work without any SQL server (except those, which are able to co-operate with SQL server, like DBMiner or SAS). In the approach with SQL server, machine learning algorithms communicate directly with an original data storage engine through a series of dynamic SQL queries and do not store all the necessary data in the local memory.

The discussion above was a starting point for further Inlen 3.0 development [Kaufman 97]. Especially, it was necessary to select appropriate database format and to develop a new database structure, which would be able to store all components of a knowledge system, i.e. attribute descriptors, examples, rules and parameters for learning algorithms. The format of data archives (a txt file format) of Inlen 3.0 was insufficient to satisfy new demands standing before the developed software. A new system called InlenStar, as the ancestor of Inlen 3.0 has had to be constructed with respect to the current database and data-mining technologies.

InlenStar database

Inlen 3.0 system is a system for extracting knowledge from databases. It provides tools for discovering rules characterising sets of data, generating meaningful conceptual classifications, detecting similarities and formulating explanations for the rules, generating rules and equations characterising data, selecting and/or generating new relevant variables or representative examples, and testing the discovered rules on new data [mli].

Examples, rules, and all parameters of implemented algorithms for every knowledge system of Inlen 3.0 are stored in text files (19 files for a knowledge system). The system consists of a set of modules organised into a system by an additional module, which realises tasks of communication with a user. The modules read selected files, perform their processes and write results into another text files. Knowledge systems data are available through editors, i.e. example editor, variable editor, and rule editor. Data in the files are organised with an Inlen internal data format.

Inlen is a system implemented for DOS platform and with Borland Turbo C programming environment. Limitations of these systems became an integral part of developed application. A new InlenStar system is developed for Win32 system platform and with Borland Builder C++ 4.0 programming environment, and thus most of limitations were able to overcome. List of the most important of them is presented in Table 1.

One of the main differences between Inlen and InlenStar is a database. InlenStar's database stores learning and testing examples, definitions of their attributes, rules and other data, e.g. actual and default parameters of a system. However, in the new system all system data are integrated in a relational database. Schema of the new database organises all information, make it independent from functional layer of the system, eliminates data redundancy present in the Inlen data and knowledge file set. It is open, sound and easy to modify, and makes available a large group of tools and methods specific to relational databases. Data and knowledge are organised in a set of related tables to make the access to requested data simple and relatively fast. Data structure is ready to introduce rules with attributional calculus [Michalski 00b].

Limitation	Inlen	InlenStar
Maximum Number of Knowledge Systems	30	Practically unlimited
Maximum Number of Application Domains	20	Practically unlimited
Maximum Number of Variables	95	Respectively to applied database (e.g. 255 for Access database, 1024 for MS SQL, etc.)
Maximum Number of Values per Variable	200	Practically unlimited (limited by available memory capacity)
Maximum Number of Examples	650	Respectively to applied database (practically unlimited)
Range of Integer Variable	0-50	Respectively to applied database (according to Integer data type implementation)
Maximum Value of Max-star Learning Parameter	30	Practically unlimited (limited by available memory capacity)
Maximum nuber of Rules	200	Respectively to applied database (practically unlimited)

Table 1. Limitations of Inlen and InlenStar systems.

In the new system, information is stored in the relational database (in the old system, it is stored in a set of files). However, in the current version, InlenStar modules sometimes have to work with redundant data structures (relational database and multi-file database), because most of migrated source code of the old system (especially aq15 code) is included into a new system without changes in database interface. For translation of old multi-file structures into relational database structures and inversely, a new Data Translation Module is implemented.

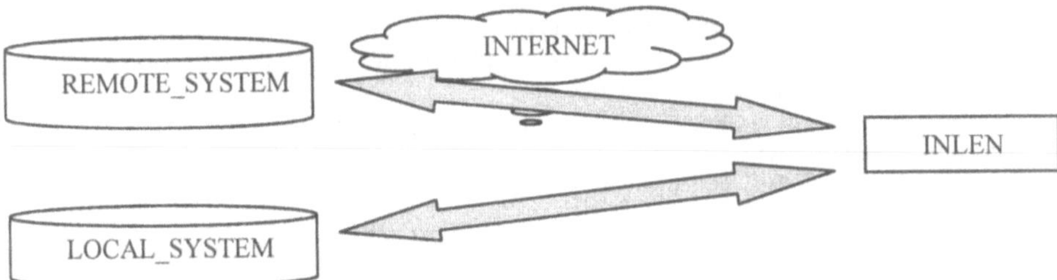

Fig. 1. Architecture of the new system

Inlen databases can be local or accessed through the internet on remote hosts as well. However, current version of the system works with local databases only. Architecture of the new system is presented in the Figure 1.

Architecture of the new system database is presented below (Figure 2).

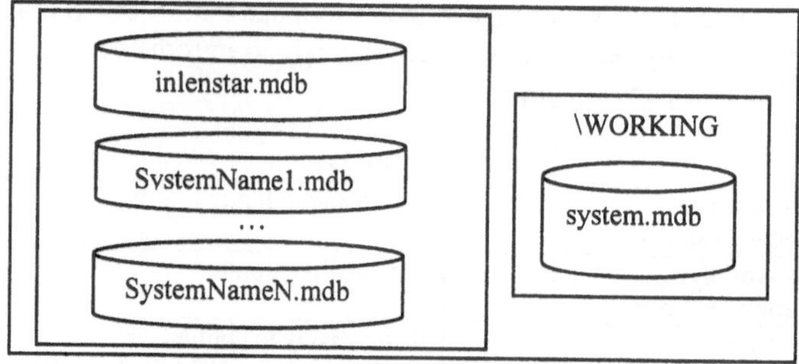

Fig. 2. Architecture of the new system database

Database structure consists of following databases:

1. INLENSTAR.mdb – contains information about all registered knowledge systems and all global parameters, i.e. common for all knowledge systems, or default values for the system modules (e.g. learning, optimisation, etc.)
2. SystemName.mdb – database, containing data structures for registered systems saved with InlenStar specific table structure (*SystemName* is unique name of a knowledge system).

Old Inlen's database contains the following set of files assigned with knowledge systems:

1. Systems.aur – contains information about all systems
2. Learn.aur – contains default learning parameters

and files associated with particular system:

1. <ks>.dta – contains learning examples
2. <ks>.dtm – contains copy of learning system (copy of <ks>.dta)
3. <ks>.gem – input file to AQ submodule
4. <ks>.inf – contains inference parameters for advisor system
5. <ks>.lrn – contains learning parameters for learning system
6. <ks>.rlp – contains last set of rules formatted for printing
7. <ks>.tst – contains output of ATEST module
8. <ks>.tta – contains set of training examples
9. <ks>.ttm – contains copy of training examples (copy of <ks>.tta)
10. <ks>.var – contains table of variables
11. <ks>.vtm – contains copy of table of variables (copy of <ks>.var)

and files associated with particular system and particular decision:

1. KB\<ks>\<da>.adv – contains cross-reference table for advisor system
2. KB\<ks>\<da>.cin – contains index for rule-compiled file
3. KB\<ks>\<da>.crl – contains rules intended to be compiled
4. KB\<ks>\<da>.old – previous set of learning examples in AQ format
5. KB\<ks>\<da>.rle – contains rules
6. KB\<ks>\<da>.stc – contains statistical data

The following two opposite solutions have been discussed for Data Translation Module (eventually, solution #1 was accepted):

Solution #1 (Figure 3) – common data assigned to all systems are stored in one database (INLENSTAR.mdb), while the data assigned to particular knowledge system (<ks>) are stored in separated database with the name same as the name of knowledge system (<ks>).

Good points:

a. Good decomposition and object ordering
b. Each knowledge system is stored in separate file – systems are easy to separate and portable
c. The database translation (from multi-file database to relational database and inversely) is much more natural (simply)

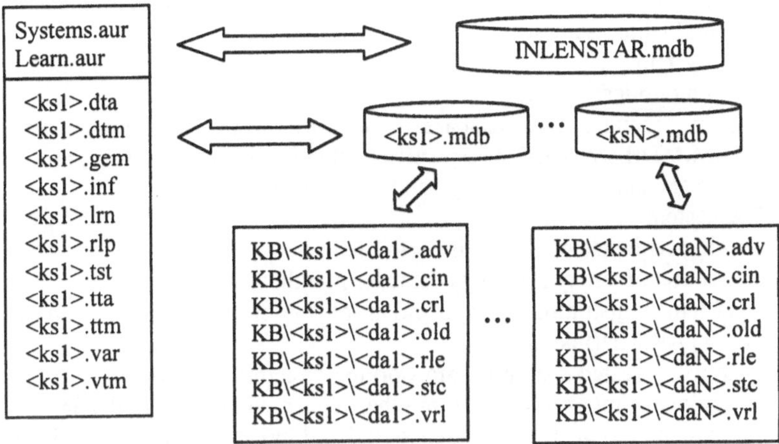

Fig. 3. Translation of particular files to relational schemas (tables) – Solution 1.

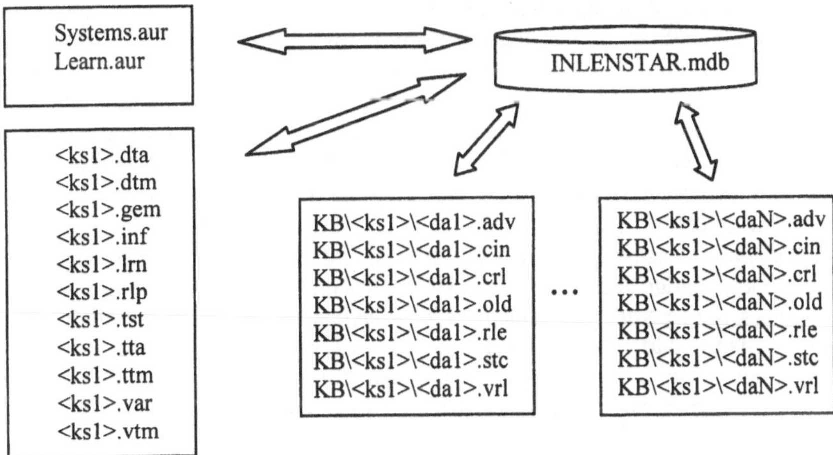

Fig. 4. Translation of particular files to relational schemas (tables) – Solution 2.

Solution #2 (Figure 4) – all systems <ks> (<ks> - knowledge system) are transformed to one relational database. Moreover, common data assigned to all systems are also collected in the same database.
A weak point: problems with system portability (all ks systems are collected in one large database)

The following actions to be performed on database are defined:
1. OPEN existing, registered system
   a) local system; b) Remote system.

When the system is opened, the copy of data structures (assigned to opened system) are created in the \WORKING directory. All operations assigned to system are performed on system's copy (this fact refers to both: relational database and temporary multi-file database)
2. SAVE system

There are two options:
   a) save changes – database structures from temporary database SYSTEM.MDB are saved in respective SystemName.mdb database, or
   b) cancel changes – temporary database content is lost.
3. NEW system

The following sequence of actions is performed:
   a) creation of empty relational database in indicated place,
   b) system registration – registration of the new knowledge system in INLENSTAR.MDB database,
   c) copy of created databases into working directory /WORKING,
   d) (optional) import of data from other registered system (tables from other system are coped) or remote database (wizard mode – creates tables for input data based on SQL query)
4. EXPORT/IMPORT – (1) export of data to old Inlen multi-file database from the opened relational database, and (2) import of data from old Inlen multi-file database to the opened relational database.

In the INLENStar, we can register many knowledge systems. Full list of them is available at INLENSTAR.MDB database. However, INLENStar user can open and work with one knowledge system at a time only. By default, database INLENSTAR.mdb and all registered local systems are stored in main system directory. In the current version, all data are stored locally as an MS Access Database files. Access to databases is realised through DAO (Data Access Objects by Microsoft) interface.

Database *inlenstar.mdb* contains general information about all registered (known) knowledge systems (such as system's name, description and domain) and default learning parameters. Database *<systemname>.mdb* contains all information assigned to particular knowledge systems. Each file of the old knowledge system is assigned with one table or a few related tables in the new one. This solution makes translation from multi-files database to relational database more simply. The general schema of InlenStar's database is presented in Figure 5.

Table DTA contains training examples and table TTA contains testing ones. Each example from Inlen 3.0 database is translated to one record in proper table.

DTM and TTM tables have identical structure like DTA and TTA tables. The tables are copies of above tables. The role of these tables is to save data and compatibility assertion to the old Inlen structures. The names of particular variables are identical to fields' names of input data.

Table INF_PARAMETERS consists of inference parameters for particular system. Similarly table LEARN_PARAMETERS consists learning parameters for particular system (knowledge system). Structure of this file is identical to structure of file learn.aur. Table LEARN_ACTUAL refers to actual learn parameters. Table KS_LEARN_PARAMETERS contains learn parameters used to generate knowledge (rules).

Table VARIABLES defines a variable set for a given system. With each variable is associated a domain of value. This domain is stored in table KS_VALUES. Regarding fact that the system supports several types of variables, we decided to take it into consideration and projected respective structure of a database.
Decision (value of decision attribute) is assigned to each set of rules (table RULES). Set of complexes is assigned to a decision (table DECISION). Every complex is a conjunction of selectors. Each selector has three parts: attribute's name, operator's name and list of values[1]. Each complex is associated with examples (table EXAMPLES) which supports the complex. An idea of decomposition of selector's list of values was also discussed, but because of significantly increasing complexity of the data structure, the idea was rejected.

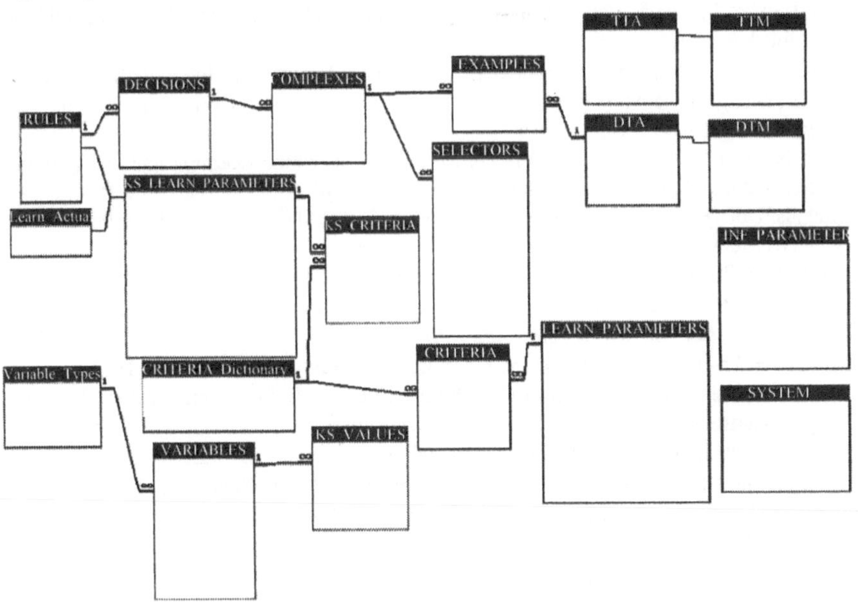

Fig. 5. General schema of InlenStar database

[1] The support of attributional calculus requires more complex structure of table COMPLEX. However, the left part of schema does not need to be modified.

Conclusions

In further work, we are going to make the system able to work with other database systems than desktop databases (MS Access database, Paradox, Xbase, etc.), i.e. MS SQL, ORACLE Database, Borland InterBase. The communication with new databases will be performed through a new interface, ADO (ActiveX® Data Objects). The new interface provides access to many kinds of data sources, especially OLE DB including Online Analytical Processing (OLAP) functionality. This will open doors to most of databases and database servers, and thus the InlenStar will be able to work with remote databases and perform In-Place Data Mining. In-Place Data Mining is an approach that allows the user to overcome the RAM size limitation and mine huge volumes of data through a series of dynamic SQL queries without necessity of storing all data locally. Proposed modification will also improve information exchange between other KDD systems.

Bibliography

[Fayyad 96] Fayyad U.M., Piatetsky-Shapiro G., Smith P., Uthurusamy R.: "Advances in Knowledge Discovery and Data Mining", MIT Press, Cambridge, MA 1996.

[Han 01] Han J., Kamber M.: "Data Mining: Concepts and Techniques" Morgan Kaufmann Publishers, 2001.

[Kaufman 97] Kaufman, K.A.: "INLEN: A Methodology and Integrated System for Knowledge Discovery in Databases," *Ph.D. Dissertation*, George Mason University Report MLI 97-15, 1997.

[Michalski 98] Michalski R.S., I. Bratko, M. Kubat: „Machine Learning and Data Mining; Method and Applications", John Wiley & Sons, 1998

[Michalski 00a] Michalski, R.S. and Kaufman, K., "Building Knowledge Scouts Using KGL Metalanguage" Fundamenta Informaticae 40, pp. 433-447, 2000.

[Michalski 00b] Michalski, R.S., "Attributional Calculus, A Logic for Deriving Human Knowledge from Computer Data", to be published in the *Reports of Machine Learning and Inference Laboratory*

[Mitchell 97] Mitchell T.M: "Machine Learning", McGraw-Hill Companies, 1997.

[Weiss 98] Weiss M. S., Indurkhya N.: „Predictive Data Mining. A practical guide", Morgan Kaufmann Publishers, San Francisco CA 1998.

[Witten 99] Witten H.I, Frank E.F.: "Data Mining: Practical machine learning tools and techniques with java implementations", Morgan Kaufmann Publishers, 1999.

[kdnuggets] http://www.kdnuggets.com/software/index.html

[megaputer] http://www.megaputer.com/

[azmy] http://www.azmy.com/

[salford-systems] http://www.salford-systems.com/

[dbminer] http://www.dbminer.com/

[sas] http://www.sas.com/

[mli] http://www.mli.gmu.edu/projects/inlen.html

Content Extraction Based on MPEG-7 Audio Representation

Alicja A. Wieczorkowska

Polish-Japanese Institute of Information Technology,
ul. Koszykowa 86, 02-008 Warsaw, Poland
e-mails: alicja@pjwstk.edu.pl or awieczor@uncc.edu

Abstract: Growth of amount of multimedia data that are stored and used nowadays requires tools for intelligent searching and management. MPEG-7 standard, which is being currently developed, provides unified representation and set of tools for multimedia content description. However, only low-level features of sound signal in MPEG-7 can be extracted automatically, whereas high-level information like sound recognition, musical instrument timbre, etc. requires manual insertion or further data analysis. In this paper, low-level sound descriptors from MPEG-7 standard are a basis for extraction of high-level information. Obtained descriptors can supplement audio data representation and facilitate content-based search of sound and multimedia databases.

Keywords: multimedia databases, audio content description

1. Introduction

Content-based representation and searching of multimedia databases became one of the main topics of interest in multimedia domain. Signal processing techniques are being developed intensively and progress in signal compression is just amazing. However, content-based searching of multimedia data, especially sound, still must be performed manually. This problem is addressed in "Multimedia Content Description Interface", called MPEG-7, by Moving Picture Experts Group. MPEG-7 standard (still under development) describes the multimedia content data, supporting some degree of interpretation of the information's meaning, which can be passed onto, or accessed by, a device or a computer code [1]. The descriptive features will be different for different user domains and different applications: a lower abstraction level would be a description of e.g. key, tempo, tempo changes, position in sound space, whereas the highest level would give semantic information. The level of abstraction is related to the way the features can be extracted: many low-level features can be extracted in fully automatic ways, whereas high level features need (much) more human interaction [2]. MPEG-7 provides a set of methods and tools for the different viewpoints of the description of audiovisual content. This representation can be used for various purposes, including content based searching, and facilitate interoperability in the future. However, MPEG will not standardize or evaluate applications, and neither automatic nor semi-automatic feature extraction algorithms, search engines, filter agents etc. will be inside the scope of the standard to leave space for industry competition and to allow making good use of the expected improvements in these technical areas. Therefore, efficient feature extraction and classification algorithms are of interest to allow extensive content-based multimedia database searching.

Some of high-level sound descriptors are frequently created in the production process, e.g. title, performer etc. However, many features that can facilitate content-based searching must be extracted directly from signal. For instance, timbre description is not produced automatically and requires preprocessing of sound. Sound processing can be based on direct signal analysis. In this paper, sound timbre description is based on MPEG-7 low-level audio data representation.

2. MPEG-7 Audio

There are 17 sound descriptors in MPEG-7 standard. These temporal and spectral descriptors can be roughly divided into the following groups [1], [2], [3]:

- Silence - no significant sound
- Basic: AudioWaveform - audio waveform envelope (minimum and maximum), AudioPower - temporally-smoothed instantaneous power
- Basic Spectral: AudioSpectrumEnvelope - logarithmic-frequency spectrum, AudioSpectrumCentroid - center of gravity of the log-frequency power spectrum, AudioSpectrumSpread – 2nd moment of the log-frequency power spectrum, and AudioSpectrumFlatness - flatness properties of the spectrum of an audio signal for each of a number of frequency bands
- Signal parameters: AudioFundamentalFrequency - fundamental frequency of an audio signal, and AudioHarmonicity - represents the harmonicity of a signal
- Timbral Temporal: LogAttackTime - the time it takes for the signal to rise from silence to the maximum amplitude, and TemporalCentroid - represents where in time the energy of a signal is focused (weighted mean of the time of the signal)
- Timbral Spectral: specialized spectral features in a linear-frequency space (SpectralCentroid - power-weighted average of the frequency of the bins in the linear power spectrum) and specific to the harmonic portions of signals:
    - HarmonicSpectralCentroid - amplitude-weighted mean of the harmonic peaks of the spectrum
    - HarmonicSpectralDeviation – average over the sound duration of the deviation of the amplitude (linear scale) of the harmonic peaks of the spectrum from a global spectral envelope
    - HarmonicSpectralSpread - amplitude-weighted standard deviation of the harmonic peaks of the spectrum, normalized by the instantaneous HarmonicSpectralCentroid
    - HarmonicSpectralVariation - normalized correlation between the amplitude of the harmonic peaks between 2 subsequent time-slices of the signal

- Spectral Basis: AudioSpectrumBasis - series of (potentially time-varying and/or statistically independent) basis functions derived from the singular value decomposition of a normalized power spectrum, and AudioSpectrumProjection - low-dimensional spectral features after projection upon a reduced rank basis.

The above features represent basic properties of sound signal. MPEG-7 also provides 5 sets of high-level audio description tools: audio signature, general sound recognition and indexing, musical instrument timbre, spoken content, and melody description. The paper focus is on sound description for musical instrument timbre classification purposes, based on low-level MPEG-7 descriptors (recognition tools in MPEG-7 use spectral basis descriptors as their foundation).

3. Descriptors Based on Low-level Representation

Both temporal and spectral features are important for identification of musical timbre. In the research on automatic musical instrument sound classification performed so far [4], [5], [6] spectra of singular sounds as well as time envelope of these sounds were characterized. The sound descriptors chosen for musical timbre representation in MPEG-7 are based on results of this research [7]. However, audio descriptors in MPEG-7 standard include only some of numerous parameters used in musical research, and high-level description is also very general - only 4 classes of instrument sounds are recognized (probabilistic classifiers that may be applied can be trained to identify narrower categories). Additionally, any descriptors are not provided with MPEG-7, but must be calculated, and preprocessing should be performed to extract reasonable segments (silence, consequent sounds) or user may set them. In specification described in this paper, analyzing window is moved through the audio signal and low-level audio descriptors are used to characterize consecutive portions of the signal for classification purposes.

The most universal way of sound description for any purposes is to observe evolution of sound descriptors [8]. Some low-level descriptors in MPEG-7 require separation of a singular sound and determination of its phases, which is unambiguous and involves preprocessing (for instance, limits of sustained part of the sound must be determined); therefore simple basic descriptors were chosen to allow fully automated feature extraction.

To observe evolution of any sound parameters, the length of analyzing frame must be established first. To analyze sound features correctly, the frame should include at least 2 periods of sound (if it is a periodic sound at all). On the other hand, analyzing frame must be as short as possible, to reflect changes in very quickly evolving (and short) sounds, like pizzicato strings. The lowest audible, hence of the longest period sound is 16Hz, so analyzing frame should be of length $f_s/16$ samples (f_s – sampling frequency). Window function should be applied as well with relatively simple function, like Hamming window proposed here. Sound analyses are usually performed with overlapping frames, with half frame overlap being the most common, thus $f_s/32$ samples overlap was chosen here. At the end of the recording, missing part of the last frame should be zero-padded.

AudioWaveform and AudioSpectrumEnvelope vector have been chosen to observe the signal; most of parameters used in musical sound description are based on these ones. Since the analyzing window and step are always the same, differences between consequent values of these descriptors characterize precisely signal evolution. To reduce the feature vector size, number of frequency bins can be limited in such way that number of frequency values in each octave is the same.

These descriptors and the differences can be calculated for any signal, without initial preprocessing like separation of sound events or pitch extraction than can introduce errors and do not have clear algorithmic definitions. Next, any learning on searching algorithms can be run on the obtained parameters.

4. Conclusions

The scope of this paper was to use and expand MPEG-7 sound description, starting from low-level audio descriptors used in this standard. The proposed method parameterizes evolution of low-level sound descriptors, and no preprocessing is needed. Moreover, observation of sound parameters' evolution also reflects properties of human hearing system that is sensitive to changes of sound (and any signal) features. The new description can supplement any audio database of musical recordings and facilitate searching of the data.

References

1. ISO/IEC JTC1/SC29/WG11, Overview of the MPEG-7 Standard (version 6.0), Int. Org. for Standardisation, Coding of Moving Pictures and Audio, N4509, Pattaya, 2001
2. Herre J., MPEG-7 Audio: What is it about? AES 110th Convention, Workshop W-6, Amsterdam, May 13th, 2001
3. Lindsay A., Herre J., MPEG-7 and MPEG-7 audio--an overview, J. Audio Eng. Soc., vol. 49, no. 7/8, pp. 589-594, 2001
4. Herrera P., Amatriain X., Batlle E., Serra X., Towards instrument segmentation for music content description: a critical review of instrument classification techniques, Int. Symp. on Music Information Retrieval ISMIR 2000, October 23-25, Plymouth, MA
5. Martin K. D., Kim Y. E., Musical instrument identification: A pattern-recognition approach, 136 meeting of the Acoustical Society of America, October 13, 1998
6. Wieczorkowska A., The recognition efficiency of musical instrument sounds depending on parameterization and type of a classifier (in Polish), Ph.D. Dissertation, Technical University of Gdańsk, 1999
7. Peeters G., McAdams S., Herrera P., Instrument Sound Description in Context of MPEG-7, Proceedings of ICMC (International Computer Music Conference), Berlin, Germany, August 27-September 1, 2000
8. Slezak D., Synak P., Wieczorkowska A., Wroblewski J., KDD-based approach to musical instrument sound recognition, Proceedings of ISMIS (International Symposium on Methodologies for Intelligent Systems), Lyon, France, June 26-29, 2002 (to appear)

Neural Network and Biologically Motivated Systems

Ant Colony Programming for Approximation Problems *

Mariusz Boryczka

Institute of Computer Science, Silesia University, Sosnowiec, Poland, e-mail: boryczka@us.edu.pl

Abstract. A successful approach to automatic programming, called genetic programming, assumes that the desired program is found by using a genetic algorithm. We propose an idea of ant colony programming in which instead of a genetic algorithm an ant colony algorithm is applied to search for the program. The ant colony programming system we define is used for approximation problems. The test results demonstrate that the proposed approach is effective.

Key words. Automatic programming, genetic programming, ant colony programming, ant colony systems, approximation problems

1 Introduction

Given a problem one usually builds an appropriate computer program to solve the problem. Automatic programming (AP) makes possible to avoid a tedious task of creating such a program. In AP the program is obtained by specifying first the goals which are to be realized by the program. Then, based on this specification, the program is constructed automatically.

A successful approach to AP, called genetic programming, was proposed by Koza [11–13]. In genetic programming a desired program is found by using a genetic algorithm. This work introduces an idea of ant colony programming (ACP) in which instead of a genetic algorithm, an ant colony algorithm is applied to search for the program. We consider approximation problems in which the need for generating arithmetic expressions arises. An approximation problem consists in a choice of an optimum function from some class of functions. Such a function should approximate in a best way another, known function, or some values of an unknown function specified in a limited number of points. Approximation problems are encountered in analysis of experimental data, modeling physical phenomena, analysis of statistical observations etc.

While solving an approximation problem by making use of an ant colony programming system we search for arithmetic expressions of a single variable represented in the Polish (prefix) notation. Note that finding an expression

* This work was carried out under the State Committee for Scientific Research grant no 7 T11C 021 21.

is in fact equivalent to finding the program, as having an expression one can easily establish the program evaluating this expression.

As mentioned above genetic programming proved a successful approach to approximation problems. Another approaches include neural networks [10] and their fuzzy variants [9,15]. To date the ant colony approach has not been applied to automatic programming, and in particular to approximation problems.

This work consists of six sections. In section 2 the idea of genetic programming is described. Section 3 characterizes ant colony systems. Section 4, which is a core part of this work, describes the idea of ant colony programming applied for generating arithmetic expressions. Section 5 contains test results, and section 6 concludes the work.

2 Genetic programming

Idea of genetic programming. The genetic programming idea [11–13] uses genetic algorithms whose work is modeled upon the natural evolution of organisms. The evolution proceeds in accordance to the Darwinian principle of survival and reproduction of the fittest. A population in genetic algorithms is a set of problem solutions (individuals) usually represented as sequences of bits. Such a population evolves as the result of repeatedly executed operations: the selection of best solutions and creation new ones out of them. While creating new solutions the operators of recombination known from genetic algorithms, such as crossover and mutation, are used. The new solutions replace other solutions in the population. In genetic programming the individuals of a population are computer programs. In order to create new programs from the two parent-programs they are represented as trees. New programs are built by removing a selected subtree from one tree and inserting it to another. The cycle of recurrent operations in genetic programming is the same as in genetic algorithms.

Preparatory steps. There are five preparatory steps which must be accomplished before a searching process for a program to solve the problem can begin. These are as follows: (a) choice of terminal symbols constituting the set $T = \{t_1, t_2, \ldots, t_m\}$, (b) choice of functions constituting the set $F = \{f_1, f_2, \ldots, f_n\}$, (c) defining the fitness function, (d) defining the control parameters, (e) defining the termination criterion.

The terminal symbols, $t_i \in T$, and functions, $f_i \in F$, are the program components. The choice of program components, i.e. the terminal symbols and functions, and a definition of the fitness function determine to a large extent a solution space (i.e. a space of computer programs) which will be searched. The control parameters include a population size, the probabilities of crossover and mutation, a maximum tree size, etc.

Choice of terminal symbols and functions. A terminal symbol $t_i \in T$ can be a constant, for example $t_i = 3$, or a variable representing an input datum or a measurement value coming from a gauge in an object under control. Every function $f_i \in F$ of a fixed arity can be an arithmetic operator (+, −, ∗, etc.), an arithmetic function (e.g. *sin*, *cos*, *exp*), a boolean operator (**and**, **or**, **not**), an alternative (**if-then-else**), an iterative operator (**while**), an arbitrarily defined function appropriate to the problem under consideration.

The crucial point in selecting the terminal symbols and functions is that using them one may express a solution to the problem. Furthermore, a closure condition is to be satisfied. We say that sets T and F satisfy the closure condition if every function from F accepts as its arguments the values returned by other functions from F (including itself) and arbitrary symbols from the set T.

Fitness function. The aim of the fitness function is to provide a basis for competition among individuals of a population. It is important that not only the correct solutions should obtain a high assessment (reward), but also every improvement of an individual should result in increasing of that reward.

There are several measures of fitness. One of them is a raw fitness. Its definition depends on the problem of interest. For most problems the raw fitness is defined as the sum of distances (errors) in all tests between the output result produced by a program for the test data and the expected value for that test. The raw fitness of an i-th program in a population in time t is defined as $r(i, t) = \sum_{j=1}^{N} |W(i, j) - C(j)|$ where $W(i, j)$ is the value returned by the i-th program for the j-the test, $C(j)$ is the correct answer for test j, and N is a number of tests. If the values returned by the programs are not numbers, but boolean values *true* or *false*, then the sum of distances is equivalent to a number of encountered errors. For certain problems the raw fitness may not have an error form. For example in problems of optimal control the raw fitness may be the cost of particular control strategies (expressed as time, distance, profit etc.). For other problems the raw fitness may be a gained result, e.g. a number of points scored, an amount of food found, etc.

3 Ant colony systems

An ant colony system (ACS) derives from research on systems inspired by the behavior of real ants. Originally it has been proposed by Dorigo, Maniezzo and Colorni in 1991 as an ant system for solving the traveling salesman problem [7]. The ACS is inspired by behavior of colonies of real ants, therefore artificial ants (agents) used in the ACS have some features taken from the behavior of real ants, e.g. (a) choice of a route of an ant depends on the amount of pheromone — a chemical substance deposited by an ant, (b) ants co-operate in order to achieve the best result, (c) ants move in a random fashion. Additionally, in the artificial ant colony systems the following assumptions are made:

1. Each artificial ant in the ACS has a memory of limited capacity, called the tabu list, in which e.g. a set of visited cities for the traveling salesman problem is stored.
2. Artificial ants are not completely blind. They move according to some probability function determining the next move. Like in the colonies of real ants it depends on the parameters corresponding to the distance of an ant colony's nest from a source of food, and the amount of (artificial) pheromone deposited on the route.
3. Artificial ants live in an environment in which time is discrete.

In the following we use the terms 'ant' and 'pheromone' as shorthands for 'artificial ant' and 'artificial pheromone'. The aim of a single ant in the traveling salesman problem is to find a salesman tour in the graph, whose nodes are the cities, and the edges connecting the cities have been initialized with some amount of pheromone trail, τ_0. Each ant located at time t at city i makes the decision regarding the next city on its tour using a probability rule of transfer. For this goal it generates a random number q, $0 \leq q \leq 1$. If $q \leq q_0$, where q_0 is a parameter of the algorithm, then the "best" available edge is chosen. Otherwise the edge is chosen in a random fashion:

$$j = \begin{cases} \arg\max\{[\tau_{ij}(t)] \cdot [\eta_{ij}]^{\beta}\} & \text{if } q \leq q_0 \text{ (exploration)}, \\ S & \text{otherwise (exploitation)}, \end{cases}$$

where $\tau_{ij}(t)$ is the amount of pheromone trail on edge (i, j) at time t, η_{ij} is the visibility of city j from city i equals $1/d_{ij}$, where d_{ij} is the distance between cities i and j, and β is a parameter which controls the relative weight of the pheromone trail and visibility, S is a city drawn by using the probabilities:

$$p_{ij}^{k}(t) = \begin{cases} \dfrac{\tau_{ij}(t) \cdot [\eta_{ij}]^{\beta}}{\sum\limits_{r \in J_i^k} [\tau_{ir}(t)] \cdot [\eta_{ir}]^{\beta}} & \text{if } j \in J_i^k, \\ 0 & \text{otherwise}, \end{cases}$$

where J_i^k is the set of the cities to which ant k can move to being located in city i (i.e. the set of unvisited cities).

After having found a salesman tour, an ant deposits pheromone information on the edges through which it went. It constitutes a local update of the pheromone trail, which also comprises partial evaporation of the trail. The local update proceeds according to the formula $\tau_{ij}(t+1) = (1-\rho) \cdot \tau_{ij}(t) + \rho \cdot \tau_0$, where $\rho \in (0, 1]$ is the pheromone decay coefficient, and τ_0 is the initial amount of pheromone on edge (i, j).

After all ants have completed their tours, a global update of pheromone trail takes place. The level of pheromone is then changed as follows: $\tau_{ij}(t + n) = (1 - \rho) \cdot \tau_{ij}(t) + \rho \cdot \frac{1}{L^+}$, where edges (i, j) belong to the shortest tour found so far, and L^+ is the length of this tour.

On the updated graph the consecutive cycles are carried out. The number of cycles is the parameter of the algorithm. The output of the algorithm is the shortest salesman tour found by the ants during the whole experiment.

Ant colony algorithms are one of the most successful examples of swarm intelligent systems and have been applied to many types of problems, including the traveling salesman problem [7,5,6], the problem of task allocation [1], the problems of discrete optimization [3,4], the vehicle routing problem [8], the graph coloring problem [2], the graph partitioning problem [14].

4 Ant colony programming for generating arithmetic expressions

We apply ant colony programming for generating arithmetic expressions of a single variable which are represented in the prefix notation. An ant colony system as the basis of ant colony programming is modified in the following way:

1. The elements of graph $G = (N, E)$ have the meaning: N is the set of nodes, where each of them can be either a terminal symbol, $t_i \in T$, or a function, $f_i \in F$, of an arithmetic expression (cf. section 1); E is the set of edges representing connections between elements of an arithmetic expression given in the form of the tree.
2. The tabu list is not used, since the multiple occurrences of a node (in the expression) which has been already visited are not prohibited.
3. The probability of moving ant k located in node r to node s in time t equals:
$$p^k_{rs}(t) = \frac{\tau_{rs}(t) \cdot [\gamma_s]^\beta}{\sum\limits_{i \in J^k_r} [\tau_{ri}(t)] \cdot [\gamma_i]^\beta}.$$
Here $\gamma_s = (1/(2+\pi_s))^d$, where π_s is the power of symbol s which can be either a terminal symbol or a function, and d is the current length of the arithmetic expression.

As mentioned above, arithmetic expressions created by ants are represented in the prefix notation. During the creation process one has to recognize if the expression is closed, i.e. if it can be evaluated. An expression is closed if all its functions, f_i, have their arguments in the form of terminal symbols or closed expressions. For example, expression $+ * * - x / - 1x51x5$ is closed and can be evaluated (Fig. 1a), whereas expression $+ * * - x / - 1x51x$ is not, since function "+" does not have its right argument (Fig. 1b).

In order to check the closure of the expression we introduce a notion of the power of the expression. This notion is defined by using the power (arity) of terminal symbols and functions (Table 1). The expression created by a single ant is initiated with symbol F which is the starting node of the power equals 1. When the expression is expanded by a terminal symbol or function, the power of the expression is increased by the power of this terminal symbol or function. The expression becomes closed when its power equals 0. The

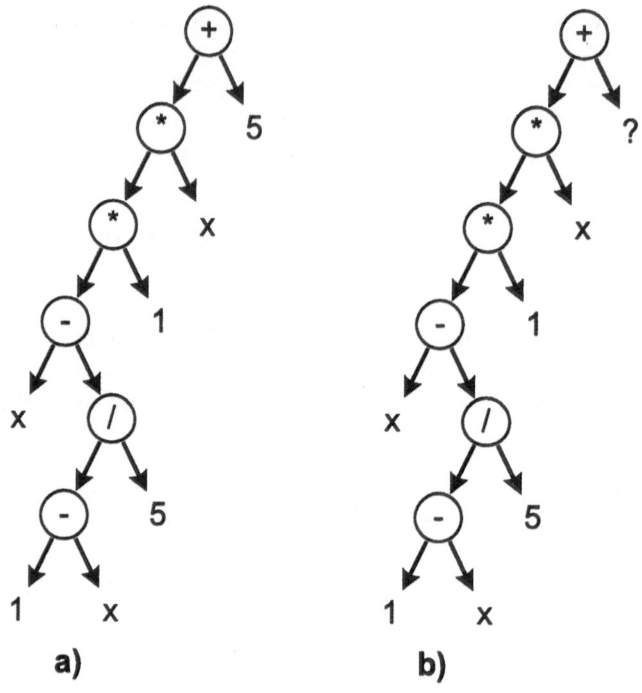

Fig. 1. Trees representing expressions in prefix notation; (a) closed expression, (b) not closed expression

Terminal symbol or function	Number of arguments	Power
constant, variable	0	-1
NOT, N, 1-argument functions	1	0
$+, -, *, /$, AND, OR, XOR	2	1

Table 1. Power of terminal symbols and functions

process of determining the power of the expression is illustrated in Fig. 2 for a sample expression $+x + 11$. As mentioned earlier the ants communicate with each other only in an indirect way, i.e. through the pheromone trails which encode information collected by the ants during the search process. In our approach the nodes of the graph can be visited by the ants many times, therefore pheromone is deposited on the edges also many times. It is because the created expression corresponds to the path in the tree built out of terminal symbols and functions (see the dotted line in Fig. 3a). This in turn can be considered as the path in the pseudo-tree obtained through "winding up" the branches of the original tree (Fig. 3b).

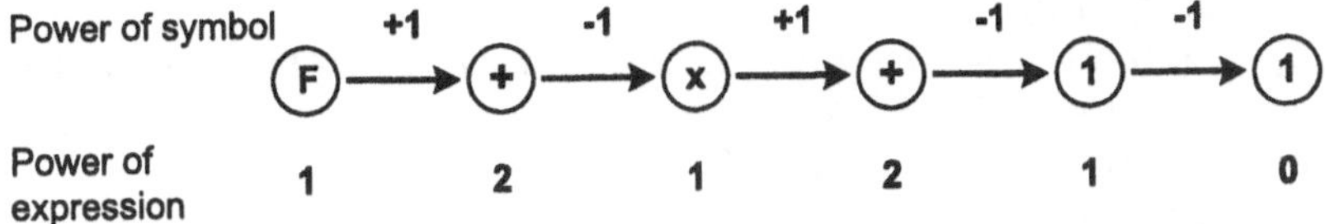

Fig. 2. Determining the power of the expression

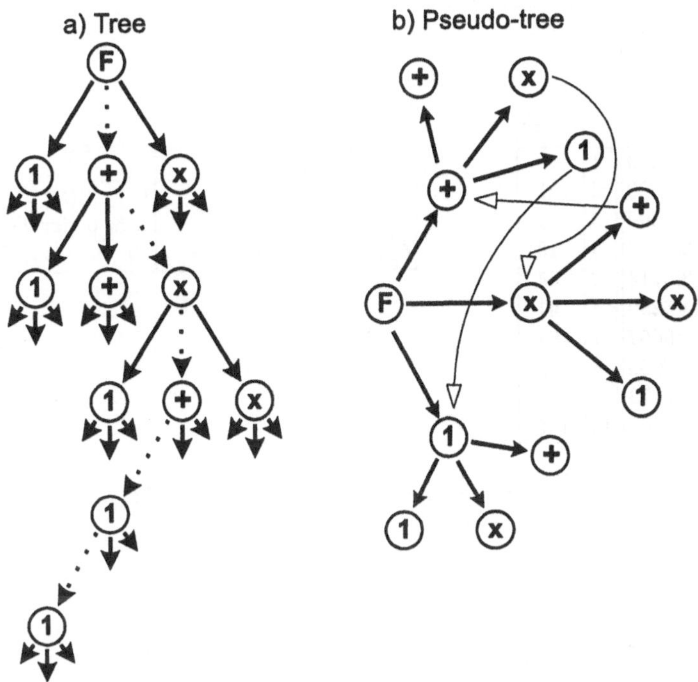

Fig. 3. Tree and pseudo-tree

5 Test results

The approach to the automatic generation of arithmetic expressions by making use of ant colony programming is illustrated on two sample functions:

$$F_1 \colon y = \frac{x-1}{x+2} + 3 \quad \text{and} \quad F_2 \colon y = 2x^2 - 6x + 5.$$

The test sets for these functions are shown in Table 2a. Two sets of symbols (Table 2b) and the following values of parameters were used for the experiments: $\tau_0 = 1$, $\beta = 20$, $q_0 = 0.05$, $\rho = 0.9$. Overall, 50 experiments with 10000 cycles of the ACP algorithm each were conducted. The sample approximate functions generated during the experiments are as follows:

- For function F_1:
  A_1: $1 + NN1 - + + / - xN - 1Nx - *N1x + /xx1N1x - 1 - Nx1N1$,
  A_2: $- + /3N + x2 + 3 + 1xx$,
  A_3: $*1 + 1N - /3 + x/ + 33NN33$,
- For function F_2:
  A_4: $+/ * 1 * - - x11 + * * -x + / - 111 + 1 * 1111x11$,
  A_5: $-5 * *2 - /62xx$,
  A_6: $+ * * - x + -1x51x5$.

(a)

x	$F_1(x)$	x	$F_2(x)$
1	3.0000	1	1
2	3.2500	2	1
3	3.4000	3	5
4	3.5000	4	13
5	3.5714	5	25
6	3.6250	6	41
7	3.6667	7	61
8	3.7000	8	85
9	3.7273	9	113
10	3.7500	10	145

(b)

Symbol	Set 1	Set 2
variable	x	x
constants	1	1, 2, 3 (for F_1) 2, 5, 6 (for F_2)
functions	N, +, −, *, /	N, +, −, *, /

Table 2. (a) Test sets for functions F_1 and F_2, (b) Sets of symbols in the ACP system (N stands for unary minus)

The values of functions F_1 and F_2 for x's from Table 2a were compared with the values of generated, approximate functions. The fractions of approximate functions (out of 50 obtained in our experiments) which gave identical values of functions F_1 and F_2 for x's from Table 2a, for two different sets of constants used in the ACP system, are shown in Figure 4.

6 Conclusions

We proposed the idea of ant colony programming for generating arithmetic expressions in approximation problems. The test results demonstrated that the proposed approach is effective. However there are still some issues which remain to be solved. The most important among them are: (a) the issue of constants, and (b) the issue of simplification of generated expressions, i.e. the need for post-processing.

The first issue regards the choice of constants which are to be enclosed in the set of terminal symbols. These constants can be crucial for the work of the ant colony algorithm. However it is difficult to predict which constants are most useful for a given approximation problem. There are at least three

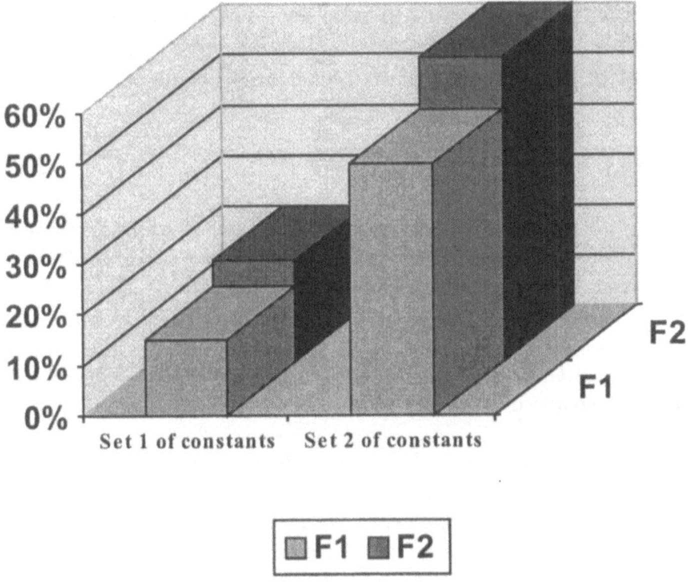

Fig. 4. Fractions of functions for two sets of constants (cf. Table 2b)

approaches in solving this issue: first, to introduce only constant 1 from which the algorithm can derive other constants using the available functions; second, to use a set of constants given explicitly or as the range of values; third, to generate randomly some number of constants at the beginning or during the course of the algorithm. Preliminary experiments show that a mixture of these approaches gives the best results. Furthermore, it was observed that a proper balance between the number of constants and other terminal symbols must be maintained. This balance guarantees that the generated expressions have reasonable lengths and high approximating quality. The large number of constants causes fast closing of expressions because the constants, of the power equal -1, are then drawn quite often.

The second issue, rather of technical nature, is the need for post-processing which simplifies the generated expressions. This need arises since the generated expressions have a tendency to grow longer and longer, in particular for complex approximated functions or in the case where some constants are to be computed. The high complexity of expressions decreases their readability and increases their evaluation time because of redundant computations. During post-processing one has to recognize and remove expressions of constant value (e.g. $+12$), expressions of value 0 (e.g. $*0x$, $-xx$), parts of expressions which do not influence their values, e.g. multiplication or division by 1, the occurrence of an even number of unary minuses or negations etc.

The works on these issues are in progress. The future plans include an extension of our solutions to multiple variable approximation problems and an enhancement of the efficiency of the ant colony programming system.

References

1. A. Colorni, M. Dorigo, V. Maniezzo, and M. Trubian. Ant System for Job-Shop Scheduling. *JORBEL — Belgian Journal of Operations Research, Statistics and Computer Science*, 34(1):39–53, 1994.
2. D. Costa and A. Hertz. Ants can colour graphs. *Journal of the Operational Research Society*, 48:295–305, 1997.
3. M. Dorigo, G. Di Caro, and L. M. Gambardella. Ant algorithms for discrete optimization. *Technical Report IRIDIA/98-10, Universit Libre de Bruxelles, Belgium*, 10, 1999.
4. M. Dorigo, G. Di Caro, and L. M. Gambardella. Ant algorithms for discrete optimization. *Artificial Life*, 5(2):137–172, 1999.
5. M. Dorigo and L. M. Gambardella. Ant Colony System: A cooperative learning approach to the Traveling Salesman Problem. *Technical Report TR/IRIDIA/1996-5, Universit Libre de Bruxelles, Belgium*, 5, 1996.
6. M. Dorigo and L. M. Gambardella. Ant Colony System: A cooperative learning approach to the Traveling Salesman Problem. *TEEE Trans. Evol. Comp.*, 1:53–66, 1997.
7. M. Dorigo, V. Maniezzo, and A. Colorni. Positive feedback as a search strategy. *Tech. Rep. Politechnico di Milano, Italy*, No. 91–016, 1991.
8. L. M. Gambardella, E. Taillard, and G. Agazzi. ACS–VRPTW: A Multiple Ant Colony System for Vehicle Routing Problems with Time Windows. In D. Corne, M. Dorigo, and F. Glover, editors, *New ideas in optimization*, pages 63–77. McGraw-Hill, 1999.
9. S. Horikawa, T. Furuhashi, and Y. Uchikawa. On fuzzy modeling using fuzzy neural networks with the back propagation algorithm. *IEEE Transaction on Neural Networks*, 3(5):801–806, September, 1992.
10. W. Kosinski and M. Weigl. Sieci neuronowe w problemach aproksymacji. *Prace IPPT PAN*, B–4, 1999.
11. J. R. Koza. *Genetic Programming: On the Programming of Computers by Natural Selection*. MIT Press, Cambridge, MA, 1992.
12. J. R. Koza. *Genetic Programming II: Automatic Discovery of Reusable Programs*. MIT Press, 1994.
13. J. R. Koza, F. H. Bennet III, D. Andre, and M. A. Keane. *Genetic Programming III: Darwinian Invention and Problem Solving*. Morgan Kaufmann, 1999.
14. P. Kuntz P. and D. Snyers. Emergent colonization and graph partitioning. In *Proceedings of the Third International Conference on Simulation of Adaptive Behavior: From Animals to Animats 3*. MIT Press, Cambridge, MA, 1994.
15. M. Sugeno and G. Kang. Structure identification of fuzzy model. *Fuzzy Sets and Systems*, 28:15–33, 1988.

Modification of Method of Least Squares for Tutoring a Neural Networks

Alexander P. Grinko, Michal M. Karpuk

Koszalin Technical University, Koszalin, Poland

e-mail: mikarpuk@.wp.pl

Abstract: *The feasibility of function of errors with fractional exponent for solving of a problem of optimization and tutoring of neural networks was theoretically explored. The analytical expressions for estimation of parameters of the models or weight factors were obtained. The algorithms were designed and the numerical experiment on actual economic datas was held, where the efficiency of an offered procedure is shown.*

Keywords: neural networks, optimization, method of least squares, function of errors, fractional integrals and derivatives..

1. Introduction

In algorithms of tutoring of neural networks the most spread method is the method of least squares. For k input datas the root-mean-square error of diversions of an output signal of a web from a true value is minimized. For example, for delta - the Widrow - Hoff's rule of tutoring of a neural networks [1]

$$E = \sum_{i=1}^{k} E(i) = \sum_{i=1}^{k} (y_i - t_i)^2 , \tag{1}$$

where $E(i)$ - is a root-mean-square error for the i-th output signal, $y_i = \sum_{j=1}^{n} \omega_j x_j - T$, t_i - is accordingly the value of an output signal of a neural networks during its tutoring process and true ("theoretical") value of the i-th output signal, x_j - the input signal for j-th neuron of a neural networks, j =1, 2... n, ω_j - weight value for the j-th neuron, T - threshold of activation of a neuron.

The choice of functions like (1) for minimization is stipulated by a relative simplicity of calculation of weight coefficients $\omega_j, j = 1, 2, \ldots n$ [2], and completeness of space l_2 [3].

However at minimization of a root-mean-square error (1) we inevitably interfere with some problems. Firstly, at usage of tutoring series of signals k the influence of unbiased errors grows. It follows from expression (1), when the minimization of squares of diversions is yielded, and the square of diversion for a unbiased error can essentially influence the function of minimization and, accordingly, the theoretical curve. In practice the methods of elimination of unbiased errors from tutoring algorithms are used, but they are not always effective.

Secondly, the minimization (1) is reduced to deriving and solution of combined equations concerning weight coefficients $\omega_j, j = 1, 2, \ldots n$ for a local minimum of a function of diversions(1). For simple "theoretical" dependences this system solves rather easy. For more complicated theoretical dependences the finding of a local minimum of a function(1) is usually possible only numerically.

Thus the examination of other types of functions of minimization of errors, the development of theoretical methods of research of local extremes and their usage in algorithms of optimization and tutoring of neural networks represents the practical concern.

Theory

In this work we consider the function of errors like

$$E = \sum_{i=1}^{k} E(i) = \sum_{i=1}^{k} (y_i - t_i)^{\beta}, \quad 0 < \beta \leq 1, \tag{2}$$

In this case there is no first derivative in points $y_i = t_i$. For examination of functions of that type the application of the functionals of fractional differentiation of order α of Reimann-Liouville [3, 4] or their modifications is possible

$$\left(D_{0+}^{\alpha}\varphi\right)(x) = \frac{1}{\Gamma(1-\alpha)} \frac{d}{dx} \int_{0}^{x} (x-t)^{-\alpha} \varphi(t) dt, \tag{3}$$

$$0 < \alpha < 1, \quad 0 < x < b < +\infty$$

$$\left(D_{b-}^{\alpha}\varphi\right)(x) = -\frac{1}{\Gamma(1-\alpha)} \frac{d}{dx} \int_{x}^{b} (t-x)^{-\alpha} \varphi(t) dt, \tag{4}$$

$$0 < \alpha < 1, \quad 0 < x < b < +\infty$$

and fractional derivatives of the Marcheau

$$\left(D_{0+}^{\alpha}\varphi\right)(x) = \frac{\varphi(x)}{\Gamma(1-\alpha)x^{\alpha}} + \frac{\alpha}{\Gamma(1-\alpha)} \int_{0}^{x} \frac{\varphi(x)-\varphi(t)}{(x-t)^{\alpha+1}} dt, \tag{5}$$

$$0 < \alpha < 1, \quad 0 < x < b < +\infty$$

$$\left(D_{b-}^{\alpha}\varphi\right)(x)=\frac{\varphi(x)}{\Gamma(1-\alpha)(b-x)^{\alpha}}+\frac{\alpha}{\Gamma(1-\alpha)}\int_{x}^{b}\frac{\varphi(x)-\varphi(t)}{(t-x)^{\alpha+1}}dt, \qquad (6)$$

$$0<\alpha<1, \quad 0<x<b<+\infty$$

For continuously - differentiable functions the functionals (3) - (4) are reduced to the functionals (5) - (6) [5]. For example, the fractional derivative (5) for $\varphi(x)=x^{\upsilon}$, $\upsilon>-1$ equals:

$$\left(D_{0+}^{\alpha}\varphi\right)(x)=\frac{\Gamma(1+\upsilon)}{\Gamma(1-\alpha+\upsilon)}x^{\upsilon-\alpha}.$$

Let's designate $H^{\lambda}([0,\ b])$ as a set of functions satisfying the condition of Holder:

$$\left|\varphi(t_1)-\varphi(t_2)\right|\le A\left|t_1-t_2\right|^{\lambda},\ 0<\lambda<1,\ t_1,\ t_2\in[0,\ b].$$

The following principle of an extreme for the functionals $\left(D_{0+}^{\alpha}\varphi\right)(x)$ and $\left(D_{b-}^{\alpha}\varphi\right)(x)$ is known.

Let's assume that we are given a nondecreasing, non-negative function $\omega(t)$ that's not to equal to zero identically and function $f(t)$ continuous on a segment $[0,\ x]$ and in an extremly small range $0<t\le x$ of a point $t=x$ the product $\omega(t)f(t)\in H^{\lambda}([0,\ b])$, $\lambda>\alpha$. Then, if on a segment $[0,\ x]$ the function $f(t)$ reaches a positive maximum (negative minimum) in a point $t=x$, then $\left(D_{0+}^{\alpha}\varphi\right)(x)>0$ ($\left(D_{0+}^{\alpha}\varphi\right)(x)>0$).

In the work the results of improving the principle of an extreme for the functionals $\left(D_{0+}^{\alpha}\varphi\right)(x)$ are obtained.

Theorem 1. Let $f(t)\in H^{\lambda}([0,\ b])$, $\lambda>\alpha$. If for all $\varepsilon\in[0,\ x]$

$$\frac{\alpha}{\Gamma(1-\alpha)}\int_{x-\varepsilon}^{x}\frac{\varphi(x)-\varphi(t)}{(x-t)^{\alpha+1}}dt>0\ \left(\frac{\alpha}{\Gamma(1-\alpha)}\int_{x-\varepsilon}^{x}\frac{\varphi(x)-\varphi(t)}{(x-t)^{\alpha+1}}dt<0\right), \qquad (7)$$

or

$$\frac{\alpha}{\Gamma(1-\alpha)}\int_{0}^{x-\varepsilon}\frac{\varphi(x-\varepsilon)-\varphi(t)}{(x-\varepsilon-t)^{\alpha+1}}dt>0$$
$$\left(\frac{\alpha}{\Gamma(1-\alpha)}\int_{0}^{x-\varepsilon}\frac{\varphi(x-\varepsilon)-\varphi(t)}{(x-\varepsilon-t)^{\alpha+1}}dt<0\right), \qquad (8)$$

then the function $f(t)$ is monotonically increasing (monotonically decreasing) on $[0, x]$.

Theorem 2. Let $\varphi(t)\in H^{\lambda}([0, b])$, $\lambda>\alpha$. The decomposition takes place:

$$\frac{\alpha}{\Gamma(1-\alpha)}\int_{x_0-\varepsilon}^{x_0}\frac{\varphi(x_0)-\varphi(t)}{(x_0-t)^{\alpha+1}}dt=f_1(\varphi(x_0))\varepsilon^{1-\theta}+\ldots+$$
$$+f_2(\varphi(x_0))\varepsilon^{2-\theta}+\ldots+f_n(\varphi(x_0))\varepsilon^{n-\theta}+\ldots,\quad 0<\theta<1, \qquad (9).$$

Then if in a point x_0 $f_1(\varphi(x_0))=0$ and the function $f(t)$ is monotonically increasing (monotonically decreasing) on $[x_0-\varepsilon, x_0]$ and monotonically decreasing(monotonically increasing) on $[x_0, x_0+\varepsilon]$,then in a point x_0 $\varphi(t)$ reaches a local maximum (minimum).

The proof of theorems 1 - 2 is obtained by estimations.

Modeling and the Results.

The expressions (5) - (9) allow to explore functions of errors like(2). As an example we shall consider the generalization of a classic method of least squares in which the criteria of a diversion of direct model

$$y'_i=a_0+a_1x_i \qquad (10)$$

from observations (x_i, y_i) is

$$Err(\upsilon,a_0,a_1)=\sum_{i=1}^{n}\frac{|y_i-y'_i|^{\upsilon+1}}{(y_i-y'_i)}\to\min,\ \upsilon>0.$$

For function $\varphi(x)=a+bx$ the equality (6) will take view:

$$\frac{\alpha}{\Gamma(1-\alpha)}\int_{x_0-\varepsilon}^{x_0}\frac{\frac{|a+bx|^{\upsilon+1}}{(a+bx)}-\frac{|a+bt|^{\upsilon+1}}{(a+bt)}}{(x_0-t)^{\alpha+1}}dt=\frac{|a+bx|^{\upsilon+1}}{\Gamma(1-\alpha)\varepsilon^{\alpha}(a+bx)}\Box$$

$$\Box\left({}_2F_1\left(-\upsilon,-\alpha;1-\alpha;\frac{b\varepsilon}{a+bx}\right)-1\right)= \qquad , \quad (11)$$

$$=\frac{|a+bx|^{\upsilon+1}}{\Gamma(1-\alpha)\varepsilon^{\alpha}(a+bx)}\sum_{i=1}^{+\infty}\frac{(-\upsilon)_i(-\alpha)_i}{(1-\alpha)_i\, i!}\frac{(b\varepsilon)^i}{(a+bx)^i}$$

where

$${}_2F_1(\gamma,\beta;\ \alpha;\ z)=\sum_{i=0}^{+\infty}\frac{(\gamma)_i(\beta)_i}{(\alpha)_i}\frac{z^i}{i!}= \qquad , |z|<1,\ \upsilon>-1,$$

$$=\frac{\Gamma(\alpha)}{\Gamma(\gamma)\Gamma(\alpha-\gamma)}\int_0^1 u^{\gamma-1}(1-u)^{\alpha-\gamma-1}(1-uw)^{-\beta}du$$

$0<\operatorname{Re}\gamma<\operatorname{Re}\alpha$ - Gauss hypergeometric function,

$(\beta)_0=1,\ (\beta)_k=\beta(\beta+1),\dots,(\beta+k-1),\ k=1,\ 2,\dots,$

$\alpha\neq 0,\ -1,\ -2,\ \dots$ - Pohhammer's index.

Applying the theorem 2 in equality (10) we can write the analog of normal combined equations:

$$\begin{cases}\sum_{i=1}^{n}\frac{|y_i-a_0-a_1x_i|^{\upsilon}}{y_i-a_0-a_1x_i}x_i=0\\ \sum_{i=1}^{n}\frac{|y_i-a_0-a_1x_i|^{\upsilon}}{y_i-a_0-a_1x_i}=0\end{cases}. \qquad (12)$$

For estimation of parameters a_0, a_1 and calculation of structural parameters of linear model (10) it is necessary to solve combined equations (12). The solution was carried out numerically on the basis of algorithm of conjugate lapse rates of minimization of function of errors like (2). The program for model operation is written on C++ [6, 7]. The numerical experiment was conducted on the ground of dates on unemployment in Poland in 1997 - 2000 years. (GUS dates). The criteria for measurement for different a was function (2).

The obtained results of estimations of parameters a_0, a_1 are represented in the Table 1 and in Figure 1. The results of a numerical modeling allows to make deductions, that at criteria (2) the best objective function is the function with an exponent $0<\upsilon<1$. Selection of parameter a can be held during the optimization process or in process of tutoring of a neural networks. For obtained dates the optimal value of a is υ=0,7. Thus a_0 =9,735, a_1 = 0,072.

υ	3	2,5	2	1,5	1	0,9	0,8
a_0	10,5364	10,4781	10,3692	10,1618	9,7333	9,7303	9,7272
a_1	0,0315	0,0346	0,0412	0,0534	0,0722	0,0725	0,0727
Err(υ)	49,962	41,307	34,966	30,234	26,911	26,447	26,133

υ	0,7	0,6	0,5	0,4	0,2	0,1	0,01
a_0	9,7351	9,5636	9,4562	9,3636	9,3030	9,4459	0,0227
a_1	0,0720	0,0818	0,0831	0,0945	0,1082	0,0854	0,3805
Err(υ)	25,992	26,242	26,474	26,978	30,626	31,494	35,196

Table 1. Estimates of parameters of linear model a_0, a_1 and value of function of errors Err (υ) (2)

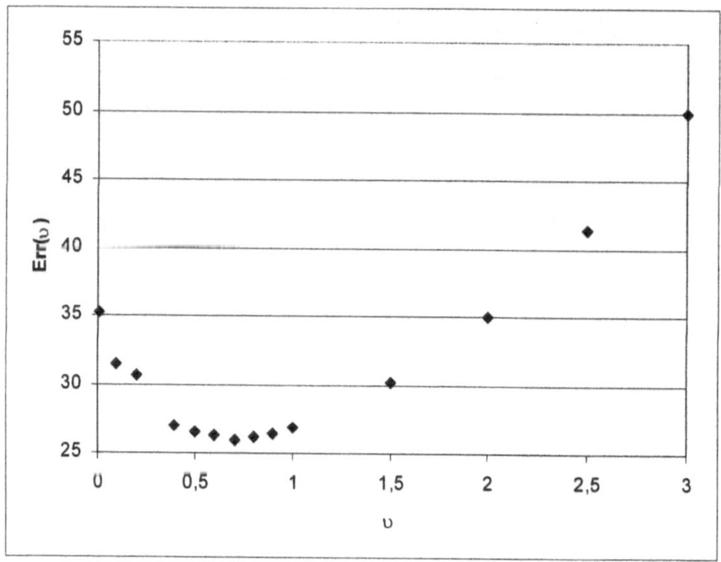

Fig.1. Dependence of function of errors *Err* (υ) from quantity of an exponent υ in (2) for linear model.

The obtained values of estimation of parameters were used for a dot estimation of the prognoses (Fig. 2). In a figure actual values of percent of unemployment on the following time intervals (continuous curve) and forecast values also are shown on the basis of linear model (continuous straight line).

As follows from a figure, that the prognosed values, obtained on the base of minimization function (2) are much closer to actual values, the than obtained on the base of a method of least squares. Therefore, while solving the problems of optimization or problems of tutoring of neural networks, it is expedient to conduct the examination of function of errors and modify it with the purpose of diminution of value of an objective function of optimization or function of errors of tutoring.

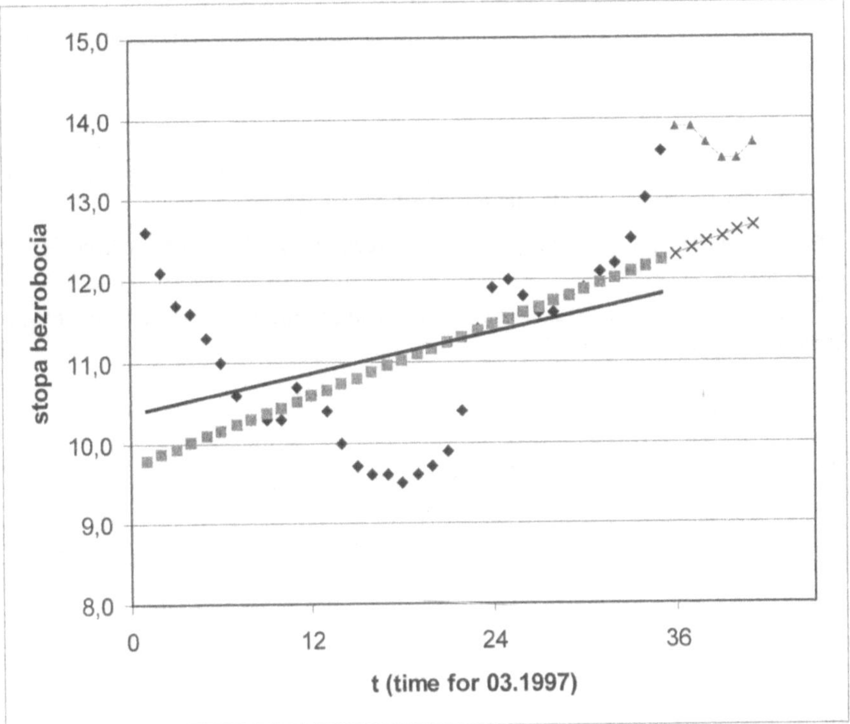

Fig.2. Dependence of a degree of unemployment on time and approximation by linear models with function of errors (2). A solid line - $\upsilon=2$ (method of least squares), dash line - $\upsilon=0,7$.

Conclusion

Thus, in the given work the following results were obtained

- On the base of application of the functionals of fractional differentiation the expressions for dot estimations of parameters of optimization of functionals or weight factors in function of tutoring of neural networks were obtained;
- The feasibilities of results for examination of models are shown;
- The numerical modeling for the test problem was carried out and it is shown, that the optimization at fractional exponents of function of errors gives the better result, than at optimization by a method of least squares.

References

1. Widrow B., Hoff M. Adaptive switching circuits // In 1960 IRE WESCON Convention Record. DUNNO. 1960. P. 96 - 104.

2. Rutkowska D., Pilicki M., Rutkowski L. (Sieci neuronowe, algorytmy genetyczne i systemy rozmyte. Warszawa. PWN. 1997. 410 S.)

3. Kolmogorov A.N., Fomin S.V. Elements of theory of functions and analyze of functions. Moskow: Nauka. 1968. 496 C.

4. Samko S. G., Kilbas A. A. and Marichev O. I. Fractional integrals and derivatives. Theory and applications. 1993. Gordon and Breach, New York, etc.

5. Erdelyi A., Magnus W., Oberhettinger F. and Tricomi F.G. Higher transcendental functions. Vol. 1. 1953. McGraw-Hill, New York, etc.

6. T. Masters. Practical neural network recipies in C ++. (Academic Press, Inc., 1993).

7. Osowski S. Sieci neuronowe w ujeciu algorytmicznym. Wydanie drugie. (Warszawa. WNT. 1996. 346 S.).

The Concept of Discoveries in Evolving Neural Net

Jerzy Tchórzewski[1)], **Mieczysław Kłopotek**[2)]
[1)]University of Podlasie, Institute of Computer Science
08-110 Siedlce, Sienkiewicza 51
[2)]Institute of Computer Science, Polish Academy of Sciences
01-237 Warsaw, Ordona 21

Abstract In this paper a concept of evolution of a neural network in the state space is presented. This evolution may be considered as another dimension of automated discoveries. As a base for building a model well known Evans' line method is used.
Keywords: Neural networks

1. Introduction

In the artificial intelligence the process of system learning is mainly understood as each autonomous change in the system over the experiments, and leading to quality improvement and its functioning (compare definition 1.1, in [1]). The system while learning acts as a 'Learner' acquiring knowledge and even making real discoveries.

Neural networks attracted the attention of many researchers not only due to their capability of learning non-trivial relationships between the input and output signals. It turns out that they may also discover knowledge useful or humans, as e.g. rules can be extracted from neural nets. Neural nets may also support knowledge discovery by serving as a "filter" for reduction of large databases. A relationship learned by a neural net from a part of the database may be used to select those cases from the database that do not fit the relationship learned so far.

In this context, one can point to at least two possible new research directions: investigation of neural network changes during the learning process (which leads to creation of a model of the phenomenon of learning as if it were a physical phenomenon) and secondly combining neural nets in order to achieve a resulting neural net describing desirable phenomenon. It seems that usage of system theory operations for synthesis and analysis of neural nets, especially the operation of subsystems and over-systems by J. Konieczny [7,13] may be vbaluable.

2. The neural net as control system

The basic structural element used for creating neural nets is the artificial neurone or neurones Hence the artificial neural net as a controlling system can be defined as follows:

$$SSN \overset{df}{=} < \{N_i\}; STR; pr >, \tag{1}$$

where:

$\{N_i\}$ – set of neurones forming the neural net,
STR – neural net structure,
pr – process occurring on the neural net consisting of a single neurone, being an elementary system presented below in the figure 1,

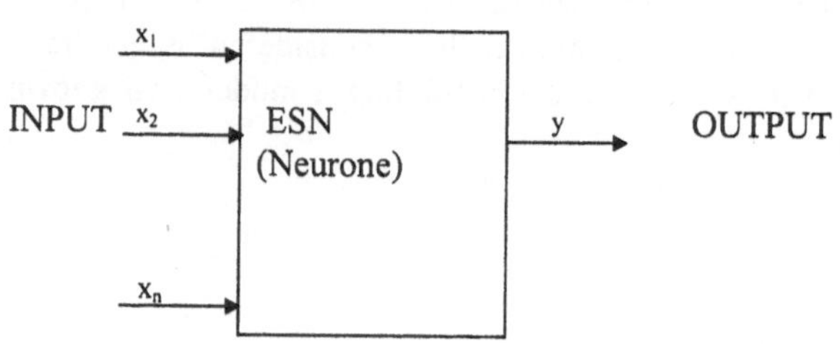

Fig. 1. Neurone as an elementary neural net

The goal of ESN is to process many inputs coming from different sources (x_i) over the one output y, which opens the possibility of setting up an equivalent scheme of elementary neural net built up from converters, which are characterised by weight and interpreted as shown in the figure 2.

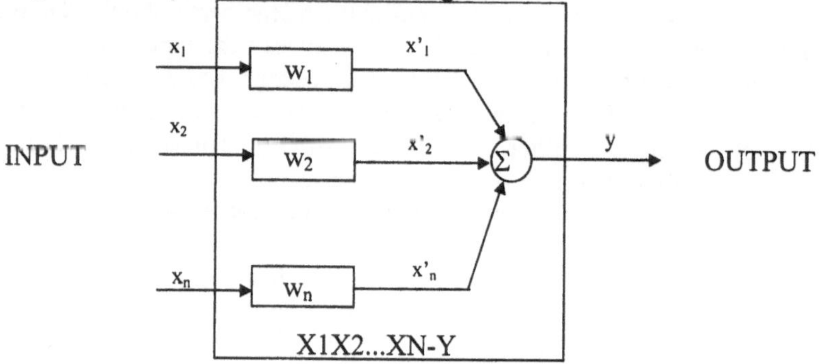

Fig. 2. Neurone converter model as a model of elementary neural net.

$$y = \sum_{i=1}^{N} w_i x_i, \tag{2}$$

where:

x_i – input signal i,
w_i – characteristic of i convector.

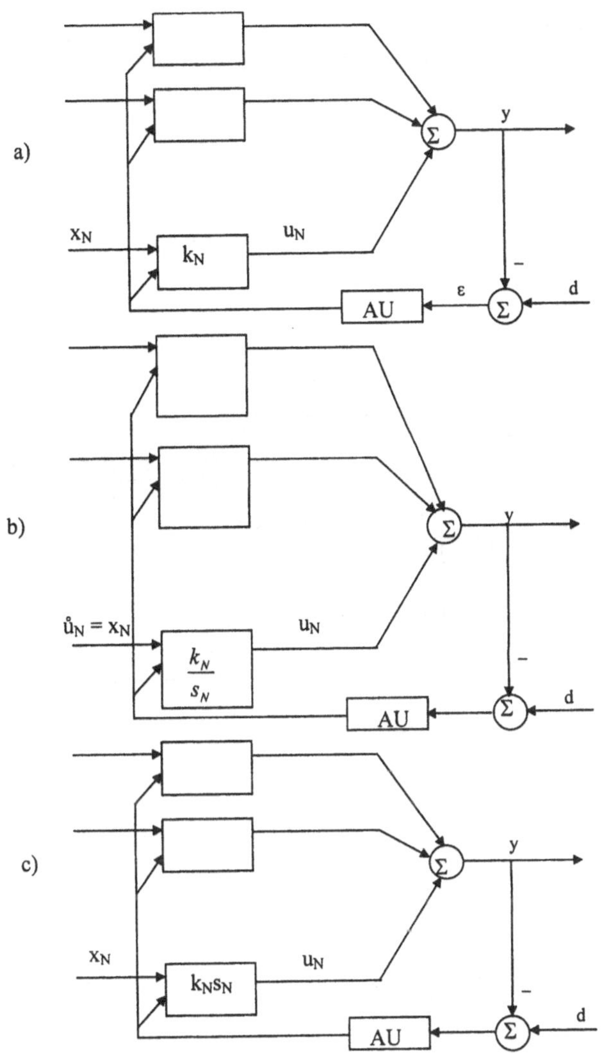

Fig. 3. Simple neurone models: a) with a proportional element; b) with an integral element ; c) with a differentiable element ; AU – learning algorithm

Presuming that characteristic of individual neurones are not only described in weight forms (by taking the level of importance of information coming from inputs), in the form of supporting units (proportional or inertial) with operational transmittance $G(s) = k = w$ but also in form of integral element $G(s)=\frac{k}{s}$ or differential element G(s) = k s (omitting here more complex dynamic elements of linear and non-linear configurations) it is received adequately:

$$\begin{aligned} &1)\quad y=\sum_{i=1}^{N} k_i x_i ,\\ &2)\quad y=\sum_{i=1}^{N} \frac{k_i}{s_i} x_i ,\\ &3)\quad y=\sum_{i=1}^{N} k_i s_i x_i , \end{aligned} \qquad (3)$$

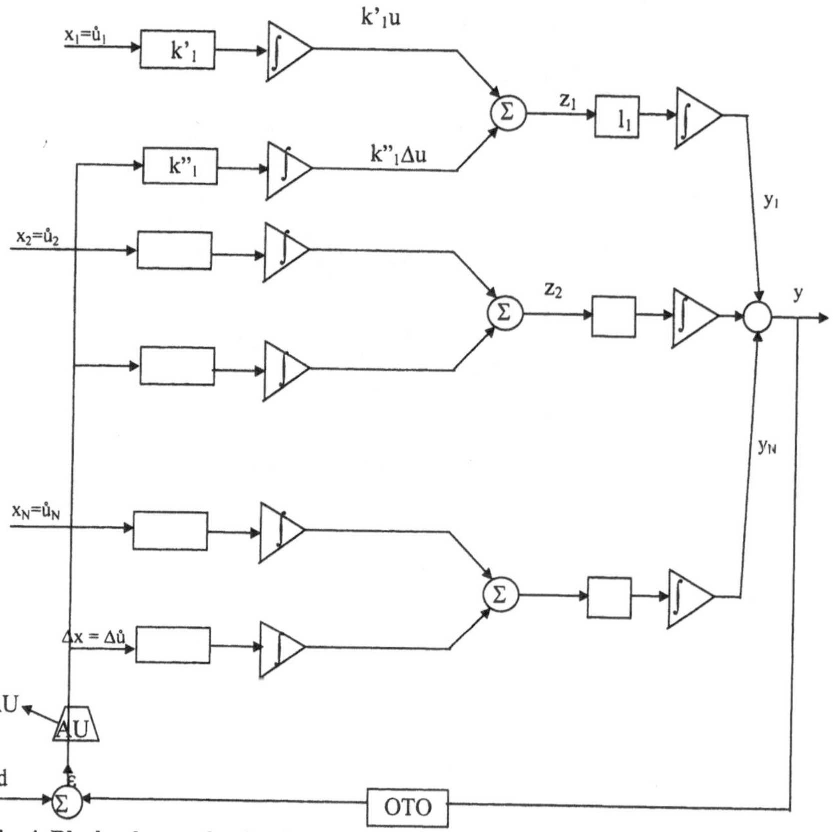

Fig. 4. Block scheme of a simple neurone characterised as integral element and algorithm of learning AU; <k'$_1$, k'$_2$, ..., k'$_N$> - characteristic of simple feed , <k"$_1$, k"$_2$,...,k"$_N$> - characteristic of feedback

Therefore there are different ways of describing the neurone converter model in a variable complex plane s, and in all three cases described by their dependence (3) it is received:

$$
\begin{aligned}
&1)\quad y = k_1x_1 + k_2x_2 + \ldots + k_Nx_N,\\
&2)\quad y = \frac{k_1x_1}{s_1} + \frac{k_2x_2}{s_2} + \ldots + \frac{k_Nx_N}{s_N},\\
&3)\quad y = k_1x_1s_1 + k_2x_2s_2 + \ldots + k_Nx_Ns_N,
\end{aligned}
\tag{4}
$$

which in cases. (3-2, 3-3) resulted with taking into account the element s: in the neurone converter model as shown in the figure 3.

Therefore in the space of state considering, that in the feedback exists an algorithm of learning with a certain characteristic AU we are getting:

$$\varepsilon(t) = d(t) - y(t),\quad \Delta x = AU \cdot \varepsilon \tag{5}$$

than for the situation like in the figure 3b we get a block scheme as in the figure 4, from where arise the following equations:

$$
\begin{aligned}
&1)\quad \varepsilon = d - OTO \cdot y,\\
&2)\quad y = f(y_1 + y_2 + \ldots + y_N),\\
&3)\quad \begin{cases} y_1 = k_1'u_1 + k_2''\Delta u,\\ y_2 = k_2'u_2 + k_2''\Delta u,\\ \ldots\\ y_N = k_N'u_N + k_N''\Delta u, \end{cases}
\end{aligned}
\tag{6}
$$

4) $\Delta\mathring{u} = \Delta x = AU \cdot \varepsilon = AU(d - OTO \cdot y) = AU[d - OTOf(y_1+y_2+\ldots+y_N)] =$

$= AU \cdot d - AU\ OTOf(k'_1u_1+k''_1\Delta u+k'_2u_2+k''_2\Delta u+\ldots+k'_Nu_N+k''_N\Delta u) =$

$$= AU \cdot d - AU \cdot OTOf(\sum_{i=1}^{N} k'_1\, u_1 + \sum_{i=1}^{N} k''_i\, \Delta u);$$

<u>After receiving a jump function of signal d finally we get:</u>

$$\mathring{d} = 0,$$

$$\Delta\mathring{u} = AU \cdot d - (AU \cdot OTO \cdot f(\sum_{i=1}^{N} k''_i)\Delta u - AU \cdot OTO \sum_{i=1}^{N} k'_i\, u_i,$$

$$y = f(y_1 + y_2 + \ldots + y_N) = f(k'_1u_1 + k''_2\Delta u + k'_2u_2 + k''_2\Delta u + \ldots + k'_1\, u_N + k''_N\Delta u) = \tag{7}$$

$$= \sum_{i=1}^{N} k'_i\, u_i + (\sum_{i=1}^{N} k''_i)\Delta u,$$

therefore:.

$$\begin{aligned}
&\mathring{d} = 0,\\
&\mathring{u}_1 = 0,\\
&\mathring{u}_2 = 0,\\
&\quad\cdot\\
&\quad\cdot\\
&\quad\cdot\\
&\mathring{u}_N = 0,\\
&\Delta\mathring{u} = AU\cdot d - AU\cdot OTO\, k'_1\cdot u_1 - AU\cdot OTO\cdot k'_2\cdot u_2 + \ldots + k'_N u_N\,(AU\cdot OTO
\end{aligned} \tag{8}$$

$\sum_{i=1}^{N} k''_i\,)\Delta u$

and

$$y = \sum_{i=1}^{N} y_i = \sum_{i=1}^{N} k'_i\, u_i + (\sum_{i=1}^{N} k''_i\,)\Delta u \tag{9}$$

or in the matrix notation:

$$\begin{bmatrix} d \\ \mathring{u}_1 \\ \mathring{u}_2 \\ \vdots \\ \mathring{u}_N \\ \Delta\mathring{u} \end{bmatrix} = \begin{bmatrix} 0 & 0 & 0 & \cdots & 0 & 0 \\ 0 & 0 & 0 & \cdots & 0 & 0 \\ 0 & 0 & 0 & \cdots & 0 & 0 \\ \vdots & \cdot & \cdot & \cdot & \cdot & \vdots \\ 0 & 0 & 0 & & 0 & 0 \\ AU & -AU\cdot OTO\cdot k'_1 & -AU\cdot OTO\cdot k'_2 & \cdots & -AU\cdot OTO\cdot k'_N & -AU\cdot OTO\cdot\sum_{i=1}^{N} k''_i \end{bmatrix} \begin{bmatrix} d \\ u_1 \\ u_2 \\ \vdots \\ u_N \\ \Delta u \end{bmatrix} \tag{10}$$

where:

- d – variable input of the model as a pattern of an output signal (of jump function)
- u_i – i-variable state as i- neurone input signal.

3. Investigating regularity of the neural net development

Let the example of our interest of a simple neural net from the figure 4 described by relationship (10) develop, so the parameters will change in the existing elements or a new element occurs like in the figure 5, and then:

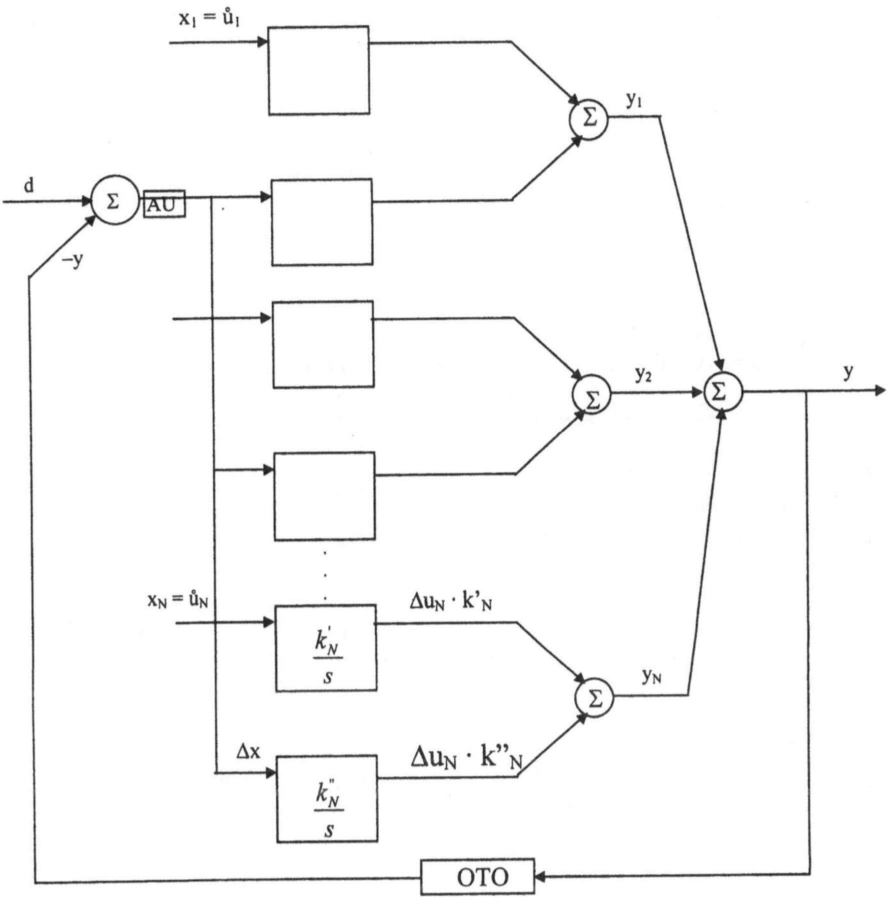

Fig. 5. Block scheme of a simple neurone characterised as integral element and algorithm of learning after the structural change connected with incorporating elements l_i

$$\varepsilon = d - OTO \cdot y,$$

$$y = \sum_{i=1}^{N} y_i, \quad y_i = l_i z_i\,,$$

$$\Delta\mathring{u} = \Delta x = AU \cdot d - AU \cdot OTO \left(\sum_{i=1}^{N} k'_i\, u_i + \sum_{i=1}^{N} k''_i\, \Delta u \right), \tag{11}$$

$$\mathring{y}_1 = l_1 z_1 = l_1(k'_1 u_1 + k''_1 \Delta u),$$

$$\mathring{y}_2 = l_2 z_2 = l_2(k'_2 u_2 + k''_2 \Delta u),$$

$$\ldots$$

$$\mathring{y}_N = l_N z_N = l_N(k'_N\, u + k''_N \Delta u).$$

Therefore:

$$
\begin{aligned}
&\mathring{d} = 0,\\
&\mathring{u}_1 = 0,\\
&\mathring{u}_2 = 0,\\
&\cdot\\
&\cdot\\
&\cdot\\
&\mathring{u}_N = 0,\\
&\mathring{y}_1 = l_1 k'_1 u_1 + l_1 k''_1 \Delta u,\\
&\mathring{y}_2 = l_2 k'_2 u_2 + l_2 k''_2 \Delta u,\\
&\quad \cdot \quad \cdot \quad \cdot\\
&\mathring{y}_N = l_N k'_N u_N + l_N k''_N \Delta u\\
&\Delta\mathring{u} = AU \cdot d - AU \cdot OTO \cdot k'_1 l_1 u_1 - AU \cdot OTO \cdot k'_1 l_2 u_2 + \ldots +\\
&\qquad - AU \cdot OTO \cdot k'_N l_N u_N - (AU \cdot OTO \cdot \sum_{i=1}^{N} l_i k''_i)\, \Delta u,
\end{aligned}
\tag{12}
$$

In the matrix registration:

$$
\begin{bmatrix} d \\ \mathring{u}_1 \\ \mathring{u}_2 \\ \vdots \\ u_N \\ y_1 \\ \mathring{y}_2 \\ \vdots \\ y_N \\ \Delta\mathring{u} \end{bmatrix}
=
\begin{bmatrix}
0 & 0 & 0 & \cdots & 0 & 0 \\
0 & 0 & 0 & & 0 & 0 \\
0 & 0 & 0 & & 0 & 0 \\
 & & \cdots & & & \\
0 & 0 & 0 & & 0 & 0 \\
0 & l_1 k'_1 & 0 & & 0 & l_1 k''_1 \\
0 & 0 & l_2 k'_2 & & 0 & l_2 k''_2 \\
 & & \cdots & & & \\
0 & 0 & 0 & & l_N k'_N & l_N k''_N \\
AU & -AU \cdot OTO \cdot k'_1 \cdot l_1 & -AU \cdot OTO \cdot k'_2 \cdot l_2 & \cdots & -AU \cdot OTO \cdot k'_N \cdot l_N & -AU \cdot OTO \cdot \sum_{i=1}^{N} l_i k''_i \,\Delta u
\end{bmatrix}
\bullet
\begin{bmatrix} d \\ u_1 \\ u_2 \\ \vdots \\ u_N \\ y_1 \\ y_2 \\ \vdots \\ y_N \\ \Delta u \end{bmatrix}
$$

(13)

and

$$
y = \sum_{i=1}^{N} y_i = \sum_{i=1}^{N} l_i z_i = \sum_{i=1}^{N} l_i (k'_i \cdot u_i + k''_i \,\Delta u) = \sum_{i=1}^{N} l_i k'_i \, u_i + \sum_{i=1}^{N} l_1 k''_i \,\Delta u \tag{14}
$$

Therefore from the analysis of dependence (10) and dependence (13) we get the regularity of the parametric-structural neural net development, due to the changing of net parameters and neural net structure (in the matrix rank **A**). Furthermore the method of the developing systems regularity presented for example in the work [13]can be successfully applied. It is essential in this respect to research the behaviour of the roots of an characteristic equation resulted from the matrix **A**, described in dependence(13) in relation to roots resulted from to dependence (10) by using evolutionary algorithms and immunological systems [13,15], subsystem and over-system operations by J.Konieczny of the information code [13] and system divergence by R.Staniszewski [11]. In this respect connecting the problem of neural net development with roots movement of characteristic equations on the variable complex plane s allows to control discoveries through the observation of development, e.g. the picture of the course of existing lines, creating new branches and contours, e.g.[3, 11, 13].

4. The development of neural net as a source of discovering knowledge

Researching the regularity of structural-parametrical changes of the neural net in the category of evolutionary algorithms results in considering the nature of the neural net development in the category of state plane, which roots movement of characteristic equation and with the opportunity of selection for practical purposes a suitable (an adequate) algorithm of learning (AU), surroundings characteristic (OTO), where for Hebba's type self-organised learning the rule determining weight values in successive learning cycles $w_{ij}(k+1) = (k) + \Delta w_{ij}(k)$ can be put forward as follow:

$$\Delta w_{ij}(k) = F(x_j, y_j), \tag{15}$$

where:

F(xj,yi) – state function of input signal x_j (presinaptic) and output signal y_j (postsinaptic).

In classical expression the Hebba's rule leads to the product function of those signals[9,12], which is written:

$$\Delta w_{ij}(k) = \eta x_j(k) y_i(k), \tag{16}$$

where:

η - learning factor determining a grade in which learning signals in the moment k influence the selection of weight values.

In consequence for

$$y\,i\,(k) = l_i(k) z_i(k) = l_i k'_i u_i + l_i k''_i \Delta u \tag{17}$$

and for

$$x_j(k) = \mathring{u}_j + \Delta u(k) = \mathring{u}_i(k) + \Delta\mathring{u}(k) \tag{18}$$

we obtein:

$$\Delta w_{ij}(k) = \eta[\mathring{u}_i(k) + \Delta\mathring{u}(k)][l_i(k)k'_i(k)u_i(k) + l_i(k)k''_i(k)\Delta u(k)], \tag{19}$$

so consequently the processes of neural net learning (its algorithm AU) are connected with the structural-parametrical changes of neural net, not only with the previous state weight.

5. Final remarks

In this paper a concept of evolution of a neural network in the state space was presented. This evolution may be considered as another dimension of automated discoveries. The presented concept of making discoveries in the neural net development, especially the graphical presentation of characteristic roots equation geometrical places on the variable complex plane s, as a specific picture of neural net may be used among others in the problem of system identification.

A numerical example illustrating the ideas presented here may be found in [14].

As a next stage we consider integration of uncertainty, and first of all the idea of Dempster-Shafer belief net [2, 4, 5, 6, 8]. However, using this theory for building Dempster-Shafer neural net, and based on this working out ways of making discoveries in its development, by using the description in the space states and the Evans roots line method, is not an easy question, because it is connected with researching the regularity of stochastic processes in non-linear systems and also with heuristic approach towards tree structures.

References

[1] Cichosz P.: Systemy uczące się. WNT, Warszawa 2000.

[2] Daniłowicz Cz., Boliński J.: Zastosowanie probabilistycznego modelu zbioru dokumentów do wyszukiwania w systemie www. Konferencja Naukowa nt. „Inżynieria wiedzy i systemy ekspertowe", PWr, Wrocław 2000.

[3] Kaczorek T.: Teoria sterowania i systemów, PWK, Warszawa 1996.

[4] Kamiński W.A., Kuczyński K.: Przydatność algorytmów drążenia baz danych naukowych na przykładzie bazy danych jądrowych, IV KKN nt. „Sztuczna Inteligencja" SzI=15'2000 (badanie-zastosowania-rozwój). Siedlce-Warszawa 2000.

[5] Kłopotek M. A: Metody identyfikacji i interpretacji struktur rozkładów przekonań w teorii Dempstera-Shafera, IPI PAN, Warszawa 1998.

[6] Kwaśnicka H: Obliczenia ewolucyjne w sztucznej inteligencji. PWr. Wrocław 1999

[7] Konieczny J.: Inżynieria systemów działania, WNT, Warszawa 1983.

[8] Lubański M.: Istota cybernetycznego myślenia.Mat.IIIoKK nt. "Sztuczna Inteligencja". CIR'98. Warszawa-Siedlce1998

[9} Osowski St.: Sieci neuronowe w ujęciu algorytmicznym, WNT, Warszawa 1996.

[10] Söderström T., Stoica P.: Identyfikacja systemów, WN PWN, Warszawa 1997.

[11] Staniszewski R.: Cybernetyka teoria projektowania, Ossolineum, Wrocław 1986.

[12] Tadeusiewicz R.: Elementarne wprowadzenie do techniki sieci neuronowych z przykładowymi programami, OW PLJ, Warszawa 1998.

[13] Tchórzewski J.: Systemowe wspomaganie procesu badania prawidłowości rozwoju elektroenergetycznej sieci przesyłowej, AP, Siedlce 1999.

[14] Tchórzewski J., Klopotek M.A.: A case study in neural network evolution. ICS PAS Reports, Warszawa, March 2002

[15]Wierzchoń S. : Sztuczne systemy immunologiczne. Teoria i zastosowania. AOW EXIT. Warszawa 2001

Searching for Memory in Artificial Immune System

Krzysztof Trojanowski[1)], Sławomir T. Wierzchoń[1,2)]

[1)] Institute of Computer Science, Polish Academy of Sciences 01-237 Warszwa, ul. Ordona 21
e-mail: {trojanow,stw}@ipipan.waw.pl

[2)] Department of Computer Science, Białystok Technical University 15-351 Białystok, ul. Wiejska 45[a]

Abstract: *In this paper an idea of the artificial immune system was used to design an algorithm for non-stationary function optimization. It was demonstrated that in the case of periodic function changes the algorithm constructively builds and uses immune memory. This result was contrasted with cases when no periodic changes occur. Further, an attempt towards the identification of optimal partitioning of the antibodies population into antibodies subjected clonal selection and programmed death of cells (apoptosis) has been done.*

Keywords: *Artificial Immune Systems, Clonal Selection, Apoptosis, Immune Memory, Non-stationary Optimization*

1. Introduction

Genetic algorithm (GA) – a probabilistic algorithm solving a wide range of problems – is in a sense a valuable instantiation of the General Problem Solver (GPS), [1], the dream of pioneers of Artificial Intelligence. It was observed by Nowell and Simon in the late fifties that the binary strings can be used for representing numbers as well as more complicated symbols. This observation gave an impulse to construct a system being able to solve general class of problems in a way similar to human problem solving. While the idea of GPS has failed (although expert systems can be viewed as its specialization), GAs still prove their usefulness and successful applications stimulate their development.

From an abstract point of view classical GA can be treated as a string evolver. Using genetic operators of crossover and mutation it modifies the population of chromosomes, represented by binary strings, to produce at least one string that is as close as possible to a target (although unknown to the algorithm) string exploiting so-called fitness function as the only information about the degree of closeness. To explain successfulness of such a search strategy, Holland formulated Schema Theorem, [2], according to which the GA assigns exponentially increasing number of trials to the observed best parts of the search space, what results in a convergence to the target string. However, this convergence is not always advantageous. As stated by Gaspar and Collard in [3], in fact it contradicts basic principle of natural evolution, where a great diversity of different species is observed. In other words, GA cannot maintain sufficient population diversity what results in its poor behavior when solving multimodal or time-dependent optimization problems.

Efficiency of GA hardly depends on the trade-off between its explorative and exploitative abilities. When exploitation dominates exploration, the algorithm finds suboptimal solutions. Otherwise the algorithm vast computer resources exploring uninterested regions of the search space. To gain the appropriate trade-off, a number of selection strategies has been proposed.

Recently, a new biologically inspired technique, so-called artificial immune systems (AIS), have been proposed to overcome the problem with finding appropriate trade-off. The learning/adaptive mechanisms used by the vertebrate immune system allows continuous generation of new species of so-called antibodies responsible for detection and destruction of foreign molecules, called antigens or pathogens. Particularly these mechanisms, described in Section 2, appear to be useful in solving multimodal, [4], and time-dependent, [3], [5], optimization problems. In this paper we trace the emergence of the immune memory and its role in solving time-dependent optimization tasks. The paper is organized as follows. Section 2 introduces basic mechanisms used by the vertebrate immune system. The immune algorithm based on these mechanisms is described in Section 3. The environment designed for our experiments is presented in Section 4 and results of these experiments are described in Section 5. Section 6 concludes the paper.

2. Immune system

While GA refers to the rules of Darwinian evolution relying upon introduction of permanent improvements in phenotypic properties of subsequent generations of living organisms, AIS refer to the mechanisms used by the adaptive layer of the immune system. The main "actors" of this system are lymphocytes or white cells of blood. We distinguish two important types of lymphocytes: B-lymphocytes (or B-cells for short) produced in *bone marrow*, and T-cells produced in *thymus*. Both the types differ in the roles fulfilled in the defense process. Roughly speaking T-cells are responsible for the detection between self and non-self substances while B-cells are involved in the production of so-called antibodies. Using military metaphor we can treat B-cell as a group of commandos equipped with selected weapon while T-cells are their commanders. From a computer science standpoint the mechanisms governing T-cells are used in designing novelty-detection systems (e.g. computer viruses detection) and the mechanisms governing B-cells are used in designing data analysis systems or optimization algorithms. Thus in the sequel we will focus on B-cells only.

B-lymphocyte is a monoclonal cell with about 10^5 receptors (antibodies) located on the cell surface. The antibodies associated with a given lymphocyte react to one type of antigen (more precisely to a small number of structurally similar antigens). When the antibodies recognize appropriate antigen they stimulate what results in intensive cloning, and the number of new clones is proportional to the degree of affinity between antibody and the antigen. This process is referred to as *clonal selection*. It is responsible for maintaining sufficient diversity of B-cells repertoire. To increase defense abilities of the immune system, the clones are subjected *somatic mutation*, i.e. mutation with very high rate. This way new, well fitted to the intruder, cells are entered to the system. Ineffective mutated clones as well as ineffective B-cells (which for a longer time do not participate in the immune response) are removed from the organism. This process is said to be *apoptosis*, or programmed death of cells. In place of ineffective cells new, almost randomly produced, cells are entered. Daily about 5% of B-lymphocytes is replaced by newly produced cells. More detailed system activity can be found in [6] or [7].

The process of production new antibodies fitted to an antigen that enters organism for the first time is referred to as *primary immune response*. It takes time (about three weeks) to produce effective antibodies. When the antigen enters organism one more time, the immune response – called *secondary immune response* – is much more efficient. The appropriate antibodies are produced very quickly and in much more amount. The effectivity of the secondary response can be explained by the existence of immune memory. Organism "memorizes" antigens entering it, and during secondary attack of an antigen, or a pathogen structurally similar to already known intruder, it quickly recalls appropriate antibodies. Interestingly, the nature of immune memory is not precisely known. According to Jerne's hypothesis, [8], B-cells are organized into so-called *idiotypic network*. Although not confirmed by immunologists this hypothesis offers an interesting and valuable metaphor for constructing systems for data analysis, [9]. The main mechanism responsible for the introduction of new cells and for maintaining efficient network is so-called *meta-dynamics* which controls the concentration of different kinds of B-cells according to the equation, [10]

$$\begin{array}{c}\textit{rate of}\\ \textit{population}\\ \textit{diversity}\end{array} = \begin{array}{c}\textit{production}\\ \textit{of new cells}\\ \end{array} - \begin{array}{c}\textit{death of}\\ \textit{ineffective}\\ \textit{cells}\end{array} + \begin{array}{c}\textit{reproduction}\\ \textit{of stimulated}\\ \textit{cells}\end{array} \qquad (1)$$

While clonal selection, somatic mutation and affinity maturation (i.e. maintaining effective B-cells) resemble mechanisms used by the evolutionary algorithms, metadynamics is the unique feature of AISs. As stated by Bersini and Varela, [11], in an ecosystem the species population densities vary according to the interactions with other members of the network as well as through environmental impacts. In addition the whole network is subjected structural perturbations through appearance and disappearance of some species. A crucial feature of AIS is the fact that the network as such, and not the environment, exerts the greatest pressure in the selection of the new cells to be integrated to the network.

3. Optimisation of non-stationary functions

The task of non-stationary function optimization is the identification of a series of optima that change their location (and possibly their height) in time. Since each optimum is located in different point of the search space that is represented by different chromosome, the algorithm designed to cope with this task can be viewed as pattern tracking algorithm. More formally we want to identify all the optima of a function $f(\mathbf{x}, t)$ where $\mathbf{x} \in D \subset \mathbf{R}^m$ and t represents time. Typically the domain D is the Cartesian product of the intervals $[x_{i,\min}, x_{i,\max}]$, $i = 1, \ldots, m$.

Evolutionary algorithms designed to cope with such stated task exploit one of the following strategies [12]: the expansion of the memory in order to build up a repertoire of ready responses for environmental changes, or the application of some mechanism for increasing population diversity in order to compensate for changes encountered in the environment. In this last case commonly used mechanisms are: random immigrants mechanism, triggered hypermutation or simply increasing the mutation rate within a standard GA to a constant high level.

1. *Fitness evaluation.* For each individual or antibody p in the population P compute its fitness i.e. the value of the objective function f_p.
2. *Clonal selection.* Choose n antibodies with highest fitness to the antigen.
3. *Somatic hypermutation.* Make c_i mutated clones of i-th antibody. The clone $c_{(i)}$ with highest fitness replaces original antibody if $f_{c(i)} > f_i$.
4. *Apoptosis.* Each $t_d \geq 1$ iterations, replace d weakest antibodies by randomly generated binary strings.

Fig. 1. Frame immune algorithm used in the experiments described later.

The first immune algorithm, called Simple Artificial Immune System or `Sais`, to cope with pattern tracking in dynamic environment was proposed in [3]. Here population consists of B-cells represented as binary strings, that is the `Sais` is so-called binary immune system. There is no distinction among a B-cell and the antibodies located on its surface (in fact all these antibodies recognize the same antigens). Thus we can use interchangeably the term "antibody" and "B-cell". The algorithm uses mechanisms described in Section 2. Particularly, to measure the affinity of an antibody to currently presented antigen (i.e. optimum at given iteration) so-called exogenic activation is used (defined as the Hamming distance between antigen and an antibody) and the affinity of an antibody to other antibodies is measured in terms of so-called endogenic activation. Later these authors proposed `YaSais` (Yet another Sais) in which only exogenic activation was taken into account. In this paper we use the algorithm tested already in [5]. It is also a binary immune system and its pseudocode is given in Figure 1.

Choosing of antibodies for somatic hypermutation in step 2 of this algorithm can be realized in many ways. In our case we used fitness values of antibodies, modified with a success register factor as a selection criterion. The succes register is a kind of counter present in every antibody, which is incremented every time the antibody is the best among all other antibodies in the population. This sort of prize is awarded every iteration.

4. Experiments

We performed a set of experiments with the algorithm described in previous section. We did three groups of experiments with two types of environments. Our test-bed was a test-case generator proposed in [13]. The generator creates a convex search space, which is a multidimensional hypercube. It is divided into a number of disjoint subspaces of the same size with defined simple unimodal functions of the same shape but possibly different value of optimum. In case of two-dimensional search space we simply have a patchy landscape, i.e. a chess-board with a hill in the middle of every field. Hills do not move but cyclically change their heights what makes the landscape varying in time. The goal is to find the current highest hill.

0.1	0.1	0.1	0.5_4
0.1	0.1	0_3	0.1
0.1	0.5_2	0.1	0.1
1_1	0.1	0.1	0.1

0.546_8	0.1	0.1	0.146_4
0.1	0.5_7	0.5_3	0.1
0.1	0.546_2	0.146_6	0.1
1_1	0.1	0.1	0_5

Fig. 2. Environments #1 (left), #2 (right) - shapes of the sequence of non-stationary fields in testing environments.

In our experiments there was a sequence of fields with varying hills' heights. Other fields of the space were static. We did experiments with two-dimensional search space where the chess-boards were of size 4 by 4, i.e. with 16 fields. Thus the search spaces consisted of 15 local optima and one global optimum in the first case. We tested four shapes of the sequence of non-stationary fields presented in Figure 3. In the figure, values in cells are weights of unimodal fuctions of the respective fields, which control heights of the hills. In other words the function located at the (i,j)-field is of the form $f_{ij}(x,y) = w_{ij} \cdot g(x-a_i, y-b_j)$, where g is a fixed unimodal function and (a_i, b_j) is the center of this field. Lower index at the value in the cell represents the position of the field in the sequence of presented optima.

The environment #1 (left part of Figure 2) was a test-bed for experiments with cyclic changes, while the environment #2 (right part of Figure 2) was a test-bed for experiments with both cyclic and acyclic changes. The aim of these experiments was to trace efficiency of primary (acyclic changes) and secondary (cyclic changes) immune response to the antigens (i.e. current optima). For experiments with cyclic changes, a single epoch obeys 5 cycles of changes. In all the experiments each antigen has been presented through 10 iterations. Thus, in case of the environment #1 a single epoch took 200 iterations, in case of the environment #2 - 400 iterations. Experiments with non-cyclic changes were based on the environment #2 and a single epoch included just one cycle of changes and took 80 iterations.

For the two environments described above we did series of experiments by changing the parameters *n* (step 2 of the algorithm in Figure 1) – see Figure 3.

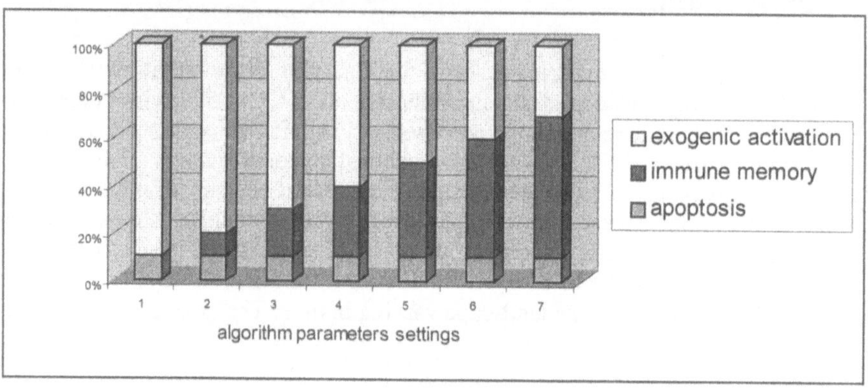

Fig. 3. Division of population into activated individuals and individuals for apoptosis. Individuals that do not belong to any of the two subgroups are supposed to be an immune memory structure.

Every experiment of the seven from the Figure 3 was repeated through 200 epochs and in the later figures we always study average values of these 200 epochs. For the results estimation we used two measures proposed in **Error! Reference source not found.**: Accuracy and Adaptability. *Accuracy* is a difference between the value of the current best individual in the population of the "just before the change" generation and the optimum value averaged over the entire run. *Adaptability* is a difference between the value of the current best individual of each generation and the optimum value averaged over the entire run. For both measures the smaller values are the better results.

4.1 Cyclic changes

The results of cyclic changes are presented in Figure 4 (env. #1) and Figure 5 (env. #2).

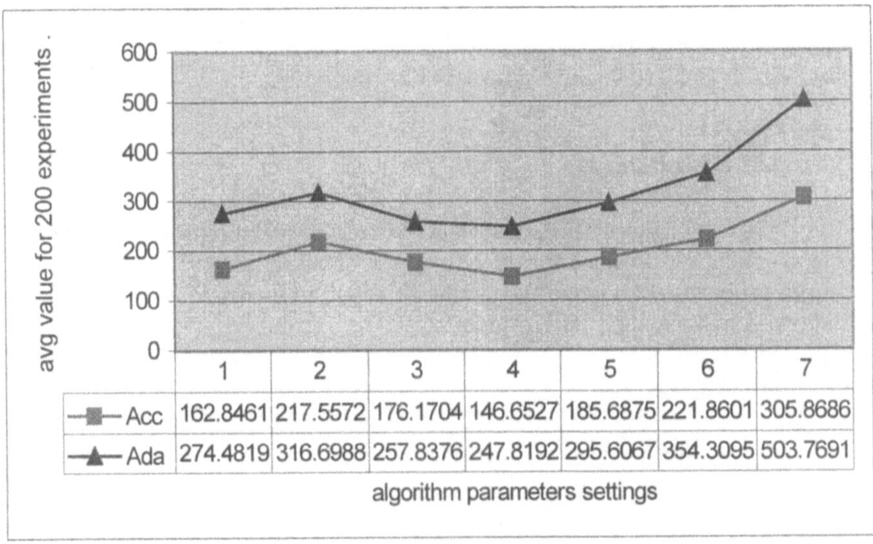

Fig. 4. Results for experiments with 7 types of parameter settings performed with environment #1 (cyclic changes).

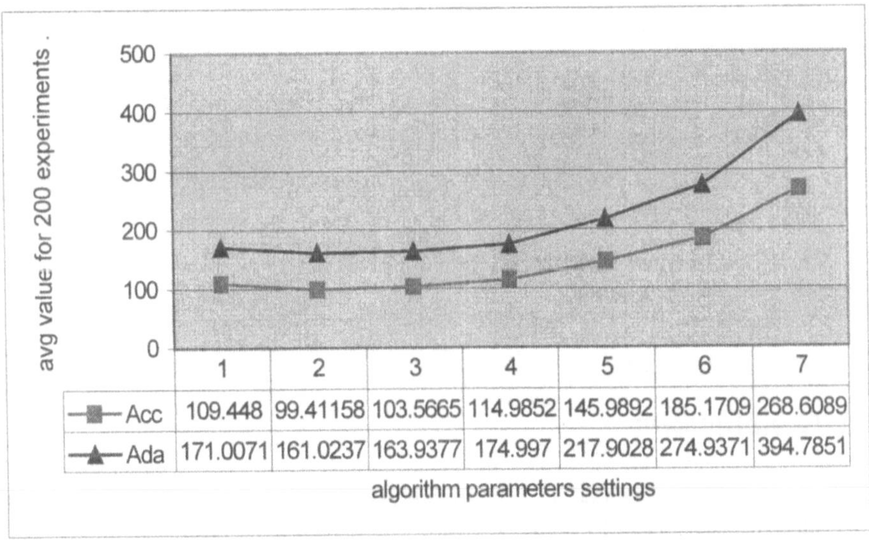

Fig. 5. Results for experiments with 7 types of parameter settings performed with environment #2 (cyclic changes).

In the Figures 4 and 5, the best results, i.e. the smallest values of Accuracy and Adaptability are obtained for different algorithm parameters settings. However, every time they are better than for the algorithm where all individuals are activated or undergo apoptosis (settings No. 1) and better than the case where the number of activated individuals is small. For the environment #1 the best case is setting No. 5, and for the environment #2 – setting No. 3.

4.2 Non-cyclic changes

The results of non-cyclic changes are presented in Figure 6. In this case the best results are obtained for the settings where all individuals are activated or undergo apoptosis (setting No. 1) and the worst are in the case where the number of activated individuals is the smallest.

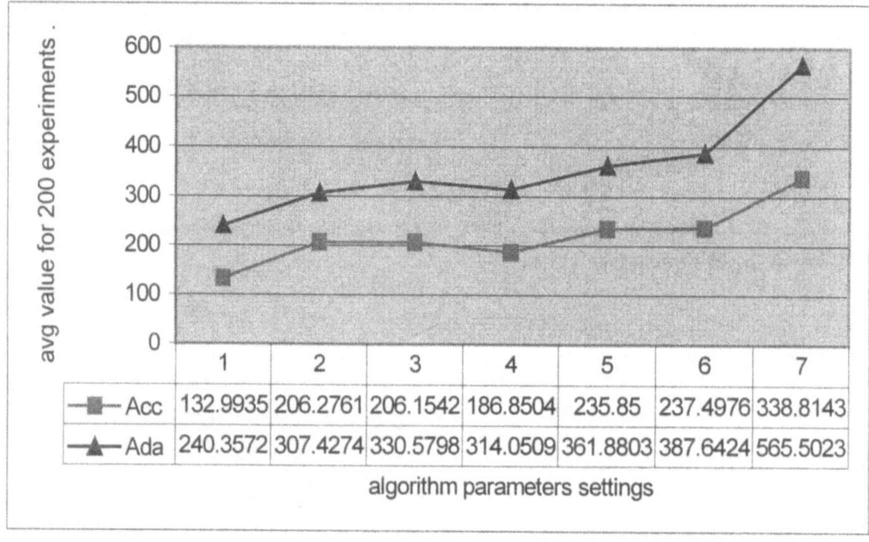

Fig. 6. Results for experiments with 7 types of parameter settings performed with environment #2 (non-cyclic changes).

5. Conclusions

Obtained results confirmed, that the individuals, which belong neither to activated group nor to the group for apoptosis can play significant role in searching for optima in problems with cyclic changes.

For environments with cyclic changes it is hard to propose one effective general proportion between the groups in a population. Differences between the best settings of algorithm parameters indicate, that the best proportion depends of the type of optimised environment and the type of changes in the environment and therefore should be tuned individually. But anyway, we can ascertain, that in case of cyclic changes, a key to a success is a balance between explorative mechanisms of the algorithm (represented by phases of activation apoptosis) and – from the other side - a form of immune memory represented by the left group of individuals, that does not take part in both phases. Now, the main difficulty is to find an effective method of management with a group of individuals that represent an immune memory of the system. This problem is the subject of our further research.

Bibliography

[1] Nowell, A., Simon, H.A. *Human Problem Solving*. Prentice Hall, NJ 1972

[2] Holland, J.H. *Adaptation in Natural and Artificial Systems*. MIT Press 1992

[3] Gaspar, A., Collard, Ph. From Gas to artificial immune systems: Improving adaptation in time dependent optimization. *Proc. of the 1999 Congress on Evolutionary Computation*, 1859-1866

[4] Wierzchoń, S.T. Multimodal optimization with artificial immune systems. M.A. Kłopotek, M.Michalewicz, S.T.Wierzchoń, eds, *Intelligent Information Systems 2001*. Physica-Verlag 2001, 167-179

[5] Wierzchoń, S.T. Artificial immune systems in action: Optimization of non-stationary functions (in Polish). Proc. of the Workshop "Artificial Intelligence", SzI'2001, Siedlce, Poland, December

[6] Hofmeyr, S.A. An interpretative introduction to the immune system. Technical Report, Dept. of Computer Science, University of New Mexico, Albuquerque, NM, 1999

[7] Wierzchoń, S.T. *Artificial Immune Systems. Theory and Applications* (in Polish). Warszawa 2001

[8] Jerne, N.J. Towards a network theory of the immune system. *Ann. Immunol. (Inst. Pasteur)*, **125C**:373-389, 1974

[9] de Castro, L.N., von Zuben, F.J. aiNet: An artificial immune network for data analysis. In: H.A. Abbas, R. A. Sarker, Ch. S. Newton (eds.) *Data Mining: A Heuristic Approach*. Idea Group Publishing, USA, 2001

[10] Perelson, A.S. Immune network theory. *Immunological Review*, **110**: 5-36, 1989

[11] Bersini,H., Varela, F. The immune learning mechanisms: Reinforcement and recruitment and their applications. *Computing with Biological Metaphors*, Chapman Hall, 1994, 166-192

[12] Cobb, H.G., Grefenstette, J.J. Genetic algorithms for tracking changing environments. In: *Proceedings of the Fifth International Conference on Genetic Algorithms*. Morgan Kaufmann 1993

[13] Trojanowski,K., and Michalewicz, Z., Searching for optima in non-stationary environments, CEC'99, IEEE Publishing, pp.1843-1850.

Selection Schemes in Evolutionary Algorithms *

Wojciech Wieczorek[1] and Zbigniew J. Czech[2]

[1] University of Silesia, Sosnowiec, Poland, e-mail: wieczor@ultra.cto.us.edu.pl
[2] University of Silesia, Sosnowiec, and Silesia University of Technology, Gliwice, Poland, e-mail: zjc@us.edu.pl, zjc@polsl.gliwice.pl

Abstract. One of the steps of an evolutionary algorithm is selection which chooses some individuals from a current population as parents to the individuals of the next population. This work focuses on loss of population diversity defined as the proportion of population individuals which are not chosen during selection. Quantifying loss of population diversity is crucial for designing evolutionary algorithms in which the search process is directed through controlling population diversity via parameters of a selection scheme. The aim of this work is to derive closed, approximate formulas which enable to determine loss of population diversity for some selection schemes. The selection schemes under consideration are also compared with respect to effectiveness and ease of controlling population diversity.

Key words. Evolutionary algorithms, selection schemes, tournament selection, truncation selection, linear ranking selection, exponential ranking selection, loss of diversity, selective pressure

1 Introduction

Evolutionary algorithms (EAs) constitute a class of random search algorithms based on the model of organic evolution and heredity observed in nature. The well-known members of this class are genetic algorithms [Holland, 1975] [Goldberg, 1991], evolution strategies [Rechenberg, 1973] [Schwefel, 1981], evolutionary programming [Fogel, 1992], scatter search techniques [Glover, 1977].

One of the steps of an evolutionary algorithm is selection which chooses some individuals from a current population as parents to the individuals of the next population. This work focuses on loss of population diversity defined as the proportion of population individuals which are not chosen during s-election. If in a given selection scheme the best individuals are chosen very often and the worst very rarely, then loss of population diversity is high. This phenomenon is known as a strong selective pressure and can lead to the premature convergence of an evolutionary algorithm into a local optimum. Quantifying loss of population diversity is crucial for designing evolutionary

* This work was carried out under the State Committee for Scientific Research grant no 7 T11C 021 21.

algorithms in which the search process is directed through controlling population diversity via parameters of a selection scheme. The aim of this work is to derive closed, approximate formulas which enable to determine loss of population diversity for some selection schemes. The selection schemes under consideration are also compared with respect to effectiveness and ease of controlling population diversity.

Loss of population diversity is considered in [Blickle and Thiele, 1995]. However the approximate formulas for this measure given there are not accurate enough. Another measure of selective pressure of a selection scheme is takeover time which is defined as the minimum number of iterations of an EA which is needed for a single best individual to fill up the whole population. In [Goldberg and Deb, 1991] takeover time is derived for proportionate, tournament and linear ranking selection schemes. Bäck establishes this measure for truncation selection [Bäck, 1994].

This paper consists of four sections. Section 2 contains the definitions of basic notions. Section 3 is devoted to loss of population diversity in some selection schemes. We first define the measures of it (subsection 3.1) and then derive the closed, approximate formulas for loss of population diversity in tournament, truncation, linear ranking and exponential ranking selection schemes (subsections 3.2–3.5). Section 4 concludes the paper.

2 Basic notions

Evolutionary algorithms (EAs) are randomized search algorithms based on principles of organic evolution and heredity observed in nature. An EA maintains a population $P = \{a_1, a_2, \dots, a_n\}$ of potential solutions to the problem called individuals. An individual a_i represents a point in the search space, I, which contains all possible solutions, i.e. $a_i \in I$. Let I^n be the set of all subsets of n individuals taken from space I, thus a population $P \in I^n$. In the course of EAs the population, after initialization, is subsequently modified by means of randomized operators of selection, s, recombination, r, and mutation, m, defined as $s, r, m : I^n \to I^n$. The operators are executed in a loop until a termination criterion is satisfied. A single run of the loop is called a generation. Let $P(t) = \{a_1(t), a_2(t), \dots, a_n(t)\}$ denote a population at the beginning of generation t. In generation t the selection operator creates first a new population, called the mating pool [Goldberg, 1989], $s(P(t)) = P'(t)$, which in turn is transformed by the recombination and mutation operators into the population for the next generation, $m \circ r(P'(t)) = P(t+1)$.

The quality of an individual is measured by a fitness function, $f: I \to R$, which distinguishes between "good" and "bad" solutions. This function is derived from the objective of the problem to be solved. The selection operator uses the fitness information to improve the average quality of the population by favoring individuals of higher quality to transfer their "genetic material" to next generations of the evolution process. Thus, selection guides the search towards promising points of the solution space. Recombination changes the "genetic material" already available in the population. Mutation creates new "genetic material" by introducing innovations into it. Both recombination and mutation explore the search space as they create new solutions, whereas selection exploits the information contained in the population, since it focuses on the individuals of higher fitness. Experience show that in order to achieve good convergence of EAs to the optimum solutions, a proper balance between exploration and exploitation, that is between an increase and reduction of the population diversity, must be adjusted.

3 Loss of population diversity

3.1 Measures

A term selective pressure is used to characterize the intensity of selection. Strong selective pressure means that only a small fraction of best individuals are chosen for recombination and mutation. Weak selective pressure allows also less fit individuals to survive and pass their "genetic material" to next generations. If selection pressure increases the population diversity decreases, and vice versa. Thus, strong selective pressure favors the premature convergence of the EAs search, while weak selective pressure can make the search inefficient.

In order to compare the selection schemes it is desirable to quantify selective pressure. Goldberg and Deb proposed to measure selective pressure by takeover time [Goldberg and Deb, 1991]. It is defined as the minimum number of generations which is needed for a single best individual to fill up the whole population obtained during an evolution process with no recombination and mutation used. More formally, let $P(0)$ denote an initial population and $\hat{a} \in P(0)$ its best individual. Then $t^* = \min\{t \in N : a_1(t) = a_2(t) = \ldots a_n(t) = \hat{a}\}$ is called takeover time of selection operator s. To assure that $\hat{a}$ does not disappear during the evolution process, it is assumed that s is a 1-elitist selection scheme which guarantees survival of one copy of $\hat{a}$ in every population. Intuitively, larger (smaller) takeover times correspond to weaker (stronger) selective pressure.

Another measure of selective pressure given in [Blickle and Thiele, 1995] is loss of diversity, d, which is defined as the proportion of individuals of a population that is not selected during the selection operation. The larger d the stronger selective pressure. In this work we focus our attention on this measure by establishing its values for some selection schemes.

Every selection scheme is characterized by selection probabilities, $p_j = Pr(a_j \in s(P(t)) : a_j \in P(t))$, which determine the chances for individual j, $1 \leq j \leq n$, to be chosen for recombination and mutation. The probabilities p_j for all individuals j constitute the probability distribution which is based solely on fitness values of these individuals. As for every probability distribution we require that $\sum_{j=1}^{n} p_j = 1$ is held.

Selection schemes involve one or more control parameters. By varying them one may influence selective pressure of a scheme, and as the result the course of the search process in EAs. Bäck formulates the following requirements that give ground for comparison the selection schemes in this regard [Bäck, 1994]: (a) the impact of the control parameter(s) on selective pressure should be simple and predictable; (b) one single control parameter for selective pressure is preferable; (c) the range of selective pressure that can be realized by varying the control parameter should be as large as possible.

3.2 Tournament selection

Tournament selection consists in picking randomly r individuals from population $P(t)$ and copying the fittest individual from this r-element sample into $P'(t)$. (Individuals can be picked with or without replacements. We assume that the individuals picked are returned to $P(t)$.) This routine is repeated n times, where n is the size of the population. r, $1 \leq r \leq n$, is called the size of the tournament. In such a scheme of selection some individuals may appear in population $P'(t)$ many times, while others may not be present at all. Clearly, an increase of r makes selective pressure stronger.

Suppose that the goal of an EA is to find the individual with the maximum value of the fitness function, and that the individuals in population $P(t)$ are sorted in descending order of their fitness values, i.e. we have $f(a_j) \geq f(a_{j+1})$, for $1 \leq j < n$. Then the following theorem can be proved.

Theorem 1. The probability of selecting individual j into population $P'(t)$ during tournament selection equals

$$p_j = \frac{(n-j+1)^r - (n-j)^r}{n^r}. \tag{1}$$

Proof. Choosing r individuals in the tournament is equivalent to selecting randomly an r-element combination with repetitions from an n-element set. An individual a_j wins the tournament, i.e. it is copied to $P'(t)$, if a_j is contained in the subset of r individuals drawn, and there are no individuals of lower subscripts than j (in the order defined above) in the subset. We get a formula for p_j by dividing the number of tournaments in which a_j wins by the number of all possible tournaments. The number of tournaments in which individual a_j wins is counted by subtracting from the number of all combinations with repetitions for $(n-j+1)$-element set (all possible tournaments for individuals $\{a_j, a_{j+1}, \ldots, a_n\}$) the number of r-element combinations with repetitions for $(n-j)$-element set (all possible tournaments for individuals $\{a_{j+1}, a_{j+2}, \ldots, a_n\}$). Since the number of r-element combinations with repetitions for n-element set is n^r, the probability we need equals $p_j = ((n-j+1)^r - (n-j)^r)/n^r$. □

Other derivation of Equation (1) can be found in [Bäck, 1994]. The next theorem concerns loss of diversity.

Theorem 2. Loss of diversity equals

$$d = \frac{1}{n}\sum_{j=1}^{n}(1 - p_j)^n, \tag{2}$$

where p_j, $1 \leq j \leq n$, are the selection probabilities of a selection scheme.

Proof. Let the values of discrete random variable X be the numbers of individuals in the population which have not been chosen during selection. The variable X is the sum of random variables $X_1, X_2, \ldots, X_n$, where a value of X_j equals 1 when individual a_j has not been chosen, and 0 when it has been chosen at least once. Then we have $X = \sum_{j=1}^{n} X_j$, and d is the mean value, $\mathrm{E}[X]$, of variable X. Since X_j has the one-zero distribution, $\mathrm{E}[X_j] = Pr(X_j = 1)$ holds. The probability that individual a_j will not be chosen is equal to the probability of n successes in the Bernoulli sequence of n draws. By a success we mean that in a single draw individual a_j has not been chosen, what takes place with probability $1 - p_j$. Thus $Pr(X_j = 1) = \binom{n}{n}(1 - p_j)^n p_j^{n-n} = (1 - p_j)^n$. Dividing $\mathrm{E}[X]$ by n we obtain $d = \frac{1}{n}\mathrm{E}[X] = \frac{1}{n}\sum_{j=1}^{n}\mathrm{E}[X_j] = \frac{1}{n}\sum_{j=1}^{n}(1 - p_j)^n$. □

Using Theorem 1 and 2, and the method of genetic programming [Koza, 1992] [Banzhaf et al., 1998] [Wieczorek and Czech, 2000] we found the following formula which approximates loss of diversity in tournament selection:

$$d_1 \cong \frac{r + \frac{4}{r+4}}{r + 4 + \frac{r+7}{n^2}}. \tag{3}$$

The test set contained triples (n, r, d), where for $n = 2$ values of $r = \{1, 2\}$, for $n = 3$: $r = \{1..3\}$, for $n = 4$: $r = \{1..4\}$, for $n = 5$: $r = \{1..5\}$, for $n = 50$: $r = \{1 .. 10, 35, 50\}$, for $n = 200$: $r = \{2, 4 .. 10, 20, 50, 100\}$. The values of d were computed from Equations (1) and (2). The set of terminal symbols contained 1, 2, 3, 4, n and r. The set of functions consisted of operators of addition, unary minus, multiplication, division and unary $n\hat{}$ ("n to the power"). Other approximations for loss of diversity computed by applying genetic programming were $(r + 1)/(r + 5)$ and $e^{-4/(r+3)}$. In the latter case, also the exponential function was included into the set of functions.

It is easy to see that for large n loss of diversity in Equation (3) does not depend on n, so we have $d_1^* = (r + 2)^2/(r + 4)^2$. In Table 1 the values of d and d_1^* are compared.

3.3 Truncation selection

In truncation selection only a fraction $T, T \in (0, 1]$, of the best individuals can be selected. All the individuals have the same selection probability defined as:

$$p_j = \begin{cases} \frac{1}{Tn}, & \text{if } 1 \leq j \leq Tn, \\ 0, & \text{if } Tn < j \leq n. \end{cases} \tag{4}$$

r	$n=50$ d	$n=200$ d	$n=2000$ d	$n=10000$ d	d_1^*
1	0.364	0.367	0.368	0.368	0.360
2	0.429	0.432	0.432	0.432	0.444
3	0.502	0.504	0.504	0.504	0.510
4	0.559	0.561	0.561	0.561	0.563
5	0.604	0.605	0.606	0.606	0.605
6	0.640	0.641	0.642	0.642	0.640
7	0.669	0.670	0.671	0.671	0.669
8	0.694	0.695	0.695	0.695	0.694
9	0.714	0.715	0.716	0.716	0.716
10	0.732	0.733	0.733	0.733	0.735
20	0.830	0.830	0.830	0.830	0.840
50	0.912	0.913	0.913	0.913	0.927

Table 1. Comparison of values d and d_1^*.

The selection procedure consists in picking randomly n individuals from the set of individuals located at positions from 1 to Tn, assuming that the population has been sorted according to the values of fitness function with the best individual at position 1. Truncation selection is equivalent to (μ, λ)-selection used in evolution strategies with $\lambda = n$ and $T = \mu/\lambda$ [Schwefel, 1992]. From Equations (2) and (4) we get the following formula for loss of population diversity in truncation selection:

$$d_2 = \frac{1}{n}\left[\sum_{i=1}^{Tn}\left(1-\frac{1}{Tn}\right)^n + \sum_{i=Tn+1}^{n}(1-0)^n\right] = T\left[\left(1-\frac{1}{Tn}\right)^n - 1\right] + 1.$$

One can see that for large n loss of population diversity in truncation selection does not depend on n:

$$d_2^* = T\left[\left(1-\frac{1}{Tn}\right)^n - 1\right] + 1 \cong T\left[\exp\left(-\frac{1}{T}\right) - 1\right] + 1.$$

In Table 2 the values of d and d_2^* are compared.

3.4 Linear ranking selection

In linear ranking selection [Baker, 1985] [Baker, 1987] the selection probability of individual j, $1 \leq j \leq n$, is defined as follows:

$$p_j = \frac{1}{n}\left(\eta^+ - (\eta^+ - \eta^-)\frac{j-1}{n-1}\right). \tag{5}$$

Thus $\frac{\eta^+}{n}$ and $\frac{\eta^-}{n}$ are the probabilities of selecting the best and worst individuals, respectively. In order to satisfy the equation $\sum_{j=1}^{n} p_j = 1$ the value

	$n=50$	$n=200$	$n=2000$	$n=10000$	
T	d	d	d	d	d_2^*
1.0	0.364	0.367	0.368	0.368	0.368
0.9	0.393	0.395	0.396	0.396	0.396
0.8	0.426	0.428	0.429	0.429	0.429
0.7	0.464	0.467	0.468	0.468	0.468
0.6	0.510	0.513	0.513	0.513	0.513
0.5	0.565	0.567	0.568	0.568	0.568
0.4	0.631	0.632	0.633	0.633	0.633
0.3	0.710	0.710	0.711	0.711	0.711
0.2	0.801	0.801	0.801	0.801	0.801
0.1	0.900	0.900	0.900	0.900	0.900

Table 2. Comparison of values d and d_2^*.

of η^+ must be chosen from the range [1.0 .. 2.0] and $\eta^+ = 2 - \eta^-$. Usually a value of $\eta^+ = 1.1$ is recommended. Note that all individuals get a different rank, i.e. a different selection probability, even if they have the same fitness value. Loss of diversity for linear ranking selection equals

$$d_3 = \frac{1}{n}\sum_{j=1}^{n}\left(1 - \frac{\eta^+ - 2(\eta^+ - 1)\frac{j-1}{n-1}}{n}\right)^n = \frac{1}{n}\sum_{j=1}^{n}(1-z)^n.$$

For small values z one may use an asymptotic approximation [Knuth, 1969] to obtain:

$$d_3 \cong \frac{1}{n}\sum_{j=1}^{n}\left(1 - nz + \binom{n}{2}z^2\right) \cong \frac{1}{6}(\eta^+)^2 - \frac{1}{3}\eta^+ + \frac{2}{3}. \tag{6}$$

We refined approximation (6) even further by making use of Marquardt's algorithm for nonlinear regression[1] taking coefficients $\frac{1}{6}$, $-\frac{1}{3}$ and $\frac{2}{3}$ as the initial values of parameters for that algorithm. The values of independent variable d were computed from Equations (2) and (5), for $\eta^+ = 1.0, 1.05, 1.1, \ldots, 2.0$ and $n = 1000$. The following approximation was obtained $d_3^* = 0.067(\eta^+)^2 - 0.137\eta^+ + 0.438$. Table 3 compares the exact, d, and approximated values, d_3^*, of loss of population diversity for linear ranking selection.

3.5 Exponential ranking selection

The selection probability of individual j in exponential ranking selection equals

$$p_j = \frac{c-1}{c^n - 1}c^{j-1}, \tag{7}$$

[1] The Statgraphics package was used for this purpose.

η^+	$n=50$ d	$n=200$ d	$n=2000$ d	$n=10000$ d	d_3^*
1.0	0.364	0.367	0.368	0.368	0.368
1.1	0.365	0.368	0.368	0.368	0.368
1.2	0.367	0.369	0.370	0.370	0.370
...	...	...	...	...	...
1.8	0.407	0.408	0.408	0.408	0.408
1.9	0.418	0.419	0.420	0.420	0.420
2.0	0.432	0.432	0.432	0.432	0.432

Table 3. Comparison of values d and d_3^*.

where parameter c is chosen from the range (0.0 .. 1.0). The smaller c the stronger selective pressure. The exact formula for loss of population diversity in exponential ranking selection is as follows:

$$d_4 = \frac{1}{n}\sum_{j=1}^{n}\left(1-\frac{c-1}{c^n-1}c^{j-1}\right)^n = \frac{1}{n}\sum_{j=0}^{n-1}\left(1-\frac{c-1}{c^n-1}c^{j}\right)^n.$$

After expanding the function under the summation sign into the power series we get

$$d_4 = \frac{1}{n}\sum_{j=0}^{n-1}\sum_{k=0}^{n}\binom{n}{k}(-1)^k\left(\frac{c-1}{c^n-1}\right)^k c^{jk}.$$

Let $\lambda = n\frac{c-1}{c^n-1}$, then

$$d_4 = \frac{1}{n}\sum_{j=0}^{n-1}\sum_{k=0}^{n}\frac{n(n-1)(n-2)\cdots(n-k+1)}{k!}(-1)^k\frac{1}{n^k}\lambda^k c^{jk}$$

$$\cong \frac{1}{n}\sum_{j=0}^{n-1}\sum_{k=0}^{n}\frac{1}{k!}(-1)^k\lambda^k c^{jk} \cong \frac{1}{n}\sum_{j=0}^{n-1}e^{-\lambda c^j}. \tag{8}$$

The approximation (8) has been obtained using the equation $e^x = \sum_{k=0}^{\infty}\frac{x^k}{i!}$. The function under the summation sign of (8) monotonically increases with respect to j, so the sum can be bounded as below:

$$d_4 \cong \frac{1}{n}\sum_{j=0}^{n-1}e^{-\lambda c^j} \le \frac{1}{n}\int_0^n e^{-\lambda c^x}\,dx.$$

In order to compute this integral we may expand function e^x into the continued fraction, $e^x = [0, 1/1, -2x/(2+x), x^2/6, x^2/10, x^2/14, \ldots, x^2/(4k+2), \ldots]$, where the fraction has the meaning: $[a_0, b_1/a_1, b_2/a_2, b_3/a_3, \ldots] = a_0 +$

$b_1/(a_1+b_2/(a_2+b_3/(a_3+\cdots)))$. The consecutive approximations $P_n/Q_n = a_0+b_1/(a_1+b_2/(a_2+\cdots b_n/a_n)))$ can be computed from the following recurrences:

$$P_n = a_nP_{n-1}+b_nP_{n-2}, \qquad P_{-1}=1, \qquad P_0=a_0,$$
$$Q_n = a_nQ_{n-1}+b_nQ_{n-2}, \qquad Q_{-1}=0, \qquad Q_0=1.$$

Thus we have $e^x \cong \frac{P_3}{Q_3} = \frac{x^2+6x+12}{x^2-6x+12}$, and

$$d_4^* \cong \frac{1}{n}\int_0^n e^{-\lambda c^x}\,\mathrm{d}x \cong \frac{1}{n}\int_0^n \frac{(\lambda c^x)^2-6\lambda c^x+12}{(\lambda c^x)^2+6\lambda c^x+12}\,\mathrm{d}x$$
$$= \frac{4\sqrt{3}}{n\ln c}\left[\arctan\left(\frac{\sqrt{3}\lambda}{3}+\sqrt{3}\right)-\arctan\left(\frac{\sqrt{3}\lambda c^n}{3}+\sqrt{3}\right)\right]+1. \qquad (9)$$

Table 4 compares the values of d and d_4^*.

	$n=50$		$n=200$		$n=2000$		$n=10000$	
c	d	d_4^*	d	d_4^*	d	d_4^*	d	d_4^*
0.999	0.364	0.369	0.368	0.369	0.421	0.423	0.712	0.729
0.998	0.364	0.369	0.369	0.371	0.522	0.528	0.821	0.845
0.997	0.365	0.369	0.372	0.375	0.607	0.618	0.868	0.891
...	...	...	...	...	...	...	...	...
0.800	0.731	0.757	0.902	0.925	0.985	0.992	0.996	0.998
0.500	0.880	0.908	0.960	0.975	0.994	0.997	0.999	0.999
0.100	0.952	0.971	0.985	0.992	0.998	0.999	1.000	1.000

Table 4. Comparison of values d and d_4^*.

4 Conclusions

In this work we analyzed some selection schemes with respect to loss of population diversity. Based on Theorem 2 proved in section 3 the closed formulas which approximate loss of diversity for the schemes under consideration were derived. Loss of population diversity is crucial for designing an evolutionary algorithm which maintains a suitable level of population diversity by changing a control parameter (or parameters) of a given selection scheme.

To conclude we note what follows. In tournament, truncation and linear ranking selections, loss of population diversity depends on a single parameter, r, T and η^+, respectively. This is an advantage if one wants to control loss of population diversity during the course of EAs. Contrary to other schemes, linear ranking selection is characterized by a very limited range of loss of population diversity. For the values of η^+ changing from 1.0 to 2.0, loss of population diversity stays within the range [0.368 .. 0.432]. Thus among the selection schemes considered in our work, tournament and truncation selection satisfy in a best way the requirements given in subsection 3.1.

References

1. Baker, J.E., Adaptive selection methods for genetic algorithms, Proc. of the 1st International Conference on Genetic Algorithms and Their Applications, Lawrence Erlbaum Associates, (1985), 101–111.
2. Baker, J.E., Reducing bias and inefficiency in the selection algorithm, Proc. of the 2nd International Conference on Genetic Algorithms and Their Applications, Lawrence Erlbaum Associates, (1987), 14–21.
3. Banzhaf, W., Nordin, P., Keller, R.E., Francone, F.D., Genetic programming — An introduction: On the automatic evolution of computer programs and its applications, Morgan Kaufmann, (1998).
4. Bäck, T., Selective pressure in evolutionary algorithms: A characterization of selection mechanisms, Proc. of the First IEEE Conference on Evolutionary Computation, IEEE World Congress on Computational Intelligence (ICEC94), (1994), 57–62.
5. Blickle, T., Thiele, L., A comparison of selection schemes used in genetic algorithms, TIK-Report no 11, version 2, (1995).
6. Fogel, D.B., Evolving artificial intelligence, PhD thesis, University of California, San Diego, CA, (1992).
7. Glover, F., Heuristics for integer programming using surrogate constraints, Decision Sciences 8, 1 (1977), 156–166.
8. Goldberg, D.E., Genetic algorithms in search, optimization and machine learning, Addison-Wesley, Reading, Massachusetts, (1989).
9. Goldberg, D.E., Deb, K., A comparative analysis of selection schemes used in genetic algorithms, Foundations of Genetic Algorithms, Morgan Kaufmann, (1991), 69–93.
10. Graham, R.L., Knuth, D.E., Patashnik, O., Concrete mathematics: A foundation for computer science, Addison-Wesley, (1994).
11. Holland, J.H., Adaptation in natural and artificial systems, The University of Michigan Press, Ann Arbor, MI, (1975).
12. Knuth, D.E., The art of computer programming, Vol. 1: Fundamental algorithms, Addison-Wesley, (1968).
13. Koza, J.R., Genetic programming: On the programming of computers by means of natural selection, MIT Press, (1992).
14. Michalewicz, Z., Genetic algorithms + data structures = evolution programs, Springer-Verlag, (1994), 2nd ed.
15. Rechenberg, I., Evolutionsstrategie: Optimierung technischer systeme nach prinzipien der biologischen evolution, Frommann-Holzboog, Stuttgart, (1973).
16. Schwefel. H.P., Numerical optimization of computer models, Wiley, Chichester, (1981).
17. Schwefel, H.P., Natural evolution and collective optimum-seeking, Computational systems analysis: Topics and trends, Elsevier, (1992), 5–14.
18. Wieczorek, W., Czech, Z.J., Grammars in genetic programming, Control and Cybernetics 29, 4 (2000), 1019–1030.

Comparison of Crossover Operators for the State Assignment Problem

Mariusz Chyży and Witold Kosiński

Polish-Japanese Institute of Information Technology
Koszykowa 86, 02-008 Warsaw, Poland
{chyzym, wkos}@pjwstk.edu.pl

Abstract. *The paper presents a brief overview of crossover operators, along with the genotypes, applicable to the state assignment problem (SAP). Comparative experimental studies of genetic algorithms with different crossover operators applied to the SAP are described and their results are discussed.*

Keywords: *evolutionary algorithm, genetic algorithm, genetic operators, state assignment problem, finite state machine synthesis, reprogrammable devices*

Introduction

In the previous paper [Chy01] we proposed the original crossover operators for the state assignment problem (SAP) [Vill98]. State encodings found by a genetic algorithm (GA) with such operators were better up to 63% than those generated by commercially available state-of-the-art software containing a lot of domain knowledge [Alt01].

There are several other crossover operators (and genotypes) applicable to SAP [Ama95], [Alm95], [Chat98]. They are reported in different papers and, what is interesting, none of them mentions the other. Unfortunately, based on these papers it is impossible to compare the effectiveness of the crossovers. They are used in different GAs for different benchmark finite state machines (FSMs) and what is the most important - for different measures of the fitness, as e.g.: the literal count, product terms count or the fitness defined by a formula. Therefore we wished to compare known crossovers for SAP with the same testbed and experimental environment, in order to obtain the reliable comparative results.

First we make a brief overview of crossover operators (together with genotypes) applicable to SAP. Next we describe the experimental environment for the comparison of selected crossovers and in the sequel we present a set of experimental results. Final discussion and conclusions end the paper.

Crossovers in SAP solutions using GAs

In the midst of many papers on SAP (compare the monograph [Vil98] or [Per97]) there are few papers on the problem solution using GAs.

In [Ama95] chromosomes are represented by a "*pick list*" (actually it is a case of *ordinal representation* [Gre85] used earlier for the traveling salesman problem (TSP)) and are crossed-over by the classic one-point crossover operator, further on referred to as an operator *O*. Authors chose such a genotype to obtain valid offspring. Similarly in [Chat98] a part of a "state-code component" of the chromosome uses a kind of the ordinal representation. The "flip-flop component" is a bit string of the length *r*. Zero or one on *i*-th position identifies the type of the flip-flop ('D' or 'JK') that stores the *i*-th state bit (when FSM is implemented as a synchronous sequential circuit).

The next paper reporting the GA application to SAP is [Ama95]. Here the chromosome is represented by a binary matrix $m \times r$, where *m* is the number of FSM states. After the problem analysis authors propose the original crossover operator. It consists in column exchange between two chromosomes. Such a crossover can create an invalid offspring which must be corrected to represent unique state assignments.

One more crossover operator dedicated to the schedule optimisation can be applied to SAP. It is the *position-based* crossover [Sys91], in the sequel called as *P* crossover.

Since it is impossible to evaluate the effectiveness of these crossovers for a given problem based on the literature only, we have decided to compare them in the same testbed. In the next section we compare *M*1 operator [Chy01], the *O* one [Alm95] and the *P* one [Sys91].

Unfortunately, the original and interesting operator proposed by [Ama95] is not included in our experiments, since [Ama95] describes the correction of the invalid offspring generated by this crossover ambiguously and hence obtained results for the assumed crossover implementation could have been unreliable

Experimental results

The effectiveness of the selected crossover operators applicable to SAP has been checked with the use of several MCNC benchmark FSMs [Yan91]. They were synthesized by Altera Multiple Array MatriX Programmable Logic User System (MAX+PLUS II) in the device of MAX9000 family [Alt01] (actually it was the EPM9320RC208-15 device). GA called the MAX+PLUS II (further on referred to as MPII) to ascertain fitness of chromosomes. As an input parameter MPII received the text design file (*.tdf*) with the state transition table describing given FSM (in Altera Hardware Description Language - AHDL) where FSM states were encoded according to evaluated chromosome. GA got the fitness of the individual (the number of logic cells and shareable expanders utilized for implementation of

FSM in given device, with a given state assignment) from the report file (*.rpt*) generated by MPII. The optimisation aim was to minimise such a fitness.

Chromosomes were represented by integer vectors ([Chy01]). They were crossed-over with the probability p_c and mutated with the probability p_m. When the individual was to be muted, the order-based mutation was applied to permute a pair of randomly selected genes with the probability p_p or with the probability $1-p_p$, then a selected allele was substituted with an allele from among 2^r-m values not used in a chromosome.

Individuals were promoted to the next population by rank-based selection [Whi89], [Gol89], [Mich99], each individual has its rank corresponding to a position in sorted (by fitness, in descending order) vector of population individuals plus *rank_offset* (tuning the selection pressure). The elitist strategy was used. Some percentage (specified by *elitism* parameter) of the best individuals from the current population (of the size *ps*) was unconditionally copied to the new population. The rest of $ps \cdot (1\text{-}elitism)$ individuals were selected to the new population from among $ps \cdot (1\text{-}elitism + elitism')$ chromosomes of the current generation.

Such a GA was run for a given number of generations *gnrs* (Table 1).

Table 1. GA parameters for tested benchmark FSMs.

FSM	*ps*	p_c	p_m	p_p	*gnrs*	*elitism*	*elitism'*	*rank offset*
*Ex*1, *keyb*, *s*1	90	65	9	65	600	3	1	127
planet, *s*510, *s*832	100	65	9	65	700	3	1	144

The GA was run 9 times for each benchmark FSM used for the tests: three times with crossover *M*1, three times with - *O* and three times with - *P*.

The left part of Table 2 shows parameters of the tested benchmark FSMs: I - the number of FSM inputs, O - outputs, T - FSM transitions, S - FSM states. On the right side there are results of state assignments proposed by MPII and the best ones chosen from among 30 000 randomly generated. The column LCs shows the number of logic cells utilized for FSM implementation plus the number of shareable expanders multiplied by 0.001. The column T gives the information on the minimum clock period for a given FSM implementation.

Table 2. Tested benchmark FSMs characteristics, state assignment done by MAX+PLUSII and best of 30000 random state encodings.

FSM	I	O	T	S	MAX+PLUSII		random (30K)	
					LCs	T[ns]	LCs	T[ns]
Ex1	9	19	138	20	46.024	21.9	45.026	21.5
keyb	7	2	170	19	34.016	21.6	20.016	20.2
planet	7	19	115	48	84.044	21.7	82.044	21.8
s1	8	6	107	20	47.030	21.3	48.028	21.1
s510	19	7	77	47	34.017	20.8	39.020	22.0
s832	18	19	245	25	52.025	21.7	43.022	22.1

The experimental results are shown in Table 3.

Table 3. The quality of the SAP solutions found by GA with tested crossovers (*M*, *O*, *P*).

FSM	Cross.:	M		O		P	
	Fit :	LCs	T [ns]	LCs	T [ns]	LCs	T [ns]
Ex1	No. 1:	39.023	17.2	42.025	20.8	46.024	21.3
Ex1	No. 2:	39.023	17.2	40.028	17.5	44.030	21.9
Ex1	No. 3:	40.022	17.3	39.023	21.0	45.031	21.9
Ex1	SUM:	**118**	51.7	**121**	59.3	**135**	65.1
Ex1	MIN:	**39.023**	17.2	**39.023**	17.5	**44.03**	21.3
keyb	No. 1:	15.016	20.2	16.016	20.2	19.019	20.2
keyb	No. 2:	15.015	17.1	16.016	20.2	18.021	20.2
keyb	No. 3:	15.016	20.2	15.016	20.2	18.023	17.1
keyb	SUM:	**45**	57.5	**47**	60.6	**55**	57.5
keyb	MIN:	**15.015**	17.1	**15.016**	20.2	**18.021**	17.1
planet	No. 1:	67.038	21.8	71.040	21.8	81.046	21.8
planet	No. 2:	69.037	21.8	74.040	21.7	81.044	21.4
planet	No. 3:	70.042	22.4	75.041	22.3	81.046	21.8
planet	SUM:	**206**	66.0	**220**	65.8	**243**	65.0
planet	MIN:	**67.038**	21.8	**71.040**	21.7	**81.044**	21.4
s1	No. 1:	36.022	17.4	40.019	22.0	45.024	22.1
s1	No. 2:	39.024	20.8	41.028	21.5	48.023	21.3
s1	No. 3:	35.018	20.7	37.021	21.1	42.025	21.5
s1	SUM:	**110**	58.9	**118**	64.6	**135**	64.9
s1	MIN:	**35.018**	17.4	**37.021**	21.1	**42.025**	21.3
s510	No. 1:	34.019	20.3	38.021	20.3	40.022	21.6
s510	No. 2:	34.017	20.3	38.021	20.3	40.020	21.3
s510	No. 3:	36.017	21.9	40.021	21.6	40.021	22.1
s510	SUM:	**104**	62.5	**116**	62.2	**120**	65.0
s510	MIN:	**34.017**	20.3	**38.021**	20.3	**40.02**	21.3
s832	No. 1:	33.014	21.1	37.019	20.3	41.021	17.5
s832	No. 2:	34.016	20.7	35.017	20.3	41.021	20.4
s832	No. 3:	34.015	20.7	36.020	17.2	40.020	21.3
s832	SUM:	**101**	62.5	**108**	57.8	**122**	59.2
s832	MIN:	**33.014**	20.7	**35.017**	17.2	**40.02**	17.5

Discussion and conclusions

Based on Table 3 we can observe a clear relationship between summed (in rows with 'SUM' label) results of GA runs with three different, tested crossover operators. It can be seen that GA with *M*1 operator has outperformed other crossovers *for each* tested benchmark FSM.

None of experiments with the use of *O* or *P* crossover gave a better result than those generated by GA with *M*1 operator. Only in three cases of 54 experiments, results generated by GA with *O* operator were equal to those obtained with *M*1 crossover (rows No. 2, 3 for *ex*1 FSM and row No. 3 for *keyb* FSM).

The *O* crossover was worse than *M*1 but it worked far better than operator *P*. The *P* crossover was definitely the worst one in each experiment. Generally its results were comparable with the best ones from among 30 000 randomly generated state assignments (Table 2).

Such a quality relationship between these crossovers applied to SAP does not seem to be surprising. The *P* crossover was dedicated to the schedule optimisation [Sys91](i.e. it was to process totally different schemata than in SAP). The *O* operator, on the other hand, was devised to TSP but applied to this problem yielded weak experimental results [Gre85]. It seems that *O* crossover applied to the SAP gave worse results than the *M*1 one because the *O* operator was not dedicated to SAP unlike the *M*1 one. However, the *O* crossover gave better results than the *P* one because the *O* operator processed the TSP schemata more weakly than the *P* one processed the schemata of the schedule optimisation.

Based on Table 2 we can see how heavily heuristics' effectiveness depends on FSM's specificity. In four of six cases the best state assignment chosen from among 30 000 random encodings was better than proposed by MPII (*ex*1 - random 2% better than MPII, *keyb* - 41%, *planet* - 2%, *s*832 - 17%). For *s*1 FSM, random and MPII solutions were comparable. The MPII heuristics worked definitely the best for *s*510 FSM (the result was 12,8% better than the random one).

On the other hand the experimental results confirm the high stability of GAs. Firstly, in all cases except *s*510 FSM, all GA results (with any of tested crossovers) were not worse than generated by MPII (actually they were significantly better, only once - Table 3, No. 1 for *ex*1 - the GA with the weakest crossover gave result equal to the MPII's one). Secondly, it can be seen that MPII heuristics were well suited for *s*510 FSM (results of the random search and of the GA with *O* and *P* crossovers were worse). But it should be also noticed that GA with *M*1 operator, during three experiments for *s*510 FSM, has generated two solutions equal to the MPII's one, and the third result was comparable (slightly worse than MPII's and better than others such as GA with *O* and *P* crossovers, and random).

Moreover, comparing GA results against the random ones we can see the GA solutions are good as the consequence of the *evolution process* but not just because a few dozen of thousand points of the search space were evaluated (although this is only a scrap of the huge search space [Vil98]). It should be noted that GA parameters were chosen arbitrary. Moreover, the *M*1 operator can be fine-tuned.

We believe the better results can be obtained after GA and its operators' parameters are adjusted.

References

[Alt01] Altera Digital Library 2001, Ver. 2.

[Ama95] Amaral J.N. et al., Designing Genetic Algorithms for the State Assignment Problem, IEEE Trans. on Sys., Man and Cybernetics, 1995, 25, (4), pp. 687-694.

[Alm95] Almaini A. E. A. et al. State assignment of finite state machines using a genetic algorithm, IEE Proc.-Comput. Digit. Tech., 1995, 142, (4), pp. 279-286.

[Chat98] Chattopadhyay S., Chaudhuri P. Pal, Genetic Algorithm Based Approach for Integrated State Assignment and Flipflop Selection in Finite State Machine Synthesis, *Proceedings of the IEEE International Conference on VLSI Design 1998*, IEEE Comp Society, Los Alamitos, CA, USA, pp. 522-527.

[Chy01] Chyży M., Kosiński W., Genetic Algorithm for the State Assignment Problem, Communications of the 10th International Symposium Intelligent Information Systems X, Zakopane, Poland, 17-21 June 2001, pp. 7-11.

[Dav91] Davis L., Handbook *of Genetic Algorithms*, Van Nostrand Reinhold, N.Y. 1991.

[Gre85] Grefenstette J.J., *Gopal* R., Rosmaita B., Van Gucht D., Genetic Algorithm for the TSP, *Proceedings of the First International Conference on Genetic Algorithms*, Lawrence Erlbaum Associates, Hillsdale, NJ, 1985, pp. 160-168.

[Mich96] Michalewicz Z., Genetic *Algorithms + Data Structures = Evolution Programs*, Springer-Verlag, Berlin Heidelberg 1996, 3rd edition.

[Per97] Perkowski M., *Digital Design Automation: Finite State Machine Design,* http://www.ee.pdx.edu/~mperkows/=FSM/finite-sm/finite-sm.html

[Sys91] Syswerda G., Schedule Optimization Using Genetic Algorithms, in [Dav91], pp. 332-349.

[Vil98] Villa T., Kam T., Brayton R., Sangiovanni-Vincentelli A., Synthesis of Finite State Machines: Logic Optimization, Kluwer Academic Publishers, Boston/London/Dordrecht 1998.

[Whi89] Whitley D., The GENITOR Algorithm and Selective Pressure: Why Rank-Based Allocation of reproductive Trials is Best, *Proceedings of the 3rd International Conference on Genetic Algorithms*, D. Schaffer, ed., pp. 116-121, Morgan Kaufmann, 1989.

[Yan91] Yang S., Logic Synthesis and Optimization Benchmarks User Guide, Microelectronics Center of North Carolina, Research Triangle Park, North Carolina 1991.

QSPR Analysis of Boiling Point of Chemical Compounds

Barbara Dębska

Department of Computer Chemistry, Rzeszów University of Technology, 6 Powstańców Warszawy Av., 35-041 Rzeszów
e-mail: bjdebska@prz.rzeszow.pl

Abstract: A selected data mining methods have been developed to model the relationships between the structure of organic compounds and their properties. Molecular graph descriptors represent valuable structural descriptors that can be used with success in developing QSPR model. In this study we have used: four valance molecular connectivity indices (${}^1\chi^v$, ${}^2\chi^v$, ${}^3\chi^v$, ${}^4\chi^v$), a second-order Kappa shape index (${}^2\kappa$), molecular weight and dipole moment. The database included seven structural descriptors and experimental value - boiling point for each compound. The paper presents the proposed cluster analysis and neural network methods used to estimate the boiling points of chemical compounds. Back-propagation 7-4-1 neural network architecture predicted boiling points of aliphatic hydrocarbons with average absolute errors of 1,55 [K] – 4,85 [K], respectively.

Keywords: QSPR, neural network, application of system science in chemistry

Introduction

Nowadays, the quantitative property structure relations (QSPRs) approach receives enormously wide applications. It is often used routinely for predicting numerous physicochemical properties, biological activity of organic compounds and for the computer-assisted design of novel structures with given properties. The physicochemical properties of chemical compounds depend strongly on their molecular structures. Examples of the some of the more commonly reported topological indices, proposed for QSPRs, include: Randic branching indices [1], valance molecular connectivity indices [2], Wiener path number [3], Kappa shape indices [3], quantum chemical parameters (heat of formation or dipole moment) and informational indices [5]. This method have been traditionally developed by selecting, a priori, an analytical model (typically linear, polynomial or log-linear) to quantify the correlation between selected structural indices and desired physico-chemical properties, followed by regression analysis to determine model parameters (i.e. toxicity of chemicals [6]). If the model is non-linear (non-linear relationships exist between model input and output parameters) the data mining methods (i.e. cluster analysis, pattern recognition methods, neural network, rough set algorithm) are used to determine existing relationships. In recent years, a number of investigators [7] have published the results of QSPR/neural networks for predicting boiling point of chemical compounds and in our work we used the neural network as an effective tool. The success of neural networks/QSPR models will depend on the ease by which the molecular descriptors can be determined by chemist.

Data bases and molecular descriptors

Chemist tended to quantify molecular structures of compound on the basic of graph theory and relate it to their properties. In the present paper, we performed QSPR study of the analytical database using molecular descriptors include four valance molecular connectivity indices [2], a second kappa shape index [4], molecular weight and dipole moment. These seven structural descriptors are input parameters and a boiling point is a single output parameter. Raw database was obtained 284 aliphatic hydrocarbons. The set of the compounds may be grouped into two categories: *alkanes* (class no 1, containing 140 compounds) and alkenes (class no 2, containing 144 objects) by VVT system [8]. This result of cluster analysis can be perceived looking at Fig 1; two classes are well separated each other, but the class 2 (alkenes) had a highest density internal structure of this set.

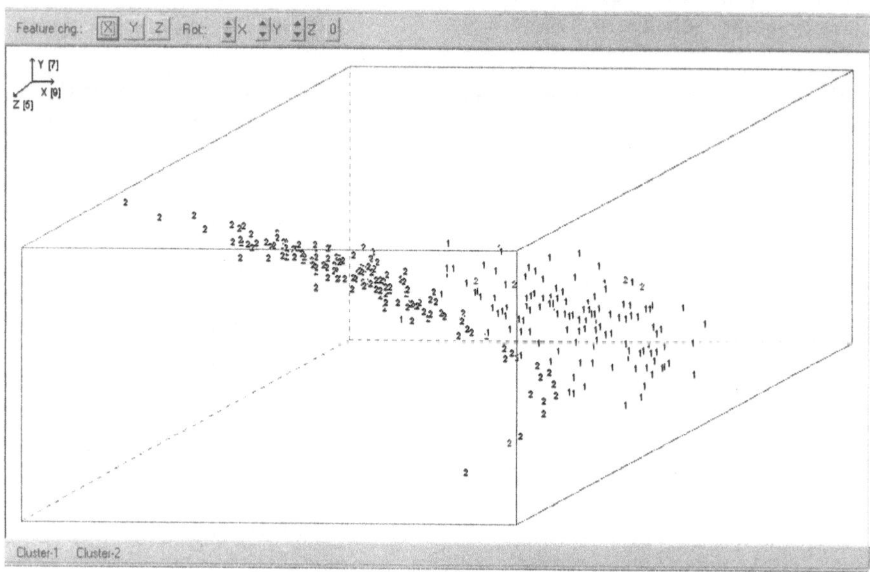

Fig. 1. Result of cluster analysis of a set of aliphatic hydrocarbons.

Neural network system

These two databases (alkane and alkene) were used separately in pre-processing process based on neural network algorythm. In our researches, the neural network/QSAR study includes the following principal steps (Fig. 2):

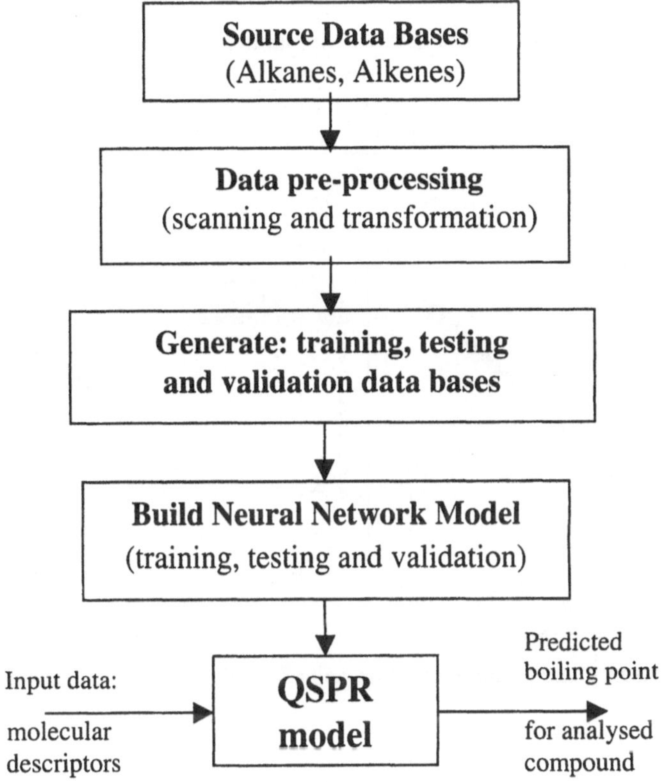

Fig. 2. The flow diagram for neural network/QSPR algorithm.

Boiling points and molecular descriptors were divided into three data sets: training, testing and validation for use with the back-propagation network models. For the alkane subset, the training, testing and validation data sets numbered 100, 20 and 20 compounds. For the alkene group the training set contain 100 compound with 24 and 20 compound for testing and validation, respectively. These sets were selected randomly using STATISTICA neural network software. The learning method used throughout was standard error back-propagation using a mean-squares-error function. A three-layer fully connected neural network with four hidden units was used as a basic model for all of the results that follow. The size of the hidden layer was computed by using the number of training examples.

Results and discussion

The optimal back-propagation 7-4-1 neural network model predicted boiling point for a set of selected analysed compounds. The computed values were compared to the experimental boiling point temperatures. The results are shown in table 1 and in figures 3.

Table 1. The errors of 7-4-1 neural network model.

	Alkanes	Alkenes
Average absolute error	1,46 [K] (0,37%)	4,53 [K] (1,27%)
Standard deviation	1,52 [K] (0,36%)	3,76 [K] (1.16%)

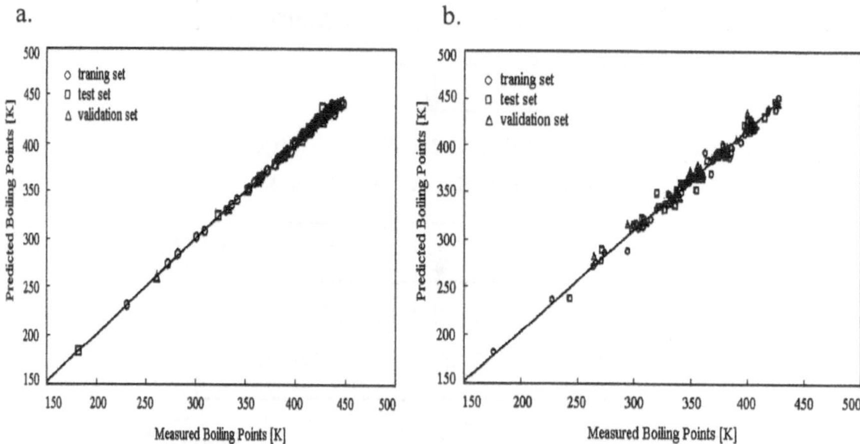

Fig. 3. Measured and predicted boiling point for: alkanes (a) and alkenes (b)

References

[1] Randic M., On characterization of molecular branching, J. Am. Chem. Soc., 97, pages 6609-6615, 1975

[2] Kier L. B., Hall L. H., Molecular Connectivity in Structure-Activity Analysis, John Wiley & Sons Inc., New York, 1985

[3] Wiener H., Prediction of isomeric difference in parafin properties, J. Am. Chem. Soc., 69, pages 17-20, 1947

[4] Kier L. B., A shape index from molecular graphs, Quant. Struct-Act. Relat. 4, pages 109-116, 1985

[5] Pyka A., Application of topological indices for chemical and chromatographical investigations, Wiadomosci Chemiczne, 51, pages 83-802, 1997

[6] Basak S. C., Grunwald G. D., Gute B. D., Balasubramanian K., Optiz D., Use of statistical and neural net approaches in predicting Toxicity of Chemicals, J. Chem. Inf. Comput. Sci., 2000, 40, 885-890

[7] Ivanciuc O., Artificial Neural Network Applications. Rev. Roum. Chim., 1998,43,885

[8] D•bska B., Defining the structure of an analytical data set using cluster analysis methods, Proc. of The Workshop VII IIS, Ustro•, 14-18 June, 1999

Clustering Methods

The Application of AI Techniques for Automatic Generation of Crowd Scenes

Peter Forte[1], Adam Szarowicz[2]

[1]School of Computing and Information Systems, Kingston University, Penrhyn Road, Kingston-upon-Thames, KT1 2EE, UK
pforte@kingston.ac.uk
[2]WhiteSpace Studio, Kingston University, Penrhyn Road, Kingston-upon-Thames, KT1 2EE, UK, tel. +44 (0) 20 8547 7984
a.szarowicz@kingston.ac.uk
www.kingston.ac.uk/whitespace/research/freewill/

Abstract. Generation of animated human figures especially in crowd scenes has many applications in such domains as the special effects industry, computer games or for the simulation of the evacuation from crowded areas. Currently such scenes have to be created by human animators using dedicated software packages. This is both expensive and time-consuming. Our "FreeWill" prototype proposes and implements a cognitive architecture designed for easy creation of animated scenes with many autonomous agents interacting in various ways. Agents maintain an internal model of the world and fulfil their goals. The design allows for easy co-operation of different software packages (geometry engine, AI engine, sensing/actuating modules, simulation managing unit and a visualisation environment). The implementation language is Java and the graphics package is 3D Studio Max. The requirements capture process and design is being conducted and documented in the Unified Modelling Language (UML).

Keywords: multi-agent systems, cognitive modelling, lifelike characters

Introduction

Animation, especially when involving human figures is a very labour-intensive task. Currently animators, using dedicated software can decrease both factors by applying a keyframing approach (the user specifies key frames and the software interpolates between them) but the process is still tedious and expensive. Those problems become especially apparent in the special effects industry, where it is necessary to generate scenes involving many interacting human figures. Most of the work in such scenes must be done manually by skilled professionals because characters still lack autonomy and self-awareness. Similar problems arise in such domains as computer games and simulations of safe evacuation of crowded areas, for example tube stations, skyscrapers, in the event of fire or other disasters.

In this paper we would like to present our FreeWill prototype which addresses these limitations by proposing and implementing an extendable cognitive architecture designed to accommodate goals, actions and knowledge, thus endowing animated characters with some degree of autonomous intelligent behaviour.

Existing architectures

The history of AI is also a history of different architectures, which were proposed to explain the working of human brain or allow for creation of sophisticated AI-based systems. One of the early examples was SOAR (Newell, 1990) - a rule-based system built to foster research into a unified theory for modelling human cognition. Together with the appearance of multi-agent systems into the main stream of the AI research many of the new proposed frameworks were based on the notion of an intelligent agent. A good example is BDI – Belief Desire Intention architecture proposed by Rao and Georgeff in 1991 (Rao and Georgeff, 1991, 1993). This architecture has its foundations in philosophy but referenced to computer-based systems tries to propose a unified framework for the development of agents in situated planning systems. Rao and Georgeff proposed also a theoretical formalism to support their findings.

Other recent proposals include C4 (Isla *et al*, 2001), SAC (Winikoff, 2001, Harland, 2001), and the cognitive architecture proposed by John Funge (Funge, 1998, Funge *et al* 1999).

C4 was developed at MIT and is based on a layered architecture consisting of distinct specialised subsystems. It allows for planning and reactive behaviour as well as learning new actions. Some of the subsystems communicate through an internal blackboard.

SAC proposed by Winikoff is an extension of the standard BDI approach. Winikoff's objective is to propose "a simplified model which retains the power (and efficiency) of the BDI model but allows more people to develop intelligent agent systems" (Winikoff, 2001) – hence the name SAC (Simplified Agent Concepts). Winikoff's concepts are much more 'implementable' than the original BDI architecture and he puts more emphasis on goals, events and construction of plans.

Another interesting recent architecture is Funge's cognitive architecture, where agents maintain knowledge about world dynamics (domain knowledge) and some representation of the internal model of the world. Funge bases his approach on situation calculus and the idea of fluents.

This project tries to synthesise the last two architectures (Funge's cognitive architecture and Winikoff's extension of the BDI concept) and consolidate ideas from both approaches while at the same time extending them. FreeWill's characters maintain internal world models, create plans, support reactive behaviour, and their internal algorithms include the sense-loop-act (Rao and Georgeff, 1991, Winikoff, 2001). FreeWill tries to merge these useful concepts with a good OO engineering. While learning and emotions are not present yet, ultimately the model will accommodate them as well.

Existing techniques

Software animation packages such as 3D Studio Max or Maya, widely used by production studios, provide limited ability to create crowd scenes using the particle systems approach or through dedicated plug-ins - e.g. Character Studio for 3DS Max. Although many film special effects were created using those techniques (example can be last year's movie "Mummy Returns") the possibilities of controlling the scene are very limited. Particle systems cannot create realistic looking human crowd and are mostly applied to modelling small animals and the abilities of the character plug-ins concentrate mainly on generation of realistically moving human figures (using inverse and forward kinematics) rather than on giving the characters some autonomy. Therefore any enhancements to the avatar behaviour repertoire are usually very specific with limited scope for extendibility or generalisation. Most of the work is still done by the animators and a limited autonomous behaviour must be hard-wired into the animation sequence. The characters do not have any self-awareness and the scene recognition (identifying objects, avoiding collisions) and decision-making processes are done by the animator.

Another but similar approach to the creation of crowd scenes leads through use of the motion capture which is a format recognised by the whole animation industry. Instead of animating each joint of the virtual figure, human motion is captured and applied to the scene. However the issues of autonomy and self-awareness still remain – applying the motion to characters and making the behaviour look natural must be done by a professional. Fig. 1 depicts capturing human motion and an example crowd scene generated using this technique ("Gladiator" – the Colosseum scene, images from Vicon, 2001).

Fig. 1. Capturing human motion (left), crowd scene (right)

The combination of AI and animation – FreeWill

FreeWill (Amiguet-Vercher *et al*, 2001, Szarowicz *et al*, 2001) addresses the shortcomings of present systems by proposing and implementing an extendable cognitive architecture designed to accommodate goals, actions and knowledge and supported by a well engineered design. The design allows for easy co-operation of different software packages – namely a geometry engine, AI engine, sensing/actuating models, simulation managing unit and a visualisation environment. Therefore FreeWill utilises the well developed features of animation packages (inverse kinematics, object modelling, virtual worlds industrial standards) and on top of these builds an extensible behavioural engine which allows for autonomous behaviour of the avatars and easy control of the parameters of the animated sequences. Each such a sequence consists of characters (avatars) interacting within a graphically defined setting.

The implementation language being used to create FreeWill is Java and the graphics package is 3D Studio Max. The requirements capture process and design is being conducted and documented in Unified Modeling Language (UML – OMG, 1999).

Each avatar comprises two main components – its body and an AI engine (so called mind). The body is the 3D representation of the avatar (with all its properties and position), whereas the "mind" supplies all functionality necessary for world representation, goal planning, sensing and acting, and emotions.

The project is divided into 5 principal subsystems:

Geometry engine – utilises the idea of bounding boxes for easy detection of collisions and also for object hiding. Further extensions of this package may include incorporation of a physics engine.

AI engine – responsible for managing the processes of space sensing and perceiving (interpretation of information), goal planning, collision avoidance, taking appropriate actions and other cognitive tasks. For example this allows an avatar to recognise "friends", initiate actions such as handshakes and update plans to achieve desired goals. Ultimately it is proposed that the AI engine should also model emotions.

Sensing/actuating modules – these components are responsible for gathering information from the environment (sensors) and physical interaction with the environment (actuators). They are not involved in any high-level information processing (perception) which is entirely performed by the AI package.

World objects – this component models all physical entities within the virtual world.

Visualisation engine – this part of the system is responsible for displaying the world model and the interacting avatars. At the moment this is performed by the package 3D Studio Max (with which the system interacts through Max Script or step files, a sample of which is depicted in Fig. 2). Currently the developers are trying to migrate into a more flexible and portable motion capture format. The visualisation engine also allows for rendering the scenes and for saving the final animation.

Finally there is a *management module* based on discrete event simulation and a queue handler enabling the autonomous behaviour to unfold within the virtual world.

```
biped.AddNewKey LarmCont3 0
biped.AddNewKey RarmCont3 0
      sliderTime = 10
rotate RForearm3 30 [-1,0,0]
biped.AddNewKey LarmCont3 10
biped.AddNewKey RarmCont3 10
      sliderTime = 20
rotate RForearm3 80 [0,0,-1]
biped.AddNewKey LarmCont3 20
biped.AddNewKey RarmCont3 20
```

Fig. 2. Sample script for generating avatar behaviour

Logic Controlling an Avatar's Behaviour

One of the key elements of the avatar's knowledge base is the internal world model. Every time an avatar performs an action, the process is initiated by first updating the avatar's world model. The avatar senses the world via a vision cone, through which it gains awareness of immediate objects in its path. The information obtained from the vision cone is then used to modify the avatar's plan and perform the next action.

An avatar's behaviour is goal directed. The primary goal is provided by the user and represents the aim of the simulation for that avatar. In the example illustrated in Fig. 4b and 5, the primary goal is to 'get to the end of the sidewalk'. However the fulfilment of this goal may be enacted with accomplishment of secondary goals which are set and assessed by the avatar. Examples are 'avoid collisions' and 'shake hands with friends'. Such goals are a part of the avatar's knowledge. The knowledge base also provides logical information about static world objects and other avatars (e.g. a list of friends).

The design of the first three subsystems is being carried out in UML (simplified class model is depicted in Fig. 3). Fig. 4 and 5 show details from the animation. A scene of walking and interacting characters with limited autonomy will be demonstrated at the Symposium. The further work will concentrate on the design of the AI engine to provide more flexible behaviour including the construction and modification of goals and plans and the reasoning process will be formalised according to the situation calculus.

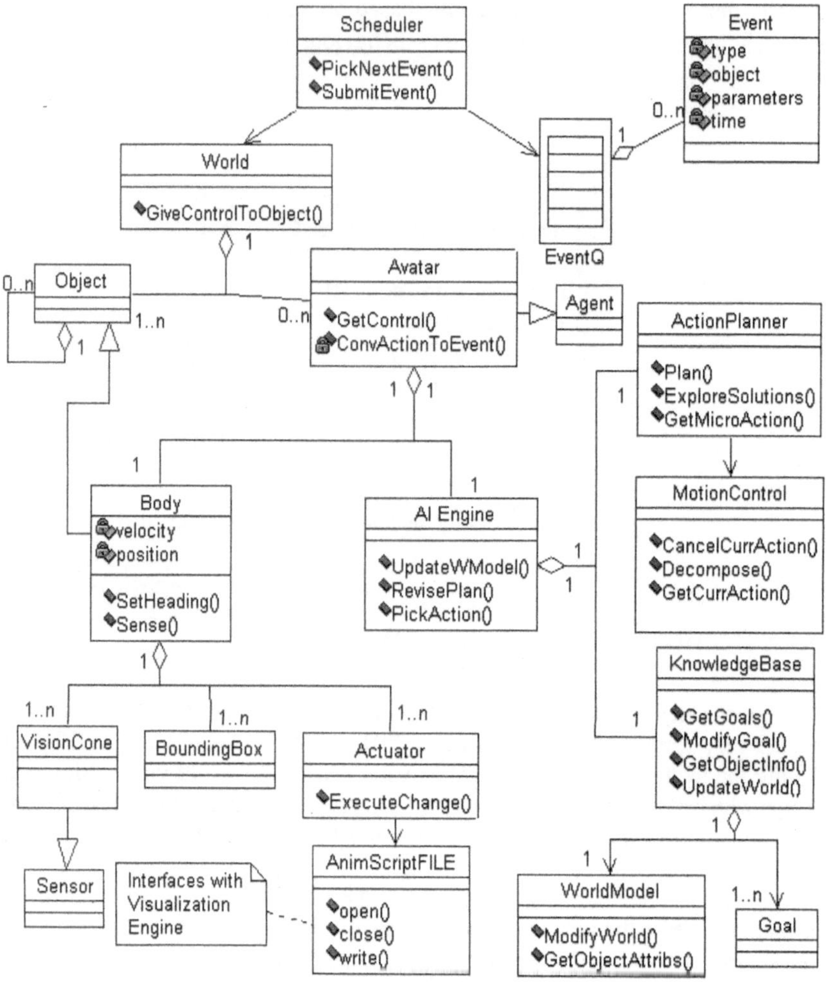

Scheduler
PickNextEvent()
SubmitEvent()

Event
type
object
parameters
time

0..n
1

World
GiveControlToObject()

EventQ

1

Object
0..n
1..n
1

Avatar
GetControl()
ConvActionToEvent()

0..n

Agent

ActionPlanner
Plan()
ExploreSolutions()
GetMicroAction()

1 1

1

1

1

Body
velocity
position
SetHeading()
Sense()

AI Engine
UpdateWModel()
RevisePlan()
PickAction()

1
1

MotionControl
CancelCurrAction()
Decompose()
GetCurrAction()

KnowledgeBase
GetGoals()
ModifyGoal()
GetObjectInfo()
UpdateWorld()

1

1

1..n
1..n
1..n

VisionCone

BoundingBox

Actuator
ExecuteChange()

Sensor

Interfaces with Visualization Engine

AnimScriptFILE
open()
close()
write()

1
1

WorldModel
ModifyWorld()
GetObjectAttribs()

1..n

Goal

Fig. 3. UML model of the system

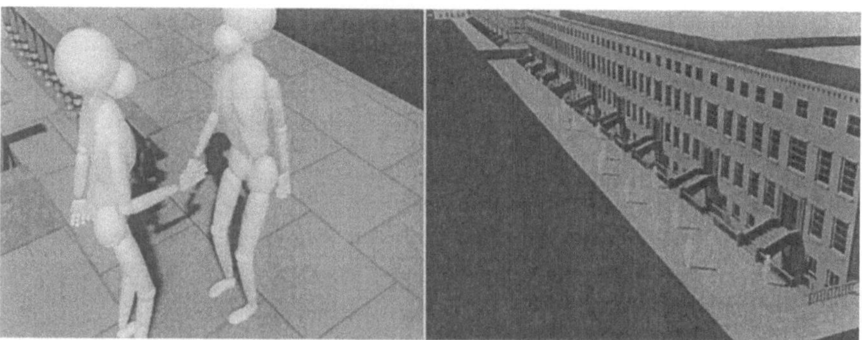

Fig. 4. Agent interaction: a) shaking hands, b) crowd scene

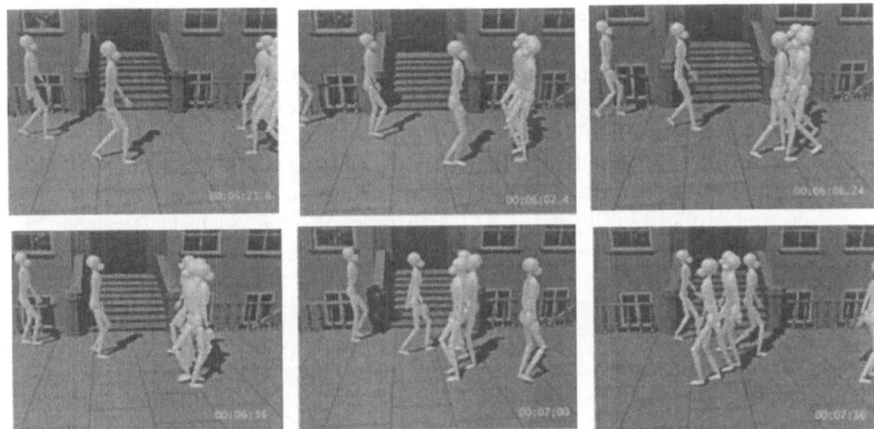

Fig. 5. Agent interaction: crowd scene

References

1. Amiguet-Vercher J., Szarowicz A., Forte P., Synchronized Multi-agent Simulations for Automated Crowd Scene Simulation, AGENT-1 Workshop Proceedings, IJCAI 2001, Aug 2001.
2. Funge J., Making Them Behave: Cognitive Models for Computer Animation, PhD thesis, Department of Computer Science, University of Toronto, 1998.
3. Funge J., Tu X., Terzopoulos D., Cognitive Modeling Knowledge, reasoning and planning for intelligent characters, Computer Graphics Proceedings: SIGGRAPH 99, Aug 1999.
4. Harland J. and Winikoff M., Agents via Mixed-mode Computation in Linear Logic: A Proposal, Proceedings of the ICLP'01 Workshop on Computational Logic in Multi-Agent Systems (CLIMA-01), Paphos, December, 2001
5. Isla D., Burke R., Downie M., Blumberg B., A Layered Brain Architecture for Synthetic Creatures, pp. 1051-1058, in Proceedings of Seventeenth Joint Conference on Artificial Conference IJCAI-01, 4-10 August, Seattle, USA, 2001.
6. Long D., The AIPS-98 Planning Competition, AI magazine, Vol. 21, No. 2, pp 13-33, 2000.
7. Object Management Group, OMG Unified Modeling Language Specification, June 1999. Version 1.3. See also http://www.omg.org
8. Newell, A. 1990, Unified Theories of Cognition, Harvard Press.
9. Rao A., Georgeff M., Modeling Rational Agents within a BDI-Architecture (1991), Proceedings of the 2nd International Conference on Principles of Knowledge Representation and Reasoning pp 473-484, Cambridge, MA, USA, April 1991. Morgan Kaufmann Publishers, 1991.
10. Rao A., Georgeff M., Intentions and Rational Commitment (1993), revised, from: http://citeseer.nj.nec.com/rao93intentions.html, accessed on 11/02/2002

11. Vicon8 Motion Capture System – Demonstration CD, presented at 3December Exhibition, London, 2001.
12. Szarowicz A., Amiguet-Vercher J., Forte P., Briggs J., Gelepithis P., Remagnino P., The Application of AI to Automatically Generated Animation, 14th Australian Joint Conference on Artificial Intelligence, AI'01, Adelaide, Dec 10-14, 2001
13. Winikoff M., Padgham L., and Harland J., Simplifying the Development of Intelligent Agents. In AI2001: Advances in Artificial Intelligence. 14th Australian Joint Conference on Artificial Intelligence. LNAI 2256, pages 557-568, Adelaide, December 2001

Unsupervised Learning Motion Models Using Dynamic Time Warping

Marek Kulbacki[1], Artur Bak[2]

[1] Systems Research Institute, Polish Academy of Sciences, PL 01-447 Warsaw, 6 Newelska St., e-mail: kulbacki@ibspan.waw.pl
[2] e-mail: abak@traf.ict.pwr.wroc.pl

Abstract. This paper concerns essential, practical problem in automatic animation human-like figures with the support of informatics technologies connected with motion capture domain. The main problem we want to solve is partition set of primitive motions into appropriate groups according to similarity between motions. Up to now, experiments in systems of this kind, appeared be not too adequate to needs. In this situation, we had been faced with the necessity of creating new methods for supporting process of managing motion data. We construct motion models to easier extract features of given motions. Using these models we propose measure of discrepancy between motions. It shows how two motions are similar to each other, normalizes length of motions and decreases high dimension of considered motion data, so clustering may take place in dimensionally reduced space.

Keywords: dynamic time warping, motion capture, computer animation, motion grouping, classification, probabilistic motion models.

1 Introduction

Currently a motion capture technique [7] is very willingly used for creation of realistic human-like figures animations. There are two most often used types of this technique. In the first case reflective markers are fixed on joints of alive actor and the motion of markers is tracked. In the latter case magnetic sensors are fixed on actor joints. These sensors are tracking disturbances of magnetic field during motion. In order to achieve realistic animation there is recorded motion of each human joint. This causes that it is necessary to describe motion with a large set of data. Such data are hard to process in some fields of applications. This problem is especially visible in use of multimedia databases. Managing the tremendous amounts of data is often supported by clustering and classification methods. It is not easy to find such methods for motion sequences.

In our approach we try to solve this problem. In consecutive sections we describe problems and propose solutions that make up the method of motions clustering and classification. At the beginning of article, we describe motion representation that is most appropriate to methods used by us. Next we show the method of motions standardization and definition of distance measure.

We base on Dynamic Time Warping method [1] modified by us. Using our distance measure and motion standardization, we describe clustering based on classical Agglomerative Clustering algorithm [4,6,5]. We also describe motion classification relying on probabilistic generic motion models defined by us. At the end we indicate proposed application of our solutions.

2 Motion Representations

We utilize several motion representations, for different levels of abstraction. A motion is a time-varying function which provides the configuration of an articulated figure at a time. Input representation is an original motion capture sequence; it is represented as Raw Data Model (RDM). We denote a RDM by $m(t) = (p_0(t), q_0(t), q_1(t), \ldots, q_L(t))^T$, where $p(t) \in \mathbb{R}^3$ and $q_1(t) \in \mathbb{R}^3$ describe the translational and rotational motion of the root segment[1], and $q_i(t) \in \mathbb{R}^3$ gives the rotational motion of the ith joint for $1 \leq i \leq L$. From RDM we extract shorter Primitive Motions (PM). Their main feature is that they are uniform. For each Primitive Motion, we generate Specific Model (SM) as a Timmer splines parameters calculated according to RDM data. We denote SM as $s(m) = (s_1(m), s_2(m), \ldots, s_M(m))^T$, where M is a number of SM parameters, and $s_i \in \mathbb{R}^3$. Specific Model is used by clustering algorithm. For every motion group a probabilistic Generic Model (GM) is evaluated. GM is a set of parameters described by Gaussian distributions over parameters of Specific Models of particular group. From these distributions new PM's can be generated (which haven't been provided as motion capture files). Fig. 1 shows the process of determining various motion representations. More detailed description of each model is described in [13].

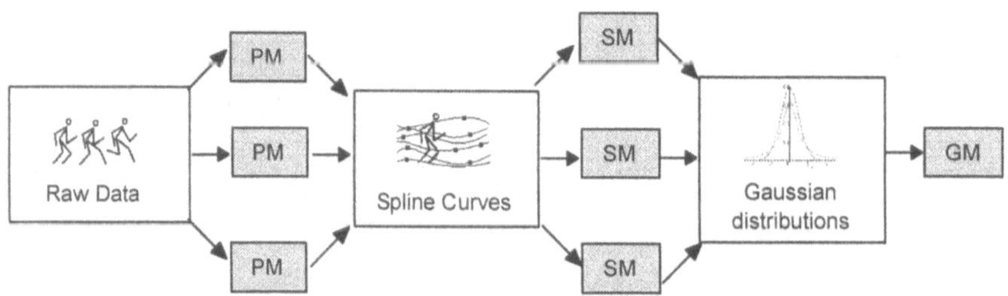

Fig. 1. Motion representations transformation process

[1] root segment - the most important joint in the human skeleton (base joint)

3 Motion Comparison and Standardization

Our motion sequences are represented as sets of time series. Several pattern matching techniques, able to deal with time sequential data, have been applied to match movement patterns: Dynamic Time Warping [1,3,8], Hidden Markov Models [9,12], Artificial Neural Networks [10].

We have chosen DTW as a tool to match motion sequences; it is conceptually simple and effective, allowing sufficient flexibility in time-alignment between test and reference motion sequence. Articulated objects such as human figures are usually represented as rotation hierarchies parameterized by a whole-body translation, a whole-body rotation, and a set of joint angles. Here motion is described by a set of motion curves, each giving the values of one of the model parameters as function of time. Using DTW we are able to solve two problems:

- find measure of discrepancy between two motion sequences,
- normalize motion sequences in the number of frames regarded.

In our case, time warping is applied in the discrete time domain to register the corresponding motion parameter signals such as joint angles. We warp each motion curve independently, so we can consider just a single curve $Q_{l,d}(t)$.[2] It represents movement of one joint for specified degree of freedom. Hereafter we call it *time series.* This definition goes for our motion sequences, because each of them is a set of motion curves at the specified period of time. As in conventional keyframing, the number of frames constraints include a set of $(Q_{l,d}[i], t[i])$ pairs each giving the value that $Q_{l,d}$ must assume at the specified time i. Thanks to it each motion curve may be represented as an *identical length* time series. For two motion sequences comparison we must warp independently each corresponding time series. Suppose we have two time series $Q_{1,x}$ and $C_{1,x}$, of length n and m respectively. To match two motion sequences using DTW we construct an n-by-m matrix where the element (i, j) of the matrix contains the distance $d(q_{l,d}[i], c_{l,d}[j])$ between two points $q_{l,d}[i]$ and $c_{l,d}[j]$ (typically the Euclidean distance is used [1]). A warping path W is a set of matrix elements that defines a mapping between $Q_{l,d}$ and $C_{l,d}$:

$$W = w_1, w_2, \ldots, w_K \qquad max(m,n) \leq K < m + n - 1 \tag{1}$$

The warping path is typically subject to several constraints: endpoint, continuity and monotonicity conditions [2]. There are exponentially many warping paths, however we are interested only in the path which minimizes the warping cost:

$$DTW(Q_{l,d}, C_{l,d}) = min\left\{ \sum_{m=0}^{K} d\big(q_{l,d}[i_m], c_{l,d}[j_m]\big) \right\} = min\left\{ \sum_{k=1}^{K} w_k \right\}. \tag{2}$$

[2] where: $l \in \{1 \ldots L\}$, L - number of joints, $d \in \{x, y, z\}$ - degree of freedom

3.1 Improved Distance Measurement

Each joint in motion sequence is defined as a set of time functions for specified degrees of freedom. To determine number of elements of all functions to be equal, we carry out normalization to the number of considered motion frames. Discrete value sequences obtained in that way, are useful as elements to compare motion sequences together. Moreover there are computed derivatives for each frame.

From previous sections we know that motion recognition is based upon the comparison of corresponding joints in two motion sequences. To do it well we have to find specified distance measure, making use of this in motion sequences comparison process. We use $d(q_{l,d}[i], c_{l,d}[j])$ to denote the distance between i^{th} and j^{th} frame of two corresponding joints to be compared. Any function that meets the above properties is a legitimate metric on the elements space. Therefore, there are many metrics, each having its own advantages and disadvantages. Standard DTW method uses Euclidean metric. This type of distance is good to compare single points but not appropriate here, where time series are compared. To find more intelligent measure, that gives consideration to adjacent values of time series, and is sensitive on the local changes among time series elements, we have invented another measure. It is composed of two components:

1. Euclidean distance between two points $q_{l,d}[i]$ and $c_{l,d}[j]$,
2. square of the difference of the estimated derivatives of $q_{l,d}[i]$ and $c_{l,d}[j]$.

The first part gives information about offset between points to be compared. The second part adds the "intelligence" to the entire measure. Thanks to this we are able to deal with situations where examinated sequences are not different enough. We use the following method for estimating derivative from joint data:

$$D_x\left[q_{l,d}[i]\right] = \left.\frac{q_{l,d}[i] - q_{l,d}[i-1]}{t[i] - t[i-1]}\right|_{t[i]-t[i-1]-1} = q_{l,d}[i] - q_{l,d}[i-1], \quad 1 < i \le n \tag{3}$$

This estimate is the slope of the line through the point $q_{l,d}[i]$ and its left neighbor. Note the estimate is not defined for the first element of the sequence. Instead we use the estimate of the second element.

On the basis of above equations we have created new measure. The full definition of this measure is

$$d(q_{l,d}[i], c_{l,d}[j]) = \sqrt{|c_{l,d}[j] - q_{l,d}[i]|^2} \cdot \left(D_x\left[c_{l,d}[j]\right] - D_x\left[q_{l,d}[i]\right]\right)^2 \tag{4}$$

As we can see this equation doesn't meet all conditions concerning distance measure, so we can't call it distance. An appropriate measure name is *measure of discrepancy* between elements $q_{l,d}[i]$ and $c_{l,d}[j]$. Standard DTW algirithm can produce pathological results. The crucial observation is that the algorithm may try to explain variability in the Y-axis by warping the X-axis. This can lead to unintuitive alignments where a single point on one time series maps onto a large subsection of another time series. An additional problem with DTW is that the algorithm may fail to find obvious, natural alignments in two sequences simply because a feature (i.e peak, valley, plateau etc.) in one sequence is slightly higher or lower than its corresponding feature in the other sequence. The weakness of DTW is in the features it considers. It only considers a datapoints Y-axis value. To prevent this problem we propose a modification of DTW that does not only consider the Y-values of the datapoints, but also considers the higher level feature of "shape". We obtain information about shape by considering the first derivative of the sequences, and thus call our algorithm Value-Derivative Dynamic Time Warping (VDTW). VDDTW's time complexity is $O(mn)$, which is the same as standard DTW. There are some added constant factors as derivative factor in distance measure. Empirically the two algorithms take approximately the same time.

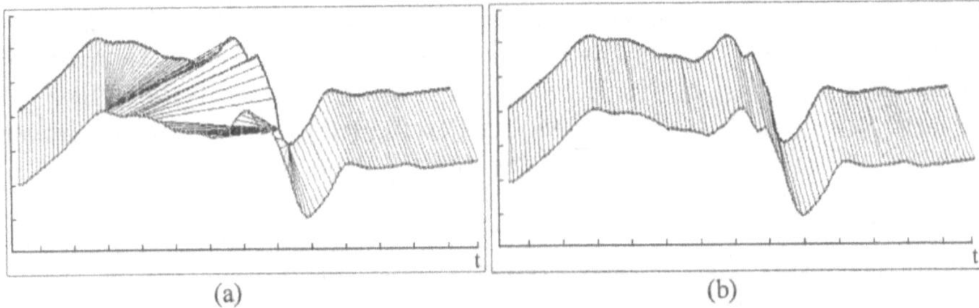

Fig. 2. Examples of some experimental datasets: **a)** the alignment produced by classic DTW **b)** the alignment produced by VDDTW

3.2 Extention VDDTW to Entire Motion Sequence

As we know the previous discussion referred to the single joint comparison for specified degree of freedom. This is only a small element of the whole motion sequence. Our skeleton is made up of eighteen joints, so this comparison operation must be applied to each joint separately, taking into consideration existing degrees of freedom. The full motion warping algorithm is shown below:

REQUIRE motion sequence A, motion sequence B
ENSURE All warping cost, Warped Sequence
for each existing joint
  for each existing degree of freedom
    TmpCost $\Leftarrow$ Least Warping Cost; TmpMotion $\Leftarrow$ Reverse Warped Path
  end for
  AllCost $\Leftarrow$ AllCost+TmpCost; update NewMotion using TmpMotion
end for

As an output we get whole cost used to warp motion sequence B into motion sequence A. Additionally this algorithm produces Warped Sequence of motion B (B_W) which have a length of motion A. This case requires explanation. The question is, how to get Warped Sequence of motion B? During the warping motion B into motion A three cases are distinguished:

1. substitution - 1:1 correspondence of successive samples;
2. deletion - multiple samples of B map to a sample of A;
3. insertion - a sample of B maps to multiple samples of A.

Of course cases discussed above concern process of single joint warping in the range of the whole motion sequences. For the following explanations, we assume that signal Q represents joint from motion B and signal C represents joint from motion A. We can say that signal Q is warped into C, and the warped signal is denoted by Q_W. Then if $q_{l,d}[i]$ and $c_{l,d}[j]$ are related by substitution it follows that $q_{l,dW}[j] = q_{l,d}[i]$. In case of a deletion, where multiple samples of $Q, (q_{l,d}[i], q_{l,d}[i+1], \ldots, q_{l,d}[i+k])$, correspond to one $c_{l,d}[j]$, $q_{l,dW}[j] = mean(q_{l,d}[i], q_{l,d}[i+1], \ldots, q_{l,d}[i+k])$. Finally, an insertion implies that one sample of $Q, q_{l,d}[i]$, maps to multiple samples of $C, (c_{l,d}[j], c_{l,d}[j+1], \ldots, c_{l,d}[j+k])$. In this case, the values for $q_{l,dW}[j], q_{l,dW}[j+1], \ldots, q_{l,dW}[j+k]$ are determined by calculating a Timmer cubic B-spline distribution around the original value $q_{l,d}[i]$.

Presented algorithm is applied in this work to normalize length of motions (Warped motion) and as a measure of discrepancy (All warping cost) used for motion clustering. Measure of discrepancy between motion m_1 and m_2 (using specific models of these motions) we denote as $\delta(s(m1), s(m2))$. Total time complexity is strictly dependent on joint number (L) and length of motion sequences A and B(respectively m and n). It is about $O(|L| \cdot |m| \cdot |n|)$ or after reduction of the searching space $O(|L| \cdot |n| \cdot |K|)$, where delimiter $K \leq \frac{m}{2}$.

4 Clustering and Classification

Clustering of motions capture sequences is not simple unless the distance measures and standardization of motions are well defined. Since when we have these mechanisms based on VDDTW the clustering algorithm itself is similar to other domains clustering methods. However we define a few specific elements that are necessary for the next classification and future use of clustered motions set. It concerns especially the clustering representation relied on probabilistic generic models.

The main goal of clustering is partition of primitive motions into appropriate clusters. It should be done according to similarity between motions. This similarity is identified with distance between motions[3] defined in previous section. The less distance between two motions the more similar these

[3] in a sense of measure of discrepancy

motions are. We have to require clustering process to divide motions set in proper way. Motions of one cluster should be similar and motions of different clusters should be dissimilar to each other. Beside the motions partition, we also need certain description of each cluster. The set of all clusters descriptions is called clustering representation. Division of motions set into clusters and clustering representation we treat as main tasks of clustering process.

4.1 Cluster Finding

The method we use to partition set of motions is classical Agglomerative Clustering algorithm. Disadvantage of this method is high time complexity. It has an impact on the fact that in every step we have to check all possible partition spaces. Solution like this is not always acceptable, especially in real time animation domain. The advantage is certainty that we find global optimal solution in respect of criterion of acceptance. Suppose we have motions set - R, that contains N primitive motions $(m_1, \ldots, m_N)$. Actual set of groups from R set we denote as X. The number of motions in any group G_i is denoted as N_i. In the first step we set number of groups equal to number of motions. Initially every motion m_n from set R belongs to separate group G_i in set X, where $n, i \in [1..N], N_i = 1$. In the consecutive steps of clustering algorithm, adjacent groups are merged into new larger group. We break algorithm when *stop condition* is satisfied. In a single step two most adjacent groups are merged so we have to define distance between these groups. It is based on internal average discrepancy between primitive motions in the group. This is not pure distance measure but hereafter we call it distance for clarity. Average internal discrepancy in a group G_i is equal to average from all possible discrepancies δ as we can compute between all primitive motions in this group:

$$\overline{\delta}_i = \text{average}\big(\{\delta(s(m_a), s(m_b)) \;\big|\; m_a, m_b \in G_i,\ a \neq b\}\big) \tag{5}$$

Distance D_{12} between two groups G_1 and G_2 is defined as discrepancy $\overline{\delta}_{12}$ between all primitive motions in new merged group $G_1 \cup G_2$. We compute distance matrix M that contains distances between all currently existing groups. Matrix M is symmetrical $(D_{12} = D_{21})$, so we have to calculate distance only $\frac{K^2-K}{2}$ times[4]. On the base of matrix M we can choose two most adjacent groups for merge. These are groups G_i and G_j for which the distance D_{ij} is the least. We break algorithm when in the given step distance D_{ij} is greater than maximal acceptable distance of merge D_{max}:

$$D_{ij} > D_{max} \quad \forall i, j \in (1, \ldots, K) \tag{6}$$

[4] K - actual number of groups in the set X

4.2 Generic Model for Group of Primitive Motions

Clustering algorithm gives partitioning, of motion set R into groups. To effective utilize the partition it is important to define appropriate clustering representation. These are appropriate descriptions of groups. In this case for every group G_i from set X we calculate exactly one probabilistic description. It is formulated as a set of gaussian distributions. These distributions are calculated over each parameter of specific model among all primitive motions in given group. All probabilistic distributions for given group are encapsulated in parametric model of this group named *generic model.* In the Fig. 3 we can see dependencies between specific motions models in the given group and generic model for this group. Parameters s_l, are description for consecutive frames, where $l \in (1, \dots, M)$ and M is the number of parameters of specific models s_m. For each of parameter s_l we evaluate Gaussian distribution over values of these parameters for all primitive motions in the given group. This distribution is denoted in generic model as two parameters: average av_l and variance v_l:

$$av_l = \frac{1}{N_i} \sum_{m_n \in G_i} s_l(m_n), \qquad v_l = \frac{1}{N_i - 1} \sum_{m_n \in G_i} [s_l(m_n) - av_l] \tag{7}$$

For given specific motion model s can be evaluated function of probability

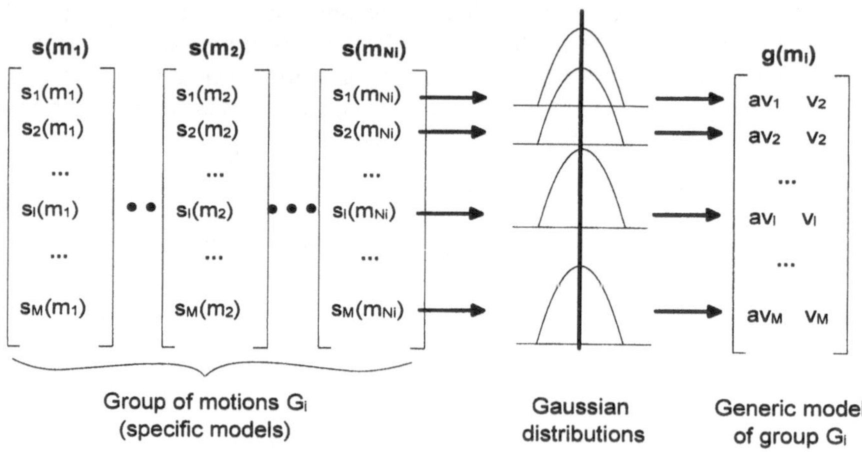

Fig. 3. Evaluation of probabilistic generic models

density for known parameter s_l according to distribution of generic model GM_i:

$$g_{i,l}(s_l(m)) = \frac{1}{\sqrt{v_l 2\pi}} \exp\Big\{ -\frac{[s_l(m) - av_l]^2}{2v_l} \Big\}. \tag{8}$$

So far we did not say about problem of different primitive motions length. In effect number of parameters M in specific models may differ between particular motions. In that case, it is difficult to compute the number of generic model parameters. We need the method of normalization all specific motions in a given group into the same number of parameters. We are finding prototypes for every group. It is similar to Oates method [6]. Prototype T_i is the most typical motion in the given group. This motion minimizes average of discrepancy with all the rest members of group G_i. In consecutive step, we normalize all specific motions from the group using VDDTW algorithm. Specific model of typical motion in the group is used as template signal in VDDTW algorithm. As a result of this operation, we get a set of specific motions in the same number of parameters. Thanks to this, it is possible to compute Gaussian distributions over values of primitive motions parameters. Generic model for the group is evaluated on the base of set of normalized specific motions. Specific models of the rest motions in the group are normalized into the lengths of specific model of typical motion.

4.3 Motion Classification

We can treat the generic model as the probabilistic generator of specific models (specific models of primitive motions that haven't been delivered in input motions set). We assume that all primitive motions that belong to one group are generated by the same generic model. We can also assume that every motion in primitive motions domain is generated by exactly one generic model. The main application of generic model is classification of motions that are outside the input motions set, into appropriate groups. To perform classification we have to choose GM that probably generates considered motion. Likelihood that given generic model GM_i generates motion m may be treated like similarity of motion m to the group connected with GM_i:

$$\theta_i\big(s(m)\big) = P(G_i)\prod_{l=1}^{M} w_l g_{i,l}\big(s_l(m)\big) \tag{9}$$

The argument of above similarity function is specific model of motion m. Weight w_l is related with the joint that is described by parameter s_l of specific model for motion m. Component $g_{i,j}$ is probability density for parameter s_l in the group G_i. Component $P(G_i)$ describes likelihood of situation that any primitive motion belongs to the group G_i (it has been generated by GM_i). This likelihood can be given *apriori* or can take into consideration relative probability of this group in motions set. Because of limited set R in regards to all primitive motions space, in this classification algorithm each group has the same likelihood $P(G_i) = \frac{1}{K}$. Before we compute measure θ we must normalize given primitive motion m according to the specific motion of typical motion T_i. To do it we utilize VDDTW algorithm. Finally primitive motion is classified into the group G_i for which similarity measure $\theta_i(s(m))$ reaches maximal value. Classification equation is given as follows:

$$h(s(m)) = \operatorname*{argmax}_{i \in \{1,2,\ldots,K\}} [\theta_i(s(m))] \tag{10}$$

4.4 Conclusions

This paper presented preliminary results of an experimental study of algorithm for human motions organization. In particular our method comprise full motion models definitions [13], algorithms of comparison and clustering of primitive motions. We did not say about problem of motions segmentation (extraction uniform motions in any motions sequences). This is very important, because it has an influence of the accuracy of our clustering algorithm. Our main goal is to expand this ideas onto automatic animation domain. The main application of presented methods is automatic motion synthesis in tools for creation realistic animations of human like figures. We were testing these algorithms on a small training set of motions. It is hard to prove efficiency of this method because it is still developed.

References

1. E.J.Keogh, M.J.Pazzani: Scaling up Dynamic Time Warping to Massive Dataset, Principles of Data Mining and Knowledge Discovery, pp. 1-11, 1999
2. E.J.Keogh, M.J.Pazzani: Derivative Dynamic Time Warping, Dep. of Information and Computer Science, University of California, Irvine, California, 1999
3. D.J.Berndt, J.Clifford: Using Dynamic Time Warping to Find Patterns in Time Series, *KDD* Workshop, pp. 359-370, 1994
4. A.K.Jain, R.C.Dubes: Algorithms for Clustering Data, Prentice Hall, Englewood Cliffs, N.J., 1988
5. T.Oates, L.Firoiu, P.R.Cohen: Clustering Time Series with Hidden Markov Models and Dynamic Time Warping, Proc. IJCAI-99, pp. 17-21
6. T.Oates: Identifying Distinctive Subsequences in Multivariate Time Series by Clustering, Proc. 5-th International Conference on Knowledge Discovery and Data Mining, pp. 322-326, 1999
7. S.Dyer, J.Martin, J.Zulauf: Motion Capture White Paper, December 1995
8. A.Witkin, Motion Warping, Computer Graphics, Vol. 29, pp. 105-108, 1995
9. M.Brand, HertzmannA.: Style machines, In The Proc. of ACM SIGGRAPH 2000, pp. 183-192, 2000
10. Y.Guo, G.Xu, S.Tsuji: Understanding Human Motion Patterns, ICPR94, pp.325-329, 1994
11. T.Darrell, A.Pentland: Space - Time Gestures, CVPR/NYC, June 15-17, 1993
12. J.Yamato, J.Ohya, K.Ishii: Recognizing Human Action in Time-Sequential Images using Hidden Markov Model, IEEE CVPR, pp. 379-385, 1992
13. M.Kulbacki: Principal methods for motion synthesis of human-like figures, MA Thesis, Wroclaw University of Technology, 2001

On Regularity of Multivariate Datasets

Wiesław Szczesny [1), 2)] and Teresa Kowalczyk [1)]

[1)] Institute of Computer Science, Polish Academy of Science, Ordona 21, 01-237 Warsaw, Poland

[2)] Department of Econometry and Computer Science, Warsaw Agricultural University, Nowoursynowska 166, 02-787 Warsaw, Poland

Abstract: *The authors propose grade irregularity measures (function-valued and numerical) for bivariate probability tables and apply them to evaluate irregularity of non-negative multivariate datasets. The results of a simulation study performed on multinormal and multiexponential data are presented and displayed graphically. This study serves not only to illustrate behavior of the irregularity measures but also to observe that in sufficiently regular datasets linear multivariate prediction is close to optimal.*

Key words: *concentration curve, concentration surface, copula, linear regression, multiexponential data, multinormal data, over-representation.*

1. Introduction

Only finite datasets T_{mxk} will be considered where m is the number of investigated objects (rows), and k is the number of variables (columns). In case of non-negative variables all cells are non-negative so that T_{mxk} can be transformed into a two-way probability table. A measurement theoretical basis of such transformation will be not discussed in this paper (the reader will find some explanations in [8] and Ch. 8 in [5]). When variables are ordinal and passage from a dataset to a probability table is not allowed or seems improper, it is still possible to transform each variable by its cumulative distribution function (cdf) and then build the probability table corresponding to the dataset T^*_{mxk}, in which values of variables are replaced by *grades* (i.e. values of the respective cdf).

Given a probability table T_{mxk} we usually try to make it *more regularly positive dependent* by a suitable permutation of its rows and columns. The Grade Correspondence Analysis (GCA – see [1] and [8]) provides such permutations which lead to tables with maximal value of one of two very popular grade

2 Model of the occurrence of an arrhythmia episode

There are two major reasons that may provoke the actual occurrence of an episode of arrhythmia. First of them is connected with negative emotional condition of patient and/or existence of recent life events that provoke his stress. We did not collect the patients' data of that kind, however.

It can be considered as a future medical research postulate: to program a collection (of data) of the pertinent variables that are connected with such a psycho-social status of patients. In our present analysis the emotional factors actually do disturb of an establishment of the main relationships. Therefore the atmospheric influence patterns (which we look for) are obscured. Nevertheless we will argue that the proposed two-stage methodology is oriented for minimization of these disturbing effects.

From the data-mining point of view we will look, besides more specific types of episodes (i.e. clusters), for so called categories of episodes. Category i.e. cluster of clusters is a basic notion while discovering a causality patterns. From other point of view category as a cluster of averages minimizes an adverse influence of disturbing psycho-social factors.

Rare configurations (very small clusters) will be rejected as outliers.

3 Variables

For any clustering procedure the definition of cases and choice of their aspects (i.e. variables) is the first and a very limiting choice. There exist analyst's decisions, however, that are comparable (in its consequences) with the first and basic decision determined by the mere availability of the actual data! In other words there are many basic alternatives that appear while looking for causality patterns. We will develop a possible basic alternative solution within the arrhythmia database.

Cases (records) correspond to episodes of arrhythmia. Data about the patient involved and the meteorological conditions of day of episode were collected. In the inference developed here we will actually obtain patterns that are connected with the meteorological conditions of surroundings of Warsaw.

We will show now variables and their transformations. It seems that the type of data we are concerned, is quite typical for any data mining process that looks for "causal-type" patterns or is a sort of unsupervised (or partially supervised) learning.

Table 1 shows in the first place the meaning of division between descriptive and explanatory variables. The latter variables measure the intensity of (a possible) influence of the causal factors. In our example these are the selected meteorological factors.

The last column of the table is connected with the following common fact that appears within the typical data mining procedures. Many variables provide the relevant information if they take the "large" values only. We mean such variables that e.g. register the existence (or no) of an influential phenomenon. Being, at the beginning, of the 0-1 type, at later stages of our procedure these variables give the values of percentage of the phenomenon.

We consider also another-type meteorological variables that are "characteristic" only partially. Absolute measure of: change or amplitude can cause cardiac episode only while taking the large value.

The information: "Characteristic values" is more important for the explanatory variables since it will be taken into account at more stages of inference. "Only +" as characteristic values (of variable) means that only large positive values can be taken into account as interesting or "characteristic" i.e. influential. It will be seen within a further development that small values of that variable play more limited role.

Table 1 Variables considered in the analysis

Variable type	Original variable	Variable name	Type of scaling	Characteristic values
Descriptive	Patient's age	Agest	Standardization	+ & -
Descriptive	Patient's sex	Sex	1-man 2-woman	+ & -
Descriptive	Ischaemic heart disease as concomitant	IHD	1-yes 0-no	Only +
Descriptive	Blood hypertension as concomitant	hiperten	1-yes 0-no	Only +
Descriptive	Complexity of the treatment procedure	thercom	1 (very easy) through 4 (very complex)	Only +
Explanatory	Atmospheric pressure of thc day of episode	p0st	Standardization	+ & -
Explanatory	Absolute change in atmospheric pressure	deltapst	Standardization	Only +
Explanatory	Is there a high air temperature?	hitemp	1-yes 0-no	Only +
Explanatory	Is there a low air temperature?	lowtemp	1-yes 0-no	Only +
Explanatory	Amplitude of daily temperature	deldiv 3	Actual difference in centigrades divided in 3	Only +
Explanatory	Is atmospheric humidity above the limit?	humlim	1-yes 0-no	Only +

Actually one can adjust Type of scaling and "Characteristic values" to the given type of dataset at hand. If analyst considers e.g. medium values as interesting it can be respected within the proposed methodology.

4 Further general remarks on the proposed clustering

We will cluster the cases and then reject some obtained groups from the main reasoning. Those of clusters, which "pass the exam" and rest in the main analysis, will enter as cases to the second clustering. The "examination" procedure will be based on explanatory variables only.

As a result of the second clustering we will obtain therefore a two-stage hierarchy. Clusters of the second clustering will be called categories.

Both hierarchical and non-hierarchical clustering methods can be applied for the first clustering. The advantage of the former method is the preparation of a structure that will be easier manageable within the second stage of our procedure. This follows from the fact that we actually impose a certain hierarchy at second stage.

Non-hierarchical method used in the first stage has another advantage. Clusters obtained through the "minimum within clusters variability vs. maximum among clusters variability" principle, are more "compact" than those obtained through the hierarchical clustering. Their members are more similar to each other and therefore further operations on more compact clusters have deeper motivation. As we will see the primary clusters will be treated as mere simple points in the scatterplots. The geometrical reasoning will be more adequate if points are modeling the "compact" sets.

In the analysis presented here we apply the second approach. We use the K-means algorithm for the first clustering. The hierarchical agglomeration will then be applied to the means of the clusters at the second stage. The between groups linkage with the square Euclidean distance (Tibshirani et al., [4] advocate this distance) will be applied at that stage. The crucial will be the decision on when to stop the agglomeration.

In literature various criterions are proposed for establishing and/or evaluating an optimal number of clusters. References can be found in [2] and [4].

In our context it would be non-practical to formulate a strict criterion while leaving other basic notions at intuitive or heuristic level. We will give indications on how to find a "basic" number of categories i.e. how to extract this number from the geometrical evidence.

5 First clustering and selection through the causality criterion

We must choose the number of primary clusters first. This is one of those very important and arbitrary decisions that have to be taken during the analysis. We give some advises in this respect.

It seems that an average size of cluster within the presented methodology should be higher than 10 and lower than 50. We have to look for "configurations-phenomenons" and these can not be very rare.

There exist methods that can cluster the samples (or sets of records) containing a large number of cases (see e.g.: [1], [5] and [6]). They can be useful but such methods are not necessary for our methodology (similar point is risen in [3]). If the number of cases is very large, the sample can be divided according to (say) 2 discrete variables. Each subsample is defined by a given (fixed) pair of values of these variables. Then the primary cluster analysis can be done for each subsample separately. The only consequence of such procedure is the fact that variables, which served for the sample division, have to play lesser (or none) role in the second stage of analysis. This can be done through the appropriate scaling of those variables.

For the present analysis we chose 40 as an initial number of clusters. This gives the number of 29 as an approximate average cluster size – since the total size of our sample is equal to 1153 (arrhythmia episodes). Clearly it is rather small database. There was no need to divide the set of cases according to some existing or additional variables: therefore all variables presented in Table 1 entered unchanged to the entire analysis.

In Table 2 we present the cluster means of the explanatory variables only. The cluster algorithm has been applied to the whole set of variables, however. We are looking for the final configurations that can be formed by all variables. Actually these primary clusters are highly influenced by the descriptive variables, as well. Nevertheless the subsequent step of reasoning will be based on the explanatory variables only. These variables determine the "borderline" that lies between the "usual" and "unusual" clusters. We will be interested in the latter ones as those that have a causal interpretation.

"Unusuality" means (for our example) that given episodes have occurred during certain, extreme meteorological conditions. Decision: if something is "extreme" or not depends on analyst. We will show through the examples how to define unusual meteorological conditions that occurred before the arrhythmia episode.

Table 2 contains cluster averages that have to be evaluated. The final decision is given in the second column.

The general averages for the cases (episodes) considered in the presented data mining analysis are given as reference values. Parameters of the variables that are standardized are equal 0 (mean) and 1 (standard deviation).

Table 2 Clusters obtained through the K-means clustering in the first step of analysis

No	Re-tained or not	Clus-ter size	p0st	del-tapst	Mean= 0,223 hitemp	Mean= 0,051. lowtemp	Mean=2,8 St.dev=1,4 deldiv3	Mean= 0,138 humlim
1	1	7	0,4637	0,9884	0	0,4286	1,6143	0
2	1	54	-0,2323	-0,3643	0,037	0	2,3241	0,1481
3	1	37	1,6679	0,6322	0	0,1892	2,3892	0
4	1	57	-0,5975	-0,5053	0	0,0526	1,5433	0,0175
5	1	57	-0,2137	-0,6398	0,4035	0	4,5292	0,2281
6	1	19	0,0723	1,0797	0	0	4,0509	0
7	1	31	0,3641	-0,4531	0	0,0968	1,6796	0,1613
8	1	60	0,6815	-0,4268	0	0,1167	1,1567	0,0833
9	1	57	0,0554	0,3354	0,1754	0	3,3906	0,2105
10	1	16	-0,7461	0,6434	0,125	0	3,5896	0,125
11	1	15	-0,9809	-0,4655	0	0,0667	0,8756	0
12	1	28	-1,827	-0,1615	0	0,0357	1,1298	0
13	0	31	0,6876	-0,5124	0	0,0645	0,9892	0,0645
14	1	34	-1,1759	-0,2877	0,2353	0	3,7725	0,2647
15	1	45	0,5015	-0,3642	0,5333	0,0222	4,48	0,3111
16	1	18	0,4575	0,5975	0	0,1111	2,4204	0,0556
17	1	5	-1,151	3,391	0	0,4	1,4	0
18	0	3	-2,2077	1,7898	1	0	6,9333	0
19	1	45	-0,5603	-0,4495	0,2	0	2,9059	0,4444
20	1	32	-1,0992	-0,488	0	0	1,8635	0,0625
21	1	29	0,8279	0,7869	0	0,2069	1,0299	0
22	1	17	-0,9014	2,5734	0	0,1765	2,9529	0,0588
23	1	35	1,3591	-0,5926	0,1429	0,0571	4,3438	0
24	0	1	2,1291	3,5821	0	0	1,4	0
25	1	18	-0,9633	1,2261	0	0	1,7333	0,1667
26	0	22	0,204	-0,7525	0,0455	0,0455	2,7318	0,0909
27	1	17	0,4164	-0,7414	0,6471	0	4,9549	0,1765
28	1	37	-1,1438	1,5966	0	0,1622	1,982	0,0541
29	1	36	-1,4082	-0,4912	0,0278	0	2,6685	0,1111
30	0	1	-2,9715	-0,5535	0	1	2,9	0
31	0	1	-1,0182	-0,4891	0	0	2,3	1
32	1	46	-0,1215	0,8542	0	0	1,85	0,0435
33	1	16	2,067	-0,3659	0	0,1875	2,3667	0
34	0	1	0,2785	-0,8754	1	0	4,8333	1
35	1	91	0,5372	-0,7403	0,1319	0,022	2,8344	0,2967

36	0	2	0,9223	5,412	0	0	1,1667	0
37	1	29	-0,1209	0,979	0,3103	0	5,1207	0,1034
38	1	3	1,8916	2,1404	0	0	2,5333	0
39	1	81	0,226	-0,5342	0,5062	0	4,6852	0,1975
40	1	19	1,1038	2,6548	0	0,1579	1,9368	0

First cluster in the Table 2 is rather small (7 episodes) so we must examine its characteristic quite thoroughly before this cluster will be retained for the subsequent analysis. The means of this cluster (as – clearly - of all others) describe the average atmospheric conditions of the day of the episode. These conditions (for some variables) take into account up to two days that proceed the episode day.

There exists (for the first cluster) a remarkable change in air pressure and very high percentage of the days with low temperature. This latter characteristic is not necessarily negative but in configuration with the first one (change in atmospheric pressure) can form "unusual" conditions that may provoke arrhythmia episode.

Decision on retaining the next 3 clusters is somewhat controversial (may be it is too "liberal"). It is based on a fact that the general mean of atmospheric pressure of an episode's days is remarkably lower than the average pressure in Warsaw. One can (but not has to) subtract actually: 0,5 from all values in p0st column to evaluate them as deviates from the "normal" atmospheric conditions. With that in mind we retained these clusters for the next stage of analysis.

13-th cluster has either average values or small ones for the variables with "Only +" characteristic values. It can not be retained for further analysis therefore.

Similar reasoning is made for the rest of clusters at this stage of analysis.

6 Categories

For the second clustering the average linkage hierarchical method was applied. The Euclidean metric was employed to be in accordance with the forthcoming intensive review of scatterplots. For these same reasons the K-means clustering used in the first stage seems to be appropriate, too.

There is a very important decision to take at this second stage: when to stop the hierarchical agglomeration? Our reasoning that addresses this issue is determined by a certain finding. We present a development connected with this finding. The analysis is typical, however, for all possible considerations that can be done at this stage.

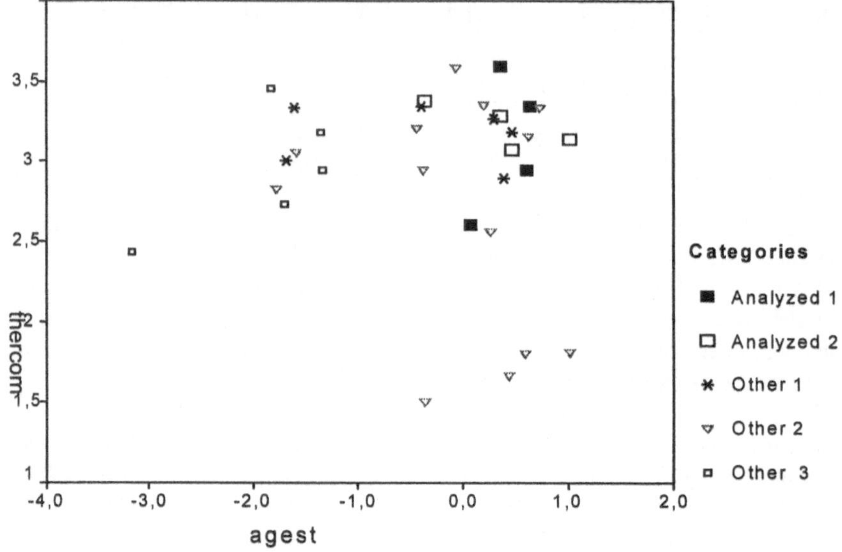

Fig. 1 Scatterplot for patient's age and complexity of his therapy

Our finding appears at the stage of agglomeration when we have 5 second-level clusters and the possibility: if to join two of them or not, is considered. These clusters, which we call categories, are specially marked at diagrams.

First of them: "Analyzed 1" is the group of the following first level clusters i.e. those that were partially been presented in Table 2. Numbers of primary clusters in this group are the following: 17, 22, 28 and 32. A second group ("Analyzed 2" category) is formed by the following clusters: 4, 12, 20 and 29. Fig. 1 displays the configuration for descriptive variables i.e. aspects not presented in Table 2.

Fig. 1 shows nearly a perfect closeness of both analyzed categories within the "characteristic" area of age and therapy complexity (variables).

Fig.2 shows a very important similarity: both categories belong to the set of episodes that occur during a low atmospheric pressure period. In category 1 a 100%-women-formed cluster may be treated as a subcategory.

In the next step of hierarchical agglomeration procedure our two Analyzed categories are going to be joined. This would be an inappropriate step of reasoning, however. These two groups differ extremely in one respect: within the variable deltapst (see Fig. 3). There was no change in atmospheric pressure (during the day, which preceded the arrhythmia episode) in the second Analyzed category. In contrast, episodes of the first Analyzed category took place after a radical change in the atmospheric pressure.

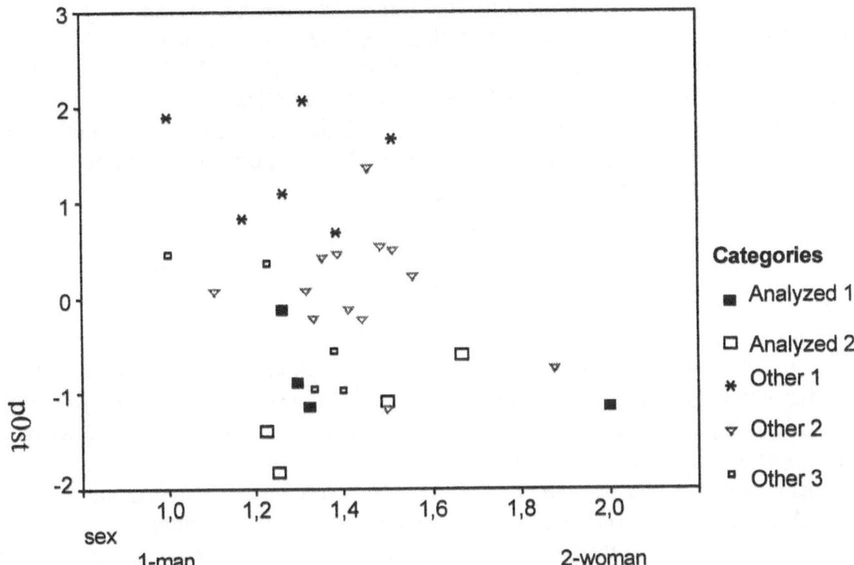

Fig. 2 Scatterplot for patient's sex and episode's atmospheric pressure

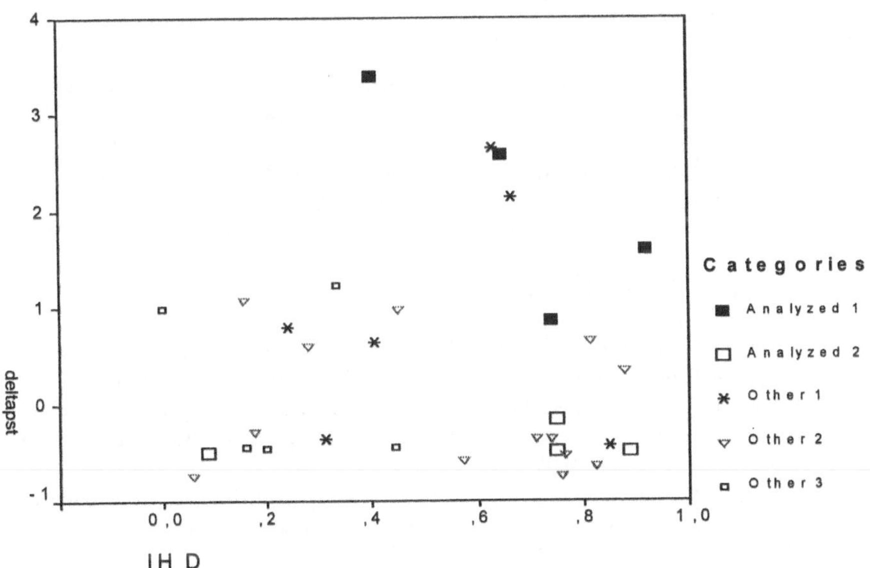

Fig. 3 Scatterplot for ischaemic heart disease and absolute change in atmospheric pressure

One cannot reject the possibility that this radical change was the major reason that provoked the occurrence of arrhythmia episode. We see at Fig.2 that atmospheric pressure does influence patients involved in Analyzed 1. Therefore we must stop the procedure at this step i.e. before the agglomeration.

Other 3 categories need a specific interpretation that is based on analysis of other scatterplots. Nevertheless the solution with 5 categories seems to be the most appropriate initial choice.

7 Further steps of analysis

Once the final configuration of categories is obtained a number of additional analyses and graphical presentations are usually necessary. Categories and their specific clusters (subcategories) can be named, taking into account the extreme means observed within those categories.

Reviews must be done that compare categories within the originally scaled variables (recall: a principal part of the analysis needs rescaling of variables). Clusters rejected after the first stage of analysis (but not outliers!) can serve as reference group for the categories. This reference group is a model of episodes that are not affected by causal factors under consideration.

References

1. Eddy W.F., Mockus A., Oue S., "Approximate single linkage cluster analysis of large data sets in high-dimensional spaces, Comp. Statist. And Data Analysis, 23, Number 1, pp.29-45, 1996.
2. Podani J., "Explanatory variables in classifications and detection of the optimum number of clusters", Data Science, Classification and Related Methods, Proceedings of the 5-th Conference of the International federation of Classification Societies, pp.125-132, 1998.
3. Posse C. "Hierarchical model-based clustering for large datasets", Journal of Computational & Graphical Statistics, 10, Number: 3, pp. 464 – 486, 2001.
4. Tibshirani R., Walther G., Hastle T., Estimating the number of clusters in a data set via the gap statistics", J. Royal, Statist. Soc., B, 63, Part 2, pp. 411-423, 2001.
5. Wishart D., "Efficient hierachical cluster analysis for data mining and knowledge discovery", Computing Science and Statistics, Proceedings of the 30th Symposium on the Interface, pp. 257-263, 1998.
6. Zhou A., Qian W., Qian H., Wen J., Zhou S., Fan Y., "A hybrid approach to clustering in very large databases" in: D.Cheung, G.J. Williams and Q. Li (Eds.), PAKDD 2001, Spriger-Verlag, LNAI 2035, pp. 519-524, 2001.

On Regularity of Multivariate Datasets

Wiesław Szczesny [1), 2)] and Teresa Kowalczyk [1)]

[1)] Institute of Computer Science, Polish Academy of Science, Ordona 21, 01-237 Warsaw, Poland

[2)] Department of Econometry and Computer Science, Warsaw Agricultural University, Nowoursynowska 166, 02-787 Warsaw, Poland

Abstract: *The authors propose grade irregularity measures (function-valued and numerical) for bivariate probability tables and apply them to evaluate irregularity of non-negative multivariate datasets. The results of a simulation study performed on multinormal and multiexponential data are presented and displayed graphically. This study serves not only to illustrate behavior of the irregularity measures but also to observe that in sufficiently regular datasets linear multivariate prediction is close to optimal.*

Key words: *concentration curve, concentration surface, copula, linear regression, multiexponential data, multinormal data, over-representation.*

1. Introduction

Only finite datasets T_{mxk} will be considered where *m* is the number of investigated objects (rows), and *k* is the number of variables (columns). In case of non-negative variables all cells are non-negative so that T_{mxk} can be transformed into a two-way probability table. A measurement theoretical basis of such transformation will be not discussed in this paper (the reader will find some explanations in [8] and Ch. 8 in [5]). When variables are ordinal and passage from a dataset to a probability table is not allowed or seems improper, it is still possible to transform each variable by its cumulative distribution function (cdf) and then build the probability table corresponding to the dataset T^*_{mxk}, in which values of variables are replaced by *grades* (i.e. values of the respective cdf).

Given a probability table T_{mxk} we usually try to make it *more regularly positive dependent* by a suitable permutation of its rows and columns. The Grade Correspondence Analysis (GCA – see [1] and [8]) provides such permutations which lead to tables with maximal value of one of two very popular grade measures of dependence: Spearman's *rho* (ρ^*) or, at choice, Kendall's *tau* (τ). It has been argued in [2] and [7] that after GCA performed according to τ the permuted table is in a sense the most close to one with regular dependence called TP_2 (total positivity of order two). Members of family TP_2 have smooth regular positive dependence, no matter how strong it is ([4]). Kowalczyk in [2] proposed an index $\tau_{abs} \in [\tau_{max}, 1]$ which is equal to τ_{max} (i.e. to the maximal value of τ) if and only if the considered probability table P_{mxk} belongs to family TP_2. Therefore the expression

$$\kappa(P_{m\times k}) = \frac{\tau_{abs}(P_{m\times k}) - \tau_{max}(P_{m\times k})}{\tau_{abs}(P_{m\times k})}$$

evaluates the departure of P_{mxk} from the family TP_2 and measures therefore *irregularity of positive dependence* due to P_{mxk}. Irregularity κ in a TP_2 table is null.

However, a small value of κ (even κ=0) can be obtained for tables with relatively poor regularity. To find a *more sensitive evaluation of irregularity*, we refer to the fact that total positivity can be measured on various levels: there is a sequence of gradually more and more regular families TP_i such that $TP_i \supset TP_j$, i=2,3,..., j=3,4,...i<j;. a continuous bivariate distribution is said to be TP *of infinite order* if for any m and k its discretizations with m rows and k columns are *totally positive of order min(m,k)* (see [6]). That property is possessed by binormal distributions $N_2(\rho)$, and this is why we conctruct a regular analog $N(P_{mxk})$ of P_{mxk}. This analog is a discretized binormal table related to $P^{GCA}_{m\times k}$ so that both marginal distributions and also index ρ^* are in $P^{GCA}_{m\times k}$ and $N(P_{mxk})$ the same. Then we compare $P^{GCA}_{m\times k}$ with $N(P_{mxk})$ as described in the next section.

2. Concentration surface of $P^{GCA}_{m\times k}$ on $N(P_{m\times k})$

The calculations leading to a concentration surface of $P^{GCA}_{m\times k}$ on $N(P_{m\times k})$ will be illustrated step by step for table $P_{3\times 4}$ presented in Table 1. This probability table remains unchanged after GCA, with $\tau(P_{3\times 4})=\tau_{max}(P_{3\times 4})=0.2068$ (and $\rho^*(P_{3\times 4})=\rho^*_{max}(P_{3\times 4})=0.316$). Since κ is close to 0 ($\tau_{abs}(P_{3\times 4})=0.236$, κ=0.1237), table $P_{3\times 4}$ is almost TP_2. However, will be shown that it is not very regular.

Similarity of $P_{3\times 4}$ and its binormal counterpart $N(P_{3\times 4})$ is directly seen from Tables 1 and 2 and also from their graphical displays (called overrepresentation maps), presented in Figs 1 and 2.

Table 1. Probability table $P_{3\times4}$

	1	2	3	4
1	0.16	0.08	0.12	0.04
2	0.07	0.03	0.07	0.08
3	0.02	0.08	0.13	0.12
Total	0.25	0.19	0.32	0.24

Table 2. Probability table $N(P_{3\times4})$

	1	2	3	4
1	0.1549	0.0881	0.1104	0.0466
2	0.0551	0.0505	0.0875	0.0569
3	0.0401	0.0513	0.1221	0.1365
Total	0.25	0.19	0.32	0.24

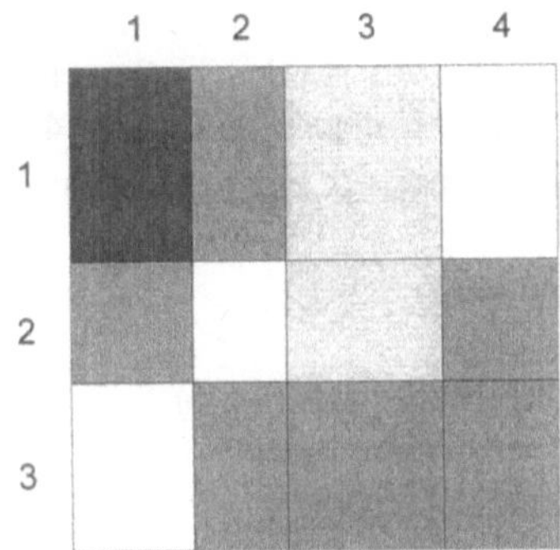

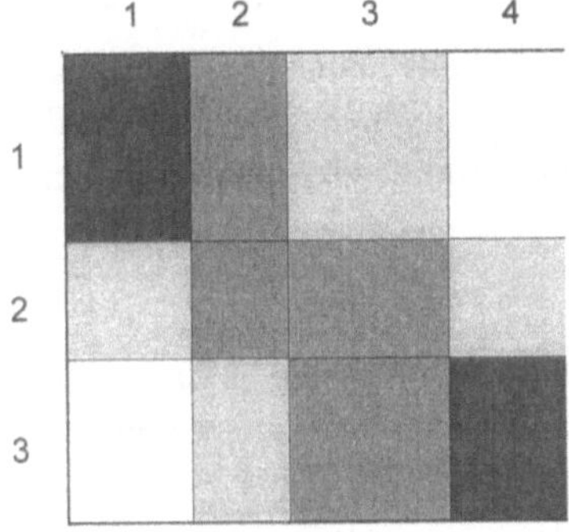

Fig 1. Overrepresentation map of $P_{3\times4}$ Fig 2. Overrepresentation map of $N(P_{3\times4})$

Let us recall shortly what an overrepresentation map is (see e.g. [8]). In grade statistics probability tables $P_{m\times k}$ are often decomposed into a pair of vectors of marginal distributions and a *copula* (denoted $\mathbf{C}(P_{m\times k})$) which is a transformation of $P_{m\times k}$ onto a continuous distribution on the unit square. The unit square consists of $m\times k$ rectangles formed by the horizontal and vertical lines, which divide the sides of the square according to the widths of marginal probabilities of rows (horizontal lines) and columns (vertical lines). The rectangle corresponding to cell (i,j) of $P_{m\times k}$ has constant frequency $f_{ij}=p_{ij}/p_{i+}p_{+j}$, called the *overrepresentation* of p_{ij} over the probability $p_{i+}p_{+j}$, where the latter is due to independence of marginal variables. A copula can be presented as a map with different shades of grey, from white corresponding to $f_{ij}<2/3$, through light grey, grey ($0.98<f_{ij}<1.02$), dark grey, to black ($f_{ij}>2/3$).

The map in Fig 2 is visibly more regular than the map in Fig 1; in particular, white rectangles appear only in two opposite corners of the square and are separated from the dark rectangles by light grey ones.

We shall now find the concentration surface which evaluates differences between $P_{3\times4}$ and $N(P_{3\times4})$. To this aim, we consider four pairs of conditional column distributions in $P_{3\times4}$ and $N(P_{3\times4})$, and calculate the respective concentration curves

C1, C2, C3, C4 presented in Fig. 3. For instance, the concentration curve C1 for the first column in $P_{3\times4}$ with respect to $N(P_{3\times4})$ is the set of linearly interpolated points

$$\{(0,0),(q_{11}/q_{+1},p_{11}/p_{+1}),((q_{11}+q_{21})/q_{+1},(p_{11}+p_{21})/p_{+1}),(1,1)\},$$

where $\{p_{ij}\}$ and $\{q_{ij}\}$ correspond to probability tables $P_{3\times4}$ and $N(P_{3\times4})$, respectively. Curves C1,...,C4 serve as conditional column distributions in a continuous distribution constructed on the unit square, which will be called the *concentration surface* of $P_{3\times4}$ on $N(P_{3\times4})$ and denoted $\mathbf{C}(P_{3\times4}:N(P_{3\times4}))$. The marginal column distribution of the concentration surface **C** is uniform on interval [0,1]; curve C1 corresponds to points in the interval (0,0.25), C2 corresponds to points in (0.25,0.44),...,C4 corresponds to points in (0.76,1).

The probability table of $\mathbf{C}(P_{3\times4}:N(P_{3\times4}))$ is shown in Table 3, the related overrepresentation map is presented in Fig 4. According to Figs 3 and 4, the largest departures of $P_{3\times4}$ from its binormal analog appear for the first and second column.

Table 3. Probability table of the concentration surface $\mathbf{C}(P_{3\times4}:N(P_{3\times4}))$

	1	**2**	**3**	**4**	**Total**
1	0.0502	0.0335	0.0676	0.040	0.1913
2	0.0389	0.026	0.0524	0.0509	0.1682
3	0.0223	0.0149	0.0221	0.0291	0.0884
4	0.0084	0.0056	0.0083	0.0069	0.0292
5	0.0399	0.0174	0.0396	0.0326	0.1295
6	0.0003	0.0001	0.0004	0.0002	0.001
7	0.0350	0.0124	0.0376	0.0233	0.1083
8	0.0350	0.0326	0.0375	0.0232	0.1283
9	0.0200	0.0474	0.0546	0.0338	0.1558
Total	0.25	0.19	0.32	0.24	1.0000

Clearly, the concentration surface $\mathbf{C}(P_{3\times4}:N(P_{3\times4}))$ is a function-valued measure of irregularity of $P_{3\times4}$: the more close it is to a uniform distribution on the unit square, the more regular is $P_{3\times4}$. The corresponding numerical measures of irregularity are $\rho^*(\mathbf{C})=0.0156$ and $\rho^*_{max}(\mathbf{C})=0.1512$.

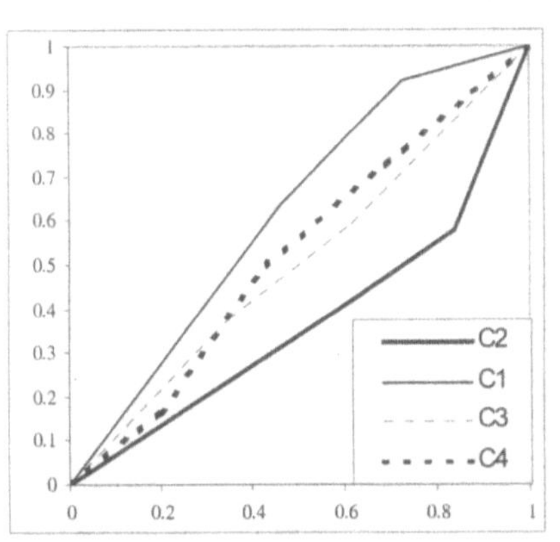

Fig 3. The concentration curves C1,...,C4

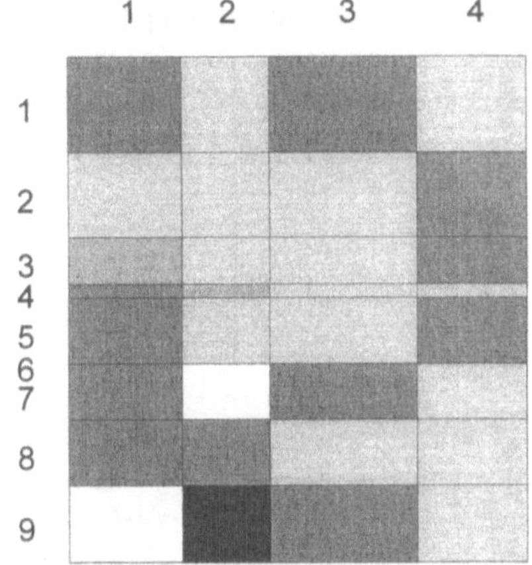

Fig. 4. The overrepresentation map of $\mathbf{C}(P_{3\times4}:N(P_{3\times4}))$

3. Application of $\mathbf{C}(P_{m\times k}:N(P_{m\times k}))$ to multivariate datasets

3.1. Trinormal data

A sample of size 100 was drawn from a vector (Y,X_1,X_2), distributed according to trinormal distribution with means (3,3,3) and unit variances, and with covariances

$$\text{cov}(Y,X_1)=0.85,\ \text{cov}(Y,X_2)=0.72,\ \text{cov}(X_1,X_2)=0.30.$$

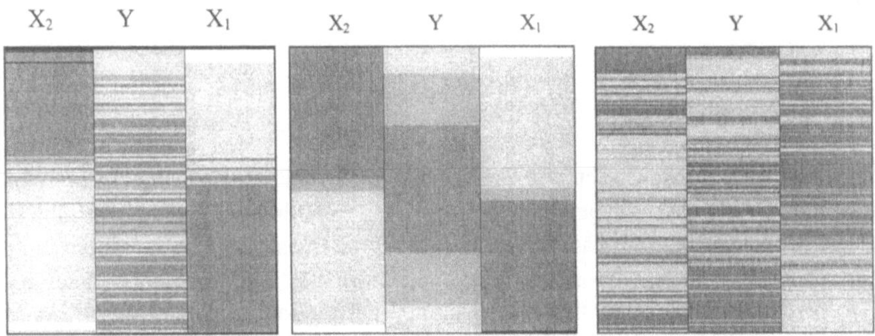

Fig. 5. Overrepresentation maps for $P_{100\times3}$, $N(P_{100\times3})$ and $\mathbf{C}(P_{100\times3}:N(P_{100\times3}))$, where $P_{100\times3}$ denotes the trinormal dataset transformed by GCA.

The overrepresentation maps for the dataset $P_{100\times3}$ (transformed by GCA), for its binormal counterpart and for their concentration surface **C** are presented in Fig 5. We have $\rho^*(\mathbf{C})$=-0.0009, $\rho^*_{max}(\mathbf{C})$=0.032.

3.2. Grade trinormal data

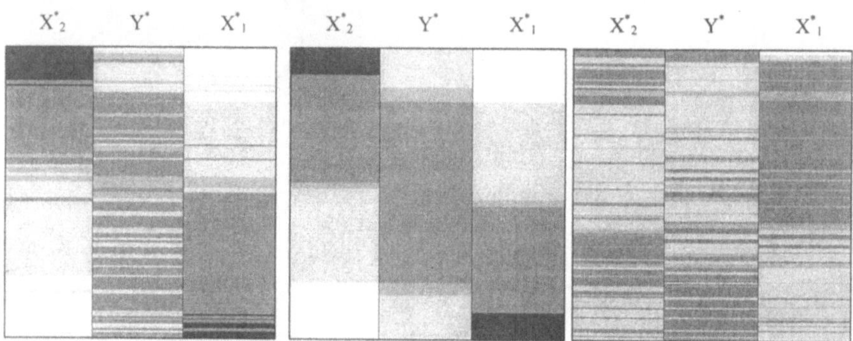

Fig. 6. Overrepresentation maps for $P_{100\times3}$, $N(P_{100\times3})$ and $\mathbf{C}(P_{100\times3}:N(P_{100\times3}))$, where $P_{100\times3}$ denotes the grade trinormal dataset transformed by GCA.

The sample considered in Sec. 3.1 was replaced by a sample of (Y^*,X^*_1,X^*_2), where $Y^*=F_Y(Y)$, $X^*_1=F_{X1}(X_1)$, $X^*_2=F_{X2}(X_2)$, and F_Y,F_{X1}, F_{X2} are, respectively, the cdf's of Y, X_1,X_2. This new sample was investigated in the same way as the previous one in Sec. 3.1; Fig 6 presents the respective overrepresentation maps; the values of ρ^* and ρ^*_{max} for the concentration surface are –0.0064 and 0.061.

3.3. Triexponential data

A special triexponential vector Z,W_1,W_2 is considered which arises from two identically distributed independent vectors of standardized trinormal variables (V,V_1,V_2) and (V',V'_1,V'_2) as a sum of squares of respective components (e.g., $Z=(V^2+V'^2)/2$). The correlation matrix of the trinormal (V,V_1,V_2), used to generate (Z,W_1,W_2), was chosen so that the resulting correlation matrix of (Z,W_1,W_2) appeared identical to that of (Y,X_1,X_2) (considered in Sec. 3.1). The three overrepresentation maps obtained for the sample of size 100 are shown in Fig 7; the values of ρ^* and ρ^*_{max} for the concentration surface are -0.011and 0.103.

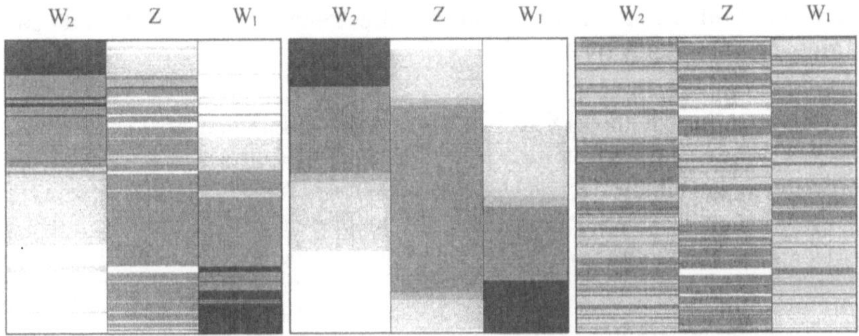

Fig. 7. Overrepresentation maps for $P_{100\times3}$, $N(P_{100\times3})$ and $\mathbf{C}(P_{100\times3}:N(P_{100\times3}))$, where $P_{100\times3}$ denotes the triexponential dataset transformed by GCA.

3.4. Grade triexponential data

The vector (Z,W_1,W_2) from Sec. 3.3 is transformed to the respective grade vector $(Z^*,W^*_1,W^*_2)=(F_Z(Z), F_{W_1}(W_1), F_{W_2}(W_2))$. The respective overrepresentation maps are shown in Fig 8; the values of ρ^* and ρ^*_{max} for the concentration surface are -0.0045 and 0.091.

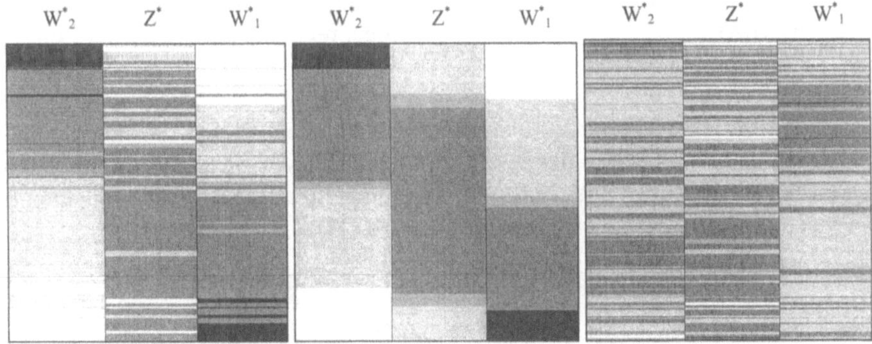

Fig. 8. Overrepresentation maps for $P_{100\times3}$, $N(P_{100\times3})$ and $\mathbf{C}(P_{100\times3}:N(P_{100\times3}))$, where $P_{100\times3}$ denotes the grade triexponential dataset transformed by GCA.

4. Behavior of linear regression of the response variable on two explanatory variables

In the trinormal distribution (Y,X_1,X_2), the regression function $E(Y|\mathbf{X}=(x_1,x_2))$ is linear, and the fit between the response variable Y and its linear prediction LR depends on the strength of dependence between Y and $\mathbf{X}=(X_1,X_2)$. The scatterplot for Y and $LR(x_1,x_2)= E(Y|\mathbf{X}=(x_1,x_2))$, i.e. the set of points $(Y, E(Y|\mathbf{X}=(x_1,x_2)))$, is presented in Fig. 9, together with the scatterplots for other pairs of variables.

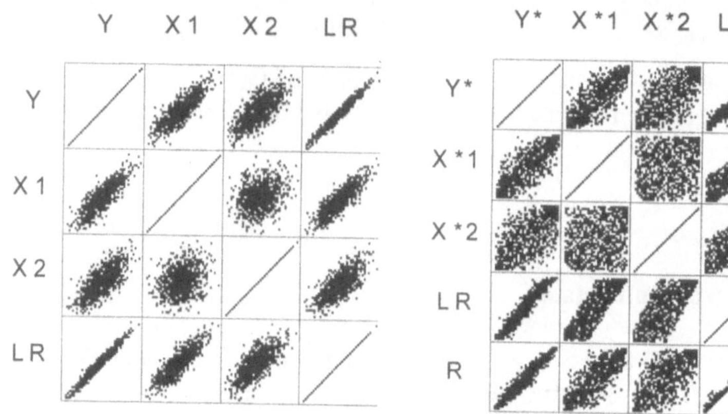

Fig. 9. Scatterplots for all pairs from the vector (Y,X_1,X_2,LR), where LR is the linear regression of Y on (X_1,X_2)

Fig. 10. Scatterplots for all pairs from the vector (Y^*,X^*_1,X^*_2,LR,R), where LR and R are the linear regression and the proper regression of Y^* on (X^*_1,X^*_2)

It is interesting to compare this scatterplot with that in Fig. 10 for the pair $(Y^*,LR(Y^*|\mathbf{X}^*))$. It seems that linear regression behaves relatively well, the more so when compared with the behavior of the proper ("true") regression function of Y^* on (X^*_1,X^*_2), given by the formula (Ch. 7 in [5]):

$$R(u_1,u_2)=\Phi\left(\frac{\rho'_1\Phi^{-1}(u_1)+\rho'_2\Phi^{-1}(u_2)}{\sqrt{2-\rho_1\rho'_1-\rho_2\rho'_2}}\right),$$

where $\rho_1 = corr(Y,X_1)$, $\rho_2 = corr(Y,X_2)$, $\rho_{12} = corr(X_1,X_2)$,

$$\rho'_1=\frac{\rho_1-\rho_2\rho_{12}}{1-\rho_{12}^2},\quad \rho'_2=\frac{\rho_2-\rho_1\rho_{12}}{1-\rho_{12}^2}.$$

The scatterplot of LR and R is also presented in Fig. 10. The points concentrate along the diagonal in a remarkable way.

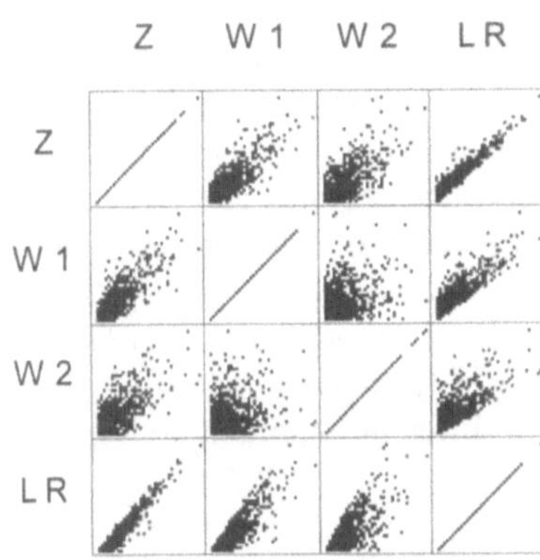

Fig. 11. Scatterplots for all pairs from the vector (Z,W_1,W_2,LR), where LR is the linear regression of Z on (W_1,W_2)

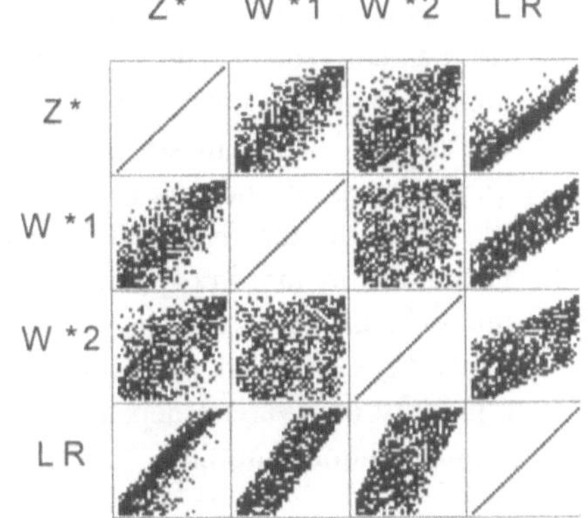

Fig. 12. Scatterplots for all pairs from the vector (Z^*,W^*_1,W^*_2,LR), where LR is the linear regression of Z^* on (W^*_1,W^*_2)

Fig. 11 compared with Fig. 9 shows that linear regression of Z on (W_1,W_2) is only slightly worse as an estimator of Z than linear regression of Y on (X_1,X_2) as an estimator of Y. Here, the correlation matrices of (Y,X_1,X_2) and (Z,W_1,W_2) are identical. This is not the case for the respective triples of grade variables: the correlations are respectively smaller for (Z^*,W^*_1,W^*_2) than, respectively, for (Y^*,X^*_1,X^*_2). Therefore linear regression LR in Fig. 12 seems worse than that in Fig. 10 but the two cases are not legitimately comparable (although $\rho^*_{max}(Y^*,X^*_1,X^*_2) \cong \rho^*_{max}(Y^*,X^*_1,X^*_2) \cong 0.267$).

5. Final remarks

(i) One of the desirable features of multinormal distribution is that the regression function of any subset of variables on another subset is linear. In the past, researches looked for transformations, which aimed at producing data “close to multinormal”; they are also constantly trying to remove outliers from multinormality, but these efforts are rarely effective in practice. On the other hand, we believe that removing records and variables, which outlie from a total positivity pattern (see [7] and [8]), should be the first step in analyzing any multivariate dataset.

(ii) The results contained in this paper suggest that grade transformations of ordinal and interval variables might be very useful, and that regular grade datasets transformed by GCA are worth attention.

(iii) The paper is addressed to data analysts. Probabilistic distributions are only used as convenient patterns of data sets regularity. Our aim is to introduce some irregularity measures and let researchers be aware of their importance and properties. Let us stress that not only measures of regularity but also its very concept are not yet established in statistics and data analysis. Lehman did not name the feature that ordered the classes of bivariate distributions introduced by him in [4] (from *quadrant dependence* to *total positivity*). This hierarchical set of models was called *ordered according to regularity* by Kowalczyk et al in [3]. The authors of [3] stressed that strength and regularity of bivariate dependence are two different important concepts that supplement one another.

References

1. Ciok A., Kowalczyk T., Pleszczyńska T. (1995): Algorithms of grade correspondence-cluster analysis, The Collected Papers on Theoretical and Applied Computer Science, 7, 5-22.
2. Kowalczyk T. (2000). Link between grade measures of dependence and of separability in pairs of conditional distributions. Stat. Prob. Lett. 46, 371-379.
3. Kowalczyk T., Pleszczyńska E., Szczesny W. (1991): Evaluation of stochastic dependence, in Statistical Inference - Theory and Practice, Eds. Bromek T. and Pleszczyńska E., PWN – Polish Scientific Publishers in co-publication with Kluwer Academic Publishers Dordrecht/Boston/London, 106-132.
4. Lehmann E. (1966). Some concepts of dependence. Ann. Math. Stat. 37, 1137-1153.
5. Pleszczyńska E., Kowalczyk T., Ruland F. (Eds). Models and Methods of Grade Data Analysis (in preparation).
6. Schriever B. F. (1985). Order dependence. Vrije Universitet te Amsterdam.
7. Szczesny W. (2000): Detecting rows and columns of contingency table, which outlie from a total positivity pattern. Control and Cybernetics, vol. 29, no. 4, 1059-1073.
8. Szczesny W. (2001). Grade Correspondence Analysis applied to Contingency Tables and Questionnaire Data. Intelligent Data Analysis vol. 5, 1-35.

The Clusters and the Minimization of Some Nonlinear Functional

T. Bochorishvili, E. A. Grebenikov

Akademia Podlaska, Siedlce, Poland.
E-mail: *tengiz@ap.siedlce.pl*

Abstract. Many problems of practical importance bring to the nonlinear system equations, to find which solutions is possible by using iterations algorithms. It is known, that the realization of the iteration algorithm is defend on the successful selection of initial point. The choice an initial point is connected to separation of clusters from a big set of points. Where each cluster represents an heap around the point of minima.

1 Introduction

We consider the problem, pointed in the 60-th of XX century by known American mathematician C. Lanczos [1].

The problem of the separation of radioactive substances from radioactive mixture is connected with data processing obtained from the experimental measurements. The rules of decomposition of the radioactive chemical elements are described by exponential functions. It is natural that the problem of the best approximation of a finite set of measurements by the exponential functions is adequate.

It is necessary to determine the hidden exponents in processes of the radioactive disintegration, represented by massive measurements. This problem is related to so called “ill posed problems” [2] and hence if solutions exist, there are several solutions [3]. The system of equations, that one has to solve for determining the unknown parameters, is transcendental. More ever, the number of parameters also is unknown, which complicate one more the problem.

C. Lanczos has solved this problem for the simplest models: the measurements are realized on equidistant time grid and the number of parameters is known [1].

In our paper is proposed an algorithm of the pick-out of the exponential functions, based on the approximation discreet experimental measurements by exponent polynomials. It is possible to realize this algorithm on the non-equidistant time grid.

2 Methods and Solutions

Let be done N points

$$\left(t_k, y_k\right) \in R^2 \ 0 \le t_k \le T \ , \ (k=0,1,\ldots,N) \tag{1}$$

We are looking for a function $f(t)$, $t \in [0,T]$, the graph of which contains these points. More ever, this function must be of the form:

$$f(t) = \sum_{i=1}^{m} \alpha_i \cdot e^{\lambda_i t} \qquad t \in [0,T] \tag{2}$$

where $\vec{\alpha} = (\alpha_1, \alpha_2, \cdots, \alpha_m)$, $\vec{\lambda} = (\lambda_1, \lambda_2, \cdots, \lambda_m)$ and the natural number m are to be determined, usually m is much less then N, i.e. $m << N$. More ever, in order to solve this problem it is necessary to determine the lower and upper bound of m $(m_1 \le m \le m_2)$.

To find the vector of activity $\vec{\alpha}$ and the coefficients of decompositions $\vec{\lambda}$, first of all we fix the natural number $m = m_0$. In order to use the method of least squares, we must construct the functional

$$\Psi(\vec{\alpha}, \vec{\lambda}, f) = \sum_{k=0}^{N} \left(y_k - \sum_{i=1}^{m_0} \alpha_i \cdot e^{\lambda_i t_k} \right)^2 \tag{3}$$

and we have to find the minimum of that.

$$\underset{\vec{\alpha}, \vec{\lambda}}{Min}\, \Psi(\vec{\alpha}, \vec{\lambda}, f) \to 0 \tag{4}$$

Like this found solutions are supposed roots and require laborious analyses.

The problem (4) is referred to as the problem of absolute (unconditional) minimization. In such kind main difficulty consists in finding the initial point. In what follows we put in evidence an algorithm to solve this problem.

For this we generate a set of pseudo-random vectors:

$$\{\vec{\alpha}, \vec{\lambda}\}_s = \left(\alpha_1^s, \alpha_2^s, \cdots, \alpha_m^s, \lambda_1^s, \lambda_2^s, \cdots, \lambda_m^s\right), \quad s = 1,2,,,\overline{N} \tag{5}$$

where $\overline{N}$ is big number about $10^6 - 10^7$. We calculate the values of our functional in these points, and so, we obtain a finite set of values of Ψ in the points (5). Let denote them by Ψ_s, $s = 1,2,,,\overline{N}$. From this set we choose the minimal value $\Psi_{\min}$, and then we filter the set (5) in such way, that we drop out the points, which does not satisfy the following inequality:

$$\Psi_s \le \Psi_{\min} + \varepsilon \tag{6}$$

where ε is sufficiently small.

On this way we select a subset of the set (5), on which the values of the functional is small enough, and which accumulate in clusters around the points of minima. If the functional has at least one point of minimum, then there is at least one isolated cluster. We divide this cluster on other accumulations groups, enumerate them and denote by $c_1, c_2, \cdots, c_p$ (see Fig. 1), where p represents the number of these small clusters. Let $l_1, l_2, \cdots, l_p$ denote the number of points in each cluster.

After this we find for each groups C_i ,($i=1,2,\ldots,p$) the centroid (center of gravity) of the derivatives from the points of minimum and denote them by X_{c_i}.

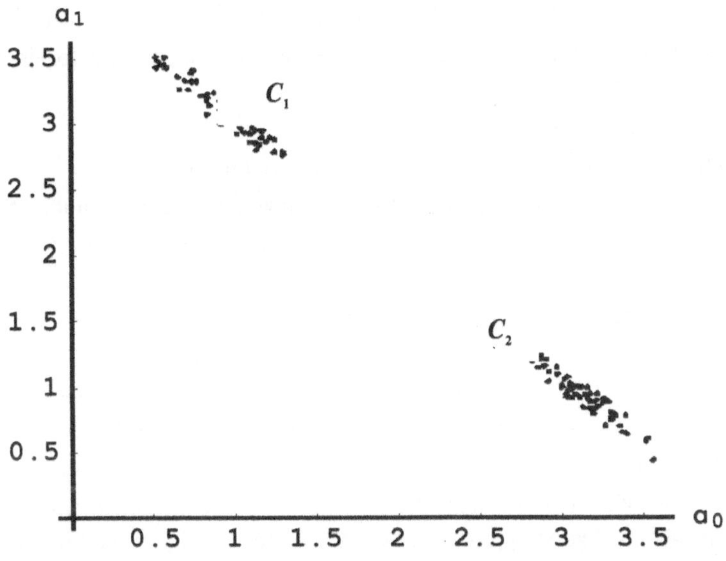

Fig. 1 The projections of clusters C_1, C_2 on the plane (α_0, α_1).

This point can be determined by formula:

$$X_{c_i} = \frac{\sum_{k=1}^{l_i} x_k \left(\Psi_{\max}^i - \Psi_k\right)^{31}}{\sum_{k=1}^{l_i} \left(\Psi_{\max}^i - \Psi_k\right)^{31}} \qquad (7)$$

where x_k ($k=1,2,\ldots,l_i$) are points of the cluster c_i, $\Psi_{\max}^i$ is the maximum value of the functional on these points. The values of X_{c_i}, found in this way, will represent the first approximation (initial point). The more exact solution will be determined by the method of steepest descent. Each solution is probably one of the problem (4).

This construction has been purposed actually for that case, when one has a very big number of measurements, and to find a good first approximation (initial point) for one of the iteration algorithm for finding the points of minima of the quadratic functional. To be certain, that the obtained values of parameters $\{\vec{\alpha}, \vec{\lambda}\}$ give us the solution we have to do further analyses.

We proposed to divide the interval $[0, T]$ into m_0 parts and for each subinterval to repeat the above algorithm all over again. If the new values of the parameters are close enough to previous one, then we can conclude, that the find solution is the correct one. If not, then we increase the number m_0 (i.e. increases the number of exponential functions in the term (2)) and we repeat the process for the new value of m_0 from the beginning.

This process one has to repeat until:

- Either after some steps of iteration we obtain desired result;
- Either we continue the calculations until we achieve the maximal number m_2;

3 Conclusions

A numerical experiment was realized to estimate an efficiency of the suggested algorithm. It was calculated the values of functional (3) at the $6 \cdot 10^6$ points. On the Fig. 1 shown the projections of clusters on the plane (α_0, α_1), which are obtained after filter of set (4). Each cluster gives one initial point for iteration algorithm. It was obtained good approximations of a vector activity $\vec{\alpha}$ and the coefficients of decomposition $\vec{\lambda}$. Based on made calculations we can conclude, that it is possible to use above algorithm for not only numerical experiments.

References

1. C. Lanczos, Applied Analysis, M.: Goc. Izdatelstvo fiz.-mat. Literatury, 1961,524 c.
2. Tihonov A.N., Arsenin B.I., Metody reshenia nekorektnyx zadach, -M,: Nauka,1986.
3. Grebenikov E.A., Kiosa M.N., Mironov C.V., Chislenno analiticheskie metody issledovania regularno vozmushennyx mnogochastotnyx system, -M.: Izd-vo MGU, 1986,184s.

Grade Decomposition of a Contingency Table into Binormal Discretized Tables

Olaf Matyja

Institute of Computer Science, Polish Academy of Science, Ordona 21, 01-237 Warsaw, Poland

Abstract:

An analogy of Correspondence Analysis called the Grade Correspondence Analysis (shortly GCA) has been introduced in [1]. Its applications cover an approximation of a contingency or probability table to a more regular model. This paper extends GCA to produce a sequence of regular (binormal) models, which after suitable permutations of rows and columns form a mixture close to the initial table. In the first part of the paper features of the Grade Correspondence Analysis (GCA) are analyzed. The second part introduces an algorithm for using GCA to decompose a table into two or more permuted binormal tables and the smallest possible residuum table.

Key words:

Binormal distribution, GCA, Grade Correspondence Analysis, decomposition.

1. Introduction

The algorithm presented in the paper is based on the Grade Correspondence Analysis algorithm introduced in [1]. In short, GCA algorithm sorts rows and columns of a table to achieve the maximal value of Spearman's ρ. The comparison of the presented approach with other approaches to the decomposition of a probability or contingency tables using grade statistics can be found in [4]. A simplified version of the algorithm was also published in [5].

In the first part of the paper we consider two or more binormal tables with different values of Spearman's ρ. Each one is then permuted in a different way (rows and columns separately) and taken to the sum with a different weight. The weights are non-negative and sum to one. For each component we introduce a parameter called **share,** equal to the product of its Spearman`s ρ (before permuting) and its weight in the mixture. A component of the mixture with the biggest share will be called **the primary component**. The resulting table will be called **mixture table** and its transformation with rows and columns permuted to achieve the maximal value of Spearman`s ρ will be called **maximal mixture table.**

Formally:

Let *T'=Perm(T)* be a table obtained from T' by a permutation of rows and/or columns. Let $P_{n\times m}$ be a probability (contingency) table. In the decomposition model we represent it as a linear combination of a binormal distribution tables:

$$P=\pi_1 Perm_1(N_2(\rho_1))+\pi_2 Perm_2(N_2(\rho_2))+\pi_k Perm_k(N_2(\rho_k)), \qquad (1)$$

where $\pi_i \geq 0$, $\sum \pi_i=1$, $Perm_i(T)$ is a permutation of rows and columns of table T, $N_2(\rho_i)$ is a discretized binormal distribution table of $\rho=\rho_i$ and the same size as P discretized in such a way to obtain uniform marginal distributions (equal sum of each row and equal sum of each column).

2. Comparing permutations

The GCA algorithm permutes rows and columns of the table to achieve the maximum dependency. In the next section we will try to determine properties of GCA applied to the composition of binormal distribution tables. This requires a metric to compare table after GCA with the components of the sum (1) in order to determine which component (or at least its approximation) has been found.

We have to take into account, that GCA in approximately half of cases reverses the order of rows and columns. We apply Pietra divergence index to tables P and P' being compared, and then apply it again, with one of the tables reversed, and take the smallest value:

$$Diff(P,P')=\min\Big(\sum_{1\leq i\leq M}\sum_{1\leq j\leq N}|P_{ij}-P'_{ij}|,\sum_{1\leq i\leq M}\sum_{1\leq j\leq N}|P_{ij}-P'_{M+1-i,N+1-j}|\Big)$$

3. Properties of the GCA algorithm

The decomposition method utilizes some unique features of GCA algorithm applied to linear combinations of permuted binormal distribution tables. We created a simulation study on 4293 cases with permutations and values of Spearman's ρ generated randomly and independently in tables 20x20 with uniform marginal distributions. The steps of the simulation were as follows:

1. The table P of size 20×20 with uniform marginal distributions, $P=\pi Perm_1(N_2(\rho_1))+(1-\pi)Perm_2(N_2(\rho_2))$ was calculated with values of π, ρ_1, ρ_2, and permutations $Perm_1$, and $Perm_2$ chosen randomly (with the same probability of each permutation). It is a special case of a combination (1) when $k=2$, $\pi_1=\pi$, and $\pi_2=1-\pi$. Values of $\tau_1=\tau(N_2(\rho_1))$, and $\tau_2=\tau(N_2(\rho_2))$ were also calculated.

2. GCA has been executed for this table, the result with the highest ρ was applied to the table P. We obtained factors ρ_{GCA}, τ_{GCA} and a permutation $Perm_{GCA}$.

3. $Perm_{GCA}$ was compared with $Perm_1$ and $Perm_2$. We obtained $Diff(Perm_{GCA}(P),Perm_1(P))$ and $Diff(Perm_{GCA}(P),Perm_2(P))$.

4. Values of π, ρ_1, ρ_2, τ_1, τ_2, ρ_{GCA}, τ_{GCA}, $Diff(Perm_{GCA}(P),Perm_1(P))$ and $Diff(Perm_{GCA}(P),Perm_2(P))$ were saved for further analysis.

Statistical analysis of the results showed the following properties:

Property (i) The best result of GCA is almost always more similar to the primary component, i.e. the component of a sum (1) with the maximum value of the share $\rho_i\pi_i$. The scatter-plot below illustrates this feature.

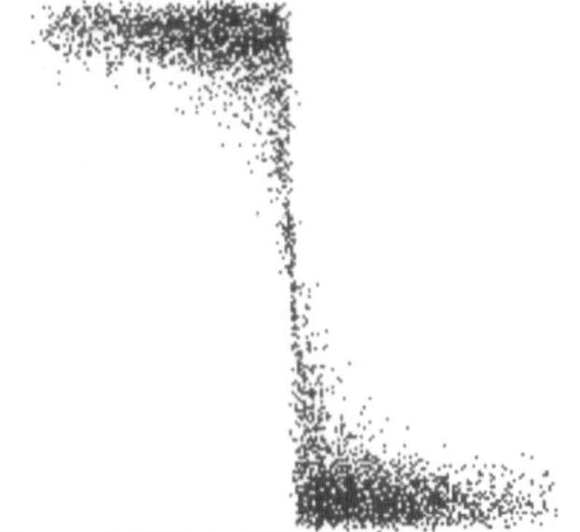

Figure 1. Values of $\pi_1\rho_1-\pi_2\rho_2=\pi\rho_1-(1-\pi)\rho_2$ lie on the horizontal axis and values of $Diff_{1\text{-}2}=Diff(Perm_{GCA}(P),Perm_1(P))-Diff(Perm_{GCA}(P),Perm_2(P))$ on the vertical axis.

Notice, signs of this expressions are almost always opposite - The difference between the best GCA permutation and permutation of a component was smaller when $\pi_i\rho_i$ for this component was larger. In fact only 39 cases (0.9% of the population) violated this rule. In all this cases $|\pi_1\rho_1 - \pi_2\rho_2| < 0.03$ – the components were almost equally important. The GCA method seems to select the most important component rather than create a combination of them. The distribution of values of $\mathrm{Diff}_{1\text{-}2}$ shown on the figure 1 seems to validate this supposition.

Property (ii) Let F be an index of the primary component, i.e. 1 if $\pi_1\rho_1 > \pi_2\rho_2$ and 2 in the opposite case in this simulation. The following expressions are almost equal: $\rho_{GCA} \approx \pi_F\rho_F$, $\tau_{GCA} \approx \pi_F\tau_F$. The Pearson's correlation between ρ_{GCA} and $\pi_F\rho_F$ is 0.9985 for this sample !

This can be easily justified for a considered model:

$$\begin{aligned}\rho_{GCA} &= \rho(Perm_{GCA}(P)) = \\ &= \rho(Perm_{GCA}(\sum \pi_i Perm_i(N_2(\rho_i)))) = \\ &= \sum \pi_i \rho(Perm_{GCA}(Perm_i(N_2(\rho_i))))\end{aligned}$$

The components of the sum for $i \neq F$ are almost zero, because conjunction of two independent permutations $Perm_{GCA}$ and $Perm_i$ for $i \neq F$) is a random permutation. Average of Spearman's ρ for random permutations of any table is equal to zero. Thus the sum can be simplified to

$$\rho_{GCA} \approx \pi_F \rho(Perm_{GCA}(Perm_F(N_2(\rho_F)))) \approx \pi_F \rho(N_2(\rho_F)) = \pi_F \rho_F$$

because GCA tends to reconstruct the order of rows and columns of the primary component, as has been shown a moment ago. The same reasoning can be provided for Kendall's τ. Notice, for both ρ and τ, the independence of permutations $Perm_i$ is required. If, for example $Perm_1 = Perm_2 = \ldots = Perm_k$, then

$$\begin{aligned}\rho_{GCA} &= \sum \pi_i \rho(Perm_{GCA}(Perm_i(N_2(\rho_i)))) = \\ &= \sum \pi_i \rho(Perm_{GCA}(Perm_F(N_2(\rho_i)))) \approx \\ &\approx \sum \pi_i \rho(N_2(\rho_i)) = \sum \pi_i \rho_i\end{aligned}$$

4. The decomposition algorithm

Step 1. Identifying primary trend.

GCA algorithm applied to table T. This step results in a table T`, being a transformation of $T$ with rows and columns permuted to achieve the maximum value of the Spearman`s ρ. According to the Property (i) the permutation of rows and columns in T` can be treated as an approximation of the permutation of the primary component. Let $RevPerm_l$ be a function that assigns rows and columns of table $T$` to the corresponding rows and columns of T. According to the Property (ii), the maximum Spearman`s $\rho$ of $T$` can be treated as a good approximation of the primary component share.

Step 2. Calculating ρ and π.

We try to split the result of step 1 (the approximated share) into its factors - Spearman`s ρ of the component and its weight. This is done by calculating Blomqvist's q index of a table, which is also proportional to weight but depends on ρ in a different way than share (π without indexes in the following equations means *3.1415...*, not weight).

Binormal distribution:

$$p(\rho, x_1, x_2) = \frac{1}{2\pi\sqrt{1-\rho^2}} \exp\left[-\frac{1}{2(1-\rho^2)}(x_1^2 - 2\rho x_1 x_2 + x_2^2)\right]$$

Integral of a quarter of binormal distribution:

$$l(\rho) = \int_0^{\frac{1}{2}}\int_0^{\frac{1}{2}} p(\rho, x_1, x_2)dx_1 dx_2$$

Integral taken from [6], page 95, equation (24):

$$l(\rho) = \frac{1}{4} + \frac{\arcsin \rho}{2\pi}$$

Blomqvist's q for a binormal distribution:

$$q = 2l(\rho) - 2l(-\rho)$$

Finally:

$$q = \frac{\arcsin(\rho) - \arcsin(-\rho)}{2\pi} = \frac{\arcsin(\rho)}{\pi}$$

We are able to approximate values of ρ (ρ_1) and weight (π_1) from the following equations:

$$\rho(T') = \rho_1 \pi_1$$

$$q(T') = \frac{\arcsin(\rho_1)}{\pi} \pi_1$$

Step 3. Idealization of the main trend

The binormal table B_1 of the same size and marginals as T` and with Spearman`s ρ equal to ρ_1 is created. Then, B_1 is permuted by $RevPerm_1$. The output table, called C_1, becomes the first component of the created mixture.

Step 4. Collecting remains

Table $R_1 = T - \pi_1 C_1$ is calculated.

Step 5. Identifing secondary trend

Steps 1...3 of the algorithm are applied to table R_1 instead of T. The second component C_2 is obtained according to Step 3, its weight is π_2. Two ways of handling negative values in R_1 are exploited. (GCA algorithm for ρ doesn't process negative data.) We can either subtract the smallest (negative) value from the whole table or treat all negative data as equal to zero. Simulations showed, the second way is better (in the first case noise added to the smallest value had too big impact on the table, moreover marginal distributions changed).

Step 6. Collecting remains of remains

Table $R_2 = R_1 - \pi_2 C_2$ is calculated.

In such a way we obtain two permuted binormal tables C_1 and C_2, their weights π_1 and π_2, and a residuum table R_2, which satisfy the condition $T = \pi_1 C_1 + \pi_2 C_2 + R_2$. The process can be continued to achieve further trends. $\sum \pi_i$ can be treated as a measure of fit of the table T with considered mixture model, and a measure of meaningfulness of the results. In an ideal case it is equal to one. Rows or columns of the residuum table with the biggest totals should be considered as potential outliers from the mixture model.

References

1. Ciok, A., Kowalczyk T., Pleszczynska E., Szczesny W.:Algorithms of grade correspondence cluster analysis. The Collected Papers of Theoretical and Applied Computer Science 7 No. 1-4 (1995) 5-22.

2. Szczesny W.: Detecting rows and columns of contingency table, which outlie from a total positivity pattern. Control and Cybernetics, vol. 29 (2000) No. 4.

3. Szczesny W.: Grade Correspondence Analysis Applied to Contingency Tables and Questionnaire Data. Intelligent Data Analysis, vol 6(1) in press.

4. O. Matyja: Smooth Grade Correspondence Analysis and the related computer system. PhD thesis. Institute of Computer Science, Polish Academy of Science, Warsaw, Poland

5. O. Matyja: Decomposition of a probability table into a mixture of permuted discretized binormal tables. CompStat 2002, Berlin.

6. N.L. Johnson, S. Kotz: Distributions in Statistics: Continuous Multivariate Distributions, ISBN 0-471-44370-0, Wiley 1972

Search Space Partitioning to Enhance Outlier Rule Discovery

Michał Okoniewski, Piotr Gawrysiak, and Łukasz Gancarz

Institute of Computer Science
Warsaw University of Technology
ul.Nowowiejska 15/19
00-665 Warszawa
{okoniews,gawrysia,lgancarz}@ii.pw.edu.pl

Summary. This paper presents an enhancement of the multidimensional quantitative rule discovery methodology presented in [9] by clustering of preselected μ-tuples. This unconventional, in KDD cycle, usage of clustering as a preprocessing step allows for significant speed-up without compromising informational value of discovered results. In that sense it is a continuation of research described in [2]. The paper presents the outcome of experiments performed with this method over datasets obtained by random sampling of graphic image files. The outcome clearly shows the advantages and applicability of proposed methodology.

Keywords: quantitative association rules, outlier rules, clustering, KDD cycle, multimedia

1 Quantitative association rules

Association rules are a highly popular data mining method. However,most of the approaches are designed for market basket analysis and operate on categorical (qualitative) data [1]. It renders them useless for learning from many common types of data based on numeric values. Special forms of association rules for quantitative attributes may be applicable here [3,8,11]. There are still relatively few mining algorithms and methodologies to deal with quantitative associations.

Data-driven algorithms are expected to be competitive to those based on discretization. An example of such algorithm is Window algorithm proposed in [6] which operates on a new form of a quantitative rule. In Window, the boundaries of ranges in the antecedent of an association rule are determined by attribute values for specific tuples. A set of these ranges, called a profile, selects a subset of tuples. The antecedent consists of a statistical measure (usually the mean), which is based on values of another numeric attribute. The measure for the sub-population is compared with the same measure for the whole dataset. The rule is significant if the difference between these two measures is high. An example of the rule discovered by this algorithm may be:

$$age \in (35, 45) \Rightarrow$$
$$mean\ Salary = 38k (overall\ mean\ Salary = 29k)$$

In [6] only rules with single numeric attribute in the antecedent are p-resented. Thesis [9] describes a generalization of this solution to multiple attributes. Such form of rules is applicable to learning associations from spatial data.

This paper discusses the aspect of such multi-dimensional quantitative rules discovery, where the approximate result may be obtained much faster by means of clustering the set of outliers in data.

2 Outliers as a base for rule discovery

Precise definitions of new quantitative association rules are presented in papers [9,10]. These papers also extend notions of irreducible and maximal rule introduced in [6] into multiple attributes in rule antecedent. Briefly, the rule has an antecedent named a profile, that consists of one or more numeric attribute ranges. Profile may be represented by a hyper-cuboid in the space of multiple continuous attributes. The consequent of the rule includes a statistical measure for the sub-population defined in the profile, which significantly differs from the same measure for the whole dataset.

In case of mean-based rules, the mean of decisive attribute in sub-population must be greater than mean of this attribute in whole dataset plus predefined constant *mindif*.

Such multidimensional rules may be well used to describe local phenomena in spatial data. For example:

$$latitude \in (49N, 50N) \wedge longitude \in (19E, 21E) \Rightarrow$$
$$avg\ temp.April = 3C(avg\ temp\ April\ Poland = 7C)$$

Furthermore, in [9,10] some important qualities of mean-based rules are proven. One of them states that on every profile boundary of irreducible rule there is an outlier tuple (called μ-tuple), that has decisive attribute value above $\mu = avg + mindif$. In fact, μ-tuples define ranges of attributes in the profile of irreducible rule.

The algorithm initially selects all μ-tuples from dataset, then combines them, creates a profile and performs a check if the rule is irreducible.

3 Computational complexity assessment

The computational complexity of the algorithm depends on the percentage p of μ-tuples in the dataset, and may be estimated [9] as $O(k(pn)^{2k})$. This assumes that the cost of selecting tuples inside a profile hyper-cuboid is small, because of effective indexing method for multiple attributes [7,4].

The complexity is polynomial, but may be considered still high. However, if we divide the attribute space into r sub-spaces, the complexity is decreased to:

$$O(rk(\frac{pn}{r})^{2k}) = O(k\frac{(pn)^{2k}}{r^{2k-1}})$$

There are several complexity reduction strategies that are based on above principle. For example μ-tuples may be divided into r disjoint groups with a clustering algorithm. Alternatively, if we assume that rules can not be found in regions where there are no μ-tuples, excluding one biggest "empty" hypercuboid [5] results in division into 2^k smaller search spaces.

However the discovery of rules with the sub-space division can not be proved to be complete. It is possible that some rules, that have profiles between clusters, are lost. Our experiments included such approximate discovery with clustering as a preprocessing step. The results obtained proved that in spite of the tradeoff between the number of rules, their quality and the efficiency of algorithm, this method is worth trying.

4 Results of experiments with multimedia data

Experiments were performed on a synthetic data, then on datasets created by random sampling of graphical images. Pixel coordinates were used to build rule profiles, while numerical values were generated from pixel colors according to RGB or HSV models for one decisive attribute. By proper choice of decisive attribute and setting $mindif$, we could direct automatical discovery of local phenomena in images, for example areas that were lighter, darker than the rest of the image or which were uniform in color.

The experimental system was implemented as a Java client with Oracle and Transbase engines as sources of data. Input images were randomly sampled. From 200 to 2000 pixels were used as an input to discover phenomena in data. K-means clustering was applied to determine fixed number of μ-tuple clusters. Then, new rule discovery [9,10] algorithm was run with an input of μ-tuples inside each cluster.

The number of rules generated from this data compared with the number of search spaces obtained by clustering is presented in Fig. 1.

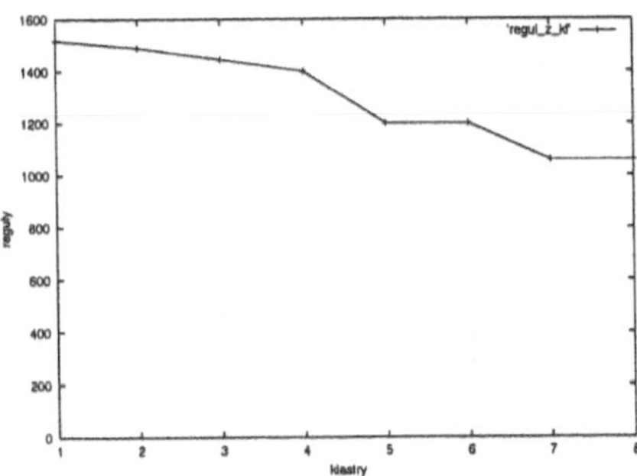

Fig. 1. Number of rules to number of clusters relationship

This proves that we do loose relatively small number of rules with the use of clustering. However, if the standard condition of minimal support for association rules is taken into account, the ratio of not discovered rules is bigger 2.

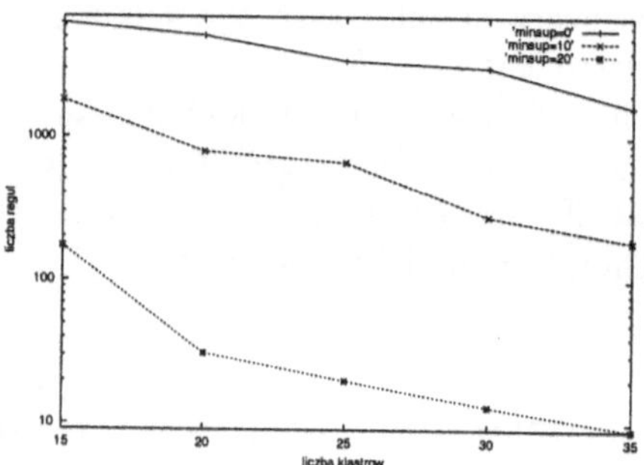

Fig. 2. Relationship between number of rules and number of clusters - support

The efficiency increase with the use of clustering is significant, especially if we search for rules with high support - Fig. 4.

Fig. 3 shows the same relationship obtained with less μ-tuples, only with irreducibility condition for rules.

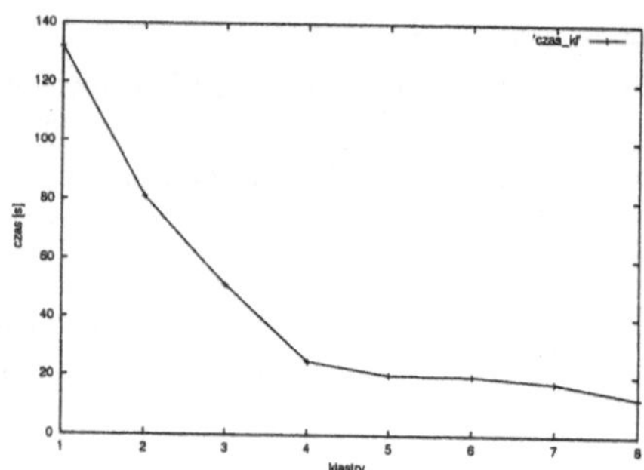

Fig. 3. Time and number of clusters relationship 1

5 Conclusions

Quantitative association rules in the form presented in this paper are applicable to spatial data and have clear advantages. Data-driven algorithms for rule discovery have polynomial complexity, and may be speeded up by heuristic strategies. Profile boundaries are determined by the data themselves, without errors inflicted by the static discretization. Input data may be sampled even

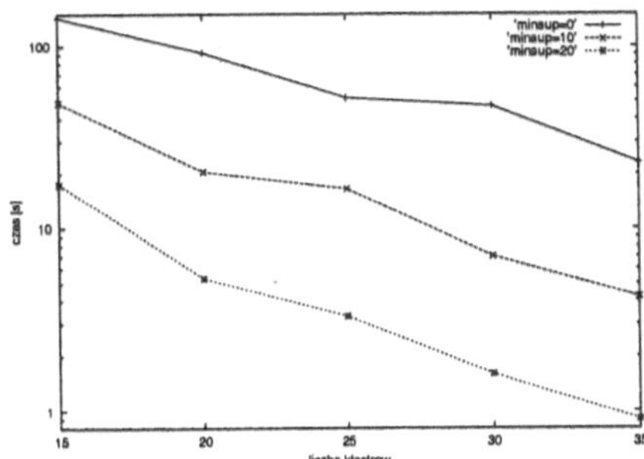

Fig. 4. Time and number of clusters relationship 2

at random. Experiments performed showed that use of clustering strategies for discovery of multidimensional rules results in significant increase of the mining process efficiency.

References

1. Gajek, M.: Comparative Analysis of Selected Association Rules Types. Intelligent Information Systems, Physica Verlag (2000)
2. Gawrysiak, P., Okoniewski, M., Rybiński, H.: Clustering with Regression as Quality Measure, Intelligent Information Systems, Physica Verlag (2001)
3. Głowiński, C.: Discovering Rules with Various Forms of Selectors, Proceedigs of Intelligent Information Systems Workshop, Malbork (1998)
4. Geade, V., Günther, O.: Multidimensioanal Access Methods, ACM Computing Surveys 30(2) (1997)
5. Gryz, J, Liang, D. and Miller, R.J.: Mining for Empty Rectangles in Large Data Sets. Proceedings of the 8th ICDT, London, UK (2001)
6. Lindell, Y., Aumann,Y.: Theory of Quantitative Association Rules with Statistical Validation, Proceedings of SIGKDD Conference, Boston (1999)
7. Markl, V.: MISTRAL: Processing Relational Queries using a Multidimensional Access Techinque, Ph.D. Thesis, TU Munchen (1999)
8. Miller, R.J.,Yang ,Y. Association Rules Over Interval Data,Proceedings of ACM SIGMOD97 Conference (1997)
9. Okoniewski M., Discovery of Multi-dimensional Quantitative Association Rules. Ph.D. Thesis. Warsaw University of Technology, Warsaw (2001)
10. Okoniewski M., Gancarz L., Gawrysiak P.: Mining Multi-dimensional Quantiatative Associations. 14th INAP Conference, Rule-Based Data Mining Workshop, Tokyo, Japan (2001)
11. Srikant, R., Agrawal, R.: Mining Quantitative Association Rules in Large Relational Tables, Proceedings of SIGMOD Conference, Montreal, Canada (1996)

Handling Imprecision and Uncertainty

Probabilistic Label Algebra for the Logic of Plausible Reasoning

Bartłomiej Śnieżyński

Institute of Computer Science
University of Mining and Metallurgy
Kraków, Poland
e-mail: sniezyn@agh.edu.pl

Abstract. This paper presents plausible algebra for the logic of plausible reasoning (LPR), which is defined as a labeled deductive system. Labels representing uncertainty of knowledge are defined in terms of probability. Examples of applying proof rules conclude the work.

Keywords: Logic of plausible reasoning, uncertain knowledge representation, probabilistic label algebra.

1 Introduction

Logic of plausible reasoning (LPR) was developed by Collins and Michalski in 1989 [3]. The main difference between this formalism and other common knowledge representation techniques (such as fuzzy logic [15], multiple-valued logic [8], certainty factors [13], Dempster-Shafer theory [12], rough sets [9] and belief networks [10]) is that it is based on human reasoning. Boehm-Davis and Michalski showed in [2], that human reasoning patterns can be represented as a sequence of LPR knowledge transformations. In this formalism several inference patterns are defined (not only Modus Ponens) and many parameters estimate certainty.

Idea of certainty parameters and using them in knowledge transformations is presented by Collins and Michalski in [3]. Up to date there were no concrete proposal known to the author, how such algebra should be defined.

Nowadays return to probability theory as a tool for representing uncertainty can be observed. It appears that it could be very useful tool not only in bayes networks, but also when it is combined with other knowledge representation formalisms (see e.g. [5,7,11]).

In this paper LPR is defined as a labeled deductive system (see [4]). In the following sections we define language, proof system and we propose the label algebra using terms of probability. Next we show some examples of applying proof rules using probability-based label algebra.

2 Logic of Plausible Reasoning

LPR language consists of a set of constant symbols C, four relational symbols and logical connectives: $\rightarrow$, $\wedge$. The relational symbols are: V, H, S, E. They are used to represent respectively: statements, hierarchy, similarity and dependency.

Statements are represented as object-attribute-value triples: $V(o, a, v)$, where $o, a, v \in C$. It is a representation of a fact that object o has an attribute a equal v. Value should be a sub-type of an attribute: if $V(o, a, v)$ is in a knowledge base, there should be also $H(v, a, c)$ (see below for H description). If object o has several values of a, there should be several appropriate statements in a knowledge base.

Relation H represents hierarchy between constant symbols. $H(o_1, o, c)$, where $o_1, o, c \in C$, means that o_1 is o in a context c. Context is used for specification of the range of inheritance. o_1 and o have the same value for all attributes which depend on attribute c of object o.

S is a similarity relation. $S(o_1, o_2, c)$ represents a fact, that o_1 is similar to o_2 ($o_1, o_2, c \in C$). Context, as above, specifies the range of similarity. Only these attributes of o_1 and o_2 have the same value which depends on attribute c.

To express dependency relation E is used. $E(o_1, a_1, o_2, a_2)$, where $o_1, a_1, o_2, a_2 \in C$, means that values of attribute a_1 of object o_1 depend on attribute a_2 of the second object. To represent bidirectional dependency (mutual dependency, see [3]) we need a pair of such expressions.

Now we are able to define *well formed formulas* of LPR. If $o, o', o_1, ..., o_n, a, a_1, ..., a_n, v, v_1, ..., v_n, c \in C$ then $V(o, a, v)$, $H(o', o, c)$, $S(o_1, o_2, o, a)$, $E(o_1, a_1, o_2, a_2)$, $o_1.a_1 = v_1 \wedge ... \wedge o_n.a_n = v_n \rightarrow o.a = v$ are well formed formulas of LPR.

As we can see, only positive statements are considered. There were two more formulas defined in [3]: dissimilarity between objects (one object is dissimilar to another in a given context) and negative statement (is not true that $o.a = v$). They are omitted in the language definition. Negative statement can be introduced using closed world assumption, see the end of section 3.

To deal with uncertainty we use labels (see [4]). Hence we need a *label algebra* $\mathcal{A} = (A, \{f_{r_i}\})$. A is a set of labels which estimate uncertainty. $\{f_r\}$ is a set of functions which are used in proof rules to generate a label of a conclusion: for every proof rule r_i an appropriate function f_{r_i} should be defined. For rule r_i with premises $p_1 : l_1, ..., p_n : l_n$ the plausible label of its conclusion is equal $f_{r_i}(l_1, ..., l_n)$.

Definitions of labels and functions are presented in the next section.

Labeled formula is a pair $f : l$ where f is a formula and l is a label. A set of labeled formulas can be considered as a knowledge base.

Having language we can define proof system. There are 5 types of proof rules: GEN, $SPEC$, SIM, $TRAN$ and MP. They correspond to the following inference patterns: generalization, specialization, similarity transformation, transitivity transformation and modus ponens. Some transformations can be applied to different types of formulas, therefore indexes are used to distinguish different versions of rules.

Rules can be divided into several groups according to type of formulas on which rules operate and types of inference patterns.

First group is *statement proof rules.* It consist of 6 rules presented in table 1. They are used to perform reasoning on statements, hence first premises and the conclusions are object-attribute-value triples. Rules indexed by o transform object argument, what correspond to generalization and specialization of the statement. Rules indexed by v operate on values. Applying these rules changes the detail level of a description and corresponds to abstraction and concretion.

Table 1. Statement proof rules.

$$GEN_o\ \frac{\begin{array}{l}V(o_1,a,v)\\ H(o_1,o,c)\\ E(o,a,o,c)\end{array}}{V(o_1,a,v)} \qquad SPEC_o\ \frac{\begin{array}{l}V(o,a,v)\\ H(o_1,o,c)\\ E(o,a,o,c)\end{array}}{V(o_1,a,v)} \qquad SIM_o\ \frac{\begin{array}{l}V(o_2,a,v)\\ S(o_1,o_2,c)\\ E(o_1,a,o_1,c)\\ E(o_2,a,o_2,c)\end{array}}{V(o_1,a,v)}$$

$$GEN_v\ \frac{\begin{array}{l}V(o,a,v_1)\\ H(v_1,v,c)\\ H(v,a,c_1)\end{array}}{o.a=v} \qquad SPEC_v\ \frac{\begin{array}{l}V(o_1,a,v)\\ H(v_1,v,o)\\ H(o_1,o,c_1)\end{array}}{V(o_1,a,v_1)} \qquad SIM_v\ \frac{\begin{array}{l}V(o_1,a,v_2)\\ S(v_1,v_2,o)\\ H(o_1,o,c_1)\end{array}}{V(o_1,a,v_1)}$$

Second group is *dependency proof rules*, which is shown in table 2. They operate on dependency formulas and allow to use generalization, specialization, analogy and transitivity inference patterns to change objects in dependency relations.

Table 2. Proof rules based on dependencies.

$$GEN_E\ \frac{\begin{array}{l}E(o_1,a_1,o_1,a_2)\\ H(o_1,o,c)\\ E(o,a_1,o,c)\end{array}}{E(o,a_1,o,a_2)} \qquad SPEC_E\ \frac{\begin{array}{l}E(o,a_1,o,a_2)\\ H(o_1,o,c)\\ E(o,a_1,o,c)\end{array}}{E(o_1,a_1,o_1,a_2)} \qquad SIM_E\ \frac{\begin{array}{l}E(o_1,a_1,o_1,a_2)\\ S(o_1,o_2,c)\\ E(o_1,a_1,o_1,c)\end{array}}{E(o_2,a_1,o_2,a_2)}$$

$$TRAN_E\ \frac{\begin{array}{l}E(o,a_1,o,a_2)\\ E(o,a_2,o,a_3)\end{array}}{E(o,a_1,o,a_3)}$$

Third group consist of one *implication proof rule* presented in table 3. It is used to transform implication formulas and can be used to represent quantification over all objects which are below of given object in the hierarchy.

Table 3. Proof rule based on implications.

$$SPEC_{o\to}\ \frac{\begin{array}{l} o.a_1 = v_1 \wedge \ldots \wedge o.a_n = v_n \to \\ \quad o.a = v \\ H(o_1, o, c) \end{array}}{\begin{array}{l} o_1.a_1 = v_1 \wedge \ldots \wedge o_1.a_n = v_n \to \\ \quad o_1.a = v \end{array}}$$

Last group, shown in table 4, consist of modus ponens rule. It is well known inference pattern.

Table 4. Modus ponens rule.

$$MP\ \frac{\begin{array}{l} o_1.a_1 = v_1 \wedge \ldots \wedge o_n.a_n = v_n \to o.a = v \\ o_1.a_1 = v_1 \\ \vdots \\ o_n.a_n = v_n \end{array}}{o.a = v}$$

Having inference rules, proof can be defined in a standard way. It allows to build complex inference chains.

3 Probability-based Plausible Algebra

In [5] Halpern defines two types of statement probabilities: for individual objects and for classes of objects. In LPR there is no explicit distinction between classes and individual objects (the only difference is a position in the hierarchy), therefore we define only one parameter which is used to represent these two types of probability. It makes inference process simpler and allows to introduce negation in an easy way (see below). But there is also a drawback of this assumption: probabilities should be carefully interpreted.

To define plausible algebra $\mathcal{A}$ (see previous section) we need a set of labels and plausible functions. Each label is a tuple of certainty parameters. We define 9 parameters, see table 5. We assume, that a domain of all parameters is $[0, 1] \cup \{\varepsilon\}$. ε value is used to represent unknown value of parameter. If ε is an argument of any arithmetical operation, the result is ε.

For each type of formula specific set of parameters is appropriate. Hence specific label for each type of formula is defined, see table 6.

Table 5. Certainty parameters

Parameter	Description
γ	Degree of certainty that a formula is true
η	Strength of dependency
σ	Degree of similarity (for objects in V relation)
σ_E	Degree of similarity (for dependency relation)
ξ	Degree of similarity (for values in V relation)
τ	Degree of typicality in a hierarchy (for objects in V relation)
τ_E	Degree of typicality in a hierarchy (for dependency relation)
α	Strength of implication
$\bar{\alpha}$	Negative strength of implication

Table 6. Plausible labels

Formula	Plausible label
$V(o, a, v)$	(γ)
$E(o_1.a_1, o_2.a_2)$	(γ)
$S(o_1, o_2, a)$	(σ, σ_E, ξ)
$H(o_1, o_2, c)$	$(\sigma, \tau, \sigma_E, \tau_E, \xi)$
$\psi_1 \wedge ... \wedge \psi_n \rightarrow \varphi$	$(\alpha, \bar{\alpha})$

Parameter γ, which is the label of formula $\varphi = V(o, a, v)$ represents a probability of φ. It can be interpreted in two ways according to o interpretation.

If o has specialization objects (lying below o in the hierarchy) and can be considered as a set of individuals, γ represents a probability that a randomly chosen element x of this set satisfies given property, i.e. $V(x, a, v)$. It represents statistical information about the world and it corresponds to probabilities used in Halpern's Type I probability logic [5].

If o is a leaf in a hierarchy and it represents a particular individual, γ represents degree of belief in φ. It can be interpreted as the probability of a set of possible worlds, where φ is true. It corresponds to probabilities used in Halpern's Type II probability logic [5].

Dependency relation E is also described by one parameter, η. It is probability of dependency between attributes of given object or objects. In inference rules we use only dependency between objects representing sets of individuals.

Similarity relation is labeled by three parameters. First one is σ. It represents a degree of similarity between objects and hence – a probability of having the same values of attributes. Similarity relation has context defined, so we are able to reason about all attributes which depend on the context. Therefore the probability of the conclusion depends on the probability of dependency between attribute and context. More formally, having $S(o_1, o_2, c) : (\sigma, \sigma_E, \xi)$, $E(o_1, a, o_1, c) : (\eta_1)$, $E(o_2, a, o_2, c) : (\eta_2)$ and $V(o_2, a, v) : (\gamma)$ we can conclude $V(o_1, a, v) : (\sigma\eta_1\eta_2\gamma)$.

Parameter σ_E is used in similar way, but with dependency relation E instead of V. Separate parameter is needed, because two objects can be more similar in dependencies then in attribute values. If we have $S(o_1, o_2, c)$: (σ, σ_E), $E(o_1, a_1, o_1, c) : (\eta_2)$ and $E(o_2, a_1, o_2, a_2) : (\eta_1)$ we can derive $E(o_1, a_1, o_1, a_2) : (\sigma\eta_2\eta_1)$.

Parameter ξ represents similarity between objects when they are values of attributes. It is used in similarity of value transformation. Let us assume that we have in knowledge base $S(v_1, v_2, o) : (\sigma, \sigma_E, \xi)$ and $V(o_1, a, v_2) : (\gamma)$, where o_1 is specialization of o. ξ is a probability, that v_2 can be replaced by v_1, therefore we can conclude $V(o_1, a, v_1) : (\xi\gamma)$.

Hierarchy relation is labeled by several parameters. σ and σ_E is very similar to parameters defined above. The difference is that, they represent similarity between object and its specialization and hence – probability of inheritance of attribute values or dependencies. Similarly as above, context is taken into consideration. More formally, having $H(o_1, o, c) : (\sigma, \tau, \xi, \sigma_E, \tau_E)$, $E(o, a, o, c) : (\eta_2)$ and $V(o, a, v) : (\gamma)$ we can infer $V(o_1, a, v) : (\sigma\eta_2\gamma)$; or given $E(o, a, o, a_1) : (\eta_1)$ we can derive $E(o_1, a, o_1, a_1) : (\sigma\eta_2\eta_1)$.

Parameters τ and τ_E represents typicality of the specialization object and they are used in generalization transformations. τ is a probability that object o has the same attribute value as its specialization o_1. Parameter τ_E, analogically, is a probability of generalizing dependency. Having hierarchy and dependency relations given above and $V(o_1, a, v) : (\gamma)$ we can conclude $V(o, a, v) : (\tau\eta_2\gamma)$; or given $E(o_1, a, o_1, a_1) : (\eta_1)$ we can derive $E(o, a, o, a_1)$: $(\tau_E\eta_2\eta_1)$.

Last parameter in H relation, ξ, is used in value specialization transformation. Let us assume that we have in knowledge base $H(v_1, v, o) : (\sigma, \tau, \xi, \sigma_E, \tau_E)$ and $V(o_1, a, v) : (\gamma)$, where o_1 is specialization of o. ξ is a probability that we can replace v by v_1, that means we can conclude $V(o_1, a, v_1) : (\xi\gamma)$.

Implication formula $\psi_1 \wedge \ldots \wedge \psi_n \rightarrow \varphi$ is labeled by two parameters: α and $\bar{\alpha}$. They are defined as conditional probabilities: $\alpha = P(\varphi|\psi_1 \cap \ldots \cap \psi_n)$, $\alpha = P(\varphi|\overline{\psi_1 \cap \ldots \cap \psi_n})$. These parameters are used in MP rule to calculate the probability of a conclusion if we know probabilities of premises. It is analogy of updating probabilities in the face of uncertain evidence which was considered by Jeffrey [6]. Events $\psi_1, \ldots, \psi_n$ should be independent.

Having plausible parameters defined as above, plausible function definitions are straightforward. They are presented in table 7.

Because object-attribute-value statements are labeled by one parameter representing its probability, it is possible to use negative statements assuming closed world. If we want to find probability $\bar{\gamma}$ of $\neg V(o, a, v)$, we should prove that $V(o, a, v) : (\gamma)$ with as big value of γ as possible and we have $\bar{\gamma} = 1 - \gamma$.

Table 7. Function definitions

Function	Arguments	Value
f_{GEN_o}	$(\gamma_1),(\sigma,\tau,\ldots),(\eta)$	$\gamma=\gamma_1\eta\tau$
f_{SPEC_o}	$(\gamma_1),(\sigma,\tau,\ldots),(\eta)$	$\gamma=\gamma_1\eta\sigma$
f_{SIM_o}	$(\gamma_1),(\sigma,\ldots),(\eta_1),(\eta_2)$	$\gamma=\gamma_1\eta_1\eta_2\sigma$
f_{GEN_v}	$(\gamma_1),(\sigma_1,\ldots),(\sigma_2,\ldots)$	$\gamma=\gamma_1$
f_{SPEC_v}	$(\gamma_1),(\sigma_1,\ldots,\xi),(\sigma_2,\ldots)$	$\gamma=\gamma_1\xi$
f_{SIM_v}	$(\gamma_1),(\sigma_1,\sigma_E,\xi),(\sigma_2,\ldots)$	$\gamma=\gamma_1\xi$
f_{GEN_E}	$(\eta_1),(\sigma,\tau,\sigma_E,\tau_E,\xi),(\eta_2)$	$\eta=\tau_E\eta_2\eta_1$
f_{SPEC_E}	$(\eta_1),(\sigma,\tau,\sigma_E,\tau_E,\xi),(\eta_2)$	$\eta=\sigma_E\eta_2\eta_1$
f_{SIM_E}	$(\eta_1),(\sigma,\sigma_E,\xi),(\eta_2)$	$\eta=\sigma_E\eta_2\eta_1$
f_{TRAN_E}	$(\eta_1),(\eta_2)$	$\eta=\eta_2\eta_1$
$f_{SPEC_{o\to}}$	$(\alpha_1,\bar{\alpha_1}),(\sigma,\tau,\sigma_E,\tau_E,\xi)$	$(\alpha=\alpha_1,\bar{\alpha}=\bar{\alpha_1})$
f_{MP}	$(\alpha,\bar{\alpha}),(\gamma_1),\ldots,(\gamma_n)$	$\gamma=\prod_i\gamma_i\alpha+(1-\prod_i\gamma_i)\bar{\alpha}$

4 Examples

In this section we present examples of proof rule applications in a battle ship domain (see [1]). Hierarchy of objects is presented in fig. 1.

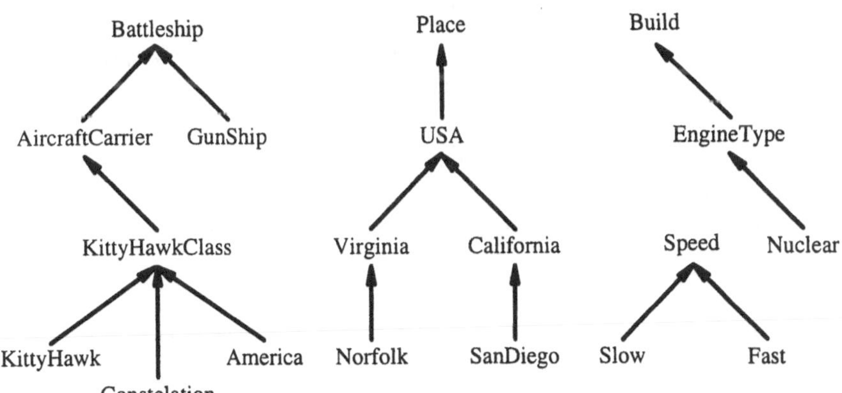

Fig. 1. Hierarchy of objects

We will start with GEN_o transformation. Let us supose, that we have information, that Kitty Hawk Class battleship is located in USA. Using object generalization, we can conclude that maybe some aircraft carrier battlesips are located there:

$$\frac{\begin{array}{l} V(KittyHawkClass, Place, USA) : (\gamma = 0.3) \\ H(KittyHawkClass, AircraftCarrier, OperateCharacteristic) \\ \quad : (\sigma = 0.33, \tau = 0.1, \sigma_E = 1, \tau_E = 0.9, \xi = \varepsilon) \\ E(AircraftCarrier, Place, AircraftCarrier, OperateCharacteristic) \\ \quad : (\eta = 0.9) \end{array}}{V(AircraftCarrier, Place, USA) : (\gamma = 0.03)}$$

Having the same information, using $SPEC_o$ rule, we can infer that maybe Constellation battleship is located in USA:

$$\frac{\begin{array}{l} V(KittyHawkClass, Place, USA) : (\gamma = 0.3) \\ H(Constellation, KittyHawkClass, OperateCharacteristic) \\ \quad : (\sigma = 0.33, \tau = 0.33, \sigma_E = 1, \tau_E = 0.9, \xi = \varepsilon) \\ E(KittyHawkClass, Place, KittyHawkClass, OperateCharacteristic) \\ \quad : (\eta = 1) \end{array}}{V(Constellation, Place, USA) : (\gamma = 0.09)}$$

Gunships are similar to aircraft carriers in the context of build. Hence from information that aircraft carriers are powered by nuclear power, we can derive, using SIM_o transformation, that maybe gunships are powered by nuclear power too:

$$\frac{\begin{array}{l} V(AircraftCarrier, EngineType, Nuclear) : (\gamma = 0.8) \\ S(Gunship, AircraftCarrier, Build) : (\sigma = 0.7, \sigma_E = 0.9, \xi = \varepsilon) \\ E(AircraftCarrier, EngineType, AircraftCarrier, Build) : (\eta = 1) \\ E(Gunship, EngineType, Gunship, Build) : (\eta = 1) \end{array}}{V(Gunship, EngineType, Nuclear) : (\gamma = 0.56)}$$

If we know that Constellation battleship is located at the Virginian coast, using GEN_v rule we can conclude, that it is anchored in USA:

$$\frac{\begin{array}{l} V(Constellation, Place, Virginia) : (\gamma = 1) \\ H(Virginia, USA, KittyHawkClass) \\ \quad : (\sigma = 0.1, \tau = 0.1, \sigma_E = \varepsilon, \tau_E = \varepsilon, \xi = 0.1) \\ H(Constellation, KittyHawkClass, OperateCharacteristic) \\ \quad : (\sigma = 0.33, \tau = 0.33, \sigma_E = 1, \tau_E = 0.9, \xi = \varepsilon) \end{array}}{V(Constellation, Place, USA) : (\gamma = 1)}$$

In the situation as above, using $SPEC_v$ we can derive, that probably it is at Norfolk:

$$\frac{\begin{array}{l} V(Constellation, Place, Virginia) : (\gamma = 1) \\ H(Norfolk, Virginia, KittyHawkClass) \\ \quad : (\sigma = \varepsilon, \tau = \varepsilon, \sigma_E = \varepsilon, \tau_E = \varepsilon, \xi = 0.9) \\ H(Constellation, KittyHawkClass, OperateCharacteristic) \\ \quad : (\sigma = 0.33, \tau = 0.33, \sigma_E = 1, \tau_E = 0.9, \xi = \varepsilon) \end{array}}{V(Constellation, Place, Norfolk) : (\gamma = 0.9)}$$

Because San Diego is similar to Norfolk in the context of battleships, if we know that some aircraft carriers can be found at Norfolk, maybe they can be found at San Diego too.

$$\frac{\begin{array}{l} V(AircraftCarrier, Place, Norfolk) : (\gamma = 0.1) \\ S(SanDiego, Norfolk, Battleship) : (\sigma = \varepsilon, \sigma_E = \varepsilon, \xi = 0.7) \\ H(AircraftCarrier, Battleship, BuildCharacteristic) \\ \quad : (\sigma = 0.9, \tau = 0.1, \sigma_E = 0.8, \tau_E = 0.7, \xi = \varepsilon) \end{array}}{V(AircraftCarrier, Place, SanDiego) : (\gamma = 0.07)}$$

To show how dependency transformation GEN_E work let us assume that speed of the aircraft carrier depends on its build. Because aircraft carrier is a battleship, we can conclude that speed of battleship depends on its build:

$$\frac{\begin{array}{l} E(AircraftCarrier, Speed, AircraftCarrier, Build) : (\eta = 0.95) \\ H(AircraftCarrier, Battleship, BuildCharacteristic) \\ \quad : (\sigma = 0.9, \tau = 0.1, \sigma_E = 0.8, \tau_E = 0.7, \xi = \varepsilon) \\ E(Battleship, Speed, Battleship, BuildCharacteristic) : (\eta = 1) \end{array}}{E(Battleship, Speed, Battleship, Build) : (\eta = 0.665)}$$

Similarly, we can specialize this dependency using $SPEC_E$ to show, that it is true for Kitty Hawk Class ships:

$$\frac{\begin{array}{l} E(AircraftCarrier, Speed, AircraftCarrier, Build) : (\eta = 0.95) \\ H(KittyHawkClass, AircraftCarrier, BuildCharacteristic) \\ \quad : (\sigma = 0.9, \tau = 0.8, \sigma_E = 1, \tau_E = 0.95, \xi = \varepsilon) \\ E(AircraftCarrier, Speed, AircraftCarrier, BuildCharacteristic) : (\eta = 1) \end{array}}{E(KittyHawkClass, Speed, Battleship, Build) : (\eta = 0.855)}$$

Using SIM_E transformation, we can show, that gunship speed depends on its build too:

$$\frac{\begin{array}{l} E(AircraftCarrier, Speed, AircraftCarrier, Build) : (\eta = 0.95) \\ S(Gunship, AircraftCarrier, BuildCharacteristic) : (\sigma = 0.4, \sigma_E = 0.8, \xi = \varepsilon) \\ E(Gunship, Speed, Gunship, BuildCharacteristic) : (\eta = 1) \end{array}}{E(Gunship, Speed, Gunship, Build) : (\eta = 0.76)}$$

If we know, that build of a aircraft carrier depends on the age of a ship, we can use $TRAN_E$ rule to conclude, that speed of aircraft carrier depends on its age:

$$\frac{\begin{array}{l} E(AircraftCarrier, Speed, AircraftCarrier, Build) : (\eta = 0.95) \\ E(AircraftCarrier, Build, AircraftCarrier, Age) : (\eta = 0.9) \end{array}}{E(AircraftCarrier, Speed, AircraftCarrier, Age) : (\eta = 0.855)}$$

Now we show implication specialization rule application. Let us suppose, that we know that if aircraft carrier has nuclear engine, it is fast. We can specialize this implication for Kitty Hawk Class aircraft carriers:

$$\frac{\begin{array}{l} V(AircraftCarrier, EngineType, Nuclear) \rightarrow V(AircraftCarrier, Speed, Fast) \\ \quad : (\alpha = 0.9, \bar{\alpha} = 0.4) \\ H(KittyHawkClass, AircraftCarrier, BuildCharacteristic) \\ \quad : (\sigma = 0.9, \tau = 0.8, \sigma_E = 1, \tau_E = 0.95, \xi = \varepsilon) \end{array}}{\begin{array}{l} V(KittyHawkClass, EngineType, Nuclear) \rightarrow V(KittyHawkClass, Speed, Fast) \\ \quad : (\alpha = 0.9, \bar{\alpha} = 0.4) \end{array}}$$

Having information that maybe Kitty Hawk Class aircraft carrier is nuclear powered, we can infer that it is fast:

$$\frac{\begin{array}{l} V(KittyHawkClass, EngineType, Nuclear) \rightarrow V(KittyHawkClass, Speed, Fast) \\ \quad : (\alpha = 0.9, \bar{\alpha} = 0.4) \\ V(KittyHawkClass, EngineType, Nuclear) : (\gamma = 0.3) \end{array}}{V(KittyHawkClass, Speed, Fast) : (\gamma = 0.55)}$$

5 Conclusions and Further Works

In the paper we have defined LPR as a labeled deductive system and presented how LPR label algebra can be constructed using probability theory. Parameters based on probability are better then one based on certainty factors, which was used in examples in [14]. Probabilities are easier to interpret and to assign.

Further research will concern formalism extensions such as adding uncertainty to other relations (e.g. hierarchy) to represent uncertain sources of knowledge; adding negation symbol to the language and developing new proof rules. Important extension would be aggregation of proofs, because the same conclusion inferred from several different sources should be more certain then formula inferred from one source.

Simultaneously computer program using this theory should be developed, what would give the possibility of testing theory on practical knowledge bases.

References

1. N. W. Alkharouf and R. S. Michalski. Multistrategy task-adaptive learning using dynamically interlaced hierarchies: A methodology and initial implementation of interlace. In *Proceedings of the Third International Workshop on Multistrategy Learning*, 1996.
2. D. Boehm-Davis, K. Dontas, and R. S. Michalski. *A Validation and Exploration of the Collins-Michalski Theory of Plausible Reasoning*. Reports of the Machine Learning and Inference Laboratory. George Mason University, 1990.
3. A. Collins and R. S. Michalski. The logic of plausible reasoning: A core theory. *Cognitive Science*, 13:1–49, 1989.
4. D. M. Gabbay. *LDS – Labeled Deductive Systems*. Oxford University Press, 1991.
5. J. Y. Halpern. An analisys of first-order logics of probability. *Artificial Intelligence*, 46:311–350, 1990.
6. R. Jeffrey. *The Logic of Decision*. Unicersity of Chicago Press, second edition, 1983.
7. D. Koller and A. Pfeffer. Probabilistic frame-based systems. In *AAAI/IAAI*, pages 580–587, 1998.
8. J. Łukasiewicz. Many-valued systems of propositional logic. In S. McCall, editor, *Polish logic*. Oxford University Press, 1967.
9. Z. Pawlak. Rough sets. *Int. J. Comp. Inf. Sci.*, 11:344–356, 1982.
10. J. Pearl. Fusion, propagation, and structuring in bayesian networks. *Artificial Intelligence*, 29:241–288, 1986.

11. D. Pool. Probabilistic horn abduction and bayesian networks. *Artificial Intelligence*, 64:81–129, 1993.
12. G. Shafer. *A Mathematical Theory of Evidence*. Princeton University Press, 1976.
13. H. Shortliffe and B. G. Buchanan. A model of inexact reasoning in medicine. *Mathematical Biosciences*, 23:351–379, 1975.
14. B. Śnieżyński. Verification of the logic of plausible reasoning. In M. Kłopotek et al., editor, *Intelligent Information Systems 2001*, Advances in Soft Computing. Physica-Verlag, Springer, 2001.
15. L. A. Zadeh. Fuzzy sets. *Information and Control*, 8:338–353, 1965.

Expert Preferences Evaluation

Zbigniew Świątnicki

Department of Logistic Management, Logistics Institute
Military University of Technology
Kaliskiego 2, 00-908 Warsaw, Poland
zswiat@wat.waw.pl

Abstract. The problem of knowledge acquisition from domain experts is discussed in this paper. It presents basic methods of knowledge acquisition, and introduces a formal description of these methods. The way of using basic methods for improvement of knowledge gathering is also described.

Keywords. AI foundations, cognitive modeling, common sense, creativity support, expert system, information gathering, knowledge acquisition.

1 Introduction

The study concerning the expert knowledge modeling is one of the branches of research concerning the artificial intelligence. It is especially used for expert system development. The expert system is usually defined as "***the computer program, which uses knowledge and inference procedures for solving such problems, which are difficult enough to require the essential human expertise for solving them***" [2].

The expert system simulates processes of problem solving performed by human experts. Designing the expert system the knowledge of one or more experts has to be grasped and gathered in such a way that it can be used to solve the problems. The expert system contains knowledge of one or more human-experts and uses this knowledge for solving the problems. Such an idea is radically different from approaching to problem solving in the traditional computer systems.

The base for problem solving is the expert knowledge about probability of future events or stages of processes. The subjective evaluation of risk is usually included.

The previous stages are the premises of future condition prediction. The statistical analysis (and similar methods) could be used. But in most cases, the expert opinions are essential.

The expert system is assumed to simulate the expert reasoning in the process of solving problems concerning a specific branch of knowledge. Human experts have some specific characteristics, which predestined them to this name:

- they learn, using acquired experience,
- they use their own common sense (even contrary to appearances),
- they have intuition,
- they may reason on the basis of analogy.

These characteristics we want to "inoculate" to the expert system. The implementation of such characteristics in the system differentiates them other, "classic" computer systems. Any activities meant to acquire knowledge characterize only the human being. Up to now the computer systems (including expert systems) do not have such characteristics. Sometimes, mastering of that knowledge in a short time by one human-expert is almost impossible, and - after all – we can employ many such experts. By replacing their knowledge through the expert systems it is possible to handle invaluable service even with the help of less qualified personnel.

"***The common sense***" is not a very precise conception, like any problems concerning with modeling of the human thinking. The common sense principles are hard to verbalize (clear presentation through using words), and harder even to formalize (records using formulas or presentation using models). An example of such a principle may be a statement "have the restricted confidence to the observed facts - they may occasionally be false". Generally the typical computer systems are designed by using the precise mathematical models without regard for such operation conditions. Thus, an expert system that is able to have the critical evaluation of the facts will be of a considerable advantage.

An extremely important problem in designing expert systems is modeling of the ***intuition***. There are many areas of human activities where the intuition has the fundamental importance for the success of affairs. For example, forecasting, the trends on the stock market requires some high intuition. The ability to associate the indefinable facts (sometimes even without specific basis) is also the proof of the high level of the thought processes. Imitating this kind of human reasoning with utilization of the computer systems is therefore especially complicated.

Designing the expert system needs the close co-operation between a designer and an expert. It is not an easy task at all. Fortunately, experts have different approaches to the problem of expert system designing. According to Keller [5], they may be: willing and clever, uninterested, incompetent or hostile.

Certainly, each designer should wish to meet only the first category of experts, but not always can one expert have so much luck. If experts are willing and clever, then even in spite of their incompetence it is possible for them to obtain much information concerning facts existing in the specific domain of knowledge[1]. Knowledge concerning reasoning (problem solving) is basically harder to get from the expert and even the willing expert (but incompetent) does not bring much to the expert knowledge on that subject.

Uninterested competent expert is a very valuable source of information for the knowledge engineer. Putting questions properly and not overloading with the sec-

---

[1] For instance, production standards do not have to be known to the expert but, generally, he knows in which document they could be found.

ond-rate information[2] it is possible to acquire essential information, especially regarding the methods of problem solving (knowledge about facts may be achieved by other means).

Unfortunately, we have no methods to deal with the expert frustration on problems of modeling the human reasoning (as well as supplementing human being in solving even some of the problems). Such experts should be avoided in the process of knowledge acquisition concerning the design of the expert system. Furthermore, for fear of deprivation of their importance they might even mislead the system designer (knowledge engineer) with intention to compromise the designed expert system.

In view of the above-mentioned problems with acquiring knowledge from experts, the knowledge engineer has to be a properly educated and experienced person. According to Feigenbaum [2] he must possess:

- experience in computer hardware and software,
- experience in computer programming,
- wide general knowledge,
- psychological experience,
- basic information concerning the branch of knowledge for which the designed system is assigned.

These characteristics and the knowledge of the expert systems engineering enable the knowledge engineer to design efficient and useful tools.

2 Methods of Expert Knowledge Acquisition

The problem of knowledge acquisition in the expert systems gains more and more importance. It results from the fact that the expert system has a limited knowledge base at its disposal. Even if it were equipped with an extended inference engine, it would be less effective than a similar one with a developed knowledge base.

Knowledge has some characteristics that are not so easy to master. For example, it is generally dispersed. Its elements are placed on different carriers and in various sources, making it almost impossible for the person not fully oriented in the specific field to acquired all the knowledge (and such a person is undoubtedly a potential designer of the expert system - the knowledge engineer). As a result of this, knowledge is difficult to gather.

It is difficult to use knowledge. Even if its basic elements are mastered, there may be substantial difficulties in utilizing them to solve a specific problem. In many cases there are difficulties in accessing (copying) the knowledge. It has to be remembered, however, that the case is not in the distribution of facts but in spreading the consciousness of relations between them and being a master in utilizing these relations.

---

2 Which usually could be achieved from a less competent expert or, for instance, from written sources.

Using the knowledge from a given domain it is often believed to be insufficient for practical purposes. Knowledge happens to be unclear or uncertain, as well as having inconsistencies occurring in it (contradictions). It could not be omitted because the knowledge is changing (its elements are seldom fixed once and for ever). Thus, this requires supplementing the knowledge base and verification both by its new elements and with those which already existed earlier in the knowledge base.

Up to the present time, the human mind has managed quite well with the above problems - however, not always to the full extent). Our mind is precise and easy to use (for its owner). The human memory is quite retentive and fast (where it concerns the speed of reproduction of knowledge and its processing). The human mind is on continuous alert and shows activity - for example, in detecting contradictions and incompleteness of knowledge.

As mentioned before, there have been difficulties in gathering and utilizing knowledge from one side, and the advantages of the human expert from the other side, causing an interest in using the human expert in the process of knowledge acquisition.

In the initial stage of development of the expert systems there was a problem of knowledge acquisition that was a margin of the interest to the knowledge engineers. As the time passed, the recognition of its value had arisen. Knowledge acquisition was found to be very time-consuming and ineffective. As a result of these studies, its acquisition has become one of the main problems of the expert system engineering.

It is important to distinguish at least a few reasons for the development of the formal methods in knowledge acquisition, and these are:

- reluctance of the experts to co-operate,
- unconsciousness of what somebody knows,
- errors in the course of verbalization of knowledge by experts,
- substantial differences between human thinking and the processing of knowledge in the expert system,
- necessity of a knowledge engineer's presence during the knowledge verbalization by the expert.

The necessity to overcome the above mentioned difficulties has brought forward the elaboration of many methods of knowledge acquisition.

The basic methods of knowledge acquisition are generally useful at the stage when being designed and during preparation of the expert system prototype. Their essence lies in gathering (from domain experts) the knowledge necessary to create the "shell" of the newly designed system. With the use of the manual methods found in the next stages of the expert system, the result is rather limited, although it cannot be excluded.

In simple cases the knowledge acquisition is reduced itself to placing the knowledge elements (represented as rules, triplets, frames, semantic networks or adequate hybrid) in the knowledge base. Such method of knowledge acquisition requires co-operation between the domain expert (who is the source of knowledge) and the knowledge engineer. The latter has to gain information and place it in an adequate knowledge base (having all the time for figuring the future functions of the system).

The most popular manual methods of knowledge acquisition are:

- interview,
- report analysis,
- going through the problem,
- questionnaire,
- expert report,
- brainstorming.

The experience gained in designing and creating the expert systems shows that the most effective pattern of knowledge acquisition is the analysis of examples and counter-examples. The examples consist of the base in the inductive process for gaining broader conclusions (rules creation). The set of examples is a sufficient base for creating the new knowledge (without any additional external sources). Nonetheless, this new knowledge may not be absolutely correct. Because of this it is necessary to verify this set, especially by comparing it with the checked knowledge gathered previously in the system.

An ***interview*** is most often an initial stage of the knowledge acquisition. It becomes a conversation between the knowledge engineer and the domain expert. Interviews may be divided into two main groups:

- □ non-structural interviews,
- □ structural interviews.

A ***non-structural interview*** is considered generally as a preliminary one. The expert is not limited by the knowledge engineer as it concerns the subject of the statement. His task is to tell the "story" about the problem using his own ideas and phrases. He may define his own conception of solving the problem, suggesting in this way to the knowledge engineer the shape of the future solutions in the expert system. In this type of interview the position of the expert is prevailing, the knowledge engineer is generally only the listener (but often he has to assist the expert to articulate his knowledge in the way that is useful later in designing of the expert system).

In a ***structural interview*** the positions of its participants are reversed - the knowledge engineer is the one directing the interview. He asks the questions about specific problems (using usually the knowledge acquired during a previously executed non-structural interview). The expert has the task to be objective in formulating his answers (the knowledge engineer should be encouraged to give appropriate answers to the selected questions)[3].

The higher form of the knowledge acquisition is called a ***report analysis***. It consists of expert's acquaintance with the reports prepared by the experts during problem solving. Reports should contain the essential steps undertaken by the ex-

---

[3] It is not possible, for example, to ask the expert, how does he make the decisions, as it is usually too general a question, and the answer will be too general. It is better to ask about the premises (bases) of the decisions, but even answers for these questions may require questions for further details. In the original shape they are not sufficient for fitting the knowledge base and designing the inference engine.

pert (for example, the analysis of the problem, evaluation of the situation and decision making). Experts may prepare the reports single-handedly or jointly, with the knowledge engineer (this second form often enables better understanding of the ways for problem solving by the expert).

There is a direct participation in the process of solving the problem (and what comes with that process is the practical acquaintance with the proceedings and rules that govern them) which secures the knowledge engineer's process for ***going through the problem***. The knowledge engineer occurres in this case as an executor (student), and the expert as a supervisor (instructor). The engineer is directed by the expert, and the consecutive steps are prompted by him. He may at the same time ask questions regarding the stages essential to solve the problems. "Going through the problem" seems to be the most effective way to acquire the knowledge about the strategy of problem solving (after it was previously oriented to the subject branch, for example during the interview).

A specific sort of the interview executed by the knowledge engineer among experts is a ***questionnaire***. Answers for the questions put in the questionnaires give the engineer a great amount of knowledge concerning the problem and its solution. They are valuable because the engineer has formulated questions forcing to extract the knowledge. Generally, answers become more valuable information if the questions are shorter. Not only at the ground of the questionnaires the knowledge engineer has the possibility to acquire new conceptions. Additionally, the expert may comment on the answers and evaluate their correctness. Thus, other questions can be suggested for making knowledge more general (which may be hard for the knowledge engineer if he should execute it incorrectly).

The ***expert report*** apart from the formal resemblance to report analyses, is a qualitative and different method of knowledge acquisition. It is not the report style of problem solving (as in the case of the report analyses). The description of data and rules necessary for solving the problem, as well as the strategy, proceeding stages and expected results are expressed[4]. The knowledge engineer may help the expert to make the report, preparing a set of some previously known facts and rules, and indicating the expected relations between them (for example concerning connections between their positive and negative features).

Brainstorming is a method that is very well known as a result of designing other types of computer systems. Its base can be gathering as many experts as possible in one place and at the same time. They should have different qualifications and various opinions on solving the related problems. During the "brainstorming", experts have the opportunity to discuss freely and exchange their opinions (ideas). The task of the knowledge engineer is a skilful registration of the needed information.

---

[4] So it perfectly suits the purpose of the diagnostic system creating process - for example for diagnosing the defects in the technique devices.

Conclusion

The basic methods of expert knowledge acquisition discussed above are the first step on the way towards the automatic methods of knowledge acquisition. We may separate them into the intermediate shape - ***semi-automatic methods***. In this case the expert has the possibility of dialogue with the system. He may in this case solve the problems (examples) or provide answers to the system questions. The whole internal structure is not "visible" either for the expert, or for the knowledge engineer. The knowledge acquisition module is able to input the knowledge introduced by the expert (for example as question-answer relations) to the base, according to the representation adapted by the knowledge engineer.

The semi-automatic methods of knowledge acquisition have as their assumption co-operation of the system with the expert (and even with a direct user - who is especially able to express knowledge not only in contact with the expert but also during the regular, standard work of the system). The system has the target to verify and arrange the knowledge gained from the user. It explores simultaneously its redundancy and possible contradictions. In doubtful cases, the system may ask additional questions. In this way the acquired knowledge is generally correct (although it may be incomplete). The semi-automatic acquisition of knowledge is connected usually with so-called machine learning. It relies on knowledge acquisition during dialogue of the expert system with the expert or user. As the knowledge acquisition is performed in this case by multiple analysis of the particular cases (examples), the semi-automatic methods of knowledge acquisition are sometimes identified as system training.

The most sophisticated methods of knowledge acquisition are the ***automatic methods***. The presence of the expert or the knowledge engineer is not necessary. The extraction of the new knowledge is performed by using knowledge previously introduced. Therefore, there is no need to make contact with the system surrounding. Procedures of knowledge acquisition may work automatically by analyzing the knowledge gathered in the knowledge base. The behavior of these procedures is directed mainly at detection and deletion of redundancies and contradictions in the knowledge base. The knowledge acquired in an automatic way is currently used in the system's activities for problem solving.

Notwithstanding the substantial progress in the area of designing and implementing the expert systems, they are still not the perfect tools. In many situations they already have ability for autonomic solutions to complicated problems, but human supervision is demanded in almost every case. A big step has been achieved in transferring features of the human being (knowledge, intuition and reasoning) to the computer systems. It was done thanks to methodological foundations of designing and implementation of expert systems. But it is still the long way to design a fully intelligent system. The expert systems are the only bridge for creating an artificial intelligence.

References

[1] Addis T.R.: *Designing Knowledge-Based Systems*, Tab Books Inc., 1986

[2] Feigenbaum E.A.: *Artificial Intelligence: An Overview of Knowledge Engineering and Expert Systems*, Artificial Intelligence Satellite Symposium, Dallas, 1985

[3] Ignizio J.: *Introduction to Expert Systems*, McGraw-Hill Inc., 1991

[4] Jackson P.: *Introduction to Expert Systems*, Addison-Wesley Publ. Comp., 1988

[5] Keller R.: *Expert System Technology*, Yourdon Press, 1987

[6] Świątnicki W., Świątnicki Z.: *Intelligent weapons* (in Polish), Bellona Pub., 1992

[7] Świątnicki Z.: *Expert Systems. Introduction*, Bellona Pub., 1997

[8] Waterman D.A.: *A Guide to Expert Systems*, Addison-Wesley Publ. Comp., 1986

A Non-monotone Logic for Reasoning about Action[1]

Marek A. Bednarczyk

Instytut Podstaw Informatyki PAN, Gdańsk
m.bednarczyk@ipipan.gda.pl

Abstract. A logic for reasoning about action is presented. The logic is based on the idea that *explicit substitutions* can be seen as atomic formulae describing basic change of state of a system. The logic is non-monotone, i.e., it does not admit weakening in its presentation as a fragment of non-commutative linear logic. Potential applications of the logic are also discussed in connection to the "Frame Problem".

1 Introduction

The need to reason about actions, for instance to be able to predict their effects, was recognized as a central issue already at the beginning of Artificial Intelligence, see [21]. The quest for an appropriate formalism continues, which indicates that the problem is not only fundamental, but also difficult. Originally, cf. [21], McCarthy and Hayes identified actions with *imperative programs*. Later, the trend moved toward more abstract formalisms, in which actions are abstract entities subject to characterization within a *logical framework*. Today, the latter approach, often based on logic programming with negation as failure ([9]), seems to underly most of the work in the area.

The aim of this paper is to present a formal system which comprises the following components.

- A *logic* to describe and to reason about changes of the world.
- A *language* to define actions.
- A *logical framework* whose judgments relate actions to the changes caused.

In AI the work in this direction has already been initiated by Gelfond and Lifschitz. Our starting point is $\mathcal{A}$, their *action calculus* developed in [12]. The calculus, and its recent extensions, is also explained in terms of logic programming. Thus, although the objectives beyond $\mathcal{A}$ are quite similar, the principles underlying the calculus are quite different.

$\mathcal{A}$ can be characterized as follows.

It is *axiomatic*. Actions, represented by action symbols, are characterized within the formal system by stipulating a number of axioms. The axioms describe the effect that an execution of an action has on the validity of certain properties.

$\mathcal{A}$ is, essentially, *propositional*, i.e., the properties are formed from propositional symbols and their negations. In fact, in some recent extensions, like $\mathcal{AR}$ ([10]), a step is taken towards descriptions based on predicate logic. Nevertheless, it is important to note that the calculus does admit a propositional presentation, whereas our logical framework relies on the first order features.

[1] Partially supported by State Committee for Scientific Research grant 8 T11C 037 16.

The formal comparison between our proposal and $\mathcal{A}$ would certainly exceed the scope of this note. Here, we use the calculus in its original form mainly as a vehicle to convey ideas. There are two kinds of judgments in $\mathcal{A}$: value propositions and effect propositions. In the sequel, the different fonts are used to distinguish between the different syntactic classes.

Value propositions postulate that F would hold after executing a sequence of actions, first action $\mathtt{A}_1$, then action $\mathtt{A}_2$, and so on, until $\mathtt{A}_n$. Write

$$F \textbf{ after } \mathtt{A}_1, \ldots, \mathtt{A}_n \qquad \textit{and} \qquad \textbf{initially } F \tag{1}$$

where F is a *fluent expression*, i.e., a propositional variable or its negation, and $\mathtt{A}_1$, ..., $\mathtt{A}_n$ a sequence, possibly empty, of *action names*. The second form is an abbreviation of the first when $n = 0$.

Effect propositions are used to capture the idea that under assumption that all *preconditions* P_1, ..., P_n hold before initiating action $\mathtt{A}$, then F holds upon its termination. They take two forms

$$\mathtt{A} \textbf{ causes } F \textbf{ if } P_1, \ldots, P_n \qquad \textit{and} \qquad \mathtt{A} \textbf{ causes } F \tag{2}$$

Again, the second abbreviates the first when $\mathtt{A}$ always causes F, i.e., when $n = 0$.

Many examples, considered as benchmarks in the area, have been represented in $\mathcal{A}$. For instance, the domain of the famous Yale Shooting problem, cf. [16], has been described in [12] as follows. There are two (propositional) fluent names: *Loaded* and *Alive*, and three action names: `Load`, `Shoot` and `Wait`.

$$\begin{array}{ll} \textbf{initially } \neg \textit{Loaded} & \mathtt{Load} \textbf{ causes } \textit{Loaded} \\ \textbf{initially } \textit{Alive} & \mathtt{Shoot} \textbf{ causes } \neg \textit{Loaded} \\ & \mathtt{Shoot} \textbf{ causes } \neg \textit{Alive} \textbf{ if } \textit{Loaded} \end{array} \tag{3}$$

Thus, in this domain we have some knowledge about the effects of performing actions `Load` and `Shoot`, but nothing is said about `Wait`.

The Frame Problem concerns the existence, within a formal framework, of a mechanism to incorporate the common sense axiom of *inertia*, viz., the property that things tend to stay as they are, and that it is the change of the state that is exceptional. Here, the Frame Problem can be readily described as the difficulty to formally describe within the framework of $\mathcal{A}$ that `Wait` does not interfere with the validity of fluents *Loaded* and *Alive*. We could, in principle, extend (3) by adding the following clauses.

$$\begin{array}{ll} \mathtt{Wait} \textbf{ causes } \textit{Loaded} \textbf{ if } \textit{Loaded} & \mathtt{Wait} \textbf{ causes } \textit{Alive} \textbf{ if } \textit{Alive} \\ \mathtt{Wait} \textbf{ causes } \neg\textit{Loaded} \textbf{ if } \neg\textit{Loaded} & \mathtt{Wait} \textbf{ causes } \neg\textit{Alive} \textbf{ if } \neg\textit{Alive} \end{array} \tag{4}$$

But this solution has several disadvantages.

The description of `Wait` is context dependent, and thus not immediately *reusable*. If, for instance, one would want to consider an extension of the Yale Shooting domain where new fluents are added, one would need to add new axioms of inertia for each new fluent.

Secondly, as argued already in [21], this leads to combinatorial explosion of the size of domain descriptions.

Above all, it is not elegant and annoying to be forced to state the obvious. That is why Gelfond and Lifschitz rejected (4). At the same time their semantics treats actions with no informative description, like `Wait`, as fully inertial. Thus, semantically, `Wait` does satisfy (4). As a byproduct, the resulting system is non-monotone: the empty description of `Wait` entails all of (4). However, changing the description of `Wait` by adding, say, just the first judgment of (4) would *decrease* the set of properties enjoyed by action `Wait`.

It remains to provide a deductive machinery sound with respect to the above semantics. For this purpose in [12] the authors propose to use extended logic programs, cf. [11, 23] as the target language in which the descriptions of $\mathcal{A}$ could be interpreted. Indeed, the main result of [12] is that the proposed interpretation is semantically sound, although not complete. But the use of logic programming as the target language introduces its limitations, despite all the recent advancements. Also, after translating judgments of $\mathcal{A}$ into logic programs one requires a backward translation in order to reinterpret the results in terms of $\mathcal{A}$.

It seems that the best solution would be to reason on the level of $\mathcal{A}$-judgments. Our aim here is to propose a deductive system that offers this potential. Section 2 introduces a logic $\mathrm{LP}_{\sigma}^{=}$ to describe changes, i.e., the effects of actions. This is a non-commutative sub-structural logic of predicates with equality and explicit substitutions, see [2]. It is also shown how the Frame Problem is tackled within $\mathrm{LP}_{\sigma}^{=}$. Section 3 presents the proof-theoretic semantics of $\mathrm{LP}_{\sigma}^{=}$. Its mathematical semantics is vaguely described, for more details the reader should consult full version of the paper. Section 4 introduces a language of actions, formalizes its semantics. It also relates the semantics of actions to the semantics of descriptions from $\mathrm{LP}_{\sigma}^{=}$, by introducing the relation of *satisfaction* between the extensions of actions and descriptions. A formal system to reason about the satisfaction is also introduced here.

It is a pleasure to thank Halina and Teodor Przymusiński for stimulating discussions.

2 Informal presentation of the logic of descriptions

Returning to the Yale Shooting problem, let us postulate, again, that there are two fluent names: `ldd` and `alv`, and three action names: `Load`, `Shoot` and `Wait`.

The first modification with respect to (3) is, seemingly, trivial. We assume that the fluents are not propositional, but (potentially) multi-valued. To recapture the original situation assume that for both fluents `alv` and `ldd` the allowed values are the same, and range over the set {`yes`, `no`}. We now have to use the *equality* predicate to formulate the facts, for instance *Loaded* becomes `ldd` = `yes`.

This small modification changes the meaning of the *effect* of an action. Before, actions directly changed the set of facts that hold. Now, they do it indirectly — each fact is a predicate that refers to some attributes. The validity of a fact changes with accord to the changes of *assignment* of values to the attributes. Thus, within this framework we can use (simple) imperative programming notation to code basic actions — just like McCarthy did in [21]. For instance, the action of loading can be succinctly *defined* by:

$$\texttt{Load}: \qquad \texttt{ldd} := \texttt{yes} \tag{5}$$

The second, and crucial novelty is to use the finer nature of fluents, and allow the substitutions to be used explicitly within the formalism. Normally, substitutions are relegated to the meta-level in the studies into logics. Here, we postulate that they should be used as the dynamic logical counterpart of actions. Notation $\left[\frac{e}{\mathtt{a}}\right]$ is used to denote the *explicit substitution* of an expression e, for an attribute $\mathtt{a}$. The usual *meta-substitution* of expression e for a fluent $\mathtt{a}$ in a fact F is denoted $F[e/\mathtt{a}]$. For instance, *Loaded*$[\mathtt{yes}/\mathtt{ldd}]$ results in $\mathtt{yes} = \mathtt{yes}$. It is convenient to introduce a special constant Υ with the same meaning as that of an *identity sybstitutions* of the form $\left[\frac{\mathtt{a}}{\mathtt{a}}\right]$. Now, with 'dynamic' formulae like substitutions on the descriptive, or logical side, we can easily capture the essence of an assignment action. Intuitively, the effect of loading (5) is fully captured by the following correspondence.

$$\mathtt{Load}\ \ \boldsymbol{sat}\ \left[\frac{\mathtt{ldd}}{\mathtt{yes}}\right] \tag{6}$$

In the sequel, judgments like (6) are used to indicate that action $\mathtt{Load}$ *satisfies* formula $\left[\frac{\mathtt{ldd}}{\mathtt{yes}}\right]$, which is called *specification* of the action.

2.1 Temporal projection

We have not discussed this issue in case of $\mathcal{A}$, but now the idea is simple. Assume action $\mathtt{A}$ and action description Φ are given such that $\mathtt{A}\ \ \boldsymbol{sat}\ \ \Phi$. Further suppose that a precondition P and a fact F are given. We can capture the intuition behind a clause $\mathtt{A}$ **causes** F **if** P in $\mathcal{A}$, see (2), with the following consequence.

$$P \vdash \Phi \odot F \tag{7}$$

Above, $\odot$ denotes the *application* of the dynamic formula Φ to a static fact F. In case Φ is an explicit substitution the application should correspond to *internalization* of the substitution:

$$\left[\frac{v}{\mathtt{a}}\right] \odot F \dashv\vdash F[v/\mathtt{a}] \quad \textit{and} \quad \Upsilon \odot F \dashv\vdash F \tag{8}$$

Thus, in the case considered above, with F equal *Loaded*, Φ equal $\left[\frac{\mathtt{ldd}}{\mathtt{yes}}\right]$, we can deduce that after loading the gun will always be loaded, since

$$\mathtt{yes} = \mathtt{yes} \dashv\vdash (\mathtt{ldd} = \mathtt{yes})[\mathtt{yes}/\mathtt{ldd}] \dashv\vdash \left[\frac{\mathtt{yes}}{\mathtt{ldd}}\right] \odot (\mathtt{ldd} = \mathtt{yes})$$

as required.

2.2 The Yale Shooting Problem revisited

The fragments of the general framework introduced so far is almost sufficient to describe a solution to the Yale Shooting Problem. Its domain can be presented as follows.

$$\vdash \neg\texttt{ldd} = \texttt{yes} \tag{9}$$

$$\vdash \texttt{alv} = \texttt{yes} \tag{10}$$

$$\texttt{Load}\ \ sat\ \left[\frac{\texttt{yes}}{\texttt{ldd}}\right] \tag{11}$$

$$\texttt{Shoot}\ \ sat\ \left((\texttt{ldd} = \texttt{yes})\ \&\ \left[\frac{\texttt{no}}{\texttt{ldd}}\right] \odot \left[\frac{\texttt{no}}{\texttt{alv}}\right]\right) \oplus ((\neg\texttt{ldd} = \texttt{yes})\ \&\ \Upsilon) \tag{12}$$

$$\texttt{Wait}\ \ sat\ \Upsilon \tag{13}$$

Condition (9) intends to capture that the gun is initially not loaded. Similarly, (10) says that the bird is initially alive. Condition (11) characterizes the action of loading. We have already discussed how the temporal projection that the gun will be loaded after loading can be derived from (11).

The remaining two conditions deserve a separate discussion. Before dwelling into it let us make a quick remark. Namely, the above presentation is equally uncommitted as to the real *nature* of actions `Load`, `Shoot` and `Wait`, as (3). It just stipulates that each of them should satisfy certain axioms.

2.3 The Frame Problem revisited

There are two important differences between (3) and (9)-(13).

The first relates to the treatment of the `Wait` action. In (3) it is simply not mentioned, and the task of making it inertial is relegated to the semantical level. Above, condition (13) provides a specification for `Wait` in the form of the *identity substitution*, which we denote Υ.

The essence of the identity substitution, partially captured by (8), is that it is the neutral element of '$\odot$'. Therefore, for any fact F, and for all those mentioned in (4) in particular, we should be able to *derive* a consequence $F \vdash \Upsilon \odot F$ for each instance of `Wait` **causes** F **if** F in (4) due to the following.

$$F \dashv\vdash \Upsilon \odot F$$

Thus, an action like `Wait` that satisfies Υ is fully inertial.

The other difference with (3) is that in our new formalization there is just one axiom (12) that describes the behavior of the shooting action. It is more complex, since it intends to capture *all* essential properties of `Shoot`. Axiom (12) is a disjunction of two formulæ. Each disjunct describing the effects of the shooting action in accord to whether the gun has been loaded or not. In the first case, if the gun was loaded, the effect is to unload it, and to make the bird dead. If, however, the gun is not loaded, nothing happens.

Again, the identity substitution comes in handy to describe inertia. What is worth stressing, the inertia kind of behavior is exhibited only under some assumptions, namely that the gun was not loaded.

Finally, let us verify that axiom (12) allows to deduce the consequences corresponding to the specification of `Shoot` in $\mathcal{A}$ with accord to the translation given by (7). Now, *Loaded* is now interpreted as $\texttt{ldd} = \texttt{yes}$, while $\neg$*Alive* is now interpreted as $\neg\texttt{alv} = \texttt{yes}$, which is equivalent to $\texttt{alv} = \texttt{no}$.

Let us impose distributivity laws between composition '$\odot$' on one hand, and disjunction and conjunctions on the other.

$$(\Phi \,\&\, \Psi) \odot \Xi \dashv\vdash \Phi \odot \Xi \,\&\, \Psi \odot \Xi \tag{14}$$

$$(\Phi \oplus \Psi) \odot \Xi \dashv\vdash \Phi \odot \Xi \oplus \Psi \odot \Xi \tag{15}$$

Also, let us assume that facts are *Platonic.* That is to say that when used in composition on the left they subsume everything on the right.

$$F \odot \Phi \dashv\vdash F \tag{16}$$

Then, under these assumptions, we can indeed derive the expected consequences.

In the sequel let Φ equal $\Phi^{+} \oplus \Phi^{-}$, with Φ^{+} and Φ^{-} equal to $(\texttt{ldd} = \texttt{yes})$ & $\left[\frac{\texttt{no}}{\texttt{ldd}}\right] \odot \left[\frac{\texttt{no}}{\texttt{alv}}\right]$ and $(\neg\texttt{ldd} = \texttt{yes})$ & Υ, respectively. Above, and in the sequel, we assume that the biding precedence is the following, from the strongest binding to the weakest: $= \prec \odot \prec \& \prec \oplus$.

Let us consider axiom **Shoot causes** $\neg$*Alive* **if** *Loaded* which seems most interesting. Here, with accord to (7), we should derive *Loaded* $\vdash \Phi \odot \neg$*Alive*.

$$\dfrac{\dfrac{\dfrac{\dfrac{\dfrac{}{\texttt{ldd=yes} \vdash \texttt{ldd=yes}}(i)}{\texttt{ldd=yes} \vdash (\texttt{ldd=yes}) \odot (\texttt{alv=no})}(c) \qquad \dfrac{\dfrac{\dfrac{}{\texttt{ldd} = \texttt{yes} \vdash \texttt{no=no}}(\top)}{\texttt{ldd} = \texttt{yes} \vdash \left[\frac{\texttt{no}}{\texttt{ldd}}\right] \odot \texttt{no=no}}}{\texttt{ldd=yes} \vdash \left[\frac{\texttt{no}}{\texttt{ldd}}\right] \odot \left[\frac{\texttt{no}}{\texttt{alv}}\right] \odot (\texttt{alv=no})}}{\texttt{ldd=yes} \vdash (\texttt{ldd=yes}) \odot (\texttt{alv=no}) \,\&\, \left[\frac{\texttt{no}}{\texttt{ldd}}\right] \odot \left[\frac{\texttt{no}}{\texttt{alv}}\right] \odot (\texttt{alv=no})}(R\&)}{\texttt{ldd=yes} \vdash \Phi^{+} \odot (\texttt{alv=no})}(b)}{\dfrac{\texttt{ldd=yes} \vdash \Phi^{+} \odot (\texttt{alv=no}) \oplus \Phi^{-} \odot (\texttt{alv=no})}{\texttt{ldd} = \texttt{yes} \vdash \Phi \odot (\texttt{alv} = \texttt{no})}(a)}$$

The justification of the above semi-formal deductions requires a formal underpinning that is presented in the subsequent section. Now, let us just remark, that for instance derivation (a) is an abbreviation of a more formal deduction which applies one of the postulated distributivity axioms, and the cut rule. Indeed, let $(\oplus\odot)$ denote the following instance of distributivity: $\Phi^{+} \odot (\texttt{alv} = \texttt{no}) \oplus \Phi^{-} \odot (\texttt{alv} = \texttt{no} \vdash (\Phi^{+} \oplus \Phi^{-}) \odot (\texttt{alv} = \texttt{no}$. Then (a) really means the following.

$$\dfrac{\texttt{ldd} = \texttt{yes} \vdash \Phi^{+} \odot (\texttt{alv} = \texttt{no}) \oplus \Phi^{-} \odot (\texttt{alv} = \texttt{no}) \qquad (\oplus\odot)}{\texttt{ldd} = \texttt{yes} \vdash \Phi \odot (\texttt{alv} = \texttt{no})}$$

Now, derivation (b) is a similar abbreviation, but this time it is concerned with the right distributivity if $\odot$ over &. Also derivation (c) corresponds to the cut applied to the stipulated axiom $F \vdash F \otimes \Gamma$, for facts F.

All the remaining derivation steps correspond to the normal proof-theoretic treatment of a logical system. Thus, (i) corresponds to the identity, or reflexivity axiom, while $(\top)$ corresponds to $\texttt{a} = \texttt{a}$ being an axiom of the usual theory based on equality. Finally, $(R\&)$ stems from application of the rule introducing conjunction on the right of a sequent. All the above is formalised in the sequel.

3 Logic of predicates with explicit substitutions

Substitution is normally considered as a part of the meta-theory of a logic. This applies not only to logics, but to λ-calculæ and type theories as well. It has been recently realized that more efficient implementations of functional languages can be achieved if one better controls the process of performing a substitution. This calls for frameworks with substitution as a *primitive operation.* Indeed, a variety of λ-calculæ with explicit substitutions have already been considered. All of them are 2-sorted — the old syntactic class of λ-*terms* is retained while a new class of *substitutions* is added.

The logic of predicates has already two sorts: the sort of *terms* and, built over terms, the sort of *formulæ.* So far nobody has considered adding explicit substitutions to it via a new syntactic sort. All attempts known to the author use the idea that substitutions behave as modal operators, see e.g., [22]. In section 2 we have given good reasons to consider substitutions as a new kind of atomic formulæ with a dynamic character. We have also postulated a new logical connective '$\odot$' which should subsume the usual operation of composition on substitutions. The idea is to follow Lambek ([18]) and Girard ([13]), and to consider a substructural logic, i.e., a logic deprived of some of the usual structural rules. Then, the usual classical connectives split into two variations: additive and multiplicative. It is time to make these ideas formal.

3.1 Syntax

Formulæ of the logic of action descriptions, which is called $\mathrm{LP}^{=}_{\sigma}$ in the sequel, are given by the following grammar.

$\Phi = \sigma$	substitutions, the *dynamic* atomic formulæ
$\mid a$	predicates, the *Platonic* atomic formulæ
$\mid \Phi \odot \Psi \mid \Upsilon$	multiplicative conjunction and truth
$\mid \Phi \,\&\, \Psi \mid \top$	additive conjunction and truth
$\mid \Phi \oplus \Psi \mid \bot$	additive disjunction and false

3.2 A sequent system for $\mathrm{LP}^{=}_{\sigma}$

A sequent-style presentation of the logic is given in Table 1. With one exception, the rules in Table 1 are the natural generalizations of the rules given by Girard for the *commutative* intuitionistic linear logic, cf. [13,14], to the non-commutative case, cf [5]. The exceptional axiom is ($\bot$). Its expected generalization is $\Gamma, \bot, \Delta \vdash A$, as in [5]. However, the stronger axiom is not consistent with our earlier discussion. For instance, `ldd` = `yes`, $\bot$, which is equivalent to `ldd` = `yes` $\odot \bot$ by (L$\odot$), would then be equivalent to $\bot$ rather than `ldd` = `yes`. Consequently, it will no be valid in our intended interpretation.

Embedding the usual logic of predicates into $\mathrm{LP}^{=}_{\sigma}$, which is also based on (16), gives another good reason for *not* assuming that having falsehood as one of the assumptions always logically implies anything.

The reader can notice at this point that some of the properties of the desired logical formalism discussed in section 2 are satisfied by $\mathrm{LP}^{=}_{\sigma}$ as a consequence of

$(\text{Refl})\ \dfrac{}{\Phi \vdash \Phi}$	$(\text{Cut})\ \dfrac{\Gamma \vdash \Phi \qquad \Delta, \Phi, \Delta' \vdash \Psi}{\Delta, \Gamma, \Delta' \vdash \Psi}$
$(\text{L}\Upsilon)\ \dfrac{\Gamma, \Delta \vdash \Phi}{\Gamma, \Upsilon, \Delta \vdash \Phi}$	$(\text{R}\Upsilon)\ \dfrac{}{\vdash \Upsilon}$
$(\text{L}\odot)\ \dfrac{\Gamma, \Phi, \Psi, \Delta \vdash \Xi}{\Gamma, \Phi \odot \Psi, \Delta \vdash \Xi}$	$(\text{R}\odot)\ \dfrac{\Gamma \vdash \Phi \qquad \Delta \vdash \Psi}{\Gamma, \Delta \vdash \Phi \odot \Psi}$
$(\text{L\&-L})\ \dfrac{\Gamma, \Phi, \Delta \vdash \Xi}{\Gamma, \Phi \,\&\, \Psi, \Delta \vdash \Xi}$	$(\top)\ \dfrac{}{\Gamma \vdash \top}$
$(\text{L\&-R})\ \dfrac{\Gamma, \Psi, \Delta \vdash \Xi}{\Gamma, \Phi \,\&\, \Psi, \Delta \vdash \Xi}$	$(\text{R\&})\ \dfrac{\Gamma \vdash \Phi \qquad \Gamma \vdash \Psi}{\Gamma \vdash \Phi \,\&\, \Psi}$
$(\bot)\ \dfrac{}{\bot, \Gamma \vdash \Phi}$	$(\text{L}\oplus)\ \dfrac{\Gamma, \Phi, \Delta \vdash \Xi \qquad \Gamma, \Psi, \Delta \vdash \Xi}{\Gamma, \Phi \oplus \Psi, \Delta \vdash \Xi}$
$(\text{R}\oplus\text{-L})\ \dfrac{\Gamma \vdash \Phi}{\Gamma \vdash \Phi \oplus \Psi}$	$(\text{R}\oplus\text{-R})\ \dfrac{\Gamma \vdash \Psi}{\Gamma \vdash \Phi \oplus \Psi}$

Table 1. A sequent system for non-commutative substructural logic.

its Gentzen-style presentation given in Table 1. This is for instance the case for $\Upsilon \odot \Phi \dashv\vdash \Phi$. But others have to be postulated by considering a suitable theories, i.e., by imposing suitable axioms.

Finally, it is important to note that the only structural rules of the logic are Cut and Reflexivity. Thus, the logic is *non-monotone.* That is the usual weakening rule

$$\frac{\Gamma, \Delta \vdash \Phi}{\Gamma, \Psi, \Delta \vdash \Phi}$$

is not part of it, and in fact it is neither admissible, nor sound. Otherwise, one would be able to derive $\top \vdash \Upsilon$, and so obtain an inconsistent system with $\top \dashv\vdash \bot$.

3.3 Platonic formulæ and axioms

Intuitively, the usual logic of predicates lives as a *Platonic sublanguage* of $\mathrm{LP}^{=}_{\sigma}$. More precisely, a formula is called Platonic if it contains neither explicit substitutions, nor $\odot$ nor Υ. To put the same statement in positive form, a Platonic formula is built from Platonic atoms and from additive conjunctions and disjunctions.

We have not included negation as a first-class citizen of our logical system. Thus, in order to retain the expressive power of (quantifier free) classical logic the usual trick is applied, i.e., one keeps negation on the level of atomic formulæ. In our case it is safe to apply the trick to platonic atomic formulæ, i.e., to predicates. Thus, for each predicate symbol R of arity $n \geq 0$, and for any sequence $\mathbf{e}$ of expressions of length n we associate two atomic formulæ: $R^{+}(\mathbf{e})$ and $R^{-}(\mathbf{e})$. Intuitively, the first is positive, while the second is its negative twin. Notation $R^{\star}(\mathbf{e})$ is used to denote either form, while $\neg R^{\star}(\mathbf{e})$ is used to denote the twin form of $R^\star(\mathbf{e})$. Thus, negation is rendered as a syntactic operation on platonic atoms of $\mathrm{LP}^{=}_{\sigma}$. The classical platonic sub-logic is equipped with the following axioms to make the usual negation rules admissible.

$$(\&\neg)\ \frac{}{R^\star(\mathbf{e})\ \&\ \neg R^\star(\mathbf{e}) \vdash \bot} \quad \textit{and} \quad (\oplus\neg)\ \frac{}{\top \vdash R^\star(\mathbf{e}) \oplus \neg R^\star(\mathbf{e})}$$

Reflexivity of equality axiom schema is coded as expected.

$$(=)\ \frac{}{\top \vdash e = e}$$

The other facet of equality, that equals can be substituted for equals, reflects the dynamic nature of substitution. This is treated in subsection 3.4.

In first order logic the conjunction distributes over disjunction, i.e.,

$$(\Phi \oplus \Psi)\ \&\ \Xi \dashv\vdash (\Phi\ \&\ \Xi) \oplus (\Psi\ \&\ \Xi) \quad \textit{and} \quad \Phi \oplus (\Psi\ \&\ \Xi) \dashv\vdash (\Phi \oplus \Psi)\ \&\ (\Phi \oplus \Xi).$$

In substructural logics not all of the above follow from the rules of Table 1. Consequently, we add those missing as axioms.

$$(\oplus\&)\ \frac{}{(\Phi \oplus \Psi)\ \&\ \Xi \vdash (\Phi\ \&\ \Xi) \oplus (\Psi\ \&\ \Xi)} \qquad (\&\oplus)\ \frac{}{\Phi \oplus (\Psi\ \&\ \Xi) \dashv (\Phi \oplus \Psi)\ \&\ (\Phi \oplus \Xi)}$$

3.4 Dynamic atoms and axioms

Additive connectives and atoms built from predicates are the Platonic ingredients of $\mathrm{LP}^{=}_{\sigma}$. The dynamic ingredients are: the substitutions, multiplicative conjunction, and multiplicative truth. The dynamic features of the logic are captured by the following set of axioms. We add them all to the theory we build.

Explicit substitutions, ranged over by σ, have the syntactic form $\left[\frac{e}{x}\right]$ where v is a multi-fluent, or attribute, and e is an expression of a type suitable for v.

Substituting equals for equals. The principal property of logics with equality that **equals can always be substituted for equals** can now be expressed as the following axiom.

$$(=\sigma)\ \frac{}{e_1 = e_2\ \&\ \left[\frac{e_1}{x}\right] \vdash \left[\frac{e_2}{x}\right]}$$

Quick comparison with its classical predecessor, which takes the form of an axiom schema $e_1 = e_2\ \&\ \varphi[e_1/x] \vdash \varphi[e_2/x]$ reveals the the simple truth. Moving to the formalism with explicit substitution amount to removing formula φ which played a *dummy*.

Pending substitutions. The general idea put forward in section 2 was that a formula $\sigma \odot \Phi$ in $\mathrm{LP}^{=}_{\sigma}$ represents substitution σ *pending* to be performed on Φ. We explain what that means by considering the structure of Φ.

Substitution pending on a Platonic atom is explained via meta-substitution.

$$(\sigma R^\star)\ \frac{}{\left[\frac{e}{x}\right] \odot R^\star(e_1, \ldots, e_k) \dashv\vdash R^\star(e_1[e/x], \ldots, e_k[e/x])}$$

One substitution pending upon another corresponds to their composition. Thus, composing two substitutions which concern the same variable results in aggregating the effects of both in a single substitution. Just as in $(\sigma R^\star)$ pending explicit substitution in the world of formulæ is reduced/explained by metalevel substitution in the world of terms. All identity substitutions are equal Υ.

$$(xx)\ \frac{}{\left[\frac{e_1}{x}\right] \odot \left[\frac{e_2}{x}\right] \dashv\vdash \left[\frac{e_2[e_1/x]}{x}\right]} \qquad (\Upsilon)\ \frac{}{\left[\frac{x}{x}\right] \dashv\vdash \Upsilon}$$

Since simultaneous substitutions are not allowed, all we can do to explain the effect of composition of two substitutions for different variables is to say how they commute. Again, the equality predicate is needed to state the axioms.

$$(xz)\ \frac{}{c_1 = e_2[e_1/x]\ \&\ e_1 = c_2[c_1/z]\ \&\ \left[\frac{e_1}{x}\right] \odot \left[\frac{e_2}{z}\right] \vdash \left[\frac{c_1}{z}\right] \odot \left[\frac{c_2}{x}\right]}\,(x \text{ different } z)$$

The side-condition of (xz) says that x and z are *syntactically different variables.*

The meaning of $\sigma \odot B$ in other cases is guided by distributivity axioms given in the sequel.

Platonic formulæ are eternal facts. Predicates, i.e., the Platonic atoms, were described as facts, i.e., formulæ the truth of which does not depend on the state. By $(\bot)$ the same property holds for $\bot$. The following axiom schemas capture the idea in other cases.

$$(R^\star\odot)\ \frac{}{R^\star(e_1,\ldots,e_k) \vdash R^\star(e_1,\ldots,e_k) \odot \bot} \qquad (\top\odot)\ \frac{}{\top \vdash \top \odot \bot}$$

Notice that axiom $(\top\odot)$ could not co-exist with the more general axiom $\Gamma, \bot, \Delta \vdash A$ for the additive false. Together they give inconsistency: $\top \vdash \bot$.

As a consequence of the above axioms one obtains the following result in which ϕ ranges over platonic formulæ of $\mathrm{LP}^{=}_{\overline{\sigma}}$.

Proposition 1. *Platonic ϕ's are a constant predicate transformers: $\phi \dashv\vdash \phi \odot B$.*

The above proposition provides a technical justification of the idea that the Platonic formulæ do not depend on the state.

The mathematical semantics of $\mathrm{LP}^{=}_{\overline{\sigma}}$, as developed in [2], is described in the full version of the paper. It substantiates the claims made above in the sense that the meaning of each formula is indeed sought in the space of *predicate transformers.*

Distributivity axioms. In the fragment of linear logic described in Table 1 the only distributivity law which is guaranteed is that of $\odot$ over binary additive disjunction $\oplus$.

In general, as exemplified by $(R^\star\odot)$ and $(\top\odot)$, $\odot$ does not distribute over nullary additive disjunction $\bot$ on the right. But it does for dynamic atoms.

$$(\sigma\bot)\ \frac{}{\sigma \odot \bot \vdash \bot}$$

Let us recall that the right-sided distributivity $\bot \odot A \vdash \bot$ always holds by $(\bot)$.

Distributivity of $\odot$ over additive conjunctions is not guaranteed in general. But we want it at least for the binary &.

$$(\odot\&)\ \frac{}{A \odot (B\ \&\ C) \dashv (A \odot B)\ \&\ (A \odot C)} \qquad (\&\odot)\ \frac{}{(A\ \&\ B) \odot C \dashv (A \odot C)\ \&\ (B \odot C)}$$

For nullary conjunction we impose left-sided distributivity only for dynamic atoms.

$$(\sigma\top)\ \frac{}{\sigma \odot \top \dashv \top}$$

Its general form is not valid, cf. prop. 1. Its right-sided form always holds by $(\top\odot)$.

Elimination of substitutions It is easy to see that the axioms provided above together with their converse, which are derivable, provide means to associate with any formula Φ and any platonic formula φ of $\mathrm{LP}^{=}_{\sigma}$ a platonic formula $\lceil \Phi \odot \varphi \rceil$ obtained by *performing* the substitution Φ upon φ.

Lemma 1. *For any Platonic φ and any Φ the formula $\lceil \Phi \odot \varphi \rceil$ is a well defined Platonic formula such that $\Phi \odot \varphi \dashv\vdash \lceil \Phi \odot \varphi \rceil$.*

3.5 Translation of Logic of Predicates to $\mathrm{LP}^{=}_{\sigma}$

In [2] it is shown that *logic of predicates with equality lives as the Platonic fragment of* $\mathrm{LP}^{=}_{\sigma}$. More formally, one can consider an embedding of a theory $\vdash_\kappa$ into $\mathrm{LP}^{=}_{\sigma}$ with the axioms from κ extending those introduced above. Then classical derivability of sequents can be mimicked in $\mathrm{LP}^{=}_{\sigma}$.

Theorem 1. *Let $\vdash_\kappa$ be a theory obtained by extending quantifier free logic of predicates with negation and equality axioms, and an arbitrary set of axioms κ. Suppose that $\vdash_\lambda$ is a $\mathrm{LP}^{=}_{\sigma}$ theory obtained by extending the logic with κ. Then*

$$\Gamma \vdash_\kappa \Delta \quad \textit{implies} \quad \&\lfloor \Gamma \rfloor \vdash_\lambda \bigoplus \lfloor \Delta \rfloor.$$

In fact, one can prove that the translation is conservative.

4 A formal system to reason about actions

Let us finish this note by presenting another formal system which has satisfaction statements π ***sat*** Φ as basic judgments. Above, π is an imperative program, thus its extension is an action, and Φ is a formula of $\mathrm{LP}^{=}_{\sigma}$.

In its most general form the system enables to reason on the level of *parametrized* non-deterministic programs with loops. Its applicability has been demonstrated in [3, 4]. We claim that it is suitable for the tasks ranging from verification, via specification, to formal program development.

It should not be difficult to realize that actually, the shooting action `Shoot` specified in (12) as

$$\texttt{Shoot}\ \ \textbf{\textit{sat}}\ \ ((\texttt{ldd} = \texttt{yes})\ \&\ \left[\frac{\texttt{no}}{\texttt{ldd}}\right] \odot \left[\frac{\texttt{no}}{\texttt{alv}}\right]) \oplus ((\neg\texttt{ldd} = \texttt{yes})\ \&\ \Upsilon)$$

corresponds to the program

$$\texttt{Shoot} \mathrel{\hat{=}} \textbf{if}\ \texttt{ldd} = \texttt{yes}\ \textbf{then}\ \texttt{ldd} := \texttt{no}; \texttt{alv} := \texttt{no}\ \textbf{else skip}.$$

That is, we claim that one can formally *prove* with the help of the formal system presented below that the above program satisfies specification (12). The system is given a sequent style presentation of consequence relation called *pLSD*, and denoted $\Vdash$.

In the rules of pLSD logic the following conventions apply.

π, ϖ range over *programs*. Programs are built from *indeterminate programs*, denoted p, q; *assignments*, denoted α; constant program **skip**; *boolean tests*, $b?$; binary *sequential composition* operation, $\pi;\varpi$; *non-deterministic choice*, $\pi \sqcup \varpi$. Finally, the *least fixed point* construction, notation $\mu\, \mathsf{p}\,.\,\pi$, is binding all free occurrences of p in π. The set of *free* indeterminate programs in π is denoted $\mathsf{PI}(\pi)$.

In what follows A, B and C range over formulae of first order logic with explicit substitution described in section 3.

Metavariables $\mathcal{C}$ and $\mathcal{D}$ range over sequences of satisfaction assumptions about indeterminate programs — each of the form p *sat* A, and such that no indeterminate occurs more than once. $\mathsf{PI}(\mathcal{C})$ is used to denote the set of all indeterminate programs in $\mathcal{C}$.

Finally, a word about semantical interpretation of the judgments. For simplicity, assume that π is a closed program. It's interpretation is sought in the domain of binary relations on the set Val of *states*, i.e., in the set of valuations of multi-fluents: $\mathsf{Val} \mathrel{\hat{=}} \mathsf{Var} \to D$, where D is a suitable domain of values.

We interpret a formula A of $\mathrm{LP}^{\equiv}_{\sigma}$ as a predicate transformer

$$\mathcal{S}_M[\![A]\!] : (\mathcal{P}ow(\mathsf{Val}) \to \mathcal{P}ow(\mathsf{Val}))$$

Then, interpretation of a judgment π *sat* A is based on the Galois connection between the two semantical domains: of binary relations on Val and predicate transformers on Val.

$$\models \pi \ \textit{sat}\ A \qquad \textit{iff} \qquad [\![\pi]\!] \supseteq (\mathcal{S}_M[\![A]\!])^*$$

where α^* denotes the relation corresponding to the predicate transformer α under the Galois connection.

Under the above interpretation the system presented below is not only relatively sound with respect to a given classical predicate language theory, but also relatively complete in the sense of Cook. These results also extend to reasoning about programs/actions with parameters.

Structural Rules

Reflexivity

$$\frac{}{\mathsf{p}\ \textit{sat}\ A \Vdash \mathsf{p}\ \textit{sat}\ A}$$

CUT

$$\frac{\mathcal{C} \Vdash \pi\ \textit{sat}\ A \qquad \mathsf{p}\ \textit{sat}\ A, \mathcal{D} \Vdash \varpi\ \textit{sat}\ B}{\mathcal{C}, \mathcal{D} \Vdash \varpi[\pi/\mathsf{p}]\ \textit{sat}\ B}\ \mathsf{PI}(\mathcal{C}) \cap \mathsf{PI}(\mathcal{D}) = \emptyset$$

Exchange

$$\frac{\mathcal{C}, \mathsf{p}\ \textit{sat}\ A, \mathsf{q}\ \textit{sat}\ B, \mathcal{D} \Vdash \pi\ \textit{sat}\ C}{\mathcal{C}, \mathsf{q}\ \textit{sat}\ B, \mathsf{p}\ \textit{sat}\ A, \mathcal{D} \Vdash \pi\ \textit{sat}\ C}$$

Weakening

$$\frac{\mathcal{C} \Vdash \pi\ \textit{sat}\ B}{\mathcal{C}, \mathsf{p}\ \textit{sat}\ A \Vdash \pi\ \textit{sat}\ B}\ \mathsf{p} \notin \mathsf{PI}(\mathcal{C})$$

Contraction

$$\frac{\mathcal{C}, \mathsf{p}_1 \;\; \textbf{\textit{sat}} \;\; A, \mathsf{p}_2 \;\; \textbf{\textit{sat}} \;\; A \Vdash \pi \;\; \textbf{\textit{sat}} \;\; B}{\mathcal{C}, \mathsf{p} \;\; \textbf{\textit{sat}} \;\; A \Vdash \pi[\mathsf{p}/\mathsf{p}_1][\mathsf{p}/\mathsf{p}_2] \;\; \textbf{\textit{sat}} \;\; B} \; \mathsf{p} \notin \mathsf{PI}(\mathcal{C})$$

Interaction Rule
Consequence

$$\frac{\mathcal{C} \Vdash \pi \;\; \textbf{\textit{sat}} \;\; A \qquad A \dashv B}{\mathcal{C} \Vdash \pi \;\; \textbf{\textit{sat}} \;\; B}$$

Connective Rules
Assignment

$$\overline{\Vdash x := e \;\; \textbf{\textit{sat}} \;\; \left[\tfrac{e}{x}\right]}$$

Test and Skip, where action **skip** is defined by: **skip** $\hat{=} \top?$

$$\overline{\Vdash b? \;\; \textbf{\textit{sat}} \;\; \neg b \oplus \Upsilon} \qquad\qquad \overline{\Vdash \textbf{skip} \;\; \textbf{\textit{sat}} \;\; \Upsilon}$$

Sequential composition

$$\frac{\mathcal{C} \Vdash \pi \;\; \textbf{\textit{sat}} \;\; A \qquad \mathcal{C} \Vdash \varpi \;\; \textbf{\textit{sat}} \;\; B}{\mathcal{C} \Vdash \pi ; \varpi \;\; \textbf{\textit{sat}} \;\; A \otimes B}$$

Nondeterministic choice

$$\frac{\mathcal{C} \Vdash \pi \;\; \textbf{\textit{sat}} \;\; A \qquad \mathcal{C} \Vdash \varpi \;\; \textbf{\textit{sat}} \;\; B}{\mathcal{C} \Vdash \pi \sqcup \varpi \;\; \textbf{\textit{sat}} \;\; A \,\&\, B}$$

Just as the rule for **skip** above one can derive as admissible other rules for some definable, more familiar action constructs. For instance
Conditional, where **if** b **then** π **else** $\varpi \;\hat{=}\; (b?;\pi) \sqcup (\neg b?;\varpi)$.

$$\frac{\mathcal{C} \Vdash \pi \;\; \textbf{\textit{sat}} \;\; A \qquad \mathcal{C} \Vdash \varpi \;\; \textbf{\textit{sat}} \;\; B}{\mathcal{C} \Vdash \textbf{if } b \textbf{ then } \pi \textbf{ else } \varpi \;\; \textbf{\textit{sat}} \;\; (b \,\&\, A) \oplus (\neg b \,\&\, B)}$$

Conclusions

A novel logical framework has been presented which, we hope, solves some of the problems encountered in AI, and related to the difficulty of formalizing the idea of *inertia* into logical descriptions of dynamic systems.

Earlier, and independently, Łukaszewicz and Madalińska-Bugaj discovered that the use of Dijkstra's calculus ([7, 8]) of predicate transformers copes with the Frame Problem, cf. [19, 20]. Whereas their approach is more general, the advantage of the framework presented here relates to its logical nature. As a result, we are able to encode our system in a general purpose theorem prover Isabelle, cf. [4]. Thus, one can solve instances of the temporal projection problem in purely deductive fashion.

The framework presented seems quite elegant and offers a solution to the Frame Problem. It even admits extensions to cope not only with non-deterministic actions as advocated here, but with repetitive actions as well. It does come, however, with its own limitations at present. Thus, further studies, and especially a thorough comparison with $\mathcal{A}$ and descendant formalisms, as well as with cf. [19, 20] should be conducted.

References

1. Apt, K., and M. Bezem. Acyclic programs. In D. Warren and P.Szeredi (Eds.), *Logic programming: Proc. 7th Int'l Conf.*, 1990, pp. 617–633.
2. Bednarczyk, M. A. Logic of predicates with explicit substitutions. Mathematical Foundations of Computer Science 1996, 21st Symposium, Cracow, Poland, Proceedings (eds. W. Penczek & A. Szalas), LNCS 1113, 192-206, 1996.
3. Bednarczyk, M. A. and T. Borzyszkowski. Towards program development with Isabelle. Proc. 1st Isabelle User Workshop, pp.101–121, Cambridge, 1995.
4. Bednarczyk, M. A. and T. Borzyszkowski. Information system development as mechanizable logical activity. Information System Development - ISD'96, 5th International Conference, Gdańsk, Poland, Proceedings (eds. S. Wrycza & J. Zupancic), 535-544, 1996.
5. Brown, C. and D. Gurr. Relations and non-commutative linear logic. *J. of Pure and Applied Algebra*, **105**, 2, pp.: 117-136, 1995.
6. Brown, F., (Ed) Proc., of the 1987 Workshop *The Frame Problem in Artificial Intelligence.* Morgan Kaufmann Publishers, 1987.
7. Dijkstra, E. W. *A Discipline of Programming.* Prentice-Hall, 1990.
8. Dijkstra, E. W. and C.S. Scholten. *Predicate Calculus and Program Semantics.* Springer-Verlag, 1990.
9. Eshghi, K., and R. Kowalski. Abduction compared with negation as failure. In G. Levi and M. Martelli (Eds.) *Logic programming: Proc. 6th Int'l Conf.*, 1989, pp. 234–255.
10. Giunchiglia, E., Neelakantan Kartha, G. and V. Lifschitz. Reprezenting action: indeterminacy and ramifications. submitted, (1997).
11. Gelfond, M. and V. Lifschitz. Classical negation in logic programs and disjunctive databases. *New Generation Computing*, 9 (1991), pp 365–385.
12. Gelfond, M. and V. Lifschitz. Reprezenting actions and change by logic programs. *Journal of Logic Programming*, 17 (1993), pp 301–322.
13. Girard, J.-Y. Linear logic. *Theoretical Computer Science*, 50 (1987), pp 1–102.
14. Girard, J.-Y., Lafont, Y. and P. Taylor. *Proofs and Types.* volume 7 of *Cambridge Tracts in Theoretical Computer Science*, Cambridge University Press, 1989.
15. Girard, J.-Y. Linear logic : its syntax and semantics. In *Advances of Linear Logic*, 1995.
16. Hanks, S., and D. McDermott. Nonmonotonic logic and temporal projection. *Artificial Intelligence*, 33(3) (1987) pp.:379–412.
17. Hoare, C. A. R. An axiomatic basis for computer programming. *Communications of the ACM*, 12, (1969).
18. Lambek, J. The mathematics of sentence structure. *American Mathematical Monthly*, 1958, vol. 65, pp.:363–386.
19. Łukaszewicz, W. and E. Madalińska-Bugaj. Reasoning about Action and Change Using Dijkstra's Semantics for Programming Languages: Preliminary Report. In: *Proc. IJCAI-95*, Montreal, Canada, 1995, pp.:1950–1955.
20. Łukaszewicz, W. and E. Madalińska-Bugaj. Reasoning about Action and Change: Actions with Abnormal Effects. In: *KI-95, Adv. in AI, Proc. 19th German AI Conference*, Springer-Verlag, LNAI, 981, 1995, pp.:209–220.
21. McCarthy, J., and P.H. Hayes. Some philosophical problems from the standpoint of Artificial Inteligence. B. Meltzer and D. Mitchie (Eds.), *Machine Intelligence* **4**, (1969) pp.:463–502.
22. Poigné, A. Basic Category Theory. In *Handbook of Logic in Computer Science. Vol I.*. Clarendon Press, Oxford, 1992.
23. Przymusiński, T. Extended stable semantics for normal and disjunctive programs. In D. Warren and P.Szeredi (Eds.), *Logic programming: Proc. 7th Int'l Conf.*, 1990, pp. 459–477.

Application of Valuation Based Systems to Optimization of Enumeration Protocols

Mieczysław A. Kłopotek[1,3)], Sławomir T. Wierzchoń[1,2)]

[1)] Institute of Computer Science, Polish Academy of Sciences,
[2)] Dept of Computer Science, Białystok University of Technology,
[3)] Institute of Mathematics, Warsaw University of Technology,
e-mail: {klopotek,stw}@ipipan.waw.pl

Abstract: The paper presents a new algorithm for the problem of an enumeration protocol for nodes in a network. The new algorithm, contrary to previous ones, is local both in information access (neighborhood only) and information stored (proportional to the number of neighbors). This property is achieved at the expense of the type of connectivity the network is assumed to exhibit.
Keywords: Reasoning, distributed computation.

1. Introduction

The problem of enumeration of nodes of a graph by local transformations appears to be interesting at least for the following reasons [9], [10]:

- Local labeling transformations are good models of distributed computation
- Enumeration is a good model for resolving global conflicts by local means
- The theoretical problem is by itself interesting

A general solution to the problem can be found in [10]. The proposed solution is general in that it is valid for most types of undirected graphs connecting the nodes in the network, except for some peculiar locally highly symmetric networks, where the decision cannot be made. It appears to have some disadvantages, however: Each node has to keep itself separately information received from all the nodes of the network, which it eventually receives. That is each node reflects the structure of the whole network. A single node has to be activated many times.

In this paper we are asking whether it is possible to invent a protocol that would assure that each node has a totally local behavior, that is:

- Each node collects information only from its neighbors
- Each node holds only an amount of information proportional to its neighborhood and not to the entire network.
- Each node is activated only at most a fixed number of times

We shall call this constrained setting as “strictly local computation problem”.

As the necessity of the solution from [10] was proven for the general case, it is obvious that we have to look for solutions under the requirement of more constraining local computation by turning to a special set of graphs.

In the past, strictly local computations have been investigated intensely in the context of computations of marginal distributions of joint probability distributions in graphical expert systems (called also Bayesian Networks). Bayesian Networks were transformed to a special representation of so-called Markov trees (hypertrees) e.g. via the so-called the trangularization process (consult [13] for details). A triangulated graph is one in which any loop with more than three nodes has a direct connection in the graph between a pair of non-neighbors in the loop. After the triangulation the computational problem, that was otherwise exponential in time and space in the total number of variables, turned to be bounded by local neighbourhood size so that computations could run in both reasonable time and reasonable space consumption.

As it turned out, triangulated graphs are applicable not only to decomposition of Bayesian networks, but also to Dempster-Shafer networks, to necessity calculus and to Spohn's disbelief function and to some reasoning problems in the fuzzy set theory [14]. So the original local reasoning engine was extended from Bayesian networks to the more general concept of "valuation based systems" (VBS). Many types of reasoning processes like conditional probabilities or belief functions computations may be carried out efficiently in the VBS framework. Also such hard tasks like finding most probable explanation or k-most-probable explanations for a hypothesis, some decision making tasks etc. may be solved efficiently using the formalism of the valuation based systems.

The idea of graphical expert systems, called also Bayesian networks (BN) was initiated by Pearl, [11], and worked-out by Lauritzen and Spiegelhalter, [8]. Its generalization to different uncertainty formalisms was proposed by Shenoy [15] under the name valuation based systems (VBS in short).

Since the VBS proved to be very efficient in diverse local computation task, we posed the question whether it can also be applied to the enumeration by local computation problem.

2. Problem formulation

Let $\mathcal{X} = \{X_1,...,X_n\}$ be a set of variables with discrete domains $D_1,..., D_n$, respectively. Each domain is a set of integers 0,1...*n*. 0 meaning the node does not possess any enumeration value assigned, otherwise it has assigned a value under enumeration. Obviously our goal is to assign each X a different natural number value. Let *D* stands for the Cartesian product of these domains, $D = D_1 \times ... \times D_n$; it represents the space of total configurations. Furthermore let $E=\{\{ X_i, X_j\} \mid X_i, X_j \in \mathcal{X}.: X_i \neq X_j \}$ be a set of undirected edges over $\mathcal{X}$. Let us call $(\mathcal{X},E)$ a network.

We are obviously interested in finding a configuration of the network in which all the values of all the variables are distinct and ranging from 1 to *n*.

For this purpose we want to elaborate a protocol for local computations that is with each node acquiring its "identity number" only by communicating its direct neighbors. For a given node X_i its neighborhood Nh(X_i) be defined as a set Nh(X_i)={ X_j | { X_i, X_j}∈ E}.We say that any subset of Nh(X_i) such that for any X_k, X_j∈ Nh(X_i) we have {X_i, X_j}∈ E is a completely connected subneighborhood of X_i. Let us say in passing that a set consisting of all sets comprising of nodes from $\mathcal{X}$ joint with their completely connected subneighborhoods constitute a hypergraph H over $\mathcal{X}$ such that it is equivalent to E.

We want now to have enumeration of nodes based on some local criterion, with limited information flow. In particular we want to distinguish one node that has the highest number assigned, and then starting from it assign numbers to all the other nodes. The problem is of course that locally no node knows how many nodes are there in the network.

One idea for choosing the starting node would be that of graph trangulation. It consists essentially in removal steps until only one node remains. This would be the winner. Then the sequential numbers should be assigned corresponding to the removal order. We want to elaborate this idea in more detail in the subsequent section.

3. Problem solution

3.1. The general idea

Imagine we create a "spanning tree" over the network such that given a node with highest value all the subtrees in the tree after removing it have values only within some range each. The same happening in all the subtrees. To have a valuation like that we would have to pick a node from the network, give it the entire range of values 1..n and to pass to it the control. The node in control would assign itself the highest rank available and give its neighbors disjoint subranges of values and pass to each of them the control as to separate subtrees. In this case the node with the highest rank node of all and in each subtree would have to possess knowledge only of the range it has been assigned to (two integers) and the number of nodes within each of subtrees originating from it (one integer per neighbor).

The problem is now to find the spanning tree based only on local properties (the actual neighborhood) of each node.

In Figure 1 you see the idea of message passing over the tree. A node A receives the whole range of values (1..7), retains the top value (7) and passes the range (1..3) to C and (4..6) to B and so forth. Of course, A would have to be informed about the cardinality of nodes in the tree sub-branch starting at B and in that starting at C.

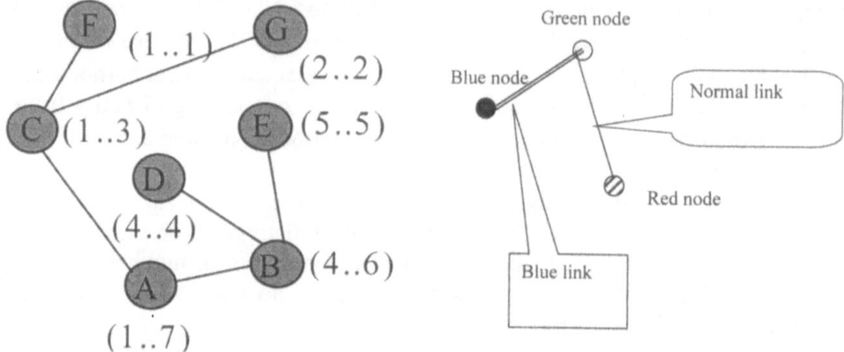

Fig. 1. The idea of range passing **Fig. 2. The denotation**

3.2. Hypergraphs and junction trees

The task to find a spanning tree may be understood as identical with finding a removal sequence of nodes such that the graph is connected all the time. How to do a thing like this based on local properties? If we remove a node only if its actual neighborhood is completely connected then we have a guarantee that the whole graph will remain connected. But is this procedure granted a success?

To find good deletion ordering Shenoy [15] proposed a metaphor being in a sense a redefinition of the graphical approach of Bertele and Brioschi [2]. Suppose $\mathcal{H} = \{H_1,...,H_k\}$ is a family of subsets of $\mathcal{X}$ (to be thought of as nodes with their completely connected neighborhoods), and $D(H_i)$ is the Cartesian product of the domains of variables in H_i.

Among hypergraphs of special importance are so-called acyclic hypergraphs, denoted $(\mathcal{X}, \mathcal{N})$, or simply $\mathcal{N}$ ($\mathcal{N}$ is the set of hypernodes). They admit two attractive properties. First, their hypernodes, denoted N_j, $j = 1,...,q$, (q is the cardinality of $\mathcal{N}$) can always be ordered in such a way that the *running intersection property*[1], or RIP for short, holds:

$$(\forall k \geq 2)(\exists j < k): N_j \supseteq N_k \cap (N_1 \cup ... \cup N_{k-1}) \quad (1)$$

This property means that the variables in node N_k also contained in previous nodes $(N_1,..., N_{k-1})$ are all members of one previous node, N_j. Second, the hypernodes of $\mathcal{N}$ can be organized into a tree, called *junction tree*. To introduce this tree we need further definitions. The set

$$S_k = N_k \cap (N_1 \cup ... \cup N_{k-1}) \quad (2)$$

is said to be separator: it separates the residual

---

[1] Precise description of all notions concerning hypergraphs can be found e.g. in [1]

$$R_k = N_k \backslash S_k \quad (3)$$

from $(N_1 \cup ... \cup N_{k-1}) \backslash S_k$. Particularly $S_1 = \varnothing$ and $R_1 = N_1$. Any node N_j containing S_k with $j < k$ is called a *parent* of N_k in the tree; similarly the node N_k is called a *child* of N_j. Hence N_1 is the root of the junction tree and N_q is a leaf node in this tree. Lemma 1 below characterizes some useful properties of the set of residuals.

Lemma 1. Let $\mathcal{N}$ be an acyclic hypergraph with nodes ordered such that the RIP holds, and let $\mathcal{T}$ be its junction tree. Denote $Ch(N_i)$ the set of indices of the children of the node N_i, $T(N_i)$ the set of indices of the nodes belonging to the subtree rooted at the node N_i. Let $De(N_i)$ be the set of indices of the descendants of the node N_i, i.e. $De(N_i) = T(N_i) \backslash \{i\}$ Then

a) if $\cup De(N_i)$ stands for the set theoretical union of all the subsets being descendants of the node N_i, then $\cup\{R_j | j \in De(N_i)\} = \cup De(N_i) \backslash N_i$,
b) the residuals $R_2,...,R_q$ form a partition of $\mathcal{X}/N_1$.

Proof: (a) We prove this identity by induction. It trivially holds if N_i is a leaf in the junction tree. If it holds for any $i > 1$, and let N_p be the parent of N_i. then

$$\cup\{R_w | w \in De(N_p)\} = \bigcup_{k \in Ch(N_p)} [R_k \cup (\cup De(N_k) \backslash N_k)] \quad (4)$$

Consider a single child, say N_k of N_p. Since $R_k \subseteq N_k$ then $R_k \cup (\cup De(N_k) \backslash N_k) = \cup De(N_k) \backslash S_k = \cup De(N_k) \backslash (N_k \cap N_p) = \cup De(N_k) \backslash N_p$. By the identity $A_1 \backslash B \cup ... \cup A_n \backslash B = (A_1 \cup ... \cup A_n) \backslash B$ we obtain the thesis.

(b) To prove this statement we must show that: (i) the residuals are mutually exclusive, and (ii) their set theoretical union equals $\mathcal{X}/N_1$. Part (ii) is just the case (a) when i=1, i.e. when N_i is the root of the junction tree. Hence we must prove only part (i). Let A^c be the complement of A in $\mathcal{X}$. Then $R_i = N_i \backslash S_i = N_i \cap (N_i \cap (N_1 \cup ... \cup N_{i-1}))^c = N_i \cap (N_1^c \cap ... \cap N_{i-1}^c)$. Let R_j, $j > i$, be another separator. Then $R_i \cap R_j = (N_1^c \cap ... \cap N_{i-1}^c \cap N_i) \cap (N_1^c \cap ... \cap N_i^c \cap ... \cap N_{j-1}^c \cap N_j) = \varnothing$. □

Graham test allows verifying if a hypergraph $\mathcal{H}$ is acyclic. It consists of two, performed in any order, rules: (i) if a variable X belongs to exactly one hypernode H, remove it from $\mathcal{X}$, i.e. $H \leftarrow H - \{X\}$, and (ii) if H_1, H_2 are two hypernodes such that $H_1 \subset H_2$, and $H_1 \neq H_2$ then delete H_1 from $\mathcal{H}$. If any of two rules cannot be applied further, and $\mathcal{H} = \varnothing$, it means that $\mathcal{H}$ is acyclic.

There is another way of finding acyclic coverage of a given hypergraph (i.e. we search for $\mathcal{N} \supset \mathcal{H}$). Define namely 2-section of a hypergraph $\mathcal{H}$ as an undirected graph $\mathcal{G}(\mathcal{H}) = (\mathcal{X},\mathcal{E})$ such that $\{X_i,X_j\} \in \mathcal{E}$ only if X_i and X_j belong to a common hypernode $H \in \mathcal{H}$. If $\mathcal{H}$ is acyclic then $\mathcal{G}(\mathcal{H})$ is triangulated and hypernodes in $\mathcal{H}$ are precisely cliques of $\mathcal{G}(\mathcal{H})$. Hence, to find an acyclic coverage of the original hypergraph, we construct its 2-section, triangulate it, and the cliques of such a graph are hypernodes in the acyclic hypergraph $(\mathcal{X},\mathcal{N})$. This explains also another name of the junction tree: *tree of cliques*

3.3. The informal algorithm specification

Let us exploit the good deletion properties of a hyper-tree for the construction of enumeration. This would be our enumeration protocol. Let us first describe the algorithm informally.

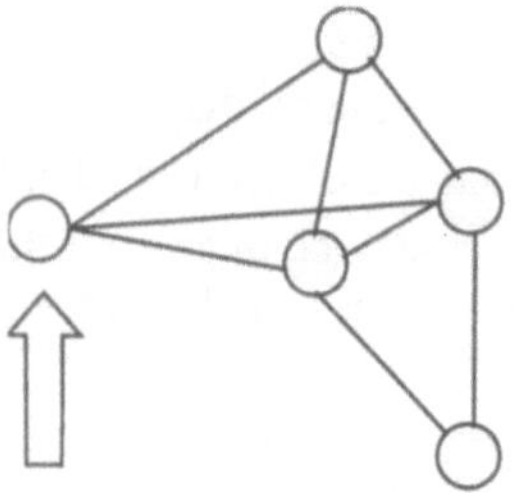

Fig. 3. The initial state

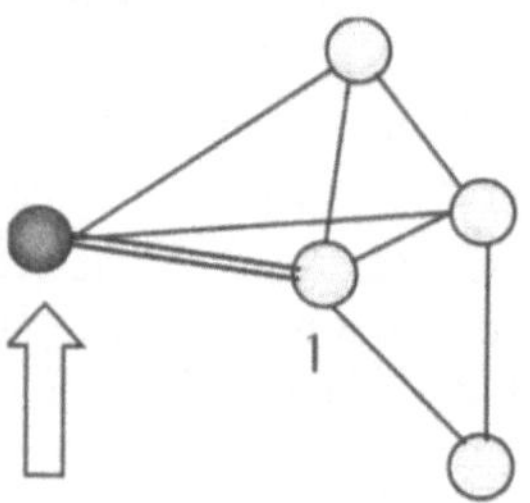

Fig. 4. One node turned blue

Each node should be characterized by a state (green, blue, red), the blue link to a distinguished neighbor (present or absent), the sum of claims to it, and the assigned enumeration value as well as the assigned range of values. The Figure 2 illustrates the graphical denotation used in the sequel.

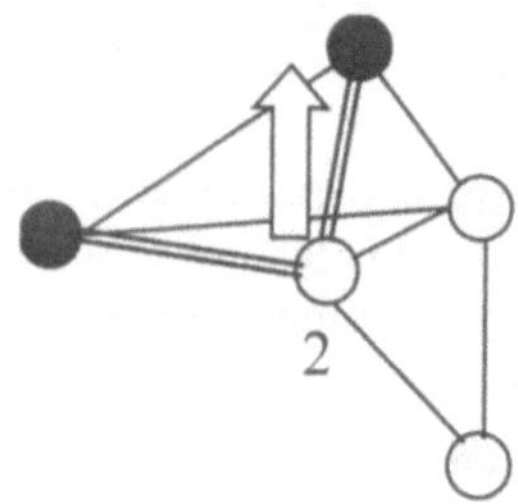

Fig. 5. The second node turned blue

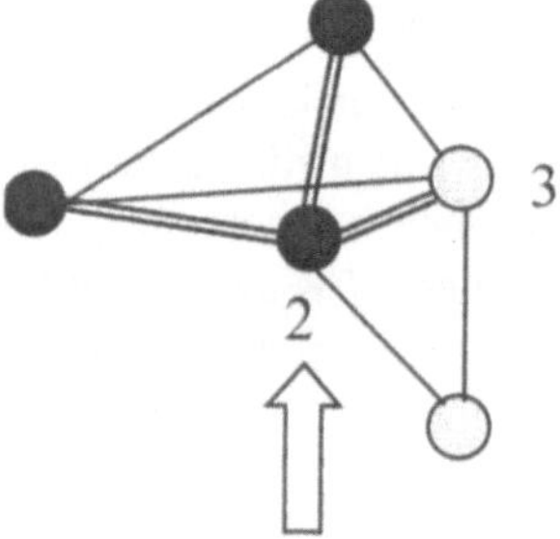

Fig. 6. Now a node turns blue that could not so before some of its neighbors turncd bluc

The initial state is green, no distinguished neighbor and the sum of claims equal zero, and there is no assigned enumeration value (Figure 3).

First a green node asks if all its neighbors in state "green" are interconnected.

If so, then it changes its state to blue and sends a message to one of the green neighbors that it requests its own sum of claims plus one and it remembers this neighbor as its "when-blue neighbor".

The when-blue neighbor receives the message and increases its sum of claims by the received number. This procedure is continued as long as there are green nodes that have more than zero green neighbors.

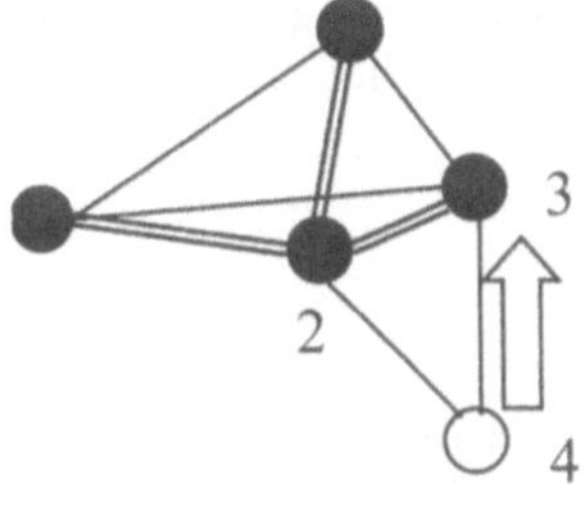

Fig. 7. Now the forth node turns blue

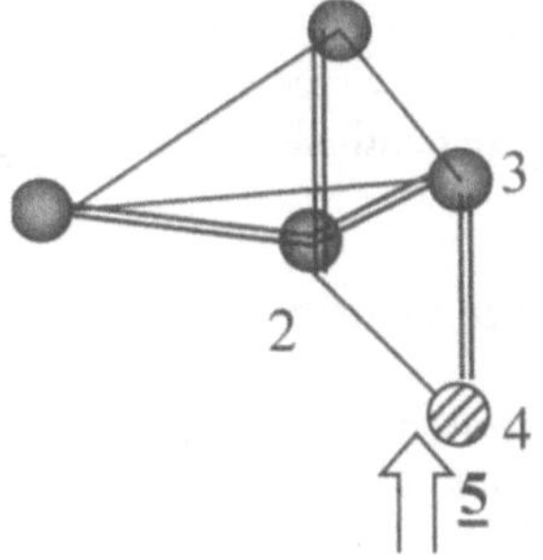

Fig. 8. The remaining green node turns red

Now the remaining (guaranteed only one) green node has no green neighbors. Then it assigns itself enumeration value equal to its sum of claims plus one and changes its state to red.

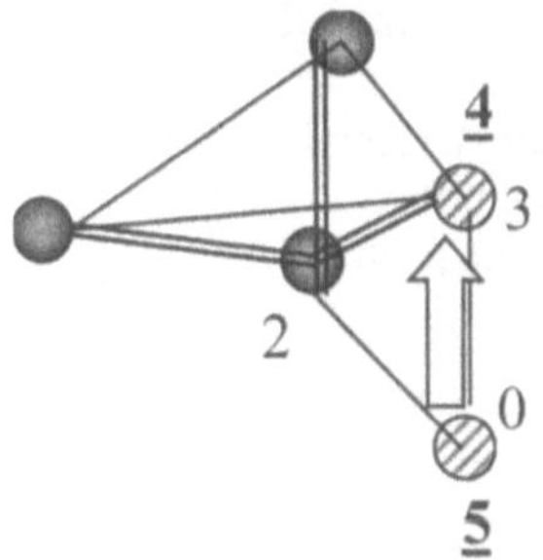

Fig. 9. The blue-link neighbor turns red

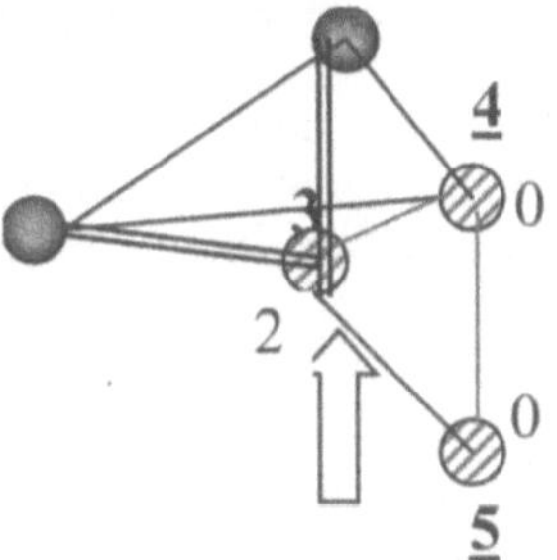

Fig. 10. Another blue-link neighbor of a red node turns red

Now the neighbor of red along the blue line requests over the blue link the sum of its claims plus one. The receiver node replies by sending back its actual sum of claims, thereafter it diminishes the sum of claims by the number actually received.

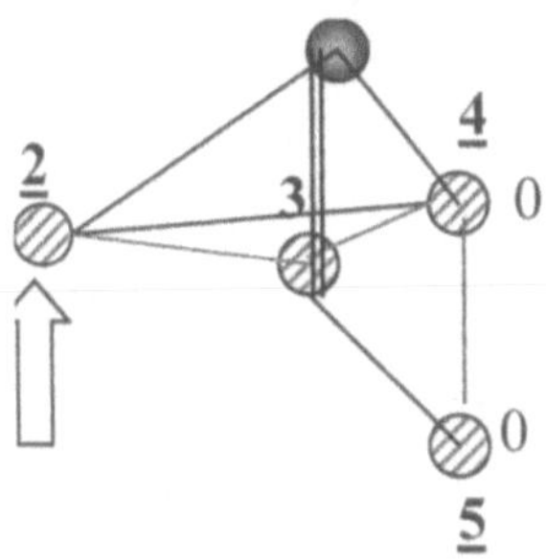

Fig. 11. Another blue-link neighbor of a red node turns red

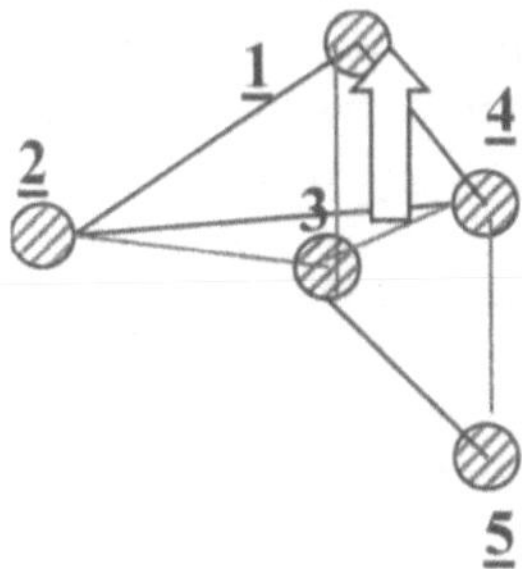

Fig. 12. Another blue-link neighbor of a red node turns red

The sender receives the number, sets it as its enumeration value and sets its sum of claims to the newly received number minus one. It changes the color to red.

The procedure continues until all nodes turn red.

3.4. The formal protocol specification

In this subsection we want to specify the protocol formally. The protocol tells not how the whole network behaves, but rather how a local node behaves. Let in this protocol the node speak of itself as "me".

Each node can send/receive the following messages:

- Request-message – the count of nodes in the subtree
- Rejection-message – refusing to accept the request-message
- Accepting-message – accepting the request message
- Range-request-message – inquiring about the assigned range of numbers in the enumeration; this message cannot be rejected
- Range-assignment-message – the actual assignment of enumeration range

The request-message and a range-request-message are targeted at some particular node. The other ones are replies back to the sending node.

Each node has local variables as described in step 0 of the protocol.

The Protocol

```
0.   Let me initialize: my_state:=green,
     my_valuation:=unknown (0), my_blue_link:=unknown,
     my_request_count:=0, my_range_upper_bound:=-1,
     my_range_lower_bound:=0
1.   If  my_state=red and
     my_range_upper_bound<my_range_lower_bound then
     STOP
2.   While my_state=red and incoming
     range_request_message queue is not empty repeat:
     x:= pop_the_range_request_message_queue(),
     send_range_assignment_message_back(my_range_upper_
     bound), my_range_upper_bound:=
     my_range_upper_bound-x
3.   While my_state=green and incoming request_message
     queue is not empty repeat: my_request_count:=
     my_request_count+pop_the_message_queue(),
     send_accepting_message_back(pop_the_message_queue(
     ))
4.   While my_state is not green and incoming re-
     quest_message queue is not empty repeat:
     send_rejection_message_back(pop_the_message_queue(
     ))
```

```
5.  If my_state=green and all my green neighbors are
    interconnected then my_blue_link:=any of the green
    neighbors,
    send_request_message(my_blue_link,my_request_count
    +1), wait_till_accepting_or_rejection_message
6.  If rejection_message received then
    my_blue_link:=unknown, goto step 1
7.  If my_state=green then my_state:=blue
8.  If my_state=blue and my_blue_link.my_state=red
    then send_range_request_message(my_blue_link,
    my_request_count+1),
    wait_till_range_assignment_message,
    my_valuation:=pop_range_message(),
    my_range_upper_bound:= my_valuation - 1,
    my_range_lower_bound:= my_valuation -
    my_request_count, my_state=red
9.  Go to step 1
```

4. Final remarks

Mazurkiewicz [10] studies the problem of "fairness" of the assignment of the enumeration values. He proves that under his settings the enumeration is fair that is all permissible configurations are actually possible.

This cannot be claimed about the algorithm of our invention. Our protocols use at a node only limited knowledge about the whole network: some cumulative statistics. In particular, the value assignments are restricted by permissible node removals in a trangularized network.

Mazurkiewicz investigates also the question of termination of the networks protocol. He shows that the network can identify whether or not the protocol may successfully terminate (that is whether or not the network matches the conditions for network structure). Our protocol, running on a network with presumably simpler structure, can only determine whether or not it can be completed successfully by setting a time-out condition. Determining whether or not the graph has a hypertree is linear in the number of nodes in the graph. Setting a reasonable high number of potential nodes in the network will do the job.

Finally, the most important thing we gain from the VBS approach (and just from the assumptions about the network structure) is that for the enumeration task we need only space linear in the number of neighbors and execution time linear in the number of variables. If you think of real applications of network protocols like those for the Internet, with a large and unpredictable number of nodes, then it may be of value to construct the network spending the money for a structure suitable for triangulation with potential revenue of linear time local network protocols.

References

[1] Beeri, C., et.al. (1983) On the desirability of acyclic database schemes. J. ACM, 30, 1983,479-513

[2] Bertele, U., and Brioschi, F., Nonserial Dynamic Programming, Academic Press, New York, 1972

[3] Cooper G. The computational complexity of probabilistic inference using Bayesian belief networks. Artif. Intell. 42,1990, 395-405

[4] Dechter, R. Bucket elimination: A unifying framework for probabilistic inference algorithms. In Uncertainty in AI (UAI-96), pp. 211-219

[5] Henrion M. An introduction to algorithm for inference in belief nets, Uncertainty in Artificial Intelligence 5(1990).

[6] Jensen, F.V. An Introduction to Bayesian Networks. University College Press, London, 1996

[7] Lauritzen, S.L., and Spiegelhalter, D.J. Local computations with probabilities on graphical structures and their application to expert systems. J. R. Statist. Soc. B-50(1988)157-224

[8] Mazurkiewicz A.: Solvability of the asynchronous ranking problem, Inform. Process. Lett. 28(1988), 221-224

[9] Mazurkiewicz A.: Distributed enumeration. Inform.Process.Lett. (in print)

[10] Pal, N., Bezdek, J., and Hemanisha, R. Uncertainty measures for evidential reasoning I: a review. Int. J.Approx. Reas. 7(1992)162-183.

[11] Pearl, J. Fusion, propagation and structuring in Bayesian networks. Artif. Intel. 28(1986), 241-288.

[12] Pearl, J. Reasoning in Intelligent Systems: Networks of Plausible Inference, Morgan Kaufmann Publishers, 1988.

[13] Shafer, G. Probabilistic Expert Systems, SIAM CBMS-NSF Regional Conference Series in Applied Mathematics, Philadelphia, 1996, vol. 67

[14] Shenoy, P.P. A valuation-based language for expert systems. Int. J. Approx. Reas., 3(1989)383-411

[15] Shenoy, P.P. Conditional independence in valuation-based systems. Int. J. Approx. Reas., 10(1993)203-234

[16] Shimony, S.E., and Charniak, E. A new algorithm for finding MAP assignments to belief networks. Proc. Conference on Uncertainty in AI, Cambridge, MA, 1990, 98-103.

[17] Wierzchoń, S.T. Constraint propagation over restricted space of configurations, and its use in optimization. In: R.R. Yager, J. Kacprzyk and M. Fedrizzi (eds.) Advances in the Dempster-Shafer Theory of Evidence, J. Wiley, New York, 1994, 375-394

[18] Wierzchoń, S.T., Kłopotek, M.A., Michalewicz, M. Reasoning and facts explanation in valuation based systems, Fundamenta Informaticae, 30(1997)359-371

[19] Wu, T. A problem decomposition method for efficient diagnosis and interpre-tation of multiple disorders, Proc. 114th. Symp.Computer Appl. in Medical Care, 1990, 86-92.

[20] Yen J. Generalizing Dempster-Shafer theory to fuzzy sets. IEEE Trans. Syst.Man.Cybern. 20(3), 1990, 559-570.

Fuzzy Reals with Algebraic Operations: Algorithmic approach

Witold Kosiński[1], Piotr Prokopowicz[2], and Dominik Ślęzak[1]

[1] Polish–Japanese Institute of Information Technology
ul. Koszykowa 86 , 02-008 Warszawa
[2] University of Bydgoszcz
Institute of Environmental Mechanics and Applied Computer Science
ul. Chodkiewicza 30, 85-064 Bydgoszcz, Poland
email: wkos@pjwstk.edu.pl, piotrekp@ab-byd.edu.pl, slezak@pjwstk.edu.pl

Abstract. Fuzzy counterpart of real numbers, called fuzzy numbers (reals), are investigated. Their membership functions satisfy conditions similar to quasi–convexity. In order to operate on them in a similar way to real numbers revised algebraic operations are introduced. At first four operations between fuzzy and real numbers are in use in a form suitable for their algorithmisations. Two operations: addition and subtraction between fuzzy numbers are proposed to omit some drawbacks of the corresponding operations originally defined by L. A. Zadeh with the help of his extension principle.

Keywords: fuzzy sets, fuzzy numbers, algebraic operations, field of numbers, quasi–convexity

1 Introduction

The last thirty years have witnessed the emergency of series of works introducing fuzzy sets into modelling control systems, decision analysis and data analysis. Fuzzy logic has already proved its applicability to a number of real-life problems of industrial applications. Fuzzy data analysis,on the other hand, understood in two different ways: the fuzzy analysis of data and the analysis of fuzzy data , requires more than fuzzy logic: it requires fuzzy arthmetic. In real problems parameters and data describing them and then used in mathematical modelling are vague. The vagueness can be described by fuzzy numbers and fuzzy sets. The development of the theory of fuzzy sets should be based on a well established theory of fuzzy sets defined on the real axis in order to build a fuzzy counterpart of real numbers.

In the classical approach for numerical handling of fuzzy quantities of fundamental importance is the so–called extension principle which gives a formal apparatus to carry over operations (e.g. arithmetic or algebraic) from sets to fuzzy sets. Namely, if $f\ : X \to Y$ is a function and A is a fuzzy set in X, then A introduces via f a fuzzy set B in Y given by

$$\mu_B(y) = \sup_{x \in f^{-1}((\{y\}))} \mu_A(x) \text{ for } y \in Y. \tag{1}$$

If $f : X \times Y \to Z$ is a two–argument operation (function) then a fuzzy set C is given in Z by

$$\mu_C(z) = \sup_{\{(x,y):h(x,y)=z\}} \min(\mu_A(x), \mu_B(y)) \text{ for } z \in Z. \tag{2}$$

Here μ_A, μ_B and μ_C are membership functions of the fuzzy sets A, B and C, respectively.

In the literature several attempts in formulating a theory of fuzzy (real) numbers can be found. The commonly accepted theory of fuzzy reals has been that set up by Dubois and Prade [1]. According to their definition, a fuzzy real is meant as a fuzzy set A defined on the real axis $\mathbb{R}$ where its membership function μ_A is normal (unimodal in cf. [2]), continuous (or at least upper semi-continuous), and convex . Then they assumed a restricted class of membership functions and introduced so-called (L, R)–numbers. The functions of the class became quite popular, because of their good interpretability and relatively easy handling for simple operations (e.g. fuzzy addition). However, already multiplication leads out of this class. So, if one wants to stay within this class and operate on their members, following the Zadeh [3] classical operations on fuzzy sets, one is forced to approximate fuzzy functions (and operations) by these numbers. Unfortunately, approximations coming from linearisation, by applying, for example series expansion, may lead to large computational errors that cannot be further controlled when applying them repeatedly (cf. [2]).

There are other drawbacks of the Zadeh's definition (see Fig. 1), e.g. the difference of two normal fuzzy sets leads to a membership function which is no more normal (value 1 is not reached for $C - B$) and moreover $C - B \neq A$ when $C = A + B$. Several modifications proposed have not succeeded to authors' knowledge in solving all drawbacks and in forming a field of fuzzy numbers. However, in many applications such a particular structure could be of a great help, for example in constructing fuzzy inference systems [4], fuzzy controllers not mentioning an effective fuzzy calculus [5].

That is why we investigate this problem and try to revise the approach of Prade and Dubois as well as our previous definitions of fuzzy numbers [6], and construct two operations on fuzzy numbers in a way that solves some drawbacks of the original ones. To do this we add to the previous definition of fuzzy number an extra feature characterizing the direction in which the graph of the membership function should be drawn.

An attempt to introduce a non–standard operations acting on fuzzy numbers has been made by Sanchez in [7], compare also [8] and cf. [2].

Dubois and Prade as well as Wagenknecht already noticed that in order to construct operation algorithms for fuzzy numbers an invertibility in a weak sense of fuzzy number's membership functions is required. That weak invertibility is known in the theory of quasi–convex functions (cf. [9]). The quasi–convexity has been assumed in some sense in the previous papers [6,10].

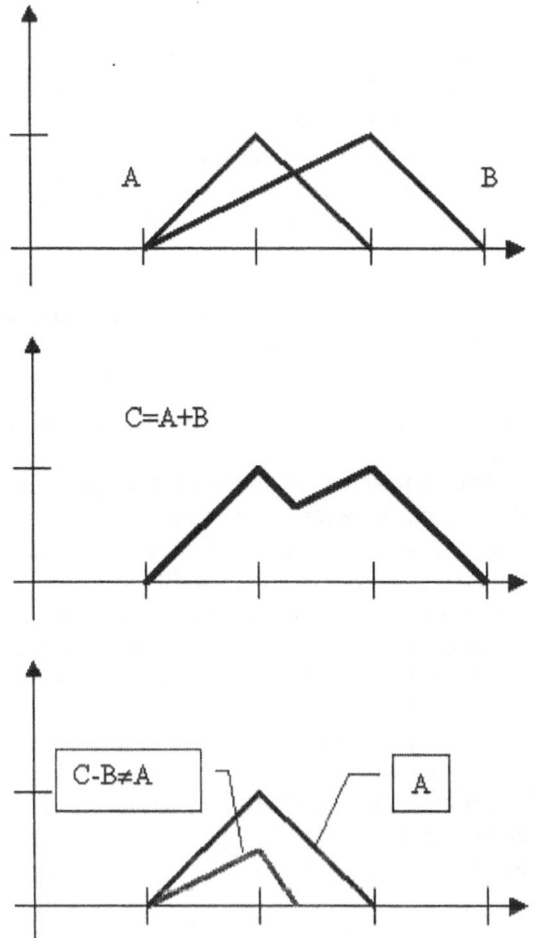

Fig. 1. Operations based on Zadeh's extension principle

To construct algorithms that will realize algebraic operations on fuzzy numbers and to have a direct contact with real (crisp) numbers regarded as characteristic functions of one-point sets, a new observation should be made. On the real axis only one zero appears. How many fuzzy zeros are possible and how to distinguish limits of two sequences of fuzzy numbers approaching crisp zero from the left and from the right side, respectively? Do we have for our disposal a feature to characterize the first sequence as a **negative fuzzy zero**, while the latter to call a **positive zero** ? This was our observation made recently.

First particular definitions of four main operations: addition, subtraction, multiplication and deviation between fuzzy and real numbers are recalled in the form suitable for their algorithmisations. Then two algebraic operations:

addition and subtraction between fuzzy numbers are introduced, different from that proposed by L. A. Zadeh by means of the extension principle [11]. The new operations solve some drawbacks of the original ones, namely in the case of triangular shaped membership functions the sum of two membership functions is a triangular shaped membership function. In the case of the subtraction, the previously noticed inconvenience (see [6]) disappear; it was related to the fact for any fuzzy number A the difference $A - A$ was a fuzzy zero, not the crisp zero.

Two operations on fuzzy numbers are programmed and implemented in the Delphi language for selected types of membership functions, namely triangular, trapezoidal and rectangular ones.

2 Operations on membership functions of reals

In [6] a set of conditions were introduced for membership functions of fuzzy sets defined on $\mathbb{R}$ in order to regard them as fuzzy reals. They were in some sense weaker than that original given by Dubois and Prade, however were similar to those proposed by Wagenknecht in [2].

We do underline that the quasi-invertibility property of membership functions plays an essential role in defining operations on such fuzzy sets. However, in order to have a unique neutral element of the operation addition, and consequently for any fuzzy number A the difference $A - A$ is a crisp zero, we are introducing the next feature to the definition of a fuzzy number, namely the orientation of the graph.

Let us start with crisp or non–fuzzy real numbers. Let $r \in \mathbb{R}$, then its representation in the set–theoretical language is the characteristic function χ_r of the one–element set $\{r\}$, and its the classical definition

$$\chi_r(x) = \begin{cases} 1 \text{ if } & x = r \\ 0 \text{ if } & x \neq r \,. \end{cases} \tag{3}$$

The space of the characteristic functions, denoted by Ξ can be equipped with the structure of an algebra with a unit, and then with the structure of a field. For any $a, b \in \mathbb{R}$ the multiplication of an element χ_r from Ξ by a scalar $a \in \mathbb{R}$ is given by

$$(a\chi_r)(x) = \chi_{ar}(x), \tag{4}$$

with the properties

$$a(\chi_r + \chi_z) = a\chi_r + a\chi_r, \ (a+b)\chi_r = a\chi_r + b\chi_r, \ 1\chi_r = \chi_r. \tag{5}$$

Let us recall four algebraic operations:

addition

$$(\chi_r + \chi_z)(x) = \chi_{r+z}(x), \quad \text{for any } r, z \in \mathbb{R}; \tag{6}$$

subtraction

$$(\chi_r - \chi_z)(x) = (\chi_r + (-1)\cdot\chi_z)(x) = \chi_{r-z}(x); \tag{7}$$

multiplication

$$(\chi_r \cdot \chi_z)(x) = \chi_r(\frac{x}{z}) = \chi_z(\frac{x}{r}) = \chi_{rz}(x) \tag{8}$$

for any real r and z, and the last operation
division

$$(\chi_r \div \chi_z)(x) = (\chi_r \cdot \frac{1}{\chi_z})(x) = (\chi_r \cdot \chi_{1/z})(x) = \chi_{r/z}(x), \tag{9}$$

for any real r and $z \neq 0$. Notice that the neutral element of the operation addition is the characteristic function of zero, i.e. χ_0 (the crisp zero), while the neutral element of the operation multiplication is the characteristic function of 1, i.e.

$$(\chi_r \cdot \chi_1)(x) = (\chi_1 \cdot \chi_r)(x) = \chi_r(x). \tag{10}$$

The space $\{\Xi, +, \cdot\}$ is a commutative algebra with a unit and the space $\{\Xi, +, -, \cdot, \div\}$ is a field.

3 Definition of fuzzy numbers

We are beginning this section with some definition. If $\mathcal{S}$ is a plane (Jordan) closed curve then it can possesses two orientations: positive – if together with the increasing parameter of the curve its running point moves counterclockwise (compatible with the orientation of the coordinate vectors), and negative – in the opposite case.

If in $\mathbb{R}^2$ one adds points belonging to the segment $[a, b] \times \{0\}$ to all points of the graph of a piecewise continuous and nonnegative function μ defined on the interval $[a, b]$, with $a < b$ and such that $\mu(a) = \mu(b) = 0$, then the resulting set C_μ can be parameterized as a plane (closed) curve. Such a curve can be equipped with two orientations, depending on the choice of the direction of parameterization of this segment. If together with the increasing parameter of the curve the running point moves along the segment from the point $(a, 0)$ (the left-end) to the point $(b, 0)$ (the right-end), then the orientation is positive. Consequently, this situation corresponds to the case when with the increasing parameter subsequent points of the graph

$$\text{graph}(\mu) = \{(x, y) \in \mathbb{R}^2 : y = \mu(x), x \in [a, b]\} \subset C_\mu \tag{11}$$

are attained starting from the right-end of the support of the function μ, i.e. the point $(a, 0)$ is reached after the point $(b, 0)$. In such a case we will say that the **orientation of the graph** of the function μ is **positive** (see Fig. 2). The negative orientation of the graph corresponds to the opposite orientation of the curve C_μ.

Let $\mathbb{R}$ be a set of reals. By a **fuzzy number** we understand a triple $A = (\mathbb{R}, \mu, \mathsf{s})$ where s denotes orientation of the graph of μ, and either μ is a characteristic function of a one–element set, as it was defined in the previous section, or $\mu : \mathbb{R} \longrightarrow [0, 1]$ is normal and the function $-\mu$ is strictly quasi–convex, i.e.

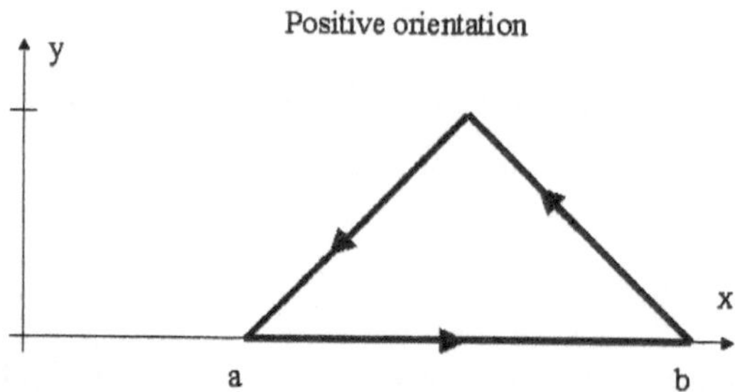

Fig. 2. Positive orientation of the graph of a triangular membership function

1. $1 \in \mu(\mathbb{R})$,
2. the support of μ is a bounded interval,
3. the support of μ can be split into three subintervals:

$$\text{supp } \mu = (l_A, 1_A^-) \cup [1_A^-, 1_A^+] \cup (1_A^+, p_A), \tag{12}$$

   with $l_A \leq 1_A^- \leq 1_A^+ \leq p_A$, such that: on the subinterval $(l_A, 1_A^-)$ the function μ is increasing, on $(1_A^-, 1_A^+)$ the function μ is constant and equal to 1, and on $(1_A^+, p_A)$ the function μ is decreasing,
4. each of the subintervals $(l_A, 1_A^-)$ and $(1_A^+, p_A)$ may be empty or may reduce to one point as well as the subinterval $[1_A^-, 1_A^+]$; in the latter case $1_A^- = 1_A^+$, and
5. $\mu(l_A) = \mu(p_A) = 0$,
6. the value of s is $+1$ if the orientation of the graph of the membership function μ is positive and is equal to -1 if the orientation is negative.

The function μ is called the **membership function of** the fuzzy number A and then denoted by μ_A. If the orientation of the graph is known then to simplify the notation we will identify a fuzzy number A with its membership function μ and write A for it. To write explicitly the orientation we will use an orientation function, denoted identically with the same letter s, i.e s(A) $= +1$ if the orientation of the graph of μ is positive, and s(A) $= -1$, in the opposite case. For simplicity we will call the value of the function s(A) the orientation of the fuzzy number A. If μ is a crisp number the orientation is unrelevant.

Let us notice that with one function, say μ, satisfying above conditions 1–5 we can attached two different fuzzy numbers, say $A^+ = (\mathbb{R}, \mu, +1)$ and $A^- = (\mathbb{R}, \mu, -1)$ which differ by their orientations, only.

Let us define four operations between fuzzy and crisp numbers:
addition

$$(A + \chi_r)(x) = A(x - r), \quad \text{for any } x \text{ and } r \in \mathbb{R}; \tag{13}$$

subtraction

$$(A - \chi_r)(x) = A(x + r) \quad \text{for any } x \text{ and } r \in \mathbb{R}; \tag{14}$$

multiplication

$$(A \cdot \chi_r)(x) = A(\frac{x}{r}) \quad \text{for } x \in \mathbb{R} \text{ and } r \in \mathbb{R}^+ = [0, \infty); \tag{15}$$

division

$$(A \div \chi_r)(x) = A(xr) \quad \text{for } x \in \mathbb{R} \text{ and } r \in \mathbb{R}^{++} = (0, \infty). \tag{16}$$

The resulting fuzzy numbers have the same orientation as that of the fuzzy number A; in particular $\mathsf{s}(\mathsf{A} \cdot \chi_r) = \mathsf{s}(\mathsf{A})$.

Now we have to define the multiplication of fuzzy numbers by negative crisp reals. To each A we relate its opposite number $-A := \chi_{-1} \cdot A$ which is a fuzzy number with its support given in terms of the support of A by supp $(-A) = (-p_A, -l_A)$ with supp $A = (l_A, p_A)$ however, with the opposite orientation, i.e.

$$\mathsf{s}(-\mathsf{A}) = -\mathsf{s}(\mathsf{A}). \tag{17}$$

In the case when supp $A \subset \mathbb{R}^+$ the function $-A$ is the mirror reflection of A with respect to y axis since $-A(x) = A(-x)$, for each x, while the orientation of the graph of μ_{-A} is opposite to the orientation of the graph of μ_A. Having this defined we can manage with the multiplication by any crisp real number and with the division by any nonvanishing crisp real number. Notice that, as before the neutral element of the operation addition is the function χ_0, while the neutral element of the operation multiplication is χ_1. Moreover, from the definition we can assume that

$$\chi_r \cdot A = A \cdot \chi_r, \quad \text{for any } r. \tag{18}$$

4 Arithmetic operations on fuzzy numbers

Let us define the operation addition between fuzzy numbers. First let us define the addition of numbers with the same orientation.

By a **sum** $A + B$ **of two fuzzy numbers** A and B **with the same orientation**, i.e. with $\mathsf{s}(\mathsf{A}) = \mathsf{s}(\mathsf{B})$, we understand a fuzzy number C for which:

1. supp $C = (l_C, p_C)$ with $l_C = l_A + l_B$ and

$$1_C^- = 1_A^- + 1_B^-, \; 1_C^+ = 1_A^+ + 1_B^+, \; p_C = p_A + p_B,$$

2. its membership function is a prolongation of three functions, such that C and its inverse C^{-1} satisfy

$$C|[1_C^-, 1_C^+] = \chi_{[1_A^- + 1_B^-, 1_A^+ + 1_B^+]}, \tag{19}$$

(i.e. on the interval $[1_C^-, 1_C^+]$ the function C is constant);

$$C^{-1}|(l_C, 1_C^-) = A^{-1}|(l_A, 1_A^-) + B^{-1}|(l_B, 1_B^-), \tag{20}$$

(i.e. on the interval $(l_C, 1_C^-)$ the function is the inverse of the sum of two functions: $A^{-1}|(l_A, 1_A^-)$ and $B^{-1}|(l_B, 1_B^-)$);

$$C^{-1}|(1_C^+, p_C) = A^{-1}|(1_A^+, p_A) + B^{-1}|(1_B^+, p_B), \tag{21}$$

(i.e. on the interval $(1_C^+, p_C)$ the function is the inverse of the sum of two functions: $A^{-1}|(1_A^+, p_A)$ and $B^{-1}|(1_B^+, p_B)$),

3. the orientation of C is the same as that of A and B , i.e. with $\mathsf{s(C)} = \mathsf{s(A)} = \mathsf{s(B)}$.

Let us notice that the definition coincides with (13) in the case when one of the components of the operation is a crisp number.

By **a sum** $A + B$ **of two fuzzy numbers** A and B with **with the opposite orientation** , i.e. with $\mathsf{s(A)} = -\mathsf{s(B)} = -1$, we understand a fuzzy number C for which:

1. supp $C = (l_C, p_C)$ with $l_C = l_A + p_B$ and

$$1_C^- = 1_A^- + 1_B^+,\ 1_C^+ = 1_A^+ + 1_B^-,\ p_C = p_A + l_B,$$

2. its membership function is a prolongation of three functions, such that C and its inverse C^{-1} satisfy

$$C|[1_C^-, 1_C^+] = \chi_{[1_A^- + 1_B^-, 1_A^+ + 1_B^+]}, \tag{22}$$

(i.e. on the interval $[1_C^-, 1_C^+]$ the function C is constant);

$$C^{-1}|(l_C, 1_C^-) = A^{-1}|(l_A, 1_A^-) + B^{-1}|(p_B, 1_B^+), \tag{23}$$

(i.e. on the interval $(l_C, 1_C^-)$ the function is the inverse of the sum of two functions: $A^{-1}|(l_A, 1_A^-)$ and $B^{-1}|(p_B, 1_B^+)$);

$$C^{-1}|(1_C^+, p_C) = A^{-1}|(1_A^+, p_A) + B^{-1}|(1_B^-, l_B), \tag{24}$$

(i.e. on the interval $(1_C^+, p_C)$ the function is the inverse of the sum of two functions: $A^{-1}|(1_A^+, p_A)$ and $B^{-1}|(1_B^-, l_B)$),

3. the orientation of C is the same as that of A , i.e. with $\mathsf{s(C)} = \mathsf{s(A)} = -\mathsf{s(B)}$.

To define the next operation – subtraction we need to notice that in an abstract field the subtraction operation of an element B from an element A is defined (regarded) as an addition to A the opposite element to B, i.e. $A - B = A + (-1) \cdot B$. We are using this to define the next operation on fuzzy numbers – the subtraction. In the previous paper [6] another method has been employed.

5 Conclusions

In the present paper next modifications of the two algebraic operation on fuzzy numbers have been proposed by confining the set of admissible membership functions to normal and strictly quasi–concave, and by introducing the next feature to any fuzzy number, namely the orientation of the graph of its membership function. In this way a fuzzy number should be regarded as a pair: membership function and orientation. Moreover, four algebraic operations between fuzzy and crisp numbers have been defined. The operation of subtraction of two fuzzy numbers lastly defined does fulfill the requirement $A - A = \chi_0$, in contrast to the previous definition which was giving rather $A - A = O$ where O is a fuzzy number "around zero". We see that the present definitions solves next drawbacks (cf. Fig. 3.) of the operations based on the Zadeh's extension principle [11]. In the further publication we will try to define the next algebraic operations.

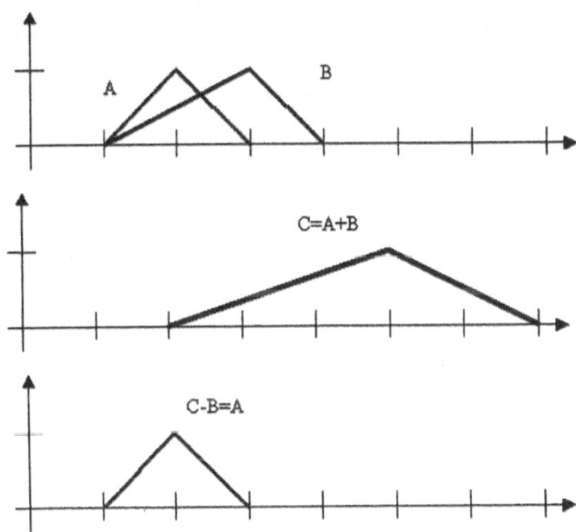

Fig. 3. Operations based on present definitions

References

1. Dubois D. and Prade H., Operations on fuzzy numbers, *Int. J. System Science*, **9** (1978) 576–578.
2. Wagenknecht M., On the approximate treatment of fuzzy arithmetics by inclusion, linear regression and information content estimation, in *Zbiory rozmyte i ich zastosowania* (Fuzzy sets and their applications) (in Polish), J. Chojcan and J. Łęski (eds.), Wydawnictwo Politechniki Śląskiej, Gliwice 2001, pp.291–310,.
3. Zadeh L. A., Fuzzy sets, *Information and Control*, **8** (1965) 338–353.

4. Kosiński W. and Weigl M ., General mapping approximation problems solving by neural networks and fuzzy inference systems, *Systems Analysis Modelling Simulation*, **30** (1), (1998) 11–28.
5. Weigl M., *Neural networks and fuzzy inference systems in approximation problems* (Sieci neuronowe i rozmyte systemy wnioskujące w problemach aproksymacji), Ph. D. Thesis (in Polish), IPPT PAN, Warszawa, czerwiec 1995.
6. Kosiński W., Piechór K., Prokopowicz P. and Tyburek K., On algorithmic approach to operations on fuzzy reals, in *Methods of Artificial Intelligence in Mechanics and Mechanical Engineering, Gliwice, October, 2001*, T. Burczyński and W. Cholewa (eds.), PACM, Gliwice, 2001, pp. 95–98.
7. Sanchez E., Solutions of fuzzy equations with extended operations, *Fuzzy Sets and Systems*, **12** (1984) 237–248.
8. Czogała E. and Pedrycz W., *Elements and methods of fuzzy set theory* (Elementy i metody teorii zbiorów rozmytych), (in Polish), PWN, Warszawa, 1985.
9. Martos B., *Nonlinear Programming. Theory and Methods* (Polish translation of the English original published by Akadémiai Kiadó, Budapest, 1975) PWN, Warszawa, 1983.
10. Kosiński W. and Słysz P., Fuzzy reals and their quotient space with algebraic operations, *Bull. Polish Acad. Scien., Sèr. Techn. Scien.*, **41**(3), (1993) 285–295.
11. Zadeh L. A., The concept of a linguistic variable and its application to approximate reasoning, Part I, *Information Sciences* **8** (1975) 199–249.

Application of Data Decomposition to Incomplete Information Systems

Rafał Latkowski

Institute of Computer Science, Warsaw University
ul. Banacha 2, 02–097 Warsaw, Poland
rlatkows@mimuw.edu.pl

Abstract. Many developed classification methods and knowledge discovery software, that were research subjects for years, suffer from the lack of possibility to handle data with missing attribute values. To adapt existing classification methods to incomplete information systems, we propose a decomposition method that allows more appropriate missing value attributes handling. The decomposition method consists of two phases. In the first step data from original decision table are partitioned into subsets. In the second step, knowledge from those subsets, that in our case is classification hypothesis, is combined to achieve a final classification based on a whole original decision table. There were carried out some experiments in order to evaluate the decomposition method.

Keywords

Missing Attribute Values, Inductive Reasoning

1 Introduction

In recent years many researchers have faced the problem of missing attribute values [2,5,6,9,19]. Nowadays data acquisition and warehousing capabilities of computer systems are sufficient for wide application of computer aided knowledge discovery. Inductive learning is employed for various domains such as images, medical data, bank transactions and others. Due to various factors, those data suffer from impreciseness and incompleteness. The hard task of dealing with data imperfection in inductive learning methods was addressed in the area of data impreciseness by Pawlak in early 80's [14]. He proposed a Rough Set approach that made possible to precisely express facts about imprecise data in a formal way. The main concept of Rough Sets, indiscernibility relation, proved to be very useful for analysis of decision problems concerning objects described in a data table by a set of conditional attributes and a decision attribute [15,18]. In practical applications, however, the data table is often not only imprecise but also not complete, because some data are missing. Missing attribute values are frequently distributed not uniformly, but generated by underlying mechanism of investigated real world domain. Many developed classification methods and knowledge discovery software, that were research subjects for years, suffer from the lack of possibility to handle data with missing attribute values. To adapt existing classification methods to incomplete information systems, we propose a decomposition method that allows more appropriate missing value attributes handling.

Missing values can reduce soundness of inductive inference and result in decrease of classification quality. We expect the proposed method to reveal the pattern that governs the appearance of missing values in dataset. Such a decomposition avoids reasoning about missing values and makes possible the application of already developed methods and software, initially incapable of incomplete information systems processing. This method was experimentally compared with Quinaln's C4.5 method [17]. C4.5 is an example of inductive learning method that tries to deal with missing attribute values problem [16].

2 Method Description

The decomposition method was developed to meet certain assumptions. The primary aim of search for another method that could deal with missing attribute values was to find a possibility of adaptation for many of existing, well-known classification methods, that are not able to handle incomplete data. A development of solution, which makes possible to analyze incomplete information systems by already known and implemented classification methods, will reduce an effort necessary to construct a new software and framework for such data analysis from the beginning. The secondary aim was to cope with the problem of incomplete information systems without making an assumption of independent random distribution of missing values and without data imputation [4,7]. Many real world applications have showed that appearance of missing values is governed by very complicated dependencies, similar to the ones that we used to searching between decision and conditional attributes. This problem potentially could be solved by application of classification methods to predict value of missing data. However, the application of arbitrary method for data imputation produce a cycle of inductive reasoning steps and the feedback from such a cycle can drastically increase error rate of the classifier.

To meet those assumptions we created a decomposition method that allows for processing of incomplete information systems with use of methods that originally cannot handle missing attribute values. Roughly, the decomposition method consists of two phases. In the first phase incomplete information system, describing entire real-world interest domain, is decomposed into a number of complete information systems, consisting of objects and attributes that are taken from original information system. By accomplishing certain *filling patterns* we expect those complete information subsystems to describe some subproblems of investigated real-world problem, in which the mechanism of missing values appearance is similar. In the second phase some knowledge fusion is necessary in order to merge hypotheses about approximated real-world concept previously decomposed into subproblems. Application of conflict resolving methods is required to merge knowledge from a number of classifiers. As an example of conflict resolving method one may take voting mechanism or similar classifier to the one used in classification of decision subtables obtained from the decomposition phase.

3 Algorithm Description

The decomposition method consists of two phases. In the first one data from original decision table are partitioned into subsets. In the second step, knowledge from those subsets, that in our case is classification hypothesis, is combined to achieve a final classification based on a whole original decision table.

The aim of the first step is to decompose data according to regularities in missing value distribution in data table. The result of decomposition is a number of subtables that are free from missing values and contain as much meaningful data as possible. To provide a mechanism for extraction of data regularities we must apply some kind of pattern extraction that is customized for this task.

Definition 1. Filling pattern.
Let $a_i \neq *$ be a *filling descriptor.* An object satisfies filling descriptor $a_i \neq *$, if value of the attribute a_i for this object is not missing, otherwise object does not satisfy filling descriptor. *Filling pattern* is a conjunction of filling descriptors. An object satisfies filling pattern $a_{k_1} \neq * \wedge \ldots \wedge a_{k_n} \neq *$ if values of attributes $a_{k_1} \ldots a_{k_n}$ for this object are not missing.

Filling patterns are used to discover regular areas in data that contain no missing values. Once we have a filling pattern, we can identify it with a subtable of original data table. Such a subtable consists of attributes that are elements of filling pattern and contains all objects that satisfy this pattern. With such a unique assignment of filling patterns and subtables of original data we can think of result of decomposition step as of set of filling patterns. The decomposition itself becomes a problem of covering data table with patterns, as investigated in [12,13].

Standard approach to generation of covering pattern set is based on greedy strategy. The set of patterns is iteratively extended until all objects from data table are *covered.* The object is covered when exists at least one pattern in generated set that is satisfied by this object. We can outline this algorithm as follows:

1. Extract best filling pattern according to some criteria,
2. Remove objects that satisfy extracted pattern from data table,
3. Repeat 1–2 until all objects are covered by some pattern.

Extraction of best pattern is subordinate to some criteria. In experiments we used a number of criteria that are described in the next section. Also, we carried out some experiments with modified algorithm, where object removal was replaced by various object's weighting techniques. Such a modifications, however, do not improve results so in the final experiments only the above algorithm was used. Pattern extraction was performed with the help of a genetic algorithm that was customized for this task [11]. Deterministic methods [12] were not applicable. Criteria used for selection of best filling patterns are based not only on width and height of pattern, as described in the next section. Customization of genetic algorithm, some data compression and partial result caching permitted results comparable to results of deterministic pattern extraction methods.

Decomposition provides a set of subtables uniquely determined by filling patterns. Those subtables consist of a subset of attributes from original decision table and a subset of objects. Sets of objects and attributes in such subtables are different, but usually not disjoint. Data subtables are free from missing attribute values, so in such tables a classifier that is not able to handle missing values can be applied. We expect that discovered regularities in missing values' distribution are meaningful for inductive learning and partition of interest domain into subproblems in accordance to its hidden nature. The classifier induced over such subset of data should be able to appropriately classify new objects satisfying its filling pattern. When new object is classified, there may occur a situation that more than one, previously selected in decomposition phase, filling pattern is satisfied. Thus, there exists more then one classifier that is capable of classifying such object. In the second phase of decomposition a knowledge integration is required in order to obtain a classifier valid for a whole domain of objects. The problem is how to combine knowledge from different classifiers to obtain one decision. The first approach to this problem is to apply a voting mechanism. However, due to reduction of positive region (see [8]) in decision subtables voting mechanism is not enough. This fact became apparent during the early stage experiments. The more precise method is to apply a classifier induction algorithm similar to the one that is used for subtables. Application of another classifier at the top of subtable-based classifiers allows to fine tune system's answer in a non-linear way. We can imagine a situation that this top classifier can completely change assignment of object's decision obtained from subtable based classifiers. With such a proceeding confidence level of a particular subclassifier depends on filling patterns that are satisfied.

We can briefly summarize the algorithm of classifier induction as follows:

1. Decomposition: Greedy generate filling patterns that meet certain properties,
2. Split data into subtables according to filling patterns,
3. Induce classifier from subtables,
4. Integration: Induce classifier from answers of classifiers based on subtables.

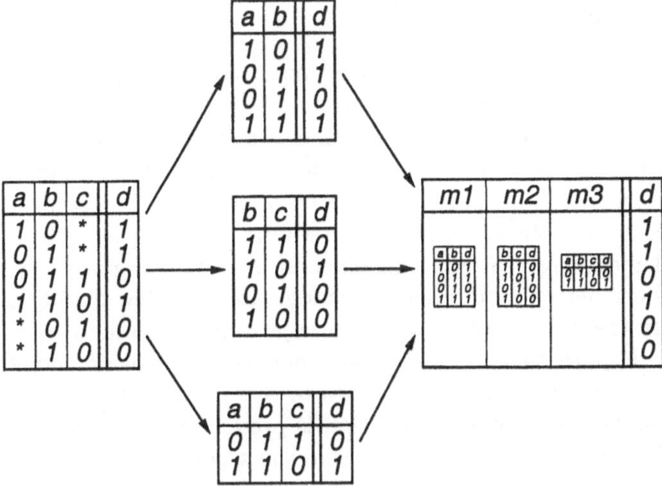

Fig. 1. Illustration of the decomposition method idea.

The classification of new objects is a two step process that requires both layers of previously induced classifiers. Objects that are classified could have missing attribute values, so we have to apply processing scheme similar to the previous one. Classification of such an object proceeds as follows:

1. Check, which filling patterns are satisfied,
2. Compute answers from subclassifiers (i.e. classifiers based on subtables),
3. Compute final decision from top classifier that bounds answers from subclassifiers.

The classification employs methods that are originally unable by itself to process data with missing attribute values. However, the described decomposition method allows to work around this problem. The presented solution does not completely eliminate problem of missing values, because missing values return as missing answers coming from classifiers based on subtables. This problem could be eliminated by using another method of resolving conflict between subtable based classifiers. It is our strong believe that discovered blocks of complete data are relevant and helpful for inductive learning of dependencies between conditional attributes and decision attribute. Missing answers contain information not exactly about missing attribute values, but rather about patterns in missing data distribution. In such patterns missing attribute values should be more comparable, than in whole data. Empirical results showed that this assumption can by correct, but we should cautiously choose proper methods of filling pattern generation.

4 Decomposition Criteria

Subsets of original decision table must meet some requirements in order to achieve good quality of inductive reasoning as well as to be applicable in case of methods that cannot deal with missing attribute values. Original decision table is partitioned into smaller decision tables. Those smaller tables are not necessarily disjoint, but we expect them to exhaustively cover input table. They should contain no missing attribute values. It is obvious, that the quality of inductive reasoning depends on a particular partition and some partitions are better than others. From one point of view quality of learning depends on the number of examples. It is proven that inductive construction of concept hypothesis is only feasible, when we can provide enough number of concept examples. A strict approach to this problem can be found in [20] where Vapnik-Chervonenkis dimension is presented as a tool for evaluation of examples number requirements. From the second point of view inductive learning tries to discover a relationship between decision attribute and conditional attributes. A precise description of concepts in terms of conditional attributes values is required to achieve good quality of classification. Without an attribute, which value is important to concept description it is impossible to accurately approximate a concept. This yields an assumption that subtables derived from partition should also have sufficient number of attributes for inductive learning. It clearly suggests that we should not blindly select partition, especially because the partition has strong influence on reasoning quality.

We should have some measurements in order to compare each partition to others and select the best one. By measuring some properties of decision subtables we can evaluate correspondence between such tables and the decomposition of real world problem into subproblems. Several approaches were applied to estimate the filling pattern correspondence. Among them are:

- Traditional size based evaluation,
- Predictive quality — a real reasoning quality factor that can be evaluated by applying classification algorithm to a subtable.

Traditional size based evaluation is related to width and height of generated subtable. By width we understand a number of attributes in such a table and by height a number of objects. These values correspond to width and height of generated filling pattern. We can combine these two values into fitness function that can be used in genetic algorithm. Standard approach is to evaluate fitness of pattern as a product of width and height ($q = w \cdot h$, where w stands for width of pattern and stands h for height). We can also apply modified fitness function from family $q = w^{\alpha} \cdot h$. However empirical evaluation showed, that there are no big differences between such functions. The observation was, that in searched space of filling patterns there were several patterns with similar size based fitness value, but with drastically different results in quality of classification. This implies the second approach.

	all	exact	$w \cdot h$	$w \cdot h \cdot p$	$w \cdot h \cdot p^2$	$w \cdot h \cdot p^4$	$w \cdot h \cdot p^8$	p
att	17.15	3.90	3.94	4.00	4.10	4.15	4.09	5.35
ban	56.80		5.33	8.09	8.28	9.01	10.08	22.14
cmc2	6.96	2.00	2.00	2.41	2.59	2.91	3.51	3.92
dna2	7.80		1.06	2.54	2.63	2.61	3.55	7.08
hab2	5.00	3.83	3.69	3.20	3.01	2.78	2.50	1.84
hco	164.65	5.03	5.46	5.80	6.16	6.89	9.70	67.54
hep	18.48	3.84	4.03	4.12	4.30	4.70	5.30	8.27
hin	25.97	4.11	3.83	4.91	5.74	7.21	8.77	13.22
hyp	17.96	2.00	2.01	2.01	2.02	2.01	2.01	4.55
pid2	6.77	2.97	2.98	2.99	3.11	3.41	3.48	3.89
smo2	4.00	2.00	2.00	2.42	1.80	1.33	1.39	2.14
tumor	6.40	1.99	2.17	2.53	3.03	3.58	3.84	4.37

Table 1. Average number of filling patterns.

The size based fitness function is only an estimation of relevance for classifier induction. Instead of size based fitness function we can estimate relevance by measuring predictive quality — quality of classifier induced from subset of data determined by this filling pattern. We can easily incorporate such a factor into fitness function of filling pattern. To measure the influence of predictive quality on decomposition relevancy we can test some functions from family $q = w \cdot h \cdot p^{\alpha}$, where p stands for predictive quality and α is the tuning coefficient. We can also completely eliminate a size based factor and put $q = p$ fitness function. Empirical evaluation shows that this last function behaves best.

5 Empirical Evaluation

There were carried out some experiments in order to evaluate decomposition method and its components, such as genetic algorithm for binary pattern extraction. Results were obtained from the average of classification quality from 100 times repeated five-fold Cross-Validation (CV5) evaluation. This testing method was introduced to assure preciseness in measuring the number of generated patterns. The *C4.5* method was used as a classifier and tests were performed with different decomposition approaches as well as without using decomposition method at all. The *WEKA* software system [3], which contains re-implementation of Quinlan's C4.5 Release 8 algorithm in Java, was utilized in experiments. Data sets from UCI [1] machine learning repository were used for evaluation of the decomposition method Selected data sets contain missing values in range from 14.1% to 89.4% of all values in data.

First group of results, presented in Table 1, shows efficiency of filling pattern generation. The numbers in the table are averages over 100 CV5 steps

	C4.5	$w \cdot h$	$w \cdot h \cdot p$	$w \cdot h \cdot p^2$	$w \cdot h \cdot p^4$	$w \cdot h \cdot p^8$	p
att	52.55	+2.39	+3.22	+5.23	+7.79	+9.39	+10.78
ban	62.14	+3.68	+6.37	+8.29	+10.55	+12.77	+14.16
cmc2	45.72	-0.80	+1.56	+2.89	+4.37	+5.61	+5.69
dna2	86.84	-6.11	-0.64	+0.11	+0.32	+1.55	+2.23
hab2	71.54	-3.47	-2.40	-0.83	+1.36	+3.13	+4.44
hco	81.68	-2.18	+0.28	+1.92	+3.34	+4.31	+4.32
hep	80.12	-4.24	-0.59	+1.36	+3.58	+5.17	+6.41
hin	70.47	-0.51	-0.31	+0.02	+0.51	+0.63	+0.06
hyp	95.82	+0.90	+0.94	+0.97	+0.98	+0.99	+1.27
pid2	60.81	+1.17	+1.38	+3.03	+5.43	+6.30	+7.48
smo2	60.75	-4.61	-2.83	+4.73	+7.72	+8.20	+8.91
tumor	38.89	-2.61	+1.28	+3.31	+4.16	+5.00	+4.41

Table 2. Comparison of experiments' results.

of the numbers of patterns generated. The column entitled *exact* corresponds to a method, which is an implementation of exhaustive exact method that checks all 2^n possible patterns and selects the best one. Such a exhaustive search is very time-consuming and therefore was evaluated only for $q = w \cdot h$ fitness function and data that contain no more than 25 attributes. The results presented in following columns were obtained with the help of genetic algorithm using various fitness functions. The corresponding fitness function is described in the header of each column. To make comparison easier we also provide the number of *all* filling patterns that were present in the data. As we can see, the results of exhaustive search are similar to those of genetic algorithm with the same fitness function. Results for other fitness function show that — at least for some data sets — the use of predictive quality does not drastically increase the number of selected patterns.

The second group of results presents a classification qualities in comparison with the C4.5 method. The decomposition method, which uses the predictive quality as a fitness function overcomes results of the C4.5 method. As the importance of predictive quality in filling pattern's evaluation function increases, we can observe a continuous increase of the classification quality. For some data sets other fitness functions achieve good results too. We should consider that evaluation of predictive quality is very time-consuming, in spite of partial results' caching and other optimizations. The last presented column corresponds to experiments with predictive quality as a fitness function. These results nearly overcome all other approaches, including the one the is embed in the C4.5 method of missing attribute values handling.

6 Conclusions

Most of existing methods are incapable of incomplete information systems processing. The decomposition method proved that it is an efficient tool for adapting existing methods to data with missing attribute values. It can be applied to various algorithms of classifier induction to enrich them with capabilities of incomplete information systems processing. In comparison with other approaches to missing attribute values handling [10,21], this method can be applied to a broad group of inductive reasoning algorithms. This unique property of the decomposition method allows an efficient transforming of already developed software systems that could not handle missing data. The week point of this method is the computational complexity of predictive quality evaluation. The answer how to better and less time-consuming evaluate a filling pattern suitability to the decomposition process, remains an open question for a further research.

Acknowledgments

I wish to thank professor Andrzej Skowron for a great support while writing this paper. This work was partially supported by the Polish State Committee for Scientific Research grant No. 8T11C02519.

References

1. C. L. Blake and C. J. Merz. *UCI Repository of machine learning databases.* http://www.ics.uci.edu/~mlearn/MLRepository.html, Univerity of California, Departament of Information and Computer Science, Irvine, CA, 1998.
2. N. H. Bshouty and D. K. Wilson. On learning in the presence of unspecified attribute values. In *Proceedings of the Twelfth Annual Conference on Computational Learning Theory, COLT'99*, pages 81–87. ACM, 1999.
3. E. Frank, L. Trigg, and M. Hall. *Weka 3.1.9, Waikato Environment for Knowledge Analysis.* http://www.cs.waikato.ac.nz/ml/weka, The University of Waikato, Hamilton, New Zealand, 2000.
4. Y. Fujikawa and T. Ho. Scalable algorithms for dealing with missing values. 2001.
5. S. A. Goldman, S. Kwek, and S. D. Scott. Learning from examples with unspecified attribute values. In *Proceedings of the Tenth Annual Conference on Computational Learning Theory*, pages 231–242, 1997.
6. S. Greco, B. Matarazzo, and R. Słowiński. Rough sets processing of vague information using fuzzy similarity relations. In C. S. Caldue and G. Paun, editors, *Finite vs. infinite: contribution to an eternal dilemma*, pages 149–173, Berlin, 2000. Springer-Verlag.
7. J. W. Grzymała-Busse and M. Hu. A comparison of several approaches to missing attribute values in data mining. In W. Ziarko and Y. Y. Yao, *Proceedings of 2nd International Conference on Rough Sets and Current Trends in Computing, RSCTC-2000*, pages 180–187, 2000.

8. J. Komorowski, Z. Pawlak, L. Polkowski, and A. Skowron. Rough sets: A tutorial. In S. K. Pal and A. Skowron, editors, *Rough Fuzzy Hybridization. A New Trend in Decision Making*, pages 3–98. Springer-Verlag, 1998.
9. M. Kryszkiewicz. Properties of incomplete information systems in the framework of rough sets. In L. Polkowski and A. Skowron, editors, *Rough Sets in Data Mining and Knowledge Discovery*, pages 422–450. Physica-Verlag, 1998.
10. W. Z. Liu, A. P. White, S. G. Thompson, and M. A. Bramer. Techniques for dealing with missing values in classification. In X. Liu, P. Cohen, and M. R. Berthold, editors, *Advances in Intelligent Data Analysis*, pages 527–536. Springer-Verlag, 1997.
11. Z. Michalewicz. *Algorytmy genetyczne + struktury danych = programy ewolucyjne*. WNT, 1999.
12. S. H. Nguyen. *Regularity Analysis and its Application in Data Mining*. Praca doktorska, Warsaw University, Faculty of Mathematics, Computer Science and Mechanics, 1999.
13. S. H. Nguyen, A. Skowron, and P. Synak. Discovery of data patterns with applications to decomposition and classification problems. In L. Polkowski and A. Skowron, editors, *Rough Sets in Knowledge Discovery*, volume 2, pages 55–97, Heidelberg, 1998. Physica-Verlag.
14. Z. Pawlak. *Rough sets: Theoretical aspects of reasoning about data*. Kluwer, Dordrecht, 1991.
15. L. Polkowski, A. Skowron, and J. M. Żytkow. Tolerance based rough sets. In T. Y. Lin and A. M. Wildberger, editors, *Soft Computing*, pages 55–58. San Diego Simulation Councils Inc., 1995.
16. J. R. Quinlan. Unknown attribute values in induction. In A. M. Segre, editor, *Proceedings of the Sixth International Machine Learning Workshop*, pages 31–37. Morgan Kaufmann, 1989.
17. J. R. Quinlan. *C4.5: Programs for Machine Learning*. Morgan Kaufman, San Mateo, 1993.
18. A. Skowron. Boolean reasoning for decision rules generation. In J. Komorowski and Z. Ra, editors, *Proceedings of the 7th International Symposium ISMIS'93, Trondheim, Norway*, pages 295–305. Springer-Verlag, 1993.
19. A. Skowron. Extracting laws from decision tables. *Computational Intelligence*, 11 (2):371–388, 1995.
20. V. N. Vapnik. *The Nature of Statistical Learning Theory*. Springer-Verlag, New York, 1995.
21. S. M. Weiss and N. Indurkhya. Decision-rule solutions for data mining with missing values. IBM Research Report RC-21783, IBM T. J. Watson Research Center, 2000.

Granular Sets and Granular Relations: Towards a Higher Abstraction Level in Knowledge Representation

Antoni Ligęza

Institute of Automatics AGH, al. Mickiewicza 30, 30-059 Kraków, Poland
e-mail: ligeza@agh.edu.pl

Abstract. In this paper some ideas about granularity of data and knowledge are put forward. The concepts of a *granular set* and *granular relation* are defined and some algebraic operations on them are outlined. Granular data representation with a varying preciseness is a key issue in moving the knowledge representation and manipulation operations to a higher level of abstraction.
Keywords: *granular sets, granular relations, semi-partitions, granular relational algebra*

1 Introduction

Knowledge representation and manipulation can be performed at various levels of abstraction. In this paper some ideas about granularity of data and knowledge are put forward. The concepts of a *granular set* and *granular relation* are defined and some algebraic operations on them are outlined. Granular data representation with an adjustable preciseness is a key issue in moving knowledge representation and manipulation to a higher level of abstraction.

In intelligent information analysis, data mining and machine learning the use of *partition calculus* can be observed [1,6]. The approach presented here make use of a weakened version of set partition concept. The paper puts forward the idea of a *semi-partition* into granular values and a calculus based on this idea. A semi-partition of a set (e.g. the domain of an attribute) is a set of disjoint subsets of it. The sets forming a semi-partition need not to cover the whole universe. Algebraic operations on semi-partitions, granular sets and granular relations are defined. The level of granularity changes according to details of knowledge representation and operations performed.

The aim of the paper is to present a concept of granularity in sets and relational tables. An extended version of *Relational Algebra*, applied in *Relational Database Systems* is outlined. The proposed extension consists in admitting non-atomic, granular values, so the formalism is kept close to the original relational algebra. The results are called *Extended Attributive Decision Tables* and *Granular Relational Algebra*. Roughly speaking, the proposed modification allows to represent and manipulate 'blocks' of data rather than single data items.

2 Basic mathematical notions

Consider some universe **U** of atomic objects or values under interest. This can be both a set of numerical values or vectors, such as $\mathbf{R}$ or $\mathbf{R}^n$ or a finite or infinite set of symbolic values. Let S denote any set being a subset of **U**. It is usual to consider such a set either as *extensionally specified* collection of elements (in this case one writes $S = \{s_1, s_2, \ldots, s_m\}$ if S is a finite discrete set), or as *intensionally specified* area in **U** (in such a case one writes $S = \{s \in U : \phi_S(s)\}$, where $\phi_S(s)$ is the so-called characteristic formula of S).

In analysis of certain sets it may be the case that some of its elements are in certain sense 'equivalent' or 'indiscernible' while some other may be distinguished landmarks or characteristic values. In such a case it may be useful to consider the elements of such sets from the standpoint of qualitative point of view. In particular, some values may be 'glued' together to form bigger 'granules' while some values may stay untouched.

Consider the simplest case of set T of possible discrete water temperatures. Let $T = \{-25, -24, \ldots -2, -1, 0, 1, 2, \ldots, 99, 100, 101, \ldots, 119, 120\}$. Note that there are two characteristic landmark values, i.e. 0 (the water turns into ice) and 100 (the temperature of boiling water). Below 0 we have normally ice, and the temperature of it is usually not of interest. Between 0 and 100 we have just water. Above 100 we have steam. For certain qualitative analysis it may be useful to consider a structure $G(T) = (T, \sigma(T))$, where $\sigma(T)$ is the partition of T into the following sets: $T_1 = \{-25, -24, \ldots -2, -1\}$, $T_2 = \{0\}$, $T_3 = \{1, 2, \ldots, 99\}$, $T_4 = \{100\}$ and $T_5 = \{101, 102, \ldots, 120\}$. Further, if we do not insist to be very accurate, we may disregard the landmark values (as ones rarely met in practice), and consider only an incomplete partition of T, say T_1, T_3 and T_5. As in fact we consider a set with some of its elements 'glued' together and forming "granules" of values, a structure like $G(T) = (T, \{T_1, T_3, T_5\}$ will be called a *granular set*, and the set of disjoint granules $\{T_1, T_3, T_5\}$ will be called a *sigma-partition* or a *semi partition* of T.

3 Set partitions and semi-partitions

Recall that if S is a collection of individual elements and $S_1, S_2, \ldots S_k$ are some subsets of S, then the sets $S_1, S_2, \ldots S_k$ form a *partition* of S, if and only if (iff): (i) $S_1 \cup S_2 \cup \ldots \cup S_k = S$ (i.e. partition satisfies the completeness condition), and (ii) $S_i \cap S_j = \emptyset$ for any $i \neq j$ (i.e. partition satisfies the separation condition). Obviously, partitions can be defined for ordered and nominal sets; the sets $S_1, S_2, \ldots S_k$ are called *blocks*.

Although from theoretical point of view the concept of partition provides a convenient tool for analysis of sets at an abstraction level higher than a single element [6,1], in practice it is often the case that one does not have the possibility to consider all the subsets necessary to form a partition; in such a case the completeness condition is not satisfied. Consider a set V and several subsets of it, say $V_1, V_2, \ldots, V_k$. We shall say that sets $V_1, V_2, \ldots, V_k$ form a *semi-partition* of V iff $V_i \cap V_j = \emptyset$ for $i \neq j$. A semi-partition will be also called an *incomplete partition*, or an s-partition for short. An s-partition of V will be denoted as $\sigma(V)$.

In case of an ordered set L any s-partition of it is a set of disjoint intervals covered by L (the intervals are ordered), and in case of a nominal set N any s-partition of it is just a collection of disjoint subsets of N. The case of a lattice is specific; an s-partition of a partially ordered set K is $\sigma(K) = \{K_1, K_2, \ldots, K_k\}$, such that $K_1, K_2, \ldots, K_k \in K$ and for any $K_i \neq K_j$, $K_i \sqcap K_j = \top$. For intuition, in case of lattice a semi-partition is formed by incomparable, separate elements of the set.

If $\sigma(V)$ is an s-partition, $\sigma(V) = \{V_1, V_2, \ldots, V_k\}$, then the set of all the elements of V occurring in the s-partition $\sigma(V)$ will be called the ***support*** of it and it will be denoted as $[\![\sigma(V)]\!]$; of course, $[\![\sigma(V)]\!] = V_1 \cup V_2 \cup \ldots \cup V_k$.

A nice thing about s-partitions is that any family of subsets of some set V can be transformed into an 'equivalent' (having the same support) s-partition of V. Let us consider an arbitrary collection of subsets of V, say $V' = \{V'_1, V'_2, \ldots, V'_m\}$ (not necessarily disjoint ones). By subsequent replacing any two sets V'_i and V'_j of V' (ones having nonempty intersection) with three sets: $V'_i \setminus V'_j$, $V'_j \setminus V_i$ and $V'_i \cap V'_j$ one can generate an s-partition $\sigma(V) = \{V_1, V_2, \ldots, V_k\}$ of V as the fixed point of this replacement operation. More formally, for any two sets $V'_i, V'_j \subseteq V'$ one may define the following partition generation operation as $V'_i \sqcap V'_j = \{V'_i \setminus V'_j, V'_j \setminus V'_i, V'_i \cap V'_j\}$. Further, let $\Pi(V') = \{V_1, V_2, \ldots, V_k\}$, where $V_i \cap V_j = \emptyset$ for $i \neq j$, $V_1 \cup V_2 \cup \ldots \cup V_k = V'_1 \cup V'_2 \cup \ldots \cup V'_m$, and $\Pi(V')$ is the fixed point of the $V'_i \sqcap V'_j$ operation over the subsets of V' and derived from them sets. Note that the $\Pi()$ transformation to s-partition is constructive if only the operations $\cap$ and $\setminus$ are defined.

4 Granular sets

Let S be any set. A granular set over S can be defined as follows.

Definition 1 *A granular set $G(S)$ is a pair $G(S) = (S, \sigma(S))$, where $\sigma(S)$ is any s-partition defined on S. The set S is called the* domain *of the granular set, while the s-partition $\sigma(S)$ defines the so-called* signature of granularity.

A granular set can be defined in an arbitrary way. In a number of practical applications, however, its structure can be *induced* in a natural way. Let there be some finite set of classes or decisions of the form $C = \{c_1, c_2, \ldots c_k\}$; usually, in tasks such as pattern recognition or decision making the set contains just a few elements. Let there be a (partial) mapping h defining the classification or decision procedure of the form $h: S \longrightarrow C$; a decision $c_i \in C$ is assigned to an element of S. As in general case h is not a one-to-one mapping, consider an inverse mapping h^{-1} of the form $h^{-1}: C \longrightarrow 2^S$. Note that for any two different elements $c_i, c_j \in C$ there is $h^{-1}(c_i) \cap h^{-1}(c_j) = \emptyset$

(in other case h would not be a function). Thus in fact the co-domain of h^{-1} is an s-partition over S. In such a case we would say that being given a set S, a set C and a functional mapping $h: S \longrightarrow C$, the mapping h *induces* an s-partition over S. Even in the case the mapping in undefined for some values of S, a granular set of the form $G(S) = (S, h^{-1}(C))$ is properly defined. This explains the idea and potential origin of granular sets.

Granular sets can be compared among themselves. From now on, assume for simplicity that only sets of exactly the same domains are compared. Hence, a granular set can provide finer or more rough signature of granularity. Consider some two granular sets $G(S) = (S, \{S_1, S_2, \ldots, S_k\})$ and $G'(S) = (S, \{V_1, V_2, \ldots, V_m\})$. An s-partition $\sigma'(S) = \{V_1, V_2, \ldots, V_m\}$ is finer the an s-partition $\sigma(S) = \{S_1, S_2, \ldots, S_k\}$ iff any set $S_i \in \sigma(S)$ can be expressed as $S_i = V^1 \cup V^2 \cup \ldots V^{n_i}$, where $V^1, V^2, \ldots V^{n_i} \in \sigma'(S)$. In other words, a finer granular set (or s-partition) is build from smaller blocks and can be used to re-build the more rough one. In this way a partial order relation w.r.t. *finer granularity* can be introduced.

Another partial order relation w.r.t. *blocks covering* can be introduced as follows. For intuition, a more general granular set (its signature) covers a less general one iff any block of the latter is covered by some block of the former one. Consider two granular sets $G(S) = (S, \sigma(S))$ and $G'(S) = (S, \sigma'(S))$. Then $G(S) \leq G'(S)$ iff $\sigma(S) \leq \sigma'(S)$; the latter condition means that $\forall S_i \in \sigma(S)\ \exists V_j \in \sigma'(S) : S_i \subseteq V_j$, i.e. any block of $\sigma(S)$ is covered by some (single) block of $\sigma'(V)$. The s-partition $\sigma'(V)$ will be called *more general* as one operating at more general level of granularity.

5 Elements of an algebra of s-partitions

The simplest algebraic operations can be performed directly over s-partitions. Note that since s-partitions are sets of blocks (of set-elements), the usual set-algebraic operations ($\cup$, $\cap$, $\setminus$, etc.) over s-partitions can be applied. However, in order to make sense of such operations, the s-partitions must be based on the same signature of the universe, i.e. they must use the same universe of blocks. Below some further specific operations are outlined in brief.

Consider a set V and two s-partitions of it, say $\sigma(V)$ and $\sigma'(V)$. The *product* of such two s-partitions is defined as $\sigma(V) \cdot \sigma'(V) = \{V_{ij} : V_{ij} = V_i \cap V_j, V_i \in \sigma(V), V_j \in \sigma'(V)\}$. Obviously, the product of two s-partitions is an s-partition. Note that the product of two s-partitions defines the maximal common parts from both s-partitions covered by any of them (in certain cases it can be the empty file). Roughly speaking, the product of two s-partitions is the s-partition composed of all nonempty intersections of their blocks. The product of two s-partitions is less general than any of them.

In a similar way a *composition* of s-partitions can be defined; $\sigma(V) \circ \sigma'(V) = \Pi(\sigma(V) \cup \sigma'(V))$. Note that the s-partitioning is necessary if one wants to preserve the 'structure' of original partitions (e.g. the boundaries of the initial intervals), since some elements of the partitions may be overlapping; in such a case the result might not be an s-partition. The composition of any two s-partitions is one of finer granularity than any of the initial ones and in most cases contain more elements. The elements of $\sigma(V) \circ \sigma'(V) \setminus \sigma(V) \cdot \sigma'(V)$ will be called *residuals.*

Any two s-partitions $\sigma(V)$ and $\sigma'(V)$ define also a *cover* $\Sigma(\sigma(V), \sigma'(V))$, i.e. an s-partition covering all the elements of V belonging to some component set of at least one of them. The construction of a cover can be analogous to the one of s-partition operation. Consider the set $\sigma(V) \cup \sigma'(V)$; by subsequent replacing of any two elements V_i and V_j of it having a non-empty intersection by $V_i \cup V_j$ one obtains the cover $\Sigma(\sigma(V) \cup \sigma'(V))$ being still an s-partition of V. Note that $\sigma(V) \cdot \sigma'(V) \leq \sigma(V) \circ \sigma'(V) = \Pi(\sigma(V) \cup \sigma'(V)) \leq \Sigma(\sigma(V) \cup \sigma'(V))$.

For intuition, both s-partitioning with the $\Pi()$ operator and generating a cover with the $\Sigma()$ are kinds of operations preserving the support, but changing the signature. In case of s-partitioning one preserves also in some way the definition of the initial signatures (structuring) (e.g. the boundaries of intervals of characteristic subsets of V), while in the case of cover generation a kind of maximal reduction of the subsets is performed.

Consider also *reduction* operation transforming an s-partition into another, more general one, by *gluing* some of its elements; this operation will be called *reduction* of the s-partition. Let $\sigma(V)$ be an s-partition of V. Let $\{V^1, V^2, \ldots, V^k\}$ be some selected blocks of it, and let $W = \{V^1 \cup V^2 \cup \ldots \cup V^k\}$. Reduction is defined as $\rho(\sigma(V)) = \sigma(V) \setminus \{\{V^1, V^2, \ldots, V^k\}\} \cup W$. The reduction of an s-partition consists in replacing several blocks with an equivalent single block. The generated output must be an s-partition, so in the case of intervals, gluing is allowed only for intervals which meet or overlap. The generated s-partition is equivalent w.r.t the support, but simultaneously it is more general than the input one.

Finally, consider the problem of checking if $[\![\sigma(V)]\!] \subseteq [\![\sigma'(V)]\!]$ having given two s-partitions of V and the so-called *induced split* operation. An obvious sufficient condition is that $\sigma'(V)$ is more general than $\sigma(V)$; however this is not a necessary condition.

Consider the set $V = \{a, b, c, d, e, f, g, h\}$, and the following s-partitions: $\sigma(V) = \{\{a, b, c\}, \{d, e, f\}\}$ and $\sigma'(V) = \{\{a, b\}, \{c, d, e\}, \{f, g\}\}$. Although $\sigma'(V)$ covers all the elements of V occurring in $\sigma(V)$ (i.e. $[\![\sigma(V)]\!] \subseteq [\![\sigma'(V)]\!]$), the generalization $\leq$ defined as above does not hold. This means that verification if $[\![\sigma(V)]\!] \subseteq [\![\sigma'(V)]\!]$ cannot be easily performed at the abstract level by checking that $\sigma(V) \leq \sigma'(V)$. In such a case, instead of going down the the most detailed level of single elements of V, it seems reasonable to perform some further reduction of $\sigma'(V)$ or *split* of the s-partition $\sigma(V)$; for simplicity we consider only the latter case. In our example, $\sigma(V)$ should be split into an s-partition of the form $\{\{a, b\}, \{c\}, \{d, e\}, \{f\}\}$, since we want to perform some *minimal split.* Such an operation will be called an *induced split* of $\sigma(V)$

generated according to the structure of $\sigma'(V)$. More formally, the *split* of $\sigma(V)$ *induced* by $\sigma'(V)$ is performed according to the following principles:

- any block $V_i \in \sigma(V)$ is processed in turn; if the block is a subset of some $V_j \in \sigma'(V)$, then it is left untouched,
- for any other block, its (nonempty) intersections with every blocks of $\sigma'(V)$ are generated and deleted from V_i, and placed in the resulting s-partition of the split operation (i.e. $\{V_i\} \cdot \sigma'(V)$),
- the residual C_i being the rest of V_i (uncovered by any of the elements of $\sigma'(V)$ is added to the result (if nonempty).

From the procedure above, one can see that a satisfactory condition for $[\![\sigma(V)]\!] \subseteq [\![\sigma'(V)]\!]$ is that any residual C_i should be empty. In fact, it is equivalent to check that $\Pi(\sigma(V) \cup \sigma'(V)) \leq \sigma'(V)$.

6 Basic knowledge representation model : extended attributive tables

The basic knowledge representation model accepted here is defined as the so-called *Extended Attributive Decision Table* [4]. The scheme of a table consists of a sequence of (distinct) attributes, say $A_1, A_2, \ldots, A_n$, selected as common characteristics of data items. For any attribute A_i there is defined its domain D_j, for $j = 1, 2, \ldots, n$. The basic data and knowledge representation structure is just a table $T = [t_{ij}]$, $j = 1, 2, \ldots, n$, $i = 1, 2, \ldots, m$ with the columns labelled with the attributes and the rows being records (or specifying rules).

Note that, if attributes $A_1, A_2, \ldots, A_n$ constitute names of some characteristics such that their domains are linearly ordered sets (e.g. subsets of integer or real numbers) and the t_{ij} are atomic ones, it is convenient to imagine any object described with some record as a *point* in the n-th dimensional space defined by the attributes (to be called the *conceptual space*). This leads to an idea of more powerful representation admitting some *regions* rather than points. In fact this idea is almost omnipresent in the philosophy of science, in mathematics and in various areas of computer science. In his recent work on *Conceptual Space Logic* [5] Nilsson provides a formal account for a *conceptual space* and the idea that "*...concepts occupy or are identified with regions within the space...*" is explored. The geometrical interpretation of formal representation of concepts was also pursued in [3,4].

The basic extension considered in this paper consists in removing the constraint imposed by the requirement of atomic values of attributes, while keeping the external structure the ones of RDBs. In Extended Attributive Decision Tables instead of atomic point values it is proposed to admit t_{ij} to be *interval values*, *set values* and *lattice elements*. Note that looking at each column j of the table we have the domain D_j and a number of sets (intervals) $t_{1j}, t_{2j}, \ldots, t_{mj}$. For intuition, the key issue about such tables and granular sets is that the data covered by any column of such table can be transformed to a granular set of the form $G(D_j) = (D_j, \Pi(t_{1j} \cup t_{2j} \cup \ldots \cup t_{mj}))$. This should allow to introduce data representation and manipulation with algebraic operations at the level of higher granularity.

In these paper three basic types of domains are considered: ones being *linearly ordered sets* (for simplicity, we assume discrete sets only, although it is not crucial for this approach), partially ordered sets forming a lattice structure (with difference operation defined for elements), and ones being *nominal sets* (with no order or partial order relation established). Further, three basic operations must be defined, i.e. $\cup$, $\cap$, and $\setminus$. To be consistent, we admit use of non-convex intervals (e.g. as defined by Ladkin in [2]).

Finally, the definition of *Granular Relation* providing mathematical core of an extended attributive table can be defined.

Definition 2 *Let $G_1 = (D_1, \sigma_1(D_1))$,..., $G_n = (D_n, \sigma_n(D_n))$ be some granular sets. A* granular relation *$R(G_1, G_2, \ldots, G_n)$ is any set R_G such that $R_G \subseteq U$ where*

$$U = \sigma_1(D_1) \times \sigma_2(D_2) \times \ldots \times \sigma_n(D_n). \tag{1}$$

The elements (rows) of a granular relation will be called *boxes*. Note that in fact a granular relation defines and extended attributive table; however, there are tables which are not expressed with granular relations. This will be the case if the subsets of at least one domain overlaps; we shall show how to 'normalize' such a table so that it takes the form of a granular relation.

7 Towards an algebra for knowledge manipulation

Consider two tables, say T_1 and T_2, both of them being granular relations having the same scheme of attributes. Let $[\![T]\!]$ denote the extensional form of T, i.e. an appropriate subset of $\mathbf{U} = D_1 \times D_2 \times \ldots D_n$ of atomic data records, such that all of them and only they satisfy the specification given by T. Now one can specify the following definitions of basic operations:

- *union*: $T = T_1 \cup T_2$ iff $[\![T]\!] = [\![T_1]\!] \cup [\![T_2]\!]$,
- *intersection*: $T = T_1 \cap T_2$ iff $[\![T]\!] = [\![T_1]\!] \cap [\![T_2]\!]$,
- *set-minus*: $T = T_1 \setminus T_2$ iff $[\![T]\!] = [\![T_1]\!] \setminus [\![T_2]\!]$,
- *covering*: $T_1 \subseteq T_2$ iff $[\![T_1]\!] \subseteq [\![T_2]\!]$.
- *complement*: $T_1 = \overline{T_2}$ iff $[\![T_1]\!] = [\![U]\!] \setminus [\![T_2]\!]$.

In order to perform operations necessary to various knowledge manipulation and verification operations [4] the above set of basic operations over the Extended Attributive Tables must be defined.

Consider two tables T_1 and T_2. Before approaching any algebraic operation on them it is crucial to accomplish an agreement among them with respect to the granules of knowledge they use, i.e. they must make use of the same s-partition of the conceptual space. If so, the tables use the same set of potential boxes, and in such a case the algebraic operations can be applied at the meta-level in an efficient way.

The first step should consists in decomposing both of the tables into the so-called *canonical forms* based on the same s-partition.

Definition 3 *A granular relation is in* canonical form *iff no projection (on a column) of any two boxes described with some rows overlap. Two (or more) granular relations are in consistent canonical forms, iff they are both in canonical form, and they use the same partition (signature) of the universe.*

For simplicity, maximal canonical forms are preferred. Consider first the case of a single table T, perhaps not being a granular relation (having overlapping values). Consider projection operation[1] $\pi_j(T)$, i.e. the projection on attribute A_j. We obtain a family of subsets of the domain of this attribute. The subsets, each of them corresponding to one row, are not necessarily disjoint. Using the partitioning algorithm one is to generate an appropriate s-partition $\sigma(D_j) = \Pi(\pi_j(T))$, preserving the support. Assume the s-partition for domain D_j is given by $\sigma(D_j) = \{V_1, V_2, \ldots, V_k\}$.

At the second stage the initial table must be split so that the values of the attribute A_j are only the ones of $\sigma(D_j)$. This can be done by replacing any attribute value t_{ij} with the sum of components belonging to $\sigma(D_j)$ only. Let $t_{ij} = V^1 \cup V^2 \cup \ldots \cup V^r$, where $V^1, V^2, \ldots, V^r \in \sigma(D_j)$. The i-the row of the table is now replaced by r rows of the form:

A_1	A_2	$\ldots$	A_j	$\ldots$	A_n
t_{i1}	t_{i2}	$\ldots$	V^1	$\ldots$	t_{in}
t_{i1}	t_{i2}	$\ldots$	V^2	$\ldots$	t_{in}
t_{i1}	t_{i2}	$\ldots$	$\vdots$	$\ldots$	t_{in}
t_{i1}	t_{i2}	$\ldots$	V^r	$\ldots$	t_{in}

(2)

The split operation must be performed for any row i, such that t_{ij} is not an element of the s-partition $\sigma(D_j)$. In such a way the initial table is transformed to an equivalent form, but such that in the j-th column only the blocks of the appropriate s-partition are used. The split operation must be performed for any column of the table, i.e. for $j = 1, 2, \ldots, n$.

Observe that, after the split operation one obtains a table T^* equivalent to the initial one (covering the same area in the conceptual space) but covering only disjoint boxes of the space. Note that if $\sigma(D_j)$ is the s-partition of the domain of the j-th attribute, then the resulting table is composed of the elements of the Cartesian product of the s-partitions, i.e. $T^* \subseteq U$, where U is defined by (1). The picture one can have in mind is as follows: table T^* represents separate boxes in the conceptual spaces. Due to using s-partitions to represent the values in columns, the resulting table is in its canonical form.

[1] As in classical RDBS, projection is a mapping of the table onto a specific column(s).

Now, in the case of two tables T_1 and T_2 one has to apply the same procedure in parallel. The only difference is that at the beginning one has to take the sum of projections on attribute A_j for both of the tables, i.e. the initial family of sets for the j-th column is given by $\pi_j(T_1) \cup \pi_j(T_2)$. This family is split then into the s-partition $\sigma_j(D_j) = \Pi(\pi_j(T_1) \cup \pi_j(T_2)) = \{V_1, V_2, \ldots, V_k\}$, which is now common for both of the tables. The process of row splitting goes as before, and as before the procedure is repeated for any column of the tables. As the result one obtains the canonical forms of the initial tables, T_1^* and T_2^*, such that:

$$T_i^* \subseteq \sigma_1(D_1) \times \sigma_2(D_2) \times \ldots \sigma_j(D_j) \times \ldots \sigma_n(D_n) \tag{3}$$

for $i = 1, 2$. Obviously, both the canonical forms are embedded in the same meta-space of boxes; they share the same signatures (structure of granularity) of the conceptual space. Any two boxes are disjoint, and any box is represented with one row of some table. This enables the straightforward definition of algebraic operations to be performed at the meta-level.

In fact, the definitions of *union*, *intersection*, *set difference*, *covering* and complement are the same as for classical databases. In case of *union* duplicates are eliminated. The complement operation, defined as $\overline{T^*} = \sigma_1(D_1) \times \sigma_2(D_2) \times \ldots \times \sigma_n(D_n) \setminus T^*$ is defined in a constructive way, although an attempt at executing it may lead to a large number of rows – as in the case of classical RDBS. Note, however, that in comparison to classical RDBs, the number of elements in the complement will be reduced to the degree following from the reduction of the initial detailed space $D_1 \times D_2 \times \ldots \times D_n$ to $\sigma_1(D_1) \times \sigma_2(D_2) \times \ldots \times \sigma_n(D_n)$.

Finally, one can consider *reduction* of the resulting table to some minimal form. The reduction operation consists in gluing 'similar' rows into one, equivalent to the original ones; in the conceptual space reduction can be illustrated as joining some neighboring boxes. More formally, consider two or several rows of some table of the form given by (2), where $V_{ij} = V^1 \cup V^2 \cup \ldots \cup V^r$ (this time the sets V^l are not necessarily disjoint). The rows can be replaced with a single row of the form:

A_1	A_2	$\ldots$	A_j	$\ldots$	A_n
t_{i1}	t_{i2}	$\ldots$	V_{ij}	$\ldots$	t_{in}

(4)

The reduction operation leads to a simpler form; some boxes are replaced with one bigger. Therefore, it is crucial operation for knowledge abstraction, i.e. moving to a more abstract level or thicker granularity of the conceptual space. The reduction may be applied in a way that the canonical form is obtained (note that after certain operations, the result may be not in the canonical form, although both inputs were; the simplest example is the union of two boxes which can be glued into a single box). If one wants to reduce to canonical form only, the reduction of table should be applied in such a way that a projection over any column is always an s-partition of the domain of the attribute assigned to this column. More precisely, if $\pi_j(T)$ is the family of sets observed in the j-th column of T, after reduction to some table T', projection $\pi_j(T')$ should be an s-partition of D_j. Referring to the reduction operation ρ, reduction can be performed by finding $\rho(\pi_j(T))$ for rows identical on any attributes apart A_j; such reduction leads to a number of rows equal to the number of elements of the s-partition $\rho(\pi_j(T))$.

Reduction to canonical form leads to a unique result T^*. It can be also continued, leading to some minimal forms of T (having less rows than the canonical form). In such a case, however, the final form is not necessarily unique. Further, $\pi_j(T)$ may be no longer an s-partition.

8 Concluding remarks

The paper presented an approach to algebraic management of intensional knowledge specification with use of granular sets and granular relations. The key notion introduced is the one of s-partition of a set. The knowledge itself is represented with Extended Attributive Tables. The approach follows the ideas presented in [3,4] and it is based on classical RDBs. The main difference consist in admitting non-atomic, granular values of attributes. Special attention was paid to sets, lattice elements and intervals. Such extension leads to a more abstract level of knowledge representation and manipulation.
Acknowledgment The research was carried out within a KBN Grant No.: 8 T11C 019 17.

References

1. Daniłowicz Cz., Nguyen N. T. (2001) Criteria and Function for Expert Information Representation Choice. In: Kłopotek M.A., Michalewicz M., Wierzchoń S. (Eds.) Advances in Soft Computing – Intelligent Information Systems. Physica Verlag, Heidelberg, 227-237
2. Ladkin P. (1986) Time Representation: a Taxonomy of Interval Relations. In: Proceedings of of AAAI'86, 360–366
3. Ligęza A. (1999) Intelligent Data and Knowledge Analysis and Verification; Towards a Taxonomy of Specific Problems, In: Vermesan A., Coenen F. (Eds.) Validation and Verification of Knowledge Based Systems: Theory, Tools and Practice. Kluwer Academic Publishers, Boston/Dordrecht/London, 313-325
4. Ligęza A. (2001) Toward Logical Analysis of Tabular Rule-Based Systems. Int J of Intelligent Systems 16:333-360
5. Nilsson J.F. (1999) A Conceptual Space Logic. In: Kangassalo H. et al. (Eds.) Information Modelling and Knowledge Bases IX. IOS Press, Amsterdam, 1999, 39–53
6. Traczyk W. (1997) How to Learn From Diversified Examples. In: Bubnicki Z., Grzech A. (Eds.) Knowledge Engineering and Expert Systems, Wrocław, 21-28 (in Polish)

Reducing Memory Requirements of Scope Approximator in Reinforcement Learning

Artur Michalski

Institute of Computing Science, Poznan University of Technology, Piotrowo 3A, 60-965 Poznan

Abstract. Scope classification is an instance-based technique, which can be used as a function approximator in reinforcement learning system. However, without any storage management mechanism, its memory requirements can be huge. This paper presents modified version of scope approximator using density threshold to control memory usage. Computational experiments investigating the performance of the system and results achieved are reported.

1 Introduction

Reinforcement learning is a learning paradigm in which there is no teacher or trainer. The only information available to the agent is sparse feedback generated by its environment. The agent learns how to achieve its goal in sequential fashion by trial-and-error interactions with environment. The agent progressively learns optimal value function. This function represents agent's knowledge about the best long-term outcome it could receive in a given state when a specific action is applied and then the optimal policy is followed.

In reinforcement learning system value function is defined over the state or state-action pairs space and usually represented by function approximator [1, 2, 6]. The most important property of learning in continuous spaces that must be considered, is that it often begins without knowing the size and/or granularity of the state space. Thus, resource requirements are also unknown. However, when designing function approximators only limited resources are available. Choosing the way the function approximator represents the value of state-action pairs is an important decision, because it affects both memory requirements and learning efficiency [7]. The more memory is available to store state-action pairs, the higher the resolution of the function approximator. On the other hand, if the number of allocated state-action pairs grows, the time required to establish the value of the function for every pair increases. Given fixed amount of resources, a function approximator, which enables to control its resolution may lead to better performance and learning efficiency. We present below new method of reducing memory requirements of scope approximator and results of its experimental evaluation.

2 Scope classification

The scope classification is a new approach to learning from examples [3]. Thus, it is a supervised learning method. However, the scope algorithm as a kind of instance-based learning technique can be also used as a function approximator in reinforcement learning methods [4, 5, 6]. Within the scope algorithm, every new object is classified according to the examples in the training set that are "closer" to the object than any example labeled with another class. However, in contrast to standard distance-based classifiers, scope classification relies on partial pre-orderings between examples, indexed by objects. As a result, the number of neighbors of a given object is not fixed.

Let us introduce the basic definitions of the scope classification more formally.

2.1 Basic concepts

Let T be a training set and o be an object to be classified, described by a set of attributes $\{atr_i\}$. Our aim is to derive a classifiers that best approximates the target function i.e., maps every object to its right class denoted $class(o)$. Specifically, we are interested in classification rules, which are relevant and consistent for the training set.

Let $C(o_1, o_2)$ denote the smallest hyper-rectangle containing objects o_1 and o_2. $C(o_1, o_2)$ is defined as the conjunction of conditions (selectors) $C_i(o_1, o_2)$ on each attribute i:

- if the value of attribute i is missing in o_1 or in o_2 then $C_i(o_1, o_2)=True$,
- if i is nominal and $atr_i(o_1) = atr_i(o_2)$ then $C_i(o_1, o_2) = atr_i(o_1)$ else $C_i(o_1, o_2)=True$,
- if i is numerical or ordered then $C_i(o_1, o_2) = [min(atr_i(o_1), atr_i(o_2)), max(atr_i(o_1), atr_i(o_2))]$,

  where $atr_i(o_1)$ and $atr_i(o_2)$ are values of ith attribute of o_1 and o_2 respectively.

Thus, the most specific rule covering an object o to be classified and example e of the training set is:

$$R(o, e) \equiv C(o, e) \Rightarrow (\, y=class(e)\,),$$

if example e is labeled with $class(e)$.

For every object o, let $\prec_o$ denote the partial pre-ordering defined by, for every o_1 and o_2, o_1 is closer to o than o_2, if and only if o_1 satisfies $C(o, o_2)$, denoted $o_1 \models C(o, o_2)$

Thus, the rule $R(o, e)$ is consistent for T if and only if there is no example e_1 of T labeled with a class different from $class(e)$ such that $e_1 \prec_o e$. More formally, the neighborhood can be expressed as follows:

Let e be an example of T and o be an object to be classified. Let $CE(e, T)$ denote the set of examples e' of T such that $class(e') \neq class(e)$. e is a neighbor of o w.r.t. T, denoted $e \in scn(T, \prec_o)$, if and only if $\neg\exists\, e' \in CE(e, T)$ such that $e' \prec_o e$.

Let us emphasize, that by above definition, e is not required to be closer to o than all examples labeled with class different from *class*(e) to belong to $scn(T, \prec_o)$. What is needed is that no "counter-example" ce is closer to o than e (see Fig. 1). This means that either e is closer to o than ce, or that e and ce are not comparable w.r.t. $\prec_o$, that is the most frequent case.

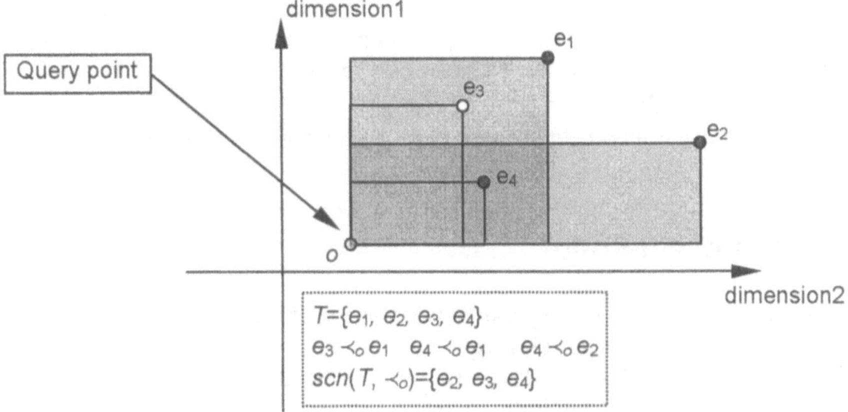

Fig. 1. Example of scope classification neighborhood in bidimensional space

An immediate consequence of the definition of $scn(T, \prec_o)$ is that, there exists a consistent and relevant rule $R=c \Rightarrow (y = v_y)$ for T that covers o if and only if there exists $e \in scn(T, \prec_o)$ such that $class(e)=v_y$, and $C(o, e) \models c$.

Based on this theorem we can avoid generation of relevant and consistent rules by computing $scn(T, \prec_o)$ instead. Certainly, rules can be easily derived on as-needed basis.

2.2 Parameterized scope classification

The logical basements of scope classification presented above are very strict. They must be relaxed to be useful in real data computations. Actually, a rule satisfied by a few counter-examples should not be ignored automatically. The consistency requirement can be relaxed by accepting at most ε counter-examples. Let $NI(e, T)$ be the number of examples ce from different class than e and closer to o than e, that is:

$$NI(e, T) = |\{ce \in CE(e, T) \mid ce \prec_o e\}|^1$$

An example e is an ε-neighbor of o w.r.t. T if and only if $NI(e, T) \leq \varepsilon \times |T|$.

Not all attributes must be interesting in areas of the space, so forgetting some of them (at most M) can turn out to be valuable. Formally, an object o_1 is closer to an

[1] For any set E, $|E|$ denotes its cardinality.

object o than an object o_2 except on (at most) M attributes, denoted $o_1 \prec_o^M o_2$, if and only if

$$|\{\text{attribute } i \mid atr_i(o_1) \not\models C_i(o, o_2)\}| < M.$$

An example e is an M-neighbor of o w.r.t. T, denoted $e \in M\text{-}scn(T, \prec_o)$, if and only if $e \in scn(T, \prec_o^M)$.

We can also strengthen the relevance requirement in order to consider only strong rules (rules satisfied by at least δ examples). Let $NC(e, T)$ be the number of examples f from the same class as e and closer to o that e, that is:

$$NC(e, T) = |\{f \in T \mid class(f) = class(e) \wedge f \prec_o e\}|$$

An example e is an δ-neighbor of o w.r.t. T if and only if $NC(e, T) > \delta \times |T|$.

3 Learning algorithm

Although not designed for approximation scope classifier can be used as a function approximator [4]. Since class equality or inequality tests can be preformed for both discrete and continuous classes (class/decision attribute value), no modifications of algorithm are required. Moreover, like all instance-based algorithms, scope classification is an incremental method. Therefore it can be used as a function representation mechanism in reinforcement learning system [5, 6].

Our main idea is to maintain a set of all agent's experiences in memory. Each memory element is a record of state-action pair the agent experienced before together with the approximated function value. Such historical information represents our training set. The memory expands dynamically and on demand as new regions of the state-action space are being explored. All instances in memory are used to determine the neighbors of the query point (new instance added) according to scope classification algorithm. The application of scope classification consists of three parts: a) recording each experience, b) using scope classification approach to find neighbors of the current query point, c) extracting output values from retrieved neighbors.

We applied these three parts to Q-learning [8] as follows:

1. The agent records the state and action it makes for each step in the environment by adding a new instance to memory. The instances in our memory-based function approximator have a simple structure. Every instance is a combination of a state s_j and action a_j the agent has performed in the past together with the approximated q_j-value for such combination, that is, $e_j=(s_j, a_j, q_j)$.
2. When the agent is about to choose action, it finds instances considered to be similar according to scope classification approach.
3. Using these instances, the agent calculates Q-value by averaging together the expected future reward values associated with the adjacent states for each action (q_i-values). The agent then chooses the action with the highest Q-value. The regular Q-learning update rule is used to update the instances that voted for the chosen action.

$P \equiv \{e_i \mid e_i \equiv \langle s_i, a_i, q_i \rangle\}$

$SCN(P, \varepsilon, \prec^{M}_{s_t,a_t}, \delta) \equiv \{e_i \in P \mid o \equiv (s, a) \wedge e_i \in scn(P, \prec^{M}_{o}) \wedge$
$NI(e_i, P) \leq \varepsilon \times |P| \wedge NC(e_i, P) > \delta \times |P|\}$

$N(s, a) \equiv |SCN(P, \varepsilon, \prec^{M}_{s_t,a_t}, \delta)|$

$$Q(s,a) \equiv \begin{cases} \dfrac{1}{N(s,a)} \displaystyle\sum_{e_i \in SCN(P,\varepsilon,\prec^{M}_{s,a},\delta)} q_i & \text{if } N(s,a) > 0 \\ Q_{init} & \text{otherwise} \end{cases}$$

$P := \varnothing$

for each time step t **do**:

1. observe current state s_t
2. select an action a_t for state s_t (using $Q(s_t, a)$ for each action a)
3. execute chosen action a_t; observe new state s_{t+1} and immediate reinforcement r_t
4. modify q-values of all neighbors i.e. $\forall e_i \in SCN(P, \varepsilon, \prec^{M}_{s_t,a_t}, \delta)$:

   $\Delta q_i := \alpha\, [r_t + \gamma\, max_a\, Q(s_{t+1}, a) - Q(s_t, a_t)]$
5. **for** each neighbor i.e. $\forall e_i \in SCN(P, \varepsilon, \prec^{M}_{s_t,a_t}, \delta)$ **do**
6. create two new objects em_i i ep_i according to the following rule:
7. $\forall r\ \ \Delta_r(\tau) = [max(\text{atr}_r) - \min(\text{atr}_r)]\, \tau$
8. $\forall r\ \ \text{atr}_r(em_i) = \text{atr}_r(e_i) - \Delta_r(\tau)$
9. $\forall r\ \ \text{atr}_r(ep_i) = \text{atr}_r(e_i) + \Delta_r(\tau)$
10. **endfor**
11. **if** $\neg\exists e_i \in SCN(P, \varepsilon, \prec^{M}_{s_t,a_t}, \delta)$ such that $\langle s_t, a_t, Q(s_t, a_t)\rangle \in \text{C}(em_i, ep_i)$ **then**
12. $P := P \cup \{\langle s_t, a_t, Q(s_t, a_t)\rangle\}$
13. **endif**

endfor

Fig. 2. Q-learning algorithm with scope approximator and new memory management mechanism

Our learning algorithm is based on two learning paradigms. Like all memory-based methods, it learns by storing examples, which are samples of its input space. However, these samples are not obtained from the teacher or trainer. They are generated in experiment (just running). Unlike most other memory-based methods, our system also performs reinforcement learning on values that are not directly available from experience. These required output values are Q-values. They are however closely related to another experimental data, namely the rewards. Detailed algorithm description is presented in Fig. 2.

3.1 Density adjustment

In order to reduce memory requirements of scope approximator we extended it with a new mechanism of storing instances in memory. Whereas in standard scope approximator each new object is added into memory, in our modified version of algorithm new instance can be stored only if a special condition is satisfied. The condition verification requires all neighbors of a new instance to be examined. For each neighbor hyper-rectangle surrounding it is created and then the test whether new object is contained in it or not is performed. The condition is fulfilled if there is no neighbor of new instance whose hyper-rectangle contains it (see Fig. 3). The size of the hyper-rectangle depends on the size of the state space and the value of the parameter called *density threshold.* The bigger the size of the state space, the larger the hyper-rectangle surrounding each neighbor. The density threshold is a scale coefficient whose values range from 0 to 1. The lower the value of the coefficient, the higher density of instances of the state space.

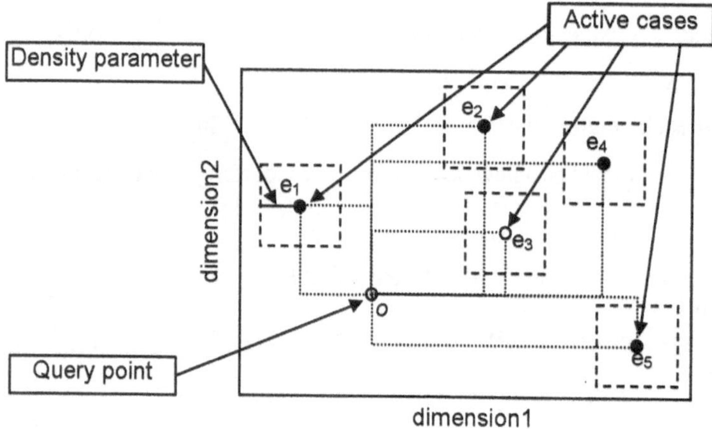

Fig. 3. Modified scope approximator with density threshold

4 An empirical evaluation

This section describes the results of using modified version of scope approximator in control problem with continuous state and action spaces. The problem studied is the double integrator. This is a linear dynamic system ,with quadratic costs that depends both on the state and action values.

4.1 Double integrator problem

The double integrator problem is represented by a car of unit mass moving in a flat terrain and subject to the application of a single force (see Fig. 4). The car is allowed to move along one-dimensional track. The controller applies either a left or right force (acceleration, a) of changing magnitude (bounded to be in the range between a_{min}=-1 and a_{max}=1) to the car at each time step. The objective is to place the car in the target position starting from a given state in such a way that the sum of the rewards is maximized.

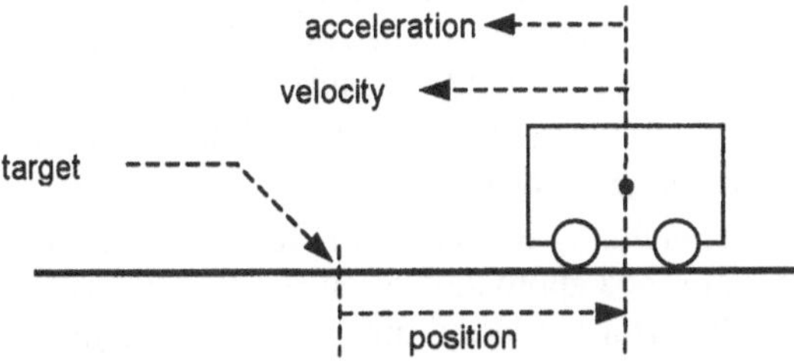

Fig. 4. Double integrator problem

The double integrator is a system with linear dynamics and bidimensional state. The state of the system consists of the current position, p, and velocity, v, of the car. The dynamic of the system is described by the following equations:

$$\frac{dp}{dt} = v$$

$$\frac{dv}{dt} = a$$

In order to use a reinforcement learning system as a controller for the double integrator problem, an appropriate reinforcement function must be used. The one-step reward function is a negative quadratic function of the difference between the current and desired position, p_t, and the acceleration applied, a_t, $r_{t+1} = (p_t^2 + a_t^2)$. Thus, the agent is penalized more heavily when the distance between the current and desired states is large and also when the action applied is large.

The double integrator problem is an instance of more general class of linear dynamics systems with quadratic cost function, which have a simple closed-form solution for the optimal policy known as *Linear-Quadratic Regulator* [7]. The optimal policy is given by equation $a^*=-(\sqrt{2}\ v + p)$, where v and p are the instantaneous velocity and position, respectively.

4.2 Experimental design

Our experiment consisted of 10 runs with different initial values of seed of the random number generator. Each run continued for 50 trials, measuring the number of time steps, cumulative cost (i.e., negative sum of rewards) and the number of instances in memory for each run after each trial. During simulation we used a time step of Δt = 0.05 seconds and a new control actions were performed every four time steps. Each trial consisted of starting the system at position p = 1 with velocity $v = 0$ and continued until either 200 decision steps had elapsed (i.e. 40 simulated seconds) or the state gets out of bounds (i.e., when $|p|>1$ or $|v|>1$), whichever comes first. In the latter case, the agent received a negative reward (i.e., a punishment) of 50 units to discourage it from going out of bounds. The averages number of time steps, cumulative costs and number of instances in memory across runs were used as measures of performance.

Action utilities of new state-action pairs (Q_{init}) were initialized to 0. The values of learning parameters were roughly optimized by a small number of preliminary runs and equal $\alpha = 0.9$, $\gamma = 0.99$, respectively. The stochastic exploration strategy used was ϵ-greedy policy with $\epsilon = 0$.

The density threshold, τ, was changed from 0.001 to 0.10. The influence of other parameters of scope approximator on learning process was also studied, but results presented below are selected only for values giving the best performance level.

In order to deal with continuous action space an adequate action selection mechanism based on one-step search [7] was used. According to this the action space was divided into 12 equally spaced acceleration values between a_{min} and a_{max}.

4.3 Computational results

The best results obtained for both standard and modified version of scope approximator are presented on Fig. 5. As we see, extending scope approximator with additional mechanism of storing new instance in memory yields positive results. Our method achieved much lower memory utilization than standard scope approximator. While the number of instances allocated in memory grows linearly in standard approximator (Fig. 5a), memory requirements of our method are logarithmic and two orders of magnitude smaller (Fig. 5b). However, the quality of policy obtained is worse than in standard scope approximator (Fig. 5d). This is obviously the effect of reduction in the density of instances in state space. The learning speed is also lower than in standard scope approximator, but both methods were able to stabilize their performance around the same trial (Fig. 5c). Interestingly enough, however, if we consider computational time requirements of modified approximator (not presented on graphs), it is still possible to achieve better performance level of learning than with standard scope approximator. Like the number of instances stored in memory (Fig. 5b), these requirements are also two orders of magnitude smaller than in standard algorithm. Given the fact that the reinforcement learning systems are able to improve their knowledge permanently, we can obtain better policy simply by extending the number of decision steps. In reinforcement learning systems time required to determine the neighbors of an instance and evaluating its Q-value is crucial because the agent performs these two operations extensively during the action selection and learning. Thus, due to limited number of instances stored in memory, these time requirements are significantly decreased and therefore the portion of time devoted only to learning process can be increased.

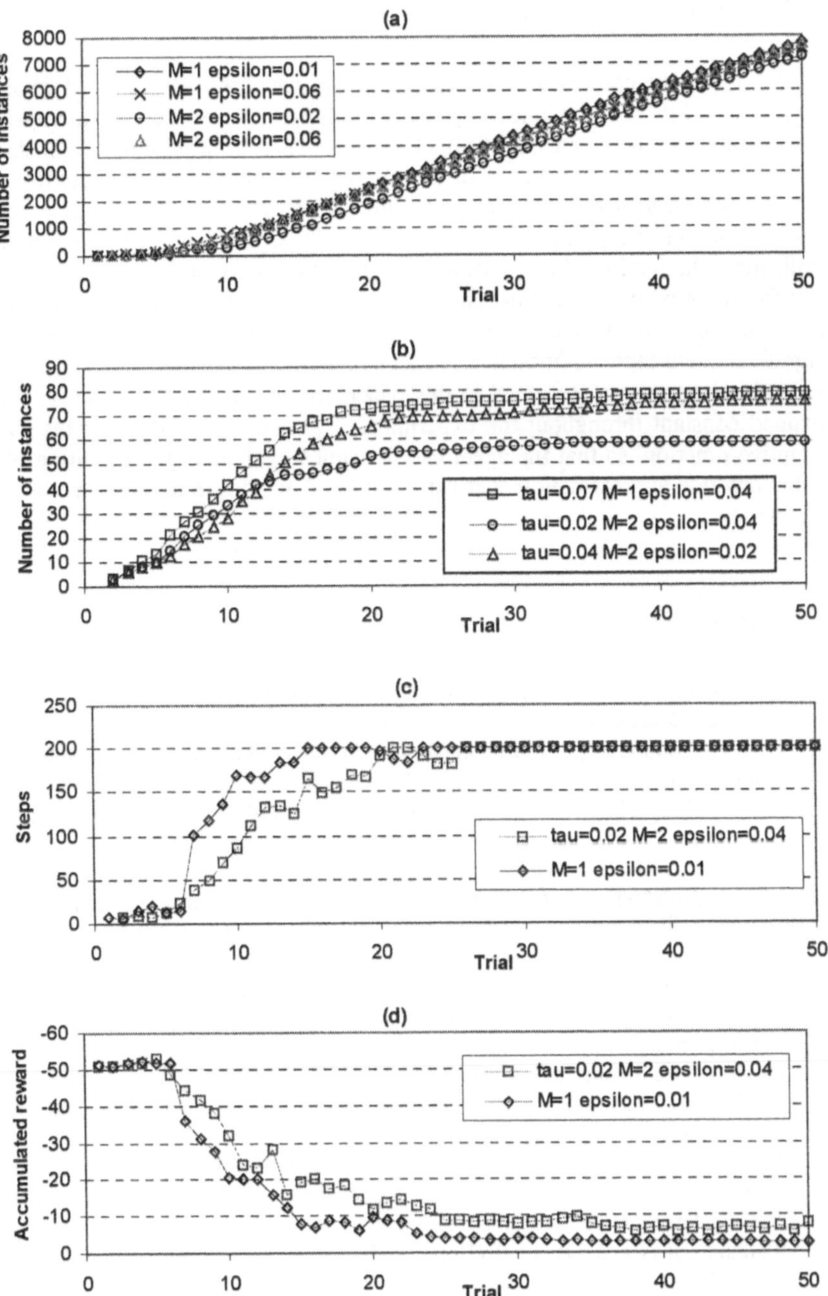

Fig. 5. Double integrator problem: memory utilization and best learning curves for standard and modified version of scope approximator

5 Concluding remarks

In this paper we described scope approximator, which have been used so far to represent value function and proposed modification to reduce its memory requirements. The idea consists of attaching new criterion of adding new instances to memory. The main advantage of this approach is that it enables to control density of instances in the state space by means of density threshold. The results achieved tend to support the idea of using density adjustment to manage memory utilization, though in order to ensure such a good quality of the final policy as in standard approximator we must perform more learning steps. However, reduction in the computational time requirements obtained by attaching the criterion is so significant, that these additional costs can be ignored.

In the experiments presented in this paper, we used density parameter that remained constant throughout the experiment. However, it is also possible to use adaptive function, so that the agent can dynamically change the resolution of the value function approximation as it gathers more data. Future research will address this issue.

References

1. Atkeson CG, (1991) Memory-based learning control. In: Proceedings of the 1991 American Control Conference, volume 3, Boston, pp 2131-2136
2. Barto AG, Sutton RS, & Anderson CW (1983) Neuronlike elements that can solve difficult learning control problems. IEEE SMC, 13:835-846
3. Lachiche N and Marquis P (1998) Scope Classification: An Instance-Based Learning Algorithm with a Rule-Based Characterisation. In: Proceedings of the 10th European Conference on Machine Learning, Chemnitz, Germany. Springer-Verlag, LNAI 1398
4. Michalski A (2000) An Application of Scope Classification in Reinforcement Learning. In: Proceedings of the 9th International Workshop on Intelligent Information Systems, Bystra, Poland 2000. IPI PAN, Warsaw, pp 89-93
5. McCallum RA (1996) Hidden state and reinforcement learning with instance-based state identification. IEEE Tans. on System, Man, and Cybernetics (special issue on Robot Learning)
6. Moore AW and Atkeson CG (1992) An investigation of memory-based function approximators for learning control. Technical Report, MIT Artificial Intelligence Laboratory
7. Santamaria JC, Sutton RS, Ram A (1996) Experiments with Reinforcement Learning in Problems with Continuous State and Action Spaces. COINS Technical Report 96-088. University of Massachusetts, Amherst
8. Watkins CJCH and Dayan P (1992) Technical Note: Q-learning. Machine Learning 8:279-292

An Experimental Comparison of Methods for Handling Incomplete Data in Learning Parameters of Bayesian Networks

Agnieszka Oniśko[1], Marek J. Druzdzel[2], and Hanna Wasyluk[3]

[1] Faculty of Computer Science, Białystok University of Technology, ul. Wiejska 45-A, 15–351 Białystok, Poland, aonisko@ii.pb.bialystok.pl

[2] Decision Systems Laboratory, School of Information Sciences, Intelligent Systems Program, and Center for Biomedical Informatics, University of Pittsburgh, Pittsburgh, PA 15260, USA, marek@sis.pitt.edu

[3] The Medical Center of Postgraduate Education, and Institute of Biocybernetics and Biomedical Engineering, Polish Academy of Sciences, Marymoncka 99, 01–813 Warsaw, Poland, hwasyluk@cmkp.edu.pl

Abstract. Missing values of attributes in data sets, also referred to as incomplete data, pose difficulties in learning tasks, such as classification, data mining, or learning Bayesian network structure and its numerical parameters. Because of the predominance of incomplete data in practice, many methods have been proposed to deal with them while there are few studies that compare their performance. The HEPAR II project presents an excellent opportunity to test experimentally how these methods perform on a real data set. We briefly review several popular methods for handling incomplete data and then compare them on the task of learning conditional probability distributions of a Bayesian network model, where the comparison criterion is the resulting diagnostic accuracy. While substitution of "normal" values of missing attributes seemed to perform best, we observed only a small difference in performance among the studied methods.

1 Introduction

It is a fact of life that most practical databases of measurements or cases contain missing values of some of their attributes. There are many reasons for missing data. Sometimes they result from human errors of omission (e.g., a nurse forgetting to record the result of a measurement) sometimes the value of the attribute in question was not known (e.g., a patient forgetting whether or not she had chicken pox as a child). At other times, the value might have not made sense (e.g., presence or absence of pregnancy in a male patient). While the causes of missing values may be of interest in choosing how to handle them, the fact that a measurement is missing is uniformly a complication in any algorithm that analyzes the data.

Cowell *et. al* [3] define a database to be complete when all cases that it contains are complete. In turn, a case is complete if every random variable has a state or a value assigned to it. A database is incomplete, if it contains at least one incomplete case. A case is incomplete, if one or more of the random variables has no value associated with it.

The data in an incomplete case can be missing, unobserved, or censored at random, but there may also be some structure, known or unknown, in why some values are missing. Little and Rubin [11,17] define three kinds of possible mechanisms that account for missing data. The first account is referred to as the missing at random (MAR) property. One way to formulate the MAR property is that while cases with incomplete data differ from cases with complete data, the pattern of data missingness is predictable from other variables in the database rather than being due to the specific variable on which the data is missing. The second mechanism is related to a situation when the data are missing completely at random (MCAR), i.e., when cases with complete data are indistinguishable from cases with incomplete data. The third type of missing data mechanism involves non-ignorable (NI) property, i.e., when the pattern of data missingness is not random and it is not predictable from other variables in the database. In case of medical data sets, both the MAR and the MCAR assumptions seem invalid. There are typically identifiable reasons why a measurement is missing.

Little and Rubin [11] offer an extensive review of various statistical approaches to handle missing data. The first group of methods involves listwise or casewise data deletion, pairwise data deletion, mean substitution, or hot deck imputation. There are also more sophisticated approaches involving regression methods, Expectation Maximization (EM) approach, raw maximum likelihood methods, or multiple imputation. All these methods require that the data meet the MAR assumption. For cases with non-ignorable mechanisms for missing data, a pattern-mixture model was developed [9,10,12].

Various approaches have been developed for learning parameters in probabilistic systems from incomplete data. These techniques include iterative methods like stochastic Gibbs Sampling [8], EM algorithm [5], and methods based on probability intervals, for example, deterministic method Bound and Collapse [16], or methods presented in [1,4]. Most of these methods assume usually the MAR property for all incomplete cases, however, Bound and Collapse algorithm proved to be robust also for NI data.

There seems to be little in terms of comparative studies that would test the proposed approaches in practical settings. Many approaches are typically tested on artificial data (or artificially introduced missing values to real world data, e.g., [16]). The HEPAR II project and its underlying HEPAR data set have provided us with an opportunity to test various approaches to handle missing data on a real data set. It has given us also a natural and fairly objective criterion for such a comparison — the quality of the resulting model. We test the diagnostic accuracy of the HEPAR II model for various methods and present the results of experimental comparison.

The remainder of this paper is structured as follows. Section 2 describes briefly the HEPAR data set and the HEPAR II model. Section 3 reviews several methods for handling incomplete data. Section 4 reports the results of an experimental comparison of selected methods that we tested on the HEPAR data set and the HEPAR II model. Finally, Section 5 discusses general issues related to the performed study and directions for further work.

2 The HEPAR data set and the HEPAR II model

Our work on the HEPAR II system is a continuation of the HEPAR project [2,18], conducted in the Institute of Biocybernetics and Biomedical Engineering of the Polish Academy of Sciences in collaboration with physicians at the Medical Center of Postgraduate Education in Warsaw. The HEPAR system was designed for gathering and processing of clinical data of patients with liver disorders and aimed at reducing the need for hepatic biopsy by modern computer-based diagnostic tools. An integral part of the HEPAR system is its database, created in 1990 and thoroughly maintained since then at the Gastroentorogical Clinic of the Institute of Food and Feeding in Warsaw. The current database contains over 800 patient records and its size is steadily growing. Each hepatological case is described by over 160 different medical findings, such as patient self-reported data, results of physical examination, laboratory tests, and finally a histopathologically verified diagnosis.

The version of the HEPAR data set, available to us, consisted of 699 patient records. The HEPAR data set contains many missing values. While there may be some randomly missing values that can be attributed to errors of omission, these are not very likely, as the data set is well maintained and utmost care is exercised in keeping it complete and correct. One of the main reasons for missing values is sheer economics. There are more than 40 variables that represent laboratory tests. It is obvious that not every patient will undergo all the possible tests since not all of them are relevant to a particular diagnostic situation. Also, performing a laboratory test is often expensive.

The HEPAR II project [13,14] aims at applying decision-theoretic techniques to diagnosis of liver disorders. Its main component is a Bayesian network model involving a subset of over 70 variables included in the HEPAR database. The model covers 11 different liver diseases and 61 feature nodes encoding medical findings such as patient self-reported data, signs, symptoms and laboratory tests results. The structure of the model, (i.e., the nodes of the graph along with arcs among them) was built based on medical literature and conversations with our domain expert, a hepatologist Dr. Hanna Wasyluk (third author of the current paper) and two American experts, a pathologist, Dr. Daniel Schwartz, and a specialist in infectious diseases, Dr. John N. Dowling, from the University of Pittsburgh. The elicitation of the structure took approximately 50 hours of interviews with the experts, of which roughly 40 hours were spent with Dr. Wasyluk and roughly 10 hours spent with Drs. Schwartz and Dowling. This includes model refinement sessions, where previously elicited structure was reevaluated in a group setting. The numerical parameters of the model, i.e., the prior and conditional probability distributions, were learned from the HEPAR database. All continuous variables in the database were discretized by our expert.

Missing values in the HEPAR database have been a major problem in our work on the HEPAR II project. We counted that there were 7,792 missing values (15.9% of all entries!) in the learning data set. Figure 1 presents the cumulative distribution of the number of cases in the HEPAR data set as a function of the number of missing values per patient case. For example, there were 200 records in the HEPAR data set where each case had at most nine missing values. Please, note that there were no records that are complete.

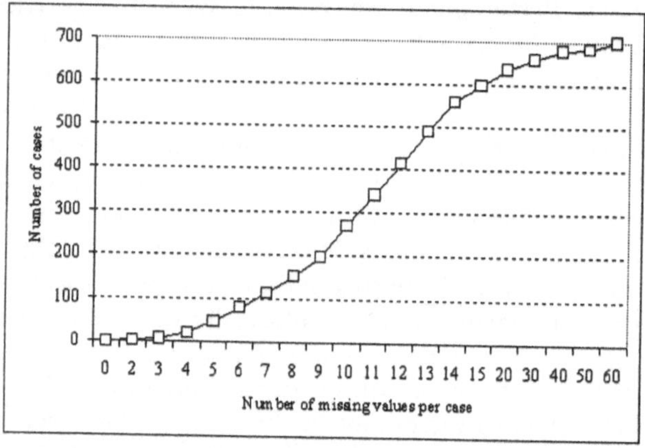

Fig. 1. Number of cases as a function of the number of missing values per case

We have tried several approaches to handle incomplete data when learning conditional probability distribution of the HEPAR II model, the choice of which was based on conversations with our expert and understanding that resulted from these.

3 Methods for handling missing data

The following section describes briefly several simple approaches to handling missing values in databases. We applied some of these methods in the course of the HEPAR II project.

3.1 Discarding records with missing data

The simplest way of dealing with missing data involves *listwise or casewise data deletion* approach. The method simply omits entire records if they have missing values for any of the variables. In those cases where only a small fraction of records contain missing values, this is a simple method that works well. An underlying assumption in this approach is that the values are missing at random and, thus, discarding records with missing data will not bias the remaining data set. When many records contain missing values, this method becomes unreliable. For example, in the HEPAR data set, no single record contained all values. Application of this method would thus result in an empty data set.

3.2 Missing as an additional state

A simple approach to handling incomplete data is treating a missing value of an attribute as an additional state of the attribute, i.e., the missing measurements are interpreted as possible values of the variables in question. This interpretation requires some care when using the system. It is assumed namely that the fact that a measurement was not taken is meaningful — for example, in case of a medical database, the physician did not find taking the measurement appropriate. The meaning of the thus construed outcome *unmeasured* can be in this way equivalent to a measured value of the variable. This approach does not assume that data are missing at random.

3.3 Replacement by "normal" values

The third approach for handling missing values is based on the suggestions of Peot and Shachter [15] on the interpretation of missing values in medical data sets. They argued convincingly that data in medical data sets is not missing at random and that there are two important factors influencing the probability of reporting a finding. The first factor is a preference for reporting present symptoms over absent symptoms. The second factor is a preference for reporting more severe symptoms before those that are less severe. In other words, if a symptom is absent, there is a high chance that it is not reported, i.e., it is missing from the patient record. And conversely, a missing value suggests that the symptom was absent. Then, in learning the model parameters, missing values for discrete variables are assigned to state *absent* (e.g., a missing value for *Jaundice* is interpreted as *absent*). In case of continuous variables, a missing value is assigned as a typical value for a healthy patient elicited from the expert (e.g., a missing value for *Bilirubin* is interpreted as being in the range of 0–1 *mg/dl*). Similarly to the previous approach, this method assumes that the pattern of data missingness is not random.

3.4 Replacement by mean values

Replacement by mean values approach relates to filling in missing data values with a variable's mean that is computed from available cases. In case of discrete binary variables, a missing value is substituted by the outcome that occurs most frequently in the data.

3.5 Hot deck imputation

Hot deck imputation approach [6] examines the cases with complete records and identifies the most similar case to the case with a missing value. Then, it substitutes a missing value with the most similar case's variable value. More sophisticated hot deck algorithms identify more than one similar record and then randomly select one of those available donor records to impute the missing value or use an average value if that were appropriate.

3.6 K-NN techniques

The distance weighted k-Nearest Neighbor techniques (k-NN) [7] are widely used in many practical research problems. The k-NN techniques involve searching for k nearest neighbors of a given data point, i.e., in case of a medical data set, it would consist in looking for neighboring patient cases. One practical issue in applying k-NN approach is that the distance between instances is calculated based on all attributes of the instance. The k-NN approach can be also used in the imputation of incomplete data, where it involves imputation of missing values based on the neighboring patient records.

4 Experimental comparison of the approaches

Our experiments involved learning conditional probability distributions of the HEPAR II model from the HEPAR data set. We compared the diagnostic accuracy of HEPAR II for each of the methods dealing with missing data. In each case, the model had the same graphical structure elicited from the experts. In other words, the various approaches to deal with missing data had impact only on the numerical parameters of the model and not on its structure. The diagnostic accuracy was defined as the percentage of correct diagnoses and was determined by cross-validation using the leave-one-out method. When testing the diagnostic accuracy of HEPAR II, we were interested in both (1) whether the most probable diagnosis indicated by the model is indeed the correct diagnosis, and (2) whether the set of w most probable diagnoses contains the correct diagnosis for small values of w (we chose a "window" of w=1, 2, 3, and 4). The latter focus is of interest in diagnostic settings, where a decision support system only suggest possible diagnoses to a physician. The physician, who is the ultimate decision maker, may want to see several alternative diagnoses before focusing on one.

In our comparison we have taken into account the methods described in Sections 3.2 through 3.6. We could not include approaches that are based on discarding records with missing data (Section 3.1) because there was not even one complete record in our data set (see Figure 1). In case of the *replacement be mean values* approach, we noticed that most of mean values that were calculated for the variables representing laboratory tests were significantly higher/lower than normal values. For example, a mean value for AST was equal to $111U/L$[1] while the normal value for this finding is between 5 and $35U/L$. When analyzing the HEPAR data set, we found that there were only three binary variables, for which "present" value was the most frequent occurring value. In case of the ***hot deck imputation*** approach, we defined the most similar case as a case that has the highest number of similar or equal values for corresponding variables. We also employed the k-nearest neighbor method for $k = 1, 5$. We chose the Euclidean distance as a metric. For $k = 1$, we substituted missing values with the values of the nearest neighbor, in case of the five nearest neighbors, we have calculated mean values based on the neighboring cases and replaced with them missing values. Because the results were similar for both values of k, we present the results only for $k = 5$.

In addition, we have included the following three methods that played the function of the baseline, i.e., we expected that they would perform poorly.

Replacement by "abnormal" values

This method is the opposite of replacement by "normal" values described in Section 3.3 and involves replacing missing values with values that are considered "abnormal." Missing values for discrete variables are replaced by "present" value and for continuous variables are replaced by the values indicating most abnormal result (elicited from the expert).

Proportional random replacement

In this method we replaced missing values by a random drawing from the set of possible states of the variable. The probability of drawing a state was proportional to the probability of that state.

Replacement at random

In this method, we replaced missing values by a random drawing from the set of possible states of the variable. The probability of drawing a state was uniform, i.e., each state was equally likely to be drawn.

Table 1 captures the results of the diagnostic accuracy of HEPAR II for different approaches to handle missing values. The methods marked by an asterisk are also presented graphically in Figure 2.

5 Discussion

We tested the diagnostic accuracy of HEPAR II for several methods dealing with incomplete data. In each case, the model had the same graphical structure elicited from the experts. The accuracy for most of the methods that

[1] An abbreviation U/L stands for units/liter.

Table 1. The diagnostic accuracy of HEPAR II for different approaches to handle incomplete data for window size equal $w = 1, 2, 3, 4$

Approach	w=1	w=2	w=3	w=4
Replacement by "normal" values*	0.57	0.69	0.75	0.79
Missing as an additional state*	0.54	0.67	0.75	0.82
Replacement by mean values*	0.49	0.63	0.72	0.77
Hot deck imputation	0.51	0.64	0.72	0.77
k-NN	0.51	0.63	0.71	0.77
Replacement by "abnormal" values*	0.51	0.65	0.72	0.78
Proportional random replacement	0.52	0.66	0.74	0.79
Replacement at random*	0.49	0.64	0.72	0.78

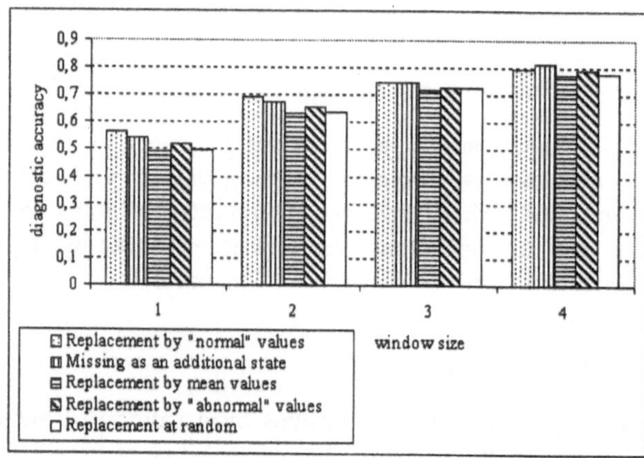

Fig. 2. The diagnostic accuracy of HEPAR II as a function of the window size for selected approaches to handling missing data.

we have tested was similar, with *replacement by "normal" values* and *missing as an additional state* performing slightly better than other approaches. It is interesting that while there are some performance differences between the methods, they are minimal. Even though the data set contained many incomplete values and one would expect even small performance differences to be amplified, this did not happen. It will be interesting to probe this issue further by performing tests on another real medical data set.

Our expert was able to predict a-priori which method would perform best on the data or, in other words, which of the assumptions was the most reasonable, even though the performance difference turned out to be minimal. Our advice to those knowledge engineers who encounter data sets with missing values is to reflect on the data and find out what the reasons are for missing values. In case of medical data sets, the assumption postulated by Peot and

Shachter [15] seems very reasonable. Even in this case, however, we advise to run it through the expert.

Acknowledgments

Marek Druzdzel was supported by the Air Force Office of Scientific Research grant F49620–00–1–0112, Hanna Wasyluk was supported by Medical Center of Postgraduate Education grant 501–2–1–02–59/02, and by Institute of Biocybernetics and Biomedical Engineering PAS grant 16/ST/02. Our collaboration was enhanced by travel funds from the NATO Collaborative Linkage Grant PST.CLG.976167.

The HEPAR II model was created and tested using SMILE, an inference engine, and GeNIe, a development environment for reasoning in graphical probabilistic models, both developed at the Decision Systems Laboratory, University of Pittsburgh and available at `http://www2.sis.pitt.edu/~genie`.

References

1. Silvia Acid, Luis M. de Campos, and Juan F. Huete. Estimating probability values from an incomplete dataset. *International Journal of Approximate Reasoning*, 27(2):183–204, 2001.
2. Leon Bobrowski. HEPAR: Computer system for diagnosis support and data analysis. Prace IBIB 31, Institute of Biocybernetics and Biomedical Engineering, Polish Academy of Sciences, Warsaw, Poland, 1992.
3. Robert G. Cowell, A. Philip Dawid, Steffen L. Lauritzen, and David J. Spiegelhalter. *Probabilistic Networks and Expert Systems.* Springer Verlag, New York, 1999.
4. Luis M. de Campos, Juan F. Huete, and Serafin Moral. Probability Intervals: A tool for uncertain reasoning. *International Journal of Uncertainty, Fuzziness and Knowledge-Based Systems*, 2:167–196, 1994.
5. A. Dempster, D. Laird, and D. Rubin. Maximum likelihood from incomplete data via the EM algorithm. *Journal of the Royal Statistical Society*, 39:1–38, 1977.
6. B. L. Ford. An overview of hot-deck procedures. In Rubin D. B. Madow W. G., Olkin I., editor, *Incomplete data in sample surveys*, pages 185–207. Academic Press, New York, 1983.
7. K. Fukunaga. *Introduction to Statistical Pattern Recognition.* Academic Press, New York, 1972.
8. S. Geman and D. Geman. Stochastic relaxation, Gibbs distributions and the Bayesian restoration of images. *IEEE Transactions on Pattern Analysis and Machine Intelligence*, 6:721–741, 1984.
9. D. Hedeker and R.D. Gibbons. Application of random-effects pattern-mixture models for missing data in longitudinal studies. *Psychological Methods*, 2(1):64–78, 1997.
10. R.J.A. Little. Pattern-mixture models for multivariate incomplete data. *Journal of the American Statistical Association*, 88:125–134, 1993.

11. R.J.A. Little and D. B. Rubin. *Statistical analysis with missing data.* John Wiley and Sons, New York, 1987.
12. R.J.A. Little and N. Schenker. Missing data. In C.C. Clogg G. Arminger and M.E. Sobel, editors, *Handbook for Statistical Modeling in the Social and Behavioral Sciences*, pages 39–75. New York Plenum, 1994.
13. Agnieszka Oniśko, Marek J. Druzdzel, and Hanna Wasyluk. Extension of the Hepar II model to multiple-disorder diagnosis. In S.T. Wierzchoń M. Kłopotek, M. Michalewicz, editor, *Intelligent Information Systems,* Advances in Soft Computing *Series*, pages 303–313, Heidelberg, 2000. Physica-Verlag (A Springer-Verlag Company).
14. Agnieszka Oniśko, Marek J. Druzdzel, and Hanna Wasyluk. Learning Bayesian network parameters from small data sets: Application of Noisy-OR gates. *International Journal of Approximate Reasoning*, 27(2):165–182, 2001.
15. Mark Peot and Ross Shachter. Learning from what you don't observe. In *Proceedings of the Fourteenth Annual Conference on Uncertainty in Artificial Intelligence (UAI–98)*, pages 439–446, San Francisco, CA, 1998. Morgan Kaufmann Publishers.
16. Marco Ramoni and Paola Sebastiani. Learning conditional probabilities from incomplete data: An experimental comparison. In *Proceedings of the The Seventh International Workshop on Artificial Intelligence and Statistics*, pages 260–265, San Francisco, CA, 1999. Morgan Kaufmann Publishers, Inc.
17. D.B. Rubin. Inference and missing data. *Biometrika*, 63:581–592, 1976.
18. Hanna Wasyluk. The four year's experience with HEPAR-computer assisted diagnostic program. In *Proceedings of the Eighth World Congress on Medical Informatics (MEDINFO–95)*, pages 1033–1034, Vancouver, BC, July 23–27 1995.

Feasibility Studies of Quality of Knowledge Mined from Multiple Secondary Sources

Zdzisław S. Hippe, Maksymilian Knap, and Wiesław Paja

Department of Expert Systems and Artificial Intelligence, University of Technology and Management, Sucharskiego 2, 35-225 Rzeszów, Poland
e-mail: {zhippe, mknap, wpaja}@wenus.wsiz.rzeszow.pl

Abstract. A new algorithm, aimed at evaluation of learning models developed by inductive machine learning from examples, was developed and tested. The evaluated learning models are treated here as ***secondary sources of information***, giving an indirect insight into the ***primary source of information***, being the standard decision table. It was found, that after application of the developed algorithm, the number of rules generated for an investigated decision table, was reduced from **45** (on average, depending on the method of quantization of continuous attributes) to **4**, without increasing the error rate.

Key words: machine learning, learning from examples, a posteriori knowledge, quality of knowledge

1 Introduction

In our previous research on machine learning we attempted at studying the accuracy and truth of knowledge, contained in learning models obtained by inductive learning from ***primary sources of information***. This paper presents recent results obtained in the subsequent steps of our research, devoted now to a problem of quality of knowledge gained from ***multiple secondary sources of information***. By *secondary sources* we understand a set of learning models explaining the same *primary source*, being for example, an information system formalized (according to Pawlak [1]) in the form of a decision table. The main paradigm used in our research is an assumption, that in the machine learning it is necessary to apply different learning methods (algorithms) in order to develop a ***set of models*** that explain the same primary source of information (see Fig.1). In the next phase of the process of knowledge discovery, this set of models can be used to infer about class-membership of unseen objects. The main problem, essential for our research, is directly connected with a trial to develop a reliable and versatile algorithm for improvement and simplification of learning models, being in fact the secondary sources of knowledge. It is assumed that the simplification (in a general sense) of learning models developed has to flow without losses of knowledge and information contained. Thus it should be emphasized, that this element of our research is directly devoted to estimation of accuracy and truth of knowledge, gained by the analysis of a set of developed learning models.

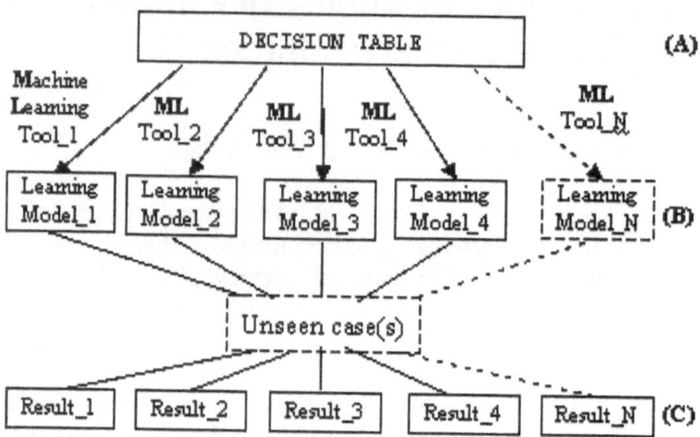

Fig. 1. Information system (**A**) is a primary source of information and knowledge, used for development of various learning models, regarded here as a secondary source of knowledge (**B**) by using different tools. Using these models for classification of unseen cases, the set of results (**C**) is obtained.

2 Machine learning tools used. Standardization of the investigated information system

Development of secondary knowledge sources was performed using three different tools for learning from examples, namely: **LERS** [2], **GTS** system (a new type of covering algorithm, enhanced by recursive reduction of the number of rules induced for a given information system [3]), and the **1stClass** program. The first two tools generate learning models in the form of a set of production rules, but in completely different format. For this reason, special programming tool for conversion of rules from **LERS**-format to **GTS**-format was developed (the **R-Convert** program). In this way, the **GTS**-format of decision rules was set up as a standard for their comparison. However, the third tool used in our research (**1stClass**), generates learning models in the form of decision trees, applying R. Quinlan's **ID3**-algorithm [4]. Therefore, learning models developed in the form of decision trees, to facilitate qualitative comparisons, were converted into a standard format of production rules, using another developed by us module (**TreeRul**). It should be stressed that preparation of original information system (primary source of knowledge) for the research, consisted on removals of typographic errors (in manual way), filling of missing data (automatically), detection and removals of conflicting data, and finally development of N-pairs of files (in each pair is one file for training and one for testing), to execute N-fold-cross-validation [5]. Creation of these pairs of files for validation of learning models was done using another module developed in our research, namely the **Shuffle** program. Its additional function is to insert a special steering line (at the very beginning of testing files) in the format required for processing either by **LERS** or by **GTS**. The investigated information system, described in details in [6], contained 250 cases with almost equal distribution of four classes of objects.

3 Algorithm of optimization of secondary sources of knowledge. Introduction to research on quality of knowledge hidden in learning models

In the initial step of our investigations, we focus attention on development of an effective algorithm for quasi-optimal decreasing the number of decision rules generated within each learning model. It was found, that the evaluation of knowledge hidden in the secondary sources of information should be performed in two-step process. In the first step, all learning models (in our case, three models) were carefully checked applying testing files provided by the **Shuffle**-module. For each model, the error rate was estimated and used in the second step, as a criterion for the improvement and preliminary optimization of a given model. The learning model being investigated, was in the second step considered in context of: **(i)** contribution of each rule separately to the inference process, and **(ii)** significance of the entire set of rules for the conclusive process. In this point of our discussion it is necessary to emphasize that the algorithm devised, at least in its initial shape, was set up with the default value of confidence factor (for all conditions in rules) as equal to 1. However, the contribution of each rule to the inference process was evaluated somewhat differently in models generated by **LERS** and in models generated by **GTS** system. Analysis of the entire set of rules was conducted using some generic operations on decision rules, namely:

1. *removing redundancy*: the data (primary source of information) may be overdetermined, that is, some rules may explain the same cases. Redundant (excessive) rules were analyzed, and the redundant rule(s) was(were) removed, provided this operation did not increase the error rate;
2. *merging rules*: sometimes a set of rules, taken together, explain a pool of cases that can be accounted for by a single, slightly more general, rule which includes all the positive evidence, but not any negative evidence;
3. *making rules more specific*: in some cases, rules developed by the induction systems used were too general, and therefore made incorrect classifications. As a remedy for these cases general rule was split into two more specific rules, having - for example - some numerical regions of selected attributes properly changed;
4. *making rules more general*: in some circumstances generated learning models contained rules that are more specific than they should be. In these cases, more general rule(s) were applied, so that they cover the same investigated cases, without making any incorrect classifications;
5. *selecting the final rules*: it was found, that in some cases redundancies have been introduced by the generalization and/or specialization procedures. Consequently, the selection procedure of step 1 was applied again to remove them.

4 Conclusions

The algorithm described in paragraph 3, was used in analysis of quality of knowledge contained in learning models developed for the information system (the primary source of information), briefly mentioned in the paragraph 2. This information system, treated by us as a test bed for the research, is described in details in [7]. Learning model(s) generated in the research consisted - on average – of **45** rules. After application of the developed algorithm, the number of rules was reduced to **4**, without increasing the error rate. It should be emphasized, that the main goal of our research seems to be very challenging, and very difficult. In fact, searching throughout various learning models, aimed at evaluation of quality of the knowledge discovered, touches the question of precision and truth of an a posteriori knowledge.

5 Acknowledgements

Financial support of our research project No 7 T11E 030 21, obtained from the State Committee for Scientific Research (Warsaw), is greatefully acknowledged.

References

[1] Z. Pawlak: Knowledge and Rough Sets. In: W. Traczyk (Ed.) Problems in Artifical Intelligence, Wiedza i Życie, Warsaw 1995, pp. 9-21 (in Polish).

[2] J.W. Grzymała-Busse: A New Version of the Rule Induction System LERS. **Fundamenta Informaticae** 31(1997)27-39.

[3] Z.S. Hippe: Machine Learning - A promising strategy for business information processing ? In: W. Abramowicz (Ed.) Business Information Systems'97, Academy of Economy Edit. Office, Poznań 1997, pp. 603-622.

[4] J.R. Quinlan: C4.5: Programs for Machine Learning. Morgan Kaufmann Publishers, San Mateo (CA) 1993.

[5] S. Weiss and C.A. Kulikowski: Computer Systems That Lean - Classification and Prediction Methods from Statistics, Neural Nets, Machine Learning, and Expert Systems. Morgan Kaufmann Publishers, Inc., San Francisco 1991. (How to Estimate True Performance of a Learning System, pp. 17-49)

[6] J.W. Grzymała-Busse, and Z.S. Hippe: Application of Covering Algorithm for Classification of Melanoid Marks on the Skin. In: Szczepaniak P.S. (Ed.). System-Modelling-Control, Inst. Comp. Sci., Technical University, Łódź 2001, pp. 261-265.

Well-structured Program Graphs and the Issue of Local Computations

Mieczysław A. Kłopotek[1,2)]

[1)] Institute of Computer Science, Polish Academy of Sciences,
[2)] Dept. of Computer Science, University of Podlasie,
e-mail: klopotek@ipipan.waw.pl

Abstract: The paper presents a proof of the famous claim about no-go-to-programs and analyses its impact onto reasoning in Bayesian networks
Keywords: Reasoning, distributed computation.

1. Introduction

One of the most hotly discussed problems in the early years of programming theory was the issue of well-structuring of programs. By a well-structured program one understood a program consisting of nested sequences, alternatives and loops, that is a program without "labels" and "go-to" instructions. Beside the obvious esthetical reasons one of the important points was whether or not each "dirty" program can be written also in a well-structured manner. Below we present one of the unpublished proofs that this is always possible. From the proof we can easily guess that the pure transformation to a go-to-free program nothing is gained in terms of program clarity. But, nonetheless, we can see that in practice not only programs, but also most of graphical structures used intensely in AI can be subject to a transformation like this, including e.g. Bayesian networks. Surprisingly, we can gain something from "well-structuring" of Bayesian networks: a new distributed reasoning method.

2. Well-structured programs

Assume the program graph consists of the following types of instructions: (1) one node of the start type, (2) one node of the stop type, (3) nodes of type "execution instruction", (4) nodes of type "branching", (5) and nodes of type "junction"

Let us define the following collapsing operators: a collapsing operator substitutes structures visible in Fig.1 with one execution instruction node.

Our goal is now to modify the structure in such a way as to achieve a program carrying out exactly the same operations, but possessing the following "collapsing" property: the collapsing operators can be recursively applied until the structure consisting of a starting node, execution node and a stop node is achieved.

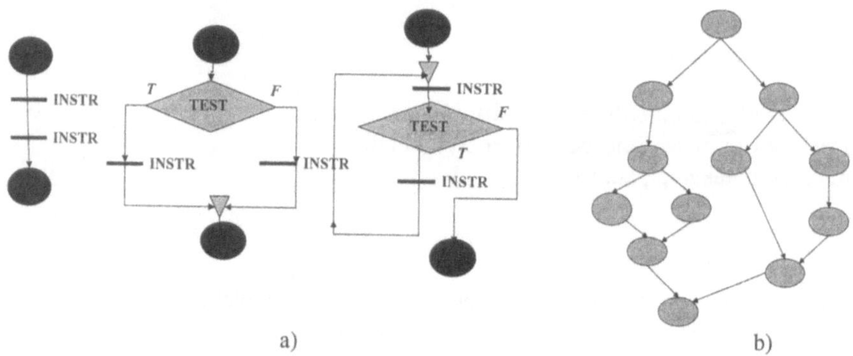

Fig. 1 a) Structural elements in a program, b) a structured Bayesian network

.

Let us first turn to the problem of programs having a directed acyclic graph structures (no loops) - see Fig. 2. We can always find the "earliest" junction point (that is one where there is no preceding junction point on every path from the root to this point), and the corresponding branching point, say T1. Assume now that the test T2 is the closest test (branching point) preceding this junction point on the path from T1. To obtain a structured program we have to move this branching outside of the T1-alternative. For this purpose we introduce an auxiliary variable Z initiating it to False before T1. Before the test T2, with truth leading outside of the T1 alternative, we set Z to the value of T2. Instead of T2 we test on Z and introduce a junction point before T1 junction point where the True branch of the Z-test is directed. Thus, the Z alternative can be collapsed. Behind the T1 junction a next Z branching is introduced with the False path being the original successor of T1 junction and True branch being the original T2 alternative true branch. (Fig.2). After eliminating in this way all branchings between T1 branching and T1 junction we can collapse the T1 alternative. Notice that in this way the number of junctions was reduced by 1 and no loops were introduced. So the process will terminate with collapsing the whole structure. .

Now to the more delicate problems of loops. Let us identify a loop (Fig.4). The first instruction of a loop be the junction point and the last the one from which the arrow goes to this junction point. First we eliminate all ingoing arrows of the loop (all junction points inside it beside the starting one). We eliminate always the earliest such branching point. We introduce an auxiliary variable Z and initialize it on the ingoing arrow to false and on the entry arrow of the loop to true. We move the junction point before the loop entry junction and by alternatives tested on Z we prevent all simple instructions of the loop before the original ingoing arrow from executing, and all branching instructions from leaving the loop on false Z (Fig.5).

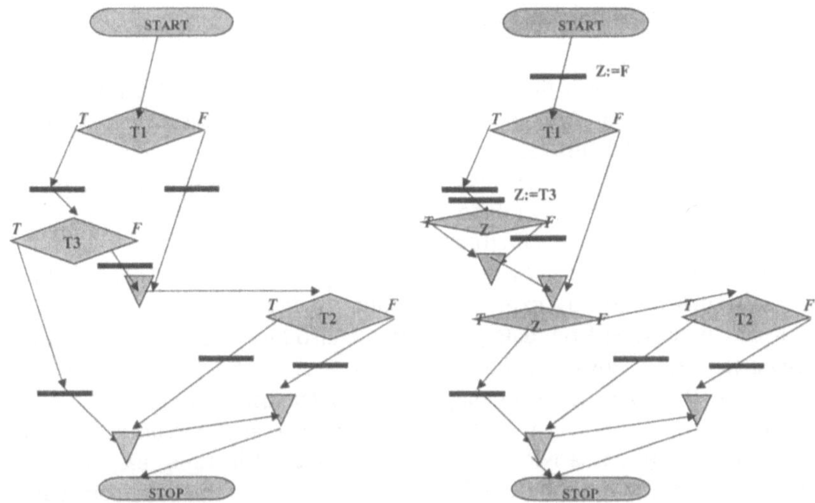

Fig. 2 Treatments of dags – removal of a branching in an alternative

Thereafter we collapse all branchings within the loop to a single one (substituting the last one) using auxiliary variables and preventing execution of unwanted instructions within the loop by appropriate testing on auxiliary variables and after the loop-leaving branch of the final test we conduct subbranching into the appropriate leaving branches. Thereafter the loop is "clean?" and we can collapse it to a single instruction. Notice that in the process after this collapsing the number of junctions is reduced by one. So the process will terminate in a finite number of steps leaving a loop-less structure (dag structure) which can be processed further in the way outlined earlier.

Hence we can always obtain a well-structured program. Clearly, this program is not necessarily more readable than the original chaos program, but this is a proof that we do not need to write chaotic programs.

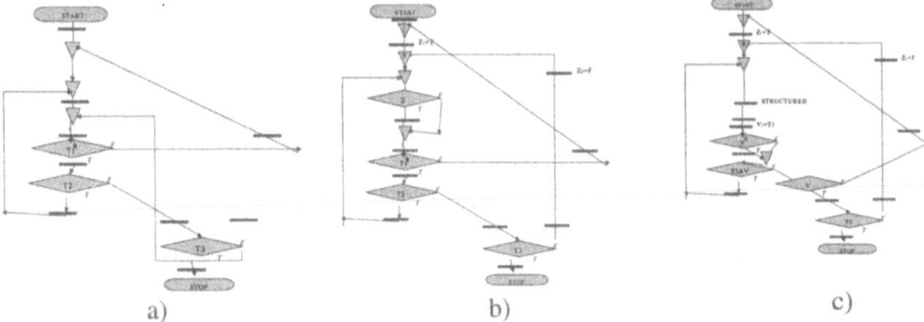

Fig. 3 Treatments of loops a) original graph, b) ingoing arrows removed c) branchings collapsed

3. Well-structured Bayesian networks

We can easily discover that similar transformations are possible on many other graphical structures of AI. One important example is Bayesian networks. With "auxiliary variables" being just extensions of the original node valuations, we can really get "well-structured" Bayesian networks. With well-structured programs we had the advantage of better understanding the contents, easier optimization etc. What is the advantage of "well-structured" Bayesian networks?

Bayesian networks are known for their ability to represent compactly the joint probability distribution by exploiting conditional independence information [2], which may be learned from data [3]. They are also known for efficient reasoning mechanisms [2,3]. However, these mechanisms are applicable to special representation of Bayesian networks only: the so-called triangular graphs, or hypertrees or Markov-trees. The transformation of a general Bayesian network to an optimal Markov tree is a NP hard task. Hence special learning procedures were developed to learn Markov-tree-like Bayesian networks directly from data [1]. Regrettably, the Markov-tree representations may ignore quite a large number of conditional independences; hence we lose some compactness of representation. On the other hand, general-type Bayesian networks are NP hard for reasoning [2]. Hence new reasoning mechanisms finding a way in-between would be needed, so that both reasoning and learning are kept tractable.

Here we would like to point at the possibility of an efficient reasoning mechanism for well-structured Bayesian networks. Let us concentrate only on marginal distribution calculations. A node with only one predecessor ("execution" node or "branching node") would require only the marginal distribution of its predecessor to calculate its own marginal. A node with two predecessors ("junction" node) would require conditional distributions of its predecessors on the corresponding junction node and the marginal of that junction node. This would imply propagation of conditional and marginal distributions over the net (twice the effort of Markov tress) which is still tractable during reasoning. The structured Bayesian network on the other hand is not so restrictive for learning and has the advantage of an elegant hierarchical representation.

References

[1] Cercone N., Wong S.K.M., Xiang Y.: A 'Microscopic' study of minimum entropy search in learning decomposable Markov networks. *Machine Learning*, 1997, vol. 26, nr 1. .65-92

[2] Jensen J., *An Introduction to Bayesian Networks*, Springer Verlag, 1996

[3] M.A. Kłopotek, S.T. Wierzchoń, M. Michalewicz, M. Bednarczyk, W. Pawłowski, A. Wąsowski. Bayesian network mining system. M.A. Kłopotek, M. Michalewicz, S.T. Wierzchoń, eds. *Intelligent Information Systems 2001*. Physica/Springer Verlag, 2001, 180-193

Deductive, Distributed and Agent-based Systems

On Multiprocessor Scheduling with Cellular Automata

Anna Święcicka[1], Franciszek Seredyński[2]

[1] Department of Computer Science, Białystok University of Technology, Wiejska 45A, 15-351 Białystok, Poland, e-mail: amzs@ii.pb.bialystok.pl

[2] Polish-Japanese Institute of Information Technologies, Koszykowa 86, 02-008 Warsaw, Poland and Institute of Computer Science, Polish Academy of Sciences Ordona 21, 01-237 Warsaw, Poland e-mail: sered@ipipan.waw.pl

Abstract: *In this paper we propose using cellular automata (CAs) to perform distributed scheduling tasks of a parallel program in a multiprocessor system. We consider a program graph as a CA with elementary cells interacting locally according to a certain rule which must be found. Effective rules for a CA are discovered by a genetic algorithm (GA). With these rules, CA-based scheduler is able to find allocations which minimize the total execution time of the parallel program in the two processor system. We analyse different modes of operating of the scheduler in the case of two processors. We also show how our algorithm works in the case of more than two processors.*

Keywords: *multiprocessor scheduling, cellular automata, genetic algorithms*

1. Introduction

Scheduling tasks of parallel programs represented by directed acyclic graphs in a parallel architecture is NP-complete problem in its general form [gar79]. Therefore effective solutions of the problem are proposed in the form of heuristics [ElRew94, kwo98, sal98, wan97] based on different mathematical platforms. On one hand heuristics using techniques such as list scheduling, critical path or clustering [kwo98, ElRew94] have been proposed, and on the other hand techniques derived from nature, such as simulated annealing, GA or neural networks [sal98, wan97] have been successfully applied. We follow this latter line of research and propose in the paper to use a hybrid technique combining CAs and GA to create distributed scheduling algorithm.

CAs are discrete dynamical systems made up of a large number of cells which behave according to a local rule. It is an interesting feature of these systems that although these cells only interact locally, complex global behaviour can emerge. This is very similar to the behaviour of many systems in the real world, so CAs are often used to model such systems. In particular, they can be considered as models of higly parallel and distributed computations in multiprocessor and distributed systems. Results described in the literature [das94, sip97] show that CAs combined with evolutionary techniques can be effectively used to find parallel and distributed solutions of complex problems, such as density classification task or synchronization task.

It has been shown recently [sw00, ser01] that such a hybrid technique can be applied to discover scheduling algorithms. In this paper we analyse different modes of operating of the scheduler in the case of two processors. We also extend our algorithm on the case of more than two processors.

This paper is organized as follows. Section 2 discusses accepted models of a parallel program and a parallel system in the context of the scheduling problem. Section 3 presents a concept of CAs. The next section explains our scheduling algorithm and discovering interesting rules with use of a GA. Section 5 contains results of our experiments. Last section contains conclusions.

2. Scheduling problem

A multiprocessor system is represented by an undirected unweighted graph $G_s = (V_s, E_s)$, called a *system graph*. V_s is the set of N_s nodes of the system graph representing processors with their local memories of a parallel computer of MIMD architecture. E_s is the set of edges representing bidirectional channels between processors and defines a topology of the multiprocessor system. Figure 1a shows an example of a system graph representing a multiprocessor system consisting of two processors *P0* and *P1*. It is assumed that all processors have the same computational power and a communication via the links does not consume any processor time.

A parallel program (see Figure 1b) is represented by a weighted directed acyclic graph $G_p = (V_p, E_p)$, called a *precedence task graph* or a *program graph*. V_p is the set of N_p nodes of the graph representing elementary tasks, which are indivisible computational units. Weights b_k of the nodes (marked on the nodes) describe the processing time needed to execute a given task on any processor of a multiprocessor system. There exists a precedence constraint relation between the tasks *k* and *l* in the program graph if the result produced by task *k* has to be send to task *l*. E_p is the set of edges of the precedence task graph describing the communication time between the tasks. Weights a_{kl} of the edges (marked on the edges) describe a communication time between pairs of tasks *k* and *l*, when they are located in neighbour processors. If the tasks k and l are located in the same processor than the communication time between them is equal to 0.

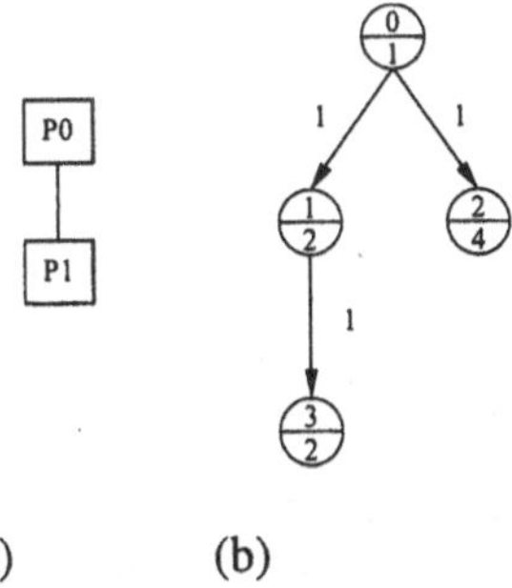

a) (b)

Fig. 1: Examples of a system graph (a) and a precedence task graph (b).

The purpose of *scheduling* is to distribute the tasks among the processors in such a way that the precedence constraints are preserved and the total execution time T is minimized. The value of T depends on the given allocation of tasks and some *scheduling policy* applied to tasks:

$$T = f(allocation, scheduling\_policy). \tag{1}$$

While allocations of tasks are changed by the algorithm, a scheduling policy remains constant. It defines an order of processing tasks, ready to run in a given processor. We will assume that a scheduling policy is the same for all processors of the system.

3. Cellular automata

CAs [sip97, wol84] are dynamical systems in which space and time are discrete. The cellular array is n-dimensional, where $n = 1, 2, 3$ is used in practice. In this paper we shall concentrate on one-dimensional CAs.

A one-dimensional CA consists of a spatial lattice of N cells, each of which, at time t, can be in one of k states. The collection of all local states is called the *configuration*. A CA has a single fixed rule, which is used to update each cell. The rule maps from the states in a neighbourhood of a cell to a single state, which is the update value for that cell. In a one-dimensional CA, the neighbourhood of a cell includes the cell itself and some *radius* r of neighbours on either side of the cell.

The equations of motion for a CA are often expressed in the form of a *rule table*: a look-up table listing each of the neighbourhood patterns and the state to which the central cell in that neighbourhood is mapped. For example, Table 1 presents one possible rule table for a one-dimensional, binary-state CA with radius $r = 1$. Each possible neighbourhood η is given, along with the "output bit" a to which the central cell is updated.

Tab. 1: An example of a rule table for a one-dimensional, binary state CA with r=1.

η	000	001	010	011	100	101	110	111
a	0	1	1	1	0	1	1	0

The CA starts out with some initial configuration (IC) of cell states. To run the CA, the look-up table is applied, usually synchronously, to each neighbourhood in the current lattice configuration, respecting the choice of boundary conditions, to produce the configuration at the next time step.

4. Scheduling algorithm

We assume that we approximate a program graph by a one-dimensional CA of size N_p, with null boundary conditions [sw00, sw00a, sw01]. In the case of k processors, we use a CA with k states. For example, let us consider a system consisting of two processors. In this case, our automaton is a binary one. We use state 0 (1) of a cell to indicate that the corresponding task is allocated to processor $P0$ ($P1$). Each configuration corresponds to the allocation of tasks in the system graph. To calculate the value of T for the given allocation of tasks we use the scheduling policy of the type: "a task with the biggest dynamic level first" [sw00a].

CA corresponding to our program graph evolves according to its rule. Initial states of CA correspond to an initial allocation of tasks in the two processor system. Changing states of CA results in changing an allocation of tasks in the system. It results in changing the response time T. We want to know if exists a rule for CA providing for any initial allocation of tasks converging CA to an allocation which minimizes T.

There are three phases of our algorithm: a phase of learning rules, a phase of normal operating and a phase of reusing discovered rules. The purpose of the learning phase is discovery effective rules for scheduling. Searching effective rules is conducted with use of a GA [sw00, sw00a, sw01]. In the phase of normal operating, when a program graph is initially randomly allocated, CA is initiated and equipped with a rule taken from the set of discovered rules. We expect in this phase that for any initial allocation of tasks of a given program graph, CA will be able to find allocation of tasks, providing the minimal or near minimal value of T. The third phase, called „immune system", enables a potential reusibility of discovered CA rules [ssw01].

5. Results of experiments

A number of experiments with various program graphs available in the literature has been conducted [sw00, sw00a, ssw01]. In this paper we will describe in details results obtained for the program graph refered as *g40* (see Figure 2), scheduled in the two processors system. Computational costs are all the same and equal 4 while communication costs are all equal 1. The optimal response time T for this program graph in the two processor system is equal 80.

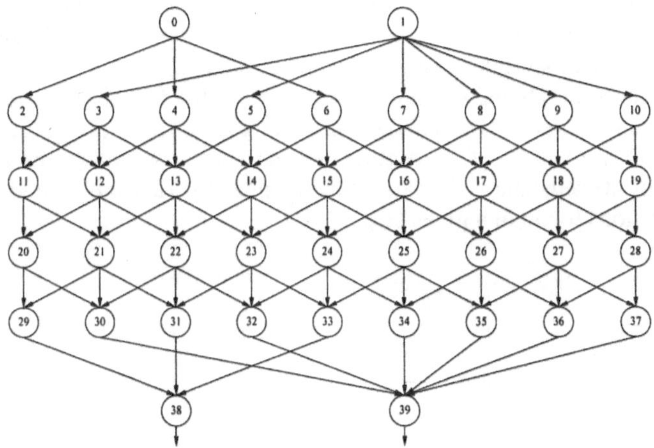

Fig. 2: Program graph *g40*.

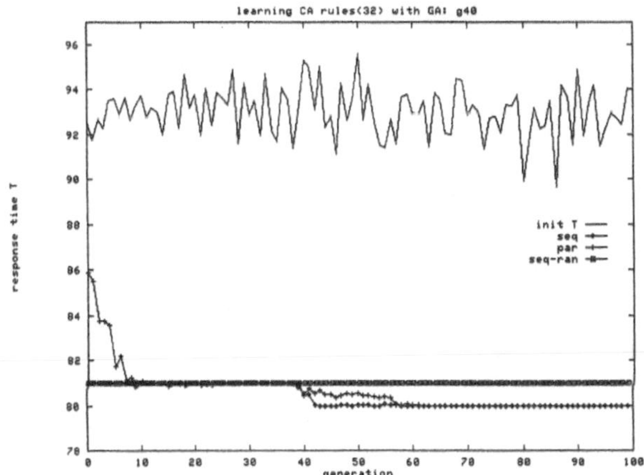

Fig. 3: CA-based scheduler for the *g40* - learning mode.

The first problem is to fix the value of r. In our experiments we tested two values of r: 1 and 2, what resulted in 8 and 32 bit long CA rules (in the case of other program graphs, the maximal value of r, we tested, was 3). The minimal value of r which allows converging to optimum is 2. We also tested different modes of operating of the CA: parallel (par), sequential (an order of updating states by cells is defined by their order number corresponding to tasks in the program graph - seq) and sequential with a random order of updating states by cells (seq-ran). The last mode is the most expensive because it requires generation of many random numbers. Figure 3 shows typical runs of the GA for $r = 2$ and for three modes of operating of the CA described above. This figure presents the average initial time (init T) and the average response time T (computed for 50 initial configurations). One can see that two modes of operating of the CA: parallel and sequential, allow converging to optimal value of T equal 80.

Figures 4a, 4b and 4c show typical runs of the CA-based scheduler with the best rules found after 100 generations, starting from randomly generated initial configuration. Left parts of the figures present space-time diagrams of the CA consisting of 40 cells and right parts show graphically values of T corresponding to the allocations found in a given step.

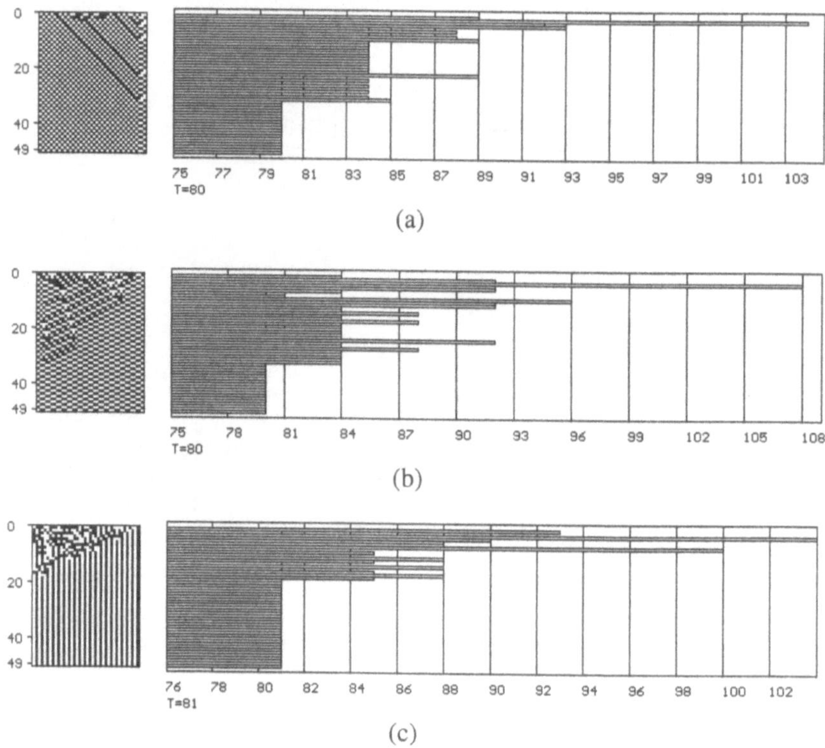

Fig. 4: Space-time diagrams of the CA-based scheduler in the case of different modes of operating of the CA: sequential (a), parallel (b) and sequential with a random order of updating states by cells (c).

Let us, for example, consider Figure 4a. One can see that in the step 0, cells of the CA are in some states corresponding to the allocation of tasks (white cell – a corresponding task is allocated to $P0$, black cell – a task is allocated to $P1$) and the value of T corresponding to this allocation is equal 89. Then the CA starts to change its states what results in changing values of T. One can see that the CA needs about 30 time steps to converge to tasks' allocation corresponding to the minimal value of T equal 80.

Quality of discovered rules we can find out in the normal operating mode. We generate 1000 random initial configurations and use them to test each of found rules. Figures 5a and 5b show results obtained for two modes of operating of the CA: parallel and sequential. Each figure presents frequency of finding an optimal solution by every rule in the population. One can see that, in both cases, there is a lof of rules which are able to find an optimal scheduling for each representative of the test.

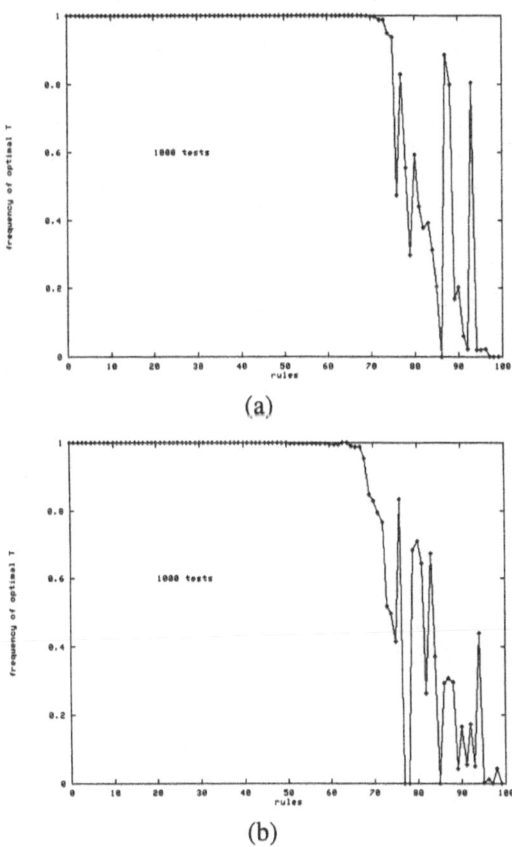

(a)

(b)

Fig. 5: Normal operating of CA-based scheduler: sequential mode (a), parallel mode (b).

When considering scheduling problem in the case of more than two processors, we are faced with the problem of the length of the rule. The length of the rule is calculated as k^{2r+1} - it grows very quickly with k and r. Table 2 shows lengths of rules for various k and r.

Tab. 2: Lengths of rules for various k and r.

k	r	the length of a rule
2	1	8
2	2	32
2	3	128
3	1	27
3	2	243
3	3	2187
4	1	64
4	2	1024
4	3	16384

In general, it is very difficult for the GA to search such vast spaces. In fact, preliminary results of conducted experiments confirm it. The next table presents results obtained for some program graphs in the case of more than two processors (we assume a fully connected system). They are compared with results obtained by a standard GA (with a chromosome of a given individual coding an allocation of tasks to processors). These results are given in brackets. All experiments were conducted for $r = 1$ and sequential mode of operating of the CA.

Tab. 3: The best average response time T received for program graphs – learning mode (20 tests).

program graph	$k = 3$	$k = 4$
tree7	5.0 (5)	5.0 (5)
tree15	7.0 (7)	7.0 (7)
intree7	5.0 (5)	5.0 (5)
intree15	7.0 (7)	7.0 (7)
g18	38.0 (36)	27.0 (26)
gauss18	53.0 (44)	53.0 (44)

We can see that in the case of program graphs from tree family results obtained by the CA-based scheduler are the same as these obtained by a standard GA. However, for other program graphs obtained results are worse. How to improve the efficiency of the algorithm in the case of more than two processors is the subject of our current research.

6. Conclusions

In this paper we presented results of research on the CA-based scheduler. The results of conducted experiments (see also [ssw01, sw00, sw01]) show that genetic algorithm is able to discover effective rules for the scheduler. It is worth to notice that decisions concerning scheduling are fully distributed. In subsequent steps of operating of a CA none estimation of T is calculated. We have also shown [ssw01] that discovered rules may be used to find optimal or suboptimal solutions of other, not known in advance instances of the problem.
How to improve the efficiency of the algorithm in the case of more than two processors is the subject of our current research.

References

[das94] R. Das, M. Mitchell, J. P. Crutchfield: A genetic algorithm discovers particle-based computation in cellular automata. In Y. Davidor, H.-P. Schwefel, R. Männer (eds.): Parallel Problem Solving from Nature - PPSN III, LNCS 866, Springer, 344-353, 1994.

[ElRew94] H. El-Rewini, T. G. Lewis, H. H. Ali: Task Scheduling in Parallel and Distributed Systems. PTR Prentice Hall, Englewood Cliffs, New Jersey, 1994.

[gar79] M. R. Gary, D. S. Johnson: Computers and Intractability: A Guide to the Theory of NP-Completeness. W. H. Freeman and Company, 1979.

[kwo98] Y. K. Kwok, I. Ahmad: Benchmarking the Task Graph Scheduling Algorithms. In Proceedings of 1998 IPPS/SPDP Symposium, Orlando, Florida, 531-537, 1998.

[sal98] S. Saleh, A. Y. Zomaya: Multiprocessor Scheduling Using Mean-Field Annealing. In Parallel and Distributed Processing, LNCS 1388, Springer, 288-296, 1998.

[ser01] F. Seredyński: Evolving Cellular Automata - based Algorithms for Multiprocessor Scheduling. In A. Y. Zomaya, F. Ercal, S. Olariu (eds.): Solutions to Parallel and Distributed Computing Problems: Lessons from Biological Sciences, John Wiley & Sons, Inc., 179-207, 2001.

[ssw01] F. Seredyński, A. Święcicka: Immune-like System Approach to Cellular Automata - based Scheduling. In Proceedings of the Fourth International Conference on Parallel Processing and Applied Mathematics (PPAM'2001), Częstochowa, Poland, 2001.

[sip97] M. Sipper: Evolution of Parallel Cellular Machines. The Cellular Programming Approach, LNCS 1194, Springer, 1997.

[sw00a] A. Święcicka, F. Seredyński: Evolving Cellular Automata Structures to Solve Multiprocessor Scheduling Problem. In Proceedings of The Ninth International Symposium on Intelligent Information Systems, 2000, Bystra, Poland, 115-119, 2000.

[sw00] A. Święcicka, F. Seredyński: Cellular Automata Approach to Scheduling Problem. In Proceedings of International Conference on Parallel Computing in Electrical Engineering: PARELEC 2000, IEEE Computer Society, 29-33, 2000.

[sw01] A. Święcicka, F. Seredyński, M. Jażdżyk: Cellular Automata Approach to Scheduling Problem in Case of Modifications of a Program Graph. In Proceedings of The Tenth International Symposium on Intelligent Information Systems, Zakopane, Poland, 155-166, 2001.

[wan97] L. Wang, H. J. Siegel, V. P. Roychowolhury, A. A. Maciejewski: Task Matching and Scheduling in Heterogeneous Computing Environments Using a Genetic-Algorithm-Based Approach. Journal of Parallel and Distributed Computing 47, 8-22, 1997.

[wol84] S. Wolfram: Universality and complexity in cellular automata. Physica D, 10, 1-35, 1984.

Agent Based Infrastructure for Web Service Integration

Stanislaw Ambroszkiewicz[1] *, Leszek Rozwadowski[2], and Dariusz Mikulowski[2]

[1] Institute of Computer Science, Polish Academy of Sciences,
al. Ordona 21, PL-01-237 Warsaw,
[2] Institute of Informatics, University of Podlasie,
al. Sienkiewicza 51, PL-08-110 Siedlce, Poland
sambrosz@ipipan.waw.pl; www.ipipan.waw.pl/mas/

Abstract. A new simple minimum language Entish is proposed for automatic web service integration. The integration is done by autonomous software agents. The new language is fully declarative although it corresponds functionally to WSFL, XLANG, XAML, and DAML-S which are procedural languages. This is achieved by separating the essential data of the integration process (agent) from execution and reasoning machinery (that must be realized procedurally), and moving it outside Entish to a dedicated service (i.e., BodyService). The essential data are expressed in Entish (as agent soul) and serve as control data of the agent process responsible for web service integration. Entish is implemented on HTTP+SOAP, however, it may be also implemented on the top of SOAP+WSDL+UDDI stack if the syntax of WSDL is adopted.

1 Introduction

What are Web services? Perhaps the best definition can be found in IBM's tutorial [4]:
Web services are self-contained, self - describing, modular applications that can be published, located, and invoked across the Web. Web services perform functions that can be anything from simple requests to complicated business processes ... Once a Web service is deployed, other applications (and other Web services) can discover and invoke the deployed service.
What infrastructure and standards are necessary to realize this vision? It is clear that simplicity and ubiquity of the infrastructure are the key factors here. From a service provider's point of view, if they can setup a web site they can join global community. From a client's point of view, if you can type, you can access services. Let us see what solutions are proposed by the prominent vendors: IBM, Microsoft, Sun, HP, and others.

Web services are getting to mean just UDDI, WSDL, and SOAP. SOAP (Simple Object Access Protocol) is a standard for applications to exchange

* The work was supported partially by KBN project No. 7 T11C 040 20

XML-formatted messages over HTTP. WSDL (Web Service Description Language) describes *what* a web service does, *where* it resides, and *how* to invoke it. WSDL is a general purpose XML language for describing the interface, protocol bindings and the deployment details of network services. UDDI (Universal Description, Discovery and Integration) is a standard for publishing information about web services in a global registry as well as for finding out web services.

Does the stack of standards mentioned above provide sufficient means for automatic service invocation, composition, and integration? It seems that the problem is hard. UDDI aims at automatic service discovery of potential business partners. At the moment, it is supposed that after service discovery, programmers affiliated with the business partners program their own systems to interact with the services discovered.

Automatic Web service integration requires more complex functionality than SOAP, WSDL, and UDDI provide. The functionality includes: Transactions, workflow, negotiation, management, and security.

There are several efforts that aim at providing such functionality, for example, WSCL, WSFL, XLANG, BTP, and XAML. All these languages are based on SOAP+WSDL+UDDI stack.

WSCL (Web Service Conversation Language of uddi.org) is a language for defining conversations, i.e., the order in which WSDL messages can be sent between interacting services. WSCL specifies the public interface to web services, but it does not specify how the conversation participants will handle and produce the documents received and sent. Conversation definition is service independent, and can be used by any number of services with completely different implementations. A conversation developer can create a WSDL description of a conversation, and publish it in a UDDI directory. In order to interact automatically, services must implement the same conversation.

WSFL (Web Services Flow Language of IBM) is an XML language for the description of web service compositions. Composition is a specification of the execution sequence of functionalities provided by the composed services. Execution orders are specified by defining the flow of control and data between the services.

Similar technology is proposed by Microsoft, it is XLANG that aims at formal specification of business process as long-running interactions of web services. Business process is defined as a contract between two or more services. A contract includes flow of control and data, transactions with compensation, handling of internal and external exceptions.

WSFL as well as XLANG use WSDL for the description of service interfaces and their protocol bindings. They are procedural languages, i.e.,, they use actions as well as process constructors that combine actions together, e.g., *switch, while*.

XAML (Transaction Authority Markup Language) has not been published yet. Citation from www.xaml.org:

XAML is a set of XML interfaces that allows web service providers to participate in business transactions on the web. These business transactions coordinate the interactions among distributed web services.

OASIS BTP (Business Transaction Protocol) specifies an XML-based interoperation protocol for managing complex, B2B transactions over the Internet. BTP is designed to allow transactional coordination of participants which are a part of services offered by multiple autonomous organizations. The coordination is done by software agents. The protocol defines the roles which software agents (actors) may occupy, the messages that pass between such actors, and the obligations upon and commitments made by actors-in-roles. According to BEA, BTP is to be placed between UDDI and ebXML in the web service protocol stack.

There is a consensus between prominent vendors that SOAP+WSDL+UDDI is the basic standard stack for automatic web service discovery. However, there is no agreement what should be the next standard in the stack necessary for automatic composition, and integration of web services; see the approaches presented briefly above. They are complex and it is not clear how to implement them efficiently.

The standards described (briefly) above are the basis for realizing the idea of new emerging technology: B2Bi. The current B2Bi standards initiatives include: RosettaNet, BizTalk and .NET, ebXML, Sun ONE and many others. On the other hand there is an academic and government supported effort called DAML-S. It is a part of the larger project called DAML (DARPA Agent Markup Language) which aims at realizing the idea of Semantic Web. DAML-S (S for services) is based on semantic description of services. In DAML-S, a service is described by the three components: *ServiceProfile, ServiceModel, ServiceGrounding.* Generally speaking, *ServiceProfile* provides the information needed for an agent to discover a service. *ServiceModel* and *ServiceGrounding* provide enough information for an agent to make use of a service. According to DAML-S, (composed) service can be viewed as a process. DAML-S is augmented with process ontology, as well as with control process ontology, and a simple time ontology. This makes DAML-S a procedural language, because the composition templates such as **If-Then-Else** and **Repeat-Until** are introduced to the language. Also temporal process properties are introduced. Since the current published version of DAML-S is not completed, it is not clear how to implement automatic service integration. DAML-S is supposed to be a content language, so that it can be compared with WSDL+(WSCL, WSFL, BTP, XLANG, or XAML). DAML-S delegates the tasks of service publishing and discovery to the Semantic Web to be realized by DAML.

2 Troublesome questions

The basic question is whether the proposed technologies are *simple and ubiquitous*, and which one is the right one. Perhaps the technologies are appropriate for development of serious large application such as B2Bi. However, if a group of students and our friends wants to present their own applications as web services, use and compose them in an automatic way, do they have to employ all that heavy and complex machinery?

As we see above, the landscape of solutions for new emerging technology is rich and complex so that it is not easy to find the right path to the one common standard. It seems that the path starts with the basic stack SOAP+WSDL+UDDI, however, it is not clear how to go further. Perhaps the basic stack is not appropriate, i.e., it is too complex so that the next protocols (based on the initial stack) accumulate the initial complexity.

On the other hand: Is the formal semantics of services and tasks necessary for automatic web service integration ?

We are not going to give simple answers to these tedious questions. Instead, we suggest going back to the roots and asking again: What are web services ? Once we grasp the idea of web service properly, let us define a minimum protocol stack necessary and sufficient for automatic web service integration.

The following items seem to be important for web service definition:

1. A way to find and register interest in a service.
2. A transport mechanism to access a service.
3. A way to define what the input and the output parameters are for such a service.
4. A way for remote applications (services) to locate and invoke a service.
5. A way to provide transparency between users and services, i.e., a user should only formulate a task. The task performance (i.e., boring and time consuming jobs of discovering, composing, integrating, and invoking the needed services) should be done automatically.

The items should be realized in a simple way so that:

- anyone who is able to set up a web site, can also deploy and register interest in a service.
- anyone who is able to type in the Web, can realize its task.
- the realization is scalable.

Let us notice that there are two sides to be connected: Users who formulate tasks, and service providers who present their services on the Web. The tasks should be realized by the services (composition). Every user should know what she/he wants. On the other hand, service provider must know what service he/she provides. It would be great if both the users and service providers used the same language and agreed on the meaning of that language. Moreover, service discovery, invocation, and integration should be done in the same language.

Is it necessary for the users to express the task semantics explicitly in a formal way? Is it necessary for a service provider to present a formal semantic of the operation performed by his/her service? Do we really need multiple formal ontologies and translations between them in order to realize the semantic interoperability, i.e., the agreement on the meaning of concepts used in our language? Our answer is NO. Semantic interoperability between service providers and users is realized in the course of language development, and caused by the way the language is used. Let us quote L. Wittgenstein [5]: *Don't ask what it means, bur rather how it is used.* Hence, first of all, a simple open and scalable infrastructure for language use and development should be realized. Then, the understanding (i.e., semantic interoperability) will emerge in a natural way. It seems that this is the core of the original idea of Semantic Web proposed by T. Berners-Lee in 1998.

Is it necessary to introduce actions and process constructors to the language (making the language procedural) in order to realize automatic service integration? Again, our answer is NO. Let us try to design a simple fully declarative language for web service integration by applying the Principle of Least Power (T. Berners-Lee [3]):
When expressing something, use the least powerful language you can.

3 Entish

Let us call our language Entish (an abbreviation of e-Language). Web service is fully described by its **name** and **the type of operation** it performs. Service name is a URI that determines the communication address as well as the transport protocol for providing communication with the service in the very similar way as it is done for URL, for example,
hermes://ipipan.waw.pl/node/my-service is a URI where *hermes* is a transport protocol, *ipipan.waw.pl* is the name of a host whereas */node/my-service* is the path to the service whose short name is *my-service*. Service names are elements of type *Service* in Entish.

The type of operation (performed by service) is constituted by well specified input condition and output condition, i.e., operation type is a pair of Entish formulas: *form_in* and *form_out*. The pair is an element of the type *Operation_type*. Once the formula *form_in* is satisfied, the service is invoked, the operation is performed, and the result is that the formula *form_out* is satisfied.

What does an operation perform? Generally, it processes resources, that is, it performs a function on resources. Variables of that function denote input resources whereas the function value denotes the output resource. Hence, we must introduce names for functions as well as names for resource types to Entish.

There are spatial and temporal relations to be expressed in Entish, e.g., "a resource is in a service by a time". So that let us introduce names for expressing time, i.e., the type *Time* defined according to the format **datetime** (see www.w3c.org/TR/NOTE-datetime). Since GMT time is available at any host, let us introduce the function *gmt()* that, when evaluated at a host, returns the current GMT time at the host. To express temporal relations, let us introduce the relation of the form "t1 is before (less or equal) t2", formally *(leq, t1, t2)*. For example, relation *(leq, gmt(), 2001-11-13T13:15:30)* evaluated at a place denotes that the current GMT time at that place is less or equal 2001-11-13T13:15:30. This is supposed to be the general form of timeouts for task and commitment realizations in Entish.

In order to express spatial relations let us introduce to Entish the relation symbol *is_in*, so that *(is_in, res, ser)* denotes that the resource *res* is in the service *ser*.

Let us follow the idea of T. Berners-Lee of webizing language [2], and webize Entish. Let all Entish names be URI, and let us keep Entish development open and distributed, i.e., new names for services, resources types, functions, relations can be introduced in an open and distributed way. For this purpose, let us specify distributed DictionaryService where everyone can create and manage his / her own dictionary consistent with the Entish syntax. The dictionary should have a form of a collection of read-only documents created according to one specific XML format.

To sum up what has been done so far, it seems that the Entish is a minimum language for service description by service providers as well as for task formulation by users. Service invocation is realized by satisfying the formula *form_in* of the type of operation the service performs. The idea of service invocation appears to be great, however, the question is: Who or what is responsible for realizing this satisfaction. Who or what is responsible for realizing service composition and integration if it is needed? The answer is *agent*, i.e., there must be a process (called agent) responsible for task realization. Hence, we introduce the type *Agent* to Entish .

For any task issued by a user there must be an agent responsible for the task realization. In order to do so a user needs a GUI that is called SecretaryService. For any task there is a timeout for its realization. The task with a timeout is written down as the agent's goal. The agent is dedicated only to its goal realization, so that when it succeeded or the timeout is over, the agent notifies the SecretaryService about that, and terminates its process. Hence, we introduce to Entish the first agent attribute: *goals(agent)*.

What is the agent supposed to do after receiving the goal? It starts with its main goal as its first intention. It asks any service by sending the following message: "My intention is ϕ", where ϕ is an Entish formula describing the goal of the agent. Hence, we introduce to Entish the next agent attribute *intentions(agent)*. If the service is able to realize the agent intention, it replies to the agents a commitment that has the following form: "I commit to realize your intention, if the conditions *con1 and con2* are satisfied." These conditions describe the input resources the agent is obliged to deliver to the service as well the timeout for the delivery. Hence, we introduce to Entish the attribute *commitments(service)*, that is a pair of *form_in, form_out* formulas, where *form_in* is equal to *(con1 and con2)* whereas *form_out* is equal to *intentions(agent)*. The information about the commitment must be saved in agent's knowledge, so that we introduce to Entish the next agent attribute: *knows(agent)*. Usually, agent is equipped by the SercretaryService with initial knowledge. Let us note that agent can also commit to a service (particularly to its SecretaryService) to perform a task, so that we introduce also the following agent attribute: *commitments(agent)*.

Service invocation is realized in the following six steps: In the first step an agent sends its intention to the service. In the second step a commitment is sent to the agent by the service. In the third step the formula *form_in* of the commitment is satisfied by the agent or by another service. In the fourth step an operation is performed by the service. In the fifth step the formula *form_out* of the commitment is satisfied. Let us note that there may occur failures in the steps: second, third, and fourth one if, for example, the timeout is over. In the final sixth step the agent is notified by the service about either success or failure. The service invocation constitutes the first crucial point of our approach.

Generally, if agent's goal can not be realized by a single service, the agent looks for a plan (called workflow plan) that decomposes the main goal into sub goals (sub tasks). Once it has got a plan, it must find out services that can realize the sub tasks, and arrange the workflow. How can it be done? The simplest solution is to introduce a special service (called InfoService) for providing agents with workflow plans and info about services performing operations needed for the workflow. However, the workflow arrangement, execution and control, as well as reconfiguring and recovery in the case of failure is delegated to agents. Workflow plan is an element of type *Operation* in Entish , and it is a sequence of Entish formulas to be adopted by agent as its intentions. The last formula of the sequence describes the final result of the workflow execution, whereas the first formula describes what initial resources are needed to start an execution. The rest formulas describe intermediate situations and correspond to operations to be performed in the workflow.

The way the agent constructs a workflow on the basis of a fixed workflow plan is the following. The agent starts with the last formula in the workflow plan sequence as its first intention. It is supposed that the agent's goal follows from that last formula. The service **SER-0** that agrees conditionally to realize the first intention, gives to the agent an appropriate commitment where the *form_in* formula of the commitment determines (together with the work plan) the next intentions of the agent. The next move of the agent is to find out service(s) that can realize the next intentions. Once the agent finds out an appropriate service, say **SER-1**, that commits to realize the intentions, the satisfaction of the *form_in* formula of the service **SER-0** is delegated to the service **SER-1**. (**It is the critical point for understanding our idea of automatic service integration.**) Supposing that the agent finds out the service **SER-1** that agrees to realize its intention, the service **SER-1** returns to the agent a commitment with another *form_in* formula that determines the next intentions of the agent. Once the agent finds out an appropriate service, say **SER-2**, that commits to realize the intentions, the satisfaction of the *form_in* formula of the service **SER-1** is delegated to the service **SER-2**. And so on. The process goes on until the agent collects all commitments needed to construct a workflow according to the adopted plan. The commitments include appropriate timeouts that synchronize the workflow. Once the agent computes (on the basis of its knowledge) that it itself can satisfy initial formulas in the workflow plan, it can start the workflow execution. Usually, the initial formulas correspond to the initial resources (data) provided by the SecretaryService for the task realization. The satisfaction of the initial formulas starts the workflow execution; it looks like domino effect. If the process is completed before the timeout set for the task realization, the agent can execute the workflow, and then notifies the SecretaryService about that. The method of constructing and executing workflows by the agent constitutes the second crucial point of our approach.

InfoService is crucial for task realization by the agents. From the point of view of system functioning it is a distributed database, and it is not important how it is implemented. The only requirement is that InfoService implements simple conversation protocol for providing info about operations (workflow plans), and about services having specified operation type. This is done in response to agent's request that is always of the form: "My intention is ϕ". InfoService is also used for publishing info by service providers. Service provider can send an info (as Entish formula), describing the type of operation his/her service provides, to InfoService. InfoService can joint this info to its database. So that, the conversation protocol for InfoService is extremely simple. InfoService corresponds to UDDI, however, it seems to be simpler. Agent is dedicated only to one task performance, but its experience is supposed to be saved in an InfoService where it is processed and the results help other agents that have tasks of the same type. The idea of InfoService constitutes the third crucial point of our approach to service integration.

The idea presented above seems to be nice, but the problem is how to create an agent that could perform tasks by arranging and executing workflows. How should such agent react to failures of some workflow elements? What if the agent process is killed by an accident or if the host of the agent process is down? The solution is quite simple: The essential data of agent process must be separated from execution machinery of the process. Surprisingly, these data correspond to agent (mental) attributes. Let these data be called `soul` in Entish. The execution machinery should be delegated to the special dedicated service called BodyService. Agent process is created if the data structure `soul` is sent to a BodyService. BodyService is responsible for agent's reasoning, planing, communication, and action execution on the basis of the soul data. If the process is killed by an accident, then it can be fully reconstructed from the `soul`, because the `soul` stores (by definition) all essential data of the process. Since the `soul` is expressed in Entish, it is implementation independent. This constitutes the fourth crucial point of our approach.

To sum up, Entish is fully declarative language although it corresponds functionally to WSFL, XLANG, XAML, and DAML-S which are procedural languages. To be more precise, Entish (being declarative) supports automatic service integration which is also the intended goal of WSFL, XLANG, XAML, and DAML-S. It is the concept of separation of the essential data (i.e., soul) of the agent process from the process execution and reasoning machinery that allows to keep Entish as a declarative language. The essential data are expressed in Entish and serve as control data of the service integration process. The execution and reasoning machinery (that must be realized procedurally) is moved outside Entish to the dedicated service, i.e., BodyService. BodyService is viewed as an application implementing the appropriate interface for communication in Entish. However, we impose several conditions on the BodyService behavior, for example, agent's goals and commitments can not be canceled unless the associated timeouts are over, an agent can not take intentions that contradict its goal or commitments, and finally agent must be rational whatever it means. These requirements are not formal but are necessary for assuring intended system behavior.

Of course, Entish could be extended by introducing actions and process constructors, so that execution, reasoning and control could be described. However, the design motto was: *When expressing something, use the least powerful language you can.* Hence, we have designed a minimum language. What was unnecessary was moved outside, that is, the functionality associated with service publishing and discovery was moved to InfoService, whereas execution and reasoning machinery was moved to BodyService. As a result, Entish is a simple declarative and action independent language for web service integration.

Let us compare Entish to the existing web service integration efforts. The point of inventing Entish was not to create a new better language for service description. Entish as a web service description language is simple, perhaps too simple so that WSDL should rather be adopted as the basis for developing Entish idea. The novelty the Entish proposes is a new technique for automatic service invocation and service integration. It corresponds to the efforts of WSFL, XLANG, XAML, and DAML-S. Hence, the idea of Entish could be applied to built the layer on the top of SOAP+WSDL+UDDI stack. In order to do so the syntax of WSDL should be adopted. However, the syntax of Entish seems to be easier for presentation as well as for implementing. For this very reason we decided to adopt only SOAP as the transport layer, and to implement Entish on SOAP.

A detailed syntax of Entish with explanation is available on request from `sambrosz@ipipan.waw.pl`
The first prototype of Entish implementation was done on HTTP+SOAP transport. Simple instances of SecretaryService, InfoService, DictionaryService, BodyService and a number of ordinary services were implemented. Most of the ordinary services are for converting data formats, e.g., gif to jpg, pdf to ps, latex to html, etc.. There are also other services like PhoneNumberService that returns the phone number of a person given his/her personal data (name, address), and a lot more will be implemented as student projects shortly. Now, we are testing the prototype and collecting experience. One corollary is obvious: More services are needed.

A preliminary version of Entish has been published in [1]. For sources and reports on the progress of Entish specification and implementation, see our web sites `www.ipipan.waw.pl/mas`

References

1. S. Ambroszkiewicz and T. Nowak. Agentspace as a Middleware for Service Integration. In Proc. ESAW'2001. Springer-Verlag LNAI, vol. 2203.
2. T. Berners-Lee - www.w3.org/DesignIssues/Webize.html -and- /DesignIssues/Logic.html
3. The Principle of Least Power (T. Berners-Lee) www.w3.org/DesignIssues/Evolution.html
4. IBM's tutorial www-4.ibm.com/software/solutions/webservices/
5. L. Wittgenstein. *Philosophical Investigations.* Basil Blackwell, pp. 20–21, 1958.
6. AML-S www.daml.org/services
7. OASIS BTP www.oasis-open.org/committees/business-transactions/
8. UDDI www.uddi.org
9. SOAP and XMLP www.w3.org/2000/xp/
10. XAML www.xaml.org
11. XLANG www.gotdotnet.com/team/xml_wsspecs/xlang-c/default.htm
12. ebXML www.ebxml.org/
13. WSFL www-4.ibm.com/software/solutions/webservices/

Numerical Schemes for Exploring Delayed Nonlinear Feedback

Victor F. Dailyudenko

Institute of Engineering Cybernetics AS of Belarus,
Surganov St. 6, 220012, Minsk, Belarus

Abstract: We propose to use characteristic exponents of averaged instability for diagnostics of complex systems. It is shown that these exponents can be calculated from eigenvalues of the product matrix obtained from Jacobian-matrixes of the multi-step transformation. The effective scheme for calculating the product matrix in a finite time interval is developed, it allows to reduce calculation complexity (about by an order) due to exact factorization of the Jacobian-matrix in restricted time intervals. The detailed analytical analysis of the reconstruction process is implemented with respect to delay nonlinear equations for both Runge - Kutta and Euler approaches.
Keywords: complex system, nonlinear feedback, delayed differential equation, stability analysis, multidimensional map, characteristic exponents, Runge - Kutta scheme, Euler approximation

Investigation of delayed feedback for a complex system (CS) using nonlinear differential equations with delayed variables has become an object of a very attractive attention in many problems of physics, especially in researching dynamics of lasers and nonlinear optical systems [1], as well as in neural networks exploration [2,3], in biology, ecology and medicine [4,5]. In submitted paper we propose to implement diagnostics of delayed CS by averaged estimation of its stability in a finite time interval, the problem of CS's stability is of a great significance for many tasks of diagnostics and control [6]. We describe averaged instability of the CS with delayed feedback through characteristic exponents [7,8] calculated from eigenvalues of Jacobian-matrix product for the averaged multidimensional map (MM), that provides reconstruction of temporal evolution for the CS. The two numerical approaches for reconstruction of MM from a delay equation are explored in this paper: (i) by Euler approximation of the differential operator and (ii) with using the Runge - Kutta scheme (the four-parametric version). The detailed analytical description for each method is presented, that allows to obtain the product matrix with minimal computer expenses (the product matrix describes the averaged MM obtained from the delay differential equation). The results of numerical simulations show the good convergence and accuracy of proposed analytical methods. The proposed methods are shown to reduce the calculation complexity in comparison with the approach based on successive orthogonalization of multiplied matrixes with using QR-decomposition [8].

Let us consider the following nonlinear delay differential equation (DDE)

$$x'(t) = G(x(t), x(t-\Delta T)) \tag{1}$$

with initial conditions $x(t) = f_0(t)$ at $0 \le t \le \Delta T$. Considering (1) from standpoint of Euler approximation, where $x'(t_n) \cong \frac{x_{n+1} - x_n}{h}$, one can obtain the formula defining the difference equation

$$x_{n+1} = x_n + hG(X_n) \tag{2}$$

where $X_n = (x_n, \bar{x}_n)$; $x_n = x(t_n)$; $\bar{x}_n = x(t_n - \Delta\widetilde{T})$; $\Delta\widetilde{T} = \frac{\Delta T}{\Delta t}$; initial conditions of (2) are given by $x(t_n) = f_0(t_n)$ at $1 \le n \le \Delta\widetilde{T} + 1$; and h is a constant interval of discretization. Very effective way for enlarging accuracy is just applying many-parametric Runge-Kutta schemes [9]. In this paper, we use the four-parametric scheme, because it provides the high accuracy and is of a compact form of its parameters definition. Such type of Runge-Kutta classical methods are widely developed for nonlinear both ordinary and partially differential equations [9]. At the same time, exploration of these approaches for DDE's is not so deep, especially that concerns stability of corresponding functional maps. So, in this paper we compare in detail the Runge-Kutta many-parametric schemes for ordinary differential equations without delay and those for DDE's. We show that though these both approaches are of the similar form of parametric reconstruction, the specific feature of DDE's scheme is enlarging the order of a common delay time (defining the depth of recurrent reconstruction), proportionally to the scheme's order.

The Runge-Kutta approach implies the following decomposition at reconstruction of solution (for a second order):

$$x_{n+1} = x(t_n + h) = x_n + hx'_n + \frac{h^2}{2}x''_n + o(h^2) \tag{3}$$

Note that an increase of a derivative order results in growth of a common delay interval of the reconstruction scheme for DDE. Really, corresponding derivatives can be written as

$$x'_n = \left.\frac{dx(t)}{dt}\right|_{t=t_n} = G(X_n);\; x''_n = \frac{\partial G(X_n)}{\partial x_n}G(X_n) + \frac{\partial G(X_n)}{\partial \bar{x}_n}G(\bar{X}_n) \tag{4}$$

where $\bar{X}_n = (\bar{x}_n, \overset{2}{\bar{x}}_n)$; $\overset{l}{\bar{x}}_n = x(t_n - l\Delta T)$. Taking into account (3), (4), one can suppose that because of enlarging the temporal depth, the two-parametric Runge-Kutta scheme is to be of a form

$$x_{n+1} = x_n + h(p_1k_1 + p_2k_2) + o(h^2); \tag{5}$$

where $k_1 = G(X_n)$; $k_2 = G(u,\bar{u})$; $u = x_n + \alpha_1 hk_1$; $\bar{u} = \bar{x}_n + \alpha_2 h\bar{k}_1$; $\bar{k}_1 = G(\bar{X}_n)$. The scheme (5) can be used for calculating all samples x_n, where $n > \Delta\widetilde{T} + 1$. The proof of (5) can be implemented by the decomposition (3). Really, k_2 in (5) and x''_n in (3) are expressed through partial derivatives of $G(X_n)$ as follows (we suppose $\alpha_1 = \alpha_2 = \alpha$)

$$x''_n = \frac{\partial G(X_n)}{\partial x_n} k_1 + \frac{\partial G(X_n)}{\partial \bar{x}_n} \bar{k}_1 \tag{6}$$

$$k_2 = k_1 + \frac{\partial G(X_n)}{\partial x_n} \alpha hk_1 + \frac{\partial G(X_n)}{\partial \bar{x}_n} \alpha h\bar{k}_1 + o(h) \tag{7}$$

For background of (5), from (3) - (7) we obtain the expression

$$\frac{x_{n+1} - x_n}{h} - (p_1 k_1 + p_2 k_2) = k_1(1 - (p_1 + p_2)) + h\left[\frac{\partial G(X_n)}{\partial x_n} k_1 + \frac{\partial G(X_n)}{\partial \bar{x}_n} \bar{k}_1\right](½ - \alpha p_2) + o(h) \tag{8}$$

In order to (5) be valid, the following conditions are to be true

$$p_1 + p_2 = 1; \qquad \alpha p_2 = ½ \tag{9}$$

For simplicity, suppose that in (9) $\alpha = 1$; $p_1 = p_2 = ½$. Such equations as (9) for definition of parameters in (5) completely coincide with ones in conventional Runge-Kutta scheme for ordinary differential equations without delay [9]. Consequently, because of similarity of the two schemes, one can suppose that four-parametric Runge-Kutta scheme for (1) can be constructed using the structure and coefficients of the conventional one, namely

$$x_{n+1} = x_n + h\sum_{i=1}^{4} p_i k_i + o(h^4); \tag{10}$$

where still $k_1 = G(X_n)$; and $k_2 = G(Y_n)$; $k_3 = G(Z_n)$; $k_4 = G(W_n)$; while two-dimensional points are defined as $Y_n = (L_2, \bar{L}_2)$; $Z_n = (L_3, \bar{L}_3)$; $W_n = (L_4, \bar{L}_4)$; and for $l>1$ we have that $k_l = G(L_l, \bar{L}_l)$; $L_2 = x_n + \alpha hk_1$; $L_3 = x_n + \beta hk_2$; $L_4 = x_n + \gamma hk_3$; coefficients values are given by

$$\alpha = \beta = ½; \; \gamma = 1; \; p_1 = p_4 = ⅙; \; p_2 = p_3 = ⅓. \tag{11}$$

In (10) $\bar{L}_2 = \bar{x}_n + \alpha h \bar{k}_1$, i.e. it is formed from L_2 by additional delay at ΔT, $\bar{L}_3$ and $\bar{L}_4$ are formed analogously.

For background of the scheme (10), let us consider it with unknown coefficients $\alpha, \beta, \gamma, p_i$. Then the error of (10) is written through its components as follows:

$$\varphi_4(h) = x(t_n + h) - x_n - h(\sum_{i=1}^{4} p_i k_i) \tag{12}$$

So far as $\varphi_4(0) = 0$, for validness of accuracy condition for the scheme (10) (i.e. for $\varphi_4(h) = o(h^4)$), the following terms of above explored decomposition, expressed through derivative of error function in zero point, are to be equal zero

$$\varphi_4'(0) = 0;\ \varphi_4''(0) = 0;\ \varphi_4'''(0) = 0;\ \varphi_4^{IV}(0) = 0. \tag{13}$$

The first derivation of (12) is given by the relationship

$$\varphi_4'(h) = (x_{n+1})_h' - \sum_{i=1}^{4} p_i k_i \ - h(p_2 k_2' + p_3 k_3' + p_4 k_4') \tag{14}$$

and from the first condition of (13) it immediately follows that $k_1(1 - \sum_{i=1}^{4} p_i) = 0$, and thus we obtain the first equation for p_i coefficients in (10)

$$\sum_{i=1}^{4} p_i = 1. \tag{15}$$

The second derivation of (12) can be calculated from (14) and has a following form

$$\varphi_4''(h) = (x_{n+1})_h'' - \sum_{i=2}^{4} p_i [2k_i'(h) + hk_i''(h)] \tag{16}$$

where $k_2'(h) = \alpha[G_{(1)}'(Y_n)k_1 + G_{(2)}'(Y_n)\bar{k}_1]$;

$$k_3'(h) = \beta[G_{(1)}'(Z_n)(k_2 + hk_2') + G_{(2)}'(Z_n)(\bar{k}_2 + h\bar{k}_2')];$$

$$k_4'(h) = \gamma[G_{(1)}'(W_n)(k_3 + hk_3') + G_{(2)}'(W_n)(\bar{k}_3 + h\bar{k}_3')];$$

$$(x_{n+1})_h'' = G_{(1)}'(X_{n+1})G(X_{n+1}) + G_{(2)}'(X_{n+1})G(\bar{X}_{n+1})$$

In these formulae $G_{(1)}'$ means a partial derivative on the first argument (in the other words, on the first coordinate of the point), while $G_{(2)}'$ means a derivative on the second one. Calculating (16) for h=0, one can obtain, after some transformations, the expression

$$\varphi_4''(0) = [1-2(p_2\alpha+p_3\beta+p_4\gamma)]\,[G'_{(1)}(X_n)k_1+G'_{(2)}(X_n)\bar{k}_1] \tag{17}$$

From (17) we have a second equation for coefficients in (10)

$$p_2\alpha+p_3\beta+p_4\gamma=\tfrac{1}{2}. \tag{18}$$

It is evidently that equations (15) and (18) have a form, very similar to relations (9) in two-parametric scheme. The subsequent equations for coefficients are obtained by differentiation of (16) and calculation of both $\varphi_4'''(h)$ and derivative included by that, namely

$$\varphi_4'''(h) = (x_{n+1})_h''' - \sum_{i=2}^{4} p_i[3k_i''(h)+hk_i'''(h)], \tag{19}$$

where

$$(x_{n+1})_h''' = G''_{(1)(1)}(X_{n+1})G^2(X_{n+1}) + 2G''_{(1)(2)}(X_{n+1})G(X_{n+1})G(\bar{X}_{n+1}) + G''_{(2)(2)}(X_{n+1})G^2(\bar{X}_{n+1}) +$$
$$(G_{(1)}(X_{n+1}))^2G(X_{n+1}) + 2G_{(1)}(X_{n+1})G_{(2)}(X_{n+1})G(\bar{X}_{n+1}) + G_{(2)}(X_{n+1})G_{(2)}(\bar{X}_{n+1})\overset{2}{G(\bar{X}_{n+1})}; \tag{20}$$

$$k_2''(h) = \alpha^2[G''_{(1)(1)}(Y_n)k_1^2 + 2G''_{(1)(2)}(Y_n)k_1\bar{k}_1 + G''_{(2)(2)}(Y_n)\bar{k}_1^2]; \tag{21}$$

$$k_3''(h) = \beta[\beta G''_{(1)(1)}(Z_n)(k_2+hk_2')^2 + 2\beta G''_{(1)(2)}(Z_n)(k_2+hk_2')(\bar{k}_2+h\bar{k}_2') + \beta G''_{(2)(2)}(Z_n)(\bar{k}_2+h\bar{k}_2')^2 +$$
$$G'_{(1)}(Z_n)(2k_2'+hk_2'') + G'_{(2)}(Z_n)(2\bar{k}_2'+h\bar{k}_2'')]; \tag{22}$$

$$k_4''(h) = \gamma[\gamma G''_{(1)(1)}(W_n)(k_3+hk_3')^2 + 2\gamma G''_{(1)(2)}(W_n)(k_3+hk_3')(\bar{k}_3+h\bar{k}_3') + \gamma G''_{(2)(2)}(W_n)(\bar{k}_3+h\bar{k}_3')^2 +$$
$$G'_{(1)}(W_n)(2k_3'+hk_3'') + G'_{(2)}(W_n)(2\bar{k}_3'+h\bar{k}_3'')] \tag{23}$$

From these formulae, one can derive the expression for $\varphi_4'''(0)$, and the following two equations are obtained directly from (19)-(23), taking into account condition that $\varphi_4'''(0)=0$:

$$p_2\alpha^2+p_3\beta^2+p_4\gamma^2=\tfrac{1}{3} \tag{24}$$

$$\beta(\alpha p_3+\gamma p_4)=\tfrac{1}{6} \tag{25}$$

At last, for the fourth derivative we can write from differentiating of (19) the expression

$$\varphi_4^{IV}(h) = (x_{n+1})_h^{IV} - \sum_{i=2}^{4} p_i[4k_i'''(h)+hk_i^{IV}(h)], \tag{26}$$

where corresponding derivatives are obtained from (20)-(23) by additional differentiation. After some algebraic transformations, one can obtain four equations with respect to defining parameters, analogously above obtained (15), (18), (24), (25). Let us note that such equations completely coincide with those for conventional Runge-Kutta scheme [9], values of parameters in (10) properly corresponding to such equations. So, the scheme (10) can be really used for modeling DDE (1) in its general form.

In this paper, we investigate the partially nonlinear DDE (PN DDE), that is given by

$$\xi'(t) = -b\xi(t) + \Phi(\bar{\xi}(t)) \tag{27}$$

with the same initial conditions as in (1), where $\bar{\xi}(t) = \xi(t - \Delta T)$. The equations of the type such as (27) describe a wide class of nonlinear processes with delayed action in physics, cybernetics, ecology and medicine [2-6]. The behavior of a single neuron in a well-known Hopfield model can be described by equation similarly (27) with sigmoidal nonlinearity expressed through hyperbolic tangent tanh($\beta\,\xi$), β is the neuron gain (see [2] and references therein).

As a model for numerical experiments, we use the Mackey-Glass equation [5], where

$$\Phi(\xi) = \frac{a\xi}{1+\xi^{c}}, \tag{28}$$

$f_0(t) = 0.9$, b=0.1, a=0.2, c=10. Using initial conditions $\xi(t) = s$ in the segment $0 \le t \le \Delta T$, after integration of (27) for $\Delta T \le t \le 2\Delta T$ we obtain the relationship

$$\xi(t) = \frac{A}{b} + (s - \frac{A}{b})\exp[-b(t - \Delta T)] \tag{29}$$

where $A = \Phi(s)$. Unfortunately, the exact integration in subsequent segments seems to be impossible, because for deriving exact solution of the equation (27), (28), the integrals of the following form are to be found: $\int \frac{d\eta}{(\eta-\alpha)^{M_1}(1+\eta^{10})}$, the complexity of formulae under integration essentially growing for every subsequent segment. So, the only way for solving (27) in subsequent time intervals is the approximation of (27), (28) by numerical methods. So, at reconstruction of the third segment ($2\Delta T < t \le 3\,\Delta T$) of solution time series (TS), we use the two-parametric Runge-Kutta scheme (5), (9). At the fourth segment ($3\Delta T < t \le 4\,\Delta T$), we apply Runge-Kutta method of the third order. After those three steps, we obtain the approximate solution of (27), (28) at the region $0 \le t \le 4\,\Delta T$, and for further reconstruction the four-parametric scheme (10) is used. The obtained time series (TS) (n=1, 2, …, N) are shown in the fig.1. One can see that ones display a process with growing chaoticity and are very similar to obtained by the direct Euler approximation [10]. By computer experiments, we have proved that essential difference between TS obtained by these two methods (Euler and Runge-Kutta) is detected only for enough large N (N□3 $\times$ 10^4), that is in a good coincidence with results of the other authors (see references in [10]).

Estimation of instability with respect to CS is of a great significance for many tasks of diagnostics and control [2 - 4, 6]. The present paper is devoted to exploring CS with complex stochastic behavior, so the analysis of stability in Lyapunov sense [7-8] is applied. Lyapunov stability analysis allows calculating characteristic exponents, those describe global properties of attractor.

Applying to (27)-(28) approximation (2), one can show that modeling temporal evolution of CS with delayed feedback in the phase space of fixed dimension can be implemented by the m-dimensional vector map $\vec{G}^{(k)}$ ($\mathfrak{R}^m \Rightarrow \mathfrak{R}^m$), m= $\Delta\tilde{T}+1$, where $\vec{\varsigma}(n+k)=\vec{G}^{(k)}(\vec{\varsigma}(n))$, the coordinates of $\vec{\varsigma}(n)$ are written as $\vec{\varsigma}(n)=(\xi(n), \xi(n+1),...,\xi(n+\Delta\tilde{T}))$. In [11-12] we showed the k $=\Delta\tilde{T}$ is very suitable for exact factorization (as well as for reducing operations) in the matrix multiplication, in such a case functional matrix of the multi-step map $\vec{G}^{(\Delta\tilde{T})}$ is of the form for Euler approximation

$$J_n^{(\Delta\tilde{T})}=B_\Delta\ F\ \Phi_n^D, \tag{30}$$

where the triangle Toeplietz matrix B_Δ describes liner transformations in PN DDE and is given by

$$B_\Delta=\begin{pmatrix} 1 & 0 & \cdots & 0 \\ \beta & 1 & \cdots & 0 \\ \cdot & \cdot & \cdot & \cdot \\ \beta^{\Delta\tilde{T}-1} & \beta^{\Delta\tilde{T}-2} & & 0 \\ \beta^{\Delta\tilde{T}} & \beta^{\Delta\tilde{T}-1} & \cdots & 1 \end{pmatrix}, \tag{31}$$

the diagonal matrix Φ_n^D presents nonlinear transformations through corresponding derivatives $\Phi_n^D=\mathrm{diag}[\psi_n,\psi_{n+1},...,\psi_{n+\Delta\tilde{T}-1},1\ ]$, where $\beta = 1- h\ b;$ $\psi_n=h\dfrac{d\Phi(\xi(n))}{d\xi(n)}$, and F is a matrix of cyclic unit shift (in the other words, permutation matrix). In accordance with [7,8], calculation of Lyapunov exponents for the MM $\vec{G}^{(\Delta\tilde{T})}$ can be implemented as follows

$$\nu_k \cong \frac{1}{M}\ln|\lambda_k| \tag{32}$$

where λ_k is the *k-th* eigenvalue of the product $P^{(M)}$ defining the resulting transformation of the MM's

$$P^{(M)} = \prod_{j=0}^{M-1} J^{(\Delta\tilde{T})}_{(M-j-1)\Delta\tilde{T}} \,, \tag{33}$$

For long time regions, computational process requires enormous computer resources (especially for large m) for one-step transformation derived directly from (2), so the minimization of matrix multiplications in (33) obtained due to MM $\vec{G}^{(\Delta\tilde{T})}$ and its decomposition, instead of one-element reconstruction (2), is very helpful in such a case. The results of numerical computation of the characteristic exponents for $\vec{G}^{(\Delta\tilde{T})}$ by (30)-(33) are displayed in fig. 2, in this computation we used M=100, TS was obtained from (27), (28) at h=0.25, its length was $N=M\cdot\Delta\tilde{T}$. As follows from calculated dependence in fig.2, positive Lyapunov exponents display growth (in the other words, growth of chaoticity) with increase of ΔT. One can conclude from fig.2 that this growth is especially sharp near "critical" point ΔT =16.8, where the chaos onset takes place, that displays a good coincidence with results of linearized analysis of (27), (28) [4]. The results in fig. 3 display influence of localization extent to the structure of a profile of calculated exponents (i.e. dependence ν_k versus k), for this aim we calculated the eigenvalues of the product

$$P^{(\Delta m)} = \prod_{j=0}^{\Delta m-1} J^{(\Delta\tilde{T})}_{(M-j-1)\Delta\tilde{T}} \,, \tag{34}$$

where Δm defines an extent of locality. One can explicitly see the lost of smoothness in profile curves with extending a temporal region Δm of investigations, as well as growth of positive exponents level. The instability analysis for Runge-Kutta scheme is implemented analogously Euler's one with using (10), we obtained that an angle of the slope corresponding to the negative exponents is larger for the Runge-Kutta method

In comparison with the widely applied scheme of successive mutual orthogonalization (SO), the proposed method of Jacobian-matrix product for multistep MM provides essential reduction of computational operations, because mutual orthogonalization operations are absent in proposed method, while matrix multiplications are involved in the both approaches. Let us note that coefficients μ_i defined at every step of SO [8] depend on all previous steps, and only if partial eigenvalues μ_i are replaced by the singular values, those will define the local properties of Jacobian-matrix at the certain time step (because of orthogonality of corresponding matrixes involved into SO process).

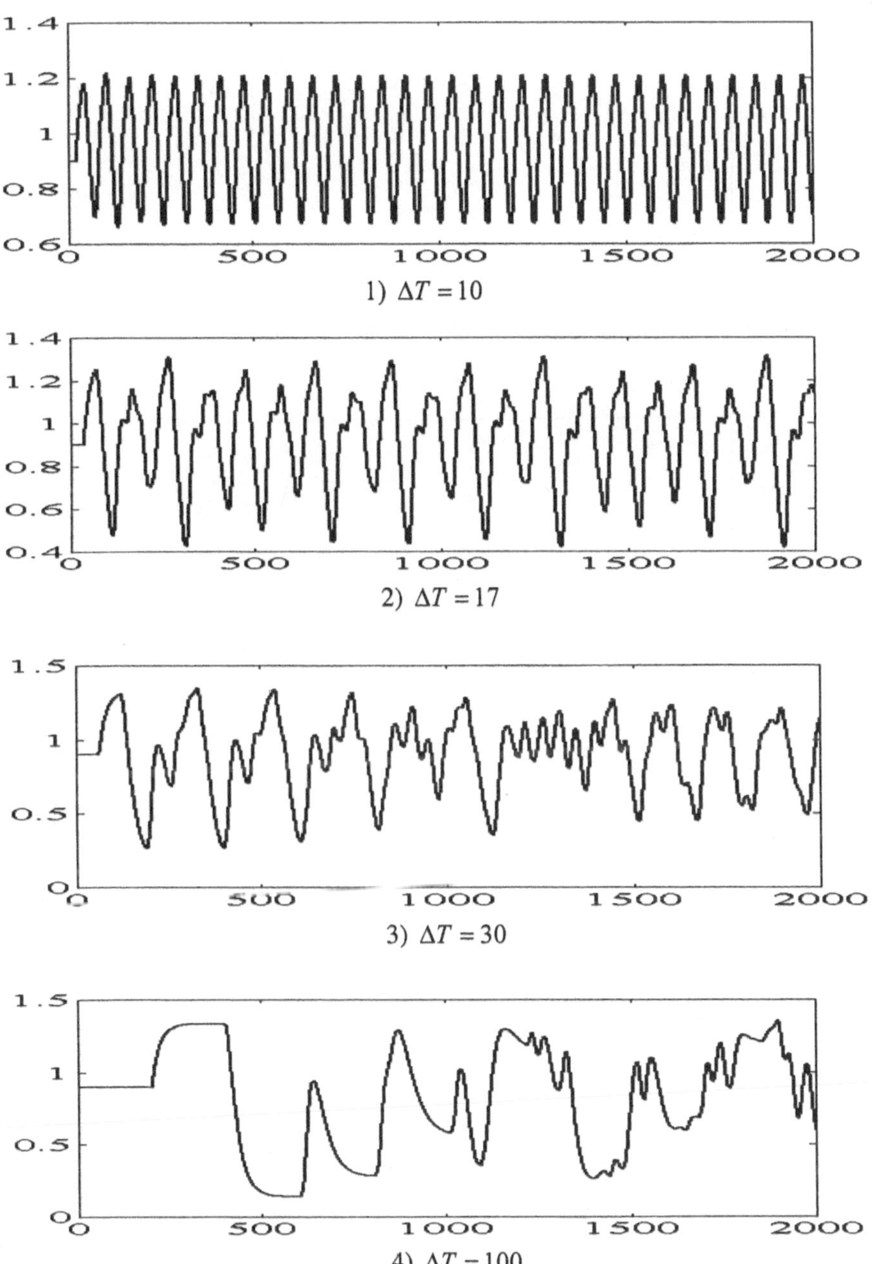

Fig. 1. Time series samples obtained according to four-parametric Runge-Kutta method are shown as plot points level $\xi(i)$ versus point number i ; h=0.5.

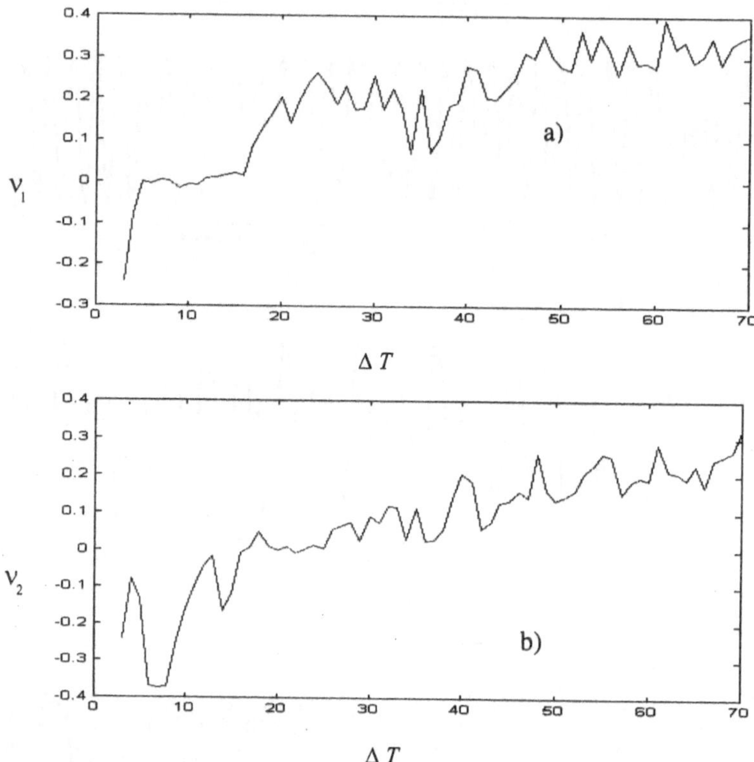

Fig. 2. The plot of the largest Lyapunov exponents vs delay time ΔT (Euler approximation); a), b), correspond to the first and second exponents respectively

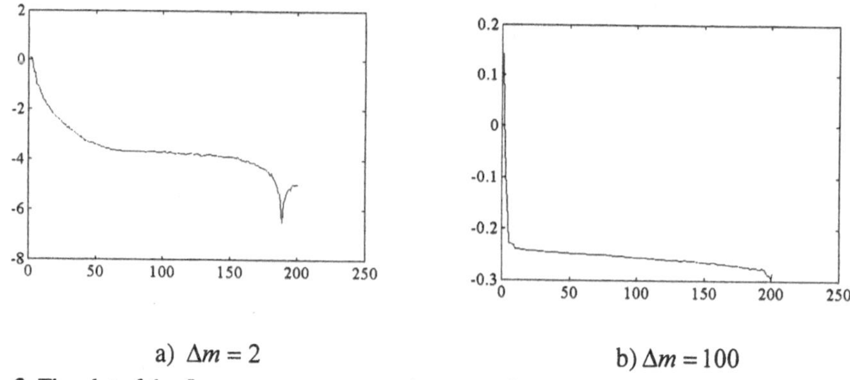

a) $\Delta m = 2$ b) $\Delta m = 100$

Fig. 3. The plot of the Lyapunov exponents value ν_i vs its number i (Euler approximation) for changing temporal region Δm; $\Delta T = 40$; h=0.2; M=200

References

1. Arecchi, F.T. (1991): Space-time complexity in nonlinear optics. Physica D 51, 450-464.
2. Ye, H., Michel, A. N., Wang, K. (1994): Global stability and local stability of Hopfield neural network with delays. Phys. Rev. E 50, 4206- 4213.
3. Van den Driessche, P., Wu, J., Zou, X. (2001): Stabilization role of inhibitory self-connections in a delayed neural network. Physica D 150, 84 - 90.
4. Farmer, J.D. (1982): Chaotic attractors of an infinite-dimensional dynamical system. Physica D 4, 366-393.
5. Mackey, M.C., Glass, L. (1977): Oscillation and chaos in physiological control systems. Science 197, 287 - 289.
6. Trinh, H., Aldeen, M. (1995): Robust stability of singularity perturbed discrete-delay system. IEEE Trans. Automat. Contr. 40, 1620 – 1623.
7. Stefanski, A. (2000): Estimation of the largest Lyapunov exponent in systems with impacts. Chaos, Solitons and Fractals 11, 2443-2451.
8. Eckman, J.-P., Ruelle, D. (1985): Ergodic theory of chaos and strange attractors. Rev. Mod. Phys. 57, 617-656.
9. Hairer, E., Norsett, S.P. (1987): Solving Ordinary Differential Equations I. Nonstiff Problems. Springer-Verlag.
10. Dailyudenko, V.F. (2000): Nonlinear model for stochastic minelike objects based on delay differential equations. In: Proc. of the SPIE's 14-th Ann. Int. Symp. (Apr. 2000, Orlando, Florida, USA) 4038, 1294 - 1305.
11. Dailyudenko, V.F. (2000): Characterization of the topological structure and stability for a vector map derived from a delay differential equation. Nonlinear Phenomena in Complex Systems (Minsk) 3, 231 - 241.
12. Dailyudenko, V.F. (2001): Global stability of nonlinear systems with temporal multi-dimensionality. In: Proc. of the SPIE's •onf. on Applications and Science of Computational Intelligence IV (Apr. 2001, Orlando, Florida, USA) 4390, 281-292.

References

Migration of Multi-class Objects in Information Systems

Król D., Nguyen N.T., Daniłowicz C.,

Wroclaw University of Technology, Department of Information Systems, Wybrzeze S. Wyspiańskiego 27, 50-370 Wroclaw, Poland
{krol, thanh, danilowicz}@zsi.pwr.wroc.pl

Abstract: This paper concerns object migration in object-oriented information systems. For this aim a model of multi-class objects which enables object dynamics, is presented. Two aspects of object dynamics are analyzed in detail. The first aspect refers to multi-class feature of objects, and the second is related to the migration of multi-class objects. This model is an expanded version of the basic object model. The expanding is relied on standardizing the elementary notions: object and class. Owing to this concept it is possible to realize migration operations on objects, that is the object dynamics. Migration operators and an object migration language (OML) are also presented.

Key words: object database, multi-class object, data dynamics, object migration.

1. Introduction

In relation to the fact that the first object-oriented databases arose at the end of the 80-th years of the 20-th century, it seems to be obvious that the full object theory is still incomplete. Up to now objects databases have been applied in such fields as CAD, CAM, CASE and OIS [3], [5], [6], [9]. The characteristic of these fields is relied on the complexity and large numbers of processed data.

In known object-oriented models [1], [14], [17], [21] the dynamics of objects has been done in a very small degree. Most often the authors have dealt with the evolution of classes and objects. In the basic object model [6], [19] a class is understood as a collection of objects of the same structure. Thus the evolution on class level relies on class modification, for example, attribute domain modification or method modification [12]. The evolution on the object level consists of such operation as object moving or object adding. Note that between classes and objects different relationships, such as inheritance or preference etc., may occur. Because of these relationships an object database mentions a complicated and nested net in which the nodes represent classes and objects, and the edges – different relationships between them. One should note that in this kind of nets each operation which moves or adds elements requires a very expensive reconstruction.

In existing object models multi-class objects appear only in the inheritance relation. For example, if class *Student* inherits class *Person* then an object which belongs to class *Student* belongs also to class *Person*. Thus if class *Student* does not inherit class *Employee* then for storing information about a working student (or a studding employee) it is necessary to define in the system two different objects (referring to the same real world object), one of which belongs to class *Student*, and the second belongs to class *Employee*.

In the basic object model an object is defined as a pair (*identifier*, *value*), and a class is a triple (*class_name*, *set_of_attributes*, *set_of_methods*). The first component of an object is unique and invariable, thus the dynamics if exists, refers only to the second component. However, objects of this type cannot change their structures and behavior; cannot migrate among classes and cannot occur in several classes which are not in inheritance relationships. The migration of an object can be realized only by moving this object from one class and adding it to another [2], [4], [13], [15], [18].

A question may arise: Assuming non-deviation from the object ideology is it possible to define such notions as class and object and their relations in another way so that the data dynamics may be performed more effectively? In this work the authors present an object model, owing to which the answer for the above question is positive. In this aim the notions of class and object are unified. The following assumptions are made:

- An object may belong to many classes simultaneously (multi-class object).
- Objects and classes have unified structure, owing to which a class may be treated as an object and vice versa.

In this work a model of multi-class objects is presented. This model enables the following three aspects: the first concerns treating objects in the same category as classes; the second refers to belonging of an object to several classes simultaneously and the third – possibility for defining operators for object migration. An object manipulation language is also presented.

2. Multi-class Object Model

At first, we assume that in the model an object does not necessarily belong to one class. An object may be created as an instance of one class or more classes. However, when considering objects with several classes new problems may arise, because an object does not have to belong to a single class, but rather to a set of classes. In such a case, an object takes the union of the features of all the classes to which it belongs. Conflicts among different definitions may however take place.

The second main assumption of our model is relied on eliminating the difference between an object and a class. This means that an object may be treated as a class and vice versa. Also in this case we may come across on potential conflicts. In this section we will discuss how these conflicts may be solved taking into account the structural components of objects. Conflicts referring to object behavior will be the goal of the future research.

Definition 1. By a multi-class object x we call an expression

$$(\mathrm{id}(x), \mathrm{Sub}(x), \mathrm{Sup}(x), \mathrm{A}_{\mathrm{Sub}}(x), \mathrm{v}(x), \mathrm{M}(x)),$$

where id(x) – object identifier of x, Sub(x) – set of sub-objects identifiers of x, Sup(x) - set of sup-objects identifiers of x, $\mathrm{A}_{\mathrm{Sub}}(x)$ – set of attributes described sub-objects of x, v(x) - value of x, M(x) – set of methods of x, where:

$$(\forall x, y \in \mathrm{OBJ})\begin{pmatrix}\mathrm{id}(x) = \mathrm{id}(y) \Leftrightarrow \mathrm{v}(x) = \mathrm{v}(y) \wedge \mathrm{Sub}(x) = \mathrm{Sub}(y) \wedge \mathrm{Sup}(x) = \mathrm{Sup}(y) \\ \wedge \mathrm{M}(x) = \mathrm{M}(y) \wedge \mathrm{A}_{\mathrm{Sub}}(x) = \mathrm{A}_{\mathrm{Sub}}(y)\end{pmatrix}$$

$$(\forall x, y \in \mathrm{OBJ})(\mathrm{id}(y) \in \mathrm{Sub}(x) \Rightarrow \mathrm{id}(x) \notin \mathrm{Sub}(y)),$$

$$(\forall x, y \in \mathrm{OBJ})(\mathrm{id}(y) \in \mathrm{Sup}(x) \Rightarrow \mathrm{id}(x) \notin \mathrm{Sup}(y)),$$

$$(\forall x, y \in \mathrm{OBJ})(\mathrm{id}(y) \in \mathrm{Sub}(x) \Leftrightarrow \mathrm{id}(x) \in \mathrm{Sup}(y)),$$

$$(\forall x, y \in \mathrm{OBJ})(\mathrm{id}(y) \in \mathrm{Sub}(x) \Rightarrow \mathrm{A}(y) \supseteq \mathrm{A}_{\mathrm{Sub}}(x) \vee \mathrm{A}_{\mathrm{Sub}}(y) \supseteq \mathrm{A}_{\mathrm{Sub}}(x)),$$

v(x): $\mathrm{A}(x) \rightarrow \mathrm{V}(x)$ where $a \in \mathrm{A}(x)$, $v \in \mathrm{V}_a(x)$. ♦

The multi-class object notion needs some additional requirements. We introduce the notions of local attribute, attribute origin and attributes sum.

Definition 2. Local attribute of an object x is attribute $a \in \mathrm{A}(x)$ as follows: $\neg\exists$ ($y \in$ OBJ), id(y) $\in$ Sup(x) where $a \in \mathrm{A}(y)$. Set of local attributes object x we denote as $\bar{\mathrm{A}}(x)$. ♦

We now define the attribute origin notion.

Definition 3. By an attribute origin for $a \in \mathrm{A}$ of an object x we call an object y, for which $a \in \bar{\mathrm{A}}(y)$. ♦

Definition 4. The attributes sum of objects x and y, denoted as $\mathrm{A}(x) \oplus \mathrm{A}(y)$, is defined as follows: $\{\mathrm{A}(x) \div \mathrm{A}(y)\} \cup \{\mathrm{A}(x) \cap \mathrm{A}(y) \wedge (a,x) = (a,y)\}$. ♦

The above definition states that for $a \in \mathrm{A}(x) \cap \mathrm{A}(y)$, if $(a, x) \neq (a, y)$ then we create two new attributes, denoted adequately $x \perp a$ and $y \perp a$. In the case where the attributes sum applies to many sets we use the short notation $\oplus \mathrm{A}(y_i)$ which is equal to $\mathrm{A}(y_1) \oplus \mathrm{A}(y_2) \oplus \ldots \oplus \mathrm{A}(y_n)$.

Thus, the following conditions formally state these concepts.

$$\mathrm{A}(x) = \bigoplus_{\mathrm{id}(y) \in Sup(x)} \mathrm{A}_{\mathrm{Sub}}(y) \oplus \bar{\mathrm{A}}(x),$$

$$\mathrm{A}_{\mathrm{Sub}}(x) = \bigoplus_{\mathrm{id}(y) \in Sup(x)} \mathrm{A}_{\mathrm{Sub}}(y) \oplus \bar{\mathrm{A}}_{\mathrm{Sub}}(x)$$

where x is object-class.

Next we introduce two common notations: object-instance and object-class.

Definition 5. A multi-class object x is an object-instance, if $\mathrm{A}_{\mathrm{Sub}}(x) = \varnothing$ and $\mathrm{Sub}(x) = \varnothing$. ♦

Definition 6. A multi-class object x is an object-class, if $A_{Sub}(x) \neq \varnothing$. ♦

Example 1. Consider the database for local department of education. Suppose that objects are two types: object-class and object-instance. First type contains sub-objects, sup-objects and local attributes.

Id(x)	Sub(x)	Sup(x)	$A_{Sub}(x)$	v(x)	M(x)
School_11	Class_2a, Class_2b, Math_circle,	Dolny_Śląsk	Unit_name, Number_of_ pupils	<School_nr: 11, Director: Teacher_1, Number_of_ pupils: 122>	∅

By contrast, consider object-class with null value.

Id(x)	Sub(x)	Sup(x)	$A_{Sub}(x)$	v(x)	M(x)
Dolny_Śląsk	School_11, School_12	∅	School_number, Director, Number_of_pupils	<∅>	∅

Second type object-instance does not contain sub-objects and set of attributes for sub-objects is empty.

Id(x)	Sub(x)	Sup(x)	$A_{Sub}(x)$	v(x)	M(x)
Pupil_1	∅	Class_2a, Pupil, Person	∅	<Surname: Maciej, Name: Kruk, Born: 1990, Sex: M, Grade: {5.0, 4.0, 3.5}>	∅

The object algebra presented in works [7], [11], [20] includes the following operators: select (σ), associate (τ), project (π), join (χ), sum ($\cup$), difference (–), intersection ($\cap$), flatten (ε), nest (γ), unnest (μ), dupeliminate (θ). To limit the paper we do not present detailed definitions for these operators.

We are now able to give the definitions of evolution operators.

1. Changes to object: (a) add a new attribute, (b) drop an existing attribute, (c) change the name of an existing attribute, (d) change the domain of an existing attribute, (e) add a new method, (f) drop an existing method, (g) change the name of an existing method.
2. Changes to object schema: (h) add a new object, (i) drop an existing object, (j) change the name of an existing object, (k) add an object to the set of sub-objects, (l) drop an object from the set of sub-objects, (m) add an object to the set of sup-objects, (n) drop an object from the set of sup-objects.

For these evolution operators some of them are considered as the basic while the others are derivable. The basic evolution operators are: (a) add a new attribute, (b) drop an existing attribute, (e) add a new method, (f) drop an existing method,

(h) add a new object, (i) drop an existing object, (k) add an object to the set of sub-objects, (l) drop an object from the set of sub-objects, (m) add an object to the set of sup-objects and (n) drop an object from the set of sup-objects.

The rest of the evolution operators are derivable in terms of the basic operators. The derivation is the following: (c) is derivable as (b) followed by (a), (d) is derivable as (b) followed by (a), (g) is derivable as (f) followed by (e), (j) is derivable as (i) followed by (h).

In the rest of this section, we show how the basic operators can be handled using the operators of the object algebra described earlier.

Definition 7.

1. Add local attribute a_i to x is specified to be
$$x = \gamma\,(x, a_i).$$
2. Drop local attribute a_i from x is specified to be
$$x = \pi\,(x, a_1, \ldots, a_{i-1}, a_{i+1}, \ldots, a_n).$$
3. Add attribute a_i described sub-objects to x is specified to be
$$A_{Sub}(x) = \{a_i\} \oplus A_{Sub}(x)$$
and for all sub-object y_i of x is specified to be
$$A(y_i) = \{a_i\} \oplus A(y_i).$$
4. Drop attribute a_i described sub-objects to x is specified to be
$$A_{Sub}(x) = A_{Sub}(x) - \{a_i\}$$
and for all sub-object y_i of x is specified to be
$$A(y_i) = A(y_i) - \{a_i\}.$$
5. Add method m_i to x is specified to be
$$M(x) = \{m_i\} \cup M(x).$$
6. Drop method m_i from x is specified to be
$$M(x) = M(x) - \{m_i\}.$$
7. Add object x to Sub(y) is specified to be
$$Sub(y) = \{id(x)\} \cup Sub(y) \text{ and } Sup(x) = \{id(y)\} \cup Sup(x).$$
8. Drop object x from Sub(y) is specified to be
$$Sub(y) = Sub(y) - \{id(x)\} \text{ and } Sup(x) = Sup(x)) - \{id(y)\}.$$
9. Add object x to Sup(y) is specified to be
$$Sup(y) = \{id(x)\} \cup Sup(y) \text{ and } Sup(x) = \{id(y)\} \cup Sub(x).$$
10. Drop object x from Sup(y) is specified to be
$$Sup(y) = Sup(y) - \{id(x)\} \text{ and } Sup(x) = Sub(x)) - \{id(y)\}.$$
11. Add a new object x is specified to be a sequence of operators:
    - add local attributes $x = \gamma\,(\gamma\,(\gamma\,(\gamma(\text{object}, a_1), a_2), \ldots)\, a_n)$, where $a_1, a_2, \ldots, a_n$ are attributes of x and object is system super object for all objects,
    - add objects to set of sub-objects x,
    - add objects to set sup-objects x,
    - add attributes described sub-objects x,
    - set values for attributes of x,
    - add methods to x.
12. Drop object x is specified to be a sequence of operators:

- drop x from set of sub-objects for each sup-object of x,
- drop x from set of sup-objects for each sub-object of x,
- drop identifier x from values others objects,
- formulation v(x) = Sup(x) = Sub(x) = ∅. ♦

3. Object Migration

We now integrate the notions of multi-class object and evolution operators introduced in the previous section. Our model can be developed on the base of three basic migration operators: **move, add** and **delete**.

Definition 8. Move operator $\frac{\mathrm{id}(x)}{\mathbf{move}}$ is an operator of the form

$$\mathrm{id}(x_1), \mathrm{id}(x_2), \ldots, \mathrm{id}(x_n) \frac{\mathrm{id}(x)}{\mathbf{move}} \mathrm{id}(y_1), \mathrm{id}(y_2), \ldots, \mathrm{id}(y_m),$$

where x is migrating object, $\mathrm{id}(x_1), \mathrm{id}(x_2), \ldots, \mathrm{id}(x_n) \in \mathrm{Sup}(x)$ and $y_1, y_2, \ldots, y_m \in$ OBJ, such that after executing:

(1) drop $x_1, x_2, \ldots, x_n$ from the set of sup-objects x,

(2) drop attributes described sub-objects $x_1, x_2, \ldots, x_n$,

(3) add objects $y_1, y_2, \ldots, y_m$ to set sup-objects x,

(4) add attributes described sub-objects $y_1, y_2, \ldots, y_m$,

(5) set values for each attribute x. ♦

Example 2.

$$\text{School\_11} \frac{\text{Class\_2a}}{\mathbf{move}} \text{School\_12}.$$

Definition 9. Add operator $\frac{\mathrm{id}(x)}{\mathbf{add}}$ is an operator of the form

$$\frac{\mathrm{id}(x)}{\mathbf{add}} \mathrm{id}(y_1), \mathrm{id}(y_2), \ldots, \mathrm{id}(y_m),$$

where x is migrating object and $y_1, y_2, \ldots, y_m \in$ OBJ, such that after executing:

(1) add objects $y_1, y_2, \ldots, y_m$ to set sup-objects x,

(2) add attributes described sub-objects $y_1, y_2, \ldots, y_m$,

(3) set values for each attribute x. ♦

Example 3.

$$\frac{\text{Pupil\_1}}{\mathbf{add}} \text{Math\_circle}$$

Definition 10. Delete operator $\frac{\mathrm{id}(x)}{\mathbf{delete}}$ is an operator of the form

$$\mathrm{id}(x_1), \mathrm{id}(x_2), \ldots, \mathrm{id}(x_n) \ \frac{\mathrm{id}(x)}{\textbf{delete}}$$

where x is migrating object and $\mathrm{id}(x_1), \mathrm{id}(x_2), \ldots, \mathrm{id}(x_n) \in \mathrm{Sup}(x)$, such that after executing:

(1) drop $x_1, x_2, \ldots, x_n$ from the set of sup-objects x,

(2) drop attributes described sub-objects $x_1, x_2, \ldots, x_n$. ♦

4. Object Migration Language

4.1. Insert instruction

BNF syntax for insert instruction in OML is the following:

<Insert instruction> :: = insert <Oid> | insert <Oid> into <Oid> {, <Oid>}
| insert <Oid> into <Select_instruction>

Thus we have two cases:

1. Object creation

   insert (Dolny Śląsk, ∅, ∅, {School_nr, Director, Number_of_pupils}, <∅>, ∅)

   insert (Teacher_1, ∅, ∅, ∅, <Surname: Beata, Name: Bąk, Born: 1960, Course: Polish language, Suplement: 100>, ∅)

   insert (School_11, ∅, {Dolny Śląsk}, {Unit_name, Numer_of_pupils}, <School_nr: 11, Director: Teacher_1, Number_of_pupils: 2>, ∅)

2. Add object to set of sub-objects another object

   insert Pupil_1 into Math_circle

4.2. Delete instruction

BNF syntax for delete instruction in OML is the following:

<Delete instruction> :: = delete <Oid> | delete <Oid> from <Oid> {, <Oid>}
| delete <Oid> from <Select_instruction>

Also here we have two cases:

1. Object deletion

   delete Pupil_1

2. Object deletion from set of sub-objects another object

   delete Pupil_2 from Math_circle, Class_2b

4.3. Update instruction

BNF syntax for update instruction in OML is the following:

<Update instruction> :: = <Value update instruction> | <Attributes update instruction> | <Object update instruction>

<Value update instruction> :: = update <Oid> set <<Attribute> : <Value> {,<Attribute> : <Value>}>

<Attributes update instruction> :: = update <Oid> del <Attribute> {,<Attribute>}

<Object update instruction> :: = update <Oid> from <Oid> {,<Oid>} into <Oid> {, <Oid>} | update <Oid> from <Oid> {,<Oid>} into <Select_instruction> | update <Oid> from <Select_instruction> into <Oid> {, <Oid>} | update <Oid> from <Select_instruction> into <Select_instruction>

Now we have three cases:

1. Value update

   update Pupil_1 set <Name: Król, Born: 1991, Height: 140>

2. Attribute deletion

   update Pupil _1 del Height

3. Association update

   update Class_2a from School_11 into School_12

   update Teacher_1 from Teacher into Person

   update Teacher_1 from Teacher into Director

4.4. Translation OML instructions to object algebra

Given the instruction syntax described in the previous section, this section presents the translation process for queries to algebra equivalents.

1. Object creation

   insert (id(x), Sub(x), Sup(x), A_{Sub}(x), v(x), M(x)) is translated into operator 11 from def. 7.

2. Add object to set of sub-objects another object

   insert id(x) into id(y_1), id(y_2), ..., id(y_m) is translated into add operator: $\frac{\text{id}(x)}{\textbf{add}}$ id(y_1), id(y_2), ..., id(y_m).

3. Object deletion

   delete id(x) is translated into operator 12 from def. 7.

4. Object deletion from set of sub-objects another object

   delete id(x) from id(x_1), id(x_2), ..., id(x_n) is translated into delete operator id(x_1), id(x_2), ..., id(x_n) $\frac{\text{id}(x)}{\textbf{delete}}$.

5. Association update

update id(x) from $id(x_1), id(x_2), ..., id(x_n)$ into $id(y_1), id(y_2), ..., id(y_m)$ is translated into move operator $id(x_1), id(x_2), ..., id(x_n) \xrightarrow[\textbf{move}]{id(x)} id(y_1), id(y_2), ..., id(y_m)$.

5. Conclusions

In this paper a novel object-oriented model which enables objects migration is presented. As it is shown, this model is an expanded version of the basic object model, which could be realized by small costs, but its benefit is large because of its dynamics features. Different from the traditional object processing, the dynamic object algebra proposed here allows multi-class objects to be directly manipulated using the original concept of attribute origin. Some formal properties of multi-class objects were investigated. The influence and significance of these new ideas were also discussed.

The future works should concern creating automatic interfaces for users to satisfy their needs in realizing database evolution. Such interfaces should be done in a simple way owing to defined migration operators. It is necessary to get to know what can be done not only with object structures but also with object behavior. These works then should include defining specific methods for algebra operators, proving their completeness and incorporating new techniques for query language optimization.

References

1. Abiteboul S., Hull R., Vianu V. (1995): Foundations of Databases. Addison-Wesley Publishing Company.
2. Abano A., Bergamini R., Ghelli G., Orsini R. (1993): An Object Data Model with Roles. In Proceedings of the 19th International VLDB Conference, 39-51.
3. Delobel C., Lecluse Ch., Richard P. (1995): Databases: From Relational to Object-Oriented Systems. International Thomson Publishing.
4. Ferrandina F., Ferran G. (1995): Schema and Database Evolution in the O2 Object Database System. In Proceedings of the 21th International VLDB Conference, 170-181.
5. Kemper A., Moerkotte G. (1994): Object-Oriented Database Management: Applications in Engineering and Computer Science. Prentice Hall International.
6. Kim W. (1992): Introduction to Object-Oriented Databases. Massachusetts Institute of Technology.
7. Król D. (2001): Data Dynamic in an Object Model (PhD thesis). Wroclaw University of Technology.
8. Król D. (1995): Dynamic bibliographic object in Digital Libraries. In Proceedings of the International Symposium on Digital Libraries, University of Library and Information, Tsukuba Science City, Japan, August 22-25, 1995, 233-238.

9. Król D. (1995): Modeling Bibliographic Database Dynamics on the Base of an Object-Oriented Approach. In Proceedings of the Tenth International Symposium on Computer and Information Sciences, Istanbul Technical University, Ephesus, Turkey, October 30- November 1, 1995, 265-266.
10. Król D., Nguyen N. T. (1995): A data model for dynamic object-oriented information system. In Bazewicz (ed.): Proceedings of the ISAT '95, Informatics Library of Universities, Wroclaw, 126-131.
11. Król D., Nguyen N. T. (1996): A query language for dynamic object-oriented information system. In Bazewicz (ed.): Proceedings of the ISAT '96, Informatics Library of Universities, Wroclaw, 184-189.
12. Król D., Nguyen N. T. (2000): Dynamic aspects into object-oriented information system. In Grzech, Wilimowska (ed.): Proceedings of the ISAT '2000, Informatics Library of Universities, Wroclaw, 203-207.
13. Li Q., Dong G.: A framework for object migration in object-oriented databases. Data and Knowledge Engineering (1994), 13, 221-242.
14. Li Q., Lochovsky F. (1998): ADOME: An Advanced Object Modeling Environment. IEEE Transactions on Knowledge and Data Engineering, March/April, 255-275.
15. Mendelzon A., Milo T., Waller E. (1994): Object Migration. In Proceedings of the ACM SIGMOD/PODS 94, USA, 232-242.
16. Mitchell G. A. (1993): Extensible Query processing in an Object-Oriented Database (PhD thesis). Brown University.
17. Papazoglou M.P., Kraemer B.J. (1997): A database model for object dynamics. The VLDB Journal, 6, 73-96.
18. Su J. (1991): Dynamic Constraints and Object Migration. In Proceedings of the 17th International VLDB Conference, 233-242.
19. Subieta K. (1998): Obiektowość w projektowaniu i bazach danych. Akademicka Oficyna Wydawnicza PLJ, Warszawa.
20. Urban S., Lai Ch., Saxena S. (1994): The Design and Translation of ORL: An Object Retrieval Language. Journal Systems Software, 24, 187-206.
21. Wieringa R. J., Jonge W., Spruit P. (1995): Using Dynamic Classes and Role Classes to Model Object Migration. Theory and Practice of Object Systems, 1, 61-83.

System for Automated Deduction (SAD): Linguistic and Deductive Peculiarities

Alexander Lyaletski[1], Konstantine Verchinine[2], Anatoli Degtyarev[3], and Andrey Paskevich[1]

[1] Faculty of Cybernetics, Kyiv National Taras Shevchenko University
2, Glushkov avenue, building 6, 03022 Kyiv, Ukraine
E-mail: lav@tc.unicyb.kiev.ua, andrey@raptor.kiev.ua

[2] Math-Info Department, Paris 12 University
61, avenue du General De Gaulle, 94010 Creteil, France
E-mail: verko@logique.jussieu.fr

[3] Department of Computer Science, University of Liverpool
Liverpool L69 7ZF, United Kingdom
E-mail: a.degtyarev@cs.man.ac.uk

Abstract. In this paper a state-of-the-art of a system for automated deduction called SAD is described *. An architecture of SAD corresponds well to a modern vision of the Evidence Algorithm programme advanced by Academician V.Glushkov. The system is intended for accumulating mathematical knowledge and using it in a regular and efficient manner for processing a self-contained mathematical text in order to prove a given statement that always is considered as a part of the text. Two peculiarities are inherent in SAD: (a) mathematical texts under consideration are formalized using a specific formal language, which is close to natural languages from usual mathematical publications; (b) proof search is based on a specific sequent-type calculus, which gives a possibility to formalize "natural reasoning style". The language may be used as a tool to write and to verify mathematical papers, theorems, and formal specifications, to perform model checking, and so on. The calculus is oriented to constructing some natural proof search methods such as definition and auxiliary proposition applications.

1 Introduction

In this paper some linguistic and deductive peculiarities of the System for Automated Deduction, SAD, are described. These peculiarities satisfy well to the main principles of the realization of the Evidence Algorithm, or EA.

The Evidence Algorithm was advanced by Academician V.Glushkov as a programme of investigations into automated theorem proving. Its main objective was to help to working mathematicians in mathematical text processing, i.e. in computer-aided constructing and verifying long, but in some sense "evident" proofs. That is why V. Glushkov proposed to explore simultaneously: formalized languages for presenting mathematical texts in the

* Investigations are supported partly by INTAS 2000-447.

form most appropriate for a user, a formal notion of evolutionary developing computer-made proof step, EA information environment that has influence on the evidence of a proof step, and man-assisted search for a proof.

An idea underlying SAD corresponds well to the contemporary trends of the construction of computer mathematical services. In this connection, we must draw your attention to the following.

A specific feature of SAD is that proof search of a theorem T under consideration is done in a framework of a self-contained mathematical text Txt written in a formal language close to natural languages used in mathematical papers. The term "Txt is a self-contained text (w.r.t. T)" denotes that Txt contains all the necessary for proving T. So, this language should have a formalized syntax and semantics. It should permit to write theory axioms, definitions, lemmas, theorems, and proofs in order to provide self-contained texts. Accordingly, a thesaurus of the language should be separated from its grammar in order to be extendible. Besides, the language should permit to imitate mathematical texts in a "natural" form (this provides a user-friendly interface for creating a text or processing it in an interactive mode).

According to EA, the core of a mathematical text processing technique is a so-called "evidence routine" that establishes the evidence of a proven (verified) step in terms of some deductive formalism, which should permit: to preserve a structure of an initial problem; to search for an inference in a signature of an initial theory; to reduce a "goal" under consideration to a number of new auxiliary "subgoals"; to separate a deductive process from finding solutions for "equations" (for systems of "equations"); to use a specific equality handling technique; to build-in human-like methods of theorem proving such as, for example, definition and auxiliary proposition applications; to organize a flexible interactive search mode.

To achieve the above, various tools enforcing the "evidence routine" should be provided: search for auxiliary information, use of analytical transformations, application of a proof technique usual for a man, and so on. It is clear that first of all, both the tools and the "evidence routine" should be able to exchange data using a certain formalized language (languages). That is why this paper reflects a current state of investigations relating to a linguistic and deductive support of SAD in accordance with the EA programme.

2 Linguistic Tools

A number of languages has been constructed for EA (see, for example, [1,2]). By now, ForTheL (FORmal THEory Language) [3] is the last representative of this languages family. The main objective of the construction of ForTheL is to provide an initial environment for the evolutionary development of the "evidence routine" and to enforce proving tools of SAD depending on a problem to be solved and a mathematical text to be processed. Thus, ForTheL can be used as a tool to write and verify mathematical publications and formal specifications. Also, it can be used as a universal interface of declarative mathematical knowledge bases and as a tool for integration of mathematical services.

According to a current approach, the processing of a mathematical text in the EA-style is made in conformity with the following scheme.

First of all, a text to be processed should be written as a ForTheL-text. Then, the ForTheL-text must be automatically translated into a so-called ForTheL1-text. Any ForTheL1-text consists of sentences, which, on the one hand, are analogs of 1st-order logic formulas, and, on the other hand, preserve a signature of an original ForTheL-text, its syntax and structure, i.e. partitioning into sections such as definitions, auxiliary propositions, and a theorem to be proved. After transforming a ForTheL-text into its ForTheL1-representation, the construction of a ForTheL1-environment for proof search procedures must be made.

In the frame of this ForTheL1-environment, a user formulates some problem to be solve: for example, he asks to prove a selected theorem. After this, the "evidence routine" begins to work. Since the information environment preserves a signature of an initial ForTheL-text and natural-type proof methods may be used by the "routine", the user has a possibility to control a search process.

At present, some units of such a "chain" of transformations already are constructed: a translator from ForTheL to ForTheL1 and proving tools for first-order logic are implemented. Units providing a proof representation, interactive search, and control of an information environment is under development now.

Let us give an example of a correct ForTheL-text, which deals with some elementary notions of the non-standard analysis taken from [4]. We omit definitions which are not necessary for the proof of a given theorem. We just note that `nst[A]` represents a set A in a non-standard universe $^*\mathbf{U}$, and a predicate "`x is close to y`" affirms that a point `x` from $^*\mathbf{U}$ is close to a point `y` from the standard universe.

```
If set _ A is a subset of the set _ B
        then nst[A] is a subset of nst[B].
Definition 1. A is a subset of B iff all elements
        of the set _ A belong to the set _ B.
Definition 2. M is closed iff for all t if some element of
        nst[M] is close to t then t belongs to the set _ M.
Definition 3. M is compact iff every element of nst[M]
        is close to some element of the set _ M.
Theorem 1. Closed subset of a compact set is compact.
```

(In ForTheL, a underscore symbol declares a variable following it.)

Given the text above, the translator generates the following ForTheL1-text. (Note that there are new variables in it of the form $\_i$. These variables are implicitly introduced by the quantifying words "`some`", "`every`", "`all`".)

```
FORALL A (set[A] THEN FORALL B (set[B] THEN (subset[A, B]
        THEN subset[nst[A], nst[B]]))).
DEFINITION 1. FORALL A (set[A] THEN FORALL B (set[B]
              THEN (subset[A, B] IFF FORALL _1 (in[_1, A]
              THEN in[_1, B])))).
DEFINITION 2. FORALL M (set[M] THEN (closed[M] IFF
              FORALL t (EXISTS _2 (in[_2, nst[M]]
              AND close[_2, t]) THEN in[t, M]))).
DEFINITION 3. FORALL M (set[M] THEN (compact[M] IFF
              FORALL _3 (in[_3, nst[M]] THEN EXISTS _4
              (in[_4, M] AND close[_3, _4])))).
THEOREM 1. FORALL _6 ((set[_6] AND compact[_6]) THEN
           FORALL _5 ((subset[_5, _6] AND closed[_5])
           THEN compact[_5])).
```

3 Deductive Technique

Deduction in EA-style requires a special sequent formalism using a proof environment constructed on the base of a ForTheL1-text containing definitions, auxiliary propositions, and a theorem to be proven. Here we note that the first paper on an EA-style heuristic procedure for theorem proof search in Group Theory appeared in 1966 [5]. In that paper an attempt was done to make allowance for some proof search methods used in mathematical papers at an informal level. Then that formal technique was extended to certain fragments of Set Theory. Its final completion appeared as a specific calculus [6], which was meant for ascertaining the validity of 1st-order classical logic formulas. Its further development gave arise to the first representative [7] of an EA-style family of a-sequent calculi, which later was "extended" to a number of a-sequent calculi (see, for example, [8,9]). That is why a deductive technique of SAD is based on a subsequent modification of the sequent formalism.

3.1 Goal-Driven Sequent Inferring

By now, an original prover using a computer-oriented modification of the a-sequent formalism has been constructed and has been implemented. The prover handles ForTheL1-sections, which can be treated as 1st-order logical formulas. It bases on a special calculus GD described below, which is a modification of the calculus gS from [8], has some changes in comparison with it, and reflects the main approach to the construction of the prover. Note that one of basic objects of GD is an e-sequent.

The most important changes in the modification concern quantifiers rules and handling the premises of e-sequents. In comparison with gS, an initial set of premises stays the same during the whole inference search in the modification. So, new premises cannot be added to an e-sequent in GD, though a set of equations is changed every time, when auxiliary goal rule applications are made. As to quantifier rules, we must note that to avoid the irrelevant duplications of premises, which are observed in gS, a special technique of bound variables processing is developed for the modification.

To do the description of this modification self-contained enough and independent from [8], here we introduce all the necessary notions.

PRELIMINARIES. We consider classical first-order logic with the universal and existential quantifiers and with the propositional connectives of implication ($\supset$), disjunction ($\vee$), conjunction ($\wedge$), and negation ($\neg$). Below, atomic formulas and literals are denoted by L or M, formulas are denoted by F, G, or P, and the empty formula denotes by $\#$. All letters can be subscripted.

The expression $F^{\neg}$ denotes the result of one-step carrying of the negation into a formula F.

We define *positive* ($P\lfloor F^{+}\rfloor$) *and negative* ($P\lfloor F^{-}\rfloor$) *occurences* of a formula F in a formula P in the usual manner.

In what follows, W denotes a set of first-order formulas. We assume that no two quantifiers in formulas from W contain the same variable. Also, we assume that the notion of the scope of a quantifier is known to a reader.

For every variable v from W, we introduce a countable set of new variables of the form ${}^{k}v$, where $k = 0, 1, 2, \ldots$ These new variables are called *indexed.*

Any expression under consideration can contain both an indexed and unindexed variables.

A variable v is said to be *unknown w.r.t.* W if there exists a formula $P \in W$ such that $P\lfloor(\forall vF)^{+}\rfloor$ or $P\lfloor(\exists vF)^{-}\rfloor$ holds. Correspondingly, v is said to be *fixed w.r.t.* W if there exists $P \in W$ such that $P\lfloor(\forall vF)^{-}\rfloor$ or $P\lfloor(\exists vF)^{+}\rfloor$ holds. Obviously, all variables in formulas from W are either unknown or fixed (in [10] they are called "dummies" and "parameters").

A set W of formulas induces an antisymmetric relation $\prec_W$ on a set of bound variables from W by the following: $u \prec_W w$ holds if and only if for some formula F from W, a quantifier from F containing w occurs in the scope of a quantifier from F containing u.

We treat the notion of a substitution as in [11]. Any substitution component is considered to have the form t/x, where x is a variable (denominator), and t is a term (numerator) of a substitution. Also, we assume that a reader is familiar with the notion of a simultaneous unifier of sets of expressions.

For a substitution σ we define an *antisymmetric relation* $\ll_W^{\sigma}$ as follows. Assume $t/u \in \sigma$, where u is an unknown variable w.r.t. W and t is a term containing a variable w, fixed w.r.t. W. Then $w \ll_W^{\sigma} u$.

A substitution s is said to be *admissible* for a set W of formulas if and only if (i) denominators of σ are unknown variables w.r.t. W and (ii) the transitive closure of $\prec_W \cup \ll_W^{\sigma}$ is an antisymmetric relation.

Remark. It may be checked that the above admissible substitution notion is equivalent to the one from [12] (also, see [8]).

A *pasting substitution* for a set W of formulas is a substitution π, which satisfies the following condition: every its component has the form ${}^m v/{}^k v$ and for every variable $u \prec_W v$, it is true that ${}^m u/{}^k u \in \pi$.

An *equation* is a pair of terms s, t, which is written as $s \approx t$.

Let L be a literal of the form $R(t_1, \ldots, t_n)$ $(\neg R(t_1, \ldots, t_n))$ and M be a literal of the form $R(s_1, \ldots, s_n)$ $(\neg R(s_1, \ldots, s_n))$, where R is a predicate symbol. Then $\Sigma(L, M)$ denotes the set of equations $\{t_1 \approx s_1, \ldots, t_n \approx s_n\}$. In this case L and M are said to be *equal modulo* $\Sigma(L, M)$.

THE CALCULUS GD. A basic object of the goal-driven calculus GD under consideration is an e-sequent, which may be considered as a special generalization of the standard notion of sequents and which is closely connected with the notion of a-sequents from [8].

An *e-sequent* is an expression of the form $\Gamma \to \Delta, [\Lambda]\ \langle E \rangle$, where Γ and Δ are sequences of formulas, Λ is a sequence of literals, and E is a set of equations. The formulas from Γ are called *premises*, the formulas from Δ are called *goals*, and the literals from Λ are called *framed literals.* Here we consider e-sequents containing only one goal. We assume also that all variables occurring in Λ, Δ, and E are indexed, and all variables occurring in Γ are unindexed.

Below we are interested in e-sequent trees, which are considered to grow "from top to bottom".

Axioms of GD are e-sequents of the form $\Gamma \to \#, [\Lambda]\ \langle E \rangle$.

Inference Rules. The calculus GD contains the following *inference rules* applied "from top to bottom":

Goal-Splitting Rules (GS):

$(\to \supset)_1$: $$\frac{\Gamma \to F \supset G, [\Lambda]\ \langle E \rangle}{\Gamma \to G, [\Lambda]\ \langle E \rangle}$$

$(\to \supset)_2$: $$\frac{\Gamma \to F \supset G, [\Lambda]\ \langle E \rangle}{\Gamma \to \neg F, [\Lambda]\ \langle E \rangle}$$

$(\to \vee)_1$: $$\frac{\Gamma \to F \vee G, [\Lambda]\ \langle E \rangle}{\Gamma \to G, [\Lambda]\ \langle E \rangle}$$

$(\to \vee)_2$: $$\frac{\Gamma \to F \vee G, [\Lambda]\ \langle E \rangle}{\Gamma \to F, [\Lambda]\ \langle E \rangle}$$

$(\to \wedge)$: $$\frac{\Gamma \to F \wedge G, [\Lambda]\ \langle E \rangle}{\Gamma \to F, [\Lambda]\ \langle E \rangle \quad \Gamma \to G, [\Lambda]\ \langle E \rangle}$$

$(\to \neg)$: $$\frac{\Gamma \to \neg F, [\Lambda]\ \langle E \rangle}{\Gamma \to F^{\neg}, [\Lambda]\ \langle E \rangle}$$

$(\to \forall)$: $$\frac{\Gamma \to \forall\, {}^k v\, F, [\Lambda]\ \langle E \rangle}{\Gamma \to F, [\Lambda]\ \langle E \rangle}$$

$(\to \exists)$: $$\frac{\Gamma \to \exists\, {}^k v\, F, [\Lambda]\ \langle E \rangle}{\Gamma \to F, [\Lambda]\ \langle E \rangle}$$

Auxiliary-Goal Rule (AG): $$\frac{\Gamma_1, F\lfloor M^+ \rfloor, \Gamma_2 \to L, [\Lambda]\ \langle E\rangle}{\Gamma_1, F, \Gamma_2 \to {}^l(\neg F), [L, \Lambda]\ \langle E \cup \Sigma(L, {}^l M)\rangle}$$

Termination Rule 1 (T1): $$\frac{\Gamma_1, M, \Gamma_2 \to L, [\Lambda]\ \langle E\rangle}{\Gamma_1, M, \Gamma_2 \to \#, [\Lambda]\ \langle E \cup \Sigma(L, {}^l M)\rangle}$$

Termination Rule 2 (T2): $$\frac{\Gamma \to L, [\Lambda_1, M, \Lambda_2]\ \langle E\rangle}{\Gamma \to \#, [\Lambda_1, M, \Lambda_2]\ \langle E \cup \Sigma(\widetilde{L}, M)\rangle}$$

In AG, the formula F is not a literal. (So, T1 is necessary for the completeness of GD.) In AG and T1, the literals L and ${}^l M$ are equal modulo $\Sigma(L, {}^l M)$, where the index l is a new index. In T2, the literals $\widetilde{L}$ and M are equal modulo $\Sigma(\widetilde{L}, M)$, where $\widetilde{L}$ denotes a literal L', if L is $\neg L'$, and $\widetilde{L}$ denotes $\neg L$ otherwise.

The requirement to GD "to be goal-driven" denotes that whenever the AG rule is applied to some e-sequent with a literal-goal L, some positive occurrence M of L (modulo $\Sigma(L, M)$) is fixed in some premise F and all subsequent rules applications are performed w.r.t. the fixed occurrence M until it is possible.

We consider that every usual sequent $P_1, \ldots, P_n \to G$ induces the *initial e-sequent* $P_1, \ldots, P_n, \neg G \to {}^0G, [\ ]\ \langle\ \rangle$. (It is supposed that the formulas $P_1, \ldots, P_n$, and G do not contain indexed variables).

When a proof of an initial e-sequent S is searching, an *inference tree* Tr w.r.t. S is constructing. At the beginning of search, Tr contains only S. The subsequent nodes are generated by means of the rules of GD.

Let Tr be an inference tree and W be a set of formulas occurring in succedents of all e-sequents obtained by *AG*-rule applications in Tr. A substitution σ is *admissible for* Tr if and only if σ is admissible for W.

An inference tree Tr is considered to be a *proof tree w.r.t.* S if and only if the following conditions are satisfied: (i) every leaf of Tr is an axiom and (ii) if E is a union of sets of equations from of all the leaves of Tr, then there are a pasting substitution π and a substitution σ such that σ is a simultaneous unifier of all the equations from $E \circ \pi$ and σ is admissible for $Tr \circ \pi$, where $E \circ \pi$ and $Tr \circ \pi$ denote the results of applying π to all terms from E and to all expressions from Tr, respectively.

Proposition 1. *Let $P_1, \ldots, P_n$ form a consistent set of formulas and G be a formula. The sequent $P_1, \ldots, P_n \to G$ is deducible in Gentzen's calculus **LK** [13] if and only if there exists a proof tree w.r.t. the initial e-sequent $P_1, \ldots, P_n, \neg G \to {}^0G, [\ ]\ \langle\ \rangle$ in the calculus GD.*

Proof. A proof of this proposition may be obtained by extending a proof of the soundness and completeness of a calculus GD-2 [14] to the case of 1st order logic, taking into account peculiarities of admissible substitutions pointed in [12].

Proposition 2. *A formula G is valid if and only if there exists a proof tree w.r.t. the initial e-sequent $\neg G \rightarrow {}^0G, [\ ] \langle\ \rangle$ in the calculus GD.*

Proof. It follows from the completeness of **LK** and Prop. 1.

3.2 Deduction in a ForTheL1-environment

We remind that after translating a ForTheL-text to be processed into a correspondent ForTheL1-text, an assertion T to be proved is represented as a substantive ForTheL1-section "theorem", in which conditions Txt (including assumptions, definitions and auxiliary propositions) are separated from a conclusion T, and an initial e-sequent induced by T and Txt is constructed with Txt and T in its antecedent and succedent, respectively. It was noted above that any ForTheL1-sentence can be treated as an analog of some 1st-order classical logic formula. This enables to construct formula images of such units of a ForTheL1-text as a theorem to be proved, definitions, and auxiliary propositions, and to treat a self-contained ForTheL1-text as a set of 1st-order formulas. So, it is possible to understand unambiguously such terms as "ForTheL1-text consistency", "logical consequence of a theorem from a given ForTheL1-text", and "validity" (of a theorem to be proved) without special defining a semantics of the ForTheL1-language. Keeping this in mind, we obtain the following main results about GD, when inference search is made in a ForTheL1-environment.

Corollary 1. *A ForTheL1-theorem T is a logical consequence of a consistent ForTheL1-text Txt (which does not include T) if and only if a proof tree w.r.t. an initial sequent induced by T and Txt can be constructed in the calculus GD.*

Corollary 2. *A ForTheL1-theorem T is valid if and only if a proof tree w.r.t. an initial sequent induced by T only can be constructed in the calculus GD.*

As a side result, we can note that a rather rich collection of rules in GD enables to construct various proof search strategies, which reflect proofs constructions from usual mathematical texts and allow to a user to has an influence in theorem proving, when an interactive mode of proof search is used. If these strategies (with or without participation of a human) ensure an exhaustive search, then the corollaries 1 and 2 guarantee the soundness and completeness of a strategy under consideration.

4 Related Work

Now, there exists a number of projects and systems, which have common feartures with the EA programme or which are close to it in their ideas. Below, we give only a brief remark on such projects and systems.

The project MIZAR [15] has the most closed relation to the EA programme. The objective of that project is the construction of computer systems for mathematical texts processing. A collection of mathematical languages, which are convenient both for mathematicians and computer processing, forms a basis for the MIZAR system. The core of a MIZAR mathematical language is some king of a language of 1st-order classical logic. The soundness of mathematical texts can be checked by the system.

The main objective of the THEOREMA project [16] is to construct an unified environment (for both logical methods and program mathematical tools) for solving mathematical problems (including numeric computations, algebraic transformations, and theorem proving). Project THEOREMA is designed to offer such an environment for a mathematician that enables to pass through the whole cycle of problem solving.

The system OMEGA [17] is developed in order to support theorem proving in mathematics and mathematical education. The system includes a proof planner and a unified collection of tools for the forming subproblems, for searching for proofs for subproblems, and for representing proofs. Both a computer algebra system and well-known general-purpose theorem provers are integrated into OMEGA as external units.

The system ISABELLE [18] is used as a tool for creating an environment for interactive theorem proving. A mathematical knowledge base, which includes a library of concrete mathematics and various packages for advanced mathematical concepts, is used. The system supports a "fashion" of theorem proving usual for mathematicians by reasoning in terms of a given application domain.

A number of the above and some other projects, systems, and groups (for example, the DReaM group, Mechanized Reasoning Group, CAAR group, etc.) are members of the CALCULEMUS project [19] interested in the integration of the deductive and computational power of both deduction systems and computer algebra systems.

5 Conclusion

The linguistic and deductive peculiarities of SAD show that SAD has a specific technique of mathematical text processing, which takes into account expressive features of ForTheL as well as a "fashion" of theorem proving.

The language ForTheL can be used as a tool to write and to verify mathematical papers and formal specifications, to perform model checking, and so on. It also can be used both as a universal interface for declarative knowledge bases and as a tool for the integration of computer mathematical services.

As for the deductive technique of SAD, the calculus GD can serve as a good base for the further development of EA-style theorem proving in the direction of efficiency improvement by means of formalizing some natural proof search methods such as, for example, definition and auxiliary proposition applications.

In this connection, the authors hope for that results obtained in the frame of investigations connected with SAD can be helpful in attacking the following problems: distributed automated theorem proving, checking self-contained mathematical texts for soundness, remote training in the mathematical disciplines, extracting knowledge from mathematical papers, and constructing knowledge bases for mathematical theories.

References

1. Glushkov, V., Kostyrko, V., et al. (1970) On a language for description of formal theories (in Russian). In: Teoreticheskaya kibernetika **3**
2. Glushkov, V., Vershinin, K., et al. (1974) On a formal language for description of mathematical texts (in Russian). In: Avtomatizatsiya poiska dokazatel'stv teorem v matematike. Institute of Cybernetics, Kiev, 3–36.
3. Vershinin, K., Paskevich, A. (2000) ForTheL — the language of formal theories. IJ Information Theories and Applications **7-3**, 121–127.
4. Davis, M. (1980) Applied non-standard analysis (Translated from English). Mir, Moskva.
5. Anufriyev, F., Fediurko, V., et al. (1966) On one algorithm of theorem proof search in Group Theory (in Russian). Kibernetika **1**, 23–29.
6. Anufriyev, F. (1969) An algorithm of theorem proof search in logical calculi (in Russian). In: Teoriya avtomatov **1**. Institute of Cybernetics, Kiev.
7. Degtyarev, A., Lyaletski, A. (1981) Logical inference in SAD (in Russian). In: Matematicheskiye osnovy sistem iskusstvennogo intellekta. Institute of Cybernetics, Kiev.
8. Degtyarev, A., Lyaletski, A., Morokhovets, M. (1999) Evidence Algorithm and Sequent Logical Inference Search. In: LNAI **1705** 44–61.
9. Degtyarev, A., Lyaletski, A., Morokhovets, M. (2000) On the EA-style integrated processing of self-contained mathematical texts. Proc. of the Intern. Workshop CALCULEMUS'2000, Great Britain.
10. Kanger, S. (1963) Simplified proof method for elementary logic. In: Comp. Program. and Form. Sys.: Stud. in Logic, North-Holl., Publ. Co.
11. Robinson, J. (1965) A machine-oriented logic based on resolution principle. In: J. of the ACM, 23–41.
12. Lyaletski, A. (1991) Gentzen calculi and admissible substitutions. In: Actes preliminaries, du Simposium Franco-Sovetique "Informatika-91". Grenoble, France, 99–111.
13. Gentzen, G. (1934) Untersuchungen uber das Logische Schliessen. Math. Zeit. **39**, 176–210.
14. Lyaletski, A., Paskevich, A. (2001) Goal-Driven Inference Search in Classical Propositional Logic. In: Proc. of the Inter. Workshop STRATEGIES'2001. Siena, Italy.
15. http://mizar.org/
16. http://www.theorema.org/HomePage.html
17. http://www.ags.uni-sb.de/~omega/
18. http://www.cl.cam.ac.uk/Research/HVG/Isabelle/
19. http://www.mathweb.org/calculemus/

Specification of Distributed Systems with Actors Using Object Oriented Petri Nets

Boleslaw Mikolajczak and Artur Ottlik
Computer and Information Science Department
College of Engineering
University of Massachusetts
Dartmouth, MA 02747, USA
bmikolajczak@umassd.edu

Abstract The aim of this paper is to combine three methodologies and related technologies: distributed computing with actors, concurrent object-oriented programming, and Petri nets. A final outcome is a formal specification of a distributed software system with actors by means of object-oriented Petri nets. In particular, PNTalk tool and related methodology are applied to specify a distributed stack.
Keywords: Distributed computing with Actors, Concurrent object-oriented programming, Petri nets

1. Object Oriented Petri Nets and PNTalk

Object Oriented Petri Nets are based on Colored Petri Nets and enriched by the object oriented paradigm. One can use the natural way of modeling parallelism, formal semantics and analysis methods of Petri nets. Concepts of abstraction, encapsulation and inheritance are inherently related to object orientation. Several different methodologies and software tools, that combine Petri nets and object-orientation, have been developed [2,3,6].

We adopted PNTalk tool that uses Smalltalk as an inscription language. A class consists of an object net, method nets, and predicates. The object net describes the behavior of the class, whereas method nets correspond to methods. Predicates test places for a specific condition. In PNTalk not only objects' own behavior is described by Petri nets but also the methods. Ceska et al. developed a formal model, Object Oriented Petri Net (OOPN), which serves as a base for the tool PNtalk [2]. This formalism is characterized by a Smalltalk based object orientation enriched by concurrency and polymorphic transition execution which allow message sending waiting for and accepting responses, creating new objects, and performing primitive computations. OOPNs are based on viewing objects as active servers. A class consists of an object net describing the internal activity and several method nets describing the services the class provides to other classes. A token represents an object. Method nets represent services. Every method has parameter places and a return place. Each object is an instance of a class and consists of an instance of its object net and several instances of its method nets. A service of an object is requested by sending this object a message. When an object receives a message, an instance of the corresponding method net is created, parameter tokens are put in the input places of the method and this instance is executed concurrently to the other services. When the method net places a token in the return place, this token is passed to the object that called the method and this instance of the method is deleted. Every object has its own independent activities that are represented by the object net. The object net can be used by all the methods of the class; i. e. the places of the object net can be accessed by the method nets. The attributes of objects can be represented as places in the object net.

Inscriptions: A term in the PNTalk language can be one of the following: Literals, Numbers, Characters, Strings, Symbols, Boolean literals, Undefined object (identifier nil), Variables. There are reserved names of identifiers *true*, *false*, *nil*, *self* and *super*. Pseudovariables - *self* and *super*; the first one refers to the object itself and the second one to the super class of this object.

Expressions: can be terms, message sending or variable assignments. Messages are sent by <receiver><blank><message>. A message specifies the requested service and its parameters. There are three types of messages: unary messages, binary messages with one argument, key word messages which have at least one argument. The first argument's name is the method's name. Variable assignments have the form <variable> := <expression>, e.g. y := x+1. To sequentialize expressions they are separated by a dot. Arc expressions represent multisets. They are represented as h_1, h_2, h_3, . h_n. Lists can be represented as (h_1, h_2, .., h_m | t), where t stands for another list, that will be added at the end of h_1, h_2, .. h_m.

Places and Transitions: Every place is specified by its name, initial marking, and initial action. If a place holds initially a variable, then this variable must be assigned a value in the initial action. A transition is specified by its name, guard and an action. A transition guard is a set of conditions that must be evaluated to true in order to enable the transition. The conditions must be atomically evaluable. In the action part we can define several actions which can be non-atomic. Arcs interconnect places and transitions. Arcs have expressions. There are input and output arcs. There is a new kind of arcs, dialog arcs, which only tests if there are available tokens in the place. Such an arc does not remove any token from a place.

Predicates: Predicates allow atomic testing of object states. A predicate can have parameters and a guard. It returns true or false regarding to the evaluation of the guard. It is connected to at least one place of the object net. Predicates can be invoked by a transition and by other predicate guards.

Constructors: A class can have a constructor, which is a special method that describes initial actions when an instance of this class is created. The constructor method of a class can be as well called in an instance of this class. The system provides a standard constructor *new*.

Inheritance: A class consists of an object net, several method nets, a constructor and several predicates. An OOPN consists of several classes. One of them is the primary class that will be instantiated at the beginning. Every class has exactly one ancestor. On top of the inheritance hierarchy there is the class 'Object'. Then there are two types of classes, primitive and non-primitive ones. Primitive classes are literals. The non-primitive classes are OOPNs. On top of all OOPNs there is the class PN that is not described as a Petri Net.

A class inherits everything from its ancestor. Redefining a method, the constructor or a predicate can be achieved by introducing a method, constructor or predicate with the same name and parameters. Object nets can be redefined by redefining single transitions and/or places. Redefinition of a transition removes all originally connected arcs, whereas the redefinition of a place keeps all the inherited arcs and one can add some new ones.

Dynamic Behavior of OOPNs: A transition can fire if there is a binding of variables present, such that there are enough tokens in its input places with regard to its arc expressions and the guard is satisfied by the binding. If transition fires the tokens will be removed from the input places and tokens will be placed in the output places of the transition. An action within a transition corresponds to the sending of a message. An action is described as $y := x_0.msg(x_1, ..., x_n)$, where y is a variable, x_0 the receiver of the message, msg the message selector, i.e. the method name and $x_1, ..., x_n$ the parameters. Performing the action depends on the receiver:

a) If the receiver is a primitive class, the transition is performed atomically.
b) If the receiver is a class and the message is a constructor, an instance of this class will be created and an instance of the constructor method will be instantiated and executed. The identification of the new instance will be stored in y. Classes are treated as special objects that never change their state.
c) If the receiver is a non-primitive object, tokens are removed from the input place of a transition according to the binding. An instance of the receiver's method is created and the tokens are placed into the parameter places of the method. The method will be executed concurrently to other methods. After placing a token in the result place, this token will be assigned to y and the method instance will be deleted. Finally tokens are placed into the output places of the transition. In this case the transition is said to be non-atomic, and the execution of the action is an invocation.

The user has to declare one class explicitly as the primary class. An instance of this will automatically be created at the start of the evolution of the OOPN. After that all dynamics is then performing transition firings. All evolution steps have the form of atomic events. They can be classified into four classes as A, N, F and J-events. The A and the N event are atomic transition firings, where an A-event represents an execution inside one net instance, which corresponds to the firing in colored Petri nets. The N-event describes the creation of a new object by the method 'new'. If we use a self-defined constructor, the N, F and J-event occur. The non-atomic transition firing is divided into the F and the J part. The F-event describes an execution of the transition input part and a creation of a new method net instance, whereas the J-event deletes the created method instance and performs the output part of the transition. A state of the system is defined as a set of objects composed of running net instances. The states of these instances are markings, which specify for every place a multiset of tokens and for every transition a set of invocation.

Example of an OOPN: The example above involves the described features (Fig. 1). It has a predicate 'example_predicate' that is used in the guard of transition T4 and a method 'calculate' called in the action part of T4. If one wants to invoke a method within the class itself, it has to specify the receiver with 'self' (see T4). The method 'calculate' takes one input parameter y. It is connected to the place P4 and thus will remove a token from P4 when invoked. The method net 'calculate' is specified as in Figure 2. The product of x and y is calculated and put into the return place.

Figure 3 illustrates inheritance. The class 'Example2' inherits from 'Example'. The inherited parts are displayed in gray, new or redefined elements in black. The predicate places P3 and P7 and transition T2 is redefined. It is connected to two places. Furthermore there is a constructor 'create', which is when creating this class. If another class wants to create a new object of this class, it does it by performing the action 'var1 := Example2: init: var2', where var1 is a variable assigned to the new object and var2 is any value that will be put into the input parameter place of the method 'init'. There is another new method 'Additional' with two parameters x and y. An invocation of this method would be 'var Additional: 5 with 7', where 'var' stands for a variable that was assigned an instance of the class 'Example2'. The class inherited the method 'calculate' as well, but it is not displayed, because it is not redefined.

2. Distributed Computations with Actors

Actor systems were introduced by Agha [1]. Computation in an actor system is a result of processing communications that are contained in tasks. A task consists of a tag, which uniquely identifies it, a target, i.e. a mail address of another actor, and a communication. An incoming communication will be mapped by an actor to a 3-tuple consisting of: a finite set of communications sent to other actors, a finite set of new actors created, a new behavior specifying the response to the next message. In order to process the incoming message, an actor can send messages to other actors, create new actors and change its behavior to react properly to the next messages. Incoming messages are stored in the actors mail queue. The behavior of an actor specifies which messages the actor will accept. Because the behavior of an actor can change after every received message the actor's behavior can be history sensitive. One could compare the behavior to an object's public interface in object-oriented programming. An actor is described by the following properties: Unique mail address, Mail queue to store incoming messages, Set of acquaintances (other actors), Behavior, specifying the messages the actor accepts at the moment Actors communicate with each other via asynchronous message passing. While processing an accepted message, an actor can send messages to its acquaintances, create new actors and change its behavior.Mail queue and acquaintances: Every actor has a mail queue where incoming messages are stored until the actor processes them. The mail queue should be in a FIFO order and guarantee that a sent message will finally be delivered. Every actor has a list of acquaintances. An actor A gets to know actor B's mail address because actor A created actor B or because B's address was passed to A in a message. Behavior: A behavior is described by the set of methods that can be currently invoked by a message. This set is a subset of all methods. It is dependent on the local state and activity of an actor. The behavior can change after every processing of a message, which is done by the *become* operation. A new message can only be accepted after a *become* operation is executed. Executing *become* operation after the processing of a message, leads to a serialized actor. This is because the next message has to wait for the *become* operation in order to be processed. If the *become* operation would be executed after receiving a message and prior to the processing of this message, then the next message could be received and processed concurrently to the first message. Agha describes a special behavior called *forward*. An actor with this behavior will delegate the message it receives to an acquaintance.

3. Specification of an actor with PNTalk

In order to specify an actor we use the PNTalk. The object-oriented nature of OOPNs supports the specification since an actor is defined as a self contained and active object. Every actor has a *create* method, used to create an instance of this actor class. Moreover there is a *send* method, that allows an actor to send another actor a message. The behavior and its change (i.e. the *become* operation) is modeled in the object net.

Processing of a message: When the actor X_n accepts the message n, it will create a new actor machine X_{n+1} that will carry out the replacement behavior of the actor. The new machine will point to the message n+1. It is important to note that X_n and X_{n+1} will not affect each other behavior though they could potentially work concurrently. X_n will never receive any further message nor specify any other replacement.

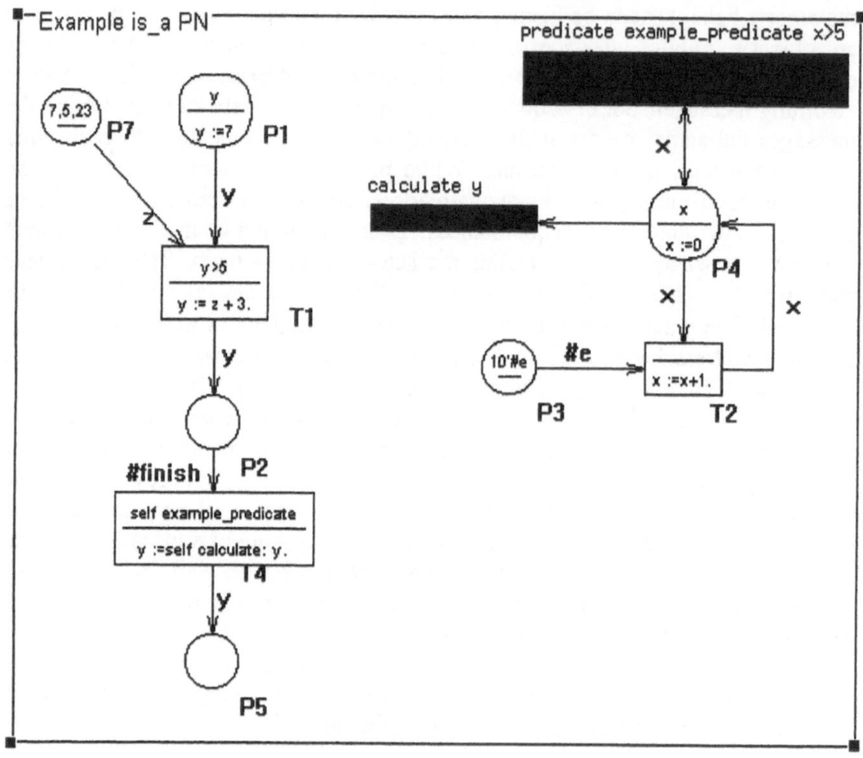

Figure 1. A class in PNTalk

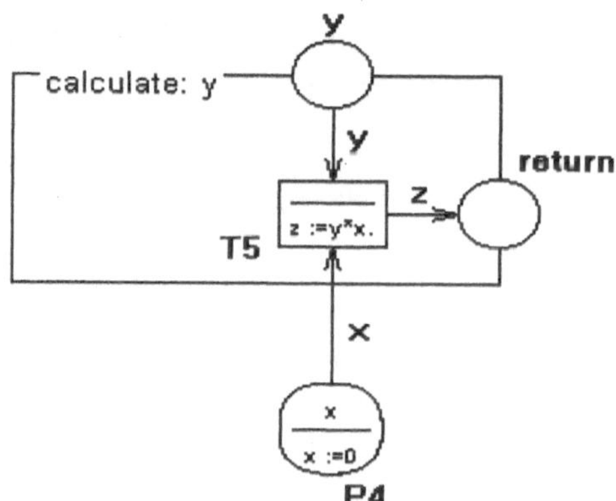

Figure 2. Method net of the method *calculate* from the example class.

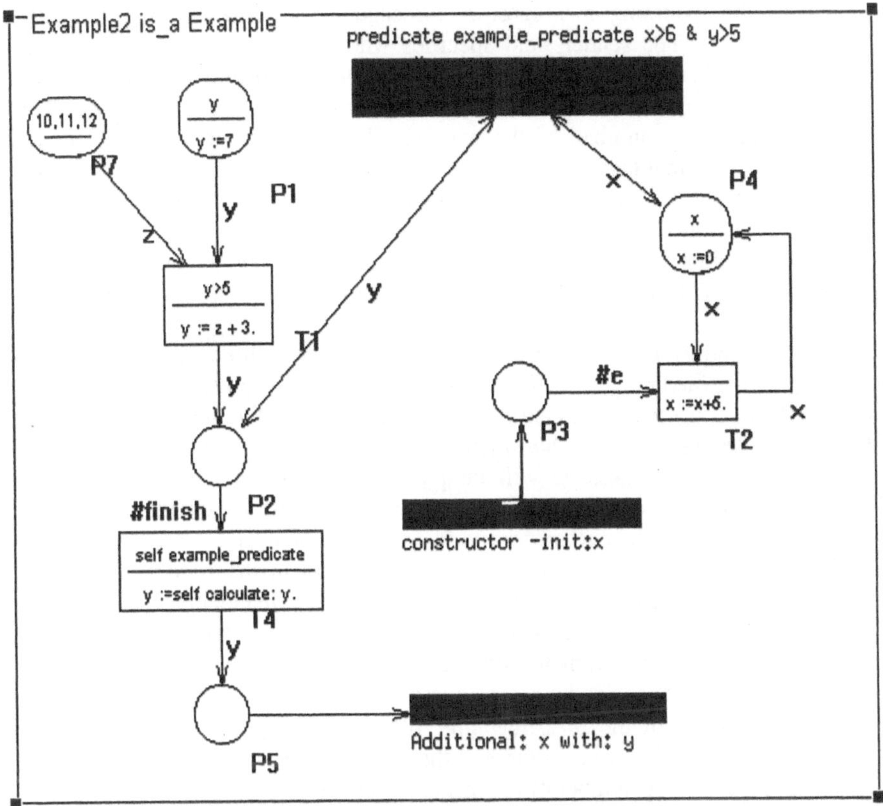

Figure 3 . Example of inheritance.

Basic Constructs: A minimal actor language consists of the following basic constructs: *New:* used to create a new actor. It returns the address of the mail queue of the new actor. *Send:* operation to send a message to another actor asynchronously. *Become:* allows the actor to change its behavior according to the last processed message.

In order to specify an actor we use the PNTalk. The object-oriented nature of OOPNs supports the specification since an actor is defined as a self contained and active object. Every actor has a *create* method, used to create an instance of this actor class. Moreover there is a *send* method, that allows an actor to send another actor a message. The behavior and its change (i.e. the *become* operation) is modeled in the object net.

For communication purposes we introduced several additional methods*: call, receive, reply and forward*. Furthermore there are two places *current_tag* and *Messagebuffer*. *Current_tag* is a number to identify a message. *Messagebuffer* stores all the incoming messages. A message is a 4-tuple (*sender, request, parameter, tag*). The sender field specifies who sent the message, the request field tells us what the message is all about, and the parameter field may contain one item or a tuple of items, which are used as a parameter for the request. The tag determines the number of the message. Messages from the same sender always have different tags.

Figure 5 shows the method net for the method *send*. This method returns the tag of the message. The tag for a message is taken of the *current_tag* place and incremented, thus a new message will have a different tag. A message will be assembled as a 4-tuple and the sending is achieved by invoking the *receive* method.

Figure 6 shows the *receive* method net. This is a net with only one transition, which puts the incoming message into the *Messagebuffer* place. A new instance of a method net is created and executed upon invocation of a method. That means that whenever an actor's *send* method invokes the *receive* method of the receiving actor, this message will be placed in the receiver's *Messagebuffer* place. Thus the delivery of messages is guaranteed. Based on the method as above we introduced the *call, reply* and *forward* method nets.

A response is indicated by the keyword *#reply* in the *request* field of a message. The parameter field is a tuple itself, where the first element specifies the tag of the original message and the other elements the response. The transition *assemble* creates the parameter entry for the response message. The call operation is for synchronized message passing. We send a message and wait until a response arrives in the *Messagebuffer* place. The response has to have the keyword *#reply* in the request field and the parameter must be a tuple, where the first element is the tag number of the original message.

Whenever an actor uses the *call* method to send a request it will wait until the other actor has processed the message and replied to it. Thus this is a synchronized communication. Finally we added another method which is *forward*. When an actor forwards a message, the actor simply sends it to another actor without processing the message at all. Thus we do not use the *send* method here, but directly invoke the other actor's *receive* method. The methods *forward, reply* and *call* are not necessary since they are based on the *send* and *receive* methods.

One could ask now why to model an actor with a message buffer and explicit methods for communication whereas PNTalk already supports invocation of methods. We could have decided that any class in PNTalk is an actor that behavior is presented by the object net. Messages could be sent in the form of invoking the specific method in another actor. We decided not to do so for two reasons. First, the method invocation in PNTalk is a synchronized form of communication whereas actors should be able to communicate asynchronously. The second reason was that one might specify aspects of communication more thoroughly, e.g. communication protocols, in order to test them as well.

Example of a stack as an actor: We modeled a stack actor. Figure 8 illustrates a simple stack, which is represented as a chain of stack node actors, where every actor contains only one element. After creation a stack node has one element in its content field and its behavior is *FILLED*. If a new element should be pushed on top of the stack (message request: *#push*), a new actor is created with the element and link of the old actor, and the old actor will now contain the new element and the link to the newly created actor. If the first element of the stack is requested (request: *#pop*), the actor returns its element and becomes a forwarder, i.e. it forwards every other incoming mail to the next stack actor in the chain.

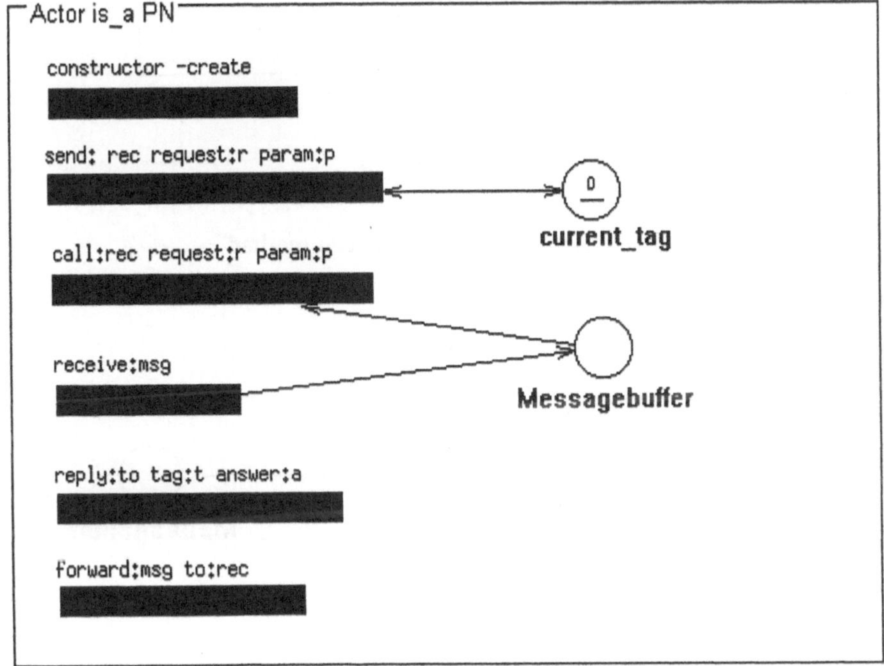

Figure 4 – Class *Actor*.

Conclusions

We have shown a modeling and formal specification of distributed software systems with actors using object-oriented Petri nets. In particular, we applied the PNTalk tool to specifiy a distributed stack with actors. This combination of traditional informal approaches to object-oriented design with formal computational models of actors and Petri nets allows rapid prototyping of concurrent systems with verification and validation mechanisms supported by Petri nets.

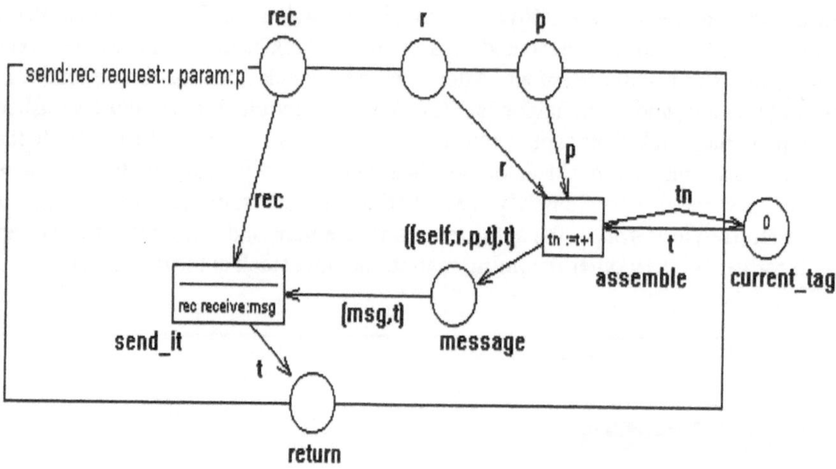

Figure 5. Method net of the *send* method

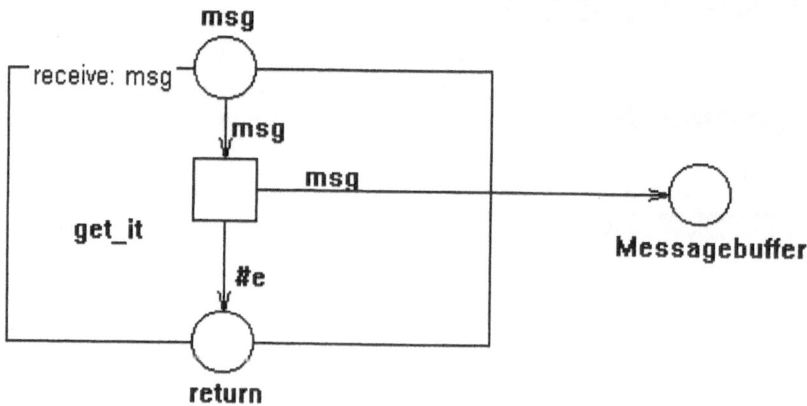

Figure 6 – *receive* method net.

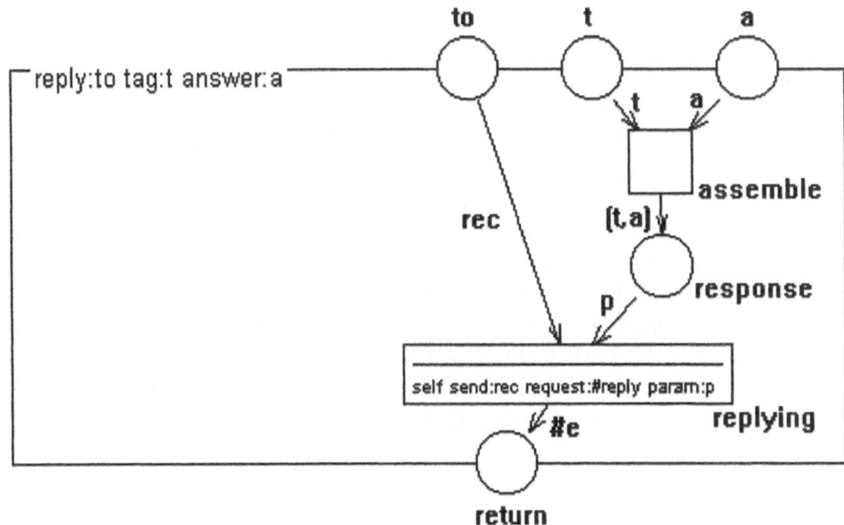

Figure 7 – *reply* method net.

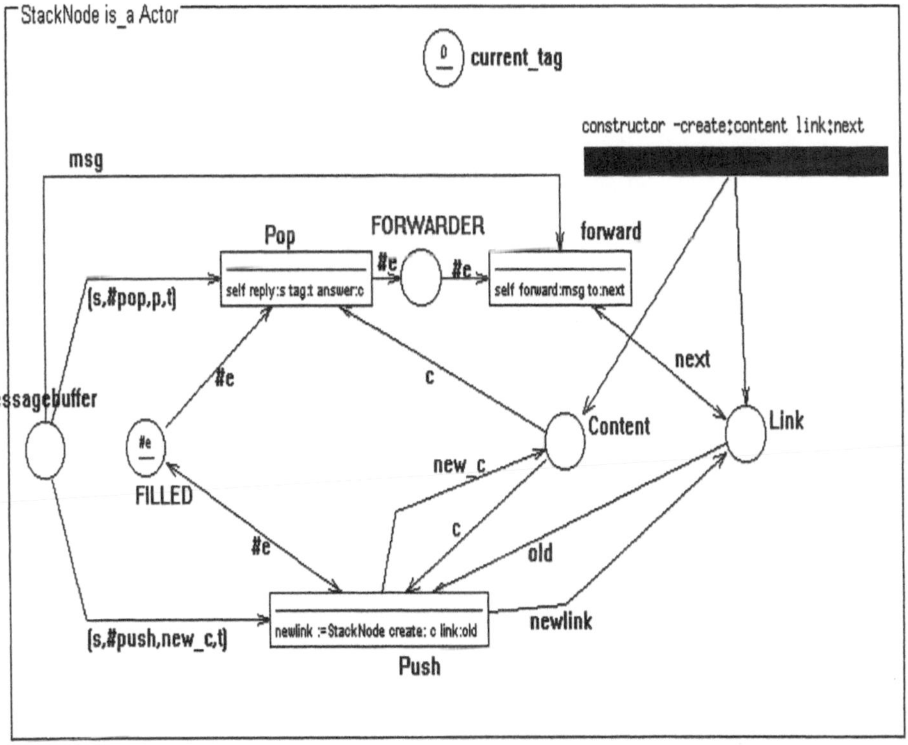

StackNode is_a Actor
current_tag
constructor -create:content link:next
msg
Pop
FORWARDER
forward
(s,#pop,p,t)
self reply:s tag:t answer:c
#e
#e
self forward:msg to:next
next
#e
c
Messagebuffer
#e
Content
Link
FILLED
new_c
c
#e
old
newlink := StackNode create: c link:old
newlink
(s,#push,new_c,t)
Push

Figure 8 – *stack* as an actor.

References

[1]. G. Agha, Actors, Model of Concurrent Computation in Distributed Systems, The MIT Press, 1986.

[2]. M. Ceska, V. Janousek, A formal Model for Object-Oriented Petri Net Modeling, Advances in Systems Science and Applications, Special Issue, pp. 119-124, 1997.

[3]. B. Mikolajczak, A.Ottlik, Specification of Distributed systems with Actors Using Object-Oriented Petri Nets, Proc. of the International Conference SMC 2000, Nashville, Tennessee, IEEE Press.

[4]. A. Omicini et al. (eds), Coordination of Internet Agents, Models, Technologies, and Applications, Springer Verlag, 2001, ISBN 3-540-41613-7.

[5]. A. Ottlik, Specification of Actors with Object Oriented Petri Nets", University of Massachusetts, Dartmouth, 2000.

Cost-based Sequential Pattern Query Optimization in Presence of Materialized Results of Previous Queries

Mikolaj Morzy, Marek Wojciechowski, Maciej Zakrzewicz

Poznan University of Technology
Institute of Computing Science
ul. Piotrowo 3a, 60-965 Poznan, Poland
{mmorzy, marek, mzakrz}@cs.put.poznan.pl

Abstract. Data mining is very often regarded as an interactive and iterative process. Users interacting with the data mining system specify the class of patterns of their interest by means of data mining queries involving various types of constraints. It is very likely that a user will execute a series of similar queries, before he or she gets satisfying results. Unfortunately, data mining algorithms currently available suffer from long processing times, which is unacceptable in case of interactive mining. One possible solution, applicable in certain cases, is exploiting materialized results of previous queries when answering a new query. In this paper we discuss cost-based data mining query optimization in presence of materialized results of previous queries, focusing on one of the popular data mining techniques, called discovery of sequential patterns.

Keywords: data mining, sequential patterns, query optimization

1 Introduction

Data mining aims at discovery of useful patterns from large databases or warehouses. One of the well-known data mining methods is sequential pattern discovery introduced in [2]. Informally, sequential patterns are the most frequently occurring subsequences in sequences of sets of items. Typical sequential pattern mining algorithms discover all patterns whose support exceeds a user-specified threshold. Some of them allow users to specify time constraints [10] to be used when checking if a given source sequence contains a given pattern.

From a user's point of view, data mining can be seen as an interactive and iterative process of advanced querying: a user specifies the source dataset and the requested class of patterns, the system chooses the appropriate data mining algorithm and returns discovered patterns to the user [5][6]. A user interacting with a data mining system has to specify several constraints on patterns to be discovered. However, usually it is not trivial to find a set of constraints leading to the satisfying set of patterns. Thus, users are likely to execute a series of similar data mining queries before they find what they need. Unfortunately, data mining algorithms require long processing times, which makes such interaction difficult.

One possible solution to that problem is exploiting materialized results of previous queries when answering a new query [3][7][9]. A data mining system should be able to determine which materialized query results can be used to answer the current query, and then to choose the one leading to the shortest response time. In has been observed [3] that the three particularly interesting relationships between two mining queries DMQ_1 and DMQ_2 extracting patterns from the same data are equivalence, inclusion, and dominance. The three relationships refer to results of the queries, not to their syntax, and are interesting since they represent situations, where one data mining query can be efficiently answered using the results of another query with no actual mining process. Equivalence, inclusion, and dominance relationships were introduced in the context of association rules. Nevertheless, they are general relationships applicable to many pattern types and constraint models.

Previous research on exploiting materialized patterns focused on identification of queries whose materialized results can be used to answer the current query. It has been shown experimentally that using materialized results of one of the previous queries is usually much more efficient than running a complete mining algorithm. However, none of the works addressed the problem of estimating the cost of answering a data mining query using materialized results of another query. Cost estimation is necessary in order to choose the optimal query answering plan when many possible strategies are applicable. In this paper, we discuss cost-based sequential pattern query optimization in the presence of materialized results of previous sequential pattern queries. The only goal of the optimization that we consider is minimizing the query execution time. We build on our previous work [11] where we identified situations in which one sequential pattern query can be answered using the results of another sequential pattern query. In this paper, we discuss strategies that can be used by a data mining query optimizer exploiting materialized results of previous queries. We provide cost functions for query answering algorithms exploiting materialized patterns. These cost functions are then used to choose an optimal (in terms of the execution time) query execution plan when many applicable materialized sets of patterns are available.

1.1 Related Work

To facilitate interactive and iterative pattern discovery, [9] proposed to materialize patterns discovered with the least restrictive selection criteria, and answer incoming queries by filtering the materialized pattern collection. In [7], the idea of caching intermediate results of association rule queries was discussed. In the approach, materialization of frequent itemsets instead of rules was proposed. However, in some cases it was required to materialize also some of the infrequent itemsets.

Cost-based query optimization is widely used in database management systems (see e.g. [4] for a review). One of the techniques used by query optimizers is exploiting results of previous queries available in the form of materialized views (see e.g. [8]). The cost-based optimizer chooses the query execution plan with the lowest estimated cost. The cost of a given execution strategy is estimated using known cost functions for the algorithms being used and certain statistics maintained for the database.

2 Basic Definitions

2.1 Sequential Patterns

Let $L = \{l_1, l_2, ..., l_m\}$ be a set of literals called items. An *itemset* is a non-empty set of items. A *sequence* is an ordered list of itemsets and is denoted as $<X_1 X_2 ... X_n>$, where X_i is an itemset ($X_i \subseteq L$). X_i is called an *element* of the sequence. The *size* of a sequence is the number of items in the sequence. The *length* of a sequence is the number of elements in the sequence. Let D be a set of variable length sequences (called *data-sequences*), where for each sequence $S = <X_1 X_2 ... X_n>$, a timestamp is associated with each X_i.

With no time constraints we say that a sequence $X = <X_1 X_2 ... X_n>$ is *contained* in a data-sequence $Y = <Y_1 Y_2 ... Y_m>$ if there exist integers $i_1 < i_2 < ... < i_n$ such that $X_1 \subseteq Y_{i1}$, $X_2 \subseteq Y_{i2}$, ..., $X_n \subseteq Y_{in}$. We call $<Y_{i1} Y_{i2} ... Y_{in}>$ an *occurrence* of X in Y. We consider the following user-specified time constraints while looking for occurrences of a given sequence: minimal and maximal gap allowed between consecutive elements of an occurrence of the sequence (called *min-gap* and *max-gap*), and time window that allows a group of consecutive elements of a data-sequence to be merged and treated as a single element as long as their timestamps are within the user-specified *window-size*.

The support of a sequence $<X_1 X_2 ... X_n>$ in D is the fraction of data-sequences in D that contain the sequence. A *sequential pattern* is a sequence whose support in D is above the user-specified threshold.

2.2 Relationships between Results of Data Mining Queries

Two data mining queries are *equivalent* if for all datasets they both return the same set of patterns and the values of statistical significance measures (e.g. support) for each pattern are the same in both cases. A data mining query DMQ_1 *includes* a data mining query DMQ_2 if for all datasets each pattern in the results of DMQ_2 is also returned by DMQ_1 with the same values of the statistical significance measures. A data mining query DMQ_1 *dominates* a data mining query DMQ_2 if for all datasets each pattern in the results of DMQ_2 is also returned by DMQ_1, and for each pattern returned by both queries its values of the statistical significance measures evaluated by DMQ_1 are not less than is case of DMQ_2.

Equivalence is a particular case of inclusion, and inclusion is a particular case of dominance. Equivalence, inclusion, and dominance meet the transitivity property.

If for a given query, results of a query equivalent to it, including it, or dominating it are available, the query can be answered without running a costly mining algorithm. In case of equivalence no processing is required, since the queries have the same results. In case of inclusion, one scan of the materialized query results is necessary to filter out patterns that do not satisfy constraints of the included query. In case of dominance, one scan of the source dataset is necessary to evaluate the statistical significance of materialized patterns (filtering out the patterns that do not satisfy constraints of the dominated query is also required).

3 Sequential Pattern Queries

In constraint-based sequential pattern mining, we identify three classes of constraints: database, pattern, and time constraints. Database constraints are used to specify the source dataset. Pattern constraints specify which patterns are interesting and should be returned by the query. Finally, time constraints influence the process of checking whether a given data-sequence contains a given pattern.

The basic formulation of the sequential pattern discovery problem introduces three time constraints: max-gap, min-gap, and time window, and assumes only one pattern constraint (expressed by means of the minimum support threshold). We model pattern constraints as complex Boolean predicates having the form of a conjunction of basic Boolean predicates of types presented below:

- π(**SPG**, α, pattern) – true if pattern support is greater than α, false otherwise;
- π(**SL**, α, pattern) – true if pattern size is less than α, false otherwise;
- π(**SG**, α, pattern) – true if pattern size is greater than α, false otherwise;
- π(**LL**, α, pattern) – true if pattern length is less than α, false otherwise;
- π(**LG**, α, pattern) – true if pattern length is greater than α, false otherwise;
- π(**C**, β, pattern) – true if β is a subsequence of the pattern, false otherwise;
- π(**NC**, β, pattern) – true if β is not a subsequence of the pattern, false otherwise.

Analyzing syntactic differences between sequential pattern queries leading to equivalence, inclusion, and dominance relationships between the queries, in [11] we identified two useful relationships regarding pattern and time constraints of sequential pattern queries, which can be informally defined as follows:

- *DMQ_2 extends pattern constraints* of DMQ_1 if pattern constraints of DMQ_1 can be transformed into pattern constraints of DMQ_2 by appending new basic Boolean pattern predicates or replacing basic Boolean pattern predicates with more selective predicates of the same types.
- *DMQ_2 extends time constraints* of DMQ_1 if it restricts at least one of the time parameters and does not relax any time parameters.

The following three theorems (proved in [11]) capture the influence of syntactic differences between queries on the differences between query results:

Theorem 1 Let DMQ_1 and DMQ_2 be two sequential pattern queries, operating on the same dataset and having the same time constraints. If DMQ_2 extends pattern constraints of DMQ_1, then DMQ_1 includes DMQ_2.
Theorem 2 Let DMQ_1 and DMQ_2 be two sequential pattern queries, operating on the same dataset and having the same pattern constraints. If DMQ_2 extends time constraints of DMQ_1, then DMQ_1 dominates DMQ_2.
Theorem 3 Let DMQ_1 and DMQ_2 be two sequential pattern queries, operating on the same dataset. If DMQ_2 extends pattern constraints of DMQ_1 and DMQ_2 extends time constraints of DMQ_1, then DMQ_1 dominates DMQ_2.

4 Cost Analysis of Sequential Pattern Query Execution Plans Exploiting Materialized Results of Another Query

Given a sequential pattern query *DMQ* and materialized results of a sequential pattern query DMQ_V operating on the same dataset, there are four classes of syntactic differences between the queries resulting in situations where *DMQ* can be answered efficiently using the materialized results of DMQ_V since they correspond to equivalence, inclusion, and dominance relationships between DMQ_V and *DMQ*. These cases are listed below:

1. If DMQ_V and *DMQ* have the same pattern and time constraints, then the results of *DMQ* are equal to the results of DMQ_V (equivalence);
2. If DMQ_V and *DMQ* have the same time constraints, and *DMQ* extends pattern constraints of DMQ_V, then *DMQ* can be answered by filtering out the patterns returned by DMQ_V not satisfying pattern constraints of *DMQ* (inclusion according to the Theorem 1);
3. If DMQ_V and *DMQ* have the same pattern constraints, and *DMQ* extends time constraints of DMQ_V, then *DMQ* can be answered by evaluating the support of the patterns returned by DMQ_V using the time constraints of *DMQ*, and filtering out patterns not satisfying the minimum support threshold of *DMQ*. (dominance according to the Theorem 2);
4. If *DMQ* extends both pattern and time constraints of DMQ_V, then *DMQ* can be answered by evaluating the support of the patterns returned by DMQ_V using the time constraints of *DMQ*, and filtering out patterns not satisfying the pattern constraints of *DMQ*. (dominance according to the Theorem 3).

In all the cases we assume that the results of the user-specified query are to be written to disk. Answering the query in the case of equivalence is trivial (the results are already known and stored on the disk), therefore we concentrate on details concerning inclusion and dominance relationships.

In all algorithms presented below, *DMQ* represents the sequential pattern query issued by a user, DMQ_V is a query whose results are stored on disk, and *D* is the source dataset (a collection of data-sequences). Analyzing the cost (in terms of execution time) of the proposed algorithms, we assume that the following values are known: the number of data-sequences in the dataset (r_D) and the number of patterns in materialized query results (r_P); the number of disk blocks occupied by the dataset (b_D) and materialized query results (b_P). The following costs of disk and memory operations also appear in our cost formulas: the average cost of access to a disk block (c_D); the cost of checking if a pattern support exceeds a given threshold (c_S); the average cost of checking if a pattern satisfies given pattern constraints (c_F); the average cost of checking if a pattern is contained in a given data-sequence (c_C). For simplicity's sake, we treat checking pattern constraints and the containment test as elementary operations and use their average costs. We do not expect exact values of the last four parameters to be known. However, we believe that certain assumptions can made e.g. c_D is significantly larger than c_S, c_F, and c_C, c_C is greater than c_S, etc.

The overall cost of a given algorithm includes the cost of disk operations (reading the materialized patterns and the source dataset as well as writing the results) and computations in main memory. Operations in main memory concern individual data-sequences and patterns. The atomic portion of data read from or written to the disk is one disk block, which usually contains a number of patterns or data-sequences.

For the second case (inclusion due to extending pattern constraints) we propose an algorithm that performs one sequential scan of the materialized patterns, processing one pattern at a time. Each pattern is tested if it satisfies these basic Boolean pattern predicates from the pattern constraints of *DMQ* that were not in DMQ_V. All the basic Boolean pattern predicates of *DMQ* that were in DMQ_V must be satisfied by all the materialized patterns since pattern constraints in our model have the form of a conjunction of basic predicates. The algorithm for the second case is presented below.

Algorithm 1 (Result **F**iltering)

```
Answer = results of DMQV;
for each p ∈ results of DMQV do
begin
  for each basic Boolean pattern predicate b such that
    b is in pattern constraints of DMQ and
    b is not in pattern constraints of DMQV do
      if not (p satisfies b) then
        Answer = Answer \ {p};
        break;
      end if;
end;
output Answer;
```

The cost of Algorithm 1 can be expressed by the following formula (b_P" is the number of disk blocks to be occupied by the results of the query being answered):

$$C_F = b_P * c_D + r_P * c_F + b_P'' * c_D \quad (1)$$

Algorithms for the third and fourth cases (both leading to the dominance relationship) have to scan the source dataset once in order to re-evaluate the support of materialized patterns. In the third case, all that has to be done after the support re-evaluation is checking if new support values exceed the minimum support threshold of *DMQ*. The algorithm for the third case is presented below.

Algorithm 2 (Result Verification)

```
Answer = results of DMQV;
scan D once evaluating the support of patterns
in Answer using time constraints of DMQ;
for each p ∈ Answer do
  if p exceeds the minimum support threshold of DMQ
  then output p; end if;
```

The cost of Algorithm 2 can be expressed by the following formula:

$$C_V = (b_P + b_D) * c_D + r_D * r_P * c_C + r_P * c_S + b_P'' * c_D \qquad (2)$$

The above formula is based on the assumption that the set of materialized patterns fits into main memory. Thus, the collection of materialized patterns is read only once. It should be noted that we do not make similar assumptions regarding the size of the source dataset. While scanning the source dataset, data-sequences can be read and processed one at a time.

For the fourth case (domination due to extending time and pattern constraints) we propose two algorithms. Algorithm 3, before scanning the source dataset, filters out patterns that do not satisfy pattern constraints of *DMQ* (including the minimum support threshold) using Algorithm 1. After the scan of the dataset, the minimum support threshold is checked again (it is the only one of predicate types that for a given pattern could by true before the support re-evaluation, and false after that operation). Algorithm 4 is a straightforward solution. It first re-evaluates the support of patterns being the results of DMQ_V, and then filters out patterns that do not satisfy pattern constraints of *DMQ*. The two algorithms exploiting results of a dominating query extending pattern constraints of the query to be answered are presented below:

Algorithm 3 (Result Filtering and Verification)

```
Answer = patterns in results of DMQV satisfying
         pattern constraints of DMQ; /* Algorithm 1 */
scan D once evaluating the support of patterns
in Answer using time constraints of DMQ;
for each p ∈ Answer do
  if p exceeds the minimum support threshold of DMQ
  then output p; end if;
```

The cost of Algorithm 3 can be expressed by the following formula (r_P' is the number of patterns whose support has to be re-evaluated during the dataset scan):

$$C_{FV} = (b_P + b_D) * c_D + r_P * c_F + r_D * r_P' * c_C + r_P' * c_S + b_P'' * c_D \qquad (3)$$

Algorithm 4 (Result Verification and Filtering)

```
Answer = results of DMQV;
scan D once evaluating the support of patterns
in Answer using time constraints of DMQ;
for each p ∈ Answer do
  if p satisfies pattern constraints of DMQ
  then output p; end if;
```

The cost of Algorithm 4 can be expressed by the following formula:

$$C_{VF} = (b_P + b_D) * c_D + r_D * r_P * c_C + r_P * c_F + b_P'' * c_D \quad (4)$$

The advantage of the Algorithm 3 over the Algorithm 4 is the possible reduction of the number of patterns whose support has to be re-evaluated. However, Algorithm 3 compares supports of some patterns with the minimum support threshold twice (before and after the support re-evaluation). Let us evaluate the difference between the cost of applying the Algorithms 3 and 4 for the same query and exploiting the same materialized results of a previous dominating query:

$$C_{FV} - C_{VF} = r_D * r_P' * c_C + r_P' * c_S - r_D * r_P * c_C \quad (5)$$

If we assume that the Algorithm 3 during its initial pattern filtering phase filters out *x* patterns ($r_P - r_P' = x$), then we have:

$$C_{FV} - C_{VF} = (r_P - x) * c_S - r_D * x * c_C \quad (6)$$

Assuming that the number of materialized patterns used is smaller than the number of data-sequences in the source dataset ($r_P < r_D$), and the cost of pattern containment test is larger than the cost of comparing pattern's support with the minimum support threshold ($c_C > c_S$), the above formula states that if the initial filtering phase of the Algorithm 3 filters out at least one pattern ($x > 0$), then the Algorithm 3 outperforms the Algorithm 4. Thus, generating possible execution plans we do not consider application of the Algorithm 4 at all.

5 Cost-Based Optimization of Sequential Pattern Queries in Presence of Materialized Results of Previous Queries

A cost-based query optimizer works as follows. First, it generates all possible query execution plans. Next, the cost of each plan is estimated. Finally, based on the estimation, the plan with the lowest estimated cost is chosen. Since the decision is made using estimated cost values, the plan chosen may actually not be optimal. The quality of optimizer decisions depends on the complexity and accuracy of cost functions used. Cost functions that are used in practice usually do not take into consideration all the factors contributing to the execution costs. Cost estimation procedures have to be relatively simple, so that the time spent on optimization does not contribute significantly to the overall processing time.

We observe that the cost formulas that we provided in the previous section are not appropriate for the cost-based optimization for two major reasons. Firstly, the costs of disk and memory operations depend on a particular machine configuration. Secondly, the number of patterns after initial filtration in the cost formula for the Algorithm 3 is not known a priori. While the ratio between cost of disk and memory operations can be easily determined, estimating the size of materialized pattern collection after filtration according to a given pattern predicate is not trivial. The actual problem is that the selectivity of a given pattern predicate depends not only on the predicate itself but also on the patterns being filtered. To be able to estimate the selectivity of a given predicate on a given collection of patterns, the system could apply the predicate to a random sample of patterns. However, this would clearly result in more time spent on optimization, which is not desirable. Taking all this into account, we propose to use simplified cost functions expressed in terms of the number of disk blocks accessed. Since for a given query all correct execution plans have to lead to the same set of resulting patterns, in the simplified cost formulas we omit the blocks written while storing the results on disk. Thus, the new cost functions for the Algorithm 1 (F), Algorithm 2 (V), and Algorithm 3 (FV) look as follows:

$$C_F = b_P \qquad C_V = b_P + b_D \qquad C_{FV} = b_P + b_D \tag{7}$$

Our optimizer performs the cost analysis only if there is more than one previous query including or dominating the current query, and no equivalent query can be found among the queries whose materialized results are available. The number of considered execution plans is equal to the number of including and dominating queries (Algorithm 1 is used for including queries, Algorithm 2 for dominating queries having the same pattern constraints, and Algorithm 3 for dominating queries extending pattern constraints of the current query). If the optimizer finds more than one including or dominating query, the cost of each execution plan has to be estimated using the cost formulas presented above. Then, the query is answered according to the plan with the lowest estimated cost. Of course, if no equivalent, including, or dominating query can be found, a complete sequential pattern mining algorithm has to be run.

6 Experimental Results

To support and verify our theoretical analysis, we performed several experiments on synthetic datasets generated by means of the *GEN* generator from the *Quest* project [1]. The size of the source dataset used in our experiments ranged from 1000 to 100000 data-sequences. For all datasets the total number of different items was 1000, average size of a data-sequence was 8 items, and the data distribution was the same. The time gap between two adjacent elements of each data-sequence was always equal to one time unit. The materialized collections of patterns contained from 800 to more than 6000 patterns. The source datasets and materialized query results were stored in a local *Oracle8i* database.

The first goal of the experiments was to verify whether disk activity is really a dominant contributor to the cost (expressed in terms of execution time) of the algorithms exploiting materialized patterns. For Algorithm 1, time spent on disk operations was on average 97% of the total time. However, in case of Algorithms 2 and 3 the average value of the above ratio was 78% and 92% respectively. The percentage of time spent on disk operations in case of Algorithm 3 varied significantly (from 75% to 98%) with the selectivity of pattern constraints used in queries. The experimental results prove that simplifying the cost formulas to the number of disk blocks accessed was justified. Nevertheless, it can lead to underestimating the cost of execution plans involving Algorithms 2 and 3.

The second goal was to check if the execution strategy chosen as the one resulting in the smallest number of disk accesses is really the optimal one. In general, minimizing disk accesses led to optimal execution plans. However, when we provided two materialized collections of patterns slightly differing in the number of occupied disk blocks, minimizing disk activity sometimes resulted in a non-optimal plan if at least one of the materialized collections of patterns required the application of the Algorithm 2 or 3. This is no surprise, since in case of those algorithms, main memory computations (not consider by simplified cost functions) are much more significant than in case of Algorithm 1. Nevertheless, the actual cost of the chosen strategy was never higher than the cost of the actual optimal strategy by more than 30%, which seems to be acceptable.

7 Conclusions

We addressed the problem of efficient answering sequential pattern queries in the presence of materialized results of previous sequential pattern queries. We focused on estimating the cost of execution strategies involving materialized collection of patterns. By comparing estimated costs of all execution strategies available for a given sequential pattern query, the data mining system can choose the execution plan that is optimal or close to optimal.

References

1. Agrawal R., Mehta M., Shafer J., Srikant R., Arning A., Bollinger T.: The Quest Data Mining System. Proc. of the 2nd KDD Conference (1996)
2. Agrawal R., Srikant R.: Mining Sequential Patterns. Proc. 11th ICDE Conf. (1995)
3. Baralis E., Psaila G.: Incremental Refinement of Mining Queries. Proc. of the 1st DaWaK Conference (1999)
4. Elmasri R., Navathe S.B.: Fundamentals of Database Systems, Second Edition (1994)
5. Han J., Lakshmanan L., Ng R.: Constraint-Based Multidimensional Data Mining. IEEE Computer, Vol. 32, No. 8 (1999)
6. Imielinski T., Mannila H.: A Database Perspective on Knowledge Discovery. Communications of the ACM, Vol. 39, No. 11 (1996)
7. Nag B., Deshpande P.M., DeWitt D.J.: Using a Knowledge Cache for Interactive Discovery of Association Rules. Proc. of the 5th KDD Conference (1999)
8. Oracle9i Database Performance Guide and Reference. Oracle Corporation (2001)
9. Parthasarathy S., Zaki M.J., Ogihara M., Dwarkadas S.: Incremental and Interactive Sequence Mining. Proc. of the 8th CIKM Conference (1999)
10. Srikant R., Agrawal R.: Mining Sequential Patterns: Generalizations and Performance Improvements. Proc. of the 5th EDBT Conference (1996)
11. Wojciechowski M.: Interactive Constraint-Based Sequential Pattern Mining. Proc. of the 5th ADBIS Conference (2001)

Computer Aided Design of Learning Systems in PROLOG

Dominik Ryżko

Institute of Computer Science, Warsaw University of Technology,
e-mail: dryzko@yahoo.com

Abstract: The paper describes an approach to computer aided design of symbol based machine learning programs in Prolog. By embedding Prolog clauses of previously prepared programs with special instructions a generator is able to generate fully functional solutions according to the data passed to it. The paper shows why such generation might be useful for machine learning programs. The approach is compared with other works in the field of automatic generation of logic programs. The use of some symbolic learning methods in different areas of AI is also described.
Keywords: Artificial intelligence; Machine learning; Logic programming; Automatic programming

1. Introduction

Learning systems have been subject of dynamic research since the very beginning of AI research. For different areas of AI several unique algorithms and approaches have been developed, e.g. rote learning [11], decision trees generation [8], inductive inference [8], learning from analogies [11], EBL (explanation based learning) [2], unsupervised learning [2], reinforcement learning [8]. One of the most popular is learning from examples introduced by Winston [1]. It allows learning of a new concept form a series of positive and negative examples prepared by a teacher. If examples are properly chosen, then only a small set of them is needed to perform the learning task.

Other approaches take advantage of statistical properties of a large set of examples rather then few carefully chosen instances of the concept. Among such methods is decision trees generation. Its objective is a construction of decision tree for classification of instances of some domain. In order to generate an efficient tree, theory of information is used.

Another group of learning algorithms use explicit knowledge in order to learn new concepts. Good examples of such approach are analogy learning and EBL (explanation based learning). The first of these methods is based on drawing analogies between a training example and some stored pieces of knowledge. In the second of the two previously stored knowledge is used to perform a proof of new concept and the constructed proof tree is added to the data base.

One of the important branch of machine learning is inductive inference. The significant work in this field has been done in [12]. In particular this research led to discovery of the systems that today can be called "classical", such as AQ and CN2 [12, 13]. The algorithms have initiated development of a large family of learning systems e.g. [14].

All the learning systems are very difficult to design and develop. Each specific case requires a unique approach. Therefore it's not easy to reuse the code developed for one application in another one, even if for example the same learning method is used in both cases. This is why there is a great need for methods of automatic code generation, as it would drastically reduce efforts of building new learning systems.

One can distinguish two major approaches to automated program synthesis, referring to deductive and inductive reasoning. Most of research so far has been concentrated on deduction. The reason for this is that the task of program synthesis is perceived as requiring sound reasoning. Deduction-based synthesis is a translation of some higher level specification language into an algorithm.

On the other hand induction is an example of non-sound reasoning method. In the context of automated program generation induction is a generalization of some formal specification into an algorithm. There are two basic approaches to this task: trace-based synthesis and model-based synthesis. The first one is based on explanation of positive examples which are then generalized to obtain the final program. In the second approach both positive and negative examples are used to "debug" the program.

In [9] an analysis of these two approaches can be found. The authors show that sound reasoning methods, like deduction, should not be considered as superior over non-sound methods, such as induction, analogy or other. In addition, since both of the approaches have advantages and drawbacks it might be a good idea to use combination of them in order to achieve the best results.

Prolog is a very good environment to perform reasoning and proof procedures. Therefore many works can be found where various logical structures are transformed into Prolog programs in order to perform some reasoning tasks. In [6] You, Wang and Yuan show a way of compiling defeasible inheritance networks into logic programs. Another idea can be found in [5] where Shaub and Bruning describe how translation of default theory into Prolog program allows efficient query answering within this theory. Tinkham in [4] introduces generalization and refinement operators on logic programs which define schema-hierarchy graph. Such a graph containing previously seen Prolog programs can be used to construct new ones. All these ideas benefit from the logical structure of Prolog.

In this paper we propose to consider syntactic level of a logic program. To this end we define a special meta language for specifying how to reuse pieces of the Prolog program. Reusable blocks of Prolog code are embedded in a "specification" expressed in the language. It allows generating a fully usable code using suitable code generator. In [7] this idea has been implemented and tested. The generator is equipped with GUI for easy generation of appropriate code for specific cases. In this paper the idea is extended towards interactive generation dialogue. The new version of the system communicates with the "learning program designer", requesting for particular data while processing input file.

In order to verify the applicability of the proposed approach various symbolic learning methods known from different areas of AI have been implemented. Two of these methods have been implemented in their general form, independently of the field of application, namely (1) the ID3 algorithm for decision trees generation [15], and (2) the algorithm for learning from positive and negative examples [1]. Other implemented methods refer to planning, natural language understanding and game playing.

In Section 2 a general concept of the proposed approach is described. Section 3 introduces the meta language with some examples of its use. In Section 5 with examples of using various symbolic learning algorithms in different areas of AI we illustrate how the system can be generated. Finally Section 6 brings the conclusions and possible further extensions of this approach.

2. General concept

Because of their declarative foundations Prolog programs have modular structure. Clauses with the same predicates on the left side can be treated as separate pieces of code and therefore easily substituted by another implementation of this particular predicate. Sometimes it is not obvious which version of the predicate will be needed later in the system. For example developing the general structure of decision tree generation algorithm is well known. However there can be various predicates responsible for choosing an attribute which should be tested in particular node of the tree.

Many symbolic learning algorithms require a number of repeating predicates for declarations. Manual generation of such predicates from other data structures could be tiresome. For example learning from examples as described by Winston in [1] requires previously prepared class hierarchy tree. For every arc of such a tree one predicate has to be added to the Prolog program. If the structure of such a tree is changed these predicates have to be generated anew.

The principle of the approach described here is to generate fully usable logic programs from previously prepared programs stored in files. The files contain blocks of Prolog code embedded in simple macro language which allows usage of variables, lists, loops and conditional instructions. If the generator finds Prolog instructions in the input file, then it is written to the output without change. If it encounters a macro instruction the data passed to the module has to be checked to determine the correct substitution or outcome of a condition.

In [7] a simple application was built, which allows generation of Prolog code for various symbolic learning methods. This application includes also a selection of tutorials which describe learning methods which were used. The program consists of forms which are grouped in sets. For each algorithm there are two series of forms one for tutorial and one for setting parameters required for code generation.

The data specified by the user is stored in special data structures and passed to the code generator. This generator can operate independently of the rest of the application. It requires specification of input and output files and a pointer to data structures. The generator runs through the specified file and depending on its contents and data passed in data structures generates output.

This application however can only be used for demonstration. To allow processing of new files a general utility should be built. The best solution would be an interactive generator which would ask for required data when it is needed. The source could be strings entered by user, files or even database queries. For example encountering a condition it would ask user to take a choice. If generator finds a loop it will ask for source of records to fill variables and lists in each of loop turns. Such a tool could then be used to process any file prepared according to the rules described in section 3.

The main idea of the solution described above is to write source code only once and then use conditions and variables so that only blocks of code needed will find themselves in the output file. If the same predicate has to be repeated several times in the program then we can write it only once with variables and use loops to multiply it with different substitutions.

3. Description of special macro language used

Each of the instructions of the macro language described here starts and ends with a '$' sign. The following instructions are allowed:

3.1. Variable

$<*var_name*>$

where *var_name* is the name of the variable to be substituted. The value of the variable *var_name* is written to the output file.

3.2. List

$list(*list_name*)$

where *list_name* is the name of the list to be substituted. Elements of the list *list_name* embedded in '[' and ']' signs and separated by commas are written to the output file.

3.3. Condition

$if(*conditon*)$

...

$endif$

where *condition* is like *variable=constant*. The variable is substituted as in 3.1. and then the condition is checked. If its true the input file is read as usually. In the opposite case all the code until the instruction *$endif$* is ignored. In its basic version conditions cannot be nested, however the generator could be easily extended to allow nested loops.

3.4. Loop

$loop(*loop_name*)$

...

$endloop$

where *loop_name* is the name of the loop to be executed. All the code between loop instructions is repeated as many times as there are records for this particular loop. Each record has its own variables so all the substitutions can be different in each loop turn.

3.5. Example

Here is a simple example of special instructions in input file

```
$if(examples=Y)$
$loop(examples)$
example($<classname>$,$list(attnameval)$).
$endloop$
$endif$
```

If variable **examples** has value 'Y' the following sequence of PROLOG causes will be generated:

$\textbf{example (class}_1\textbf{, [elt}_{11}\textbf{, elt}_{12}\textbf{, ..., elt}_{1n}\textbf{]).}$
$\textbf{example (class}_2\textbf{, [elt}_{21}\textbf{, elt}_{22}\textbf{, ..., elt}_{2m}\textbf{]).}$
...
$\textbf{example (class}_k\textbf{, [elt}_{k1}\textbf{, elt}_{k2}\textbf{, ..., elt}_{ki}\textbf{]).}$

4. Examples

4.1. Explanation Based Learning in the game Go

Here is a description of implementation of explanation based learning in game playing and usage of the program described above to generate the source code for this method.

The game of go takes place on a board with 19 horizontal and 19 vertical lines intersecting in 361 places. During the game pieces called stones are put on these intersections by both players. Once put stones cannot be moved during the game. The object of the game is to control territory. The enemy stones can also be captured if they have no liberties (free line intersections connected to them).

Explanation Based Learning (EBL) is a symbolic learning method which requires explicit knowledge on the domain of its operations. Based on this knowledge and examples passed to it, the reasoning (explanation) process is performed. The resulting proof tree is processed and stored for future use. A detailed description of EBL can be found in [2]. As the field of experiment the game of Go has been chosen. This game is very interesting from AI point of view because so far the best programs designed for playing it are hardly able to defeat a novice. The way of *brute force* is just not good enough, so its a good field to understand how humans think and to try to simulate similar processes in computer programs.

The main problem with implementation of EBL in Go was translation of board positions into predicates required for reasoning. This problem has been solved as follows. The examples are parts of the go board 5x5 lines. Before the main algorithm starts the example is compared with a series of patterns. If its possible to unify the particular example with a pattern, a predicate connected with this pattern is added to the knowledge base for this example. After all facts about a particular example are gathered the reasoning takes place.

An example is represented in PROLOG as:

```
pos([[-1,-1,-1,-1,-1],
    [-1, 0, 0, 1, 2],
    [-1, 1, 1, 1, 2],
    [-1, 2, 2, 2, 2],
    [-1, 0, 0, 0, 0]
    ]).
```

where symbols '-1' represent board edge, '0' - free intersections, '1' - black stones and '2' - white stones.

A pattern is represented as:

```
is_fact(X,[[-1,-1,-1,-1,-1],
```

```
[-1, _, _, _, _],
[-1, _, _, _, _],
[-1, _ , _, _, _],
[-1, _, _, _, _]],
in_corner(X)).
```

This approach has its limitations, because some of the situations can occur in many variations and would require various patterns for each of them. However pattern matching is the simplest way to build Prolog programs. Moreover the number of patterns can be reduced in other ways. For example the problem of mirror situations can be handled by special rotation predicates. The following predicate rotates the given position clockwise by 90 degrees:

```
turn([[X11, X12, X13, X14, X15],
      [X21, X22, X23, X24, X25],
      [X31, X32, X33, X34, X35],
      [X41, X42, X43, X44, X45],
      [X51, X52, X53, X54, X55]],
   [[X11, X21, X31, X41, X51],
      [X12, X22, X32, X42, X52],
      [X13, X23, X33, X43, X53],
      [X14, X24, X34, X44, X54],
      [X51, X25, X35, X45, X55]]).
```

To generate all needed variations of these predicates special instructions from section 3 can be used. Here come the most important pieces of code prepared for generator:

```
start(Pos,NT, Map) :-  pos(Pos),
                       learn_go(Pos,T)$if(gen=Y)$,
                       generalize(T, NT, [] ,Map)$endif$.

learn_go(Pos, conc(killed(group), Trace)) :-
                       bagof(P/F, is_fact(group,P,F), IsFacts),
                       facts(Pos,Facts,IsFacts),!,
                       proof(Facts,Trace,killed(group))$if(writetree=Y)$,
                       writeTree(conc(killed(group),Trace), 0)$endif$.
```

In this approach killing of a group is always the objective of the proof. The user can specify if he wants to view the proof tree and if the generalization procedure should be used to substitute constants with variables.

In this program there are many repeating predicates describing patterns and rules required by the algorithm. They are declared as follows:

```
$loop(facts)$
is_fact(X,$list(board)$,$<predicates>$).
$endloop$

$loop(rules)$
rule($list(left)$,$<right>$).
$endloop$
```

4.2. Learning from examples in natural language understanding.

The method of learning from positive and negative examples has been used to learn synthactics and semathics of natural language. In this chapter the second of this issues will be shown.

The learning program developed here concerns one stage of semanthic processing called transformation into *logical form (LF)*. This is the first stage of semantic processing introduced by *Allen* [3]. For example LF for sentence "The hammer broke the window" will be the following

```
(? b1 BREAK [INST (DEF/SING h1 HAMMER)]
            [THEME (DEF/SING w1 WINDOW)])
```

In Prolog this can be represented as:

```
lf (?, b1, break, [inst(def_sing, h1, hammer), theme(def_sing, w1, window)]).
```

This structure can now be used for the learning algorithm. The learning process uses positive and negative examples which can look like this:

```
example(rule(pos, syn(np, [det(a), adj(green), head([+apple])]),
  lf(?,c1,apple,[color(c1,gr137)]))).
```

Predicate *rule* has three parameters from which the first one describes whether the example is positive or negative and following two are left and right side of the rule which is to be learned, respectively.

The main predicate of the algorithm is as follows:

```
process_examples(CurDesc, [Example|Examples], FinDesc) :-
      object_type(Example, Object, Type),
      adapt(Object, NObject),
      update(Type, NObject, CurDesc, NewDesc),
      process_examples(NewDesc, Examples, FinDesc).
```

Function **update** divides examples into parts which are processed separately by more detailed procedures.

```
update(Type, rule(syn(S, SL), lf(L, VAR, MV, List)), rule(syn(S, SLx),
lf(Lx, VARx, MVx, Listx)), rule(syn(S, SLn), lf(Ln, VARn, MVn, Listn))) :-
    update_syn(SL, SLx, SLn, Type),
    update_sem1(L, Lx, Ln, Type),
    update_sem2(VAR, VARx, VARn, Type),
    update_sem3(MV, MVx, MVn,Type),
    update_sem4(List, Listx, Listn, Type).
```

Here our special instructions are useful to generate a large number of predicates describing class hierarchy tree and examples for learning:

```
$loop(classes)$
ako($<class>$, $<subclass>$).
$endloop$

$loop(examples)$
example(rule($<posneg>$, $<syntax>$, $<lf>$).
$endloop$
```

5. Conclusions

One should observe that the idea described in this paper is not supposed to substitute other methods of automatic code generation which take advantage of logic structure of Prolog. These methods are well suited for generation of particular predicates, but not big systems. On the other hand the approach of this paper allows generation of fully usable code, however for specific needs one has to extend it further or manually integrate into larger system. The advantage of this approach is that the core of a learning method once written and tested can be embedded in the special macro language described here and produce different variations of the algorithm from one unmodified source file.

These advantages make this system very useful for purposes of comparing various algorithms or efficiency testing.

Further extensions of this approach should be considered. Most obvious is extension of the macro language with new constructions. Another interesting possibility is to allow taking data for learning from files or even better directly from data base. This could be done by adding special interface to the designed tool which would allow for specifying SQL queries and pack the data into Prolog clauses.

A system incorporating both of these approaches should be considered in which logical structure of Prolog would be used for construction of particular predicates and the general framework and supply for input data would be taken care by macro instructions described above.

An example of a system implementing ideas described above can be found in [7].

6. Bibliography

[1] P.Winston, Artificial Intelligence, 1992, Addison-Wesley

[2] G.F.Luger, Artificial Intelligence: Structures and Strategies for Complex Problem Solving, 2001, Addison-Wesley

[3] J.Allen, Natural language Understanding, 2nd ed, 1994, Addison-Wesley

[4] N.L. Tinkham, Schema induction for logic program synthesis, Artificial Intelligence 98 (1998) 1-47

[5] T.Schaub, S.Bruning, Prolog technology for default reasoning: proof theory and compilation techniques, Artificial Intelligence 106 (1998) 1-75

[6] J.H.You, X.Wang, L.Y.Yuan, Compiling defeasible inheritance networks to generate logic programs, Artificial Intelligence 113 (1999) 247-268

[7] D.Ryżko, Project of an educational tool for designing machine learning programs in PROLOG, Master thesis, Warsaw University of Technology 2001

[8] P.Cichosz, Systemy uczące się, WNT Warszawa 2000

[9] P.Flener, L.Popelinsky, On the use of Inductive Reasoning in Program Synthesis: Prejudice and Prospects, Proceedings LOPSTR'94 69-87, Springer-Verlag 1994

[10] I.Bratko, PROLOG – Programming for artificial intelligence, Addison-Wesley 1986

[11] E.Charniak, D.McDermott, Introduction to Artificial Intelligence, Addison-Wesley 1985

[12] R.S.Michalski, On the quasi-optimal solution of the general covering problem. In: Proceedings of the First International Symposium on Information Processing, Bled, 1969

[13] P.Clark, T.Niblett, The CN2 induction algorithm. Machine learning 3, 1989, 261-283

[14] R.S.Michalski, I.Mozetic, J.Hong, N.Lavrac, The multi-purpose incremental learning system AQ15 and its testing application to three medical domains. In: Proceedings of the Fifth National Conference on Artificial Intelligence (AAAI-86), MIT Press, 1986

[15] J.R.Quinlan, Induction of decision trees, Machine Learning, 3, 1986, 81-106

FIPA Compliant Agent-based Decentralised Expert System

Paweł Skrzyński, Michał Turek, Bartłomiej Śnieżyński, and Marek Kisiel-Dorohinicki

Department of Computer Science
University of Mining and Metallurgy, Kraków, Poland
e-mail: {sniezyn, doroh}@agh.edu.pl

Abstract. The paper presents the agent-oriented architecture of a decentralised expert system based on FIPA standard. Each agent in the framework can use its own knowledge representation and reasoning strategy, which makes the system flexible and extensible. Interoperability of heterogeneous agents is ensured via common communication protocols, as well as identification and location facilities provided by an agent platform. Realisation of the proposed architecture is based on JADE platform and its description concludes the work.

Keywords: expert systems, multi-agent systems, agent standards

1 Introduction

For over thirty years expert systems have been successfully used in almost every field of human activity. An expert system is a knowledge-based computer system that contains expert knowledge and thus is able to provide expertise for solving problems in selected domains in the way human experts do. Initially expert systems had rather simple architecture – a typical expert system consisted of a knowledge base and an inference engine – they became complex and difficult to maintain applications because of more and more complicated problem domains (a huge amount of information to be processed), the need for approximate reasoning, representation of incomplete, ambiguous, corrupted or even contradictory knowledge, and – last but not least – the necessity of co-operation of systems (exploitation of knowledge or services) delivered by different vendors.

The natural way of overcoming the last problem seems the application of multi-agent technology. Multi-agent systems (MAS) stemmed from the field of Distributed Artificial Intelligence (DAI). They provide concepts and tools for building intelligent decentralised software systems [12,3]. They were also used to support development of expert systems — several projects has been done in this field and various architectures have been proposed (e.g. [1,6,16]). Yet none of these approaches make use of existing standards – such as FIPA [5] – allowing for agent-based systems interoperability. In the paper a FIPA-compliant architecture dedicated for distributed expert system development

(FIPA-DES) is proposed. While the agent framework is defined by the standard and dedicated communication protocols are generally sketched by FIPA-DES, knowledge representation and inference technique is not fixed and can be accommodated to the problem domain. Such approach gives more flexibility and allows for extensibility of the system.

The paper is organised as follows. In two following sections a brief outlook of distributed expert systems is presented and FIPA standard is described. Then the proposed FIPA-DES (i.e. system architecture and communication protocols) is introduced. Description of the implementation of rule-based FIPA-DES concludes the work.

2 Distributed Expert Systems

During the last decade the idea of an intelligent autonomous agent and an agent-based system gains more and more interest both in academic community and industry. Agent technology is used in various domains, providing concepts and tools for development of intelligent decentralised systems [10]. Yet this technology is still so immature that there is no consensus on what an agent really is [12,8]. By now this should not be considered a problem since "the notion of an agent is meant to be a tool for analysing systems, not an absolute characterization that divides the world into agents and non-agents" [14].

Agent technology seem to be a suitable tool for a distributed expert system development since:

- it is easy to extend the system by adding appropriate agent(s),
- agents can be developed by different developers (they are autonomous),
- inference engine can be specialized for given agent task – it is not necessary to build universal and thus complex inference engine,
- every agent has a knowledge base, which is necessary for his goals so it is small and thus easy to create and maintain,
- it is possible to sell problem solving abilities, not a complete system with a knowledge base.

Distributed expert systems, which are known to authors propose their own architecture for distributed system.

Ex-W-Pert [6] is a system with shared and distributed knowledge bases, which can be used for groupware design. Separate system units can be used by different users and have knowledge about different device models. Ex-W-Pert uses model-based reasoning and frames to represent knowledge. Units are similar to standard expert systems: they have a local knowledge base and inference engine. Additionally they have communication engine which is used to acquire appropriate knowledge and data from other sites. Communication is based on specialised protocol using NFS and HTTP.

MAPS (Multi-Agent Problem Solver) is a programming environment which allows to design distributed expert systems [1]. Two types of agents are proposed: knowledge server and knowledge processor. Knowledge server if responsible for maintenance and transmission of knowledge. It uses rule-based knowledge to send or request information from other agents. It can also request knowledge processor agents to solve specified problems. Knowledge processor agent is responsible for processing supplied information. Its knowledge base consist of a set of action rules and analysis procedures.

Another system, CIDIM [4] is an agent-based electricity distribution manager. It helps control engineers to ensure electricity supply. In this system ARCHON framework is used [16], which specifies agents architecture. Every agent can monitor external (intelligent) system and is able to communicate with other agents. The agents use the Agent Acquaintance Models [15] to represent other agents and their roles in the system.

3 Standards for Agent Technology

Facing progressive development of network technologies during the last years, special attention should be paid to distributed software architectures, which allow for efficient access and exchange of resources and services. In open environments it means that heterogeneous information systems supplied by multiple vendors should be able to interoperate with each other. The agent-based technologies seem to be a promising answer to facilitate the realisation of such systems. Yet, agent-based software cannot realise its full potential until standards to support interoperability are available and widely used by developers [5,13].

Even though a key role within standardisation efforts of agent-based software plays communication [7], a common communication language (agent communication language – ACL) is not enough to support interoperability between different agent systems: also some management infrastructure seems indispensable. Considering practical applications a minimum set of standards should provide [13]:

- a means by which agents can exchange information, negotiate for services, or delegate tasks (communication language),
- a unique way of agent identification (globally unique names),
- facilities whereby agents can locate each other (directory services),
- a secure and trusted environment where agents can operate and exchange confidential messages (platforms),
- if necessary, a means of migrating from one platform to another.

Several research groups are working towards the standardisation of agent technologies (for example KSE – Knowledge Sharing Effort, OMG – Object Management Group, and FIPA). The Foundation for Intelligent Physical Agents is a non-profit organisation which purpose is *the promotion of technologies and interoperability specifications that facilitate the end-to-end interworking of intelligent agent systems in modern commercial and industrial settings* (FIPA mission statement). At the same time contributors may produce their own implementations of software frameworks as long as their construction and operation complies with the published FIPA specifications, which makes that the individual software frameworks are interoperable.

FIPA specifications neither describe how developers should implement their agent-based systems, nor specify the internal architectures of agents. Instead, they provide the interfaces through which agents communicate. Each specification belongs to a one of five parts of FIPA specification structure [5]:

Abstract Architecture specification identifies the key elements of the architecture that must be codified. It makes a distinction between elements which can be defined in an abstract manner, such as agent message transport, FIPA ACL, directory services and content languages, and those elements that cannot, such as agent management and agent mobility. These are considered too close to the concrete realisation (implementation) of an agent system and may have very little in common. They have to be addressed by developers and the abstract architecture will provide a number of guidelines for specific implementation technologies.

Agent Message Transport specifications deal with the delivery and representation of messages across different network transport protocols. At this level, a message consists of an envelope and a body. The envelope contains specific transport requirements and information that is used by the Message Transport Service (MTS) on each agent platform to route and handle messages. The message body is usually expressed in FIPA ACL but is opaque to the MTS since it may be compressed or encoded.

Agent Management specification provides the framework for the creation, registration, location, communication, migration and retirement of agents. It describes the primitives and ontologies necessary to support:

- agent location, naming and control access services provided by the Agent Management System (AMS) – *white pages*,
- service location and registration services provided by the Directory Facilitator (DF) – yellow pages,
- message transport services as described previously.

Agent Communication is realised through the use of communicative acts (performatives) based on speech act theory (such as: request, inform, and refuse), that are independent from the overall content of the message. The message that is supplied with a communicative act is wrapped in an envelope called an agent communication language (ACL). An ACL provides mechanisms for describing some context of the message, such as identifying the sender and receiver, and the ontology and interaction protocol of the message. The FIPA ACL was originally based upon ARCOL with a number of revisions from KQML. The actual content of a message is expressed in a content language.

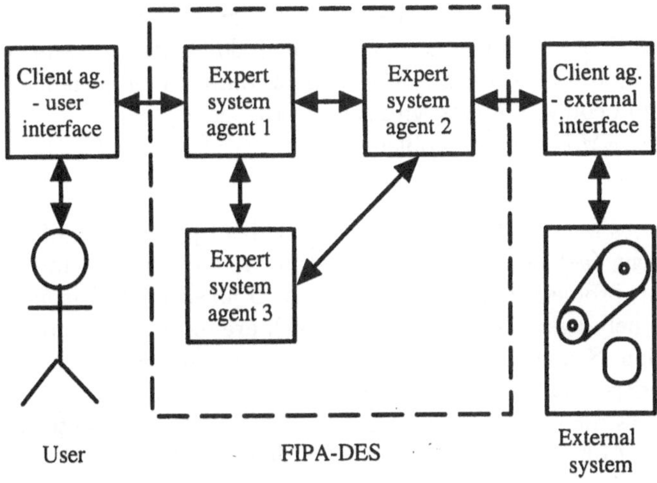

Fig. 1. System architecture

Agent Applications. FIPA has also developed specifications of four agent-based applications that contain service and ontology descriptions as well as case scenarios for travel assistance, audio-visual entertainment and broadcasting, network management and provisioning, and personal assistant.

Additionally, the *Agent Software Integration* specification contains a guide for integrating legacy software, that does not communicate using FIPA ACL.

4 FIPA Compliant Decentralised Expert System

A general system architecture is presented in fig. 1. The main element of FIPA-DES is an Expert System Agent (ESA). There may be many ESA registered in the platform. Each ESA serves expert services from given domain and communicates with other agents if necessary. Client Agents (CA) are able to use ESA knowledge processing abilities. Depending on the task, they may be used by a human user (e.g. in a diagnostic system) or some external system (e.g. in monitoring or control system). All the communication (between two ESA and between ESA and CA) is based on FIPA-ACL.

To achieve full independence of the modules no specific internal architecture of the agents is assumed. Each ESA may use its own knowledge representation and inference technique appropriate to the domain. Cooperation of agents is achieved by using a common communication language.

When ESA is added to the agent platform it registers in a directory service the following entries:

- *INFORMATION* – a brief description of an expert system,
- *DOMAIN* – a list of keywords describing domain(s) of a knowledge base,
- *DOMAIN-ONTOLOGY* – the name of ontology used in the knowledge base and content of messages sent by the agent,
- *PROBLEMS* – main problems (in terms of *DOMAIN-ONTOLOGY*), which may be solved by the agent.

These entries are used by other agents to find out possibilities of cooperation. If any agent (a_i) needs more information, it looks for agents which offer solving this problem in *PROBLEMS* entry. If no such agent is found, a_i tries to ask for help agents with keywords which are most similar to the problem specification. Search is limited to agents using appropriate ontologies: they should understand ontology used by a_i.

As it was mentioned above, communication between agents is performed by sending ACL messages. In FIPA-DES there are 5 types of communicates defined which may be sent to an agent:

prove message may be used by ESA and CA (the sender) to get information from other agents: it contains a hypothesis which should be confirmed or rejected by the receiver (hypothesis may contain free variables, which values should be fixed) and additional information that could be useful in such task (e.g. facts known to sender),

answer message contains information about results of knowledge processing (in case of confirmation it may contain free variable assignments),

ask message is very similar to the **prove** message – the only difference is that it is used by the receiver to get additional information from the sender; it is introduced to avoid loops in distributed knowledge processing,

explain message is used by CA to ask ESA for explanation how hypothesis was confirmed, why additional information is needed or what system knows about a given problem (standard WHAT, WHY and HOW questions),

explanation message is a reply for the **explain** message: information should be presented in a form readable for user.

Representation of knowledge and questions in content of ACL communicates is based on patterns (knowledge representation technique used e.g. in CLIPS programming language [9]). This formalism is general enough to support communication between systems using different internal representation of knowledge.

5 Rule-Based FIPA-DES and Distributed Backward Chaining Inference Technique

In currently realised FIPA-DES an expert system agent has rule-based knowledge base and uses backward chaining inference technique. Each ESA provides services for proving given goals based on its knowledge that could be used by other agents (both other ESA and CA).

The cooperation of ESA in proving a specific goal is based on the distributed backward chaining algorithm, which is simply a distributed version of classical backward chaining inference technique.

The difference appears, if there is no rule which can be used to confirm current goal in the knowledge base. ESA first tries to ask the agent which asked him for help by sending **ask** message. If there is no possibility to ask or there is no reply, it tries to locate other servers (by sending query to directory service) and ask them to prove this hypothesis by sending **prove** message.

When ESA receives the **ask** message, if first tries to use its own knowledge base to find a solution. If unsuccessful, it can transfer questions to the "previous" agent.

A draft of distributed backward chaining algorithm is presented below.

1. Find a rule which conclusion matches the current goal and create a binding set (or extend the existing binding set).
2. Using the existing binding set, look for a way to deal with the first antecedent:
   (a) try to match the antecedent with any stored fact,
   (b) change the current goal to the antecedent and try to support it by backward chaining using the existing binding set.
3. Repeat the previous step for each antecedent, accumulating variable bindings, until
   - there is no match with any stored fact or rule consequence using the binding set established so far. In this case, back up to the most recent match with unexplored bindings, looking for an alternative match that produces a workable binding set,
   - there are no more antecedents to be matched. In this case, the binding set in hand supports the current goal:
     (a) if all possible binding sets are desired, report the current binding set, and back up, as if there were no match,
     (b) if only one possible binding set is desired, report the current binding set and quit.
4. If there are no more alternative matches to be explored at any level try to ask the "previous" agent. If unsuccessful, locate other expert system server agents and ask them to prove the hypotheses (if more than one such server exists choose one using ontology and problem domain entries).

6 FIPA-DES Implementation

Current implementation of FIPA-DES is based on JADE (Java Agent Development Framework) – a software development framework aimed at agent-based systems conforming to FIPA specifications [2]. It includes a FIPA-compliant agent platform and a package to develop agents. JADE is realised in Java

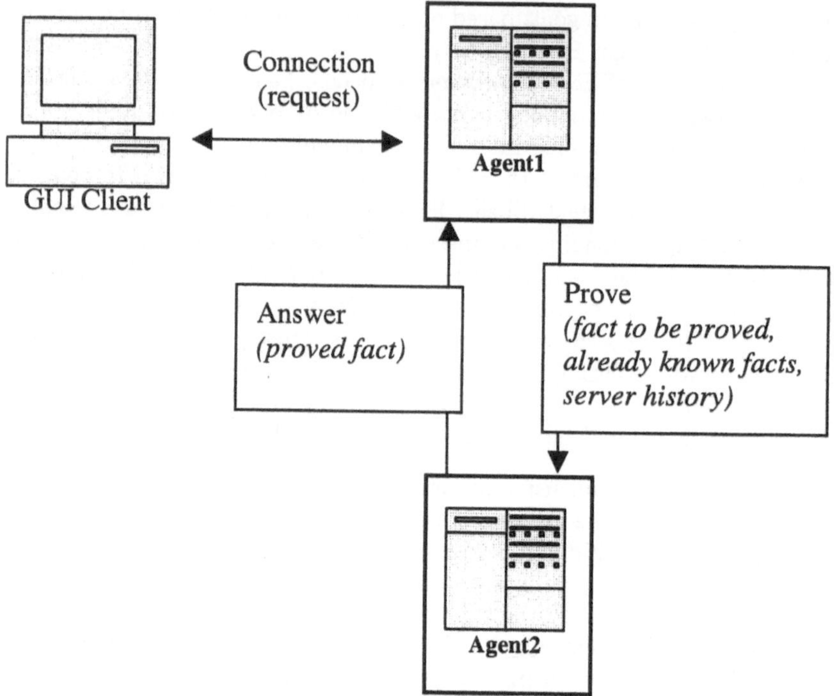

Fig. 2. Communication example

language and gives application programmers both ready-made pieces of functionality and abstract interfaces for custom, application dependent tasks.

Both ESA and CA are implemented as JADE agents. Expert system agents work as described in the previous section. Client agents play role of an interface between user and FIPA-DES. They are responsible for displaying questions, html, photos and other information send by ESA during expertise.

The communication between agents is performed by sending ACL messages (see fig. 2). All actions in the system depend on the message content. For example let's assume we have two expert system agents called Agent1 and Agent2. The user wants to ask Agent1 a question – request for fact proving (via GUI client). Agent1 cannot prove requested fact, but it can prove other facts, which could be useful when proving the requested fact. Agent1 can also communicate with Agent2, so passes the deduction process to this server by sending a request with facts already proved, deduction history and the fact to be proved. Agent2 proves the requested fact, and returns the result for the user GUI through Agent1.

7 Concluding Remarks

Interoperability between heterogenous knowledge-based systems seems to be of vast importance for development of intelligent information systems working in the global network environment. The proposed FIPA-DES may be considered as a step towards an open framework supporting cooperation of expert systems produced by different vendors and providing information and services in agent-oriented manner.

Further research work in the field will concern three main directions:

1. taking into consideration possibility of communication between agents with different ontologies,
2. extending knowledge representation techniques used in the implemented system,
3. applying FIPA-DES to casting defects diagnosis (see [11]).

References

1. O. Baujard and C. Garbay. A programming environment for distributed expert system design. *Cognitive Science*, 13:1–49, 1989.
2. F. Bellifemine, G. Rimassa, and A. Poggi. JADE – A FIPA-compliant agent framework. In *Proceedings of the 4th International Conference and Exhibition on the Practical Application of Intelligent Agents and Multi-Agents (PAAM'99)*, London, UK, 1999.
3. J. M. Bradshaw, editor. *Software Agents.* AAAI/MIT Press, 1997.
4. D. Cockburn and N. R. Jennings. Archon: A distributed artifficial intelligence system for industrial applications. In G. M. P. O'Hare and N. R. Jennings, editors, *Fundations of Distributed Arificial Intelligence.* Wiley, 1995.
5. J. Dale and E. Mamdani. Open standards for interoperating agent-based systems. *Software Focus*, 1(2), 2001.
6. B. H. Far and Z. Koono. Ex-w-pert system: A web-based distributed expert system for groupware design. In J. K. L. et al., editor, *Critical Technology: Proceedings of the Third World Congress on Expert Systems.* Cognizant Communication Corporation, 1995.
7. T. Finin, Y. Labrou, and J. Mayfield. KQML as an agent communication language. In Bradshaw [3].
8. S. Franklin and A. Graesser. Is it an agent, or just a program?: A taxonomy for autonomous agents. In J. P. Müller, M. Wooldridge, and N. R. Jennings, editors, *Intelligent Agents III*, volume 1193 of *Lecture Notes in Artificial Intelligence.* Springer-Verlag, 1997.
9. J. Giarrantano and G. Riley, editors. *Expert Systems: Principles and Programming.* MA: PWS-Kent, 1989.
10. N. R. Jennings, K. Sycara, and M. Wooldridge. A roadmap of agent research and development. *Journal of Autonomous Agents and Multi-Agent Systems*, 1(1):7–38, 1998.
11. S. Kluska-Nawarecka, T. Wjcik, G. Dobrowolski, and R. Marcjan. Learning analysis of casting defects using the expert system. In S. K.-N. et al., editor, *Simulation Designing and Control of Foundry Processes*, pages 165–174. Foundry Research Institute, 1999.

12. H. S. Nwana. Software agents: An overview. *The Knowledge Engineering Review*, 11(3):205–244, 1996.
13. P. O'Brien and R. Nicol. FIPA – Towards a standard for software agents. *BT Technology Journal*, 16(3):51–59, 1998.
14. S. J. Russell and P. Norvig. *Artificial Intelligence: A Modern Approach.* Prentice Hall, 1995.
15. T. Wittig, editor. *ARCHON: An Architecture for Multi-Agent Systems.* Ellis Horwood, 1992.
16. T. Wittig, N. R. Jennings, and E. H. Mamdani. ARCHON — A framework for intelligent cooperation. *IEE-BCS Journal of Intelligent Systems Engineering — Special Issue on Real-time Intelligent Systems in ESPRIT*, 3(3):168–179, 1994.

The Concept of the Web Expert System with Intelligent Web Search Engines for Market Analysis

Roman Wantoch-Rekowski

Military University of Technology, Institute of Computer Science, Warsaw Poland, email: rekowski@isi.wat.waw.pl, http://www.isi.wat.waw.pl

Abstract. The paper presents the concept of using expert system, which is working in the Web. Experts in area of market analysis proposed the idea of that Web expert system. The main task of the system is to support the expert during the market analysis. The main idea of the expert system in the Web was the access to information about the market in the Web. It is difficult for expert to search an information about certain company in many places in the Web, newspaper, TV news and from databases. Expert should new all that information if he wants to make a good decision. The expert system gives the expert all information in one place – one HTML page (e.g. using Internet Explorer or Netscape Navigator) and it supports expert to make good decision. The main element of the system is the knowledge base with rule representation – this is the procedural knowledge. The second part of the knowledge base – facts – are created using intelligent Web search engines. The problem is how to find important parameters (from acquired information) and how to calculate values of all parameters for inference engine of expert system. This problem is the main task for intelligent Web search engines.

Keywords. Expert systems, intelligent Web search engines, Web expert systems, knowledge representation, knowledge acquisition, Internet

1. Main idea of the Web expert system

The main problem of creating expert system is problem of knowledge acquisition. It is necessary to find (in the Web) the following information: stock exchange indexes in Warsaw WGW (all history), stock exchange indexes in other countries WGS (all history), exchange rates KW (all history), stock exchange rates of X company NFX (all history), financial reports of X company SFFX, co-owners of X company WSX, market indices published by Central Statistical Office, Central Board of Customs, Ministry of Finance, National Bank of Poland WGK, short information about X company from Polish Press Agency and Emitent KIP, information from newspaper and TV about X company IPIT, other information about X company created by experts (information about: cooperation, contracts, and so on). It is possible to find in the Web all above information, of course it is necessary to have access to the digital form of that information.

Figure 1 shows the main idea of the Web Expert System. It consists of: knowledge base, inference engine, user's interface, expert's interface, intelligent Web search engines.

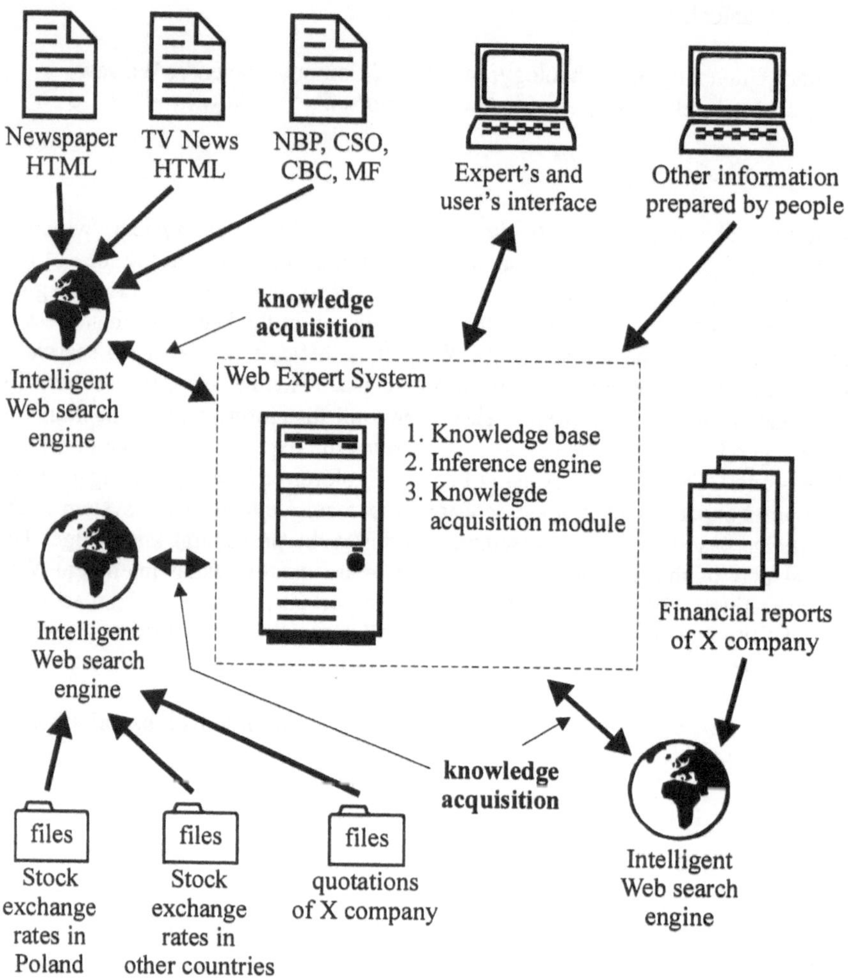

Fig. 1. Main idea of the Web Expert System

2. Main problems

1. Knowledge acquisition. This is the main task for intelligent Web search engines. Most of information is stored as HTML pages, so it is necessary to

prepare intelligent engines for knowledge acquisition from HTML form. Results of intelligent Web search engines work are values of selected parameters. It is necessary to calculate values of parameters all the time as quick as possible.

2. Reasoning. The values of selected parameters are the base of inference engine activity. The inference engine should support expert by taking into consideration all known parameters. The expert can't do that because there is so much information and some information is changing all the time, sometimes very quick.

3. Why the problem of using WEB Expert System is important?

- There are so many sources of information in the Web (including commercial information) - good source of knowledge acquisition for expert system.
- People from one team can work all over the world as sources of knowledge acquisition for one expert system.
- Information in the Web is changing all the time because reality changes all the time.
- Sometimes information is changing very quick and experts system should calculate new solution all the time.
- Sometimes short news (e.g. from Polish Press Agency) is more important than advanced analysis of stock exchange rates.
- All information for expert should be located in one place e.g. as HTML page.
- It is possible to use experience from typical expert systems.
- Expert System located in the Web can be used in any place in the world.
- Expert System located in the Web can be run using any operating system. If you wont to use Web expert system you should run Web browser (e. g. Netscape Navigator or Internet Explorer).
- One expert system can use some Web Servers.
- WEB Expert System (located in the Web) is the real time system – current information changes all the time.
- WEB Expert System may be located on some Web Servers - it is distributed system – more sources of knowledge acquisition.
- Web Expert System works permanently so if there is an important information it can inform expert about it (e.g. using cellular phone – SMS or email.)

References

1. Bliźniuk G., Wantoch-Rekowski R., Nowak M., (1999) Budowa aplikacji WWW z wykorzystaniem Oracle Designer/2000, VI Konferencja „Systemy Czasu Rzeczywistego", Zakopane

2. Calves J.P., (1992) Embedded Real-Time Systems, Willey & Sons, Willey Series in Software Engineering Practice
3. Edwards J., Deborah DV., (1997) 3-Tier Client/Server At Work, John Wiley&Sons Inc., New York
4. Musliner D.J., (1995) The Challenges of Real-Time AI, IEEE Computer Society, Vol. 28, No. 1, New York
5. Nielsen K., (1988) Designing Large Real-Time Systems with Ada, Multiscience Press Inc., New York
6. Orfali R., Harkey D., Edward J., (1996) The Essential Client/Srver Survival Guide. Second Edition, New York
7. Świątnicki Z., (1995) Artificial Intelligence in the Battlefield. Military Expert Systems. Warsaw, Bellona Pub.
8. Świątnicki Z., Wantoch-Rekowski R., (1994) Distributed Expert Systems (in Polish), In proceedings of „Decision Analyze, Expert Systems, Computer Systems Applications", Warsaw, May 25-27
9. Świątnicki Z., Wantoch-Rekowski R., (1994) Expert System for Orthodontic Diagnosis, 70th Congress of the European Orthodontic Society, Graz
10. Świątnicki Z., Wantoch-Rekowski R., (1996) Expert System for Orthodontic Application (Seksdiam), The Third World Congress on Expert Systems, Seul
11. Świątnicki Z., Wantoch-Rekowski R., (1996) Hybrid Expert System for Flying Object Recognition, The Third World Congress on Expert Systems, Seul
12. Świątnicki Z., Wantoch-Rekowski R., (1996) Using Knowledge-Based System for Air Force Development Planning, First Polish Conference on Theory and Applications of Artificial Intelligence
13. Świątnicki Z., Wantoch-Rekowski R., (1999) Expert System Application in Production Logistcs, International Conference on Logistic Interchange, Warsaw, pp.93-100, ISBN 83-900632-9-8
14. Świątnicki Z., Wantoch-Rekowski R., (1999) The Air Force Development Using Experts' Knowledge and Common Sense, „Computational Intelligence and Applications" Springer-Verlag, Edited by P.S. Szczepaniak, vol. XIV 1999, ISBN 3-7908-1161-0, pp 317-326
15. Wantoch-Rekowski R., (1997) The Neural Network As A Classifier Of Objects Located In Convex Sets, III Konferencja „Sieci neuronowe i ich zastosowania"
16. Wantoch-Rekowski R., (1999) Radial Base Function Neural Network for Wheeled Vehicles Classification, VIII Międzynarodowe Sympozjum „Intelligent Information Systems", ISBN 83-910948-1-2, pp 241-246
17. Wantoch-Rekowski R., (1999) Using Rbf Neural Network For Wheeled Vehicle Classification On The Base Of Ground Vibration, IV Konferencja „Sieci neuronowe i ich zastosowania", Zakopane, ISBN 83-908587-1-1, pp 238-243